THE WORLD'S BEST

the Ultimate Book
for the
International Traveler

Prepared by the staff of International Living | *www.InternationalLiving.com*

The World's Best—The Ultimate Book for the International Traveler
9th edition
Publisher: Jackie Flynn
Editor: Nazareen Heazle
This edition updated by: Serena Bifolchi
Design: Marsha Swan
Cover photo: ©iStockPhoto.com/Borut Trdina
978-1-905720-50-7   120B000461

CONTENTS

INTRODUCTION

*To my mind, the greatest reward and luxury of travel is to
be able to experience everyday things as if for the first time,
to be in a position in which almost nothing is so familiar it
is taken for granted.*

—Bill Bryson

Consider for a moment how much bigger the world is today than it was in 1986, when we published the first edition of *The World's Best*. How many more people there are. How many more places open to foreign travelers. How many more opportunities. The original *World's Best* was just 207 pages. The book you are now reading is 800 pages. And still I would caution that this new and expanded *World's Best* is far from comprehensive.

We have tried to include bests in every corner of the globe...in Bucharest and Buenos Aires...in Nepal and Nova Scotia...in Washington, DC and Wales... but we realize that we have but skimmed the surface.

To create this new 2012 edition, we called upon our regular correspondents all over the world (more than 200 of them), as well as our readers all around the globe, and asked that they send us their personal world's bests—their picks for the world's best art museum, sunset, surfing, scuba diving, opera house, ski resort, canyon, champagne, castle, nightclub, island, garden, market, train ride, travel bargains, restaurants, cafés, and neighborhoods. To their lists we added our own superlatives—our choices for the biggest, the oldest, the smallest, the cheapest, the grandest, the prettiest, the tallest, the coziest, the most remarkable...

Anyone who sets out to name the world's best this or the world's best that, does indeed have a "grievous charge." Who's to say what's best? We are, we decided. And on that authority, we offer a collection that is neither complete nor objective.

What we have attempted to do is to draw forth for you a small sampling of the wealth our world has to offer.

Enjoy.

Sincerely,

Jackie Flynn

Publisher, *International Living*

P.S. Details, details.

Prices throughout this book are, for the most part, given in U.S. dollars based on the current exchange rate at the time of going to press. This is meant only to give you an idea of the current pricing. Remember, exchange rates fluctuate daily. Furthermore, hotels and restaurants typically raise their prices every season. And inflation in some countries rages wildly.

SECTION ONE

THE WORLD'S BEST DESTINATIONS

THE BEST OF
AFRICA

To see once is worth more than hearing a hundred times.
—African proverb

Before you begin your travels through Africa, prepare yourself for an astonishing level of corruption. (The local term for bribes is dash.) A word about currencies…Many West African countries use the CFA franc (guaranteed by the French Treasury); Nigeria uses the naira (N); and South Africa uses the rand (calculated at both a commercial and a financial rate). Airports are usually good places to exchange your money.

THE WORLD'S BEST SAFARIS

East Africa, one of the last strongholds of the lion, the elephant, the gorilla, and other exotic beasts, is the best place in the world to go on safari. Enormous national parks where the great beasts roam freely, uninhibited by the progress of mankind, have been established throughout the region.

Kenya and **Tanzania** are the best countries for viewing wildlife; they offer comfortable accommodation and have mild climates with warm, sunny days and cool nights. Hunting is now banned in Kenya and many other African countries, where the typical safari has been replaced with a viewing safari. Plan your adventure for July through March to avoid the rainy season.

Zambia is also a good safari destination; it is less known by Westerners and therefore less spoiled. Zambia is the only country where walking safaris are still common.

The most accessible game park is **Masai Mara;** *website: www.masai-mara. com*, on the border between Kenya and Tanzania, in the **Rift Valley**. It has the largest diversity of game—rolling hills dotted with herds of elephants, antelopes, baboons, and lions. Masai tribes people, who wear beautiful colored cloth garments, also inhabit the area.

The **Ngorongoro Crater** and **Serengeti Plain** are part of the **Ngorongoro Conservation Area,** *website: www.ngorongorocrater.org,* a 3,200-square-mile tract of Masai land. Together, these two areas have the largest concentration of game in the world.

KENYA: THE MOST INVITING COUNTRY

Kenya's 225,000 square miles of mountains, plains, and coastline provide an extraordinary variety of terrain. This country is beautiful and—once you have arrived—inexpensive. Kenya is perhaps the most inviting country in Africa—it is English-speaking, and easily accessible.

Not only valued for its beauty, the land includes some of the most fertile tropical soil in the world. Although famous for its large exportation of coffee and tea, Kenya is also one of the world's leading horticultural countries. Germany and the Netherlands are among the biggest customers for its carnations and many varieties of roses. Fruits and vegetables flourish as well.

In Kenya, you can experience both the sophistication of the big city and the excitement of the bush country. The population of this nation defies generalization, composed of British colonial descendants, black Muslims with a Middle Eastern culture, Luo and Kikuyu farmers, Somali nomads and tall, inscrutable Masai warriors. The majority of the population is now Christian—but this general category comprises extreme Pentecostalism and a mélange of Christianity with indigenous religions as well as traditional Roman Catholicism and Episcopalianism.

Before a Kenyan football team will play a game, a witch doctor must be hired to set up nail fetishes around the goalposts to stop the opposing team from scoring any goals. In 1987, Kenyan courts were hearing a case involving a widow's suit against her brothers-in-law, who wanted to bury her late husband according to tribal ritual. Had his brothers-in-law buried him under the Luo ritual, the dead man's property would have gone to the tribe—and not his family.

Swahili, the official language of Kenya, combines African grammar with Arabic words. Because it is the language of trade, you will hear it in the markets and on the streets of Kenya. However, English is spoken by government officials, bankers, and international businessmen.

The best place to view the heavens

Because of its location across the equator, Kenya is one of the best places in the world to stargaze. The cloudless deserts and high, isolated Mount Kenya also contribute. Being on the equator means that every constellation in the sky is visible every night of the year. They simply change positions. What was on the western horizon at sunrise is on the eastern horizon 12 hours later, along with the sun. Mount Kenya and Lake Turkana in the northern Kenya are the best viewing sites.

Africa's metropolis: Nairobi

"Nairobi is the Paris of the East African coast" said Negley Farsoin in *Behind God's Back* (1940). The towers of the city shine in the hot noon sun and stand guard in the cool cascades of bougainvillea (a genus of South American climbing shrub), clumps of carnations, and banks of orchids. Residents harmonize with this tropical gaiety in brightly printed and tie-dyed garments.

Kenya's best museum

The **National Museum of Nairobi**, *Museum Hill; website: www.museums.or.ke*, has the world's foremost collection of fossils of human evolution. The museum houses many archeological discoveries of the late Dr. Richard Leakey, as well as 184 watercolor paintings by Joy Adamson, author of *Born Free*. Children can enjoy a special "please touch" exhibit. Also, if you want to see stuffed animals and birds this is the place to go. All of Kenya's wildlife has been stuffed and mounted over the years. There's quite a bit of tribal paraphernalia.

Snake Park, across the street from the National Museum, is also of interest to nature enthusiasts, containing more than 200 species of snakes. However, if you fear snakes there is also an aquarium at the park with all sorts of fish, crocodiles, alligators, birds, lizards, monitor lizards, turtles and tortoises that can be enjoyed.

Kenya's best art gallery

Paintings, sculptures, batiks, and photos by the best artists in Kenya and other African countries can be seen at **Gallery Watatu**, *Lonrho House, Standard Street; tel. +254 (722) 721-847; website: www.gallerywatatu.com*. The gallery displays and sells works.

The best animal viewing

A visit to the Animal Orphanage in **Nairobi National Park***; website: www.kws.org/ nairobi,* five miles outside town is a good way to prepare for a wilderness safari. The park is one of Kenya's most successful black rhino sanctuaries and so is one of the few parks where visitors are guaranteed a glimpse at these endangered beasts.

The best way to send a message

By the Thorn Tree Café at the **New Stanley Hotel**, *Kimathi Street; website: www. sarovahotels.com/stanley/*, is a thorn tree with bulletin boards affixed on four sides. You can fill out blank message forms with personal messages, advertisements, or announcements. This well-known meeting place has been here since 1959.

The most exotic meals

Food is a bargain in Nairobi. Foods of all nationalities are served, as well as local specialties, such as *ugali*, a corn and bean dish, and *ino*, a mixture of seeds. The best restaurant in town is **Carnivore**, *Langata Road*, where the specialty is—you guessed it—meat. You can try an unlimited amount of exotic skewered meats, anything from antelope to zebra washed down with a "dawa", the infamous Kenyan cocktail.

The **Mount Kenya Safari Club**, *P.O. Box 35, Mount Kenya, Nairobi; tel. +254 (20) 2265000 website: www.fairmont.com/kenyasafariclub/*, is the most elegant place to dine and enjoy a meal of pan-fried Nile perch, potatoes, and salad. Former members include Bing Crosby and Winston Churchill.

Good Indian curry, made with African ingredients, can be found in restaurants throughout Kenya. Many of the Indians, imported by British colonialists as administrators, were Muslims, which is why the curries are made with beef (which Hindus are not allowed to eat). Curry is usually served with a proliferation of accompaniments: chutneys and fried and roasted breads as in India; bananas, coconuts, mangoes, and other fruits; very hot red pepper sauce; peanuts; and even soy sauce.

Nairobi's best beds

Nairobi's best hotel is a remnant of the colonial days called the **Norfolk**, *Harry Thuku Road, P.O. Box 58581 tel. +254 (20) 226-5000; website: www.fairmont. com/norfolkhotel/.* It is Kenya's answer to the famous Singapore Raffles Hotel, with individual bungalows in a tropical formal garden.

Another good place to stay—if you can arrange an invitation—is the private **Muthaiga Country Club**; *website: www.mcc.co.ke*, where members can arrange accommodation for their friends.

The **Hotel InterContinental**, *City Hall Way, P.O. Box 30353; tel. +254 (20) 320-0000; website: www.ichotelsgroup.com/intercontinental/en/gb/locations/ overview/nairobi,* and **Mount Kenya Safari Club**, *P.O. Box 58581, Mount Kenya, Nairobi; tel. +254 (20) 226-5000; website: www.fairmont.com/kenyasafariclub/,* are also good bets.

The least expensive place to stay is the **Hotel Ambassadeur**, *P.O. Box 30399; tel. +254 (20) 224-6615; website: www.hotelambassadeurkenya.com.* A notable regular resident at the hotel was the late Mzee Jomo Kenyatta—Kenya's first president.

The best java

Kenya produces the best coffee in the world and is one of the world's leading exporters of Arabica coffee. Coffee was first introduced to Kenya by the French Holy Ghost Fathers (who liked a good cup of coffee) in the 1890s. It was developed in the region north of Nairobi. African farmers were forbidden from growing coffee until 1954. It is now Kenya's main export crop (which causes problems when the coffee crop fails). The berries are handpicked twice a year.

The second leading export crop is tea—another crop Africans were forbidden from growing. Today the region around Limuru supports more than 100,000 African smallholders, who grow enough tea to make Kenya the third-largest producer in the world, after India and Sri Lanka.

The country's best dancers

The best places to watch tribal dancing in Kenya are the country's *bomas*, miniature replicas of Kenya's 40 tribal villages, located seven miles outside Nairobi, on Langata Road. They are also good places to shop for woodcarvings.

A bird watcher's best

Lake Nakuru Park; *website: www.kws.org/nakuru*, 100 miles northwest of Nairobi, is the habitat of more species of birds than all the British Isles; it is also home to millions of pink flamingos. The best accommodation here is at the **Lake Nakuru Lodge**, *P.O. Box 561, Nakuru; tel. +254 (20) 286-7056; website: www.lakenakurulodge.com.*

Lake Naivasha is also an excellent place for bird watching. More than 340 species can be spotted near this beautifully situated lake. Dominated by the shadow of Mount Logonot, an extinct volcano, Lake Naivasha also provides water sports and hiking opportunities. Joy Adamson wrote her best-selling novel *Born Free* here.

Accommodation is available at the Lake Naivasha Resort, *South Lake Road; tel. +254 (050)-203-0298; website: www.lakenaivasharesort.net*, which is an old colonial farmhouse set on the shores of the lake.

World-class craftsmanship

Kenya has become one of the leading exporters of handicrafts, including soapstone, stone and woodcarvings, and sisal baskets (popularly known as *kiondos*). Woodcarvings, however, top the list. **Wamunyu**, a small township about 60 miles east of Nairobi, is the birthplace of this growing industry. It began with Mutisya Munge in the early 1840s and today over half of Wamunyu's population of 20,000 are wood-carvers.

You can visit woodcarving studios in Wamunyu, Mombasa, and Nairobi, where you watch rows of men effortlessly creating exquisite statues. Visitors can buy items at wholesale prices.

Mombasa: Gateway to the coast

Mombasa, gateway to the coast, is Kenya's second-largest city, combining African, Indian, and Arab cultures. Its narrow side streets, impassable by car, are lined with Indian temples, bazaars, and houses decorated with intricately carved wood doors. Curry scents the air, and the Muslim women are veiled in black buibuis.

The best way to get to the beach

Although it is possible to fly to Mombasa with Kenya Airways, old-timers prefer to take the overnight train from Nairobi. This train offers a good meal, a private sleeper, and a porter who wakes you up at 6.30 a.m. with a delicious cup of locally grown tea or coffee.

Malindi: the best modern beach resort

Malindi, an island 74 miles north of Mombasa, is known for its modern hotels, lively nightclubs, and ocean sports, including big-game fishing, sailing, water-skiing, skin and scuba diving, and underwater photography. It also has a half-dozen nature preserves; the Malindi Marine National Park, where you can see technicolor fish, the moray eel, and octopi; and Gedi, the ruin of an abandoned Islamic settlement in a thick tropical forest inland. The best hotel on Malindi is **Lawford's**, *Lamu Road, Malindi; tel. +254 422-126; website: www.malindi.info/index.php?id=Lawfords* (in German), which offers two restaurants and two swimming pools.

The best way to get to Malindi is by plane—taxis are expensive and buses are slow.

The least-developed islands

From Malindi, you can take a boat to the barely developed and sparsely inhabited islands of **Manda**, **Kuwayuu**, and **Pate**. Pate Town can be reached only if the tide is right. Faza and Siyu, also on Pate Island, are more accessible.

The best-preserved Swahili town

The island of **Lamu** is a perfectly preserved 18th-century Swahili town, where men and women still wear the traditional dress—women are veiled and men wear *kofia* (white embroidered caps). This World Heritage Site's port has been in existence for at least a thousand years. Don't expect to tour Lamu by car. The only car in town is reserved for use by the island's government representative. The best way to travel is by *dhow* (handmade sailboats).

Africa's deepest valley

The **Rift Valley**, a geological fault that originates in Syria and runs to South Africa, is best seen in Kenya. Sheer cliffs several thousand feet high rise above the valley floor, which is 50 miles wide in places. Changes in climate and topography when one descends the valley slopes are abrupt. Coffee plantations are everywhere. Large herds of relatively tame animals graze along the valley edges.

Kenya's best watering holes

Comfortable (even luxurious) lodges have been built near many of the country's watering holes. If you don't think you're up to a safari, opt for a holiday at one of these lodges. Instead of roughing it in the wilds, you'll be relaxing, while elephants, lions, hippos, and monkeys come up to you. All you need is a pair of binoculars.

The best watering hole is **Kilaguni**, 200 miles south of Nairobi in the giant Tsavo National Park. Animals can be viewed day and night, game drives and walks around Mzima Springs are offered, and camping facilities are available for true adventurers. **Kilaguni Serena Safari Lodge**; *tel. +254 (20) 284-2000*; *website: www.serenahotels.com/kenya/kilaguni/home.asp*, is the first lodge to be built in the park and has a restaurant and bar overlooking the watering hole.

The most famous of the watering holes is Kenya's original, **Treetops**, *website: www.aberdaresafarihotels.com*, 80 miles north of Nairobi in the Aberdares Mountains. You climb (slowly) to cedar huts where you are welcomed by servants, who spoil you, and by baboons, which pester you if you don't keep the windows shut. As night falls, wild animals visit the water hole below the lodge; the scene is periodically floodlit. Treetops is most famously known as the place where Princess Elizabeth of England learned of her father's death and her accession to the British throne in 1952.

The Ark, *Nyeri*; *website: www.thearkkenya.com*, near Treetops, is comparable in amenities to its more famous counterpart—but it's slightly less expensive. In addition, many argue that the game viewing is better at The Ark than at Treetops; a tunnel leads you to a hide right next to the watering hole.

Africa's most spectacular peaks

Kenya is home to the two most spectacular mountain peaks in Africa: **Mount Kilimanjaro** and **Mount Kenya** (known as Nyandarua among the Kikuyu). The eternal snows of these equatorial peaks seem like the stuff of legend even after you climb them. Mount Kilimanjaro can be climbed from the Tanzanian side of the border or the Kenyan. A five-day trip from the base to the peak, Mount Kilimanjaro is the most challenging.

The **Uhuru Park** (20,000 feet) can give climbers quite a rush of success. Tourist agencies in Tanzania will organize a climb of the mountain. No climbing is allowed during the rainy season in April and May.

In the language of the Masai, who live in its shadow, Kilimanjaro means *White Mountain*. The Masai climb only to an altitude of 10,000 feet, where the air gets thin. It's another 9,340 feet from there to the top. It can be done, thanks to an easy trail, encouraging Tanzanian guides, and comfortable Norwegian huts.

The standard hike to the top takes five days, from the park entrance at 6,000 feet, the first day's hike is along a gently rising trail for three to four hours until you reach Mandara Hut. Tropical forest animals inhabit this lower altitude. After five to seven hours of walking, you come to Horombo Hut at 12,000 feet. It has one notable difference from the first hut: the view of the snow-capped Kibo Peak above and the ocean of clouds washing the base of the mountains below.

The third day demands a climb to 14,000 feet over a stream marked "Last Water" and across wind-blown dusty terrain. It takes another three hours to climb to 15,600 feet, where the cold, dark, and uncomfortable Kibo Hut awaits you.

By tradition, you must reach the mountaintop in time to see the sunrise. So at 1 a.m. you will be awakened to trudge to Uhuru Peak. You will feel nauseous, lethargic, and sore. But when you see the sunrise from the mountain's peak, it will all seem worthwhile.

Mount Kenya, a snow-covered peak on the equator, is more scenic and easier to climb than Mount Kilimanjaro, due to the lower altitude. (It's 17,000 feet high.) Both are volcanoes, but unlike the case with its southern neighbor, Mount Kenya's fires have long been extinct. The two highest peaks—Batian at 17,058 feet and Nelion at 17,022 feet—are named after 19th-century Kenyan medicine men. They stand like huge black tombstones and are the domain of technical climbers of rock and ice. The average climber takes an easier route to Mount Lenana at 16,355 feet.

From the entrance gate at 9,500 feet, another 5,000-foot ascent brings you to the hut at Met Station Lodge, where a troop of Sykes monkeys entertain. Before passing the tree line the next morning, you might be able to see black and white Colobus monkeys flinging themselves madly through the trees overhead. At an area called the Vertical Bog, from 11,000 to 13,000 feet, the serpentine trail is covered with soggy peat and leads eventually to the foot of the glacier.

You sleep in the Kami Hut, made of corrugated iron, until 4 a.m., when you begin the trek across ice-coated boulders, using flashlights to light the way. A guide is essential to chop steps with an ice-ax. By dawn, you will reach the top.

Hikes of Mount Kenya must be arranged through **Alliance Naro Moru River Lodge**, *website: www.naromoruriverlodge.com.*

TANZANIA: THE BEST OF THE WILD

Tanzania is Kenya's southern neighbor. This country is the result of the fusion of the offshore island of Zanzibar, once an Arab stronghold, and the mainland (called Tanganyika in colonial days), inhabited by the Bantu and other African ethnic groups. The political unrest this fusion created was complicated by the country's adoption of Ujamaa, a form of socialism promoted by the country's first president,

Julius Nyerere. Tanzania is still suffering economic woes from its turbulent past; the country is desperately poor, hungry for tourism, and cheap.

Because it is so inexpensive (guides can be hired just a few dollars a day), Tanzania is beginning to draw tourists to its enormous game parks. Tanzania is really where the wild things are.

The famous **Serengeti Plain**, where you can witness the spring wildlife migration every year, has the largest concentration of game in the world. **Seronera Wildlife Lodge**, *website: www.hotelsandlodges-tanzania.com*, in the center of the park, has an airstrip and a swimming pool carved from natural rock. **Lobo Wildlife Lodge**, *website: www.hotelsandlodges-tanzania.com,* is an entire building carved from natural rock.

One of the undiscovered wonders of Tanzania is **Selous**, the largest game reserve in the world. This unspoiled, undeveloped wilderness is populated by more than one million animals, including Africa's greatest elephant and lion populations. Animals are less visible to visitors in this park, though, due to the immense area of the reserve.

Be cautious when visiting **Dar es Salaam**, Tanzania's capital. It is a city rife with criminals who prey on tourists.

ZIMBABWE: BEST HUNTING, BEST WATERFALL

Zimbabwe, formally Rhodesia, is the best place to go on a hunting safari (for which a hunting license is required). However, peaceable safaris are also offered.

Victoria Falls, located on the border with Zambia, is over a mile wide. The **Zambezi River** falls 300 feet here, creating a spray visible for miles. Spectacular rainbows arc over the cliffs.

RWANDA: THE BEST PLACE TO OBSERVE GORILLAS

Perched high in the Rift Valley Mountains west of Tanzania, tiny landlocked **Rwanda** is the best place in the world to see mountain gorillas. To visit the heart of gorilla country, you must hike through dense bamboo forests to an altitude of 10,000 feet. Professional guides lead small groups and carry rifles in case you meet wild buffalo, elephants, stray leopards, or poachers.

The hour-long trek begins easily, ascending through fields of flowers and potatoes before you enter the forest, where the trail becomes steep, narrow, and slippery. Just when you're out of breath, the path ambles across flat mountain meadows—but not for long before making another jungle climb. It takes a while to find the gorillas. They roam over a wide area and move more easily than humans through the dense vegetation—their physiques are better suited to bending and swinging than ours.

When the guide sights a troop of gorillas, he motions to hurry forward quietly. You can hear the gorillas snorting and cracking the vegetation beneath them. The guide makes low vocalizations to assure the gorillas' leader of friendliness before deciding if the great apes seem willing to allow visitors. If they are, you can crouch silently within feet of the primates for about 60 minutes. You are warned not to stare at the 500-pound creatures; they interpret this as a sign of aggression. In the unlikely event of an attack, the best defense is no defense—just lie flat.

The best ways to get there

Direct flights from Belgium, France, and Kenya are available to **Kigali**, the capital of Rwanda. There, you can rent a car or take an inexpensive but crowded bus to the gorillas' habitat, **Virunga Volcanoes National Park**. The most picturesque town to stay in is **Gisenyi**, which is on Lake Kivu, an hour's drive from the park.

To minimize disturbance to the gorillas' habitat, tour groups are restricted to six people. It's best to book tours through operators in Kigali. See the Rwandan Tourism Office website (*www.rwandantourism.com*) for a list of tour operators. Bring your own food, water, and camping equipment from Kigali.

With only a few hundred of these gorillas in the wild, they are listed as an endangered species. Because gorillas are susceptible to human diseases, a visitor with even a bad cold may not be allowed to visit the troop. Children under 15 may not participate.

UGANDA: BIRTHPLACE OF THE NILE

Uganda's tourism industry is still in its infancy. Nonetheless, Uganda is worth visiting for two reasons. First, it is cheap. Second, its people are hospitable.

Fifty miles from **Kampala**, Uganda's capital, lies Lake Victoria, the largest lake in Africa and the second-largest lake in the world. Here you can witness the beginning of the Nile's long journey to the Mediterranean Sea. About 150 miles downriver, **Kabalega National Park** is home to not only hippos, crocodiles, and other aquatic life but also the famed **Murchison Falls**. Here, the great river is crammed through a 20-foot fissure in the rocks and led down a 1,000-foot drop.

While in Kampala, visit Kabaka's Palace and Kasubi's Tomb. These are where the royal chiefs of the Buganda tribes were interred. There is also a traditional marketplace where you can purchase traditional Ugandan goods. The **Kampala Serena Hotel,** *website: www.serenahotels.com/uganda/kampala/home.asp,* in Kampala is the best place to stay in Uganda. It has park-like grounds with tennis courts, swimming pools, and restaurants.

THE SEYCHELLES: PARADISE FOUND

Some say the **Seychelles**—an island country 1,000 miles east of Kenya in the Indian Ocean—was once the Garden of Eden. Because of its government's strict environmental guidelines, some of its islands are among the least spoiled on earth. Tall palms line these sandy beaches that stretch along the pale-blue Indian Ocean. The people are an exotic mixture of African, Arab, French, British, Indian, and Chinese.

Ninety percent of all Seychellese live on the island of **Mahé**. The high mountain peaks at **Morne Seychellois National Park**, in the center of the island, offer views of the other islands.

Authors Somerset Maugham, Ian Fleming, Alec Waugh, and Noel Coward have been lured by the beauty of the islands. Most of them stayed at the **Seychelles Northolme Hotel**, *Glacis, Victoria; tel. +248 4299-000; website: www1.hilton.com.* The original hotel building is no longer in use, but guests can visit it and see the rooms labeled with names of former guests. Today's visitors are housed in a new building patterned in the old style and equipped with modern conveniences. The Northolme also has a French and Creole restaurant.

The second-largest island of the Seychelles, **Praslin**, is home to the rare black bulbul parrot and the Coco-de-mer palm, which produces a large double coconut, shaped somewhat like a woman's *derriére* and is said to have special fertility powers. **Vallée de Mai** on Praslin is the best place to glimpse rare birds and see the Coco-de-mer, and **Anse Lazio** is the Seychelles' most spectacular beach. **Baie des Chevaliers** is more secluded and can be reached by boat or airplane.

The forests of **Silhouette Island** contain plants and animals found nowhere else in the world. And the island's beaches are ideal for swimming and snorkeling. The 135 islanders raise cattle, goats, coconuts, sugarcane, cinnamon, vanilla, and fruit. There are no roads, only paths.

The most picturesque and expensive place in the Seychelles is the coral **Denis Island**, only 30 minutes by plane from Mahe. You can stay in thatched cottages by the sea at **Denis Island Lodge**, *P.O. Box 404, Victoria; tel. +248 288-963; website: www.denisisland.com*. Creole food is served at the buffet.

The least developed of the inhabited Seychelles is **La Digue**, with no cars but plenty of bicycles. Enormous boulders and tall palms line the surf. And 30 pairs of rare paradise flycatchers live in the Indian almond trees. You can stay at **Gregoire's**, *website: www.ladigue.sc,* on the beach.

Cousin, Bird, and Aride islands draw flocks of rare birds. More than a million sooty terns nest on Bird Island from May to November every year. The endangered bush warbler lives on Cousin. Aride is home to the world's largest colonies of lesser noddy and roseate terns. **Bird Island Lodge**, *website: www.birdislandseychelles.com*, has cottages with private baths and terraces, and prices include a buffet breakfast of local food.

SOUTH AFRICA: A WORLD OF CONTRASTS

South Africa is opening up as a whole new paradise for international travelers. The country is a land of contrasts. **Johannesburg**, its capital, is its industrial, financial, and cultural center. The nouveau riche (and many foreigners) have settled here in droves. But this is hardly the essence of South Africa. Each direction you travel will reveal a different and beautiful landscape, and another culture. From the rocky expanses and beautiful beaches of the west coast to the subtropical forests of the east coast, South Africa is teeming with energy and beauty. And once you get there, you'll find that travel in general is very affordable.

The best beds
The best accommodation in the country is organized through **Bed 'N Breakfast**, *website: www.bnb.co.za*. It operates a network of B&Bs, through which South Africans offer their own homes to travelers.

Cape Town: South Africa's oldest city
With **Table Mountain** as its backdrop, Cape Town is not only South Africa's oldest city but also its most beautiful. In fact, it is boasted as one of the most beautiful cities in the world. Its diverse architecture reflects the city's Victorian background, as well as its 20th-century influences.

South Africa's oldest—and best—museum

The **South African Museum**, *25 Queen Victoria Street, Gardens; tel. +27 (21) 481-3800; website: www.iziko.org.za*, is South Africa's oldest museum. It features an extensive natural history collection of mammals, reptiles, birds, fish, and insects. The whale gallery, life-size Bushman models, and planetarium are also worth a look.

World-renowned wineries

The wineries east of Cape Town are world-renowned. If you're a connoisseur of the fruit of the vine, you'll want to make time to visit this region while in South Africa. Stay the night at the **Lanzerac Manor and Winery**, *Stellenbosch; tel. +27 (21) 887-1132; website: www.lanzerac.co.za*, an original Dutch homestead. Rooms are furnished with original Cape antiques.

South Africa's smallest province

Although **Natal** is South Africa's smallest province, it offers beautiful countryside, as well as bustling city life. **Durban**, Natal's capital, is known for its Golden Mile, where five-star hotels and diverse restaurants abound. You'll also find an abundance of nightclubs, discos, or concert halls, theaters, and galleries—something for everyone.

The best way to experience Zulu life

Just north of Durban is **Eshowe**, where three Zulu *kraals* accommodate visitors in authentic beehive huts, giving you the chance to experience first-hand the lifestyle, rites, and rituals of tribal life. Also visit the **Zululand Historical Museum,** *website: www.visitzululand.co.za/museum.html,* at Fort Nonquai.

The most plants

If plants are your fancy, the **Cape Peninsula** is the place for you. It has more indigenous plant species per square meter than anyplace else on earth. The **National Botanic Gardens of Kirstenbosch**, *website: www.sanbi.org/frames/kirstfram.htm*, on the eastern slopes of **Table Mountain**, is a prime viewing location.

Africa's largest game preserve

Along the northeastern border (adjacent to Mozambique) lies **Kruger National Park**, Africa's largest game preserve. The 12,000 square miles of land is home to more species of wildlife, birds, and plants than any other park in Africa. The park is less than four hours by car from Johannesburg; local flights are also available, to get you there more quickly.

The best adventure

The best nature thrill available in South Africa is underwater shark watching. Four shark spotters at one time can spend three hours in sturdy cages, watching the great whites circling in search of prey.

The best ways to see South Africa

If you're looking for flexibility and independence, the best way to see South Africa is from the driver's seat of a rented motor home. This makes a lot of sense, especially because camping space is often easier to book than cottages at national parks throughout the country.

Another adventurous way to see South Africa is on board the world's most luxurious steam train, *Rovos*. You can spend four days and three nights exploring the former gold-rush country of the eastern Transvaal. See the website *www.rovos. co.za/train.html* for more information.

MADAGASCAR: HOME OF THE RING-TAILED LEMUR

Madagascar, off the southeastern coast of Africa in the Indian Ocean, is the fourth-largest island in the world. It is also one of the least visited. Madagascar is famous primarily for its large lemur population.

The capital of Madagascar, **Antananarivo** (known locally as Tana), is a good place to start your exploration. This charming little city offers hundreds of tiny shops and the Zuma marketplace. Every Friday, this giant market overflows with people looking for bargains in leather, jewelry, and other local goods.

Also venture over to **Nosy Be Island**, off the northwest coast of Madagascar. Coffee, vanilla, and ilang-ilang trees (their oil is used to make perfumes and soaps) are grown here.

The best lemur watching

If you came to Madagascar looking for the infamous ring-tailed lemurs, visit the **Berenty Lemur Reserve** in Fort Dauphin. Large, clean guesthouses are available on the grounds, and lemurs run rampant. The furry little creatures here are so tame they take food right from your hand.

The best beds
You can find clean, convenient accommodation in Antananarivo. The **Hotel Colbert**, 29 *rue Prince Ratsimamanga; tel. +261 (20) 222-0202; website: www. hotel-luxe-madagascar.com*, has air-conditioned rooms, a restaurant, and a casino.

The best travel tips
Because of its tropical setting, Madagascar does experience a lengthy rainy season (November through March). Avoid visiting during this period, when inland travel becomes difficult. The local buses and taxis are suitable methods of getting around the island, but avoid the *proper* buses (which hold about 30 people, not very comfortably). They tend to be slow and do not handle the unsurfaced roads well.

The island trains are inexpensive and faster than buses, but you must make reservations in advance. They run daily except Sunday.

SENEGAL: A FRENCH HOLIDAY FAVORITE

Senegal is a paradise of European sun-seekers, who make up the majority of visitors to this West African country. Americans have yet to discover Senegal, although it is the African country geographically closest to the United States, a mere six-and-a-half-hour flight from New York. The Senegalese government is working to attract more American visitors by expanding the denationalized tourist industry.

Senegal offers 350 miles of beach, two national game parks (open seasonally), a bird reserve, sailing, and fishing—as well as history and a pleasant climate (relatively speaking—remember, this is West Africa). Because it juts out into the Atlantic, pleasant breezes waft through the country, and the heat is less unpleasant than in neighboring countries.

The Senegalese Dance Troupe is world-acclaimed, and the local handicrafts are beautiful: precious jewelry crafted by hand, printed and woven fabrics, and snakeskin and crocodile leather goods.

The three negative aspects of this African country are the panhandlers, the dangerous ocean currents, and the unpleasant creatures of the surf, including sharks and jellyfish.

Dakar: The Paris of Africa
Several cities claim to be the "Paris of Africa," but **Dakar** best fits the description. Good restaurants and outdoor cafés can be found throughout the French-speaking

capital. The architecture shows signs of French influences, including wrought-iron balconies and little courtyards. But mosques also punctuate the cityscape, and little dirt streets weave between the grand boulevards.

The best of Senegalese art

The best place to see the art of Senegal is the **IFAN Museum of African Arts**. The entire first floor of this museum is devoted to Senegalese culture, displaying clothing, furniture, jewels, costumes, and instruments. Local galleries also exhibit the works of contemporary Senegalese artists.

The most important monuments

Dakar's two great architectural monuments are its cathedral and the Grand Mosque. The **Cathédral**, *Boulevard de la Republique and avenue du Président Lamine Gueye*, is one of the finest examples of Senegalese architecture. The **Grand Mosque**, *Allée Coursin*, built in 1964, is one of the largest mosques in Africa. (You must be content to view it from outside, because visitors are not permitted to enter.)

The best digs in Dakar

Novotel Dakar, *Avenue Abdoulaye Fadiga; tel. +221 (33) 849-6161; website: www.novotel.com*, which belongs to the French Novotel chain, boasts two restaurants, two bars, a swimming pool, and tennis courts.

 La Croix du Sud, *20 avenue Hassan II; tel. +221 (33) 889-7878; website: www.hotel-lacroixdusud.fr*, has a view of the flower market.

Dakar's best cuisine

Senegalese food tends to be spicy, often garnished with *sauce piment* (hot pepper sauce). Most entrées consist of rice combined with meats and sauces. French cuisine is also available in Dakar. Because alcohol is forbidden to Muslims, only non-alcoholic beverages—mostly teas—are served in restaurants.

 The restaurant in the **La Croix du Sud Hotel**, is an elegant but expensive French restaurant. All produce for the meals is imported from France.

The best entertainment in Dakar

The Senegalese National Theater Company and the Mudra Dance Group, in addition to many other groups, appear at the **Theatre Daniel Sorano** (the National Theater), *boulevard de la République*.

The darkest history

Just 20 minutes from Dakar is the **Island of Gorée**, once the most important transit center for slave traders, who bought Africans for shipment to America. It was from this appalling place that hundreds of thousands of shackled prisoners were loaded onto ships for the so-called Middle Crossing. The first crossing carried rum from the American colonies to Africa to pay for black gold; the final crossing was of sugar to New England to make the rum. A small museum on the island has chilling displays of shackles, chains, and other unpleasant instruments of the trade.

The best seashells

The **Island of Fadiouth**, 60 miles from Dakar, is so covered with seashells that the populace uses them as building material. Everything here is made of shells: a cemetery, a church, granaries built on stilts. Natives follow a traditional, self-sufficient, African lifestyle, making their own clothes and growing their food. You can reach the island from the mainland region of Joal via a bridge or in a *pirogue* (a wooden canoe).

The best bird sanctuary

One of the most important bird sanctuaries in the world is the 25,000-acre **Djoudj Park**, in the Saloum Delta, where you can see 180 species, including pelicans, herons, flamingos, and egrets. You can observe from a mirador without scaring the birds away. Mauritanian Blue People camp on the edge of the park from time to time, providing a rare opportunity to see Moors.

TOGO: A MICROCOSM OF AFRICA

Togo, a small west coast country, is sub-Saharan Africa in miniature, with plains alive with game, plantations fertile with crops of cocoa and coffee, and mud-brick villages where the old traditions remain unchanged. Originally a German protectorate, and then a French colony, Togo is now an independent country. **Lomé**, the capital, offers a wide choice of restaurants, while the coast boasts idyllic beaches.

In Lomé, women hold powerful economic and political positions, and every village has a women's union. The powerful Mama Benz—made up of matronly merchants—wields considerable force in the politics of this country (and has overthrown at least one government). The women sell everything imaginable in the marketplace—from a fully equipped Mercedes Benz to a pair of plastic slippers.

Many of the older Mama Benz members are illiterate—but they can calculate their margins and execute foreign-exchange transactions in their heads. Although the language of Togo is officially French, the people also can converse in Pidgin English.

Where to go in Togo

The best way to get a taste of the native life in Togo is to visit **Le Grand Marché** in the center of Lomé, where the smell of roasting meats and tangy spices permeates the air and tie-dyed caftans and printed pagnes are sold. These colorful swaths of cloth are used to make the dresses, shirts, and headdresses worn by West Africans, but they also can be used as unique tablecloths, draperies, or sheets back home.

For an in-depth look at Togo's culture, visit the **National Museum**, housed in the headquarters of Togo's only political party, the Rassemblement du Peuple Togolais (R.P.T.), a building decorated with reliefs sculpted by a leading Togolese artist. Museum exhibits include shells (which were formerly used as currency), pottery, musical instruments, and ceremonial relics.

The best place to settle a score

Voodoo is practiced in **Bé**, a residential area on the east side of Lomé. At **Bé Market**, near the Hotel de la Paix, you can buy unusual charms—bones, little figurines, skulls—from both pagans and Muslims. The charms are said to bring success or money, to defeat a rival in love, or to attract a lover.

Togo's most interesting village

Deep in the **Tamberma Valley** live the Tamberma people, who continue a lifestyle unchanged by the passage of time. Famous for their masonry, they live in cool tata dwellings constructed by hand from clay and wood. The houses are situated in a compound that is surrounded by a circle of conical towers connected by a wall. The towers are used primarily to store grain. The Tamberma spend most of their time outdoors on patios—they even do their cooking outdoors. They wear little clothing and smoke long pipes. The women are marked by scars in intricate patterns; they are tattooed when they are eight days old to protect against miscarriages and stillbirths.

The best hotels in Togo

Hotel Mercure Sarakawa, *Boulevard du Mono, Lomé; tel. +228 227-6590; website: www.accorhotels.com,* is a favorite of the French, a three-star hotel with restaurants, a disco, and recreational facilities.

Another good choice is **L'Hotel Equateur**, *102 rue Limitimé, Lomé; tel. +228 221-9992; website: www.hotelequateur.com,* which has large and comfortable rooms. It also has a small rooftop bar/restaurant.

NIGERIA: THE MOST POPULATED AFRICAN COUNTRY

Don't spend much time in Nigeria's capital, **Lagos**. It is an appalling place. Built on a lagoon, the city has a mushrooming population, but it lacks the infrastructure to deal with it. Roads, sewage, garbage collection, and water are all becoming problems. The results are a perpetual traffic jam and generally unpleasant conditions. Telephones seldom work, and electricity is erratic. Most of the Westerners in Lagos are diplomats and businessmen, who leave for the country as quickly and as often as they can.

In the days of high oil prices, Lagos was the most expensive city in Africa; now it is cheap—the one point in its favor. Cars and airplane tickets, however, have become more expensive. (This is helping to lessen the congestion on the highways and at the airport.) Another thing in Lagos' favor is its restaurants, which are good—and cheap. Recommended restaurants are **Chez Antoine**, *61 Broad Street, Tabriz*, which serves French and Lebanese cuisine but is closed Sunday, and **Club Bagatelle**, *208/212 Broad Street*, which serves Indian and Middle Eastern cuisine.

The **Federal Palace Hotel**, *Victoria Island*, is the best place to stay in town. It has a good restaurant/nightclub, the Atlantic, which serves Italian food.

But you shouldn't let Lagos spoil your opinion of all Nigeria. The country has much more attractive cities, notably Ife, Ibadan, Jos, Onitsha, and Kano. And the new capital is Abuja, which is roughly the geographic center of the country.

Kano: The best place to explore Islamic history
In the Old City of **Kano**, an oasis on the edge of the Sahara Desert, you can step back into the Islamic past. A mud wall inscribed with Islamic scriptures and Hausa engravings here is believed to protect the faithful from intrusion from the outside world. Livestock wander freely through the streets, along with men and women in flowing, Islamic robes and headdresses. Camel caravans of the nomadic Tuareg, dressed in immaculate sheaths and tall turbans, roam the streets.

Men in pastel *baba riga* robes and women in drab wrapper dresses trot freely with goats and lambs along winding footpaths in a maze of mud huts. The only modern addition to the Old City is the heavily guarded electric gate built into the mud wall surrounding the centuries-old Emir's Palace. The towering 40-foot Nassarawa Kofar mud gate connects the Old City with Kano's hastily constructed replica of a Western commercial center, where business is transacted but aesthetics are forgotten.

Climb to the top of the Dalan or Goren Dutse hills for a view of the city skyline against the Sahara desert.

The drawbacks

Kano has been the center of much of the political turmoil that has wracked Nigeria since it became an independent country. From this city, Muslims waged holy wars against rival groups for control of the country, which has the largest population in Black Africa.

Perhaps this history explains the terrible delays and red tape at Kano's international airport. Soldiers toting submachine guns guard the hangar-like terminal, where a sea of scuffling, sweating bodies crashes against two tiny immigration desks. One correspondent reported waiting six hours to get out of the airport after landing. She finally had to pay a bribe to get through. Water is scarce and must be boiled, strained, and purified. Sometimes, running water is not available.

The best Hausa food

If you enjoy sampling unfamiliar foods, try the local *sire* or *souya*, sold every evening at dozens of food stands all over town. Watch at dusk for small flaming fires where chunks of meat, tomato, onion, and pepper roast on skewers.

You can enjoy authentic tribal food at restaurants throughout Kano. Try the **Akesan Restaurant** and restaurants in the Ikeja, at the Usman Memorial, and in the international hotels. Prices are generally expensive, but the meals are worth it.

Hotels: Smaller is better

The cost of a hotel room in Kano is usually not worth the price. The major hotels are no better than any of the smaller hotels in town (except that hotels are subject to water, electricity, and food shortages), but the smaller hotels are cleaner and offer more courteous service.

The best side trips

If you want to shake the dust of Kano off your shoes for a few days, visit one of the three ultramodern spa resorts an hour south of the city. The **Baguada** and **Tiga Lake** resorts and the **Rock Castle Hotel** offer iced drinks under the palms.

Or take a trip to **Daura**, a town two hours north of Kano, where the nomadic desert culture that once dominated the Sahara continues unchanged. Kano is an excellent base for safaris. The **Yankari Game Reserve** is a four-hour drive due south in the state of Bauchi. East of Yankari is the **Jos zoo**. Both nature reserves offer safaris that take you to see thousands of native species.

Yoruba: Best markets, best art

Yoruba cities, such as **Ibadan**, which is as large as Lagos but much nicer, are the African cities most welcoming to tourists. Ibadan boasts the best market in Nigeria, called Dugbe, and has a large Lebanese population made up of Middle Easterners who came to Africa to trade and stayed to open restaurants.

Benin City, the Yoruba capital, boasts the best market for souvenirs in Nigeria. Its other claim to fame is **Oba's Palace**, which is difficult to get into—you must apply for permission in advance. (An *oba* is a Yoruba ruler.) Far more accessible is the public **Ife Palace complex**, another former home of a Yoruba ruler. Ife is the center of a flourishing art colony, where printmakers have adapted skills once used on cloth to produce gorgeous woodcuts.

Top travel tips

Nigeria doesn't have to be the bureaucratic nightmare it is often reported to be. You just have to be prepared. Before arriving at the international airport in Lagos, make sure you have a visa, a passport, a yellow fever vaccination certificate, and a return ticket. You will have to pay a minimal airport tax when you leave.

SIERRA LEONE—THE BEST OF THE BRITISH IN WEST AFRICA

If sightseeing isn't really your cup of tea, visit West Africa's former British colony, Sierra Leone. This country has no outstanding attractions, but it does offer beautiful tropical scenery, a dry climate, and a friendly population, made up of 18 different ethnic groups. Perhaps the best part (at least if you're a foreign visitor) is that Sierra Leone has one of the unhealthiest economies in West Africa, so your foreign currency will go a long way. Although English is the official language of Sierra Leone, a form of English called Krio, enriched by several West African languages, is more widely spoken.

Safety in Sierra Leone

Contrary to popular belief, Sierra Leone is now a peaceful country, although it is still recovering from a 10-year civil war which ended in 2002. In December 2005 UN peace keeping forces withdrew from the country and Sierra Leone resumed responsibilities for its own security. The Sierra Leonean police are working to improve their professionalism and capabilities. Travelers are urged to exercise caution, especially when traveling beyond the capital of Freetown. Road conditions are hazardous and serious vehicle accidents are common. Emergency response to vehicular and other accidents ranges from slow to nonexistent.

Freetown: The heart of Sierra Leone

Freetown, the capital of Sierra Leone, offers the best opportunities for accommodation and dining in this quiet country. And its peninsula is the only place along the West African coast where mountains rise near the sea, providing beautiful views. It's also one of the few areas where the water is safe for swimming.

The best beds in Freetown

The renovated **YMCA**, *32 Fort Street; tel. +232 (22) 223-608; website: www.ymcasierraleone.org,* is the best of all the YMCAs in West Africa. You have use of a library, a TV room, and a fully equipped kitchen. There are only six rooms, so be sure to make reservations.

The best place to try African cuisine

If you're in the mood for ethnic food, and a lot of it, try **Provilac**, *Congo Cross Road*. Every Wednesday at lunch, Provilac serves an all-Sierra Leone buffet. The best dishes include potato-leaves sauce, okra sauce, palm-oil stew, groundnut stew, and pepper soup.

Freetown bests

Across the street from the City Hotel is the city's major landmark, the **Cotton Tree**, a historic symbol of Freetown. It was found growing in the town center in 1792 when a group of former African-American slaves, who had gained their freedom by escaping with the British during the American War of Independence, founded Freetown on March 11th 1792 and held a thanksgiving service there.

Next to the Cotton Tree is the **Sierra Leone National Museum,** *Pademba Road; tel. +232 (22) 223-555.*

A must for hikers is the half-hour climb to **Leicester Peak**. The highest point in Freetown (1,952 feet), this mountain offers a spectacular view of the bay area and the peninsula. The most popular beach in Sierra Leone is the **River No. 2 Beach**, 45 minutes south of Freetown. Many consider it one of the most beautiful beaches on the entire West African coast.

THE BEST OF NORTH AFRICA

North Africa is a mixture of civilizations: the pharaohs of Egypt, whose history dates back to the beginning of time; the exotic Moroccans, whose intriguing culture mystifies Westerners to this day; and the elusive Algerians, who live in a land yet to be discovered—trapped in time.

THE BEST OF EGYPT

For 4,000 years, the pharaohs of Egypt reigned over a civilization with a stability and technology that have yet to be duplicated. A team of Japanese engineers tried to build a pyramid just 35 feet high using the ancient Egyptian methods. They couldn't finish it. Thus, the pyramids of Egypt are eternal reminders of the lost wisdom of a great civilization.

A few days among the tombs and temples of Egypt will convince you that the pharaohs had something we have now lost. But a few days among the guides and the multitudes of poor asking for *baksheesh* (tips) may also convince you that what the pharaohs succeeded in building was merely a nation of the greatest tourist attractions known to man.

While Egypt is largely a desert nation, most of its people live on the water— along the banks of the Nile, by the Red Sea, or on the Mediterranean. So one of the best ways to see this country is by boat. One of the geographic peculiarities of this land is that the southern half of it is known as Upper Egypt; the northern half is Lower Egypt.

Cairo: The greatest paradox

Founded in the 10th century by invading Muslims, this noisy, crowded city thriving in the shadow of the pyramids is one of the most intriguing capitals in the world. Cairo's mixture of poverty and riches exemplifies the paradox of the Middle East, which is made up of nations straddling the Third World and the Western world. Minarets rise imperiously from 10th-century mosques, cars hurtle recklessly down narrow streets, poor families live in the graveyards of wealthy relatives, and merchants crowd the bazaars selling Arabian Night perfume and "genuine" Pharaonic scarabs.

Metropolitan Cairo, jam-packed with one-quarter of Egypt's population, is split by the Nile into two districts: Cairo on the east bank and Giza (a suburb on the edge of the Giza Plateau) on the west. In between are two small islands: Zamalek and Roda. Zamalek (also called Gezira) lies across from the northern, more upscale New City, with its Tahrir Square—Cairo's downtown—and its Islamic section and tourist bazaar of Khan el-Khalili. Roda is parallel to the southern, squalid Old Cairo, which includes the Coptic neighborhood bordered by the Fatimid Wall built in 1087.

The best view of Cairo
Most people come to Cairo to see the pyramids; in the process, they often miss the city itself. The best place to get your bearings is atop the 600-foot **Cairo Tower** in Zohria Garden on Zamalek. The view from the observation deck stretches to the pyramids. (Skip the mediocre restaurant.)

Cairo's two best museums
Two museums on the island provide insight into modern Egypt: the **Mukhtar Museum** shows the works of Mahmud Mukhtar, the father of modern Egyptian sculpture, and the **Gezira Museum** displays rare paintings, sculptures, and Islamic and Coptic artifacts.

The most fashionable neighborhood
Walk around the fashionable neighborhood of **Heliopolis** in the New City, where former Egyptian President Honsi Mubarak lived. Buildings mix Western and Islamic architecture. Notice the Palace of Prince Husayn, the arcades on Abbas Boulevard, and the Palace of Empain, a copy of a Hindu temple with an electronically controlled tower that rotates to follow the path of the sun.

In search of the *Arabian Nights*
Islamic Cairo, with its magic lanterns and flying carpets even better than those of Baghdad, has preserved the atmosphere of the *Arabian Nights*. It takes several mornings of walking to really see the area. Visit some of the 500 mosques

here—remember that not all of them are open to non-Muslims and that you won't be allowed to enter any mosque until after prayer.

When visiting a mosque, dress conservatively and don't draw attention to yourself; women should cover their heads. You must remove your shoes at the door. (Give the man who watches them a small tip.) Anyone who opens special doors or explains things in detail also should be tipped. Some mosques charge an admission in Egyptian pounds.

The world's oldest university

Cairo's most famous mosque is certainly the **Al-Azhar Mosque**, on the corner of Al-Azhar and Al-Muizz streets. Built in A.D. 972, it was the world's first university, and today it serves more than 90,000 Muslim students. Restored in bits and pieces, the *mihrab* in the center aisle is from the 10th century. You can take photographs here, as in any mosque, as long as you don't focus on any one person.

The holiest mosque

Across the street from Al-Azhar Mosque is **Sayiddna al-Husayn**, Cairo's most venerated Muslim shrine. It is closed to non-Muslims, but you can examine the finely decorated exterior walls. Inside rests the head of al-Husayn, grandson of the prophet Muhammad (transported to Cairo in a green silk bag from Iraq). Westernization has hit even Sayiddna al-Husayn. Just inside the door is a green neon light reading "Allah."

The Citadel

South of the Al-Azhar is the **Citadel**, a monolithic complex that dominates Cairo's skyline. Built in the late 12th century by Salah al-Din on the Mokattam hill range, it has a strategic view of the capital. The 19th-century ruler Muhammad Ali added a mosque to the Citadel, one of the great features of Cairo. The silver domes and marble and alabaster decorations are rivaled only by the building's vast interior. The Citadel houses the Mostafa Kamel Museum and the Military Museum.

Cairo's oldest mosque

Southwest of Salah al-Din Square is the city's oldest mosque: **Ibn Tulun**, *Calen el-Salikban Street*. It was built in A.D. 879 by Ibn Tulun, who seceded from the Islamic Empire and built himself the largest mosque in Egypt, decorating it with sweeping contours and intricate inscriptions. The mosque's courtyard covers almost 7 acres, and the building's lacy stuccowork surrounds inscriptions from the

Koran. Climb the external staircase to the top of the tower, from which you have a view of the city and the pyramids to the west.

The most beautiful windows

The mausoleum complex of **Qala'un**, *Gonar al-Qaid Street*, in northern Sharia al-Muizz, is famous for the colors in its stained-glass windows. During the times of the Crusades, Egypt was the world's center of glasswork, and the incredible craftsmanship of these windows set a standard for all Islamic tombs and Gothic churches in Europe.

The best Islamic art

The **Museum of Islamic Art**, off Ahmad Maher Square at the corner of Port Said and Muhammed Ali streets, is an overlooked treasure. This museum houses a little of everything, from Persian carpets to Islamic glassware to Kufic script wood-carvings. Because most visitors to Egypt dwell on Pharaonic art, the Museum of Islamic Art is rarely crowded. The exhibits are arranged by craft, so it's easy to trace stylistic developments over time, giving yourself a mini-art history course. Don't miss the Koran engravings.

Giza: The most tranquil district

Giza Square, in the heart of Cairo's Giza district on the west bank, marks the beginning of Pyramids Road. Cross Al-Gamaa Bridge to get to the Al-Urman Botanical Garden and the Cairo zoo. To the north is Dokki, Giza's fashionable residential neighborhood, which contains several embassies and two good museums.

The **Museum of Modern Art**, *18 Ismail Abu'l-Futuh Street*, exhibits postwar Egyptian art and has an excellent sculpture garden. The **Agricultural Museum**, at the western end of the 6th of October Bridge, contains the only remaining mummified bull.

The best of Old Cairo

South of Tahrir Square is **Old Cairo**, which surrounds the old Roman fort Babylon outside Fatimid Wall. You'll find evidence of Greco-Roman culture and early Christianity throughout the quarter. From the time of the last pharaoh to the first mosque, Egypt was part of the Greco-Roman world and Christianity, which in Egypt emerged as the Coptic Church.

The world's finest Coptic art

The **Coptic Museum**, built on the site of the Roman fort in Qasr al-Shama, has the finest Coptic art collection in the world. The buildings, courtyards, and gardens of the museum tell the story of early Christianity from the third through the seventh centuries. See the intricately woven robes and curtains for which the Copts were renowned.

The most beautiful Coptic church

In front of the Coptic Museum are the remains of the fort that took invading Muslims seven months to overpower. The **Church of al-Muallaqa** was built atop the gate of the fort, giving it the name the Hanging Church. Also known as the Church of St. Mary, this is the most beautiful of Cairo's Coptic churches. The pointed arches and carved relief are interesting changes from the Gothic style commonly associated with Christian churches. Climb the 24 stairs to see the interior. The famous pulpit stands on 13 slender columns (symbolic of the 12 apostles and Jesus, with the black column representing Judas). Unlike in mosques, *baksheesh* is not paid in churches. Photographs are prohibited.

The three most charming churches

North of al-Muallaqa, on Mari Girgis Street, is the **Church of Mari Girgis** (St. George), noted for its fine stained-glass windows. To the left of the church is a staircase descending into an old alley, at the end of which is the elegant **Church of Abu Serga**. The crypt below is supposed to be where Joseph, Mary, and baby Jesus stayed during their flight to Egypt. The crypt is 10 meters deep and often floods when the Nile's water levels rise.

To the right of Abu Serga is the **Church of St. Barbara**, an ornate structure with striped-marble steps. According to legend, the order was given to destroy one church and restore the other, but the caliph's architect couldn't decide which to destroy. He paced back and forth between the two buildings until he died of exhaustion—so the caliph restored both churches.

Egypt's oldest synagogue

Near the Church of St. Barbara is the **Ben Ezra Synagogue**, the oldest in Egypt. The interior is beautifully decorated, and the custodian is a humorous, talkative fellow. You can follow the steps to the spot where the pharaoh's daughter is said to have found the infant Moses.

The Cities of the Dead

The vast and forbidding **Cities of the Dead**, where thousands live in and around graveyards, are to the northeast and south of the Citadel. The poor use parts of mausoleums as their homes and parts of tombs as clotheslines or soccer goals. Historically Egyptians have believed that cemeteries are an active part of a community and not exclusively for the dead.

Wealthy citizens are buried in the northern cemetery, and their graves are marked with elaborate tombs. The many-ribbed dome caps an ancient pointed archway. The most impressive monument in the southern cemetery is the mausoleum of **Imam Al-Shafi'i**, *Imam Al-Shafi'i Street*. Built in 1211, the mausoleum contains an 800-year-old carved cenotaph. The nearby tomb of **Shagarat al-Durr** was built for Shagarat, the Muslim queen who poisoned two husbands and her son to remain in power. The mausoleum is decorated with Kufic carvings and a *mihrab* with Byzantine glass mosaics.

Egypt's most important museum

The **Egyptian Museum**, *Midan El Tahrir*; *website: www.egyptianmuseum.gov.eg*, like the British National Museum and the Smithsonian, exhibits an entire culture on several floors. Located in Tahrir Square just down the road from the enormous Ramses Hilton, the Egyptian Museum (commonly called the Cairo Museum) is the world's unrivaled warehouse of Pharaonic art. More than 120,000 pieces are crammed together with little order; the most exquisite are not always highlighted. The museum has enough ankhs, scarabs, and statues to fill several days of exploring.

The second floor houses the treasures found in Tutankhamun's tomb, the only one that escaped plundering, because of its hidden location. When viewing the incredible gold statues, alabaster lamps, and general ostentation, remember that Tutankhamun died young and his treasure was comparatively small.

The Cairo Museum is always crowded but less so when the tour groups break for lunch. It is open daily 9 a.m. until 4 p.m. Cameras are prohibited.

The most colorful markets

In Cairo, you can buy not only an aphrodisiac but also an anti-aphrodisiac, made from baby crocodiles. The two Arabic phrases you'll want to know when shopping are *Bikam hadha?* (How much does this cost?) and *Hatha Kathir* (That's too expensive). The main shopping areas are **Zamalek**, **Dokki** (in Giza), and **Heliopolis** (northeast of the New City).

Khan el-Khalili is the largest bazaar in Egypt, with hundreds of shops grouped by trade: gold merchants, silversmiths, and spice sellers. The 14th-century courtyards buzz with the sounds of haggling. You will find the best buys on *galabiyyas*, full-length cotton robes worn by Egyptian men, and local crafts. Don't forget to bargain…its almost rude not to!

The **Bab Zuwayla** district of Old Cairo teems with people and livestock. Peddlers transport their goods by bicycle and truck and on foot. Saffron, cumin, coriander, and hibiscus perfume the air. Along the Street of the Tentmaker, men sit cross-legged, plying their needles in the traditional art of appliqué stitchery. Also to be found are food, silk carpets, gold jewelry, clothing, ceramics, baskets, and two fez factories. Bab Zuwayla is more commercialized than Khan el Khalili, which is across the street, but just as colorful.

Finally, you can't leave Cairo without purchasing a *cartouche*, the quintessential Egyptian souvenir. These Pharaonic 18-karat gold pendants are personalized with your name or initials translated phonetically into hieroglyphics. Prices are $70 to $180. The best place to shop for a *cartouche* is in the **Egyptian Museum**.

Best place to buy a camel

Every Friday morning, Egypt's largest camel market is held in **Birqash**, a small village about 22 miles northwest of Cairo. Traders sell and swap hundreds of camels, horses, sheep, and goats, as well as food, wagons, jeans, and baskets. (You can buy a camel for about 1,500 Egyptian pounds.) The sights and smells are strong: you may witness a camel giving birth or a goat being butchered and skinned for immediate barbecue. This is not the place for the faint of heart or those with weak stomachs. Remember to bargain. And don't pet the camels—they spit and bite. The market is an easy trip (one to one-and-a-half hours) from Cairo, and one hour in the hot and dusty market is usually enough for most visitors.

Cairo's best cuisine

In a city where butchers slap flies off pieces of meat to show them to customers, only certain restaurants can be trusted. However, if you're willing to venture beyond the hotel restaurants, you will find that the food in Cairo is exotic and inexpensive. Typical Egyptian dishes include *mulokhiya*, a gelatinous soup made with a spinach-like herb; *fool*, a big brown bean; *feteer*, which resembles pizza; *taboula*, ground wheat and parsley salad; and *kofta*, tiny grilled meatballs.

Andrea, *60 Maryotteya Canal; tel. +20 (2) 383-1133*, an outdoor farm restaurant near the pyramids, serves delicious grilled chicken and some of the best *mazza* (a collection of appetizers) in Cairo.

If you are looking for a restaurant prized by the locals, not geared for tourists, a small take-out restaurant, **Sharia Talaat Harb**, lies around the corner serving exotic food at a cheap price.

Abou Shakra, *69 Kasr El-Einy; tel. +20 (2) 531-6111*, specializes in shish kebab and *kofta*.

A full-course Egyptian meal is best at **Aladin**, *26 Sherif Street; tel. +20 (2) 362-8294,* in the Sheraton Cairo Hotel, a watering hole popular among foreign journalists. Kebabs, barbecues, and *om ali*—a spicy bread pudding—are tasty and filling.

The most romantic meals in Cairo are served on Nile boats. The food is a little more expensive, but the atmosphere is worth it. The best floating restaurant is **Scarabee**, *opposite the Shepheards Hotel; tel. +20 (2) 794-3444*. Reservations are advised.

The most recommended hotels

The **Le Meridien Heliopolis**, *51 El Orouba Street; tel. +20 (2) 2290-5055; website: www.starwoodhotels.com/lemeridien/*, is a first-class hotel. It is also close to the Egyptian Museum and Cairo's Old Town.

Good hotels need not all be five-star. The **President Hotel**, *22 Taha Hussain; tel. +20 (2) 2735-0718; website: www.presidenthotelcairo.com*, in the residential section of Zamalek, is spacious and clean. The rooftop restaurant has an extensive wine cellar.

The best nightlife

At night, when the temperature drops, Cairo's nightlife gets hot. Discos are crowded, especially on Thursday nights. A popular one is **After Eight**, *6 Kasr El Nil Street; website: www.after8cairo.com*.

Surprisingly, nightlife in Cairo can be liveliest during Ramadan, a month-long holiday during which devout Muslims fast from sunrise to sunset. After dark, however, they indulge in large meals and take to the streets around al-Azhar and the Nile, where you'll find street theater performances, magic shows, and noisy crowds.

The Marriott and Sheraton hotels have casinos, where gambling takes place in American currency.

If you want glitzy belly dancing, try the **Two Seasons Supper Club** in the **Ramses Hilton**, *1115 Comiche El-Nil*. More authentic floorshows can be seen at the clubs along Pyramids Road, which cater to Egyptians.

If you'd rather spend a peaceful, romantic evening, take a *felucca* (small sailboat) on the Nile. Feluccas can be rented just south of the Kasr El-Nil Bridge on the east bank for about 20 Egyptian pounds an hour. Across the corniche from the Shepheards Hotel, boats are available from midnight to dawn for 26 to 33 Egyptian pounds. It's *felucca* etiquette to bring food for a picnic to share with your navigator.

The best ways to get around Cairo

Getting around Cairo is simultaneously easy and bothersome. Overcrowded buses (commonly called VOAs, for Voice of America—they were bought with American aid) are cheap and run everywhere, but they can be recommended only to the most adventurous. They don't stop—they only slow down for you to jump on or off.

The metro offers fast, inexpensive service, but only in the southern area of the city. The happiest traveler is the one who has mastered the art of Cairo taxis, which come either metered or unmetered. Either bargain the cost before you get into a cab or at the end of the ride pay the driver a fair amount.

Chauffeured cars can be hired for the day outside the Hilton hotel. You also can rent a car to drive yourself around. This may be practical in the rest of Egypt, but in Cairo it's dangerous. The famous race-car driver Mario Andretti said that the one place he'd never drive is Cairo. Traffic lights here were built to be ignored. Cars speed through intersections, slowing only momentarily to warn pedestrians by honking their horns or flashing their headlights.

Giza: The best and the tackiest of Egypt

Not five miles west of Cairo, the pyramids of Giza are easily reached via Pyramids Road by taxi or by bus. The best route is through Mena village. Toward the southern edge of this town is a broad plaza where tourist buses park. Here, clear of buildings, you have an uninterrupted view of the Sphinx with the pyramids behind and overhead.

The best time to visit Giza is at dawn, when sunlight makes the area glow and you feel the power that overwhelmed even Napoleon. If you show up before the tourists arrive, you can try to climb the outside of the Great Pyramid. It's necessary to hire a guide to take you up; you must pay him again to take you back down. Although technically illegal, this is common practice.

The greatest pyramid

The tallest pyramid in Egypt, the **Pyramid of Cheops** (or the Great Pyramid), was finished in 2690 B.C. and stands 448 feet tall. It contains 2.3 million separate blocks of stone, each weighing 2.5 tons. Millions have visited and climbed Cheops, from French novelist Gustave Flaubert to a Parisian wallpaper manufacturer, who left an advertisement on the top.

Scientists believe that Cheops (or Khufu) built the pyramid for some reason besides pure ostentation. Theories that the ancient Egyptians knew the earth was round and calculated the circumference are supported by the pyramid. Measurements taken in the 1930s revealed that the proportions of the Great Pyramid are the same as the proportions of the earth's Northern Hemisphere. Scientists don't know whether this information was used in ancient navigation and astronomy, but it suggests an advanced culture.

The Grand Gallery of Cheops, with its 28-foot ceiling, is unusually devoid of decoration. It is one of the main reasons for the Great Pyramid controversy—it is the largest chamber in Cheops but contains absolutely nothing to suggest worship or religion. The gallery leads to the King's Chamber, which contains the bottom half of the sarcophagus. (A lid was never found.) The king was never buried here, because the passages in the pyramid were too narrow for the sarcophagus to be brought in after the pyramid was completed.

The most beautiful pyramid

Next to Cheops is the **Pyramid of Chepren** (Khafre), Cheops' son. This pyramid is actually about 10 feet shorter than the Pyramid of Cheops, even though it seems taller because it's on higher ground. Its construction is not symbolic—only the Great Pyramid is thought to have any astronomical significance.

Chepren, however, is the most beautiful of the pyramids, because part of its limestone casing remains. The interior is spacious, and the ornate sarcophagus sinks into the floor up to its lid.

The least-crowded pyramid

The **Pyramid of Mycerinus** (Menkaure) is a 15-minute walk south of Cheops and Chepren. Because it is "only" 210 feet tall, it attracts relatively few tourists. Mycerinus, Chepren's son, began the pyramid about 2472 B.C. but died before the outermost stones were placed.

The world's oldest boat

Next to the northern face of Cheops is the museum housing the *Solar Barque*, the oldest boat in the world. Discovered in 1954, the 128-foot-long boat is presumed to have been built to carry Cheops to the Underworld. The boat's construction is ingenious. Its hull is made from hundreds of jigsaw-like pieces of wood that were fitted and then sewn together with rope. When the hull was put into water, the wet wood swelled while the rope shrunk, creating a watertight fit.

The world's greatest riddle

Northeast of the Great Pyramid crouches the most famous statue on earth: the giant **Sphinx**. Carved out of a single ridge of rock, it has the head of a man and the body of a lion and measures 240 feet long and 66 feet high. The face is missing its nose and beard. It's not known what exactly happened to the beard but the nose was an unfortunate victim of target practice by the Turks during the Turkish Occupation in the 1700s.

Because it is commonly believed that the face of the Sphinx represents Chepren, some conclude that the statue is 4,500 years old. Other scientists, however, believe it is much older. Geologists have concluded that the severe erosion of the body could not have been caused by wind and sand. Water, they say, must have been the cause. Egypt was flooded at the end of the last Ice Age, about 10,000 B.C.; therefore, the Sphinx must have been built prior to that time, which is thousands of years before mankind is thought to have had tools. The Sphinx continues to crumble—it recently lost a chunk of its shoulder. Scientists are debating how to save it. See it while you can.

Also explore the **Valley Temple of Chepren** at the foot of the Sphinx. The core contains limestone blocks, each weighing more than 100 tons; the method used to lift these huge blocks into place is unknown. The floors of the temple are made of slabs of alabaster. Though small, the temple is well-preserved, and its construction is unique in all Egypt.

The most romantic views

Perhaps the most romantic thing to do in Egypt is to ride Arabian horses around the pyramids at dusk. Two stables near the Sphinx rent and lease horses.

The hokiest show

At night you can attend a sound-and-light show on the Giza Plateau. The pyramids and Sphinx are illuminated as the narrator tells the story of Egypt. It's as hokey as you'd expect, but few people regret attending. The English shows are held daily.

The best hotels in Giza

Most people stay in Cairo and visit the pyramids from there; however, waking up to see the Great Pyramid catch the first rays of dawn outside your window is a special pleasure. The best hotel in Giza is the **Mena House Oberoi**, *Pyramids' Road, Giza, +20 (2) 3377-3222; website: www.oberoimenahouse.com*, which is within walking distance of the pyramids. It was once a weekend palace for the Khedives, the Turkish viceroys who governed the area from 1867 to 1914, then a meeting place for Churchill and Roosevelt. Since 1973, it has been a luxury hotel. The management has kept the old wooden balconies and added air conditioning, restaurants, bars, and a swimming pool.

A less expensive hotel is the **Mercure Cairo le Sphinx**, *1 Alexandria Desert Road; tel. +20 (2) 3377-6444; website: www.accorhotels.com.*

Saqqara: The world's oldest stone complex

Saqqara, a necropolis 24 miles south of Cairo, is the oldest stone complex in the world, dating back to 2611 B.C. Although they'd never before worked with stone on such a grand scale, the Egyptians created a masterpiece here. As Egyptologist John West put it, "Starting architecture off with Saqqara is like starting automobiles off with the 1984 Porsche." The complex was designed by the legendary Imhotep, an Egyptian Leonardo.

The most important sight at Saqqara is the **pyramid complex of King Zoser**, which contains the world's oldest pyramid. Predating the Great Pyramid by a century, the 200-foot **Step Pyramid** was built of six *mastabas* (traditional rectangular tombs) of diminishing size. Inside are religious inscriptions. The complex often uses stonework to imitate organic material; the ceiling of the entranceway to Zoser, for example, simulates a roof of split logs. And the colonnade contains columns that look like they're made of papyrus stalks. (These may be the first stone columns built.) The colonnade leads into the Great Court, where Zoser and his successors ran races as part of a ritual physical fitness test called *heb-sed*.

To the south of the complex are the ruins of the **Pyramid of Unas**. The dilapidated outer stones make you wonder at the people waiting in line to get in. However, once you're inside, you'll understand—the interior is decorated with the finest hieroglyphic reliefs in Egypt. The **Pyramid Texts**, as they're known, tell the story of—and give advice concerning—the trip to the afterlife. Carved delicately out of slabs of white alabaster, the outstanding hieroglyphs in the tomb chamber are highlighted in blue paint dating back to 2330 B.C.

Surrounding the Pyramid of Unas are shacks covering stairways to the Persian tombs. (During Persian rule, mummies were buried in shaft tombs to prevent robbery.) See the Tomb of Ti, with its unusual wall decorations, and the Serapium, an ornate monument where the Persians buried sacred cows.

You can catch a minibus in Cairo to take you to Abu Sir in Giza Square at 6 a.m.; it drops you off about a mile from Saqqara. Or you can take a taxi directly to the site.

Luxor: Ancient Thebes and modern city

Built on the site of ancient Thebes, **Luxor** remains one of Egypt's most popular cities. As in most Egyptian cities, the grand sights here are crowded with natives looking to hustle naive tourists.

Ancient Thebes was the capital of Egypt during the Middle Kingdom, when Amon was the most popular of the Egyptian gods. Today the metropolitan area comprises the east bank (Luxor) and the west bank (Thebes). Luxor is small enough that you can see it on foot. The three main thoroughfares are Sharia Al-Mahatta, Sharia El-Nil, and Sharia Al-Karnak.

The most noble temple

The principal sight in Luxor is the **Temple of Karnak**. Noble is the only word that aptly describes this gigantic building. Its unusual design stems from its history: From the beginning of the Middle Kingdom until the time of Alexander the Great, each pharaoh added something new to the temple's architecture. A double row of ram-headed sphinxes guards the entrance to the Great Court, the temple's largest room, built about 1000 B.C.

Pass through the mighty outer pylon (an entranceway between two flattened pyramids) into the corner of the Great Court, which is surrounded by huge columns and flanked by the Triple Shrine of Amon on one side and the Temple of Ramses III on the other.

Continue on through Hypostle Hall, which features the Obelisk of Queen Hathsheput, carved from exquisite pink granite, and enormous columns that have been imitated in several Egyptian temples. Next is Transverse Hall, with 134 mono-lithic columns. Pass the southern buildings and pylons to the sanctuary. Filled with carved reliefs covering the mammoth stone blocks, this is the heart of the Karnak Temple. Past this are rooms, sarcophagi, and a sacred lake that is overshadowed by an enormous stone scarab. Take an entire afternoon to appreciate this.

The most unusual temple

The Avenue of the Sphinxes (which, as its name suggests, is lined with sphinxes) leads from Karnak to the most unusual temple in Egypt: the **Temple of Luxor**. Built with virtually no right angles, Luxor's rooms are set crookedly against one another. Six giant statues of Ramses II mark the main doorway, which is cut into the 80-foot Pylon of Ramses. Carved reliefs on the pylon illustrate Ramses' battle with the Hittites (tribes from Asia Minor who battled Egypt for control of Syria). Beside the pylon is a huge granite obelisk, the twin of one that stands in the Place de la Concorde in Paris.

Inside the temple court is the **Mosque of Abu el-Haggag**, a small building contrasting oddly with the general splendor of the temple. You'll pass the Colonnade of Amenhotep III, with its 14 pillars, on your way to the Sanctuary of Alexander the Great, which contains bas-reliefs of Alexander worshiping Amon.

A banana best

In the late afternoon, take a felucca to **Banana Island**, a palm-studded islet three miles upriver from Luxor. Here you can indulge in all the oranges, lemons, and, of course, bananas you can eat for next to nothing.

Luxor's best hotels

One of the two best hotels in Luxor is the **Hilton Luxor Resort and Spa**, *New Karnak, Luxor 13; tel. +20 (95) 237-4933; website: www1.hilton.com*. It has eight stylish bars and restaurants, a spa, and two infinity pools that overlook the River Nile.

Another good choice is the **Winter Palace**, *Corniche El-Nil Street; tel. +20 (95) 238-0425; website: www.accorhotels.com*. Built in 1886, this hotel is on the banks of the Nile surrounded by tropical gardens, just minutes from the Luxor Temple.

Luxor's best restaurant

The best restaurant in town is **El Kababgy**, overlooking Luxor near the Winter Palace.

The greatest collection of tombs

Across the Nile, in **Thebes**, is the greatest collection of tombs on earth. You can reach the hills of the west bank from Luxor via two tourist ferries. Once in Thebes, your best bet is to hire a taxi. Or consider a donkey. Thebes is too big and too hot to visit on foot. A donkey is certainly slower than a taxi, but it is also less than half the cost and can take you through areas too narrow for cars. (Also, it's much more fun.) The trail from the Valley of the Queens over the ridges to the Valley of the Kings makes an especially memorable donkey trip.

The best way to see the Valley of the Kings

Some 64 rulers are buried in the **Valley of the Kings**. Because the locations of the graves were selected haphazardly, a little effort is needed to see the seven most impressive tombs in chronological order.

Begin with the **tomb of Tuthmosis III**, the walls of which are covered with the complete text of the *Book of the Duat*, the most important guide to the afterlife.

Next is the **tomb of Amenhotep II**. The walls here are covered with glare-producing glass.

You can skip the famous **tomb of Tutankhamun**. Although its discovery in 1922 was front-page news (and the mysterious deaths of the exploration team started the Curse of the Mummy lore), it is the smallest and plainest of all the tombs—all the treasure was moved to the Cairo Museum. In addition, this tomb is always ridiculously overcrowded.

Next are the Ramses tombs. The **tomb of Ramses I** is followed by the **tomb of Seti I**, which is possibly the best-preserved on the west bank. The lower section of the burial chamber displays an incredible vaulted ceiling decorated with the 12 signs of the zodiac.

The **tomb of Ramses III** contains 10 unusual side chambers that show scenes from daily life (which are not found in other tombs). The artwork in the **tomb of Ramses VI** is more garish and fantastic than that in earlier tombs—Ramses VI ruled during the decadent 20th dynasty. This tomb also is noted for its ancient Greek and Coptic graffiti. One marking translates roughly as "Hermogines of Amasa was here."

The best of the Valley of the Nobles

The **Valley of the Nobles** is divided into five ticket regions. To see the best tombs, buy tickets 6, 7, and 8. The **tomb of Khaemet** has some of the best detail. The **tomb of Ramose** shows the radical departure Egyptian art took under Akhnaten. Reliefs show the pharaoh in scenes from family life, displaying affection, and showing his physical deformity.

The **tomb of Nakht** contains well-preserved paintings, some biographical, some inexplicable. The **tomb of Usheret** is notable for female figures, defaced by a Christian monk who lived in the burial chamber in the seventh century. The **tomb of Intefoger** has strangely insulting portraits. One shows an adult yelling at a child, "Your mother was a female hippopotamus!"

The Ramasseum

The **Colossi of Memnon**, two 70-foot statues, guard the **Temple of Ramses II**, also known as the Ramasseum. The temple contains the fallen Colossus of Ramses, which the poet Shelley described as "two vast and trunkless legs of stone, half sunk, a shattered visage." However, even the ruins are impressive—one ear measures three-and-a-half feet. The rest of the Ramasseum is in better condition, with relics depicting the Battle of Kadesh, astronomical charts, and rituals.

The tomb of the eight primordials

According to legend, beneath the **Temple of Medinet Habu**, which contains temples of Ramses III and Thutmose III, are buried the **eight primordials**— the Egyptian gods that existed before creation (as did the Greek gods Rhea and Kronos). Ramses' temple has pictures chiseled eight inches into the stone.

"The Most Splendid of All"

North of the Ramasseum is the cliff-side **Temple of Hatsheput**, known in Arabic as **Deir El-Bahari**, which translates as "The Most Splendid of All." Considered one of the most important architectural wonders of the world, Deir El-Bahari is the only monument to have been built partly against the cliff and partly into it. This is also the only temple in Egypt, and the first building in history, made to blend with and complement the landscape. Hatsheput (circa 1473 B.C.) was the only queen to dare crown herself pharaoh. The temple's broad walkway, the chapels to Anubis and Hathor, and the inscriptions here depict her descent from the god Amon.

Hathor: The magnificent temple

About 35 miles north of Luxor lies Dendera and the magnificent **Temple of Hathor** (the cow goddess and deity of healing), built about 200 B.C. A massive gate leads into the great courtyard of the temple, where the ceilings are decorated with the signs of the zodiac. Pass into the column-filled Hypostle Hall, the walls of which are covered with reliefs carved by priests seeking to preserve secret texts when Egyptian culture fell to the Roman Empire. The results are hieroglyphics so complex that archeologists cannot decipher them. A staircase leads to two rooftop chapels. One contains the famous circular zodiac.

The Mysterious Corridor surrounds the sanctuary, opening off into 11 chapels, one of which has a small opening in the floor that leads to the crypts. The purpose of this subterranean hallway is unknown, but its highly stylized reliefs are fascinating. If the crypts are closed, a guard will open them for you if you offer *baksheesh*.

Abu-Simbel: The most remote temple

At the far end of the Nile, 150 miles south of Aswan in the Nubian desert, is an awe-inspiring temple that seems to rise out of nowhere. Four 65-foot colossi of Ramses II guard the entrance to the structure, which was originally cut out of a cliff. Between and beside his legs are smaller statues of his queens and daughters.

As remarkable as the temple itself, is the fact that it was taken apart and moved. In the 1960s, it was dissected stone by stone and moved by archeologists after they learned it would be flooded by the new High Dam at Aswan.

The still beautiful temple lost some of its magnitude with the move. Formerly, it was part of a cliff overlooking the roaring Nile. Today, it is set beside calm Lake Nasser. Scientists took great pains to place the temple exactly as its original builders did so that during equinoxes the rising sun shines directly through the entrance, lighting statues 180 feet back in the sanctuary. Unfortunately, the statues have been badly mutilated. (No one knows by whom.)

Travel like Cleopatra

The best way to explore Egypt is aboard a **felucca**, the traditional sailboat that glides along the Nile. Because the river cuts through most of Egypt's towns and villages, following it gives you a complete view of the country. As you bob along, you'll pass women washing clothes in the river, fishermen pulling in their nets, and children playing along the river's bank.

Between Aswan, where most felucca journeys begin, and Luxor, where most of them end, the Nile passes many of Egypt's most important ancient monuments and temples. During this 140-mile sail, a felucca stops at one monument a day.

Of course, on a felucca journey, you must be prepared to rough it. Usually, you have no bathroom facilities—other than the Nile. And meals, while hearty and usually tasty, are prepared over a campfire. Your bed is on board, beneath the stars.

Spring and fall are the best times to sail. Be sure to bring sunscreen, a hat, toilet paper, and a flashlight. Women should not wear bikinis or skimpy bathing suits—they cause problems in an Islamic country. It takes about three weeks to cruise the entire length of the Nile. However, the Aswan-Luxor stint takes only about five days. Feluccas can be cheap or expensive. Shop around, and don't be afraid to bargain. Feluccas line the riverfront in Aswan and Luxor. Ask around on the waterfront at the Old Cataract Hotel in Aswan. Hotel clerks often can recommend a place to rent a boat. It is a good idea to get references.

Alexandria: The least Egyptian city

Alexandria was a very un-Egyptian city when it was founded by Alexander the Great in 330 B.C. It flourished as the cultural center of the world for 300 years, until the great library accidentally burned down during the reign of Julius Caesar, destroying more than half a million irreplaceable manuscripts. Modern Alexandria is an international city, small and clean and known for its Greco-Roman relics and its sandy beaches.

The **Greco-Roman Museum**, *Mathaf El Romani Street; tel. +20 (3) 486-5820; website: www.sacred-destinations.com/egypt/alexandria-greco-roman-museum*, houses a collection of artifacts from the days of Greek and Roman rule, including bas-reliefs, pottery, statues, jewelry, and marble pieces. Don't miss Room 9, which displays relics of the cult of the crocodile god Pnepheros, including a mummified crocodile. The museum is open daily from 9 a.m. to 5 p.m.

At the western end of town are the **catacombs of Kom el-Shoqafa**, burial chambers carved into rock 100 feet below ground. Built in the second century for a wealthy family that still practiced the ancient religion, the catacombs represent the last burst of native Egyptian sacred art. However, because the artisans were trained in Italy, the Egyptian gods have unmistakably Roman bodies. Reliefs depict a Roman-style Osiris making an offering to the deceased. Lesser gods hold bunches of grapes and Medusa heads. One statue of Anubis is even dressed in Roman armor.

Near Nasr Station is a beautifully preserved white marble **Roman amphitheater**, the only known Roman era amphitheater remaining in Egypt. Behind it lies a cistern and Roman bath. In 1963, when construction workers were building the foundation of an office building, the ruins were unearthed; archeologists continue to uncover artifacts here.

A relatively modern attraction in this ancient city of Alexandria is the 19th-century summer residence of the Egyptian royal family, the **Ras el-Tin Palace**. King Farouk forfeited its Throne Room, Gothic Hall, and Marble Hall when he abdicated in 1953 for a life of exile in Italy. It is now one of the official residences of the President of Egypt.

The **Fine Arts Museum**, *18 Menasha Street; open daily from 8 a.m. to 2 p.m.*, contains both a collection of modern Egyptian art and Alexandria's public library. Not far from the Mosque of Abul Abaas, along the corniche, it is the largest Islamic building in the city and has a beautiful courtyard. According to legend, the priest Abul Abaas rose from his tomb here to catch bombs falling on Alexandria during World War II.

At the western end of the corniche, where the Lighthouse of Pharos (one of the original Seven Wonders of the World) once stood, is the **Fort of Qait Bay**. Built by Sultan Bay in the 15th century from the remains of the lighthouse, the fort commands a sweeping view of Alexandria. Inside are a scale model of the 400-foot lighthouse and a naval museum.

The best case of mistaken identity

A 98-foot granite column erected in Alexandria in 297 A.D. was named **Pompey's Pillar** by Crusaders during the 13th century. Actually, the rose-colored column is a monument to the emperor Diocletian that was built by his troops. The most famous monument of ancient Alexandria, the pillar sits in a small public park on a hill where Diocletian once had a temple dedicated to the bull god Serapis.

The best way to get to Alexandria

Located 110 miles north of Cairo, bordering the Nile Delta, Alexandria can be reached easily by bus, plane, train, or car. Golden Rocket buses carry you between Cairo's Giza Square and Alexandria's Zaghloul Square. Make reservations if you plan to use the daily air-conditioned trains that travel between Cairo's Ramses Station and Alexandria's Masr Station. Shared taxis take the same route, but they cost more. EgyptAir's flight from Cairo departs daily.

The best dining in Alexandria

Alexandria has several excellent restaurants. Try the **Seagull restaurant**, *Al Agami Road; tel. +20 (3) 220-4370; website: www.seagullegypt.com*, an elegant seafood restaurant on the shore.

Lord's Inn, *around the corner from the San Stefano Hotel; tel. +20 (3) 546-2061*, offers continental cuisine in a gourmet setting.

Santa Lucia, *40 Safia Zaghoul Street; tel. +20 (3) 486-0332*, specializes in Greek dishes.

Egypt's best seafood restaurant

For the best seafood in Egypt, drive to the small town of Abu Kir, about 10 miles east of Alexandria. Here, four blocks from the central mosque, on the waterfront, is a famous restaurant called **Zephyrion**, *tel. +20 (3) 560-1319*. In business since 1929, Zephyrion has fresh fish, large salads, imported beer, and succulent shrimp.

Alexandria's best hotels

The best hotels in Alexandria are inexpensive. You won't have as great a choice as in Cairo, but you won't have to fight the crowds either.

The **MARITIM Jolie Ville**, *544 El Gueish Street, Sidi Bishr; tel. +20 (3) 549-0935; website: www.maritim.com/en/hotels/egypt/jolie-ville-hotel-alexandria,* has a pool, great views, and air conditioning.

Two rival beachfront hotels are the **Sheraton Montazah**, *Corniche Road, El Montazah; tel. +20 (3) 548-0550; website: www.starwoodhotels.com/sheraton/,* and the **Helnan Palestine**, *Kasr El Montazah; tel. +20 (3) 547-3500; website: www.helnan.com.*

Sinai: The most unusual landscape

Four wars have been fought between Israel and Egypt on the **Sinai Peninsula**. The southern Sinai Peninsula, with its high granite mountains and deep chasms, has some of the most unusual landscapes in the world. It's also the site of two popular beaches and one of the most famous mountains in history. The Sinai is heavily militarized. Police want you to keep to the main roads, but you can obtain permission to visit parts of the desert interior with a Bedouin guide. (You might even catch a glimpse of military exercises.) The Sinai heat can be unbearable, sometimes reaching 110° F.

Buses are the most affordable way to get to the Sinai. They depart Abassiya Station in Cairo for St. Catherine, Nuweiba, and Dahab. Most stop at Sharm El Sheikh, the southernmost town on the peninsula.

A car allows you more flexibility when exploring the Sinai. The main roads are well-maintained, but the drive from Cairo to Nuweiba is a good seven hours—and you won't find anywhere to stop along the way for gas or water.

Flying is fastest and easiest. **EgyptAir,** *website: www.egyptair.com,* flies from Cairo to Sharm El Sheikh.

Dahab: A golden town

When the Israelis occupied this town, they named it **Zahav** (Gold). It is split into two parts: a terrific beach and a Bedouin village of thatched huts and palm trees. The beach is never crowded and almost always sunny. In town, you can rent scuba gear for exploring the coral reefs.

A cheap accommodation option is to stay with villagers in their huts. This is a great way to get to know the people and to experience firsthand their lifestyle. But remember, the huts have neither toilets nor running water, and Bedouins are superstitious about having their pictures taken.

More luxurious accommodation is available at the **Swiss Inn Gold Beach**, *website: www.dahab.net.*

Nuweiba: The best beach

Nuweiba, a tourist village about 10 miles north of Dahab, has an even better beach. That's good, because this town doesn't have much else to offer, and the nearby Bedouin villages don't invite visitors. The bus to Nuweiba lets you off at the tourist office. You can rent scuba gear or sailing equipment at the Sailing Club. The best reefs are along the southern part of Nuweiba's beach. For more secluded diving, walk a quarter-mile south to what the locals call the Stone House.

Mount Sinai: The most commanding mountain

God gave Moses the Ten Commandments atop **Mount Sinai**, a remote mountain in the Sinai desert. A religious landmark, the mountain is dotted with tents and small chapels. The most interesting and difficult route to the 7,000-foot peak that the Arabs call Gebal Musa is up the 3,500 **Steps of Repentance**, supposedly carved out by just one monk to fulfill his pledge of penitence. An easier way to reach the peak is to take the camel path that begins directly behind the monastery. When the path and steps meet, look down at the 500-year-old cypress tree that marks Elijah's Hollow, where the prophet Elijah heard the voice of God. (There are now two chapels in the hollow.) At the mountain's summit is a small church, usually surrounded by dozens of tourists and pilgrims in sleeping bags.

You, too, can bring a sleeping bag and sleep on the mountain (but remember—it gets chilly). When you awaken, you'll see both Africa and Asia from the peak.

A comfortable place to stay is the **Concorde El Salam Hotel**, *White Knight Beach; tel. +20 (69) 360-1460; website: http://sharmelsheikh.concorde-hotels.com*, in Sharm El Sheikh town. It has its own private beach.

A Byzantine best

At the base of Mount Sinai is **St. Catherine's Monastery**, the oldest unrestored Byzantine complex in the world. Emperor Justinian had it built in 342 A.D. on the site of the Burning Bush, where God first recruited Moses to lead the Hebrews out of Egypt. Fortress-like walls protect St. Catherine's Monastery (named after the saint martyred in Alexandria). Inside are jewel-studded crosses, hand-carved furniture, and the Chapel of the Burning Bush. The monastery's library contains enough early Christian manuscripts to rival the Vatican, and the marvelous mosaic of the *Transfiguration of Christ* is one of the great treasures of early sacred painting.

Don't miss the Ossary, a separate building containing the bones of all the monks who have died at St. Catherine's over the centuries.

The best snorkeling in the Middle East

The best snorkeling in the Middle East is at **Yemenieh Reef**, off Aqaba, a Jordanian town just across the gulf from Nuweiba. Here, you can see 40 kinds of coral not found anywhere else in the world. Scuba and skin divers commonly cross the gulf to Aqaba (captured from the Turks in 1917 by the legendary Lawrence of Arabia), which has beautiful beaches and an excellent aquarium in its Marine Research Center. Ferries depart daily from Nuweiba for Aqaba at 11 a.m. and 3 p.m. You'll need a passport, of course, to make the crossing.

Hurghada: Egypt's best coral reefs

The sleepy little town of **Hurghada**, which lies 240 miles south of Suez and about 350 miles from Cairo, is one of the best places in the world for unspoiled scuba and snorkeling expeditions. The coral reefs here are the most beautiful in Egypt, and dozens of boats are available to take you to any one of the tiny reef islands. At Giftun El Saghir, a small island off Hurghada, the water is so clear that you can see 100 feet down to the rocky bottom. At the offshore island of **Shaab Um Qamar**, divers sometimes catch lobsters at night with their bare hands.

Everything in Hurghada centers around two landmarks: **Al-Dhar Mosque** and **Ugly Mountain**, which is, indeed, ugly. Hurghada is a good place to fish; it is teeming with barracuda, swordfish, sailfish, and tuna. You can rent bikes for a few dollars a day from a shop just north of the Al-Dhar Mosque. And about two miles north of that is the Red Sea Museum, which has a large collection of sea life, including sharks and sea lions.

The most comfortable place to stay is the **Sheraton Soma Bay Resort**; *tel. +20 (65) 356-2585/9; website: www.sheraton-somabay.com*, just south of town.

Tips on *baksheesh*

Baksheesh is a way of life in Egypt. Although only a minority of Egyptians pester foreigners, those who do expect *baksheesh* for the slightest things—opening a door, for example—and even more *baksheesh* for doing nothing. In a bazaar, you will be followed by a half-dozen children with outstretched palms. You should always travel with a pocketful of loose change and one-pound notes. However, give *baksheesh* only for services rendered. Two useful terms concerning *baksheesh* are *Shukran* (Thanks) and *Emshee!* (Get lost!).

THE BEST OF MOROCCO

Morocco is a land of *casbahs* (citadels), veiled women with painted toenails, belly dancers, minarets, and ancient *souks*. Its ancient cities have modern European sections, with tree-lined avenues, Parisian boutiques, sidewalk cafés, and luxury hotels. But each also has a *medina*, or old quarter, where you must navigate your way through a maze of narrow, twisting, cobblestone streets, arabesque archways, and cluttered bazaars.

Tangier—Morocco's port city

The port of **Tangier** on the country's northwestern tip attracts French, German, British, American, and especially Spanish travelers, who come via the hover-crafts that make daily trips between Tangier and Gibraltar and southern Spain. Its commanding position on the Straits of Gibraltar has made it a strategic military state, coveted by everyone from the Phoenicians to modern-day Spanish, British, French, and Germans. In 1923, Tangier was declared an international zone. In 1957, it became part of Morocco. Ask anyone who knows Morocco well, however, and he will tell you that Tangier is not Morocco. Its customs and culture, which retain vestiges of all those who have invaded it over the centuries, are too diverse to be truly Moroccan.

In addition to cafés, where Arabs and tourists alike sit for hours over cups of strong black coffee or sweet mint tea, Tangier has miles of uncrowded, golden beaches fringed by the Mediterranean to the north and the Atlantic to the west.

The legendary Garden of Hesperides, Tangier was once a haven for black marketeers and smugglers. Today, because of its low income tax and favorable climate, it has become a refuge for the world's wealthiest citizens.

The best marketplace

Tangier's *casbah*, or walled fortress, is very much the center of life here. It is built on the highest point of the city and juts up against the *medina*. You can reach it from the **Bab el Assa**, at the end of Rue Ben Raisouli in the *medina*. The white arched gateway into the *casbah* leads to an open courtyard called **Tabor Square**, which leads to Dar al Makhzen, the former sultan's palace (now a museum).

The *casbah* is really a huge marketplace. It is packed with people—vendors, shoppers, tourists. It is noisy. And it is filled with the smells of mint, spices, fresh camel meat, and fruits and vegetables.

The best place to stay

A relaxing and intimate place to stay in Tangier is **El Minzah Tangier**, *85 Rue de la Liberte; tel. +212 (539) 333-444; website: www.elminzah.com.*

The best castles

On the outskirts of the city are the splendid villas of the late Gianni Agnelli (Italy's Fiat magnate) and the late Malcom Forbes. The dime-store heiress Barbara Hutton lived for years in a storybook palace tucked away in a corner of the mysterious *casbah*. The palace has is now a museum and one of the city's major attractions.

The most magnificent city

Rabat, the present-day capital of Morocco, is home to one of the magnificent palaces of King Mohammed VI. Its entrances are protected by the personal guard of the royal family. You can see the full splendor of the guard on Friday morning, the Muslim holy day. It escorts the king, who rides in a gilded coach drawn by four white horses, across the palace grounds to the mosque. The weekly ritual is a dramatic reminder that King Mohammed is not only the head of state but also the religious leader of the country.

Ancient Fez

The old walled city of **Fez**, wrapped in a pink fog, is four hours by car from Rabat. Founded in A.D. 800, Fez is a renowned religious center. For 11 centuries, it was the epitome of cultural, artistic, and religious life in Morocco.

The *souk* of the woodcarvers in Fez is filled with the pleasant scent of cedar. Not so the *souk* of the tanners. Here, young men in short pants, standing thigh-high in steaming cauldrons of red, yellow, and purple dye, leap from vat to vat, dipping, pulling, and kneading the sodden camel, goat, and sheepskin pelts in the noxious liquids.

The world's oldest university

Karaouine University, which dates to A.D. 859, is the oldest university in the world. Today it is a mosque that attracts Muslims in droves. They believe that seven pilgrimages to Karaouine are the spiritual equivalent of one trip to Mecca.

The best place to stay

The best place to stay in Fez is the **Sofitel Fes Palais Jamai**, *Bab Guissa; tel. +212 (535) 634-331; website: www.sofitel.com*, a former sultan's palace located at the entrance to the bustling *medina*. It is one of Morocco's most luxurious hotels. Lavish tile murals, fine cuisine, and an unbeatable situation above the city combine to produce an extraordinary hotel in a former 19th-century palace.

The biggest palace

Meknes, less than 40 miles from Fez, is home to the sultan's gigantic palace, complete with storerooms, gardens, military barracks, and stables. At the beginning of the 18th century, this unbelievable complex housed the court and the imperial family of 600 wives and 1,500 children, as well as at least 50,000 slaves, servants, and eunuchs. The stables accommodated 12,000 horses, each with its own stall and valet.

The most imperial city

The imperial city of **Marrakech** was chosen by the sultans as capital of the 1,200-year-old Sheriffien Empire, which stretched from Spain to Timbuktu. Founded on the arid Haoux plain in the 11th century, Marrakech was a caravansary, a major port of call on the Sahara desert for camel caravans that linked Ghana with Fez and Algiers.

Today Marrakech is a city of brownish-pink houses, towering ramparts, and graceful minarets. This capital city boasts a dry, warm climate, luxurious hotels, colorful marketplaces, and an old walled quarter.

The liveliest spot in town

The heart of Marrakech is a vast public square adjacent to the *medina* known as **Djemma El Fna**, or Place of the Dead, which is in fact the liveliest spot in town. Long ago, the sultans displayed the heads of criminals and enemies defeated in battle around this huge square. Today it is filled with bazaars where you can shop for almost anything.

But more than a market, Djemma is the largest outdoor show in all North Africa. Storytellers, mimes, medicine men, sword swallowers, male belly dancers, and snake charmers perform for the crowds, each competing for the small coins that spectators toss in appreciation.

The most colorful festival

One of the most striking spectacles in the Arab world takes place in Marrakech in July. The **National Festival of Popular Arts**, which draws visitors from all over the world, is held amid the red-ochre ruins of the El Badii Palace.

The performers in the National Folklore Festival are not professionals. They are villagers, country people from the Sahara desert and the Atlas Mountains who have been selected by the festival directors to take part in the two-week extravaganza. For the performances, the stage is covered with layers of intricately woven Moroccan carpets spread to create an *Arabian Nights* setting. On either side of the stage, huge striped tents are set up to house the performers waiting their turn. In the foreground, separating the stage from the audience, is the outer edge of a rectangular pool, where, centuries ago, sultans frolicked with their harem favorites.

The best mint teas

Mint, in Moroccan, means hospitality. No guest gets away from a Moroccan household without several glasses of hot mint tea. Actually a mixture of green tea, anisette, vervain, marjoram, and mint, the tea is made according to strict rules. First, two to three teaspoons of green tea are placed in a pot. The pot is held high to aerate the tea, which is then served in tiny glasses. Guests must, according to custom, have three glasses.

One of the best places for tea in Marrakech is the **Dar Marjana**, *15 Derb Ettir, Ang Bab Doukkada; tel. +212 (44) 385-110; website: www.darmarjanamarrakech.com.*

The best silver factory in Morocco

Situated south of Agadir, along a caravan crossroads in south Morocco, is **Tiznit**. This tiny town is best known for its silver jewelry, which is made by local Berbers from the silver mined nearby.

The rooms in what the townspeople refer to as their "silver factory" are filled with handmade silver jewelry, serving trays, pots, and trinkets. In the front of the rooms sit small boys, apprentices who work in the factory in the morning and go to school in the afternoon. Expect to haggle, but you'll end up with good silver at cheap prices.

The tiny, muddy passageways that make up Old Town are crowded with street vendors offering rugs, pottery, jewelry, and spices. Everything is for sale. (Nothing is refrigerated.)

THE BEST OF ALGERIA

Algeria, Africa's second-largest country, is a sea of sand drifts. It is also a place where anything Western is in high demand; Algerians are willing to pay handsomely for Western goods of all kinds. The chief black market commodity is whiskey; you can resell a bottle of whiskey for six times your purchase price.

There is still a definite discrimination against women in Algeria; men eat at the table, while women cook and remain in the kitchen, for example. Change is coming slowly here, giving travelers a rare opportunity to experience a centuries-old culture.

The most fundamentalist town

In the very fundamentalist town of **Ghardaïa**, the few women on the streets are clothed and veiled from head to foot. They have one eyehole, through which they peer cautiously. Ghardaïa is the most prosperous town in the country and is inhabited, as it has been for more than 900 years, by the Mozabites, a strict Muslim sect that broke from the mainstream of Islam in the seventh century. The people use the same underground irrigation canals, live in the same cube-like houses, and worship in the same mysterious mosques as did their ancestors.

The world's biggest sandpile

The golden sand in the west is called the **Grand Erg Occidental**. Its white counterpart in the east is called the Grand Erg Oriental. Erg can be translated as "sand sea" or "desert of sand dunes." Either way, you get the idea. The vastness of it all will overwhelm you at times.

The best way to see Algeria

The **Trans-Algerian Highway** is the only road that crosses Algeria from border to border. It passes through the Sahara desert and covers the 1,100 miles from Morocco to Tunisia. The Highway is well-maintained. Gas stations are adequately spaced along the road. (But don't ever pass one without filling up.) Spare auto parts are a rare commodity, however, so carry with you anything you think you might need. The greatest attraction of traveling the highway is the chance it gives you to see the Sahara desert. Great sand dunes, with ridges perfectly carved by the wind, seem to go on forever, dwarfing the occasional camel train or group of palm trees.

A best for horse lovers

Horse lovers can spend two weeks in the saddle in Algeria. Riding is English-style, luggage is carried by a support car, and nights are spent at hotels, inns, private homes, or camps. Most tours involve four to six hours of riding a day.

THE BEST OF
ARGENTINA

Latins are tenderly enthusiastic. In Brazil they throw
flowers at you. In Argentina they throw themselves.
—Marlene Dietrich

Argentina has historically suffered the curse of politics; Argentine politics have been characterized by cruel military dictators, pointless border disputes with Chile, civil strife, high inflation, corruption, and general instability. But the country still has its charms.

No country in the world is as naturally suited for farming as Argentina, the second-largest country in Latin America. It has more than a million square miles of territory. An extraordinary three-quarters of this is suitable for cultivation, and the topsoil is as much as a yard deep. Argentina is also an exporter of oil and gas (to Chile), and its mines offer an abundance of minerals.

THE RICHEST REGION

The richest 10% of Argentine terrain is in **La Pampa**, the only part of the country that is cultivated. (The Argentines are careful about protecting their lands and stingy about the areas they farm). La Pampa is a treeless plain of the central, temperate-climate zone, with richness other countries can only dream about.

Nobody lives in poverty with the style and flair of the Argentines; even in its impoverished areas, Buenos Aires is as full of pizzazz as Paris itself. And Buenos Aires is a city of neighborhoods—that is what makes it so hospitable.

The **Plaza Dorrego**, in the heart of San Telmo, is Buenos Aires' answer to the Latin Quarter. Weekdays it is quiet, but on the weekends it is transformed into a bustling antiques market. Walk down Avenida de Mayo to see the Casa Rosada, the pink presidential palace. It is here that thousands of workpeople cheered political leaders Juan and Evita Péron. The square is surrounded by monuments.

La Boca is the city's oldest Italian section. It is also the poorest neighborhood in the city, distinguished by its colorfully painted wooden houses. The heart of the neighborhood is a touristy walkway, El Caminito, where painters hang out. La Boca's side streets are jammed with bakeries and butcher shops.

The **Recoleta** neighborhood is one of the most desirable in **Buenos Aires**. Located in the northern part of the city, it is home to a fashionable residential area, elegant restaurants, deluxe hotels, fine museums, and some of the city's finest shops.

The best restaurants

Cabanas Las Lilas, *Av. Alicia Moreau de Justo 516; tel. +54 (11) 4313-1336, website: www.laslilas.com* (in Spanish), is an elegant restaurant with the whole menu based on beef dishes.

Café Tortoni, *Avenida de Mayo 825; tel. +54 (11) 4342-4328*, is South America's oldest coffeehouse serving good Mediterranean food.

Indulge your inner Michelangelo at **Cumana**, *Rodriguez Pena 1149, Recoleta; tel. +54 (11) 4813-9207*, and create masterpieces on the paper tablecloths with the basket of color pencils provided while you wait for your food. The food is good too…and cheap. Try the empanadas or one of their pot stews which are filled with potatoes, eggplant, squash, and beef. If there's a queue, leave your name on the waiting list and come back later.

Buenos Aires' best nightclub

The best electronic music club in Buenos Aires is **Club Pacha**, *Av. Rafael Obligado y Pampa, Costanera Norte, 1428; tel. +54 (11) 4788-4280; website: www.pachabuenosaires.com*, which takes place in a huge, pink, art deco building beside the River Plate, usually on a Saturday night. This club is not for the faint-hearted. It does not really get going until 3 a.m. (it finishes at 8.30 a.m.), and is heaving. It has a separate dance floor outside on the river, which is a bit more relaxed. You can also buy a table in the VIP area, where you can chill out with champagne and watch beautiful people dance around you. Many of the world's top DJs regularly perform at the club, which is rated by many DJs as their favorite club in the world.

The best antiques

The weekend market in Buenos Aires at **San Telmo's Plaza Dorrego** is an antique-lover's dream come true. Hundreds of vendors, many selling quality stuff, for a fraction of what you'd pay most anyplace else, gather here every Sunday from early morning until about 6 p.m.

Calle Defensa is packed with antique dealers; heirlooms of once-wealthy merchant families—their fine china, their brocade-upholstered chairs, and their fanciful English hunting prints—are for sale here. And the prices are so low that they would embarrass most antique dealers.

The best tango

The best tango can actually be found on the streets of Buenos Aires. Head to San Telmo on a Sunday afternoon to see dancers strut their stuff. Tango shows are available all over the city…most are aimed at tourists but are still very entertaining and breath taking.

THE WORLD'S SOUTHERNMOST SKIING

The southernmost skiing in the world is in **Ushuaia**, where you can choose from five small ski centers. It is a beautiful and safe place to ski. And its residents are gracious. But the best thing about skiing here is the cost. Lodging and dining are inexpensive.

THE BEST WATERFALL

Iguazu National Park has the most beautiful waterfalls in the world. Taller than Niagara Falls and twice as wide, there are over 275 individual cascades stretching across two miles of river. There are hundreds of butterflies as well as many other species of wildlife.

The **Iguazu River**, born high in Paraguay, crashes down multiple steep falls to the lower Iguazu at the border of Brazil and Argentina. The river winds up in the River Plate, just as Niagara Falls winds up in the St. Lawrence.

THE BEST OF
AUSTRALIA

*"Don't worry about the world coming to an end today.
It is already tomorrow in Australia."*
—Charles M. Schulz

The world's oldest and smallest continent, Australia offers something for everyone. Nature lovers are fascinated by the Outback, with its rugged terrain and unusual animals. Divers explore the Great Barrier Reef, the largest coral reef in the world, stretching 1,260 miles along Australia's northeast coast. This coast is also the place to enjoy the world's best surfing. Sydney and Melbourne have big-city restaurants, nightlife, and shopping. And enormous cattle stations cover the interior of the country.

Australia is the world's most isolated country. Because of this, animals, birds, insects, and plants unknown to the rest of the world have evolved here. Nowhere else will you see kangaroos and koala bears, for example.

Also because of the country's isolation, the Aborigines, who have one of the most intriguing and ancient cultures in the world, were able to continue their way of life—living in harmony with nature—for thousands of years before Europeans arrived. Still largely uninhabitable and unexplored, this continent's vast desert heartland, known as the **Red Centre**, is made up of four great deserts that together occupy 1.2 million square miles.

Australia was formed when Europe and North America were still evolving. The last great geological shifts here took place 230 million years ago. However, some places in Australia date back 1 billion years. Ancient artifacts are stored in the **Great Western Plateau**, in the heart of Australia. A rock found near Marble Bar contained the remains of 3.5 billion-year-old organisms, the oldest forms of life yet discovered. And a dinosaur left his footprint in the rock near Broome.

Only slightly more than 21 million people live in Australia, an area roughly the size of the continental U.S. Yet this is one of the most highly urbanized nations in the world—almost 85% of all Australians live in or around the cities. Furthermore, Australia boasts one of the world's highest standards of living.

SYDNEY: THE NUMBER ONE CITY

Sydney—a huge city sprawling across 670 square miles—is the largest, oldest, and most cosmopolitan city in Australia. It is also naturally beautiful, built around a harbor and cradled by the fabulous Blue Mountains. Light-colored buildings and red-tile roofs stand out against the blue water and sky. Flowers bloom year-round. And the ocean laps at 150 miles of shoreline.

Life revolves around the harbor and the sea, where thousands of boats vie for space. Scantily clad sun worshipers flock to the city's 30-odd beaches. But Sydney's beaches are never as packed as those at U.S. resorts.

During the Australian summer (from November through February), the city is hot and humidity can make it hard for visitors used to cooler climates. It's fine if you intend to spend all your time on the beach but more uncomfortable if you wish to explore the city and journey around through the Sydney hills. Make the most of the efficient public transport system that includes buses, ferries and trains. (Sydney has one of the best transport systems in Australia, particularly post 2000 Olympics). However, during the winter, Sydney is mild and pleasant.

The summer heat brings Sydneyites outdoors and encourages light, comfortable and casual dress. At night, the inner streets of Sydney are overflowing with people, who eat outdoors and often party on until dawn.

The best view of Sydney

The best view of Sydney is from the 48th-floor of the glassed-in skywalk at the **Sydney Tower**, *tel. +61 (2) 9333-9222, website: www.sydneytower.com.au*. You'll be able to see the entire city, the Blue Mountains, and Botany Bay. What's more, the tower (which isn't square but round, constructed of steel, cement, and glass) has the fastest elevators in the Southern Hemisphere.

The best climb in Sydney

If views are your thing you'll also want to take in the Guided Bridge Climbs, *tel. +61 (2) 8274-7777, website: www.bridgeclimb.com*, to the top of the world famous **Sydney Harbour Bridge**. A climb will give you a 440-foot high, birds-eye view above Sydney Harbour. Climbs are run all day from dawn until the evening, offering you glimpses of the city at all stages of the day.

The best way to see Sydney

The **Sydney Pass** is the best bargain for sightseeing in Sydney. The pass allows you three, five, or seven days of unlimited use of the Sydney Explorer bus, the harbor shuttle, three different harbor cruises, all other Sydney ferry services, all Sydney buses, and the airport express bus.

The world's most unusual opera house

When work began on Sydney's ultramodern winged **Opera House**, *tel. +61 (2) 9250-7111; website: www.sydneyoperahouse.com*, in 1957, local residents, who called it the New South Whale and the Operasaurus, said it wouldn't fly. Much to its critics' chagrin, the opera house turned out to be the most beautiful in the world, praised from London to Hong Kong.

Designed by Danish architect Joern Utzon, the A$102 million structure on Bennelong Point, surrounded by Sydney's harbor, is topped by interlocking wing-shaped roofs that glitter with more than one million Swedish ceramic tiles. The acoustics are the best in the world. Take a tour of the building to see the treated timber panels, the tinted glass through which you have a view of the harbor, and the bright blue curtains. The opera house has a total of 980 rooms, four of which are performance halls, where concerts, operas, ballets, plays, and recitals are held. Rock'n'roll groups perform as well as symphony orchestras. One hour tours are available from 9 a.m. until 5 p.m. Book through the "Tours" section on the website.

Sydney's oldest quarter

The **Rocks,** *website: www.therocks.com*, a renovated area on the west side of Circular Quay, was notorious for its rough residents in the mid-1800s. Convicts, sailors, prostitutes, soldiers, whalers, and gangsters gathered on this rocky ridge, known as the Cradle of Sydney. For a map of the no-longer-seedy area, visit the **Information Center**, *104 George Street*, near the Overseas Passenger Terminal.

At the heart of The Rocks is **Argyle Place**, a peaceful park surrounded by pastel houses dressed with wrought-iron grills and balconies. The **Church of the Holy Trinity**, better known as the Garrison Church, was built in 1840. The second-oldest church in Sydney, it is the earliest example of Gothic architecture in Australia, with Gothic arches, mullioned windows, and a red cedar pulpit.

Sydney's oldest house, **Cadman's Cottage**, built in 1816, is just off Argyle Street. Circular Cove once came nearly to the door of this little homestead, built by John Cadman, superintendent of government boats.

The **Argyle Arts Centre**, *18 Argyle Street*, was built in 1820 by convicts as a three-storey warehouse. Today the sandstone building houses craft shops and antique stores. Notice the hand-hewn timber. (Convict labor came cheap.) You can buy hand-blown glass, beeswax candles, and pottery here. The center is open from 10 a.m. until 5.30 p.m.

From Argyle Street, take the **Argyle Cut**, a dank 300-foot tunnel hollowed out of solid stone by prisoners 140 years ago. It leads to Miller's Point.

At **The Rocks Flea Market**, *L6 Harrington Street; tel. +61 (2) 9280-8717,* some of the vendors sell one-of-a-kind Aboriginal pieces at reasonable prices. Other vendors include artisans who specialize in handcrafted puzzles, ceramics, and prints; soap and candle makers; and plant and flower sellers. What's more, some of the baked goods sold here are better than mom's.

The best picnicking

The best places to get away from the cement and steel that make up Sydney are the **Domain** and the **Botanic Gardens**, separated from each other by a highway. The Domain is a park with an emerald lawn perfect for picnics and naps on Sunday afternoons. Soapbox orators harangue crowds here with their personal views of the world. The Botanic Gardens are known for their exotic flora, including giant Moreton Bay fig trees and hothouses filled with orchids and ferns.

Australia's best art gallery

Near the Botanic Gardens is the **Art Gallery of New South Wales**, *Art Gallery Road; tel. +61 (2) 9225-1744, website: www.artgallery.nsw.gov.au,* divided into two sections, one housing Renaissance to 20th-century art, the second housing Impressionist and modern works. The new wing, with its angled white walls and views of the harbor, is more attractive. Look for works by Australian artists William

Dobell, Sidney Nolan, and Russell Drysdale. Admission is free. The gallery is open every day from 10 a.m. until 5 p.m. Late closing every Wednesday: 9 p.m.

The Southern Hemisphere's best private gallery

Holdsworth Galleries, *86 Holdsworth Street*, is the biggest art gallery south of the equator, with a great collection of contemporary Australian artists that changes every three weeks. Among the displays are paintings and sculptures by Sidney Nolan, Sali Herman, Margaret Olley, and Arthur Boyd. The gallery is as lovely as the works it contains. Admission is free. It is open daily until 5 p.m.

The world's most beautifully situated zoo

Taronga Zoo and Aquarium, *Bradleys Head Road, tel. +61 (2) 9969-2777, website: www.taronga.org.au,* on a peninsula jutting into Mosman Bay, has the most beautiful setting of any zoo in the world. It offers a view of the harbor (*taronga* means "water view" to the Aborigines) and 75 acres of bushland. Among other strange creatures, you can see koala bears, emus, platypuses, dingoes, kookaburras, and wombats. A special underground part of the zoo houses nocturnal animals, which you can see under red light. The rainforest aviary is also worth seeing. The zoo is open 9 a.m. until 5 p.m. daily.

The worst prison

Fort Denison, on a little island in the harbor, was known as Pinchgut among Australia's early convicts, because of the starvation rations meted out here. The fort was never actually used to protect Sydney, although that was its original purpose when it was built in 1857. You can still see cannons and cannonballs in the round Martello Tower, which is used as a tidal observation station. Tours of the fort depart Wharf Two on Circular Quay twice daily on Monday and Tuesday and three times daily Wednesday through Sunday. To book a tour visit the Sydney Harbour National Park Information Centre, *The Rocks, tel. +61 (2) 9247-5033.*

The best times to visit

Each year, Sydney hosts a number of different festivals. The entire month of January is one big festival, with plays, exhibitions, operas in the parks, sailboat races, and food and wine fairs. Then comes the Royal Sydney Easter Show, which is a huge country fair with animal exhibitions; Royal Gardens Week; Carnivale; and the Blessing of the Fishing Fleet. And don't miss the Gay and Lesbian Mardi Gras, one of the biggest gay festivals held anywhere in the world.

Sydney's favorite pastimes

Surfing (which many schools teach as a physical-education course) and wind-surfing are the two passions of Sydneyites. A sign on trains admonishes, "Surfers, be considerate. Don't block aisles with your boards."

Australia's best restaurant

Forty minutes north of central Sydney is the **Berowra Waters Inn**, *Berowra Waters; tel. +61 (2) 9456-1027; website: www.berowrawatersinn.com*, the finest restaurant in Australia. Chef Dietmar Sawyere produces innovative Australian dishes. Unfortunately, you can't get here by road; you must fly or take a boat. The restaurant is open for lunch Friday to Sunday and dinner Thursday to Saturday.

Sydney's best dining

Sydney's best restaurant (in 2011, it came 26th on the coveted S.Pellegrino World's 50 Best Restaurant's list) is **Quay**, *Upper Level, Overseas Passenger Terminal, West Circular Quay; tel. +61 (2) 9251-5600; website: www.quay.com.au*, where you will enjoy a great view of the bridge and Opera House. Master chef Peter Gilmore will dazzle you with rare and subtle dishes. Open for lunch Tuesday through Friday and dinner Monday to Sunday.

Tetsuya's, *529 Kent Street; tel. +61 (2) 9267-2900; website: www.tetsuyas.com*. Innovative cuisine by chef Tetsuya Wakuda who succeeds in combining Eastern and Western cuisine. Since it's difficult to get a table, it is best to reserve at least one month in advance. Open for dinner Tuesday through Saturday and for lunch Saturday.

The best place for seafood is **Doyle's on the Beach**, *11 Marine Parade, Watson's Bay; tel. +61 (2) 9337-2007*. They claim this was Australia's first seafood restaurant when it opened in 1885. Enormous plates full of battered fish are served. And the setting is lovely—a sandy beach lined with little boats. The only drawback is that the restaurant's charms are known, and it's crowded. Open seven days for lunch and dinner.

Also at Watson's Bay is **Doyle's on the Wharf**, *Fisherman's Wharf, tel. +61 (2) 9337-6214*. Take your food to go or sit *al fresco* in their outdoor seating area. Open 10 a.m. to 6 p.m. daily.

Bellevue Hotel, *159 Hargrave, in Paddington; tel. +61 (2) 9363-2293; website: www.bellevuehotel.com.au*, has a history dating back to the 1880s and is one of Sydney's most popular pubs. It also has a good menu.

Sydney's top hotels

Sydney's finest hotel is the **Four Seasons Hotel**, *199 George Street; tel. +61 (2) 9250-3100; website: www.fourseasons.com/sydney.* Overlooking the Opera House and the harbor, it has luxurious rooms and an attentive staff.

Three close seconds are the **Sir Stamford**, *93 Macquaire Street; tel. +61 (2) 9252-4600; website: www.stamford.com.au,* the **InterContinental**, *117 Macquarie Street; tel. +61 (2) 9253-9000; website: www.ichotelsgroup.com,* and the **Observatory Hotel**, *89-113 Kent Street; tel. +61 (2) 9256-2222; website: www.observatoryhotel.com.au.*

Another attractive small boutique hotel in Sydney's historic Rocks, is the **Russell**, *143a George Street; tel. +61 (2) 9241-3543; website: www.therussell.com.au.*

The hottest nightlife

Although Sydney's drinking laws are strict, the local residents manage to have a rowdy good time anyway. Bars close at 11 p.m. during the week, and after midnight on weekends and holidays (depending on the area). But many Sydneyites belong to private clubs, where you can get beer into the wee hours of the morning. The clubs often have live shows, slot machines, and food.

If you want to hear good live music, your best bet is **The Basement**, *7 Macquarie Place; tel. +61 (20) 9251-2797; website: www.thebasement.com.au.*

If you'd like to barhop but don't want to drive or risk getting lost, go to the **Holiday Inn Menzies**, *14 Carrington Street*, where 20 pubs share one roof. Each has its own character and clientele, from snooty and expensive to cheap and blue-collar.

The liveliest neighborhood at night is **King's Cross**, a combination of Greenwich Village and a red-light district, where Darlinghurst, Potts Point, and Elizabeth Bay meet. Darlinghurst Road and Macleay Street are the main thoroughfares. Sydney's best bar is here, the **Bourbon and the Cross**, *Darlinghurst Road; tel. +61 (2) 9358-1144; website: www.thebourbon.com.au.* The piano bar provides entertainment in the early evening and jazz combos jam later on.

Sydney's oldest pub is in the **Hero of Waterloo Hotel**, *81 Lower Fort Street; tel. +61 (2) 9252-4553; website: www.heroofwaterloo.com.au,* in The Rocks. Built in 1804 as a jail, it became a rousing pub in the rip-roaring 1800s. Today it is a peaceful place to have a drink while sitting beside a fireplace.

The bluest mountains

The **Blue Mountains** really are a vivid blue. Oil released by the mountains' eucalyptus trees reflects the blue light rays of the sun on these saw-toothed peaks, just 50 miles from Sydney. Head for **Katoomba**, where you can take the Scenic Railway, the steepest in the world, up the mountains. Or you can ride the Scenic Skyway, a cable car dangling above a deep chasm.

Nearby are the enormous Jenolan Caves and the giant waterfall at Govett's Leap, near Blackheath.

The world's most imaginative water festival
Surf Carnivals are hosted by the Surf Lifesaver's Association. Members of clubs compete against each other in beach and rescue oriented events that can include swimming and running, kayak-like surf skis, and surf boat races. Some events are for individuals and may combine several disciplines in ironman/ironwoman races and others are team events. For more information, contact the **Surf Life Saving Association of Australia**, *website: www.slsa.asn.au.*

CAPITAL CANBERRA

Canberra, the national capital, is a city planner's dream. Designed and built to function expressly as Australia's capital, it is free of traffic and unsightly shopping malls. At its heart is a large man-made lake. Throughout the city are parks, and the broad avenues are lined with trees. An American named Walter Burley Griffin designed the city in 1913, after winning an international competition for the job. However, Australia's parliament didn't actually meet here until 1927.

While it is not on the coast and doesn't have sunny beaches, Canberra is fast becoming an artistic and intellectual enclave. It boasts the new National Gallery, one of the finest art museums in Australia, and great restaurants and bars.

Canberra's top sights
The city's best-known landmark is the **Captain Cook Memorial Water Jet**, which shoots six tons of water 450 feet into the air from 10 a.m. to noon and 2 p.m. to 4 p.m. every day. Part of the fountain is a nine-foot globe illustrating the routes followed by Captain Cook.

More important, however, is the **Australian War Memorial**, *tel. +61 (2) 6243-4211, website: www.awm.gov.au*, on Anzac Parade, a beautiful structure honoring the 100,000 Australians who died fighting in the world wars. Bronze panels inscribed with their names cover two enormous walls. The memorial contains excruciatingly realistic paintings of the wars, as well as old biplanes, tanks, and bombs.

The **Australian National Gallery**, *tel. +61 (2) 6240-6411; website: www. nga.gov.au*, on the shores of the lake, has an outstanding collection of works by both Australians and foreigners. It also has a good restaurant with a lovely view of the lake. The memorial is open daily.

There's also **Old Parliament House**, *King George Tce; tel. +61 (2) 6270-8222, website: www.oph.gov.au,* which opened in 1927. It housed the Federal Parliament until 1988 and allows visitors the chance to experience Australian democracy and history through its grounds and exhibitions. The public can also contribute to the Museum of Australian Democracy by taking part in the unique Great Badge Swap. This is where a badge is donated by the individual that has been worn to communicate an important message or special meaning. And the badge just might end up featuring in the museum's exhibition.

Canberra's **Carillon** is one of the largest in the world, with 53 bells, the largest weighing more than six tons. A gift from Britain, the tall white pillar stands at the northern end of the Kings Avenue Bridge. Recitals are given here on Sundays and Wednesdays.

The **Botanic Gardens**, *Clunies Ross Street, website: www.anbg.gov.au,* is a maze of footpaths and bridges that guide you over little ponds and through gardens with carefully labeled Australian plants and flowers. Open daily from 8.30 a.m. to 6 p.m. on weekdays and until 5 p.m. on weekends.

For a glimpse of Australia's early pioneer life, visit **Blundell's Farmhouse**, *Wendouree Drive, tel. +61 (2) 6272-2902; website: www.nationalcapital.gov. au.com,* off Constitution Avenue. Built in 1858, the cottage's three rooms are filled with pioneer furnishings. It is open from 12 p.m. until 4 p.m. Thursdays and Saturdays. Admission is free.

Twenty-five miles southwest of Canberra is the 12,000-acre **Tidbinbilla Nature Reserve,** where you can see local flora and fauna and feed the kangaroos. This unspoiled bushland is open daily from 9 a.m. to 6 p.m.

The best eating and sleeping

The Boat House by the Lake, *Grevillea Park; tel. +61 (2) 6273-5500, website: www.boathousebythelake.com.au.* Well situated on the shores of the lake, the peaceful atmosphere is complemented by excellent light dishes.

Gus's Coffee Lounge, *Bunda Street; tel. +61 (2) 6248-8118*, is a tiny place with a pleasant outdoor terrace surrounded by flower boxes. You can linger over a meal here, reading Gus' selection of magazines and newspapers. Save room for the cheesecake, which is out of this world.

Tall Trees Motel, *21 Stephen Street, Ainslie; tel. +61 (2) 6247-9200; website: www.talltrees.bestwestern.com.au*, two miles from Canberra, is an inviting lodge named for the tall trees that surround it. All rooms have views of the gorgeous gardens and are supplied with electric blankets. (It gets cold here during the winter.) The lodge has a laundry room and a lounge with a television and tea-making equipment.

THE BEST OF MELBOURNE

Melbourne rivals Sydney as Australia's most attractive city. Both coastal cities have three million residents. However, Melbourne is more of a European city and offers more cultural opportunities than Sydney; it also has fewer tourists and lower prices.

Melbourne's weather is less pleasant than Sydney's. It rains more frequently, and winters can be grim, drizzly, and gray, without the excitement of snow. While Sydney's beauty is natural, Melbourne's is man-made.

Because it is a planned city, Melbourne's road network forms a grid pattern, making travel within the city easy. The city's architecture is sophisticated, especially along wide and gracious **Collins Street**, the banking capital of Australia. Lush parks and the Yarra River add greenery to the cityscape.

Although Melbourne was founded in 1835 by a group of Tasmanian entrepreneurs, it didn't actually take off until 1851, when it became the center of Australia's biggest and longest gold rush. A product of the time, Melbourne is mostly Victorian in appearance.

Melbourne's must-sees

The **National Museum**, the **Museum of Science**, the **state library**, and **LaTrobe Library** are combined in one huge, interconnected complex between Swanston and Russell streets. The strangest sight in the entire complex is the stuffed body of a well-loved Australian racehorse, Phar Lap, who died a mysterious death in the United States. Also look for Australia's first car and first airplane.

Melbourne's creepiest sight is the **Old Melbourne Gaol**, *Russell Street; tel. +61 (3) 8663-7228; website: www.oldmelbournegaol.com.au.* Built in 1841, it was used as a prison until 1929. More than 100 prisoners were hanged here, including the infamous bushranger Ned Kelly. The somber building is now a museum, with death masks of notorious criminals and records of the early convicts transported to Australia from Britain. (Some were exiled for incredibly minor crimes.) You can also stand in the dock, sit in the judge's chair or join in the crowd in the public gallery by taking part in the iconic Old Magistrates' Court, where criminals were given their sentence.

Melbourne's best square, **Federation Square**, *website: www.federationsquare.com.au*, is the place where Melbournians meet and has become a cultural and entertainment destination as well. Juxtaposed against St Paul's Cathedral it's a modern landmark and a space where people can eat, enjoy art and concerts, protest and take in The National Gallery of Victoria (NGV), The Australian Racing Museum, The Australian Centre for the Moving Image (ACMI) and SBS Radio.

The **National Gallery**, *tel. +61 (3) 8620-2222; website: www.ngv.vic.gov.au*, housed in the Cultural Centre Complex on St. Kilda Road, has a good art collection and exhibits from overseas. The Great Hall has a beautiful stained-glass ceiling, and fountains fill the central courtyard. The gallery is closed Mondays.

King's Domain is an enormous park that houses the Shrine of Remembrance, a World War I memorial; Governor LaTrobe's cottage, the original Victorian government house prefabricated and sent from England; and the Sidney Myer Music Bowl, an outdoor concert hall.

The **Royal Botanic Gardens**, also within King's Domain, are the most beautiful in Australia. Laid out beside the Yarra River, they include lakes, a rainbow of flowers, and a surprising number of wild animals, including water fowl, cockatoos, and possums. You can have tea and scones by the lake.

The best bets for fitness freaks

On weekends, you can rent a bicycle at the Botanical Gardens or Como Park and then bike the trail along the Yarra River.

If canoeing is more your style, you can rent a canoe or a rowboat at Studley Park in Kew. The **Studley Park Boathouse**, *website: www.studleyparkboathouse. com.au,* is open from 9.30 a.m. until 5.30 p.m.

The best place to jog is the two-and-a-half-mile running track around King's Domain Park. The Tan Track, as it is known, is where Melbourne's fitness freaks race at dawn and dusk.

The world's strangest football game

Australian football—a game all of its own that is based on Gaelic football—is a strange combination of soccer and rugby. You can see this one-of-a-kind game at the Melbourne Cricket Ground, known locally as the MCG, in Yarra Park, one of

Australia's biggest sports stadiums. The best football game, if you can get tickets, is the Grand Final in September, Australia's biggest sporting event.

Best sporting destinations

Melbourne is one of Australia's best sporting destinations. Apart from the world famous MCG, mentioned above, Melbourne also hosts the Australian Open Tennis, the Australian Formula One Grand Prix, the Australian Rules Grand Final and the Spring Racing Carnival. This latter event includes the Melbourne Cup, considered one of the world's richest horseracing events, and is commonly known as "the race that stops the nation". There is also the Bells Easter Classic, a world cup surfing fixture at Torquay.

Melbourne's best restaurants

Le Restaurant, *25 Collins Street; tel. +61 (3) 9653-7744*, in the Sofitel Hotel on the 35th floor, combines a great view with a sophisticated meal.

Melbourne is famous for its ethnic cuisine and there are a number of metropolitan areas where visitors are guaranteed to find something to their liking. Try Victoria Street in Richmond, Brunswick Street in Fitzroy, Smith Street in Collingwood, Toorak Road and Chapel Street in South Yarra or Fitzroy Street and Ackland Street in St. Kilda. Chinatown (Little Bourke Street), is another popular spot and a thriving neighborhood with pagoda-style buildings. The aroma of hanging ducks and ginseng fills the air. The best restaurant here is **Flower Drum**, *17 Market Lane; tel. +61 (3) 9662-3655; website: www.flower-drum.com*. Turkish, Chinese, and Mideastern restaurants are sprinkled along Sydney Road.

The Richmond district, just east of downtown Melbourne, off Swan Street, is also heavily ethnic, with Greek, Turkish, Argentine, Indian, Vietnamese, and Mexican restaurants. Lygon Street, near the university, is a busy row of Lebanese and Italian restaurants.

The best hotels

One of the great landmarks of Melbourne is the **Windsor Hotel**, *111 Spring Street; tel. +61 (3) 9633-6000; website: www.thewindsor.com.au*. Recently restored, the Victorian hotel has a domed Grand Dining Room, decorated with silk wallpaper and crystal chandeliers. Visiting statesmen stay here.

Hotel Como, *630 Chapel Street; tel. +61 (3) 9825-2222; website: www. mirvachotels.com.au*, also has great service and good accommodation.

The best nightlife

Melbourne has very good live music at **Bennetts Lane Jazz Club**, *25 Bennetts Lane*; tel. +61 (3) 9663-2856; website: www.bennettslane.com.

You can also enjoy theater or music at **The Arts Center**, *100 St. Kilda Road;* tel. +61 (3) 9281-8000; website: www.theartscenter.net.au. Luciano Pavarotti praised the Melbourne concert hall as the finest in the world.

The Esplanade Hotel, *11 The Esplanade, St. Kilda; tel. +61 (3) 9534-0211; website: www.espy.com.au*, is a beautiful old place on the St. Kilda Esplanade that has been the home of Melbourne and possibly Australia's live music for about a century. Traditionally bathers from the beach would take the time for a few cool drinks at the "Espy" after a day out but it's now one of the best places to see live acts on any night of the week on one of three stages. Many of the acts are free. Even the website is worth a look, if you want a taste of the Epsy's style, with its uniquely quirky and artistic presentation.

Best festivals

There is such a wide range of festivals and events to enjoy in Melbourne you could be entertained here all year round. Some of the highlights include the Melbourne International Film Festival in July/August aired in beautiful old theatres of the city. There's the Melbourne Fringe Festival in September/October showcasing local and regional music, arts, comedy and dance. The Melbourne International Comedy Festival in March/April is one of the three largest comedy festivals in the world. Moomba is held in March and is a large community festival. The streets of St. Kilda, Brunswick, Lygon, and Chapel Street also host annual festivals characteristic of these different areas of Melbourne.

Most scenic drive

The route south of Melbourne on the coast towards Adelaide is known as the **Great Ocean Road** and Australia's most scenic drive. Officially it is a 150-mile stretch between Torquay and Warrnambool and passes the beautiful beach areas of Lorne and Apollo Bay and then the 12 Apostles, dramatic natural limestone stacks in the sea.

Queensland, Australia's northeastern province, is a diverse land made up of many different worlds: the fluorescent Great Barrier Reef in the Coral Sea, the Aboriginal reservations, the Daintree Rainforest, the gold and opal mines in the desert fringe, and the sacred natural art galleries in the Outback.

The best of Brisbane

Complete with a surfing subculture (at nearby Surfer's Paradise on the Gold Coast), is the city of Brisbane. Homes in Queensland's sprawling capital city sport red-tile roofs and blue swimming pools. The hot sun fosters a casual dress code—button up shirts and jeans are probably more common than suits and ties even in the workplace and singlets and thongs (flip flops) are worn widely.

Founded as a penal colony for convicts supposedly too tough to be sent to Sydney, Brisbane was originally home to Australia's mining and agricultural industries. Today, tourism is making a bid for first place in the local economy.

While in Brisbane, stop by **Queensland Aboriginal Creations**, *199 Elizabeth Stret; tel. +61 (7) 3224-5730*; run by the Department of Aboriginal and Islanders Advancement. You can buy tribal masks, musical instruments, weapons, and bark paintings.

SouthBank, *tel. +61 (7) 3867-2051; website: www.visitsouthbank.com.au*, just across the river from the CBD has become a major inner city meeting and socializing point for local families and tourists. The gardens contain a series of lovely river-side promenades, rainforests and golden sand beaches where people converge for barbecues, varied cuisine and the live performances and free events held all year round.

Brisbane also has two fabulous multi-ethnic regions in the inner city where varied dining, festivals, markets, and cultural events take place. These are the predominantly Asian-twinged **Fortitude Valley** precinct with its Chinese eateries, festivals, markets and nightclubs and **West End** in South Brisbane which has a Greek, Indian, and alternative flavor to its bookshops, shops, and organic cafes.

Brisbane Forest Park is an oasis of eucalyptus trees and tropical birds just outside Brisbane, about 7 miles from the CBD on the Mt. Nebo Road. Another park closer to the city is the Mt. Coot-tha Botanical Gardens, with its carefully designed walking paths. You can also call in to the **Sir Thomas Brisbane Planetarium** in the gardens, *tel. +61 (7) 3403-2578*, the largest in Australia.

The best place to see cuddly koalas is the **Lone Pine Sanctuary**, *Fig Tree Pocket, tel. +61 (7) 3378-1366, website: www.koala.net*, west of Brisbane. About

100 of the little bears live here, along with kangaroos, emus, and other Australian animals. You can hold the koalas and feed the kangaroos by hand.

The place to stay in Brisbane is the **Sofitel Brisbane Hotel**, *249 Turbot Street; tel. +61 (7) 3835-3535, website: www.sofitelbrisbane.com.au.* Rooms are beautifully furnished and offer views of the Brisbane River.

Another good bet is the **Hilton International Brisbane**, *190 Elizabeth Street; tel. +61 (7) 3234-2000; website: www1.hilton.com.*

CAIRNS: TROPICAL BEST

Cairns is a beautiful, fully-restored, tropical town filled with the aromas of coffee, sugarcane, and orchids. You can walk from one end of Cairns to the other. The jungle encroaches wherever someone hasn't mowed their lawn or raked pesky mangoes from their yard.

A languid town, Cairns sprawls along the northern fringes of the Great Barrier Reef, overlooking blue Trinity Bay. The ramshackle houses, surrounding jungle, and fields of sugarcane lend the town a colonial mystique. Palm trees sway in the wind, and tropical fruits are mainstays of the local diet. Cruise and reef ships line the oceanfront.

Cairns' real attraction is the nearby Great Barrier Reef, which is described below.

Cairns' best hotels
Cairns does have a celebrated hotel or two, including **Mercure Harbourside**, *209-217 The Esplanade; tel. +61 (7) 4051-8999; website: www.mercure-harbourside.com.au.*

Palm Cove, not far from Cairns, has a jet-set resort called the **Sebel Reef House**, *tel. +61 (7) 4055-3633; website: www.reefhouse.com.au*, where bougain-villea scents the air and palm trees rustle in the wind. The resort's restaurant is good.

Australia's best caravan park
Australia's best—and most exotic—caravan park is **Ellis Beach**, 15 miles north of Cairns. It is situated among coconut palms, with views of Double Island and right next to the rainforest.

The Great Barrier Reef

Extending 1,260 miles, from New Guinea to the Tropic of Capricorn, the **Great Barrier Reef** passes along the coast of Queensland. Containing more than 2,000 coral reefs, coral islands, and cays, the reef is home to the world's greatest variety of marine life, nearly 1,400 kinds of sea creatures. It is a must-see if you are in Australia. The coral forms stunning natural patterns, and clear and brightly colored fish swim in unison.

Scuba divers from around the world come here to swim among the exotic fish. If you'd rather, you can walk across much of the reef at low tide, when the water recedes. Do take care though as it can damage the coral. (Wear tennis shoes, the coral is sharp.) Or you can go beyond the danger zones around this coral paradise and swim to your heart's content.

Australia's best island

Green Island is the best place to stay while exploring the reef. You can see the submarine world through windows at the island's **Underwater Coral Observatory** or from one of the glass-bottom boats that depart the island regularly.

The beaches that edge the mile-square island are empty except for driftwood trees. Cool coconut palm groves offer refuge from the hot sun. Blue and white herons prance along the sand paths. The cheapest way to get to the island is to book a trip with Great Adventure Tours in Cairns. You get a boat ride to and from the reef.

A beautiful reef resort is **Dunk Island**, *website: www.dunk-island.com*, where you can sleep in a beachfront cottage and spend your days snorkeling, swimming, walking in the rainforest, and playing golf and tennis.

Australia's best beach

The white crescent of **Whitehaven Beach** on Whitsunday Island on the mid Queensland coast is one of the most photographed beaches in Australia. Four miles of natural, white, silica sand stretch out on a beautiful arc of coast in contrast to the blue of the sea.

Queensland's best market

Take one of Queensland's best trips on the **Historic Scenic Railway**, *website: www. ksr.qr.com.au*, from Cairns to **Kuranda** or the **Skyrail Rainforest Cableway**, *tel. +61 (7) 4038-1555, website: www.skyrail.com.au*. Kuranda has an outdoor market, *website: www.kurandamarkets.com.au*, open daily from 9 a.m. until 3 p.m. featuring the works of local artists and craft workers. Locally designed items are available such as handmade cards, souvenirs and jewelry from native opals and sapphires.

One of the best things to do in Kuranda is to follow one of its walking tracks which include a list of must-see sites. The **Kuranda Backstreets Walk**, 1,200 metres, 35 minutes, is a particularly interesting one that shows you how locals live including the Djabugay indigenous settlers and more recent arrivals. The local architecture includes tropical colonial to homemade and modern styles.

Tarzan's favorite: Queensland's rainforests

Not far from Brisbane are misty rainforests where orchids scent the air and parrots sing from thick canopies of leaves hundreds of feet in the air. More than 800 kinds of trees grow in these forests, many with buttressed trunks that form church-size caves. Giant ferns, orchids, ginger plants, and organ-pipe fungi grow together in a thick web that blocks out the sun. You can swing like Tarzan from thick vines. Butterflies, tree frogs, snakes, and bugs make their homes here. (The best time to visit is during the less-buggy dry season, from May to November.)

The rainforest closest to Brisbane is at **Mount Glorious**, a 45-minute drive away. Slightly farther on, at **Mount Tamborine**, are six rainforest parks. While hiking here, stop at the Maiala Rainforest Café to enjoy English tea served with fresh scones, jam, and thick cream, while savoring the fragrance of jasmine and watching colorful parrots. Just two-and-a-half hours south of Brisbane is the **Lamington Plateau**, where you can stay at **Binna Burra**, *tel. +61 (7) 5533-3622; website: www.binnaburralodge.com.au*, or **O'Reilly's Lodge**, *tel. +61 (7) 5502 4911; website: www.oreillys.com.au.*

The densest and least-spoiled rainforests are 1,000 miles north of Brisbane (closer to Cairns): Kurando, Lake Eachem, Lake Barrine, Daintree River, and Cape Tribulation.

A number of private bus services run from Cairns to Cape Tribulation including SunPalm, *tel. +61 (7) 4087-2900; website: www.sunpalmtransport.com*, Coral Reef Coaches, *tel. +61 (7) 4098-2800; website: www.coralreefcoaches.com. au* and Cape Trib Connections, *tel. +61 (7) 4032-0500; website: www.capetribconnections.com.*

Peacocks and parrots roam Cape Tribulation, which is also where the **Daintree Rainforest,** said to be the oldest on earth meets the Great Barrier Reef. It is the only place where two World Heritage areas meet. The controversial new road that cuts through the forest is threatened by roots reaching down from branches to reclaim the red mud.

Wear long pants, long sleeves, and a hat to protect yourself from bugs and thorny plants. (Look out for ticks, which are unusually tenacious here; the wait-a-while plant, which has savage thorns; snakes; and leeches.)

For information on transportation to the rainforests, contact the **Queensland Travel Centre**, *website: www.destinationqueensland.com.*

AUSTRALIA'S OLDEST RESIDENTS

The Aborigines lived in Australia for at least 39,000 years before Britain sent its prisoners to colonize the country. On the shores of Lake Mungo in western New South Wales, evidence remains of a cremation that took place 30,000 years ago. And caves on the Nullabor Plain and a Bass Strait island were occupied 20,000 years ago. Anthropologists estimate that 300,000 aborigines lived in Australia before 1770. They spoke 500 different languages.

The Aborigines believe in the Dreamtime, an age that existed at the dawn of creation and is still present, a timeless otherworld linking the past, present, and future. Mythological characters from the Dreamtime, painted by the Aborigines on rocks, can be seen in the **Nourlangie Rock** in the Northern Territory and at other places throughout the country.

North of Cairns, in Laura, is the **Quinkan Reserve**, which boasts three rock galleries. Some of the paintings date from 13,200 B.C. The cracked and over-hanging rocks were chosen because they face east and the rising sun.

The best of the three galleries is the **Split Rock Gallery**, a natural gallery displaying ancient Aboriginal cave paintings. Two routes lead from Cairns to the gallery. The easier of the two is through the Outback; the more interesting but riskier route is via Cape Tribulation through the jungle. You will need a GPS to find the rock walls that are decorated with the murals, because all traces are invisible from the road.

Aboriginal people still continue the artistic ways of their forefathers, decorating weapons, tools, and totems with colorful religious patterns and figures. Tribal dancers hold on to the steps and music symbolizing events in The Dreamtime. One of the best times to observe Aboriginal dance, music and costume is at a Corroborree, or ceremonial meeting of Australian Aborigines. At Corroborees Aborigines act out events from the Dreamtime. Performers often cover their bodies in white or ochre paint to aid in the story telling. One of the most popular bands in Australia in recent times has been **Yothu Yindi**, with both Aboriginal and non-Aboriginal members who combine traditional Aboriginal music with guitars and drums.

Australia's 160,000 Aborigines maintain their tribal traditions mainly in northern and central Australia. (Queensland is populated with more Aborigines than any other state.)

About two-thirds of the Aborigines are living a relatively modern lifestyle in the big cities but many remain marginalized through poor health, education standards, and alcoholism.

Wujal Wujal, an Aboriginal reserve, is in the Daintree Rainforest, 30 miles from the nearest town of Helensvale. This village of impoverished shacks is littered with crashed cars, mysteriously parked on end, nose down, against trees. This position represents the ritual return to Dreamtime in Aboriginal paintings.

The world's most mysterious rock

An island-size red monolith called **Uluru** (it's officially called Uluru/Ayers Rock, encompassing its original Aboriginal name and the English translation, but is commonly called Uluru nowadays) lies in the heart of Australia. The largest rock on earth, it draws thousands of curious visitors and is part of a national park run by Aboriginal tribal elders. Situated in the Northern Territory, 200 miles southwest of Alice Springs, it could be considered the navel of the Australian Outback.

The Pitjantjatjara people attach religious significance to Uluru. On the north surface of the rock is a series of caves and grooves known as the Skull. The Pitjantjatjara believe this area of the rock served as the camp of their ancestors in the Dreamtime before the world began. They perform initiation ceremonies here.

Resorts have been built near the rock. The **Sails in the Desert Hotel**, *Ayer's Rock, Yulara Drive; tel. +61 (2) 8296-8010; website: www.ayersrockresort.com. au,* named after the white sails that crown its roof, is the best one, with good restaurants.

The best time to visit Uluru is during the Australian winter, from May through September, when rain makes the desert flower. Temperatures are in the 70s, rather than 140° F as they can be in the summer.

A TASTE OF THE OUTBACK

Australia's great **Outback**, a vast, hot, wilderness land in the heart of the continent, is inhabited by leathery stockmen and Aborigines. A little known land, it stretches from the heart of Australia to the northwest. It is still referred to as the Back of Beyond. Cattle graze on million-acre ranches, or stations as they are known in

Australia, on dusty turf that conceals diamonds, iron, aluminum, and uranium.

To really get to know the Outback, arrange a farm or ranch stay. For more information, contact **Bed and Breakfast Australia**, *website: www.babs.com.au* or *www.bed-and-breakfast.au.com*.

Or live like a ranch hand at **Escott Lodge Resort**, *Escott Station, Burketown; tel. +61 (7) 4748-5577*, a rambling cattle ranch in the wilds of northern Queensland. You'll stay in a rustic guest cottage on the homestead, eat with the ranch hands, and get acquainted with the cattle. Don't expect a luxurious, California-style dude ranch. The place has a bar, a swimming pool, and electricity, but you are not pampered with resort-type service. You won't spend your days enjoying planned recreational activities—life on a station involves hard work. If you're up to it, tag along with the stockmen and watch the bulls being castrated. Or you can help out with more palatable jobs, such as breaking horses, catching crocodiles, and fishing. You also can canoe on the Nicholson River and go on a wild-pig shoot.

The most gem-studded land

The Outback, in places, is paved with gems. Towns in the region have such names as Sapphire, Rubyvale, and Emerald and are connected by dirt roads made from piles of earth heaped up by old-time miners. From time to time, valuable gems overlooked by miners are found in the dirt.

Finding a sapphire, emerald, or ruby could turn a vacation into a jackpot. A book on Australian gems advises that "although it's not recommended that gem hunters should begin to dig up roads in search of stones, many fine gemstones have been found on the sides of roads." The odds against finding a gem on the road are like those against winning big in Las Vegas. But in the road, you don't have to pay to play.

It's not as easy as stepping from your vehicle and picking up a rock or two along the road; however, you could get lucky. Roy Spencer, a 12-year-old boy, did. He picked up the Black Star of Queensland, a 1,156-carat sapphire, in a field. It was cut to a 733-carat star sapphire valued at $450,000.

It's hard to see stones in the road. That sparkle you spy is most likely quartz or shards of glass from countless windshields that have been shattered along the way. Giant road trains—tractor trailers that tow huge dollies packed with freight or cattle—roar along the dirt tracks, shooting up rocks that demolish windshields. Because of this, most Australian vehicles that travel through the bush are outfitted with wire windshield guards or curved plastic shields.

The best way to set off on an Outback mining journey is to rent a camper in Sydney and then head north for the gem fields. Vans are well equipped, but you will need a few extra items, such as a shovel, a block and tackle, a spare gas can, a thermos, and some plastic bowls. Small refrigerators that run on 220 volts, generators, or porta gas are provided. Finding water can be a problem. The bore water brought up by windmills is drinkable, but it acts as a laxative. Carry your own supply.

Mining licenses cost $15, but you don't need one for just a few days. Just don't try your luck on any claims you see pegged out.

Emerald is the first of the gem-field townships in Queensland. Beyond this town are the fields near the mining village of **Sapphire**, a dingy huddle of slapped together shacks and tents. The main post office is a tiny one-room shanty. The Rough and Ready Pub is just down the dirt road.

If you don't manage to find a gem on your own, you can buy some in this region and sell them in the U.S. for a fine profit. One Yankee miner recently gave up on the quest for gems and bought one instead—a star sapphire (in Sapphire, of course) for A$30. Back in the United States, the stone was appraised at twice that.

If you'd rather search for the world-famous Australian opal, head for **Coober Pedy** or **Lightning Ridge**, in the center of the country, where 90% of the world's opals are mined. Coober Pedy is an underground town on the edge of the formidable Simpson's Desert. Miners in this 120° F desert live in underground caves, where the temperature is an even 65° F.

Opal buyers throng to this settlement to buy wholesale opal rock clusters or polished opals. Dutch buyers predominate.

The best Outback festival

This honor belongs to the **Birdsville Races**, held annually in a remote town in Queensland, one of the harshest, remotest corners of the continent. But the shifting sands, perspiration, flies, and broken vehicle axles do little to dissuade more than 5,000 people from descending on the Outback town every September for a horserace. Birdsville lies on the fringe of the Simpson Desert more than 745 miles from the sea in any direction.

The races have become regarded as an iconic Outback event and a good enough reason for campervans, four-wheel-drives, and light planes to venture out in their thousands to sample a weekend of frivolity in the middle of nowhere. The races are one of those quintessential, quirky, Aussie bush events in which the actual races are really an addition to the fun.

Traveling boxing tents, rodeos, booze, sun, sand dunes, rough roads, museums, galleries, and friendly crowds form the non-stop entertainment that starts well before and ends well after the last horse has left the turf. The official race program is a two-day extravaganza that begins on the first Friday of September. Entertainment includes evening gala events with famed pop or country and western stars, bush poetry readings, a rodeo where the audience can wrestle steers themselves, and auctions selling memorabilia from previous years.

WESTERN AUSTRALIA—THE MOST FAR AWAY LAND

Western Australia, the westernmost province, is a long way geographically and culturally from Sydney and the east coast. It's a gigantic region of natural beauty and a small population. Only 300,000 people live outside the capital Perth, in an area four times the size of Texas.

The hottest town in Australia is in this province. **Marble Bar** has an average annual temperature of 96° F.

The most beautiful sights in Westralia, as this region is known in local slang, are the fields of wild flowers. These are no ordinary fields and roll to the horizon, a patchwork quilt of blue, purple, red, and orange. Between August and October, more than 7,000 native species (some not found anywhere else on earth) blossom here. The most famous fields are near Albany on the southern coast and Geraldton, north of Perth.

Westralia also houses Australia's best ghost town. **Coolgardie**, once home to 15,000 rowdy, brawling gold miners, is now deserted except for tourists. Old covered wagons remain on the main street, where 29 hotels and bars once thrived. In nearby Kalgoorlie, the **Goldfields Exhibition**, *Bayley Street; tel. +61 (8) 9026-6090*, displays memorabilia from the gold rush of the 1890s, which brought nearly 200,000 miners to Westralia.

Kalgoorlie was the area's largest mining town, with two stock exchanges, seven newspapers, and some of the most expensive real estate in the country. Kalgoorlie still mines gold, but the pace has slowed.

The **Kimberley Plateau** raises its flat head in the northern corner of Westralia, covering a region larger than California but home to only 6,000 brave souls. The green Fitzroy River carves a gorge through the limestone plateau, its water filled with sharks, crocodiles, and stingrays. Caves once used by the Aborigines as burial grounds can be seen at Windjana.

THE BEST OF PERTH

Perth, the largest city on Australia's west coast, is the most isolated city in the world. Adelaide, the closest town, is more than 1,000 miles away. It takes three days to get to Perth by train from Sydney. Because of their isolation, the one million residents of Perth are close-knit and friendly.

Perth has many parks and wide-open spaces, miles of great beaches, good hotels, and a wide variety of ethnic restaurants. But best of all, it has the most ideal weather in Australia, more like the Mediterranean than Down Under. Although it's not as hot as Sydney, it offers more continuous hours of sunshine.

Perth's pride

King's Park, *tel. +61 (8) 9480-3600*, a 1,000-acre wilderness area, tops Mount Eliza and offers panoramic views of Perth. At its heart is a fountain dedicated to pioneer women. If you lose track of the time, check the floral clock. King's Park is a place to stroll at your leisure, enjoying some of Australia's exotic flora and fauna. When you tire, stop for a snack at the park's restaurant.

Other top sights

The **Art Gallery**, *tel. +61 (8) 9492-6622; website: www.artgallery.wa.gov.au*, is one of the best art museums in Australia. It is a dramatic modern building that cost $10 million to build. Masterpieces by Van Gogh, Cézanne, Picasso, and Monet are displayed, as well as works by contemporary Australian artists. The gallery also hosts the unique Artbar, where food, drinks, and music are on offer.

Look for the "Art of the Western Desert," created by the Panunya, a tribe of Aborigines. Open 10 a.m. until 5 p.m. daily.

The **Old Mill**, at the end of Narrows Bridge in South Perth, ground flour during the gold rush in the 1800s. Today it houses colonial tools and artifacts.

Perth's best district

In Fremantle, the attractive port city of Perth, there are a number of attractions amongst the colonial architecture including many fine restaurants, colorful markets, vibrant cafes, interesting art galleries and museums.

Stop into any one of the three **Western Australian Maritime Museums**, *website: www.museum.wa.gov.au/maritime*, in this area for their relics of Dutch shipwrecks and submarine tours. There is also a historic **Round House** by the sea, the oldest building in Western Australia.

The **Fremantle Prison**, *The Terrace, tel. +61 (8) 9336-9200; website: www.fremantleprison.com.au,* has a catacomb of tunnels and you can shop in the colorful **Fremantle Markets**, *cnr Henderson St & South Tce; website: www. fremantlemarkets.com.au,* where over 150 stalls open daily in the historic Victorian building. You can also get ferries from Fremantle to **Rottnest Island,** which is a wildlife reserve 12 miles off the coast. With its world-class beaches and abundant flora and fauna, this little island is worth a visit.

Perth's best restaurants
The best place to eat in town is **Fraser's**, *Fraser Avenue; tel. +61 (8) 9481-7100; website: www.frasersrestaurant.com.au,* which boasts a panoramic view of the city from King's Park and exciting cuisine. Taste the exquisite seafood and stop by for one of the irresistible wine and cheese evenings, boasting the finest Australian wines and foreign cheeses. Excellent dining is to be had at the **Fremantle Yacht Club** and fishing boat harbor.

Perth's most pleasant hotels
Celebrities stay at the **Parmelia Hilton**, *14 Mill Street; tel. +61 (8) 9215-2000; website: www.hilton.com.* Excellent service is the main attraction.

The **Hotel Rendezvous**, *Esplanade, Scarborough; tel. +61 (8) 9245-1000; website: www.rendezvoushotels.com,* was built on the beach and has spectacular views.

Other good hotels are The Orchard, *tel. +61 (8) 9278-2222,* the Perth Parkroyal, *tel. +61 (8) 9325-3811,* and the Sheraton Perth, *tel. +61 (8) 9224-7777.*

Perth's best bets
Burswood Restaurant and Casino, *Great Eastern Highway; tel. +61 (8) 9362-7777; website: www.burswood.com.au* is the largest resort complex in the Southern Hemisphere and the second-largest gaming floor anywhere in the world.

Australia's best foods
Australia's culinary delights often have strange names—but don't let that stop you from trying them. Look for Moreton Bay bugs and Victorian yabbies (both are crustaceans, not insects); Queensland snapper, coral trout, Tasmanian scallops; and shrimp from anywhere along Australia's 35,000-mile-long coastline. If you can find it, try some kangaroo-tail soup. For dessert, order pavlova, a delicious fruit, whipped cream, and meringue concoction.

Australian wines have become world famous and been compared favorably to those produced in France. Australia has about 60 wine growing regions, but the prime producers are in the Barossa Valley near Adelaide, Swan District near Perth and Hunter Valley near Sydney.

Top travel tips

The best way to save on the cost of rail travel within Australia is to purchase an Austrailpass (similar to the Eurailpass in Europe) before you leave home. First-class and economy versions are available, and the cost depends on class and the length of your stay rather than distance traveled. For more information, check out *website: www.gsr.com.au.*

The best way to see the Outback is by train. Two routes are especially scenic.

The transcontinental **Indian-Pacific**, *website: www.railaustralia.com.au*, runs from Sydney on the Pacific Ocean to Perth on the Indian Ocean. This route cuts through the Great Dividing Range and the pasture country to the west, the mining country around Broken Hill, along the shores of the Great Australian Bight, and across the vast expanse of the dry Nullabor Plains. The trip takes three days. Book a few months in advance—berths are in demand, particularly in September and October, when the wild flowers are blooming.

The **Ghan** runs from Adelaide on the south coast to Alice Springs in the center of Australia, skirting the beautiful Simpson Desert and its dry salt lakes. The train has an entertainment car with slot machines, a hairdresser, a gift shop, VCR rentals, and video games for children.

THE BEST OF
AUSTRIA

Austria—the land of Mozart, Strauss, Schubert, and Mahler—is the music capital of Europe. Instead of "muzak", classical music is played in elevators and offices. School children learn to play musical instruments at an early age. And Austria's yearly classical music festivals draw music lovers from around the globe.

Vienna alone supports four major symphony orchestras, two opera houses, and a host of theaters.

The world's best music festivals

The **Salzburg Festival** is the world's leading and most famous festival (we'll tell you more about the Salzburg Festival on page 94). Two other charming festivals, which are held in Vienna, are the **Haydn Festival** and the **International Chamber Music Festival**. Tickets to these music festivals are cheapest if you purchase your tickets in Austria. For more information contact the Austrian National Tourist Office, *tel. (in the U.S.) +1 (212) 944-6880; website: www.austria.info.*

THE BEST OF VIENNA

Vienna, the capital of the Hapsburg Empire for 600 years, is one of the loveliest cities in the world. Magnificent palaces, theaters, and ballrooms from its days of glory remain throughout the city. The best way to explore Vienna is on foot, and the best place to begin is the **Ringstrasse**, affectionately known as the Ring.

The most beautiful avenue in Vienna

One of the most beautiful avenues in the world, the Ring circles Vienna's old quarter. Most of Vienna's major sights line this shaded, tree-lined boulevard created by Emperor Franz Josef in December 1857. You can walk the most picturesque section of the Ring in 45 minutes. (You can walk the entire Ring in two hours.)

Begin at the 600-year-old Vienna University, near the Schottentor (Scottish Gate), and work your way around the Ring past the Stadtstheater, Europe's leading German-language theater; the neo-Gothic Rathaus; the Greek-style Parliament building; the Hofburg Palace; the Natural History Museum; and the Art History Museum. Then continue past the great opera house, the Imperial Hotel, and the town parks (as well as the airline bus terminal).

Vienna's number-one attraction

The most important sight in Vienna is the **Hofburg Palace**, *Michaelerplatz 1, Burgring; website: www.hofburg-wien.at*, once the winter residence of the Hapsburgs. Built in the 13th century, it has been embellished with every architecture style up to modern day. More a city than a palace, it is now filled with museums and government offices.

The great entranceway to the Hofburg, the Michaelertor, is on the Michaelerplatz flanked by two grand fountains. On the left as you enter are the Imperial Apartments, where you can see the exercise equipment of Emperor Franz Josef's beautiful, reclusive wife Sisi, who was obsessed with her figure (more than 100 years before it was fashionable to be so).

Beyond the courtyard to the left is the gateway to the Schweizerhof, the original nucleus of the Hofburg. The 13th-century Schweizerhof was named for the Swiss Guards who watched over the ruler. The Hofburgkapelle (the chapel), where Mozart and Schubert played, is in the courtyard of the Schweizerhof. Today, the Vienna Boys' Choir sing here on Sundays during the summer and on holidays.

The Hofburg also contains the **Imperial Treasury**, where you can see the ancient Imperial Crown, encrusted with gems and dating back to 962 A.D.; objects said to be made of unicorn horn; the elaborate cradle designed for Napoleon's son; and an agate bowl once thought to be the Holy Grail.

In the Augustinerkirche of the Hofburg is the **Chapel of St. George**. It contains 56 urns holding the hearts of the Hapsburgs. However, the chapel is not just a place of death. Maria Theresa and Francis of Lorraine were married here, as was Napoleon, by proxy, to Marie Louise.

The world's best horsemanship

The **Spanish Riding School**, located in the Hofburg, trains the noble white Lipizzaner stallions that descend from the Spanish horses imported to Austria by Emperor Maximillian II in the 16th century. The horses dance to Viennese music, guided by expert riders wearing the traditional gold-buttoned brown uniform and gold-braided black hat. For a list of performance dates and to book tickets, see the website (*www.srs.at*). If you can't get tickets for an actual performace, you can still see these amazing animals during one of their morning exercise sessions, usually held between 9 a.m. and noon. **Spanische Reitschule**, *Michaelerplatz 1, A-1010 Vienna; tel. +43 (1) 533-9031; website: www.srs.at.*

Gothic architecture at its best

The most important gothic structure in Austria is the early 12th-century **St. Stephan's Cathedral**, *Stephansplatz 1; tel. +43 (1) 513-7648*. Most of the Gothic touches were added in the 14th and 15th centuries. Climb the 345 steps to the top of the 450-foot church spire for a view of Vienna.

Inside, the black marble baroque altar is carved with illustrations of St. Stephan being stoned to death. The pulpit, designed by Anton Pilgram between 1510 and 1515, is carved with the heads of the early fathers of the church (Augustine, Gregory, Jerome, and Ambrose), as well as animals symbolizing the sins. Pilgram's own face peers out from the stairs.

Another masterpiece is contained in the cathedral: the tomb of Frederick III, created by Nikolaus of Leyden from 1467 to 1513. It is covered with carvings representing good and evil and topped with a marble statue of the emperor in his coronation robes.

Beneath the cathedral in the catacombs are the internal organs of 56 Hapsburgs minus the hearts, which are in the Church of the Augustine Friars. The bodies are in the Imperial Burial Vault at the Church of the Capuchin Friars. (The reason behind separating the body parts was that if one church burned down, all the Hapsburg remains would not be lost.) You also can see the foundations of the original basilica, which burned in 1258.

Maria Theresa's favorite place

Schönbrunn Palace, west of town, *Schönbrunner Schlossstrasse; website: www.schoenbrunn.at*, was the summer home of the Hapsburgs from 1695, when it was built, to 1918, when the last Hapsburg emperor, Charles I, abdicated. Marie Theresa ruled Austria from here while raising 16 children (Marie Antoinette was one of them) and fighting a war for her right to the throne. She redesigned the palace, and today it is much as she left it.

Often compared to Versailles, the Schönbrunn contains 1,441 rooms (45 can be visited) and a vast baroque garden. The rococo palace theater, once the stage for Max Reinhardt's famous acting school, still houses a drama school. See the collection of royal carriages; the room where Napoleon stayed; the Millions Room, a highly ornate rococo room with gold-framed mirrors and Indian paintings; and the Great Gallery, with its frescoed ceilings.

The Schonbrunn is also home to the oldest zoo in Europe, designed in 1752 by Jadot. It is probably the only baroque-style zoo in the world.

The favorite park of the Viennese

Prater Park, *Prater 9; website: www.prater.wien.info*, across the Danube River, is famous for its Ferris wheel, the Riesenrad. (The best view in Vienna is from the top.) The park was the royal hunting ground until 1766, when Emperor Joseph II opened it to the public.

The three-mile-long Hauptallee leads through the center of this garden-filled park. Lined with chestnut trees, this road is a great place to bike ride. Avoid the Krieau section, where thieves lurk.

Austria's greatest museum

If you see only one museum in Vienna, make it the **Kunsthistorisches Museum** (Art History Museum), *Burgring; tel. +43 (1) 525-244-025; website: www.khm.at*, which is across the Ringstrasse from the Hofburg. The greatest museum in Austria, it houses the paintings, sculptures, jewels, and bibelots collected by the Hapsburgs from 1500 to 1918.

The Kunsthistorisches Museum looks more like a palace than a museum, with its columned windows, enormous doors, broad central staircase, heraldic patterns, painted ceilings, and high cupola. Spread through seven buildings, it can be confusing, and the easiest way to see it is to ramble. Be sure to see the works of Pieter Brueghel the Elder in Gallery X, Dürer's works in Room 15, Giuseppe Arcimboldi's surreal works in Room 19, the Titians in Gallery I, the Tintorettos in Gallery II, the Raphaels in Gallery III, and Vermeer's works in Gallery VIII.

Vienna's other top museums

The **Österreichische Galerie Belvedere**, *Prinz Eugenstrasse 27; website: www. belvedere.at*, contains modern, baroque, and church art. Located in the baroque

Belvedere Palace, which was built by Hildebrandt between 1714 and 1723, the gallery is divided into three parts. Modern artworks are kept in the Upper Belvedere. Look for the works of Gustav Klimt (1862-1918), many of which are embellished with gold. The Lower Belvedere, where the beloved Prince Eugene (who protected his country from the Turks) once lived, is now the Museum of Austrian Baroque. The Orangerie houses the Museum of Medieval Austrian Art.

Albertina, *Albertinaplatz 1; tel. +43 (1)534-830; website: www.albertina.at,* near Augustinerbastel, has the greatest collection of drawings by old masters in the world. The etchings of Durer are the biggest attractions. Also here are works by Rubens, Fragonard, and other masters. (Reproductions are usually on display, for conservation reasons.)

The **Naturhistorisches Museum** (Natural History Museum), *Burgring 7; website: www.nhm-wien.ac.at,* across the street, houses the world's oldest-known sculpture, the *Willendorf Venus,* created in Moravia about 2900 B.C. You'll find this ancient fertility figure in Room 11. The five-inch limestone carving of a plump woman represents the mother goddess.

The **Akademie der Bildenen Kunste** (Academy of Fine Arts), *Schillerplatz 3; website: www.akademiegalerie.at,* near Getreidemarkt, is the respected art school that rejected the young Adolf Hitler after he failed the entrance exams. Some say this rejection fueled Hitler's anti-Semitism. (He claimed Jewish professors kept him out.) Established in 1692, the academy houses the impressive triptych *The Last Judgment* by Hieronymus Bosch.

Neue Hofburg, a wing of the Hofburg, has a collection of Roman sculptures from the ancient city of Ephesus, which were found on the western coast of Turkey. The museum also houses musical instruments, including the pianos of Beethoven, Schubert, and Mahler.

The world's best boys' choir

The world-famous **Vienna Boys' Choir** performs every Sunday and religious holidays from January 1 through late June and mid-September through December 31. The performances are held in the Imperial Chapel of the Hofburg. Tickets range from 36 euro to 63 euro ($48 to $85) and can be purchased at *www.mondial-reisen.com/en.* Purchase your tickets in advance and get to the church early to get a good seat.

Austria's finest musical experience—and Europe's most beautiful opera house

A night at the **Staatsoper**, *Opernring 2; tel. +43 (1) 51444-2315; website: www.staatsoper.at,* is the finest musical experience you will have while traveling in Austria. This opera house is regarded as the most beautiful in Europe. The Vienna State Opera, one of the finest opera companies, is accompanied by the Vienna Philharmonic, one of the world's finest orchestras.

If you plan on attending this magical experience in May, June, September, or October, order your tickets two to three months in advance. Get tickets from the opera house website (*www.staatsoper.at*). You should pick your tickets up four days before your chosen performance time and remember to bring your passport and confirmation letter. The cheapest tickets are sold at the ticket booth an hour before the performance.

Café culture at its coziest

The Viennese have gotten the café down to an art. Cafés have been a way of life in Vienna since the Turks retreated in 1683, leaving their sacks of coffee beans outside the walls of the city. People spend hours in cafés, sipping coffee, chatting with friends, and reading newspapers. (Cafés usually supply an assortment of international newspapers.)

Café Hawelka, *Dorotheergasse 6; tel. +43 (1) 512-8230; website: www. hawelka.com,* is a dark café with black chairs, coat racks, seats upholstered in red and brown stripes, and heavy curtains. It draws an assortment of people including students, old people, artists, and businessmen. Caricatures and drawings line the walls of this café, once frequented by Trotsky and his contemporaries. Orson Welles came here to soak up the atmosphere and prepare for his role in the film *The Third Man*. English and American newspapers are available.

Café Central, *763 Herrengasse 14; tel. +43 (1) 5333-76424; website: www.wurstunddurst.com,* is another literary hotspot that was a hangout for intellectual and political figures such as Sigmund Freud and Vladimir Lenin at the turn of the century. Set in an enclosed courtyard, it is decorated with frescoes, marble columns, and fountains. It serves the best *topfenstrudel* (flaky pastry filled with sweet cheese cream) in Vienna.

Café Schwarzenberg, *93 Kärtner Ring 17; tel. +43 (1) 512-8998,* is a 120-year-old café with oak-paneled walls, mirrors, and a white tile ceiling. They have a pianist who always draws a crowd.

Vienna's best restaurants

The elegant **Mörwald**, *Kärtnerstrasse 22; tel. +43 (1) 9616-1161*, with its winter garden in the Ambassador hotel serves Viennese cuisine at its very best. Sample such delights as suckling pig with white cabbage dumpling or his breast of pigeon with beans and olives.

Sacher Hotel Restaurant, the Hotel Sacher's restaurant, *Philharmonikerstrasse 4; website: www.sacher.com*, is a lovely surprise to those who think hotel restaurants are just mediocre. The food is as good as the atmosphere is pleasing. Men should wear a tie. Reservations are advisable.

Drei Husaren, *Weihburggasse 4; tel. +43 (1) 5121-0920*, is the essence of old Vienna, serving first-rate hors d'oeuvres and desserts. Opened 50 years ago, the restaurant is decorated with stag horns, antique busts, Gobelin tapestries, and old portraits. They have the dessert to end all desserts called the Preiselbeeren omelette with praline sabayon. Reservations are necessary.

The world's best pastries

Vienna's *Konditoreien* (pastry shops/cafés) produce the world's most delectable pastries—seductive arrays of tempting cakes, dripping with icing and whipped cream. Imagine a horseshoe-shaped Kipferl with shredded almonds or a Schifferl, shaped like a small boat, with tiny strawberries as passengers. Sweet lovers can be spotted on any afternoon lingering in *Konditoreien* over savory confections and cups of coffee or tea.

Vienna's *Konditoreien* are as colorful and varied as the pastries they serve. **Demel's**, *Kohlmarkt 14; tel. +43 (1) 535-17170*, from its exalted position on the Kohlmarkt, calls itself *K.K. Hofzuckerbackerei* (imperial and royal sugar baker).

Gerstner, *Kärtnerstrasse 13-15; tel. +43 (1) 743-4422*, with its enviable position overlooking this street, also claims royal recognition: Emperor Franz Josef prophetically remarked more than 100 years ago, "Gerstner will have a great future."

Another landmark, famous for its dainty china and delicious cakes, is **Heiner's**, *Kärtnerstrasse 21-23; website: www.heiner.co.at,* with its beautiful crystal chandeliers.

The best of Viennese nightlife

The **U4**, *Schönbrunner Strasse 22; website: www.u-4.at,* is our favorite nightclub in Vienna. So named because it is downstairs from an elevated subway stop on the U4 line, it is frequented by a mature, sophisticated crowd.

Queen Anne, *Johannesgasse 12; tel. +43 (1) 994-8844*, is the most popular disco in town and patrons here have included David Bowie and the late German playboy Gunther Sachs.

Jazzland, *Franz Josef-Kai 29; tel. +43 (1) 533-25-75; website: www. jazzland.at*, is the best place for good, sultry jazz. The atmosphere is funky and smoky. Famous bands sometimes play here. Check the website for upcoming performances.

Griechenbeisl, *Fleishmarkt 11, tel. +43 (1) 533-1977*, claims to be the oldest tavern in Vienna, dating back to 1500. The local food is great and they have live music every evening. The beer is always on tap and the wine flows with ease.

Vienna's best hotels

The Imperial, *Kärtner Ring 16; tel. +43 (1) 501-100; website: www.starwoodhotels. com*, is a deluxe hotel located in a former palace. Built in 1869 for the Duke of Württemberg, it was turned into a hotel in 1874. Wagner lived here for two months during the productions of his operas around the corner. Elizabeth Taylor stayed here with her three dogs and two cats, her mother, and her servants. Other noted guests have included Ormandy, Nureyev, Fonteyn, Domingo, and Carreras. During World War II, the Nazis used the Imperial as a guesthouse, and Hitler stayed here several times. When the war was over, the hotel served as the Russian headquarters.

Rooms at the Imperial are furnished with antiques and have wall safes. The magnificent central staircase of red, yellow, and black marble is supported by reclining gods and goddesses. Gobelin tapestries and portraits of Emperor Franz Josef and Empress Elizabeth hang on the walls.

The Bristol, *Kärtner Ring; tel. +43 (1) 515-160; website: www.starwoodhotels. com*, is a luxurious, traditional hotel across the street from the opera house. It has large, beautifully furnished bedrooms and one of the best hotel bars in Europe. The Bristol's restaurant, the Korso, received a star from Michelin for its terrific food.

The Sacher, *Philharmonikerstrasse 4; tel. +43 (1) 514-560; website: www.sacher.com*, is a first-class place with lovely rooms furnished with antiques. Musicians and music lovers stay at this hotel, which is next door to the opera house. The concierge is said to be able to get tickets to almost any of Vienna's musical events—for a handsome fee of course.

The most affordable hotels

Amadeus, *Wildpretmarkt 5; tel. +43 (1) 533-8738; website: www.hotel-amadeus.at,* is consistently good and centrally located, with private baths and telephones.

Kaiserin Elisabeth, *A-1010 Wein, Weihburggasse 3, Vienna; tel. +43 (1) 515-260; website: www.kaiserinelisabeth.at.* The hotel is situated in a pleasant 14th-century building that is centrally located. Prices start at 166 euro ($238) for a double room.

The best taverns (and best views of Vienna)

The little-known *Heurigen* is a unique style of east Austrian tavern with origins that go back more than 1,200 years. In 1784, Emperor Joseph II passed a decree allowing all farmers and winegrowers in this region to sell their own produce (although he was only officially recognizing a tradition started in A.D. 795). Each winegrower would only open for business a few weeks at a time, ensuring that there was always an open tavern to be found somewhere. *Heurigen* that continue to operate this way are now called *Buschenschanken* (bushel taverns) because of the pine bushel above the doorway that tells you they're open. But most *Heurigen* can be enjoyed year round, usually in the outer districts of Vienna.

One of the best *Heurigen* is a cozy inn called **The Wine Tavern Huber**, *Roterdstrasse 5,* in Vienna's 16th district; *tel. +43 (1) 485-8180.* Its bare wooden tables and long benches are typical of *Heurigen*, as are the waiters and waitresses who wear traditional Austrian costume: Lederhosen for the men, Dirndl for the women. But this is not a show put on for tourists—all the patrons are locals, and most know the owner by name.

Food is inexpensive and plentiful; beware the huge portions served in *Heurigen*—one portion of *wiener schnitzel* is more than enough for two people (unlike most Austrian restaurants, in a *Heurigen*, it is perfectly acceptable to take food home). *Heurigen* also offer excellent table wine, usually served in an open carafe.

Heurigen are generally open from late afternoon until midnight and most have live Viennese music. In summer, sitting outside in the *Schrebergarten* is a treat. For the best views of Vienna, we recommend **Weingut am Reisenberg**, *Oberer Reisenbergweg 15; tel. +43 (1) 320-9393*, but it can get crowded on week-ends and most of the summer. If it's too busy, you'll find the second best views of Vienna at **Heuriger Leitner**, *Sprengersteig 68; tel. +43 (1) 480-0139.*

Vienna's most tragic site

A chapel in **Mayerling**, in the middle of the Vienna woods, marks the place where Crown Prince Rudolf, son of Emperor Franz Josef, and his mistress Baroness Mary Vetsera committed double suicide. The Emperor had refused to allow Prince Rudolf to end his unhappy marriage.

INNSBRUCK: THE PRETTIEST ALPINE CITY

Innsbruck, the capital of Tyrol, is one of the prettiest cities in the world. It is also one of the biggest ski centers in Europe. The towering Alps can be seen from almost every street corner. The **Nordkette**, a steep alpine headwall, is the closest and most dramatic of the mountains that surround the city. **Maria-Theresien-Strasse**, the main street, has an especially inspiring view of the mountains. For more information, check out *website: www.innsbruck.info*.

Miles of cross-country ski tracks can be found outside Innsbruck, as well as the Olympic bobsled run, a ski jump, and a large ice-skating rink and hockey arena.

Gothic architecture (the pointed, arched, and vaulted style prevalent in Europe from the 13th to 15th centuries) can be seen throughout 800-year-old Innsbruck. Much of it was built by order of Empress Maria Theresa and Emperor Maximilian I. Gothic arcades, forerunners of modern malls because they kept shoppers out of the weather, can be found off Herzog Friedrichstrasse.

Innsbruck's treasures

The **Goldenes Dachl** (Golden Roof), *Herzog-Friedrich-Strasse 15,* is the symbol of Innsbruck. The ornate Gothic balcony, built in 1500 by Maximilian I to commemorate his wedding, was used by the royal couple to watch armor-clad knights jousting below. The regal balcony has sculpted crests and heroic wall paintings. A roof made of 2,657 gold-plated tiles tops the balcony.

Innsbruck's finest inn

Next to the Golden Roof is the **Goldener Adler** (Golden Eagle Inn), *Herzog-Friedrich-Strasse 6; tel. +43 (512) 571-111; website: www.bestwestern.at/goldeneradler*. This 600-year-old inn is said to be the best in the city. Request a room with antique trappings. Andreas Hofer, the leader of the Tyrolean uprising against Napoleon, gathered his small and poorly armed troop of volunteers here.

His troops, despite their poverty, managed to defeat the well-equipped French and Bavarian armies in three battles.

Hofkirche (the court church), *Universitätsstrasse 2,* is known as the Tyrolean Westminster Abbey. It was commissioned by Emperor Ferdinand I as a cenotaph dedicated to his grandfather Maximilian I (who was buried at Wiener Neustadt). Built from 1553 to 1563, it contains a white marble tomb with a monumental bronze statue of the kneeling Maximilian on top. Standing vigil are 28 enormous bronze statues of royal figures, ancestors, and heroes…including King Arthur. It also contains the tomb of Andreas Hofer, Tirol's national hero.

Across the Inn River is the **Hungerburgbahn** (a funicular), that will carry you to the peaks with the best views of Innsbruck. It crosses the Inn and ascends the mountainside to Hungerburg, a lofty section of the city. An aerial tram continues from here to Seegrube and Hafelaker, affording breathtaking overlooks on the Nordkette.

Downhill from here is the **Alpenzoo,** *tel. +43 (512) 292-323; website: www.alpenzoo.at,* which contains species already extinct in the Eastern Alps, as well as rare animals and birds seen only by hunters in the high mountains. Wildcats, wolves, bears, bison, otters, beavers, griffons, vultures, owls, and eagles are kept in surroundings as similar as possible to their natural habitats. The zoo is open from 9 a.m. to 6 p.m. You can get here from Innsbruck via bus or tram.

The best way to explore the mountains
Club Innsbruck arranges daily hikes and ski trips in the mountains outside Innsbruck. You don't have to be a member; you get a Club Innsbruck card when you register at a hotel in town. Sign up for club Innsbruck's programs at information centers or at your hotel before 4 p.m. the day before you plan to participate (see *www.innsbruck.info* for more information).

From June to September, the club offers daily guided hikes, with a free loan of hiking boots and a rucksack. Bus transportation to the starting point of each day's tour and back from the end point is free, as are the services of experienced, licensed guides.

During the winter, the club provides free ski buses to the five main ski areas surrounding Innsbruck and a daily cross-country ski bus. Winter hiking trips with guides are scheduled Monday through Friday. If you would rather hike on your own, pick up the map called *Innsbruck and Umgebung.* Many of the best trails start at Hungerburg. The blue trails can be followed in good walking shoes, but don't try the red ones without sturdy climbing boots.

Mozart's birthplace, dominated by a 12th-century fortress called the Hohensalzburg, is a baroque city surrounded by mountains. The Salzach River divides **Salzburg** into two worlds. On the left bank are narrow streets and ancient buildings that date back to the 13th to 15th centuries. The right bank is a modern city in the shadows of the Kapuzinerberg Mountain.

The Salzburg music festival

The **Salzburg Festival** is the world's leading and most famous festival. This is a perfect time to visit this musically based town. The festival is held from late July to August. Advance ticket sales normally end by January.

For more information contact the **Austrian National Tourist Office**, *website: www.austria.info* or the Ticket Office of the Salzburg Festival, *tel. +43 (662) 804-5500; website: www.salzburgfestival.at.* You can also reserve tickets through a travel agent in the U.S.

The old quarter

The best place to begin your exploration of Salzburg is in the **old quarter**. In the shadows of the castle, it is a maze of winding old streets with little shops, medieval wrought-iron signs, and fountains. Explore on foot—cars are banned here.

The main thoroughfare, Getreidegasse, leads into **Judengasse**, once the Jewish ghetto. Today, it is a picturesque neighborhood with five- and six-story houses. Continue on to the **Alter Markt** (Market Square), where flower stalls scent the air and a 16th-century fountain splashes.

The top sights of Salzburg

Mozart's Geburtshaus (*tel. +43 (662) 844-313*): Mozart was born at *Getreidegasse 9* in 1756 and he lived here for his first 16 years. Early editions of his works (he began composing when he was five) and models of sets of his most famous operas are on display at the house, which is open every day. (The house where Mozart lived from 1773 to 1787 is on the other side of the river at *Makatplatz 8*, but it is only open in the summer.)

The **Dom** (cathedral), *Residenzplatz*, with its two towers, marble façade, and massive bronze doors, is also in the old quarter. Look for its blue terracotta dome. Consecrated in 1628, the early baroque structure was modeled on St. Peter's in Rome.

Across from the cathedral is the **Museum Residenz**, *tel. +43 (662) 840-4510;*

website: www.residenzgalerie.at, a series of buildings that once comprised the palace of the prince-archbishops. On the first floor are 15 staterooms decorated with frescoes and paintings. A gallery of European paintings from the 16th through 19th centuries on the second floor contains works by Rembrandt, Rubens, and Breughel.

The **Glockenspiel**, *Mozartpatz 1*, in front of the Residenz, is a 35-bell carillon constructed in the 18th century. The bells are played every day at 7 a.m., 11 a.m., and 6 p.m.

The magnificent **Mirabell Palace**, *Rainerstrasse,* with its elaborate formal gardens, is on the other side of the river. Built in 1606 by Archbishop Wolf Dietrick for his mistress (and the mother of his 12 children), it is known for its grand ceremonial staircase, which is decorated with marble angels and its Marble Hall. The gardens are filled with statues, pools, and flowers of every shade and variety. Candlelight chamber music concerts are held here.

Guarding Salzburg from a great rock 400 feet above the city is the **Hohensalzburg**, *Mönchsberg 34; tel. +43 (662) 8424-3011*, a fortress built between 1077 and 1681. This stronghold of the bishops of Salzburg is filled with Gothic woodcarving, coffered ceilings, and intricate ironwork. To get to the fortress, which offers the best view of the city, walk or take the funicular from Festungsgasse, near St. Peter's Churchyard. Tours of the castle are scheduled every 15 minutes.

Outside Salzburg is the 17th-century **Hellbrunn Palace**, *Fürstenweg 37; website: www.hellbrunn.at*, built by the archbishop and prankster Markus Sittikus, who used hidden nozzles in the benches, walls, sculptures, floors, and ceilings to spray unwary guests. The palace is open to the public every day from April 1st to November 1st.

The best eating in Salzburg

The two best restaurants in the Salzburg area are **Hotel Weisses Kreuz**, *Bierjodl-gasse 6; tel. +43 (662) 845-641; website: www.weisseskreuz.at,* and **Goldener Hirsch**, *Getreidegasse 37; tel. +43 (662) 80840; website: www.starwoodhotels.com*. Weisses Kreuz offers garden dining. Goldener Hirsch serves great food and boasts an impressive wine list. Try venison in season or king prawns in curry ragout served with Thai rice.

Stiftskeller Sankt Peter, *St.-Peter-Bezirk 1-4*; *tel. +43 (662) 841-2680*; *website: www.stpeter-stiftskeller.at,* is located near the cathedral. It is a 16th-century wine cellar that serves wines from its own vineyards. The restaurant is divided into eight rooms, which serve traditional Austrian dishes at a reasonable price.

Salzburg's best affordable hotels

Hotel Schone Aussicht, *Heuberg 3; website: www.salzburgpanorama.at*, is a chalet hotel on the hill with a view of Salzburg and the Alps. It has a pool, tennis courts, a sunny terrace, and a cozy, beamed bar. Some of the rooms have balconies. Service is friendly and fresh flowers decorate the rooms. However, the walk from the bus stop is up three steep hills, so it's best to have a car if you stay here.

Hotel Kasererbraeu, *Kaigasse 33; tel. +43 (662) 842-4450; website: www.kasererbraeu.at,* is a small hotel nestled in the shadows of the Hohensalzburg. The building dates back to 1342 and some of the rooms have been furnished in baroque style. Others are furnished in pinewood.

Hotel Elefant, *Sigmund-Haffner-Gasse 4; tel. +43 (662) 843-397; website: www.elefant.at,* is a medieval townhouse in the historic heart of Salzburg. The tall, narrow building is on a quiet pedestrian street five minutes from the opera house. The public rooms have inlaid furniture and old paintings. The floors on the first floor are marble, and the rooms are decorated with antiques. The upper floors are less elegant; some of the rooms are small and plain. About half have private baths.

Salzburg's castle hotels

Hotel Schloss Mönchstein, *Mönchstein Park 26; tel. +43 (662) 848-5550; website: www.monchstein.at*, is a many-tiered, ivy-covered castle on a mountaintop above Salzburg. Once a guesthouse for archbishops, it became a retreat for scholars from the University of Salzburg in 1654. Today it is a hotel as well as a great restaurant. You can take an elevator to the castle from the streets below.

Schloss Haunsperg, *Oberalm; tel. +43 624-580-662; website: www.schlosshotels.co.at*, is a 14th-century castle hotel just south of Salzburg. The spacious rooms are furnished with antiques, and guests can use the tennis courts on the grounds. The castle is near the Autobahn that runs south from Salzburg past the airport; exit at Hallein and follow the signs to Oberalm and the castle. Book in advance as there are only eight rooms on offer.

The world's best salt mines

The salt mine at **Hallein**, located 10 miles south of Salzburg, is a bit like a roller coaster. To get around inside the tunnels, you slide down a series of long wooden chutes at 40 miles per hour. To visit, you must put on a special uniform, which consists of baggy white overalls with a white hood and a leather backside.

The mine contains sketches of the 1,000-year-old body of a man found in 1666 perfectly preserved in salt. And at midlevel is a salt lake, which, during the off-season, you can raft across to see a cathedral-like cavern 270 feet long and 150 feet wide.

Europe's best tobogganing

Don't leave Austria before you visit the Lake District, an area about 30 minutes east of Salzburg. In the winter, Austria's 200 lakes are covered with ice skaters, and the surrounding mountains with skiers. In the summer, these lakes are filled with sailboats.

The area around **Wolfgangsee** is especially popular. You can't really explore the Lake District without a car. If you don't have a rental car, join a tour. If you're lucky, your guide will introduce you to the little-known sport of mountain tobogganing. To participate, you pick up a metal, saucer-like toboggan and then take a chair lift to the top of the mountain, carrying the toboggan with you. At the top, place the toboggan on the metal track that curves its way down to the bottom, sit cross-legged on the toboggan, and push off. It is like riding a roller coaster, only better because you can go as fast or slow as you want. (A stick in the front acts like a break.) It takes about five minutes to get to the bottom.

After the trip down the mountain, drive to **St. Gilgen**, a small resort town near Lake Wolfgang. It is a favorite spot among the people of Salzburg, who come here for weekend getaways. St. Gilgen is a small place with only a few restaurants and small shops—but that is as it should be. The charm of this lakeside village would be lost if someone built condominiums here.

If planning to spend time at Wolfgansee, find a room in one of the inns situated on the side of the mountain overlooking the lake. Ask when you arrive in the area; a local should be able to point the way to a good one.

Austria's strangest tradition

The men of the little town of **Landeck** climb to the top of the rocky crags that loom above Landeck and light huge bonfires that can be seen for miles. They then set fire to circles of wood dipped in tar, roll them down the hill, and then ski downhill, racing the fiery disks at insane speeds.

The highest waterfall in Europe

Krimml Waterfall splashes down 1,250 feet through the mountains, 30 miles east of Innsbruck. You know when the fall is close; it fills the valley with mist.

Kitzbühel, the prettiest ski town

A treasure of a ski village is **Kitzbühel**, a friendly, uncrowded town with slopes for skiers of all experience and enough activity to keep even snow haters happy. This is the place to go to avoid irritating crowds and the ridiculously high prices often found in the Alps. It has well-groomed slopes, a casino, and plenty of nightlife.

Kitzbühel is worth visiting even if you don't ski. An ancient walled town, it has crooked, narrow streets and Tyrolean architecture, with gabled stone-and-stucco houses that date back to the Middle Ages.

The skiable part of the Kitzbühel Alps reaches as high as 7,750 feet. The greatest vertical drop here is 4,150 feet. These heights may seem small compared with those at other Alpine resorts; however, the smooth pastures of these mountains require less snow for good skiing than the rockier slopes of other ski areas. And the weather is milder than in other areas. Kitzbühel's 60 ski lifts and trails provide an overwhelming choice of trails, all accessible by a single ski pass called the Kitzbühel Ski Circus.

THE BEST OF
BELIZE

Belize is a very diverse little nation. And because it's so small, it means you can be on the beach and very quickly get into the highlands. Belize's interior hides Mayan ruins, tall waterfalls, rainforests, and rivers you can explore. Down near Sittee Point, in fact, is a jaguar preserve where you can venture into the jungle in search of the elusive cats. Bird watching in Belize's interior is a treat; you'll be able to spot parrots, toucans, flycatchers, and herons in their natural habitat.

THE WORLD'S SECOND LARGEST REEF

No longer a secret to the adventurous traveler, Belize is most famous for its virtually unspoiled coast. Just off the shores of its beautiful beaches is a 176-mile barrier reef, the largest coral reef in the Western Hemisphere and second only to Australia's Great Barrier Reef. Belize's reef has long been a mecca for skilled divers, snorkelers, and fisherman.

YOUR BEST CONTACTS IN BELIZE

If you're planning on traveling to Belize, the best contact to make is S&L Travel. Whether you want to rent a car, book an in-country flight, find a driver to take you wherever you want to go, locate the perfect hotel, or learn which excursions are worth the trouble…this company can help you out. Contact them at **S&L Travel**; *tel. +501 227-7593; website: www.sltravelbelize.com.*

THE BELIZE CITY GUIDE

If you fly into Belize, your first taste of the country will most likely be **Belize City**. It has suffered more than its share of bad press, but not all of it is on the mark. It's true that women, especially, would be foolish to walk the streets alone at night; petty street crime is widespread, and the area is generally run-down and dirty. Still, there is a redeeming charm about this dilapidated city. The grand colonial houses rival those anywhere in Central or South America, and residents always have a kind smile for visitors.

Where to stay in Belize City
The **Radisson Fort George**, *2 Marine Parade, Belize City, Belize; tel. +501 (2) 233-333; website: www.radisson.com/belizecitybz,* is one of two larger hotels in town. This is a very hospitable hotel.

The **Great House**, *13 Cork Street; tel. +501 223-3400; website: www. greathousebelize.com,* is an elegant colonial house, that could be mistaken for a Victorian doll house with its intricate white rose décor. The house also arranges trips to the barrier reef, Mayan sites, Mountain Pine Ridge and scuba diving.

The best places to eat in Belize City
There are many good restaurants in Belize City. These include **Bob's Grill**, *164 Newton Street; tel. +501 223-6908*, which has excellent food and a nice lounge, **Macy's Cafe**, *18 Bishop Street; tel. +501 227-3419*, is a good Creole restaurant.

Belize's best shopping
If you're looking for souvenirs to bring home, walk through the **National Handcraft Center**. The selection isn't great, but some very nice, carved picture frames as well as paintings by local artists are available.

The best cigars
U.S. travelers, in particular, seem often to be in the market for Cuban cigars. You can't legally buy them in the U.S. or bring them home with you (not with the labels

on them, anyway). But they are for sale in Belize. To find them in a state-of-the-art, walk-in humidor, take a taxi to the *Aficionado* where you'll find cigars from all over Central and South America.

The zoo: A local landmark

A good way to get familiar with the wildlife of Belize would be to visit **The Belize Zoo and Tropical Education Center**, *P.O. Box 1787, Belize City, Belize; tel. +501 220-8004; website: www.belizezoo.org*. It looks as if the zookeepers have thrown nets over portions of a jungle, and many of the zoo's inhabitants were wild animals that have been domesticated or injured and nursed back to health.

THE MOST UNSPOILED CAYES

Hundreds of uninhabited, palm-lined Cayes dot the coast of Belize. Of the inhabited ones, **Ambergris Caye** is the largest and most populated. Caye Caulker, Caye Chapel, and St. George's Caye, located just south of Ambergris Caye, are less developed but just as beautiful and offer accommodation and dive packages. Southwater Caye and other islands on the lower reef, accessible by boat from Dangriga, are truly undiscovered, unspoiled treasures.

The best cave diving

Half Moon Caye Natural Monument lies in the midst of the Lighthouse Reef Atoll, 60 miles east of Belize City. The reserve features a lighthouse and sanctuary built in 1848, as well as a sanctuary for the red-footed booby and more than 100 other bird species. The Lighthouse Reef Atoll is also host to the circular Great Blue Hole, a natural phenomenon, which stretches 1,000 feet in diameter and 400 feet below the sea's surface and offers spectacular cave diving.

The best of Ambergris Caye

San Pedro, the main town on Ambergris Caye, even with its seaside restaurants, handful of souvenir shops, and three nightclubs, is an easygoing village of guides, fishermen, families, and expatriate Americans and Britons. In the evening, the main plaza is alive with strollers and volleyball players, and hermit-crab races are held at the Pier Lounge every Monday night.

The best hotels
The **Victoria House**, *tel. +501 226-2067; website: www.victoria-house.com*, is a nice, quiet, and secluded hotel with a popular beachside bar. Helicopter tours are also on offer from the hotel's trained staff.

Cayo Espanto, *tel. +1 (888) 666-4282 (from the U.S.); website: www.aprivateisland.com*, is a luxury resort on a little private island. It's very expensive to stay there, but the service is simply amazing.

Ambergris' best seafood
Elvi's Kitchen, *tel. +501 226-2404; website: www.elviskitchen.com*, has a sand floor and there is a huge tree growing out through the roof. Sample, in season, the best lobster on the planet.

Where to shop on Ambergris
Kimara's Gift Shop in town is a good one to try. Also, **Eden Art** across from the airstrip has quality products from around Belize. **Belizean Arts** has two locations, one next to the church and another under the archway at Fido's. In both you'll find top-quality products—sculptures, pottery, jewelry, as well as the largest local collection of paintings and prints by Walter Castillo whose colorful work has made him Belize's best-known artist.

THE BEST OF THE CAYO DISTRICT

The "high jungle" of the **Cayo District** is known for its broad-leaf rainforest and its slight elevation, which means few bugs and cool nights. Overflowing with pine trees, tall waterfalls, low mountains, and breathtaking views, it is a good base from which to explore the Mountain Pine Ridge (practically inaccessible to motor vehicles) and the vast Mayan ruins in the area.

San Ignacio: A favorite inland escape
San Ignacio is a town built in Cayo's hills where the Macal and Mopan Rivers converge to form the Belize River. An old metal one-way elevated bridge crosses the Macal in town—"the loudest bridge in Central America," as it is known by the locals.

The best traveler's rest

Eva's, *22 Burns Ave., San Ignacio; tel. +501 824-2267*, is the local hangout, a restaurant where every traveler in the region ends up eventually. There you can eat lunch or dinner for a few dollars or simply order a beer, have a seat, and discover all you need to know about what's going on in the region.

Where to stay in the jungle

Twelve miles south of Belmopan lies the **Caves Branch Jungle Lodge**, *Mile 41 1/2 Hummingbird Hwy., P.O. Box 356. Belmopan; tel. +501 673-3454; website: www.cavesbranch.com.* Three underground river systems allow guests to float on inner tubes through miles of river caves, where they pass magnificent stalagmites sparkling like diamonds. You can stay in a Jungle Treehouse, Jungle Bungalow or in the Bunkhouse.

Chaa Creek Inland Expeditions, *tel. +501 824-2037; website: www. chaacreek.com*, is a lovely piece of land owned by Mick and Lucy Fleming that has been turned into a sort of retreat. The cottages here range in price from $115 to $550 per night (depending on the season and the amount of people staying) and are well worth the money.

An equestrian's dream

Mountain Equestrian Trails; *website: www.metbelize.com*, is a small resort that specializes in horseback riding and offers trail rides throughout the region to visit caves, waterfalls, and the jungle. A double room, with a mountain view, rents for $94 to $132 per night, depending on the season.

The best butterflies

Green Hills Butterfly Ranch and Botanical Collection, *tel. +501 820-4017; website: http://biological-diversity.info/greenhills.htm,* is a research facility that is open to the public from 8 a.m. to 4 p.m. every day. If viewing butterflies flying freely in a net enclosure landscaped with a collection of tropical plants is your thing, then this is the place.

THE MOST CARIBBEAN

This is technically Central America, but **Placencia Village**, located on Placencia Peninsula in the south of Belize, has an easy pace of living and a laid-back vibe that feels very Caribbean. The folks are friendly, and the Maya, Gafiruna, and Creole cultures blend yet remain distinct and unique.

After just a few days biking Placencia's road or walking its sidewalks, which runs between the road and the sea, bordered by restaurants, beachside bars, gift shops, and guesthouses, local faces and places become familiar quickly. The nightlife here is casual, and when something is going on, maybe a live band one night or a DJ the next, everyone in town can be found there, because, well, that's usually the only thing going on that night. It's easy to settle in.

Placencia's best hotels

Singing Sands Inn, *tel. +501 520-8022; website: www.singingsands.com*, is a lovely hotel that sits on a perfect piece of the beach. A double costs $80 to $160 a night, depending on the season and whether you have a sea or garden view.

The Inn at Robert's Grove, *tel. +501 523-3565; website: www.robertsgrove.com*, is another great place to stay.

THE BEST OF
BRAZIL

Delight is a weak tern to express the feelings of a naturalist who, for the first time, has wandered by himself in a Brazilian forest. The elegance of the grasses, the novelty of the parasitical plants, the beauty of the flowers, the glossy green of the foliage, but above all the general luxuriance of the vegetation, filled me with admiration.

—Charles Darwin

Brazil—the largest South American country—is watered by the Amazon rainforest, the largest in the world, and drained by the Amazon River, which carries more water than any other river in the world. The country's spectacular shoreline—which is lined with broad beaches and high mountains that circle the harbors—rivals any shoreline in the world. But Brazil has more to offer than spectacular scenery. It boasts the continent's most exciting city, Rio de Janeiro, and South America's largest industrial city, São Paulo.

Brazilians are beautiful, an exotic blend of Indian, African, and European ancestry. Half the population is under 25, adding to the beauty quotient.

A fun-loving nation, Brazil has the world's best Carnival, with glittering costumes, immense processions, mesmerizing music, and gala balls. And year-round, its beaches boast the world's most scantily clad sun worshipers. Restaurants in Brazil are excellent and cheap. Food supplies are abundant and varied, and the chefs are talented. Once you have tried the national dish, *feijoada* (a spicy black-bean stew), take advantage of the international cuisine. You can enjoy gourmet meals for next to nothing.

RIO: BRAZIL'S CULTURAL CENTER

Rio de Janeiro is Brazil's most cosmopolitan city. It is famous for its pre-Lenten Carnival, but it has much more to offer than simply a festival. A beautiful city surrounded by low mountains, Rio hugs Guanabara Bay, which is rimmed with palm-lined beaches and dotted with 84 islands. Jet-setters from around the world soak in the sun all day and dance in the nightclubs all night.

The world's best carnival

People from around the world flock to Rio for its **Carnival**, a four-day extravaganza that concludes on Ash Wednesday. Poor Cariocas (residents of Rio) often put a year's savings into their costumes for the round of wild parties and balls.

Carnival officially begins when the mayor hands the key to the city to King Momo, the mock king of the festivities, who appears at all major Carnival events (parades, balls, costume contests) and orders everyone to have fun. King Momo is elected every year by the residents of Rio; the primary requirement is that he be very fat.

Samba schools are the focus of glittering processions beginning at 6 p.m. Sunday and Monday and continuing until noon on Shrove Tuesday. These enormous groups compete for prizes and go to great lengths to come up with the most fantastic and outrageous costumes and themes. The competition is always passionate, and at times it gets violent.

Traditionally, each of the city's samba schools (which number up to 5,000 members each) paraded through the streets of downtown Rio displaying their floats and gaudy costumes. A few years ago, the rowdy parades were taken off the streets and put into the **Sambo'dromo**, a stadium about half a mile long and about as wide as a street. It is the equivalent in spectacle to a half-time show at the Super Bowl, but the majorettes are topless. And the show lasts 17 hours.

If you can't get tickets to the Sambo'dromo, just walk through the streets. Bandstands are erected on street corners, where samba bands give impromptu concerts and people in skimpy costumes shake their stuff. Rio's elite, disguised in fantastic costumes, attend elaborate balls. The best are at the Canecão nightclub, the Yacht Club, the Flamenco Football Club, La Scala, and Sugarloaf Mountain. Local nightclubs also arrange elaborate parties, with samba bands and costumes. Tickets for Carnival balls and parades go on sale in November and sell out early.

The most exotic New Year's celebration

As colorful as Carnival—but less known—is Rio's New Year's celebration. Just before midnight, thousands of white-robed worshipers carrying candles gather on the city's beaches to make offerings to the goddess of the sea, Lemanja. At midnight, fireworks go off, and crying, singing worshipers rush into the ocean carrying flowers and gifts for their deity.

The best view from Christ's feet

Rio's best-known landmark is the huge statue of **Christ the Redeemer**, overlooking the harbor from the top of Corcovado Mountain, 2,250 feet above sea level. A little train takes you to the statue. From this vantage point on the top of the mountain, the view of the harbor is spectacular, particularly as the day turns to dusk, then dark, and the city below begins to glitter against the aquamarine blue of the sea. Have a drink in the café at the top of the mountain.

Another beautiful view of Rio is from the top of **Pao de Açucar** (Sugarloaf Mountain), a rock rising 390 feet above the bay. A cable car makes the trip from 8 a.m. until 10 p.m.

Rio's best garden

Rio's **Jardim Botânico** (Botanical Garden), has 7,000 varieties of tropical plants. Palm-lined paths wind their way past ponds covered with lily pads.

Rio's best museum

The **Quinta da Boa Vista** (National Museum), *Sao Cistovao*, in the former Imperial Palace, displays objects that once belonged to the royal family, along with the Bendego meteorite, one of the largest ever grounded on earth, an impressive Amazon Indian display. The lawns, flowerbeds, and hothouses that surround the Quinta da Boa Vista can be explored by horse-drawn carriage.

Brazil's best books

The **National Library**, founded in 1810, has a collection of one million volumes in various languages, including a parchment copy of the Guttenberg Bible (one of four existing) and an astonishing collection of Hebraica.

The most authentic neighborhoods

Lapa, an old, slightly crumbling neighborhood, has narrow streets with wrought-iron balconies. The old townhouses have been converted into shops and pensions.

Santa Teresa, near Corcovado Mountain, gives a glimpse of Rio as it was at the turn of the century. Beautiful old houses flank cobblestone avenues shaded by broad, ancient trees. The neighborhood has a variety of restaurants and bars. This ceased being an upper-class neighborhood a long time ago but is being revived as an artistic hotspot.

Brazil's best cuisine, two hours north of Rio

Two hours north of Rio are the beaches of **Buzios**, the playgrounds of the elite. Called the jewel of the Brazilian Riviera, Buzios is filled with expensive boutiques. The pace is languid. People sleep until noon and dine in the wee hours of the morning. You can walk to the beach from anywhere in this little fishing village. Houses have no doors, and drums can be heard everywhere.

Buzios' cuisine is considered the finest in Brazil. An elaborate dinner for two at one of the town's best restaurants can cost more than a night in a local hotel. But it's worth it. A good restaurant to try in Buzios is **Satyricon**, *500 Orla Bardot; tel. +55 (22) 2623-2691; website: www.satyricon.com.br*, which serves local fish specialties. You can enjoy a complimentary appetizer of eggplant roasted in garlic, quail eggs (hard-boiled), baked red and yellow peppers, and warm bread. Follow all of this with fresh marimba seasoned with hot red peppers you pluck from a plant on the table.

The world's largest stadium

Maracana Stadium, the largest sports arena in South America, holds more than 95,000 people, is the locale of Rio's wild soccer matches. The games are second in importance only to Carnival here. Buy a Cadierra Especial ticket—this allows you to enjoy the matches in an area fenced off from the mobs of raucous fans. Most hotels offer packages that provide transportation to and from the stadium as well as seats for the games.

Your best bet

The **Jockey Club** holds horse races Thursday nights and weekends. The most important is the Grande Premio Brasil, held the first Sunday in August. Everyone who is anyone shows up in fancy dress to watch South America's best horses run.

The best way to see the bay

The best way to see **Guanabara Bay** is to take a day or half-day cruise among its islands. Boats dock along Avenida Nestor Moreira.

Paqueta, where Rio's lovers meet, is the loveliest island. Cars aren't allowed here, only bikes and carriages. A ferry to Paqueta takes about an hour-and-a-half; the hydrofoil takes about 30 minutes.

Rio's best restaurants

Rio has an endless list of outstanding eateries. The city's best gourmet restaurants include **Le St. Honoré**, *Meridien Hotel; tel. +55 (21) 3873-8880;* **Le Pré Catalan**, *Sofitel Rio Hotel; tel. +55 (21) 2525-1232; website: ww2.leprecatelan.com.br;* and **Cipriani**, *Copacabana Palace Hotel; tel. +55 (21) 2548-7070; website: www. copacabanapalace.com.*

For authentic Brazilian food, the best restaurant in town is **Confeitaria Colombo**, *Rua Gonçalves Dias 32; tel. +55 (21) 2505-1500; website: www. confeitariacolombo.com.br.* This elegant restaurant was first opened in 1894 and serves delicious *feijoada*.

Bar d'Hotel, *Marina All Suites Hotel, Avenida Delfim 696; tel. +55 (21) 2172-1100,* serves delicious food, but the real draw here are the cocktails.

Rio also has good barbecue restaurants, called *churrascarias*. These all-you-can-eat places serve grilled meats—pork, beef, marinated chicken livers—with salad and rice. The food is inexpensive and usually superb. The best *churrascaria* is **Porcao**, *Av. Infante Dom Henrique s/n, Aterro do Flamengo; tel. +55 (21) 3389-8989.*

The city's best Portuguese restaurant is the elegant **Antiquarius**, *rua Aristides Espindola 19; tel. +55 (21) 2294-1049*, in Leblon. Inexpensive Portuguese food is served at a no-frills eatery called **Adegao**, *Campo de São Cristovão; tel. +55 (21) 2580-7288; website: www.porcao.com.br.*

Rio's best hotels

First-class hotels include the **Marriott**, *Avenida Atlantica 2600, Copacabana; tel. +55 (21) 2545-6500; website: www.marriott.com;* **Caesar Park**, *Avenida Vieira Souto 460 Ipanema; tel. +55 (21) 2525-2525; website: www.caesar-park.com;* and **Marina All Suites**, *Av. Delfim Moreira 696, Praia do Leblon; tel. +55 (21) 2172-1100; website: www.marinaallsuites.com.br.*

The **Copacabana Palace**, *Avenida Atlântica 1702; tel. +55 (21) 2548-7070; website: www.copacabanapalace.com.br*, is the grand old lady of Rio's hotels, the first major hotel built on Copacabana Beach. Open since 1923, this is where Fred Astaire and Ginger Rogers danced around the lobby in the movie *Flying Down to Rio*. Jet-setters from around the world return here year after year.

The hottest nightlife

Rio residents don't sit down to dinner until 9 p.m. or so. By the time dinner is finished, it's nearly 11 p.m. This is when the city's nightspots wake up. Discos are everywhere, with loud music, light shows, and lively crowds. Many are organized as private clubs; you need to make a reservation, and in some cases a reference, to get in. Ask the concierge at your hotel to make a reservation for you.

Rio's *gafieiras* are a better bet if you want to see authentic Brazilian nightlife. The large dance halls draw people of all ages. The places have little or no décor, the bands vary in quality, and the crowds are noisy. But the noise is distinctly Brazilian, and the crowds are charmingly unsophisticated. One of the more sophisticated *gafieiras* is **Asa Branca**, *Avenida Mem de Sa 17*.

You'll find a more sophisticated piano bar and a live band at **Rio Scenarium**, *Rua do Lavradio; tel. +55 (21) 3147-9005; website: www.rioscenarium.com.br*. The **Centro Cultural Carioca**, *Rua do Teatro 37; tel. +55 (21) 2252-6468; website: www.centroculturalcarioca.com.br*, is also a good place to dance with live local bands.

SOUTH AMERICA'S MOST MODERN CITY: BRASILIA

Brasilia is a futuristic fantasy situated in the middle of the great central plain of Brazil and the white buildings of the city are striking, as they are set against the rich red soil. The capital is laid out in the shape of an airplane, with government buildings down the middle and residential and commercial areas along the two wings.

Brasilia came into existence in 1960. President Juscelino Kubitschek decided the nation's capital should be in the center of the country, rather than on the coast, and began construction of the city, which took three years to complete. He drew on the talents of urban planner Lucio Costa, who designed the city, and architect Oscar Niemeyer, who designed the city's major buildings.

However, the seeds of Brasilia were sown in the 1800s by St. João Bosco, who wrote in his memoirs, "Repeatedly a voice spoke out, saying: When they come to excavate the mines hidden in the breasts of these mountains (between the 15th and 20th parallels), here the promised land will arise, giving forth milk and honey. It will be of unimaginable riches, and this will happen before the second generation passes…before 120 years go by." Bosco's vision inspired Brazilian leaders to stipulate in the constitution of 1891 that the new capital should be established in the area between the 15th and 20th parallels, the location of modern-day Brasilia. The saint is commemorated at **Dom Bosco Church**, which has tall and brilliant blue stained-glass windows.

Brazil's tallest tower
Brasilia has one of the tallest telecommunications towers in the world, the 600-foot **Torre de Televisão**. Take an elevator to a platform at 225 feet or another elevator to a restaurant and bar, both of which offer an extensive view of the city.

The best place to begin
Catetinho, the temporary residence of President Juscelino Kubitschek in 1956 and Brasilia's first building, is the best place to begin a tour of the city. The white, clapboard house on stilts was built in 10 days for the former president, when he and city planners were plotting the city's future. It is modestly furnished, with a bed and a plain wooden table, around which city planners gathered.

Brazil's ultramodern cathedral
The architecturally noteworthy **National Cathedral**, is an ultramodern structure designed in the shape of the crown of thorns. A statue of St. Peter is suspended from the roof in the Passage of Reflection, which leads to the underground nave. A pool, which surrounds the concrete building, is reflected in the nave's glass roof panels, giving the interior an airy brightness.

The prettiest palace
One of Brasilia's most famous buildings is the **Itamaraty Palace**, which rises out of the beautiful water gardens that hold the city's well-known sculpture, the Meteor. The reflecting pool is filled with yard-wide lily pads called Victoria Regia, native to the Amazon. Inside the palace is a splendid collection of Brazilian art, including works by Portinari, the country's premiere painter.

Brazil's boldest architecture
The **National Congress Complex**, looks more like an outer-space colony than a political center. The long, narrow building is reached by ramp-like staircases and topped by two eggshell domes (one inverted) known as the cup and saucer. The building glows at sunset.

The **Planalto Palacio** is the city's most graceful building, its roof supported by marble arches, its façade mirrored in a reflecting pool. Next door, a man-made waterfall washes the face of the Justice Ministry. It is open to the public on Sundays from 9.30 a.m. to 1.30 p.m.

The **Palacio dos Arcos** (the Ministry of Foreign Relations) is considered the city's most beautiful building.

The president's house

The **Palacio da Alvorada**, the home of the president of Brazil, is outside town on Lake Paranoá. The sumptuous building has glass walls, rosewood floors, and panels of gilded tile.

Modern masterpieces

Brasilia is known for its modern sculptures, displayed outdoors in public places. The most famous is the **Meteor**, at the Itamaraty Palace, which was mentioned above. Also important are the **Warriors**, in front of the Planalto; the **Water Nymphs**, at the Alvorada; and the **Mermaid**, in front of the Navy Ministry on the Esplanada dos Ministérios.

Brasilia's best dining

Any of the *churrascarias* (steakhouses) along the lake are good places to eat.

For a more upscale dining experience, try **Alice Brasserie**, *SHIS QI 17 Comércio Local, Ed. Fashion Park, Lago Sul; tel. +55 (61) 3248-7743; website: www.restaurantealice.com.br.*

First-class hotels

Brasilia's best hotel is the first-class **Nacional**, *Setor Hoteleiro, Sul Lote 1; tel. +55 (61) 3321-7575; website: www.hotelnacional.com.br*, which has a lovely central view of the government buildings.

Hotel Das Americas, *SHS Quadra 4 - Bloco D, CEP: 70314-000, Brasilia; tel. +55 (61) 3034-3355; website: www.hoteldasamericas.com.br*, in the southern hotel area, is air-conditioned. Rooms are supplied with refrigerators.

Brazil's best theater

The **Teatro Nacional** (National Theater) in Brasilia has one of the most flexible modern stages in South America, as well as two auditoriums. The building was designed to look like an elongated Aztec pyramid.

SÃO PAULO: SOUTH AMERICA'S RICHEST CITY

São Paulo, a city of nearly 20 million, is the industrial center of Brazil and the largest city in South America. It employs the largest labor force in Latin America, with more than 400,000 workers, and it has the highest standard of living in Brazil. Also, it has the largest number of Japanese in the world outside of Japan.

South America's biggest cathedral

The **Catedralo Mertropolitano of São Paulo** is the largest cathedral—and one of the most beautiful in South America. The vaulted neo-Gothic structure holds 8,000 worshipers and dominates the **Praça da Sé** (Cathedral Plaza), where fountains gurgle and Paulistas gather. The cathedral's extensive underground crypt contains the remains of past ecclesiastical figures.

South America's biggest zoo

The **São Paulo Zoo**, *Avenida Miguel Estefano 4241, Auga Funda; tel. +55 (11) 5073-0811*, expands across 204 acres and is home to about 2,700 animals of 366 species. The zoo is open daily from 9 a.m. until 5 p.m.

After visiting the zoo, you may find interest in stopping by the **Jardim Botanico** just down the street to view the 35,000 orchid species displayed here.

South America's best art gallery

The **Museu de Arte de São Paulo**, *Av. Paulista, 1578; tel. +55 (11) 3251-5644*, has a collection of Western art from the Gothic Age to the present, the only such collection in South America. The museum has Raphael's *Resurrection*, painted when the 16th-century artist was just 17, a Rembrandt self-portrait, and 13 works by Renoir.

The closest thing to Japan in the Americas

São Paulo's **Liberdade**—south of Praça da Sé along Praça da Liberdade and Rua Galvão Bueno—is the closest thing to Japan in the Americas. Entered through red lacquer gates, it has tranquil rock gardens, Japanese grocers, and herbal-remedy stores. To realize the importance of São Paulo's Japanese population (nearly 800,000 strong), visit the **Museu da Imigração Japonesa** (Japanese Immigration in Brazil Museum), where exhibits explain the 85-year history of Japanese immigration.

The world's second-best religious art museum

São Paulo's **Museu de Arte Sacra** (Sacred Art Museum), is second only to the Vatican when it comes to collections of Western religious art. Room after room of the museum is filled with carved altars, gold altarpieces, statues, and paintings.

The top sights

Ibirapuera Park, was built for São Paulo's fourth centennial celebration. Inside the grounds is an exact reproduction of Japan's Katura Palace. Willows border the lakes, and eucalyptus groves scent the air.

Casa do Bandeirante, *Praça Monteiro Lobato*, is an 18th-century pioneer house preserved for tourists. You can see firsthand the Spartan lifestyles of early settlers, who slept in hammocks and used trunks as tables. On the grounds are oxcarts and three mills for sugarcane and corn.

You can see how Brazil's wealthier colonists lived at the **Museu da Casa Brasileira** (Brazilian Home Museum), *Ave. Brigada Faria Lima 2705; tel. +55 (11) 3032-3727*. Built in 1945, the mansion contains photos and sketches of early homes, as well as antique furniture and religious pieces.

In the old center of town, near the financial district, several churches and a Byzantine Franciscan convent still stand, as well as São Paulo's oldest building, a Jesuit chapel built in 1554.

Another attraction (so to speak) is the largest snake farm on the continent, the **Instituto Butantã**, *Ave. Vital Brasil 1500; website: www.butantan.gov.br*, where venom is collected for medicinal uses.

The best restaurants

The best place in São Paulo for *feijoadas* is **Bolinha**, *Ave. Cidade Jardim 53; tel. +55 (11) 3061-2010; website: www.bolinha.com.br*, a popular place that usually has long lines (reservations not accepted). Have a drink at the bar and people watch while you wait.

If you tire of Brazilian food, you can have a good French meal at **Marcel's**, *Rua da Consolação, 3555; tel. +55 (11) 3064-3089*.

Terraço Italia, *Ave. Ipiranga 344; tel. +55 (11) 2189-2929; website: www.terracoitalia.com.br*, has a spectacular view of the city as well as good food.

São Paulo also has good *churrascarias* (**Rodeio**, *Rua Haddock Lobo 1498; tel. +55 (11) 3474-1333; website: www.churrascariarodeio.com.br*, which has a great cowboy atmosphere, is the best) and a great many ethnic restaurants. The city's Oriental section is five square miles and loaded with Asian restaurants. To the east is an area of typical Italian restaurants run by descendants of immigrants who came to Brazil to grow coffee and wine.

The best beds

The best hotel in São Paulo is the **Emiliano Hotel,** *Rua Oscar Freire 384; tel. +55 (11) 3069-4369; website: www.emiliano.com.br.* This small boutique hotel prides itself on the little touches such as complimentary fruit, wine, and massage. Also sample dinner in the restaurant. The food, along with the service is excellent.

Another good hotel is the **Grand Hyatt Sao Paulo**, *Avenida das Nacoes Unidas 13.301; tel. +55 (11) 2838-1234; website: http://saopaulo.grand.hyatt.com.*

The **Hilton São Paulo Morumbi**, *Av. das Nacoes Unidas, 12901; tel. +55 (11) 2845-0000; website: www1.hilton.com*, is modern and stylish, located in the modern business district of the city.

The **Quality Suites Imperial Hall**, *Rua da Consolacao, 3555; tel. +55 (11) 2137-4555; website: www.qualityinn.com/hotel-sao_paulo-brazil-BR057*, is located in the Jardins district and is close to shopping and some great restaurants.

SALVADOR—CENTER OF VOODOOISM

Salvador de Bahía is the center of the **Candomblé** cult, created by African slaves who were forced to practice Catholicism but wanted to preserve their own religion. The slaves merged their gods with Christian saints and biblical characters and worshiped both. The deity of lightning, Chong, for example, was combined with St. Barbara, also associated with lightning. And Iemanja is another name for the Virgin Mary. Candomble has become an accepted part of Roman Catholicism. Salvador has 166 churches and 4,000 Candomblé *terreiros* (temples).

You can attend a Candomblé ceremony (as long as you don't bring a camera or cross your hands or feet, which is considered unlucky). The god to be honored at the ceremony has a special costume, the colors of which are donned by Candomblé followers. Men and women are seated opposite each other. As the ritual progresses, worshipers fall to the ground in convulsions, their bodies apparently possessed by the spirits being conjured up. They speak in voices completely unlike their own. Most ceremonies begin at 8.30 p.m. and continue until 11 p.m. or midnight.

Another ritual dating back to the days of slavery is the **capoeira**, a dance-fight. This strange and beautiful performance was begun by slaves who, forbidden to fight, learned to disguise their aggressions in the graceful form of a dance.

Traditional Christianity is also colorful in Salvador. Celebrations of regional Catholic holidays, including the Procession of Our Lady of the Seamen, the Procession of Bonfim, and the Feast of the Second of July, are elaborate.

The best place to enjoy Carnival

Carnival is even more colorful in Salvador than in Rio, although it is less known. And it is longer, beginning one month before Lent. Participants pay homage to Iemanjá, the goddess of the sea, and don the *mortalha*, a costume made of bed sheets. Groups, called *afoxes*, dance to drums and throw a powder called *efu*, which is made from the horns of sheep and supposedly possesses mystical powers.

The most beautiful church

Igreja da São Francisco, *Praça Pae. Anchieta 1*, is one of the most beautiful baroque churches in the world. Built in the 18th century by Franciscans, the interior walls are covered with gold leaf and hand-carved rosewood. Portuguese stone was imported to construct the church and Portuguese tiles to illustrate the life of St. Francis. Men can visit the monastery next door, but women can only peer through the door.

Salvador's cathedral, **Terreiro de Jesus**, is massive and also covered in gold leaf. The Jesuits built the cathedral from 1657 to 1672, before they were ousted from Brazil. It is closed to the public during Carnival.

The most popular church in the city is the **Igreja de Nosso Senhor do Bonfim** (Church of Our Lord of the Good Ending), *Adro do Bonfim*. It is dedicated to Oxalá, the father of Candomblé gods and goddesses, who is also known as Jesus. Worshippers often wear silver and white, the colors of Oxalá. A tiny room in the back of the church contains creepy testimonials to the power of faith—wax castings of injured or sick human body parts that have been miraculously cured.

A beautiful little Carmelite church, **Largo do Carmo**, founded in 1585, has been made into a museum that displays religious objects in precious metals and stones and an exhibit explaining Candomblé.

Igreja da Boa Viagen (Church of the Good Voyage), *Boa Viagen Beach*, is known for its 18th-century Portuguese mosaics.

The oldest church in Salvador is **Igreja e Mosterio de Nossa Senhora da Graça**, *Largo da Graça*. The 18th-century church includes part of a monastery built in 1557.

Igreja e Convento de Santa Tereza, *Rua do Sodré 25*, was built in the 17th century for the Shoeless Carmelites' Order of St. Teresa. It has been restored and made into the Museu de Arte Sacre.

The best shopping

Mercado São Joaquim, *Avenida Jequitaia*, is the largest market in Salvador, selling everything from vegetables to magic herbs. You can find great bargains. The market is open from 6 a.m. to 6 p.m. daily except Sundays, when it closes at 1 p.m.

Mercado Modelo, *Praça Cairu*, is a great place to shop for gifts. Choose from silver and rosewood charms to ward off the evil eye, or you can buy *balagandãs*, little silver fruits once given to slave women who shared their masters' beds.

Salvador's best food

In addition to religion, African culture also has influenced local cuisine, most of which you'll find fantastic, some of which you'll find strange. It is characterized by creoles and jambalayas, spicy and served with rice. The primary ingredients are pork, seafood, and coconut.

Fogo de Chao, *Praca Colombo, 4, Rio Vermelho, Salvador; tel. +55 (71) 3555-9292*. If you're looking for an authentic Brazilian steak house you can't go wrong with Fogo de Chao. Definitely not one for vegetarians, there are 15 different types of meat on offer which will be cooked to your specifications.

The best hotels

Convento do Carmo, *Rua do Carmo 1; tel. +55 (71) 3327-8400; website: www. pestana.com/hotels/en/hotels/southamerica/BahiaHotels/ConventodoCarmo/ Home/*, is the most charming hotel in town, occupying the former convent of a 16th-century Carmelite church. Guests sleep in nuns' cells, which have been outfitted with decadent modern additions, such as air conditioning, color televisions, and refrigerator-bars. The central courtyard has a large pool. Although the hotel is not near the beaches, it is a convenient base for exploring town. The hotel restaurant serves traditional Portuguese food.

The best moderately priced hotel in Salvador is the **Grande Hotel da Barra**, *Ave. Sete de Setembro 3564; tel. +55 (71) 2106-8600; website: www.grandehoteldabarra.com.br.*

Niagara's superior

Iguaçu Falls, at the border with Argentina and even bigger than Niagara Falls, is a spectacular sight. One of the world's greatest waterfalls, it is on the Igauçu River, near its confluence with the Paraná River. Iguaçu Falls is actually made up of 275 separate falls, some very tiny. The biggest is Devil's Throat, 330 feet high. (*Igauçu* means *great waters* in the language of the local Guaraní tribes, who were once cannibalistic and the subject of the movie *Missionary*.)

To best see the falls, take the elevator down to the river's edge and walk out onto the platform that reaches into the middle. From this angle, you will see rainbows glimmering through the water. Nearby is the great **Itaipú Dam** and the world's largest hydroelectric power complex.

THE WORLD'S LARGEST RAINFOREST: THE AMAZON

The world's largest rainforest and the world's largest river share the same name: the **Amazon**. The river flows 3,550 miles, is fed by 1,000 smaller rivers and tributaries, and is home to 2,000 species of fish (including the life-threatening piranha, with its razor-sharp teeth, and the candiru, which swims up human orifices and lodges itself in the body).

The forest is home to exotic animals, such as the tapir and anaconda. You'll see colorful parrots deep in the jungle. About 158 Indian tribes live in the Amazon. When they first visited the New World, Christopher Columbus and Sir Walter Raleigh both reported hearing of Amazon warrior women, who, like the characters in Greek legend, lived independently of men.

Encompassing an area of 2.3 million square miles, the Amazon is overwhelming. The only practical way to see it is by boat—few roads make their way through the dense jungle. Don't expect to see all the Amazon's mysteries when traveling down the river—at points the river is so wide that the shore cannot be seen on both sides.

The best ways to see the Amazon

If you are not one for wilderness, cruises down the river are available with amenities such as staterooms, dining areas, and air conditioning. However, if you are willing to sleep in a hammock on deck, riverboats depart weekly and allow for truly enveloping yourself within the feel of the Amazon.

It is best to plan these adventures before you leave home. For more information contact one of the following tour operators: **LADATCO**, *3006 Aviation, Suite 3A, Coconut Grove, Florida 33133; tel. (800) 327-6162; website: www.ladatco. com;* or **Brazil Nuts**, *tel. (800) 553-9959; website: www.brazilnuts.com.*

The best medical advice

Take proper medical precautions against malaria before and during a trip to the Amazon. Anti-malaria pills. Yellow fever shots are also required for travel in the Amazon.

The best of Belém, gateway to the Amazon

Belém—the gateway to the Amazon—is a modern city with vestiges of its colonial past. Nearby, at the mouth of the Amazon, is **Marajo Island**, which is bigger than all of Denmark. Archeologists are studying burial grounds on Marajo, where remnants of a long-lost people can be seen. The island also has huge buffalo farms and herds of wild buffalo, whose ancestors escaped the captivity of earlier farms. Buffalo hunts are organized out of Belém.

The most expensive hotel in town is the **Hilton Belem**, *Ave. Presidente Vargas 882; tel. +55 (91) 4006-7000; website: www1.hilton.com*, across from the Praça da Republica.

The **Hotel Regente**, *Ave. Governador José Malcher 485; tel. +55 (91) 3181-5000; website: www.hotelregente.com.br*, is an inexpensive three-star place.

Manaus: At the heart of the rainforest

If you want to really experience the Amazon, go to **Manaus**. The architecture in this town is a mix of European styles and modern wooden structures that is blended into the jungle surroundings. The waterfront market sells live animals and birds and voodoo and Indian artifacts. Because Manaus is a free port, you can buy imported merchandise for at least two-thirds less than elsewhere in Brazil.

Manaus is the best base for taking day excursions upriver into narrow tributary channels. **Capitania do Porto** (Office of the Port Captain), *rua Marques de Santa Cruz*, has information on boat trips, including several one- and two-day trips up the River Negro. Hunting and fishing safaris also can be arranged.

The best hotel is the five-star **Tropical Manaus**, *Av. Coronel Teixeira, 1320, Ponta Negra; tel. +55 (92) 2123-5000; website: www.tropicalmanaus.com.br*, on the beach of Ponta Negra outside town. It is well worth its price. The Tropical is situated on a 10-acre site, cleared from virgin jungle, running along the River Negro from Manaus. It has a private zoo. Architect Adolpho Linden designed the hotel to look like a Portuguese colonial country house. You can arrange expeditions to explore the Amazon River and the jungle from the hotel. The hotel's restaurant is first-class, known for its superb regional fish dishes.

South America's most spectacular wildlife

Pantanal, a region similar to the Florida Everglades, is located south of the Amazon in western Brazil. Pantanal has the most spectacular concentrations of wildlife in South America, if not the world. A tremendous place for birding and fishing, Pantanal can be reached from either Campo Grande or Cuiaba via a jeep safari or riverboat trip. The same groups that arrange trips to the Amazon organize trips to Pantanal.

The world's best colored gems

Brazil is the world's major purveyor of colored gems. Aquamarine, topaz, amethyst, and turmaline stones are abundant, and they cost 20% to 25% less in Brazil than in New York, for example. Emeralds are also in great supply; settings and mountings of these gems are also tremendous bargains because of the low cost of labor.

Two good places to shop for colored gems are **H. Stern**, *website: www. hstern.com.br*, and **Amsterdam Sauer**, *website: www.amsterdamsauer.com*—the largest dealers in Brazil. H. Stern offers free round-trip transportation from all major hotels in Rio to its headquarters in Ipanema. It also conducts tours of its lapidary, goldsmith workshops, and gem museum, the latter of which features a 42-pound aquamarine.

THE BEST OF
BRITAIN

*The way to ensure summer in England is to have it framed
and glazed in a comfortable room.*

—Horace Walpole, 1774

Britain is a land of perfectionism. Shirts must be made with precision. Suits are of good English wool. Tea must be made just so. And politeness is practically law.

The land itself is a place of wonders—mighty castles, charming villages with thatched cottages, ancient cathedrals, pre-historic stone circles, misty lakes, and dramatic shorelines.

Although hundreds of regions throughout Britain demand a visit, the number-one destination is London. Here, many of the world's most famous playwrights and artists blossomed; history's most bloody and fascinating tales unfolded; and the outcome of World War II was sealed. We begin our look at the best of Britain, then, in this remarkable city.

LONDON, THE MOST MEMORABLE CITY

"What has made London the most poignantly memorable city of the world is its continuing ability to recognize the human condition," writer Richard Condon once said. "From Battersea to Woolwich, across the 32 boroughs of the city, humans reign in perpetual celebration of one of the most complex multilayered communities on the planet… Quirky, steeped in the past but actively and civilly pursuing the present, London—and Londoners—continue to honor all that is human. And 1,250 years after its founding, visitors are still drawn to the city's idiosyncrasies—all those facets that endure and enrich life."

Top sights in London

Big Ben, the most famous sight in London, is usually misidentified. Many people believe, incorrectly, that Big Ben is the clock in the Parliament tower; it is actually the 13-and-a-half-ton bell.

The home of **Parliament**, beneath Big Ben, is a huge complex of Victorian buildings that covers 8 acres and includes 1,100 rooms. The guided tour is definitely worth your time. See *www.parliament.uk* for more information.

Westminster Hall, built from 1394 to 1402, is a part of the palace. Admission is free, but donations are accepted and go toward restoration funds.

English kings and queens begin and end their careers at **Westminster Abbey**, where royal coronations and burials have been held since the time of William the Conqueror, in the 11th century. **Poets' Corner** in the south transept contains the tombs of such British literary greats as Geoffrey Chaucer, Charles Dickens, Robert Browning, and Thomas Hardy.

The **Tate Britain Gallery,** *Millbank, London SW1P 4RG, tel. +44 (20) 7887-8888; website: www.tate.org.uk*, has the best collection of works by British painters, including Turner, Blake, Hogarth, and Constable. It also contains works by French Impressionists Manet, Monet, Cézanne, and Degas, as well as sculptures by Rodin, Picasso, and Henry Moore. If your taste runs to more contemporary art, then check out the **Tate Modern**, *Bankside, London SE1 9TG, tel. +44 (20) 7887-8888; website: www.tate.org.uk.*

Whitehall, where fiery King Henry VIII once had his palace, is now an efficient, modern-day government center that runs between the Thames River and St. James' Park.

Number 10 Downing Street, where the prime minister lives, is part of Whitehall. The War Rooms at 70 Whitehall served as Churchill's subterranean headquarters during World War II. The rooms are now open to the public from 10 a.m. until 5 p.m.

The **Banqueting House** in Whitehall is where Charles I was beheaded. Today the building is used for government receptions. Rubens decorated the house's ceiling with nine allegorical paintings. A bust of Charles I on the staircase marks the position of the window the king walked through to get to the scaffolding where he was beheaded.

Surrounded by four regal lions, the mighty **Nelson Column** rises from the heart of **Trafalgar Square**, a monument to Admiral Nelson. (Nelson died in battle with the French off Cape Trafalgar. He spurred his men on to victory with the inspiring words "England expects every man to do his duty.") Concerts are held Sundays at noon in the temple-like **St.-Martin-in-the-Fields church**, also on the square.

Nearby is the **National Gallery**, *tel. +44 (20) 7747 2885; website: www. nationalgallery.org.uk,* with works by Vermeer, Turner, Botticelli, Michelangelo, Holbein, El Greco, and Delacroix. Don't miss the gallery's controversial annex.

Europe's largest medieval fortress

The **Tower of London**, *website: www.hrp.org.uk/TowerOfLondon*, the largest medieval fortress, has witnessed foul deeds and grand spectacles alike. Inside the fortress, on Tower Green, innumerable heads rolled, including those of Anne Boleyn, Lady Jane Grey, Sir Walter Raleigh, and the Earl of Essex (Queen Elizabeth I's rejected lover). In the Bloody Tower, as it is known, Richard III supposedly murdered 13-year-old King Edward V and the king's little brother.

The **Crown Jewels** are kept in the Tower of London. The Cullinan diamond here is the largest ever found. It was sent to London from Transvaal, South Africa in a brown paper package via third-class mail.

London's oldest church

Any visit to the Tower of London should include a visit to the **Chapel of St. John**. The chapel was built in 1080, making it the oldest church in London.

The most famous sea clipper

The **Cutty Sark**, the most famous sea clipper ever built, rests on the waterfront in Greenwich. Built in 1869, it was one of the few sailing ships to survive despite the dawn of the steam age. During conservation work in 2007, the ship was damaged by a major fire but restoration work is due to be complete in 2012. While the Cutty Sark Conservation Project is underway, there is no public access to the ship but for updates on the restoration process, see *www.cuttysark.org.uk.*

London's best post office

The **Trafalgar Square Post Office**, *tel. +44 (20) 7930-9580*, is London's best—and it's also open the latest. It is open until 8 p.m. Monday through Saturday, and Sunday until 5 p.m. for those late, must-go-out parcels.

The worst place to tell secrets

St. Paul's Cathedral has a **Whispering Gallery** where you can hear a word whispered on the other side of the dome as loudly as if the person were standing right beside you. Prince Charles and Lady Diana Spencer were married here.

The best changing of the guard

The best changing of the guard in London isn't at Buckingham Palace, as you might expect. It is in the middle of **Whitehall**, where the red-suited Horse Guards are stationed. The changing of the guard here is as picturesque as at Buckingham Palace and a good deal less crowded. (Tourists visit Buckingham Palace by the millions.)

The best place for repartee

The best entertainment in London is a session at the **House of Commons**, on Parliament Square, where insults are exchanged freely and with wild abandon. Florence Horsbrugh, once minister of education, suffered the following insult: "I do not know what the Right Honorable Lady, the Minister of Education, is grinning at. This is the face that sank a thousand scholarships." And Winston Churchill, when accused of being drunk by a female political foe, replied, "And you, Madam, are ugly. But tomorrow I shall be sober!"

You can observe these verbal battles from the gallery. The 156 seats are filled on a first-come, first-served basis. Check the website for sitting times of the House; *website: www.parliament.co.uk.*

London's strangest sight

Cleopatra's Needle is the most surprising monument in London. This Egyptian obelisk dates back to 1500 B.C. Set in the shadow of Waterloo Bridge on the edge of Thames embankment, it bears the carvings of two of Egypt's greatest rulers: pharaohs Thothmes III and Ramses II. Offered to England in the 19th century by the ruler of Egypt, the obelisk actually had nothing to do with Cleopatra—it was transported down the Nile into the Mediterranean aboard a boat called *Cleopatra*.

When the Needle reached the Bay of Biscay on Oct. 14, 1877, it fell overboard during a storm. Six men volunteered to recover the monument and drowned trying to save it. (Their names are inscribed on the south face of the base.) Several days later, the monument was rescued by a freighter that lugged it to London.

The world's spookiest walks

As the night sets in and the long shadows fall, travel into the crooked, cobbled alleyways of Whitechapel to follow Jack the Ripper's bloodstained trail of terror. The **Jack the Ripper Haunts Walk** takes place every night (except Dec 24th and 25th) at 7.30 p.m. and lasts about two hours. Meet the guide outside Tower Hill Underground station. No need to reserve in advance; the cost is £8 ($13) and £6 ($9) for students and over 65s. See the website for more details: *www.walks.com*.

London's liveliest corner

Piccadilly Circus is as crazy and colorful as its name. Crowded with people and filled with brightly colored billboards, the square is centered around a small statue of Eros and known as a pickup spot and favorite spot for pickpockets. But don't worry about the criminal elements—Piccadilly is also crowded with ordinary citizens and tourists and is perfectly safe. Piccadilly is also where you'll find the **Royal Academy of Fine Arts**, the **Ritz Hotel**, and **St. James' Church**, which offers concerts during the summer.

The artiest neighborhoods

Covent Garden, where professor Higgins met Eliza Doolittle in *My Fair Lady*, has become the city's favorite hangout for yuppies. It's home to the London Transport Museum, the Theatre Museum, the Theatre Royal and Royal Opera House, and a crafts market. The area is used as an impromptu stage for clowns, mimes, musicians, and other entertainers, who perform and then pass the hat.

Bloomsbury was once the home of the literary and intellectual "Bloomsbury Group," which included Virginia Woolf, John Maynard Keynes, and E.M. Forster. This charming area offers the **British Museum**, the **Courtland Institute Galleries**, and **Pollock's Toy Museum**.

Soho is home to London's red-light district, but it's also filled with little restaurants and shops. Like Piccadilly, its criminal element is rendered harmless by the plentiful crowds. Soho's **Berwick Street** has a great produce market.

Leicester Square was the home of painters Hogarth and Reynolds.

Hampstead is a writers' and artists' quarter on a hill overlooking the city. Here you can rummage through antique stores and bookshops before enjoying afternoon tea in a neighborhood café. Visit **Keats'** home on Wentworth Place and **Freud's** home at 20 Maresfield Gardens.

London's most romantic park

The most romantic park in central London is off Guilford Street in Bloomsbury. But it has a strange restriction—no adult, a sign by the gate announces, may enter unless accompanied by a child. **Coram's Fields** is 6 acres of playground on the site of the Foundling Hospital for abandoned children, set up by Captain Thomas Coram more than 250 years ago.

The best place to rant and rave

Amateur orators spout forth at **Speakers Corner** in Hyde Park every Sunday. If you feel the urge to speak from a soapbox, this is the place. If you'd rather just listen, be prepared. You never know what you might hear—anarchists, religious zealots, racists, communists…or vegetarians! Hyde Park is worth a visit even if you aren't interested in all the ranting and raving. On a pretty day, you can go boating in the park or just take a long stroll.

The world's best waxworks

Madame Tussauds, *tel. +44 (870) 999-0046; website: www.madametussauds. com*, located on Marylebone Road, is just about as touristy as you can get in London, but if you like waxworks, these are the best in the world. Madame Tussaud began her museum in Paris in the late 18th century, but revolutionary events drove her to London in 1802. The Chamber of Horrors is still the most interesting section of all, but rock stars, politicians, sports personalities, and royalty are certainly equally well-presented.

The world's best theater

London is the theater capital of the world. Most of the major theaters are in the **West End**, a short walk from Trafalgar Square, in Covent Garden, or in Leicester Square. Notable exceptions are the **National Theatre** complex on the South Bank, next to the Royal Festival Hall, and the splendid **Barbican Centre for the Arts**, permanent London home of the Royal Shakespeare Company.

You can get half-price tickets to major shows at the **Leicester Square Ticket Booth** (right in Leicester Square). Tickets are available for same-day West End shows only and you'll rarely find tickets for recent hits. What is available is posted on the boards next to the booth, but the line is normally long and the tickets go fast, so keep an eye on the board as you wait. You can also get discounted tickets by going to the theater lobby right before the performance—although you may find yourself running from theater to theater. Last-minute tickets are sometimes also available for sold-out shows, although not at discounted prices. Tickets are always discounted for students with international student identification cards and senior citizens.

The world's best fringe theater

London's so-called fringe theaters are far removed from the neon lights and star-studded marquees of the fashionable West End. Yet, these small (each seats less than 100 people), out-of-the-way theaters offer some of the city's most inspired, innovative, and imaginative theatrical performances. One of the best-known fringe theaters in London, and for good reason, is the **Albany Empire**, *tel. +44 (20) 8692-4446; website: www.thealbany.org.uk*, located on Douglas Way. It offers two plays simultaneously year-round.

The three best ways to spend a Sunday afternoon

Where should a bargain hunter in London head on a Sunday afternoon? The **Bayswater Road Art Exhibition**. From modern art to detailed still-lifes, baroque to Romantic, portraits to landscapes, watercolors to oils, copper etchings to pastels—it's all at Bayswater, one of the largest open-air exhibitions in the world. The exhibits stretch for eight-tenths of a mile, beginning at Clarendon Place and continuing until Queensway, and they are open every Sunday, rain or shine, 8 a.m. until 5 p.m. The Queensway and Lancaster Gate Underground stations bring you right to the heart of the area.

The second best place to spend a Sunday afternoon is **Camden Lock**, London's largest, gaudiest, and most unpredictably varied flea market. It's cheap and friendly—and for dedicated "people watchers," it offers a never-ending flow of exotic youth. To get there, take the Northern Line to Camden Town or Chalk Farm.

And the third best way to spend a Sunday is to take a tour of **Little Venice**. You come upon it unexpectedly—it's just a short walk from Warwick Avenue tube station to the little bridge over the canal. Here Regent's Canal meets the Grand Union Canal, forming a wider stretch of water flowing around a tree-covered island. The nickname "Little Venice" was first coined by the famous poet Robert Browning, who once lived nearby. Sycamore trees line the banks of the canals, and the Nash-designed houses, with their distinctive white stucco facades and lawns and gardens sweeping down to the water's edge, boast an 18th-century elegance.

One of the best outfits offering tours to Little Venice is *Walkers Quay, tel. +44 (20)7485- 4433; website: www.walkersquay.com,* on their *Jenny Wren* boat.

Another good tour company is **London Waterbus Company**, *tel. +44 (20) 7482-2550; website: www.londonwaterbus.com,* which departs hourly from the intersection where Grand Union Canal and Regent's Canal cross. The Waterbus Company lands at the zoo; it offers a reduced ticket price—and none of the waiting lines found at the main gate. Both tours pass Browning's Island, Regents Park, the zoo, the Maida Hill tunnel, and Camden Locks.

London's best flea market

Petticoat Lane Flea Market, held Sundays in Middlesex Street, is brimming with bargains. The lively outdoor market has antiques as well as inexpensive new goods (especially clothing and appliances), bric-a-brac, and used items. The real bargains are found before 8 a.m. Take the underground to Liverpool Street and then walk up Bishop's Gate to Middlesex Street. (You won't find Petticoat Lane on the map; it's a nickname for Middlesex Street.)

The most entertaining flea market

One of the largest and most entertaining flea markets in Europe is held every Saturday on **Portobello Road**. To get there, take the underground to Notting Hill Gate and then walk down Pembrook Road to Portobello Road. On Saturdays, the road is lined with street performers and part-time vendors selling everything from rock group buttons to antiques. Fine hats and shoes that once bedecked Britain's elite can be found here at pauper's prices. If you aren't interested in buying, just watch the people.

Antique hunting at its best

Camden Passage is a great place for antiques—it has more than 100 shops. Decorative and Victorian antiques are of especially good quality in this corner of London, so don't expect knockdown prices. Take the underground to the Angel Islington stop and then walk up Islington High Street. An early morning flea market is held here Wednesday and Saturday.

Serious antique hunters flock to the **New Caledonian Market** (Bermondsey) at the London Bridge underground station. This huge market has quality silver, china, jewelry, memorabilia, and *objets d'art*. It is open Friday 5 a.m. until 1 p.m. Arrive early for the best buys.

The best antiquarian book dealer

A Mr. Maggs still owns **Maggs Brothers**, *50 Berkeley Square, tel. +44 (20) 7493-7160; website: www.maggs.com*. This rare book dealer specializes in illuminated manuscripts, first editions, and autographed letters of English authors. Many priceless works are in stock, and the bibliophile (with clean hands) is welcome to stop in and see the treasures. For instance, you can inspect one of the original privately printed editions of T.E. Lawrence's (Lawrence of Arabia) *Seven Pillars of Wisdom*. The lover of fine books will find no worthier shrine.

The best brass rubbing center

Not surprisingly, the best place for brass rubbing in London is the **London Brass Rubbing Centre**, *6 St. Martin's Place, tel. +44 (20) 7930-9306*. Located in a magnificent 18th-century church, famous for its lunchtime concerts of chamber and choral music, this is one of the few places in London where you can still make your own brass rubbings. The center is open Monday through Wednesday, 10 a.m. until 7 p.m., Thursday to Saturday 10 a.m. until 6 p.m. and Sunday 11.30 a.m. until 6 p.m.

The world's best maze

Hampton Court Palace, *tel. +44 (20) 3166-6000; website: www.hrp.org.uk/HamptonCourtPalace,* located at East Molesey, Surrey, contains England's oldest and most popular maze. The labyrinth is bounded by high hedges and reinforced with railings to prevent cheating. Arrive by boat from Westminster Pier or by train from the Waterloo station in London (a distance of 10 miles). The palace, which dates from the early 1500s, is open Monday through Sunday 10 a.m. until 6 p.m. The last entry into the maze is at 5.15 p.m.

The best place to go fly a kite

The **Kite Store**, *tel. +44 (20) 7836-1666*, was the first shop of its kind in Europe, and it now stocks more than 200 kinds of kite, as well as boomerangs and Frisbees. Once you've purchased your kite, the best place to fly it is on Hampstead Heath, which offers a tremendous view of the city below.

The most magical toy store

Hamleys, *188-196 Regent Street; tel. +44 (871) 704-1977; website: www.hamleys.com*, is packed with every imaginable form of entertainment for both children and adults. The store is open Monday through Wednesday and Saturday 10 a.m. to 8 p.m., Thursday and Friday 10 a.m. to 9 p.m., and Sunday noon to 6 p.m.

London's oldest cheese store

Paxton & Whitfield, *93 Jermyn Street; tel. +44 (20) 7930-0259,* is the oldest and best cheese shop in London; it came to Jermyn Street in 1797. With more than 300 European cheeses (including 40 to 50 British varieties), Paxton & Whitfield assuredly will have the kind you are looking for. (The cheeses are stocked not according to price but according to tradition.) There's absolutely no risk of buying an off-brand wheel of Brie, for instance. The counters are also stacked with preserves, pickles, and fine wines.

The best stuffed shirts

The stuffed shirts of the world know the best shirt shopping is along Jermyn Street in London. Here, traditional shirts are made of Sea Island cotton or two-fold poplin. The collars are perfectly shaped and stitched, as are the cuffs. The buttons are mother-of-pearl. The cut is generous, and the shirttails are long. **Hildich & Key** (*37 and 73 Jermyn Street, London; website: www.hilditchandkey.co.uk*), produces the finest and most expensive shirts in London. Made of soft cotton, they have hand-sewn buttonholes, removable collar stays, and double cuffs.

Turnbull & Asser, *71-72 Jermyn Street, London; website: www.turnbullandasser.com*, has shirts with collars roomy enough for T&A's generous ties. And the cut of the shirts makes them extra comfortable.

The finest linens in the world

Despite its tiny interior, the **Irish Linen Company**, *35-36 Burlington Arcade; tel. +44 (20) 7493-8949; website: www.irishlinencompany.com,* has a beautiful selection of some of the finest hand-worked linens you can find anywhere. Price-conscious shoppers will be most interested in the decorative tablecloths and napkins.

London's best tailor

Stovel & Mason, *32 Old Burlington Street; tel. +44 (20) 7734-4855*, is a London tailor who offers Saville Row quality at more moderate prices. (Always have suspenders or brace buttons attached to the inside of your pants, and insist on 13-inch-deep pockets and jacket cuffs that unbutton.)

London's finest shoemakers

The two best shoemakers in London are **Lobbs**, *9 St. James Place, London SW1* (the waiting list is long); and **Tricker's**, *67 Jermyn Street; tel. +44 (20) 7930-6395; website: www.trickers.com.*

The best brollies
Swaine & Adeney, *54 St James's Street, tel. +44 (20) 7409-7277; website: www. swaineadeney.co.uk,* in Piccadilly makes umbrellas by hand. The very best brolly (a favorite in the House of Lords) is a Brigg.

The city's best lace market
Nottingham holds the best lace market at Sneinton. The market is open Monday, Wednesday, Friday, and Saturday 10 a.m. until 4 p.m. To learn about the history of lace or to see demonstrations about how lace is made, visit **Lace Hall**, *High Pavement*, or **Severn's Building**, *Council Road*. Both are open daily 10 a.m. until 5 p.m.

The best ways to explore London
Walking is the best way to see the city if you don't have money to blow on a private guide. And on foot, you can see London in greater detail and mingle with the British. You can make your own way through the city using a guidebook and map, or you can join one of London's many walking tours.

London Walks, *tel. +44 (20) 7624-3978; website: www.walks.com*, takes you in the footsteps of Jack the Ripper, Shakespeare, Dickens, Virginia Woolf, and other notables.

If your feet get tired, rest a while on a double-decker bus or London's famous subway, known as **the Tube** or the Underground. The underground is the world's oldest and most extensive rapid transit system, with more than 250 stations and 750 miles of track. Fares are set according to the length of your ride. On buses, you can pay the conductor, but you must buy an underground ticket before you get on the train. And make sure you don't throw away your ticket—you'll need it to leave the station at the other end of your journey.

A **London Travelcard** ticket allows you unlimited travel on the London bus and tube systems. It is available from travel agents, at any subway station, and at the London Regional Transport Travel Information Centre. Tour buses depart Victoria Station and Piccadilly Circus daily at 9.30 a.m., 11 a.m., and 2.30 p.m.

London double-decker bus tours are also available. The open-topped buses depart Piccadilly Circus, Victoria Station, and Marble Arch daily 9 a.m. until 4 p.m. The tours last about two hours and 20 minutes. A free map is included. Reservations aren't necessary.

The best places to take tea

In a city known for its tea, a few places stand scones and Devonshire cream above the rest. The most elegant place to enjoy a pot of hot tea with scones is the **Dorchester Hotel**; *tel. +44 (20) 7629-8888*, on Park Lane.

The coziest place for tea would be The English Tea Room in **Brown's Hotel, Albemarle Street, Mayfair; tel. +44 (20) 7493-6020; website: www.brownshotel. com**, a Victorian Hotel where Rudyard Kipling once stayed. Men must wear a tie to take tea at Brown's after 4 p.m. (And they should take a moment to glance into the men's room before they leave; the scale is an extremely rare antique.)

Another good place to take tea is the department store **Fortnum and Mason**, *181 Piccadilly; tel. +44 (20) 7734-8040; website: www.fortnumandmason.com*. If the fashionable Fountain Room is too crowded, go upstairs to the more discreet St. James's Restaurant—few people know about it.

The best restaurants in London

Restaurant Gordon Ramsey, *68 Royal Hospital Rd. SW3 4HP; tel. +44 (20) 7352 4441; website: www.gordonramsay.com/royalhospitalroad*, is by many accounts the top restaurant in London. The chef, Mr. Ramsey himself, is a mega-star on the very sophisticated horizon of London dining. As such, a four-month advance reservation is a wise idea for this popular restaurant. Try the *foie gras*, which can be prepared in three different ways, or the caramelized duck with dates. Keep in mind that whatever one chooses is bound to dazzle. Desserts are equally delectable.

Tom Aikens, *43 Elystan Street; tel. +44 (20) 7584-2003; website: www. tomaikens.co.uk*, trained by the master chef Joël Robuchon, aims to outshine his mentor in his eponymous restaurant. Only his mastery of French cooking outdoes his ambition, for this rising star seems to have no end to his talent. His dishes, from meat and game, to pasta and more delicate entrées are always conceived with characteristic flair and delicacy. Be sure to make a reservation.

The best roast beef in London

At **Simpson's in the Strand**, *100 Strand; tel. +44 (20) 7836-9112; website: www.simpsonsinthestrand.co.uk*, a *maître d'hôtel* dressed in tails ushers diners into the paneled dining room. Six 30-pound four-rib loins are roasted simultaneously. Roast beef and saddles of mutton are wheeled directly to guests' tables and carved there. The cattle are chosen by Simpson's agents at auctions in Scotland. The Duke of Wellington and Margaret Thatcher are said to prefer Simpson's.

The best Indian food

Bombay Brasserie, *140 Courtfield Road, London SW7 4Q4; tel. +44 (20) 7370-4040; website: www.bombaybrasserielondon.com,* is consistently rated as one of the best of the upscale Indian restaurants in London. Especially good are the Goan fish curry, the aromatic chicken dishes, and the bean curries.

Another contender for top spot is **Café Spice Namaste**, *16 Prescott Street; tel. +44 (20) 7488-9242; website: www.cafespice.co.uk.* You'll be hard-pressed to find Indian food with more character and imagination: ostrich and alligator have been known to show up on the menu. The food is always scrumptious; favorites include the curries and tandoori-style meats.

A more economical choice is the **Diwana Bhel Poori House**, *121 Drummond Street, NW1; tel. +44 (20) 7387-5556.* This restaurant, with its unique south Indian vegetarian menu, is open daily noon until 10 p.m. but is closed Mondays.

The best Southeast Asian restaurant

The small, comfortable room at **Nahm**, *in the Halkin Hotel, Halkin Street, Mayfair; tel. +44 (20) 7333-1234; website: http://halkin.como.bz,* is probably the most elegant and possibly the best Thai restaurant in London. The chef keeps it traditional, so if you want authentic with a dash of gourmet, this is your place.

London's best nightlife

One of the trendiest of London's bars is **Loungelover**, *1 Whitby Street; tel. +44 (20) 7012-1234; website: www.loungelover.co.uk.* Located behind its sister Les Trois Garcons restaurant and with a real hippopotamus on the wall, you know you're in for fun. With its exotic oriental interior décor and dark Victorian paneling, this place looks liked it jumped from the page of *The Picture of Dorian Grey*. The drinks menu is spectacular, with more choices than anywhere else.

If you'd prefer something more refined, the elegant **Library Bar**, *Lanesborough Hotel, Hyde Park Corner; tel. +44 (20) 7259-5599; website: www. lanesborough.com,* in the gorgeous Lanesborough Hotel, is a luxurious watering hole for the smart set. Designed in the style of a Regency library, prepare for bookcases lined with musty leather bound books and Victorian oil lamps sitting on oak coffee tables in between deep leather wing chairs. With over 200 cognacs to choose from (some priced at over $500 per glass), it is not for the casual date—and men, don't forget your jacket after 5 p.m.

The funniest place in London

The Comedy Store, *1a Oxendon Street; tel. +44 (20) 7839-6642,* hosts a great mixture of talent; it is said that the cream of the crop of stand-up London comedians have performed here and still do. Tickets can be purchased through, *website: www.thecomedystore.co.uk.*

London's best pub

London's heart is in its pubs. They are located on nearly every street corner and are an integral part of British life. Each has its own inimitable character.

Choosing London's best pub is a big task—everyone has his or her own favorite. Our favorite is **Anchor Tavern**, *34 Park Street, Southwark; tel. +44 (20) 7407-1577,* on the south side of the Thames. This cozy riverside pub was once frequented by writer Samuel Johnson, as well as smugglers, rivermen, and wardens from the nearby Clink Prison. (The slang word for prison comes from the Clink.) The Anchor Tavern originally was built near the site of Shakespeare's Globe Theater; it was rebuilt about 170 years ago. The low-beamed rooms are many and varied. Legend has it that a special brew known as Russian Imperial Stout was prepared at the pub for the empress of Russia. Besides beer, try the roast forerib of beef or the steak and mushroom pudding. The Anchor is open noon until 2 p.m. and 7 p.m. until 10 p.m. It is closed Sunday evenings.

The Flask, *77 Highgate West hill, N6 6BU; tel. +44 (20) 8348-7346,* is our second choice for best pub in London. (You couldn't expect us to pick just one.) The Flask is tremendously popular among Londoners, primarily because of its friendly atmosphere.

The best hotels in London

The **Connaught Hotel**, *16 Carlos Place, Mayfair, London W1Y 6AL; tel. +44 (20) 7499-7070; website: www.the-connaught.co.uk,* is the best in town, with old-fashioned elegance and perfect service. The exterior of the Connaught is lovely, with a gracefully curving façade. Flowers brighten the porch. The interior is cozy, with wood paneling, Oriental rugs, and upholstered chairs.

A magnificent staircase with dark wood banisters leads to bedrooms on the upper floors. The spacious rooms have cheery wallpaper, brass beds, and antique desks. And the bathrooms are luxurious, with grand tubs, fine soaps, thick towels, and a cord ring for the maid. Breakfast, including fresh orange juice, is brought to your room on a cloth-covered table and served in fine china. Write to request a room on the Carlos Place side. Book dinner reservations six weeks in advance.

Claridge's, *49 Brook Street, Mayfair London W1K 4HR; tel. +44 (20) 7629-8860; website: www.claridges.co.uk*, in the heart of Mayfair, is a close second to the Connaught Hotel. It boasts a Hungarian Quartet that has been playing in the lobby for most of this century. Liveried attendants greet you at the door, and dress-maids are available to help you choose what you'd like to wear for the evening. Rooms have fireplaces, bells to ring for the maid or valet, and royal-sized bathtubs.

The **Beaufort**, *33 Beaufort Gardens, London SW3 1PP; tel. +44 (20) 7584-5252; website: www.thebeaufort.co.uk,* is an early Victorian house converted to an elegant guest residence in 1985. Each room is decorated in a different style, but all have telephones and color televisions. It's like staying in someone's home—but enjoying the amenities of a luxury hotel, including fluffy robes, wooden and silk hangers, a dish of chocolates, a personal decanter of brandy, and a Sony Walkman.

Last, but not least, is **Brown's**, *Abbeymarle street, Mayfair W1S 2BP; tel. +44 (20)7493-6020 website: www.brownshotel.com.*The building dates back to 1660; it opened for business as Brown's in 1837. Teddy Roosevelt was married at Brown's, Kipling wrote here, and Queen Victoria visited Queen Wilhelmina here. From 1924 to 1935, it was the official court of the king of Greece. Oak paneling, 19th-century prints, antiques, and stained glass add atmosphere to the 12 connecting buildings that make up Brown's.

The oldest pub in the world

The **George and Vulture**; *tel. +44 (844) 567-2319,* is the oldest pub in the world. The original, called the George, was built in the 12th century. Sir Richard Wittington, the "thrice-round mayor of London," visited here in the 1500s, just as Chaucer (and Chaucer's father) had done earlier. Daniel Defoe, Jonathan Swift, and Charles Dickens were frequent customers at this historic pub. The Pickwick Club meets at the George and Vulture quarterly, and members quote from the many Dickens passages about the place. The fictional Mr. Pickwick, when asked where he spent his leisure time, replied that he was "at present suspended at the George and Vulture." A framed check written by Dickens to the proprietor hangs on the wall.

Other historic pubs

Ye Olde Cheshire Cheese, *145 Fleet Street,* was opened in 1538 and rebuilt in 1667 after the Great Fire of London. The Cheese was a favorite of Goldsmith and Johnson and was mentioned by Dickens in *A Tale of Two Cities.* It is one of London's few remaining 17th-century chophouses. The Cheese has sawdust on the floors (changed twice daily), and tables are boxed in, with a bench for three diners on each side. An open fire cheers the original bar in winter, which, until recently, was reserved for men only. Try the savory baked cheese and Guinness on toast, the steak and kidney pie, and the Yorkshire pudding.

One of the oldest riverfront pubs, the **Prospect of Whitby**, *57 Wapping Wall,* was popular with painters Whistler and Turner. While drinking here, Hanging Judge Jeffreys watched his sentences being carried out at the nearby Execution Dock.

The Trafalgar is located on the Thames at the place where time begins—Greenwich Mean Time, that is. The Greenwich observatory and maritime museum are also located here. The food is good but expensive. The view is superb—and free. Take a ferry from Tower Bridge to Greenwich.

Britain's smallest pub

The **Nutshell Pub**, *Bury Street, Suffolk,* is the smallest pub in Britain, holding up to six people. The rest of the customers have to take their chances with the weather and drink outside. There is also a genuine mummified cat hanging from the ceiling—a lost relic from the days of witch burning.

The best hotels for the money

11 Cadogan Gardens, *Sloane Square, Knightsbridge, London; tel. +44 (20) 7730-7000; website: www.no11london.com,* near the intersection of Sloane Square and Draycott Place, is so popular that you must book a room months in advance. Bookings from travel agents are not accepted. This Victorian hotel is filled with mahogany and silver. A butler serves breakfast and tea.

The Crowne Plaza London, *St. James, 45-51 Buckingham Gate, Westminster; tel. +44 (20) 7834-6655; website: www.london.crowneplaza.com.* Originally built in 1897, this palatial Victorian building was, over the years, the preferred residence for many visiting aristocrats from all over the world. Ideal location.

The **Inverness Court**, *1 Inverness Terrace, London W23J; tel. +44 (20) 7229-1444,* was built for Oscar Wilde's muse, Lily Langtry, by Edward VII and truly stands out from countless others in the neighborhood. For a truly royal experience, rent the Langtry Suite, which comes with a four-poster bed and a decadent sunken bath.

The best side trips from London

Most travelers to Britain see little more than London. Yet it's outside London that you see the real England. The easiest way to get to the sights outside London is by rail or bus (or coach, as the British say). London has nine main train stations, each dealing with a different region—so make sure you are leaving from the right station. Each has an information office.

Buses are the least expensive way to take side trips. London has two main bus services: **National Express** and the **Green Line**. The main station for National Express is **Victoria Coach Station** (NOT Victoria Train Station, which is nearby), *Buckingham Palace Road, London SW1.*

The main station for the Green Line is **Eccleston Bridge**, just down the street. If you are in a hurry, take a National Express bus. The Green Line makes more stops and is slower. However, the Green Line does have some express buses (called Rapid Buses).

CAMBRIDGE—THE PRETTIEST TOWN

Cambridge is the prettiest of England's two rival university towns. A serene place, Cambridge was originally a Roman crossing over the River Cam. At the time of the Domesday Book (1086), Cambridge was a small trading village. Scholars gathered here in 1209 after being ousted from Oxford by irate townspeople. They opened a series of colleges that eventually became the university. The lovely old city (in Britain, any town with a cathedral is called a city) did not always see eye to eye with the university—riots were staged in 1381. The phrase "town and gown" indicates some of the old animosity.

The most impressive Gothic structure

The magnificent architecture of Cambridge and the beautiful surrounding countryside are good reasons to spend several days here. **King's College Chapel** is one of the most impressive Gothic structures in England. Be sure to see "Evensong" on Sunday, sung by a boys' choir at the chapel.

The best punting

A punt is a kind of boat, and punting is one of the most enjoyable ways to while away a sunny summer's afternoon—drifting under the Bridge of Sighs, the Mathematical Bridge, and down the mile-long stretch of the River Cam known as "The Backs."

The Cam is one of the most glorious of England's waterways and the best views of the colleges are from the river. "The Backs" is so-called because it runs behind many of the university buildings. Plus you'll see things from another angle;

137

the imposing architecture of King's Chapel, the Wren Library at Trinity, and all those dreaming spires. Punts are a quintessential part of the Cambridge experience.

Scudamore's Punting Company, *Granta Place, Mill Lane; tel. +44 (1223) 359-750; website: www.scudamores.com*, has stations at Mill Lane (near Queen's College and Laundress Green), Jesus Green, and Magdalene Bridge, and they also offer chauffeured punts of between 45 minutes and two hours duration.

OXFORD: THE OLDEST UNIVERSITY

Oxford University, with its 34 colleges and thousands of students, draws visitors from around the world. The college's 100 acres includes lawns, gardens, water walks, and a private deer park where the famous Magdalen deer can be spotted. New College, built in the late 14th century, is one of the most inviting colleges on campus, with its medieval cloisters and peaceful gardens. A section of the old city walls can be found here.

While the university was founded in the 12th century, the town itself dates back to A.D. 912. The hero of many Dorothy Sayers' mystery stories, Lord Peter Whimsey, studied at Oxford.

Oldest museum in Britain

The oldest public museum in Britain, the **Ashmolean**, *Beaumont Street; tel. +44 (1865) 278-0002; website: www.ashmolean.org*, is located in Oxford. It has a great collection, including works by French Impressionists and Renaissance artists Raphael and Michelangelo. It also contains historical curios, such as the lantern Guy Fawkes carried when he tried to blow up Parliament in 1605.

The best inn

The **Bear Inn**, *6 Alfred Street, Oxford; tel. +44 (1865) 728-164*, is the best place to stay in Oxford. The establishment is over seven centuries old and has oak beams and low ceilings. Rooms on the upper stories have sloping floors, and the steps are uneven. The Bear Inn is an important part of Oxford tradition—students meet here to sing university songs and to hold parties. The famous collection of neckties hanging on one wall here includes more than 4,200 ties donated by customers since 1951. Each bears the owner's signature. The collection includes ties from members of rowing clubs, cricket teams, student societies, the police, and the military. The ties are displayed according to nationality.

The best cheeses—and the craziest sport

In addition to its silks, **Gloucestershire** is also world-famous for its cheeses and for its cheese-rolling rituals. Originally, these rituals were associated with the rites of Midsummer. At one time they were common throughout Gloucestershire and Wiltshire; now they are only kept up in Cooper's Hill and Randwick.

In Randwick, three cheeses play a role in two celebrations. At 10.30 a.m. on the first Sunday in May, the cheeses are taken to the village church, St. John's, for a short service. From there, they are rolled three times around the church, and then one of them is cut up and distributed among the congregation.

The other two cheeses reappear the following Saturday, known as Wap, or Mayor's Day. Displayed on litters, they occupy a place of honor in a colorful procession that also includes a Wap Queen, a band, and the Wap Mayor, accompanied by his sword-bearer and a sheriff. The entire procession makes its way to the Mayor's Pool, where the Wap Queen officially welcomes the Mayor, who is then ceremoniously thrown into the water. After the dunking, the crowd accompanies the Mayor and the Queen to the hill near the village school, where the cheeses are rolled down the slope to open the Wap Fair.

Cheese rolling at Cooper's Hill involves a much steeper slope. The ceremonies here take place on Spring Bank Holiday (in May). Races are staged at half-hour intervals, beginning at 6 p.m. For each race, six to 10 runners line up at the top of the hill, set their cheeses, (usually seven-pound Double Gloucesters) rolling downhill, and then take off after them in hot pursuit. The cheeses have been known to pick up such speed on their way down the hill that they have bounded right over the roof of the house at the bottom. The winner of the race keeps his cheese.

The best ecclesiastical maze

Grey's Court, *Rotherfield Greys, Henley-on-Thames; tel. +44 (1494) 755-564; website: www.nationaltrust.org.uk/main/w-greyscourt*, in Oxfordshire, has the best example of an ecclesiastical maze in all England. Based on an ancient pagan design, it is formed by brick paths running through turf. At its center are two crosses—one Roman, one Byzantine. Made to celebrate the enthronement of the present Archbishop of Canterbury in 1982, the maze is said to represent the path of life and to symbolize pilgrimage.

THE BEST RACETRACK IN ENGLAND

Known as the horse racing capital of the world, **Newmarket** is renowned not only for its racetrack—with some of the best flat racing to be found anywhere—but also for its many training establishments and stud farms close by. It's a charming little town just 60 miles (about two hours drive) from London and is a must for anyone interested in horses and racing.

Newmarket has two courses: the Rowley Mile and the July Course (*website: www.newmarketracecourses.co.uk*). The three major race meetings are in spring (April/May), summer (July/August), and autumn (late September/October), with the most famous events being the One Thousand and Two Thousand Guineas (late April), the Cambridgeshire (early October), and the Caesarewich (mid-October).

The town is also home to the **National Horseracing Museum**, *99 High Street, Newmarket; tel. +44 (1638) 667-333; website: www.nhrm.co.uk;* which presents exhibits that bring to life the social history of racing and includes pictures and sculptures by such masters of the genre as Stubbs and Munnings. The museum has five galleries, a coffee bar, a restaurant, a gift shop, and offers a "junior fun tour" for children visiting the museum, whereby kids can dress up in historic clothes in the practical museum. The museum also shows videos of famous races.

THE BEST ANTIQUE SHOPPING OUTSIDE LONDON

Strangers usually visit Hungerford for one reason—to browse and to buy in the many antique shops. Here the collector can concentrate on the business at hand, undistracted by any other major attractions. The **Hungerford Arcade,** *26 High Street; tel. +44 (1488) 683-701; website: www.hungerfordarcade.co.uk*, has more than 80 stalls to investigate. There's some pretty junky stuff there, but treasures can still be found. For quality antique kitchenware, try **Below Stairs**, *103 High Street; tel. +44 (1488) 682-317; website: www.belowstairs.co.uk*, across the road from the Arcade.

Over the Kennet and Avon Canal, where High Street turns into Bridge Street, is a whole collection of quality silver and Edwardian to Georgian wine labels.

A bit farther on is **Pandora's Box**, where Joan Gleave stocks mainly Victoriana and specializes in Staffordshire pottery figures. The latter were often made to commemorate historic events (note the delightful group from the Crimean War) or a famous personality (generals and royalty were favorites). On Charnham

Street is **Bow House Antiques**, where upstairs Mrs. Herrington has a nursery of toys, dolls, teddy bears, and some bewitching dollhouse furniture.

THE WORLD'S BEST ROCKING HORSE WORKSHOP

Situated in the small Shropshire village of **Wem**, about 150 miles from London, is a workshop that makes nothing but rocking horses, **The Rocking Horse Workshop**, *1 Drayton Road, Hodnet, Shropshire; tel. +44 (1630) 685-888; website: www.rockinghorses.co.uk.* These beautiful, large-eyed creatures were a popular feature of many Edwardian and Victorian nurseries. David and Noreen Kiss have made a profession out of restoring old horses from the 18th and 19th centuries, and the barn in their garden has become the world center for these wooden chargers of old. The rocking horses are made in a variety of woods, and visitors can view the entire process of reviving the rockers; everything is on display, from a basic block of timber to the full-colored model horse on its curving runners. The shop also offers unique cards reprinted from original Edwardian and Victorian photographs featuring children with their vintage rocking horses.

THE OLDEST INHABITED MANOR HOUSE IN ENGLAND

New Hall Hotel and Spa, *Walmley Road, Sutton Coldfield, Birmingham; tel. +44 (845) 072- 577; website: www.handpickedhotels.co.uk,* isn't new. It's a 12th-century manor house, destined to become a more than worthy rival to the rather soulless conference hotels in nearby Birmingham—and a pleasant relief from the hotels in London. There are 65 rooms in the house, all with private bathrooms.

BRITAIN'S MOST CHARMING VILLAGE

The village of **Shanklin**, on the Isle of Wight off the southern coast of England, is charming—just what you'd imagine a British village should be. Thatched-roof cottages, many of them restaurants, pubs, and gift shops, line the streets. St. Blasius, the old parish church, dates in part from the 14th century. Climb down into the Shanklin Chine, a narrow ravine with a waterfall.

The Isle of Wight is accessible from Portsmouth or Southampton on the mainland by hydrofoil or ferry.

THE LARGEST INHABITED CASTLE IN THE WORLD

Windsor Castle *(website: www.royalcollection.org.uk),* still used by royalty after 850 years (construction of the castle was begun by William the Conqueror in the 11th century), is the largest inhabited castle in the world. Many of Britain's kings and queens are buried in St. George's Chapel here.

Located on the River Thames, Windsor is a picturesque Victorian town. Across the river from Windsor is Eton College, the most exclusive boys' school in Britain. Founded in 1440, it has educated many of the nation's leaders.

CANTERBURY: CHAUCER'S FAVORITE

St. Augustine established Christianity in Canterbury in A.D. 597, and in 1197 the martyr Thomas Becket was murdered in the cathedral here. Canterbury has been a settlement since the Iron Age. Visit **Canterbury Cathedral**, the mother church for the Anglican faith and a center for pilgrimages (including one Chaucer wrote about). The structure was begun in 1070 and completed in 1503.

THE WORLD'S MOST FAMOUS CLIFFS

The white cliffs of **Dover** are world-famous for their brilliant white color and their sheer drop into the sea. The best view of the cliffs is from the ferry that crosses the English Channel on its way to France.

Dover is home to the **White Cliffs Experience**, an exhibit that outlines thousands of years of British history, from the Roman invasion of Britain in 55 B.C. to the air raids during World War II. It's adjacent to the **Dover Museum**, which is on Market Square; *tel. +44 (1304) 201-066; website: www.dover.gov.uk/museum.*

THE MOST PICTURESQUE REGION: THE SOUTHWEST PENINSULA

The southwest peninsula—Devon and Cornwall—is for people who like to breathe tangy sea breezes, explore fishing villages, walk harbor walls, swim in the sea, and wallow in England's maritime history. The southern coast faces the English Channel, which affords a mild climate with gentle waves softly lapping the secluded bays and ancient smugglers' coves. The northern coast of the peninsula faces the full force of the Atlantic. All along the peninsula are little villages that appear to tumble down the hillsides. Inland are the granite moors. Dartmoor, Exmoor, and Bodmin are designated National Trust areas, protected from development.

Cornwall: The least changed region

Cornwall is one of the last genuinely unchanged counties in England, located 300 miles from London. This region, the one-time hideout of smugglers and pirates, is also the location of Tintagel, the legendary home of King Arthur. The tiny village of Camelford is supposedly the original Camelot. You can partake in a medieval banquet in the Great Hall at Tintagel, surrounded by the colors and banners of the Knights of the Round Table.

The best outdoor theater

Penzance, a colorful old South Cornish town of pirates and smugglers, is nearly 300 miles from London. In the summer, open-air opera, including the apt Gilbert and Sullivan work *Pirates of Penzance*, is performed at **Minack Theatre** at Portcurno. The Minack Theater is carved out of a cliff. The audience watches the performances in the open air looking over the Atlantic. There are also morning family shows for children with a mix of puppets, songs, storytelling and cabaret. Take along a warm sweater and a blanket. For information, *tel. +44 (1736) 810-181; website: www.minack.com.* Tickets can be bought on the morning for £4 ($6) for an adult and £2 ($3) for under 16. Children under 12 are free of charge.

The prettiest Cornish town

St. Mawes, on the southern coast of Cornwall, is one of the prettiest towns in Britain. Located at the mouth of Percuil Creek, it is known for its fine sailing and its castle, which was built by King Henry VIII from 1540 to 1543. The castle is shaped like a cloverleaf for good luck.

Cornwall's best hotels

The best seaside hotel in Cornwall is the **Falmouth Hotel**, Castle Beach; *tel. +44 (1326) 312-671; website: www.falmouthhotel.com.* Overlooking Pendennis Point and Pendennis Castle, it was opened in 1865 and has accommodated Edward VII and stage stars Anna Neagle and Herbert Wilcox.

Tregoninny Farm and Woodland, *Tresillian, Truro, Cornwall; tel. +44 (1872) 520-145; website: www.tregoninny.com,* sits on a wooded hillside just outside Truro and provides both B&B and self-catering accommodation. The beautifully renovated farmhouse has open beams in the guest dining room and a conservatory with stunning views of the surrounding countryside.

The best moor: Dartmoor

In the heart of Devon is the 365-square-mile **Dartmoor National Park***; website: www.dartmoor-npa.gov.uk*, which embodies the country's mystery and beauty. Dartmoor was the setting for *The Hound of the Baskervilles*, as well as the location of the notorious Dartmoor Prison. Its desolate moors are relieved by cozy villages and rolling hills.

Wild ponies canter through Dartmoor's fields of wild flowers. Thatched cottages dot the landscape, and towns here—Widecombe-in-the-Moor, Ashburton, Okehampton, and Chagford—are all within walking distance of the moors. Try to be in the area during a village fair or stock show. You will think time has stood still.

If you want to explore the wilds of Dartmoor National Park, pick up an ordinance map of the park, don your waterproof boots, and set out. After hiking all day in the moor, stop in Chagford, where you can enjoy an authentic Devonshire tea, complete with scones, strawberry preserves, and thick Devonshire cream.

The best stone rows

Dartmoor has the country's best example of stone **rowsyard**—high rocks set in a line. The rocks are sometimes covered with circular designs. Look carefully, they are often hidden by heather. The rows lead to round barrows or cairns (burial mounds).

The best Bronze Age village

Grimspound in Manaton is one of the best examples of a fortified Bronze Age village on the moor. It is also the largest, with 24 hut circles in a 150-yard enclosure. The protecting wall was originally 10 feet high and had three entrances. The hut circles had cooking holes, stone platforms, and flat center stones that supported the roof poles.

The most luxurious hotel in Devon

The most luxurious place to stay in Dartmoor National Park is **Gidleigh Park**, *Chagford; tel. +44 (1647) 432-367; website: www.gidleigh.com.* This peaceful country manor has blazing fires, chintz-covered furniture, and oak-paneled walls. The hotel has 12 rooms, an exceptional Michelin-starred restaurant (it was voted number one in *The Sunday Times* Top 100 Restaurants 2010) is surrounded by 30 acres. The hotel is rather expensive, but worth it.

The coziest B&B by the moor

Burrator House, *Sheepstor, Yelverton, Devon; tel. +44 (1822) 855-669; website: www.burratorhouse.com*, is a Georgian house on 20 acres with a trout pool, miniature waterfall, swimming pool, and a Victorian snooker table.

THE BEST OF THE COTSWOLDS

The "Heart of England" lies just an hour and a half west and slightly north of London by train. Here, a softly rolling ribbon of hills enfolds rustic villages of another, more romantic, age. This region, known as the **Cotswolds**, was the prosperous hub of the wool trade in the 13th through 16th centuries, and you can still glimpse an occasional flock of sheep. Towns and villages nestling in these hills are made up of houses built of the local stone, with steep slate roofs.

The most charming village

Tetbury is the most charming village in the Cotswolds, an old market town with hilly streets that weave and curve around the Old Market House, built in 1655. Early in the morning, bottles of milk with cream on top sit outside the doors of the town's quaint houses. Tetbury has a beautiful 'St. Mary the Virgin' church, a few antique shops—and little else.

Shakespeare's favorite

Stratford-upon-Avon, Shakespeare's home town, sits at the northeast tip of the Cotswolds. Despite its commercialized, touristy flavor, Stratford is pretty, with authentic Tudor buildings on practically every street. You're cheating yourself if you don't make it to one of the Royal Shakespeare Company's productions. Also worth a stop is the Dirty Duck Pub, where actors hang out between shows. It is across from the theater.

    Stratford-upon-Avon Brass Rubbing Centre is the best brass rubbing center in the area. It traces the history of commemorative brasses from the 12th through 17th centuries.

The best of Cheltenham

Cheltenham, the tourist base of the Cotswolds, is a mix of old and new. Georgian terraced houses with flower-draped, wrought iron balconies stand beside gray cube-like office buildings and utilitarian storefront strips. The nicest strip is the **Promenade**, a tree-lined avenue with ornate Georgian buildings. Visit the Cheltenham Racecourse, one of England's finest steeplechase courses.

The best castle in the Cotswolds

Six miles up the A46 from Cheltenham is **Sudeley Castle;** *website: www.sudeleycastle.co.uk* in Winchcombe. Catherine Parr, the sixth wife of Henry VIII, and the only one to survive him, lived and is buried here. (Henry's fourth wife, Anne of Cleves, also survived him, but their marriage was annulled.)

Best places to stay

A hotel that make an ideal bases for touring the Cotswolds is the **Close at Tetbury,** *Long Street, Tetbury; tel. +44 (1666) 502-272*; *website: www.theclose-hotel.com*, was once the home of a 16th-century wool merchant.

The best way to get there

One of the best things about the Cotswolds is the region's proximity to London. The capital is less than two hours away by the M4 or M40 motorway.

The best place to bathe in England

The most magnificent spa in England is, appropriately, in **Bath**. According to legend, the mineral springs at Bath were first discovered by King Bladud (the father of King Lear), who had been banished into the countryside because of his leprosy. He became a swineherd, and his pigs led him to the springs, which cured him of the disease.

Visit the Roman Baths and the Pump Room, where you can drink the bubbling hot mineral water from the fountain. The Great Bath is exposed to the sky. Next door is a museum displaying Roman and prehistoric relics. Stroll along the Royal Crescent, a sweep of 30 Georgian houses joined by one façade and fronted with Ionic columns.

Visiting the **Jane Austen Centre**; *40 Gay Street, Queen Square, Bath, BA1 2NT; tel. +44 (1225) 443-000; website: www.janeausten.co.uk*, is a definite must-see for all literary buffs. Be prepared to be transported back to a time of lace bonnets, tea-sets, and traditional courting balls. As you enter the previous home of Miss Austen you are greeted by a man dressed in a regency costume offering to take your coat.

England's best-preserved town

Chester, on the west coast in Cheshire County, is one of the few English towns still encircled by a medieval wall. The thick wall doubles as an attractive promenade lined with shops. Within the walls are Tudor half-timbered houses. Founded in A.D. 60, Chester was the headquarters of the Roman XX Legion, and many Roman relics remain.

THE MOST INSPIRING REGION: YORKSHIRE

Yorkshire has inspired a number of English writers, including James Herriot and the Brontë family. Herbert Read, the poet and art critic, was a more recent Yorkshire literary light. James Herriot Country, as Yorkshire County is known, is a patchwork of undulating pastures dotted with sheep and lined with ancient stone walls, desolate moors, rugged coastlines, and medieval towns.

The best of the Brontës

The **Brontë** family lived in Haworth, a romantic town perched precariously on a hillside, commanding superb views from its cobblestone streets. You can visit the parsonage that was their home (*website: www.bronte.org.uk*).

The best place to stay in Haworth is the **Ye Sleeping House B&B**, *8 Main Street; tel. +44 (1535) 645-992; website: www.yesleepinghouse.co.uk*. Their motto is "Welcome Stranger…Goodbye Friend" and you'll certainly find a friend in owner Mike, whose local knowledge is extensive.

The best view of the area

At **Thirsk**, a charming market town in Yorkshire, a natural ridge provides a superb hang-gliding site. Visitors are welcome to take glider rides, enjoying bird's-eye views of the area.

The best guidebook

The guidebook that offers the most insight into this region is James Herriot's *Yorkshire*. The animal lover and writer knows the region inside out—and his love of the area is evident in his writing.

The coziest place to stay

The **Black Swan Hotel**, *Market Place, Hemsley; tel. +44 (1439) 770-466; website: www.blackswan-helmsley.co.uk,* is an old coaching inn on the edge of North York Moors National Park. It serves full English breakfasts, traditional teas, and traditional Sunday lunches.

THE MOST HISTORIC CITY: YORK

In A.D. 867, the Danish Vikings vanquished York, and many of the area's street names, such as Micklegate, Bootham, and Walmgate, date from this period. After the Vikings, the Normans took possession. The city's architecture bears witness to their influence. During the sixth century, the legendary King Arthur is said to have captured York, and in the seventh century the Saxons moved in. They built a small wooden church, the original **York Minster**. (A *minster* is a church that once was a monastery.) Until the 14th century, York was strategically and economically more important than London and was the nation's capital.

In the early 1970s, it was discovered that the foundations of the York Minster were on the move; draining and underpinning were urgently required. During the work, which began in 1976, evidence of a massive Roman military fortress and Roman drainage system were discovered. The drains were in such good condition that they could be used for the necessary drainage without repair—quite impressive for something built in A.D. 71.

During the excavations, one of the workmen on the site insisted that he saw the ghosts of an entire battalion of Roman soldiers marching before him. The British workman was visibly shaken. "One of the strangest things," he said, "was that they were only visible from the knees up. You couldn't see their legs." Further excavations revealed an ancient Roman road at just about the level the soldiers' feet would have been.

The best city walk

A footpath along the top of the walls that surround York provides a pleasant three-mile saunter on a warm summer evening. You can circle the entire city on the walls, coming down the stone steps at intervals to see the sights. Modern traffic runs between these steps and their ancient gatehouses. The York Minster is visible from the walls at all times. It is a delightful contrast to the black-and-white Tudor buildings that surround it.

The best sightseeing tip

Don't take a car into York. Sights are within easy walking distance of one another, public transportation is available, and parking is a nightmare not to be contemplated.

The most esteemed chocolate maker

Just southwest of Yorkshire is a renowned chocolate maker known as **Thorntons**, *www.thorntons.co.uk.* Founded in 1925, Thorntons was initially famous for its distinctive toffee, but it is now equally renowned for its chocolates. Try to visit at Easter, when you can buy a chocolate egg and then wait while it's personalized with your name in icing. You can also shop for confections made of almonds, apricots, vine fruits, and the like, all of which may be carried away in one of Thornton's edible lacy-weave chocolate baskets.

THE BRITS' FAVORITE HOLIDAY PLACE

If it came to a choice between London and the Lake District, any Briton would choose the **Lake District**. An area of outstanding natural beauty, it covers the northwestern corner of England, just south of the Scottish border. It is easily accessible via the M6 motorway, approximately a five-hour drive from London.

The Lake District is rich in literary connections. Wordsworth was born here and was visited often by Shelley and Coleridge. Robert Southey lived in Keswick for more than 40 years. And John Ruskin's name pops up everywhere, from Ruskin House Pottery in Ambleside to the cross commemorating him in the churchyard at Coniston. This is also the country of Beatrix Potter, the much-loved author of delightful children's stories.

The best way to see the Lake District

The best way to see the Lake District is leisurely. You'll absorb more of the atmosphere by sitting beside one lake for a few hours than by racing around the largest lakes and main towns and villages. The tiny roads that weave between and over the hills will defeat anyone in a hurry. Also keep in mind that wandering sheep have the right of way here, and you'll often have to leave your car to open and close sheep gates that cross the road. Head first for **Brockhole**, a country house halfway between Windermere and Ambleside on the main road. The house is an information center and has a pleasant tea room.

The best-kept secret in the Lake District
If you want to escape the crowds of tourists in the Lake District, head for the **Wasdale Head Inn**, *Wasdale Head, Near Gosforth, Cumbria; tel. +44 (1946) 726-229; website: www.wasdale.com.* This remote, secluded pub is a haven of peace set in one of Lakeland's most beautiful, unspoiled valleys. The views of Great Gable, Sca Fell, and other massive peaks are an inspiration, and nearby Wastwater is perhaps the most dramatic of the lakes. Walkers, rock climbers, and anyone interested in the great outdoors find this traditional mountain inn a real delight. And a visit to Wasdale Head will put you in good company, for Wordsworth, Coleridge, and Dickens are known to have frequented the area, and British novelist Nicholas Monsaratt bought his first glass of beer ever in the inn.

The most spectacular lake
Ullswater, which is encircled by hills and highlands rising from the water's edge, is the most spectacular of the lakes. Wordsworth immortalized the daffodils he saw here and described Ullswater as "perhaps...the happiest combination of beauty and grandeur, which any of the Lakes affords."

The best place to stay on the banks of Ullswater is the **Sharrow Bay Hotel**, *Lake Ullswater, Penrith; tel. +44 (1768) 486-301; website; www.sharrowbay. co.uk.* A roaring fire warms the lounge, and rooms are equipped with backgammon and Scrabble boards. The views are tremendous and the food is sinfully delicious.

The most beautiful stone circle
Just two miles east of Keswick is **Castlerigg Stone Circle**, the most beautifully situated stone circle in England. And unlike the famous Stonehenge, it is not inundated with tourists. You can work out a number of astrological details from this circle, which is 100 feet in diameter with 38 stones in its outer ring (almost all standing in their original positions) and 10 more within.

From Castlerigg, you can see the north Lakeland hills. Three miles away is a hill called **Threlkeld Knott**, over which the sun rises during an equinox.

Wordsworth's favorite spot
Tiny **Grasmere** village is more famous for its delightful position, nestled as it is beneath Helm Crag and Nab Scar northwest of Lake Windermere, than for its amenities. Wordsworth called it "the loveliest spot that man hath ever found." He made his first home nearby at **Dove Cottage** (*website: www.wordsworth.org.uk*). Open to the public, Dove Cottage is tiny and charming, with a museum next door.

Historian Philip Crowl says, "The management of this site is a model of graciousness combined with efficiency. Few stately homes, for all their large staffs and high entrance fees, do so well." Even the garden is a delight.

THE WORLDS' BEST GARDENS

English gardens are known worldwide for their colorful, wild abandon. Gardening is something the British do well, and the rain and mild winters, particularly in the south, provide the perfect environment for cultivating trees and plants.

Today, you don't have to be wealthy to enjoy the immense gardens of England's royal estates. Apart from financial considerations, most owners today believe that it's right to share their historic homes and gardens with the rest of us.

The most beautiful garden

Of all the gardens in England, the most beautiful is **Sissinghurst Castle Garden**; *website: www.nationaltrust.org.uk/sissinghurst,* two miles northeast of Cranbrook. Created by writer Vita Sackville-West (who wrote a gardening column for the *Daily Telegraph* for years) and her husband, diplomat Sir Harold Nicolson, Sissinghurst is a series of walled gardens located between the surviving parts of an Elizabethan mansion. The prettiest is the white garden, planted with only white flowers. Also lovely are the rose garden, with old-fashioned English roses (old-fashioned roses predate hybrids, which are what most gardens grow today), the herb garden, the yew walk, the moat walk, and the orchard. The gardens are open March through November and close on Wednesday and Thursday.

The most splendid Temple gardens

The 350 acres of **Stowe**, in Buckinghamshire, are set around the great Palladian house of the Temple family, whose punning motto *Templa quam dilecta* (how splendid are the temples!) is equally splendidly realized in the grottos, columns, bridges, arches, and monuments amid the woodlands and undulating, grassy landscape. In the Augustan era of Georgian England, these classical temples were intended to evoke ancient Rome.

The Temples had dissipated their great fortune by the end of Victoria's reign and soon thereafter had to sell their Buckinghamshire estate. Today it has become one of Britain's foremost schools.

The names of the designers give the clue to Stowe's greatness: Vanbrugh, Kent, and Givvs, three of the foremost architects of the 18th century, worked on these gardens. Lancelot "Capability" Brown, the man who developed the natural look and advocated informal planning of gardens, was the Temples' head gardener from 1741. Under his visionary eye, the garden was transformed into a spectacular, classical landscape.

The world's largest greenhouse

Near St. Austell, in southwest England, is the world's largest greenhouse. The **Eden Project,** opened in April 2001, comprises a number of domes that house plant species from around the world, each dome emulating a natural biome. Eden is open every day except December 24th and 25th. For details of special displays, workshops, artifacts, audio-visual programs, circus shows, and music festivals, contact **The Eden Project**, *tel. +44 (1726) 811-911; website: www.edenproject.com.*

ENGLAND'S BEST PALACES

Castle Howard, *tel. +44 (1653) 648-333; website: www.castlehoward.co.uk*, in the rugged north, is the most beautiful of England's castles. This 18th-century home, 15 miles north of York, was the film site for Evelyn Waugh's *Brideshead Revisited*, the renowned British television series. Actually a palace, Castle Howard was designated in 1699 for Charles Howard, third Earl of Carlisle, and is aglow with paintings by Rubens, Gainsborough, and Reynolds. Some of the furniture is by Seraton and Chippendale, and the costume galleries have displays dating from the 18th century. The grounds are extensive, with lakes, fountains, and a beautiful Temple of the Four Winds. A replica of an 18th-century rose garden has old fashioned roses that are no longer available commercially.

   Blenheim Palace, *tel. +44 (1993) 811-091; website: www.blenheimpalace. com*, in Oxfordshire, is a close second. Near the old town of Woodstock, it was the home of the 11th Duke of Marlborough and the birthplace of Sir Winston Churchill. The gardens and park were designed by Queen Anne's gardener, Henry Wise, and later added to by Capability Brown, an 18th-century landscape gardener who created Blenheim Lake. If you weren't told it was landscaped, you'd think it was all natural. Blenheim is open mid-February through November.

THE BEST ENGLISH CATHEDRAL

Salisbury Cathedral, the only English cathedral built from a single type of stone, can be seen for miles. Set in a grassy plain, the cathedral has the tallest spire in England, rising an outstanding 404 feet. Take the Tower Tour which allows you to explore the roof spaces and tower and get a birds-eye view of the town below.

The cloisters and **Chapter House** that adjoin the cathedral are also worth seeing. The walls of Chapter House are decorated with bas-reliefs of the Old Testament. Enjoy the open lawns of the Cathedral Close. (Novelist Henry Fielding once lived in one of the houses on the close.)

A requested, but voluntary, donation to the cathedral is asked of its visitors. For more information see *www.salisburycathedral.org.uk.*

THE BEST RAILWAY MUSEUM

In 1986, Britain's Great Western locomotive works at Swindon, Wiltshire, closed. But the buildings were listed Grade II and so couldn't be demolished. The former boiler works now operate as the McArthur Glen Designer Outlet Great Western—a gigantic mall containing more than 100 shops (*website: www.mcarthurglen.com*). And next door, in the former machine shop, is STEAM—the Museum of the Great Western Railway (*website: www.steam-museum.org.uk).*

THE BEST OF WALES

Wales, that poetic land to the west of England, is renowned for its mighty castles. Dozens can be visited. They perch on rocky cliffs, cling to the mountains, hide in the moors, and rise up from the sea.

Many of the finest Welsh castles were constructed by King Edward I in the 13th century. The best known and grandest Welsh castle is **Caernarfon** in the north, birthplace of Edward II, the first Prince of Wales. Enclosed by the 13th-century town walls, it is a masterpiece of medieval architecture. Prince Charles was dubbed Prince of Wales here by his mother when he turned 18. Nearby is the Roman fort **Segontium**, founded in A.D. 78.

The two best hotels in the town of Caernarfon are the **Celtic Royal Hotel**, *Bangor Street, Caernarfon; tel. +44 (1286) 674-477; website: www.celtic-royal.co.uk,* a historic coach house, and **Black Boy Inn**, *Northgate Street, Caernarfon; tel. +44 (1286) 673-604; website: www.black-boy-inn.com*, which dates back to the 14th century.

Cardiff Castle; *website: www.cardiffcastle.com*, in the Welsh capital, is the second-best castle in Wales. Built in the 11th century on the site of an old Roman camp, it was reconstructed in 1865 and given an ornate Victorian exterior. Inside, it is romantic and extravagant, especially the Arab Room and the Chaucer Room. The roof garden is colorful. Parts of the original Roman fort on which the castle was built still exist. And you still can see the Norman keep in the northwest corner.

Last but not least is **Harlech**, an enormous castle that watches over a tiny village. Actually, you should put it first on your itinerary. Because it's not as well-preserved as Caernarfon, it's spared the crowds of tourists. Built by Edward I in 1283, the castle was the last to yield to the Yorkists in 1468 during the War of the Roses. It is set high on a cliff and protected by a massive double doorway. One of the best views of Snowdonia Mountain is from the top of the castle wall. Nearby is the most gorgeous beach on the Welsh coast.

The best fortification in Wales

Offa's Dyke, the eighth-century earthwork created by King Offa to keep out the marauding Welsh, marks the English/Welsh border. The 1,200-year-old earthwork can best be seen from the cliffs near Llanymynech in Shropshire, six miles from Oswestry. (Llanymynech's other claim to fame is the Lion Hotel, which is half in England and half in Wales.)

If you have time, one of the best ways to see Wales is to follow the **Offa's Dyke Path**, a 176-mile path from Prestatyn, on the northern Welsh coast, to Sedbury Cliff, Chepstow. It leads from sea to sea through the Black Mountains, the Clun Forest, and the Vale of Clwyd. The prettiest part of the path is over the bare central uplands of the Clun Forest, where the remains of the Dyke are best preserved.

Another highlight is the beautiful ruin **Tintern Abbey**, the inspiration for Wordsworth's poem of the same name. Nearby, the devil supposedly tempted the monks. The gabled ends of the 13th-century abbey church rise out of a green meadow. The slate roof of the church was destroyed after Henry VIII dissolved the monasteries in 1537.

The best Welsh national park

Pembrokeshire Coast National Park is 150 astounding miles of immense beauty. It includes rocky cliffs that drop off into the sea, remote bays, caves, coves, strangely shaped rock formations, and tranquil islands.

Many of the rocks along this coastline are made of lava from volcanoes that erupted 600 million years ago. A marked footpath follows the coastline, passing more than 50 Iron Age fortresses, a number of Celtic churches, and Norman castles at Pembroke, Carew, Haverfordwest, Cardigan, Manorbier, and Tenby.

Visit the seaside towns nearby. Llandudno and Aberystwyth are lively, elegant resorts. Tenby and Aberaeron are quieter places with harbors and white-washed houses. Pamper yourself at the Rock Park spa in the 19th-century spa town of Llandrindod Wells. For more information contact the **Pembrokeshire Coast National Park Development Office**, *tel. +44 (845) 345-7275; website: www. pembrokeshirecoast.org.*

The highest peak in England or Wales

Mount Snowdon, in Snowdonia National Park, is the highest peak in England or Wales, at 3,560 feet. It is also the steepest and most barren mountain. A narrow-gauge railway climbs to the top. Snowdonia offers 1,000 square miles of rugged mountains and moors, lakes, and rolling green hills. The park can be visited via the Snowdon Sherpa bus service, which runs every half-hour, Monday through Thursday, July 15 through September 1. You can catch the bus in Caernarfon.

The best walled town in Wales

Tenby, a 14th-century walled town, has two sandy beaches (the best is North Beach), and a lovely harbor. The town's narrow streets lead to Castle Hill, a spit of land edged by cliffs that drop to the beach. St. Catherine's Island, which has an abandoned fort, can be seen from Castle Hill.

The nicest place to stay is the **Imperial Hotel**, *tel. +44 (1834) 843-737; website: www.coastandcountryhotels.com*, which uses the town wall as one of its walls.

The best Welsh beach resort

Aberystwyth is a popular beach resort with a lively seafront promenade, pastel-colored Victorian houses, black-and-white Welsh houses, and the ruins of a castle. It is also home to the oldest university in Wales (a neo-Gothic building opened in 1877) and the center of the revival of Welsh culture.

You can hear traditional Welsh music at the **Cooper's Arms**, *Northgate Street*.

Also stop in at the **National Library of Wales**, which houses most of the surviving Welsh medieval manuscripts.

The best book browsing in Britain
Hay-on-Wye is a charming little border town with typically narrow streets and a surprising number of bookstores, the result of one man's passion. Richard Booth's book collection overflowed from his own huge bookstore, with shelves from cellar to attic, into the town's movie theater and dozens of smaller bookstores throughout the town. It is a monument to British eccentricity and well worth a browse.

The largest weekly market
Visit **Welshpool**, the first town over the English border, on a Monday to see the largest weekly market in Wales. Farmers have been frequenting this market for more than 500 years.

The world's oldest record store
Spillers Records, *31, The Morgan Arcade, Cardiff; tel. +44 (29) 2022-4905; website: www.spillersrecords.co.uk*, the oldest record store in the world, was established in Cardiff in 1894. It originally specialized in phonographs, wax phonograph cylinders, and shellac phonograph discs, and today sells both vinyl and CDs.

The best island in Wales
Holyhead, off the coast of Aberystwyth, is the prettiest island in Wales, complete with palm trees, pastel-colored houses overlooking tranquil bays full of fishing boats and yachts, and fine restaurants.

THE BEST OF SCOTLAND

Scotland's capital, **Edinburgh**, lost its rank as Scotland's largest city to archrival Glasgow in the 19th century. The result has been to make Edinburgh the more attractive tourist destination (except for the Victorian buffs, who prefer Glasgow).

Edinburgh's **Royal Mile**, which runs along the spine of a hill from Holyrood to Edinburgh Castle, is the most beautiful section of the city. Parts of the stretch date back to the Middle Ages. Few cities in the British Isles have so well preserved a medieval quarter. The Royal Mile has survived because of the 18th-century New Town in the plains below. New Town was built to house the surplus population and to avoid demolition of the old sections.

Follow the Royal Mile beginning at the castle end. It's downhill in this direction. The castle is mostly a shrine to British militarism, complete with red-kneed and kilted Scottish guards at the entrance (the regiment changes daily) and a military museum with historic mementos of these regiments and the parade grounds where they march.

The palace, or lodging, in the castle is where Mary Queen of Scots gave birth to James I of England (also known as James VI of Scotland). The lodging was heavily restored in the last century.

The oldest building in Edinburgh, built in 1076, is the miniscule whitewashed church inside the castle walls called the **Chapel of St. Margaret**. Margaret, queen of Scotland, was canonized for her holy life. (Her immediate predecessor as queen was Lady Macbeth, so she had a hard job of it.) Margaret helped Anglicize the Scots, starting with her husband, King Malcolm III.

The main street running below the castle features historic houses associated with the city's luminaries: John Knox, Robert Burns, Walter Scott, Robert Louis Stevenson. It also provides a fascinating glimpse of historic Scottish life: old shops and breweries, an old printing press, a Presbyterian cathedral, a school, a sugar refinery, and a bakery.

One of the most interesting sites along the route is the tollbooth, which was the prison setting for Sir Walter Scott's *The Heart of Midlothian*. Another is Golfers' Land, the property purchased by a 17th-century golf champion with his winnings. John Patersone, a shoemaker, began his golfing career as a caddie and later became the partner of James II.

At the bottom of the main road, just one mile from the castle, is Holyrood, a converted abbey that was home to Scottish kings. Its style was heavily influenced by the French style Charles II learned about in exile. Charles II also commissioned a series of paintings of his ancestors that graces the picture gallery. Dutch artist Jakob de Witt knew how to please his royal patron. He made all 111 forebearers of Charles II look terribly like Charles II.

Holyrood is closely associated with Mary Queen of Scots, who lived and held court here from 1561 to 1567. She married Henry, Lord Darnley in 1565 in the Chapel Royal. You can see the room where she received John Knox (who fulminated against "a monstrous regiment of women") and the room where her secretary, David Riccio, was dragged from her presence and murdered (probably by one of her husbands).

The finest hotel in Edinburgh is the **Caledonian Hilton**, *Princes Street, Edinburgh EH1 2AB; tel. +44 (131) 222-8888; www.caledonian.hilton.com.* This grand hotel has magnificent views of the castle. With 212 rooms, three dining rooms, and three bars, is a favorite among celebrities.

Britain's best festival: The Edinburgh International

Millions of people visit Edinburgh each summer for the Edinburgh International Festival, which draws prominent musicians and theater groups from around the world. While known as one of the world's leading musical and theater festivals, the Edinburgh International Festival has a sideshow. Edinburgh also provides a stage for some of the best avant-garde productions in the English language. The Fringe, as part of the festival is called, boasts more than 1,000 events and 9,000 performances, including theater, comedy, musicals, cabaret, revues, opera, mime, dance, children's shows, folk, jazz, rock/blues, poetry, and multimedia presentations. For more information contact the festival office: *tel. +44 (131) 473-2000* or visit the *website: www.eif.co.uk.*

Edinburgh's ghostliest tour

Greyfriars Kirkyard has a reputation for being genuinely haunted. Thousands of 16th-century plague victims lie buried beneath the grassy slopes. It's also the site of the Covenanters Prison. Covenanters were Scottish Presbyterians who incurred the wrath of England's Charles I. Many were put to death and then buried in Greyfriars—as was "Bloody" Mackenzie, the Scottish Advocate General of the time who ordered their imprisonment, torture, and death.

Anybody can visit the main part of Greyfriars Kirkyard during the day. However, the only way to see the Covenanters Prison and the mausoleum-lined avenue that lies beyond the prison gates is at night—with a **City of the Dead** tour (*www.blackhart.uk.com*). The tour ends in a section of Edinburgh's legendary historic Underground City, where a population once lived in utter misery.

Also visit **Mary King's Close**, *website: www.realmarykingsclose.com*, a warren of hidden streets beneath the Royal Mile.

Scotland's top art collection

A medieval city surrounding a 13th-century cathedral, **Glasgow** houses three remarkable art collections:

The **Burrell Collection,** Pollok Country Park, 2060 Pollokshaws Road, Glasgow; *tel. +44 (141) 287-2550; website: www.glasgowmuseums.com,* is housed in a stunning building with glass walls through which you can see the landscape of Pollok Park. The collection includes Oriental ceramics, French tapestries, and medieval stained glass. Admission is free.

The **Kelingrove**, *Argyle Street, Glasgow; tel. +44 (141) 276-9599; website: www.glasgowmuseums.com*, contains masterpieces by Lippi, Rubens, and

Constable. Its pride, however, is its collection of Impressionist paintings. Works by Monet, Pissarro, Matisse, Dégas, and Van Gogh grace the walls.

When you tire of art, take tea at the **Willow Tea Room**, *217 Sauchiehall Street; tel. +44 (141) 332-0521; website: www.willowtearooms.co.uk*. Or dine at the **Ubiquitous Chip**, *12 Ashton Lane; tel. +44 (141) 334-5007; website: www.ubiquitouschip.co.uk,* off Byres Road.

The **Quality Hotel Glasgow**, *99 Gordon Street; website: www.qualityhotelglasgow.com,* is the most comfortable and old-fashioned hotel in Glasgow.

For more information on accommodation in the city, see the VisitScotland website, *www.visitscotland.com*, and click on the "Explore Scotland" tab.

The best Scottish castle

Stirling Castle in Fife, where Mary Queen of Scots was crowned in 1543, offers magnificent views of the Grampian Mountains from its cannonades. For centuries it was Scotland's only defense against English invaders. King Robert Bruce (simply known as The Bruce) and Sir William Wallace held the castle against the English for years. In 1305, however, Wallace was betrayed to the English and hanged, drawn, and quartered in London.

For atmosphere, no hotel in Stirling beats the **Golden Lion**, *8-10 King Street*; *tel. +44 (1786) 475-351; website: www.thegoldenlionstirling.com.* It offers a splendid 32-choice buffet breakfast and a timeless stunning Regency Ballroom, which has hosted Robert Burns, members of the royal family, and movie stars.

The most authentic castle stay

There are many castles available to rent for a house party throughout Scotland. In general, the farther north and more rural you go, the more authentic they are. But to find one within easy reach of Edinburgh that doesn't have tartan drapes, reproduction suits of armor, and pine floorboards is more of a challenge. They may be genuinely 16th-century outside, but some of the travesties of conservation and restoration have to be seen to be believed.

Built in 1780, **Birkhill Castle**, *www.birkhillcastle.org.uk*, in Dundee, is the real thing—the antithesis of tourist tackiness and just 50 minutes north of Edinburgh and west of St. Andrews. Set in rolling countryside on the shores of the River Tay estuary in Fife, it is the home of the Earl and Countess of Dundee. There are 12 bedrooms of varying sizes and views, each with an individual charm. The atmosphere is friendly and informal, and you feel like a houseguest rather than a tourist.

Lord Dundee is an elected peer in the House of Lords and is the Hereditary Royal Banner Bearer for Scotland. The coronation banners hang proudly in the hall. Lady Dundee runs the 2,000-acre arable farm and oversees the succession of houseguests. The house is brimming with paintings and antiques, and the family history is worth discovering. Lady Dundee will gladly bring the pictures of her ancestors to life with details of tragic deaths, misunderstandings in love, and stories from the battlefield.

You are welcomed with a substantial afternoon tea, after which you laze about until the views of the garden can be resisted no longer. Then, geared up with borrowed wellies and two of the family dogs you set off to wander until sunset. An amble through carpets of snowdrops, woodland gardens, and the family graveyard leads eventually to a stony beach on the River Tay.

Such exertion requires a couple of hours devoted to lavender-filled baths and a leisurely read before dinner. Seven o'clock and back to the drawing room for pre-dinner champagne. Dinner is a treat—soufflé, beef bourguignon, and bread and butter pudding served in a candlelit dining room with a roaring fire. After dinner, retire to the games room—complete with billiards table and an antique soccer table—with a bottle of fine port and Scottish whiskey, of course.

An angler's dream

The area around Loch Lomond, Stirling, the Trossachs, and the Firth of Clyde, in the heart of Scotland, offers some of the best fishing you'll find anywhere in the world. And the best spot in this region to drop your line is the western end of Loch Tay at Killin. If you are interested in fishing, this is the perfect place. See *www.fishing-uk-scotland.com* for more information about the area.

The best skiing in Scotland

Where should you go for the best skiing in Scotland? The **Cairngorm** mountain range, which rises 4,084 feet and offers the most developed facilities in the country. It has the greatest range of downhill runs, as well as 17 lifts and tows. Runs vary from long, easy slopes to the black-graded West Wall, for experts only. See the website *www.cairngormmountain.co.uk* for more information.

The most dramatic region: The Highlands

The desolate beauty of the Highlands should not blind you to its violent past. Over the centuries, the Gaelic Highlanders have suffered terrible defeats to the English, fought bloody battles among themselves, and been driven from their homes by wealthy landowners. During the Highland Clearances in the 18th century, crofters were driven from their homes by landowners who wanted to raise sheep. Those who refused to go had their houses and goods burned.

Today, the peaceful Highlands are known for their secluded glens, craggy peaks, and sparkling lochs. The country is virtually unspoiled. Route A82 leads from Glasgow into the Highlands, curving along the west bank of Loch Lomond. When the famed lake turns into a stream, you are in the Highlands. The country is wild, steep, and unfenced.

The bloodiest place in the Highlands

One of the most ruggedly beautiful places in the Highlands is **Glencoe**, the misty valley that was the scene of a brutal massacre on February 13th, 1692, when the MacDonald clan, which had fought for James II, was butchered by the Campbell clan, soldiers of William of Orange. The MacDonalds were stabbed to death in their beds at dawn. Their homes were burned and their cattle stolen. Nothing remains of the human inhabitants of the Glen of Weeping, as it is known today. The only residents are golden eagles and red deer.

Inverary: The prettiest Highland town

Make Inverary, on the peaceful shores of Loch Fyne, one of your stops in the Highlands. Meaning "at the mouth of the Aray River," Inverary has been inhabited by the Campbells of Argyll for 500 years. Its white-walled buildings are reflected in the water. Services are still held in Gaelic at the town's church, the Episcopal Church of All Saints, which has the world's second-heaviest ring of 10 bells, which chime every day.

Nearby **Inverary Castle** *(website: www.inveraray-castle.com)*, home to the Duke and Duchess of Argyll, is open to the public. The Armory Hall, which is 95 feet high, has an impressive display of antique weapons. The family portraits were done by such famous painters as Reynolds and Raeburn. A tour of the castle takes about an hour and is a good introduction to Highland history.

Britain's highest mountain

Ben Nevis, at 4,406 feet, is the highest peak in Great Britain. Near Inverness in the Highlands, it guards Glen Nevis. The view from the summit (where the ruins of an observatory remain) seems endless. A precipice on the northeast side drops more than 1,450 feet. Combine a trip to Inverness and Ben Nevis with a look at nearby **Loch Ness**, home of the world's most famous monster.

The best place to stay near Inverness is **Culloden House Hotel**, *tel. +44 (1463) 790-461; website: www.cullodenhouse.co.uk*, an 18th-century palace near Culloden Moor, where the final Scottish uprising was defeated in 1746. This hotel has spacious rooms, luxurious surroundings, and beautiful antiques.

The best Highland hotel
Inverlochy Castle, *Torlundy, Fort William; tel. +44 (1397) 702-177; website: www.inverlochycastlehotel.com*, near Glencoe and Ben Nevis, is the best hotel to stay in while touring the Highlands.

THE HEBRIDES: THE BEST PLACE TO ESCAPE CIVILIZATION

If you are "a mere lover of naked nature," you will be drawn to the Scottish islands as Dr. Samuel Johnson was in 1775. The **Hebrides** are the best place in Britain to escape civilization.

The most beautiful isle—Skye
The most spectacular island in the Hebrides is the Misty Isle, as **Skye** is known. Walter Scott described the Misty Isle in *The Lord of the Isles*: "The vapor which enveloped the mountain ridges obliged us by assuming a thousand shapes, varying its veils in all sorts of forms, but sometimes clearing off altogether."

Wild, still, and distant from population centers, the island is so far north that in June the sun never really sets. From 11 p.m. until 1 a.m. a period of twilight falls, but there is never real darkness.

Canadians, Americans, Australians, and New Zealanders of Scottish descent often look to the Isle of Skye with nostalgia. Boatloads of Skyemen were shipped, often unwillingly, to these new lands during the Highland Clearances. Traces of their habitations can be seen all over Skye—foundations of walls, weeds growing over rubble, the outlines of houses, the stones of a hearth.

A trip through Skye's jagged, cloud-enshrouded Cullins and down primitive roads to Glen Brittle leads to excellent hiking country. The Cullins are beautiful seen from across Portree Bay or from Tarskavaig, across the waters of Loch Slapin. The grandest view is from the summit of Bidean Druim nan Ramh or Sgurr a'Mhadaidh.

The **Three Chimneys Restaurant**, *Colbost, Dunvegan; tel. +44 (1470) 511-258; website: www.threechimneys.co.uk*, on the Isle of Skye is an exceptional place to eat and has a world-wide following. Having won multiple awards for its cuisine, this restaurant has the best of the best.

The easiest (and most embarrassing) defeat

According to British history books, John Paul Jones was scared away from the Isle of Skye by a funeral procession he mistook for an army. The American Navy captain appeared on the coast of Skye in 1779 in the Bon Homme Richard (named for Benjamin Franklin's *Poor Richard's Almanack*). He had been harrying the shipping lanes in British waters. The appearance of his gunboat caused a flurry at Dunvegan Castle, because General MacLeod was away on military service in America. But when Jones saw the funeral party bearing the body of Donald MacLeod, he thought it was the MacLeod army in full battle array. He turned and fled. (You might take this tale with a grain of salt. American history books would probably report the incident differently.)

The favorite holiday isle

The favorite holiday isle among the British is **Arran**. Fluffy Arran sheep graze on green hillsides crossed by miles of hiking trails, especially on Goatfell, the "mountain of the winds." **Brodick Castle**, once the home of the dukes of Hamilton, can be seen in Lochranza. Now a ruin, it was once the hunting lodge of Robert the Bruce, King of the Scots.

The most important sight on Arran is **Holy Island**, containing the cave of St. Molaise and runic inscriptions. It lies off Lamlash Bay.

The Queen of the Hebrides

From Kennecraig, on Kintyre, a day tour crosses to the **Isle of Islay**, known as the Queen of the Hebrides. The island's fertile soil is carpeted with bright emerald fields dotted with sleek cows and ubiquitous sheep. Good roads wind over the moors past salmon-filled lochs and farmhouses snuggled amid tidy flower and vegetable gardens. Wild cliffs tower above secluded sandy bays.

Near Port Charlotte are the graves of U.S. troops who lost their lives when the *Tuscania* and *Otranto* were torpedoed in 1918.

The most thrilling three-island hop

For a thrilling three-island hop, take the tour from Oban to **Mull**, **Staffa**, and **Iona**. Bus rides on Mull are exciting enough, with single-track roads, but the trip to Staffa takes you through six-foot troughs. Huge foaming waves dash against dark columnar rocks on the island's coast. **Fingal's Cave**, a rocky formation beaten by waves, inspired Mendelssohn to compose the *Hebrides Overture* after his visit here in 1829. On calmer days, it is possible to disembark and explore the vast cavern.

The most sacred island

The sacred island of **Iona**, burial place of Scottish kings, is renowned as the location where Christianity was introduced to Scotland by St. Columba in A.D. 563. Abbey ruins, a reconstructed cathedral, and rugged ninth-century crosses stand silently on the buffeted shore.

The best Scottish standing stones

The islands of **Harris** and **Lewis** are famous for their Harris tweeds, but most travelers have never heard of the islands' well-preserved standing stones. Yet the prehistoric Standing Stones of Callanish on Lewis Island are more complete than Stonehenge in southern England and just as impressive. The best part, of course, is that they're free of Stonehenge's crowds.

THE BEST WAY TO EXPLORE THE ISLES

See the ScotRail website, *www.scotrail.co.uk,* for details of travel passes that include travel on trains, ferries and a selection of coach services throughout Scotland.

SCOTLAND'S BEST-KNOWN BATTLE SITES

The **Scottish Lowlands** were the site of Scotland's two best-known battles: **Stirling Bridge**, where William Wallace drove back the English forces in 1297, and **Bannockburn**, where Robert the Bruce was victorious against the English in 1314.

THE MOST NORDIC REGION

The **Orkney Islands**, north of mainland Scotland, belonged to the Norse from the ninth through the 16th centuries. Eventually, they became part of Scotland. The shops here sell Nordic sweaters rather than kilts. Lush and fertile, the islands, populated by birds of all species, are popular among bird watchers. The pace of life is slow and, in the summer, the days are long.

THE WORLD'S BEST SCOTCH WHISKIES

The *New York Times Magazine* recommends Macallan and Glenfarclas-Glenlivet as the best single-malt Scotch whiskies for their "sherry-like aroma" and "intense flavor," respectively. Among blends, the *New York Times Magazine* prefers Usquabach for its "peatlike aroma and hot finish." Chivas Royal Salute is hailed for its "round elegant flavor."

Scotland's whiskey trails are also a must-do for whiskey lovers. The trail involves touring all of Scotland's distilleries that brew the famous *Uisghe Beathas* (water of life). World famous distilleries include Speyside Cooperage, Benromach, Cardhu and Glenfiddich and are located in the Scottish highlands. Be sure to take samples from each distillery you visit; *website: www.maltwhiskytrail.com.*

THE BEST OF
BULGARIA

Although Eastern Europe in general is becoming an increasingly popular travel destination, the world has yet to discover Bulgaria. The traveler to Bulgaria is something of a trailblazer, charting virgin territory, as it were. For precisely this reason, Bulgaria is the perfect destination for the intrepid and adventurous explorer, not afraid to endure a bit of discomfort. For good tourist information go to *www.bulgariatravel.org*, or for hotel reservations look up *www.bulgaria-hotels.com*.

THE WORLD'S BEST MONASTERIES

Bulgaria is home to some of the world's best monasteries, many of which are located in the mountains. Some are as much as 500 years old. Although the Turks completely subjugated Bulgaria during their occupation from 1393 to 1878, outlawing Christianity and killing off the aristocracy, they sensibly hesitated to tread deep into the mountains. And it was here that Bulgarian monks built fantastic churches, painted exquisite icons, and printed Bulgarian books.

For example, at the **Rila monastery**; *website: www.bulgarianmonastery.com/ rila_monastery.html*, which is situated high in the Rila Mountains, about an hour and a half south of Sofia, the monks printed thousands of Bulgarian books on a printing press brought down the Danube from Vienna. Built in the 10th century and expanded in the early 14th century, the Rila monastery was destroyed in 1833 by fire. To rebuild the monastery, Bulgarians from all over the country contributed jewelry, money, and even belt buckles. The result is a dazzling structure that is part Byzantine fantasy, nestled in a green valley and surrounded on all sides by mountains.

The **Bachkovo monastery**, located near the Assenitsa River; *website: www.bulgarianmonastery.com/bachkovo_monastery.html,* is about 18 miles south of Bulgaria's second-largest city, Plovdiv. Originally governed by 50 Georgian monks, the monastery's holdings stretched as far south as Salonika in modern-day Greece. Destroyed by the Turks in the 16th century, the monastery was rebuilt. It now boasts fine frescoes and a mural depicting the ancient Greeks: Aristotle, Sophocles, and Diogenes.

Perhaps the best known of Bulgaria's monasteries is the **Transfiguration**, high above the Yantra River, about four miles from Veliko Turnovo, Bulgaria's second capital. Also destroyed during the Turkish occupation, the monastery was completely rebuilt in 1825 by the self-taught national revival architect Kolyo Ficheto.

BULGARIA'S BEST SPAS

Bulgaria boasts more than 220 mineral water springs, as well as the fabled mud from the lakes along the Black Sea coast, all believed to hold extensive curative properties. (Keep in mind that there is a tremendous difference between seaside and inland spas. The seaside spas attract thousands of foreigners, looking not only for curative treatment but also for a holiday in the sun. The inland spas, frequented mostly by Bulgarians, offer fewer amenities.)

Bulgaria's warmest and sunniest town, **Sandanski**, lies about 120 miles south of Sofia, at the foot of Pirin Mountain. The climate here is believed to have an incredible recuperative effect. The best accommodation in Sandanski is at the four-star **Inter-hotel Sandanski**, *tel. +359 (746) 3116-265; website: www.interhotelsandanski.bg,* a snow-white, seven-story building set against a background of green hills. An indoor and outdoor swimming pool is also a popular feature of the hotel.

The spa in **Velingrad** is situated in one of the most beautiful parts of the Rhodope Mountains in southern Bulgaria. The high amounts of negative ions and oxygen released by the rich vegetation and the abundant sunshine account for the curative properties of this spa. The best accommodation in Velingrad is at the **Dvoretsa Hotel,** *Tosho Staikov 8; tel. +359 (359) 56-200; website: www.dvoretsa.com.*

The best place to visit nearby is the city of **Plovdiv**, which has a well-preserved Roman amphitheater and a neighborhood of 19th-century houses that are open as museums, art galleries, or cafés.

The most modern Bulgarian seaside resort, **Albena**, lies about nine miles north of Golden Sands (probably the best-known of Bulgarian seaside resorts), located on the northern part of the Bulgarian Black Sea Coast along a picturesque bay.

THE BEST SKIING IN BULGARIA

The world has yet to realize that Bulgaria offers some of the best skiing in Europe. What's more, Bulgaria's ski resorts are also the most affordable of any on the Continent. Amenities may lag behind those in Switzerland or France, especially when it comes to service, but the low cost of a package deal means you can ski much more for much less money. Add to all of this the sheer novelty of skiing in Bulgaria, which offers a natural rugged beauty you'll find nowhere else.

Bulgaria's best ski resort is **Bansko**, which lies 100 miles from Sofia, in the Pirin Mountains. Recent development has seen it overtake Borovets as the country's premier ski resort and it has the longest ski season of all the Bulgarian resorts. Investment in the area has also meant a slew of new hotels have sprung up in the last few years. See *www.bulgariaski.com* for a list.

The oldest ski resort is **Borovets**, founded in 1897 by the royal family and named after the surrounding *bor* (or pine), the resort is old and established. Snow covers the forest and slopes for an average of 100 days a year, providing excellent conditions and a long season, which stretches from late November well into May. Accommodation at Borovets ranges from a village of Finnish-built chalets to several large hotels adjacent to the slopes. **The Rila** offers balconies facing the slopes; *website: www.bulgariaski.com/borovets/rila.shtml.* You can ski directly from the hotel to the chair lift. Another good place to stay is the four-star hotel, the **Samokov;** *website: www.bulgariaski.com/borovets/samokov.shtml.*

Bulgaria's other large resort is **Pamporovo**, which lies about 52 miles south of Plovdiv, in the heart of the Rhodope Mountains. Today, Pamporovo offers seven downhill trails, as well as cross-country runs and six lifts. The season there runs from December through April. Stay at either the **Perelik Hotel** or the new **Royal Lodge Spa Hotel**. For information on both see *www.bulgariaski.com.*

Bulgaria's busiest resort is **Aleko**, on Mount Vitosha. From its slopes, you have tremendous views of the city of Sofia. The resort offers two chair lifts and a gondola, as well as six trails for cross-country skiing. It is in close proximity to Sofia, so that means that you can stay in Sofia and combine sightseeing with skiing. While skiing is great at Aleko, amenities are not. You're better off staying in Sofia and traveling every day to Aleko for your skiing.

The best hotel in Sofia is the **Sheraton Sofia Hotel Balkan,** *5 Sveta Nedelya Square; tel. +359 (2) 981-6541; website: www.starwoodhotels.com.*

THE BEST OF
CANADA

Canada is probably the most free country in the world where a man still has room to breathe, to spread out, to move forward, to move out, an open country with an open frontier.

—Valentyn Moroz

Canada, which covers 3.8 million square miles, is the second-largest country on earth. Within its wide boundaries are a rainbow of cultures and a kaleidoscope of natural sights. To the west are cloud-piercing mountain peaks, the rugged Pacific coastline, and cities with large Chinese communities.

In the east are quaint British towns, French-speaking Quebec, and secluded islands. The interior is home to cowboys, rodeos, and ranches. Canada is a nature lover's dream, offering some of the world's best skiing, fishing, boating, hiking, bird-watching, and hunting. But it offers the best of big-city life as well. Montreal, Toronto, Edmonton, and Vancouver are metropolises with fine restaurants, high-fashion boutiques, cosmopolitan populations, artistic communities, and good theater and dance companies.

Montreal is the world's second-largest French-speaking city (after Paris). Parisian sophistication and Canadian friendliness blend here. The air smells of good coffee and French cooking.

Located on Montreal Island in the St. Lawrence River, the city faces the entrance to the St. Lawrence Seaway. Dominating the city is Mont Réal (Mount Royal), for which the city is named.

The city is informally split in two: the English section in the west and the French section in the east. Street and neighborhood names reinforce this division. Both languages are spoken across the city.

The oldest section

The oldest section, which hugs the waterfront, is called, appropriately, **Vieux Montreal** (Old Montreal). The seed of the city was an Indian village called Hochelaga. French settlers took it over in 1642 and called their town Ville Marie de Montreal. The French town was surrendered to the British in 1760. For one year (1775 to 1776), Montreal was occupied by American revolutionary troops. The quarter has been patiently restored and is filled with antique shops, cafés, and boutiques. The cobblestone alleyways are lined with artists and their easels on summer evenings. It's a pleasant place to wander or stop for a snack.

A futuristic contrast

At the other end of the time scale is **Man and His World**, a permanent mini-version of the international exposition EXPO '67. Situated on an island in the St. Lawrence River, it is a fascinating, ultramodern collection of spheres and towers, some of which are slowly rusting and falling apart. Built as part of the 1967 Expo, Habitat '67, is a unique residential complex designed by architect Moshe Safdie. This building of interlocking concrete forms is made up of "354 cubes of a magnif-icent grey-beige build up one on the other to form 148 residences nestled between sky and earth, between city and river, between greenery and light."

The stunning **Musee des Beaux Arts,** *tel. +1 (514) 285-2000; website: www.mbam.qc.ca,* houses a large and beautiful collection of Canadian and inter-national art. Admission is free.

Montreal's prettiest churches

The **Basilica of Notre Dame**, *Place d'Armes*; *website: www.basiliquenddm.org*, is an elaborate neo-Gothic affair with two tall spires. Built in 1829, the church houses an immense organ with 5,772 pipes. The altar, too, is monumental. And the wood-carvings are carefully detailed. The basilica was designed by New York architect James O'Donnell, whose grave is in the church. The **Sacred Heart Chapel**, adjacent to the basilica, has stained-glass windows illustrating the history of Montreal. The church is open daily from 8 a.m. to 5 p.m.

Notre-Dame-de-Bon-Secours, *400 St. Paul Street East; tel. +1 (514) 282-8670; website: www.marguerite-bourgeoys.com,* in Vieux Montreal, is the city's oldest church, built in 1657, destroyed by fire, then rebuilt in 1771. The facade is from 1895. Located near the water, it is also known as the Sailor's Chapel. The chapel is closed mid-January through February, except for Sunday mass.

The best of Montreal at night

Montreal doesn't close until 3.30 a.m., a liberty that spoils other cities for many Montrealers. The center of the city's nighttime activity is charming and sophisticated **Crescent Street**, Montreal's version of the Latin Quarter in Paris and frequented by a younger crowd. Prince Arthur, Duluth, and St. Denis streets are also lined with bars, cafés, and restaurants. The bars on Saint Laurent near Sherbrooke are among the city's most up-market. Or visit **Casino de Montreal**.

On summer nights in early July, you can take in the jazz festival at the **Theatre St. Denis**, *1594 St-Denis Street, tel. +1 (514) 849-4211; website: http:// theatrestdenis.com*, and in late August you can enjoy the film festival at cinemas throughout the city.

For something unique, go to a *boîte à chanson*, a Quebec-style café with French folk music.

The finest French cooking

The best restaurant in Montreal is **Toqué!**, *900 place Jean-Paul-Riopelle; tel. +1 (514) 499-2084; website: www.restaurant-toque.com*. The food is superb and inventive. Try the six-course tasting menu. Open Tuesday to Saturday, 5.30 p.m. to 10.30 p.m.

Chez la Mère Michel, *1209 Guy Street; tel. +1 (514) 934-0473; website: www.chezlameremichel.ca*, is cozy, with an outstanding French provincial menu and a pretty garden patio. Try the *homard soufflé Nantua* (fresh lobster added to mousseline potatoes and served on a bed of spinach). The restaurant is closed Sundays and Monday lunchtime.

The best hotels

Montreal's best hotel is the **Ritz Carlton**, *1228 rue Sherbrooke West; tel. +1 (514) 842-4212; website: www.ritzmontreal.com*. A luxurious, Continental-style hotel, it is near fashionable boutiques, restaurants, and galleries and has been Montreal's most elegant address since 1912.

Other grand hotels are the **Fairmont Queen Elizabeth**, *900 Rene Levesque Blvd. West, tel. +1 (514) 861-3511; website: www.fairmont.com/queenelizabeth*, situated over the train station downtown, and the **Marriott Chateau Champlain**, *1 Place du Canada; tel. +1 (514) 878-9000; website: www.montrealmarriottchateauchamplain.com*, overlooking the St. Lawrence River.

Less expensive hotels include **L'Hôtel de la Montagne**, *1430, Rue de la Montagne Street; tel. +1 (514) 288-5656; website: www.hoteldelamontagne.com*, and the **Hotel Château Versailles**, *1659 Sherbrooke Street West; tel. +1 (514) 933-8111; website: www.versailleshotels.com*.

For something new, hip, and chic, there's **W Montreal**, *901 rue Square Victoria; tel. +1 (514) 395-3100; website: www.starwoodhotels.com*.

If you're into exploring Vieux Montreal, try **Auberge Bonaparte**, *447 rue St-Francois-Xavier; tel. +1 (514) 844-1448; website: www.bonaparte.com/en/auberge/*. The interior boasts Louis-Phillippe style furnishings, French windows, and intricate woodwork imbued with imperial European influence. From the rooftop terrace you look onto Notre Dame Basilica. The hotel also offers a sophisticated restaurant, oozing French chic.

But we think the best (and certainly the most affordable) accommodation in Montreal is at the city's B&Bs. For a list, contact **Downtown Bed and Breakfast**, *3458 Laval Ave., Montreal H2X 3C8; tel. +1 (514) 289-9749; website: www.bbmontreal.ca*.

QUEBEC: THE FRENCH HEART AND THE ONLY WALLED CITY

Quebec City, the capital of the French-speaking province of Quebec, is the focal point of French Canadian nationalism and culture. It is also the first French settlement in North America (95% of the population is French) and the second oldest city in the New World (after St. Johns, Newfoundland)—the walled fortress was founded by Champlain in 1608; it celebrated its 400th birthday in 2008. Quebec is the only walled city in North America. It is set high on Cape Diamond, 350 feet above the St. Lawrence River.

The best of Vieux Quebec

In **Vieux Quebec** (Old Quebec), you'll see 17th- and 18th-century stone houses similar to those in the villages of Normandy and Brittany in France. The heart of Vieux Quebec is the beautiful **Place d'Armes**.

A good introduction to the history of Quebec is the sound-and-light show at the **Musée du Fort**, *10 Sainte-Anne Street; tel. +1 (418) 692-2175; website: www.museedufort.com.* The Seminary, dating from 1663, houses a museum containing a rare collection of Canadian money, including Indian wampum and playing cards used as legal tender in colonial times.

In the museum at the **L'Hotel Dieu** (a teaching hospital), *11 Côte du Palais,* you can see the stone vaults where Augustinian nuns took refuge during the 1759 siege. The skull of French general Montcalm is on view at the **Ursuline Convent Museum,** *12 rue Donnacona.*

Looming over the Place d'Armes is the **Château Frontenac**, *1 rue des Carrières; tel. +1 (418) 692-3861; website: www.fairmont.com/Frontenac,* a magnificent Victorian hotel with turrets and towers. Built in 1892, it perches at the top of Cape Diamond, a 300-foot bluff.

Next door is the **Jardin du Gouverneur**, originally the private garden of the Château St. Louis. It is best known for its statue of General James Wolfe and Marquis de Montcalm, erected in 1828. On it is written, "Their courage gave them the same lot; history, the same fame; posterity, the same monument."

Canada's most important battlefield

The **Plains of Abraham** in Quebec were the site of a battle that determined the fate of Canada. On September 13, 1759, the British army under Wolfe defeated the French under Montcalm, and Canada was later turned over to the British. (However, the French inhabitants held on to their language and culture.) Both Wolfe and Montcalm were killed during the battle. According to legend, at the end of the battle, a voice was heard across the plains crying, "*Je me souviens*" (I remember), which became the motto of the province of Quebec.

Today the battlefield is part of the 230-acre **Parc des Champs de Bataille** (Battlefields Park). It is a place of meadows and grassy hills, Quebec's own Central Park. From the observation post, you'll have a wide view of the field and the river.

The **Quebec Museum**, *tel. +1 (418) 643-2150; website: www.mnba.qc.ca,* is also on the park grounds. It contains displays illustrating Quebec's history, paintings by Quebecois artists, and a section devoted to 17th-century decorative arts. The museum is open 10 a.m. until 5.45 p.m. daily except Monday, when it is closed. The Quebec City Museum Card ($40) gives you unlimited access to 24 museums for three days and public transport for two days.

The **Musée de la Civilisation** (Museum of Civilization), *85 rue Dalhousie; tel. +1 (418) 643-2158; website: www.mcq.org*, is in the heart of the historic district. Not only does the museum trace the history of New France, it provides a hands-on experience to help visitors learn about such things as our Earth and the human brain. In winter it's closed Mondays.

The oldest section

The oldest section of the city is around Place Royale in a district known as **Lower Town**. When Champlain started his colony here, it was a trading post, with a store, a few houses, and fortifications. In later years, Place Royale became the center of the fur-trading industry. As colonists and missionaries arrived, the settlement gradually moved uphill, to Vieux Quebec. Today, Lower Town is a busy port. Designated a historic area by the Canadian government, the section surrounding Place Royale is being restored. It has the greatest concentration of 17th- and 18th-century buildings in North America.

The oldest church in Quebec, **Notre Dame des Victoires**, is located on Place Royale. This small stone church built in 1688 is decorated inside with elaborate woodwork. The altar is carved in the shape of an old fort. The church is open daily.

A funicular will take you from Place d'Armes down to Place Royale, where you can walk along cobblestone streets past 17th-century buildings and sunny squares. **Rue de Trésor** is a narrow alley near the Chateau and is the best place to stroll where painters sell their masterpieces.

Quartier Petit Champlain offers a great shopping experience with one-of-a-kind boutiques and bistros in a romantic European atmosphere.

The best French architecture

Quebec's **Assemblée Nationale** (parliament buildings)—bounded by rue Dufferin, boulevards St. Cyrille and St. Augustin, and Le Grande Allée—are imposing French structures built in 1877 and 1886. Twelve bronze statues commemorating famous Canadians rest in niches in the facade. They are the works of the Quebec sculptor Hubert. Guided tours are conducted daily during the summer and on weekdays during the winter.

The best time to visit

The **Carnival de Quebec**, a 10-day celebration beginning on the first Thursday in February, is the most festive time to visit the city. A huge party to commemorate the end of winter, it includes two parades, fireworks, and winter sports. The official mascot is a seven-foot snowman called Le Bonhomme Carnival. If you plan to visit during Carnival, you will be competing for hotel rooms with more than a half-million people from all over North America. Make reservations.

While Quebec is beautiful in mid-summer, for a quieter time to enjoy its charms try September, after Labor Day, up to mid-October. You'll find more space on the streets of the walled city and lower town and it's still often warm enough to enjoy the outdoor cafés and restaurants.

Quebec's best restaurants

The best restaurant in town is **Laurie Raphaël**, *117 rue Dalhousie; tel. +1 (418) 692-4555, website: www.laurieraphael.com,* which serves eclectic and inventive dishes, like the delicious lobster with citrus and vanilla.

Restaurant Louis Hébert, *668 Grande Allée Est, tel. +1 (418) 525-7812; website: www.louishebert.com,* is also good, serving light French fare. Set in a 17th-century fieldstone building, it has a French provincial atmosphere, with calico lampshades and an outdoor terrace. It is open daily.

The best place for local French-Canadian fare is **Aux Anciens Canadiens**, *34 rue St. Louis; tel. +1 (418) 692-1627; website: www.auxancienscanadiens.qc.ca.* Located in the former home of the 19th-century historical novelist Philippe Aubert de Gaspé (which was built in 1675), the restaurant serves Canadian yellow pea soup, *tourtière* (meat pie), and a French-Canadian favorite, maple sugar pie with heavy cream. Reservations are suggested. The restaurant is open daily.

L'Astral, *1225, Cours du General-de-Montcalm; tel. +1 (418) 780-3602; website: www.lastral.ca*, is the revolving rooftop restaurant at Loews Le Concorde Hotel; it has won awards for best hotel restaurant for many years.

The best hotels

The most elegant place to stay is the **Fairmont Le Château Frontenac**, *1 rue des Carrières; tel. +1 (418) 692-3861; website: www.fairmont.com/Frontenac.* It is grand, historic, and expensive. The cocktail lounge and many of the rooms have views of the St. Lawrence. However, because this is a tourist hotel, expect to be one of many Americans.

Auberge du Trésor, *20 rue Ste. Anne; tel. +1 (418) 694-1876; website:*

www.aubergedutresor.com, is a 300-year-old inn on the Place d'Armes. Its 20 guest rooms have private bathrooms, televisions, and air conditioning. Prices are moderate.

Le Château de Pierre, *17 ave. Ste. Geneviève; tel. +1 (418)694-0429; website: www.chateaudepierre.com,* is a 15-room English colonial style mansion built in 1853.

For a quite different feel, try the newly opened **Hotel Premières Nations** (First Nations Hotel), *5 Place de la Rencontre Ekionkiestha; tel. +1 (418) 847-2222; website: www.hotelpremieresnations.ca,* in Wendake, a 20-minute drive from downtown. Operated by a co-operative of Quebec's aboriginal people, it is a stylish blending of the modern with traditional themes. Attached is a First Nations museum.

THE BEST OF PROVINCIAL FRENCH CANADA

Most American visitors, smitten by Quebec City's charms, overlook the nearby countryside (unless they snow ski in the Laurentides, Quebec's Little Switzerland). This is a big oversight. Farm stays are available in fascinating villages, where people wake up with the roosters.

An island lost in time

Ile d'Orléans is a lovely island with historic Quebecois homes, old farming villages, and French restaurants. Until 1935, the island could be reached only by boat. Because of this, it retained its old French ways longer than its neighbors. Many of the houses here are from the 17th and 18th centuries. Most residents are farmers and descendants of French immigrants from Normandy and Brittany.

Miraculous cures

Farther on is the village of **Ste. Anne de Beaupré**, whose massive cathedral is a famous Catholic shrine. Invalids from all over the world come here to be cured—the fountain in front of the church is said to cure many diseases. There must be something to this claim, to judge from the plethora of crutches, canes, and walkers left behind by cured believers—some of the paraphernalia is hung from the church's ceiling. Built in 1922, the cathedral holds 10,000 people.

A best for *les artistes*

Just an hour north of Quebec City, on the north shore of the St. Lawrence River, is a bustling resort for artists and patrons called **Baie St. Paul**. Dozens of galleries display works of the Group of Seven—painters who portray the Charlevoix region.

The Gaspe Peninsula

An hour northeast of Baie St. Paul, the port of Rivière du Loup marks the beginning of the **Gaspe Peninsula**, a French fishing and farming region. The Gaspe begins dramatically. Mountains plunge into the sea. Little fishing towns brave the pounding surf. Although rugged, the peninsula is accommodating—many manor houses have been converted to inns.

Gaspe is an old French fishing village, three hours north of Riviere du Loup on the northern tip of the peninsula. The French spoken here, *joual*, sounds to the French of France as Middle English would sound to us. Gaspe is where Cartier first stepped ashore in North America in 1534. A large granite cross marks the spot. The Gaspe Museum has exhibits on the history and folklore of the area.

Around the point from Gape is **Bonaventure**, founded by French-speaking Acadians fleeing British troops in 1755. Nearby are limestone rock formations that reach out of the sea—popular among small-boat sailors and seabirds. You can walk to **Percé Rock** at low tide. **Ile Bonaventure** is a boat ride away. This bird sanctuary was once a pirate hideout.

One of Quebec province's best restaurants perches 1,000 feet above Perce Rock. **L'Auberge du Gargantua**, *222 Route des Failles; tel. +1 (418) 782-2852*, serves excellent French provincial cooking. Specialties include periwinkles in court bouillon, fresh fish, and giant crab. But the best dish is the bouillabaisse Gargantua. Reservations are required.

OTTAWA, A CAPITAL CITY

Canada's capital, **Ottawa**, is a small beautiful city with only 815,000 inhabitants. Set high on a bluff overlooking the confluence of the Ottawa, Gatineau, and Rideau rivers, it has lovely views in all directions. Man has added to the scenery: the Gothic parliament buildings create a romantic skyline. The Rideau Canal is pretty, cutting through the city.

Ottawa has a bilingual flavor. The predominant language is English, although you'll hear a lot of French especially in the downtown core and east end. Established by Queen Victoria in 1858 as the capital of the United Provinces of Canada, the city is filled with elaborate Victorian architecture. It became the capital of modern Canada in 1867.

Ottawa's top sights

Parliament Hill, on a bluff over the Ottawa River, is the pedestal for the spectacular parliament buildings, with their tall copper roofs. The 302-foot **Peace Tower** forms part of the main entrance to the buildings. Inside, the Memorial Chamber is dedicated to Canada's war dead. The books of remembrance record the names of all those Canadians who died in battle. The Peace Tower contains a 53-bell carillon.

You can go to the Visitor's Galleries in the House of Commons and the Senate. Or take a tour of the Center Block, which passes through the Memorial Chamber, and the magnificently restored Library of Parliament. During the summer, you can watch the changing of the guard on the lawns of Parliament Hill daily at 10 a.m.

The **National Gallery of Canada,** *Sussex Drive; tel. +1 (613) 990-1985; website: www.national.gallery.ca*, overlooks the Ottawa River. The modern glass structure contains galleries devoted to European and Canadian art, displaying works by Canada's Group of Seven, Paul Kane's paintings of Indians and Cornelius Kreigoff's paintings of pioneers. European masters Rembrandt, Chardin, El Greco, Cézanne, Van Gogh, Monet, and Picasso are also represented. Closed Mondays during winter.

Bytown Museum, *east of Parliament Hill; tel. +1 (613) 234-4570; website: www.bytownmuseum.com,* near the junction of the Rideau Canal and the Ottawa River, tells the story of Ottawa's (originally named Bytown) first century. It is filled with artifacts of the Ottawa Indians: furniture, clothes, guns, tools, and toys.

Ottawa's best hotels

The best hotel in town is the **Fairmont Château Laurier**, *1 Rideau Street; tel. +1 (613) 241-1414; website: www.chateaulaurier.com.* An institution in Canada since 1912, it is a favorite among politicians and big-time businessmen. The hotel's restaurant, Wilfrid's, is dignified. Zoe's Lounge is a great place to people-watch through the huge glass windows and take English-style afternoon tea. The hotel is ideally situated to explore the restored Byward Market, which is packed with bars, restaurants and nightlife.

The **Hilton Lac Leamy**, *3 Boulevard du Casino; tel. +1 (819) 790-6444; website: www1.hilton.com.* The Hilton sits across the Ottawa River in Gatineau and is connected to the Casino Lac Leamy, and live performance theatre. The hotel also contains the region's best restaurant, Le Baccara.

More moderately priced is the **Lord Elgin**, *100 Elgin Street; tel. +1 (613) 235-3333; website: www.lordelginhotel.ca.* It is also in the downtown core and close to the Elgin Street restaurants and bars. Built in the 1940s, it's less regal than the nearby Chateau Laurier but recently refurbished to a high standard.

The best restaurants

Le Cordon Bleu @ Signatures, *453 Laurier Avenue East; tel. +1 (613) 236-2499; website: www.bistroatsignatures.com.* Housed in a Tudor-style heritage mansion, Signatures is the restaurant of the Cordon Bleu Culinary Arts Institute.

The Urban Pear, *151 2nd Avenue; tel. +1 (613) 569-9305; website: www.theurbanpear.com.*Casual elegance defines this minimally decorated eatery where the emphasis is on the food, not the surroundings. The Urban Pear specializes in organic and local fare with a wide variety of venison, ostrich and vegetarian plates.

Les Fougères, *783 Route 105, Chelsea, Quebec; tel. +1 (819) 827-8942; website: www.fougeres.ca.* Take a 15-minute drive from Parliament Hill to the Gatineau Hills village of Chelsea. Offers traditional recipes with a modern flair. Looking out into the garden you can easily imagine you're in the French countryside.

THE BEST OF SHAKESPEARE

Try to make it to Stratford's annual summer **Shakespearean Festival** *(website: www.stratfordfestival.ca)*. The town, which is modeled on Stratford, England, has swans, green lawns that sweep down to the river, and pretty cottages. You can picnic in **Queen's Park** beneath tall shade trees. Past the Orr Dam and the 90-year-old stone bridge is the **Shakespearean Garden**, a formal English garden with a sundial that was presented to the town by a former mayor of England's Stratford-upon-Avon. For more information, contact **Tourism Stratford**; *website: www.city.stratford.on.ca.*

The most curious place to dine in Stratford is **The Church**, *70 Brunswick Street; tel. +1 (519) 273-3424; website: www.churchrestaurant.com*, which has delicious food and churchlike décor—organ pipes, an altar, a vaulted roof, and stained-glass windows. Reservations are required.

NIAGARA FROM THE OTHER SIDE

Just 20 minutes from Niagara-on-the-Lake, down Niagara Parkway, is the Canadian side of **Niagara Falls**, which is prettier than the U.S. side and less crowded. You can take an elevator below the falls at Table Rock House. And the ship *Maid of the Mist* takes you practically under the falls. Boats leave from the dock on the parkway just down from the Rainbow Bridge.

THE BEST OF TORONTO

Toronto, situated on the Great Lakes, is the largest city in Canada. Towering buildings, such as the CN (Canadian National) Tower, the world's fifth tallest free-standing structure, punctuate the city's dramatic skyline. Canada's most modern city, Toronto boasts avant garde architecture, especially the recent additions to the Royal Ontario Museum (the Crystal), the Art Gallery of Ontario, and the new Four Seasons Opera House.

Despite its modern appearance, Toronto is 175 years old, occupying the site of a French fort (1749-1759) in an area purchased by the British from the Indians in 1787. It was settled largely by Loyalists who left the Thirteen Colonies during and just after the Revolutionary War. Americans raided the city twice, destroying parts of it during the War of 1812. Then known as York, it was renamed Toronto in 1834.

Toronto is an Indian word meaning *place of meeting*, which is appropriate considering the huge and varied ethnic groups that populate the city. Because of the diversified population, the choice of restaurants is astounding. Toronto is second only to New York in number and variety of live stage productions. It has a progressive urban spirit and a sophisticated cosmopolitan outlook, without the big city problems of Chicago and New York.

Toronto's top sights

The best place to begin exploring the city is at its heart: **City Hall**, a modern superstructure that looks something like the landing pad for a spaceship. Topped with a white dome and flanked by 20- and 27-story curved towers, the building's twin clamshell design won an international competition for Finnish architect Viljo Revell, one of 530 contestants.

The 9-acre plaza in front of City Hall, called **Nathan Phillips Square**, was named after the Toronto mayor responsible for the project. It provides a community meeting place for concerts and festivals. In the winter, the reflecting pool doubles as a skating rink. The focal point of the square is a Henry Moore sculpture called *The Archer*. When city fathers balked at buying it, the people of Toronto raised the money to buy it themselves. Moore was so touched by their enthusiasm that he donated many of his works to the Art Gallery of Toronto.

Across the street is **Old City Hall**, an imposing Romanesque fortress that houses the Provincial Courts. Built in 1899, it has marble columns, stained glass, and grained flooring from Georgia. The building is embellished with carved gargoyles, said to be furtive caricatures of city councilors with whom the architect battled in the 1890s.

In Queen's Park, the **Provincial Parliament Building** stands on the site of a former lunatic asylum. Wander through the pink sandstone complex and listen to the lawmakers, debating in the legislative chambers. This structure dominates University Avenue, the broad boulevard leading down the center of the city to Lake Ontario.

Casa Loma, *1 Austin Terrace; tel. +1 (416) 923–1171; website: www. casaloma.org,* is a 98-room, medieval-looking castle created by financier Sir Henry Pellatt. Built between 1911 and 1914, this extravagance boasts gold-plated bath fixtures, a gigantic pipe organ, and one of the largest wine cellars in North America. An 800-foot underground tunnel leads to stables furnished in marble, mahogany, and Spanish tile.

Old Fort York, *Garrison Road*, was built in 1793, destroyed during the War of 1812, and then rebuilt. The officers' quarters, center blockhouse, and battlements have been refurbished. Members of the Fort York Guard are dressed in uniforms of British troops of the era.

Also visit the city's baseball stadium, the **Rogers Centre**, home of the Toronto Blue Jays. It has a retractable roof, several restaurants—including a Hard Rock Café, and a hotel with rooms overlooking the ball field.

The finest art

The **Art Gallery of Ontario**, *317 Dundas Street West; tel. +1 (416) 979-6648; website: www.ago.net*, is renowned for its collection of works by Canadian artists and for its important collection of Henry Moore sculptures.

The **Royal Ontario Museum**, *Avenue Road and Bloor Street West; website: www.rom.on.ca*, displays Chinese art and artifacts, extensive ethnological collections, dinosaurs, fossils, minerals, and amazing dioramas. The museum also offers international vintage film showcases from time to time.

The **McMichael Canadian Collection of Art**, *10365 Islington Avenue, Kleinburg; tel. +1 (905) 893-1121; website: www.mcmichael.com*, in Kleinburg, about 25 miles north of Toronto, has 30 gallery rooms constructed from timbers that once enclosed pioneer homes and barns. More than 1,000 paintings by the Group of Seven and their contemporaries are on display, along with West Coast and Woodland Indian and Inuit works.

The most inviting parks

Toronto has 15,000 acres of parkland displaying signs that say "Please walk on the grass." **Toronto Islands Park** can be reached by ferry from across the harbor.

Exhibition Place, *Lakeshore Boulevard West*, is the site of the Canadian National Exhibition, held from the third week in August to the first Monday in September.

High Park, near the west end of the Queen streetcar route, is a lovely place for sailing, picnicking, and strolling.

The efficient public transit system includes subways from which one can see boaters and fishermen on rivers which traverse the heart of the city.

The best entertainment

Ontario Place, along the lakefront, is an overwhelming futuristic entertainment complex built over the water on three man-made islands. It includes a disco, a roller rink, a marina, numerous restaurants, and snack bars. The main attraction is the **Cinesphere**, a ball-shaped theater where IMAX films are projected on a six-story curved screen, the world's tallest.

Harbourfront, another recreational development, stretches one-and-a-half miles across downtown from York Street to just past Bathurst. Divided into four sections, the attractions include antique shops, art galleries, waterside cafés, studios, theatres, picnic facilities, and a multicultural media centre.

Toronto has its own symphony and is home to both the Canadian Opera Company and the National Ballet. The **Sony Centre for the Performing Arts**, *Front and Yonge streets; website: www.sonycentre.ca*, is a modern hall with seating for 3,200.

The **St. Lawrence Centre**, *27 Front Street East; tel. +1 (416) 366-7723; website: www.stlc.com*, contains an 830-seat theatre that accommodates a resident repertory company, visiting theatre groups, opera and dance companies.

Incomparable cooking

Canada's best Thai restaurant is **Bangkok Garden**, *18 Elm Street; tel. +1 (416) 977-6748; website: www.bangkokgarden.ca*, a beautifully decorated place. Try the steamed gingerfish or the mussels in spicy coconut sauce. The restaurant is closed Sundays.

The most charming restaurant in town is **Bistro 990**, *990 Bay Street; tel. +1 (416) 921-9990; website: www.bistro990.ca,* which serves classic French cuisine in an elegant setting and is a good spot to sight visiting movie stars working in "Hollywood North".

The best place for Continental cuisine (with a touch of California) is **Café Victoria**, *37 King Street E.; tel. +1 (416) 863-9700*, in the King Edward Hotel. Dishes are not only light and delicious but also beautifully presented. Try the tea-smoked Atlantic salmon and fruit ices.

Il Posto Nuovo, *York Square, 148 Yorkville Ave.; tel. +1 (416) 968-0469; website: www.ilposto.ca*, is one of Toronto's best Italian restaurants, with imaginatively prepared pasta dishes and seafood. The restaurant is closed Sundays.

The best hotels

The **Fairmont Royal York Hotel**, *100 Front Street W.; tel. +1 (416) 368-2511; website: www.fairmont.com/royalyork*, is the biggest hotel in the British Commonwealth. A landmark since 1929, it is a favorite among royalty, movie stars, and visiting prime ministers. Service is superb.

Toronto's most charming hotel is the **Le Meridien King Edward**, *37 King Street E.; tel. +1 (416) 863-9700; website: www.starwoodhotels.com/lemeridien*. This Edwardian-style classic was has been hosting guests for over 100 years, including Elizabeth Taylor and Richard Burton.

The **Sheraton Centre**, *123 Queen Street W.; tel. +1 (416) 361-1000; website: www.starwoodhotels.com/sheraton*, outdoes itself with imaginative décor. A three-story waterfall cascades in the lobby, and the hotel complex houses 40 stores, two theatres, 10 restaurants, and six bars. Outside are lovely gardens. And, of course, modern luxuries, such as saunas and indoor and outdoor pools, have not been forgotten.

Metropolitan Hotel, *108 Chestnut Street; tel. +1 (416) 977-5000; website: www.metropolitan.com/toronto*, is just off University Avenue. It is easy walking distance to everything downtown, and affordable.

Along **New Brunswick's** 1,400-mile shoreline are some of the oldest cities and towns in Canada, founded by Loyalist refugees from the American Revolution. The coast is also home to small Acadian French towns. Forests cover 84% of the province. Life is serene. Along the **Fundy Coast**, residents pass the time predicting the weather and discussing the price of seafood.

Campobello Island, a president's favorite

Campobello Island is where President Franklin Roosevelt retreated from the tensions of his job. His house is open to the public.

The **Roosevelt Campobello International Park** *(website: www.fdr.net),* is a joint Canadian-American preservation effort. Benedict Arnold also lived on Campobello Island for a time, at Snug Cove.

St. Andrews, a moving town

St. Andrews is a Loyalist settlement with a unique history. The first settlers built their town at Fort George (later Castine, Maine). When that area became part of the United States, the townspeople actually lifted their homes and moved them to the Canadian side of the border. Today St. Andrews is a peaceful summer haven with swimming, golfing, and tours of Passamoquoddy Bay.

St. Andrews Blockhouse National Historic Site, at the northwest end of Water Street, is the only surviving wood fortress of several built for the town's defense during the War of 1812. Also see **Greenock Church**, a pretty church built in 1824.

Visit the aquarium at Huntsman Marine Laboratories; *website: www. huntsmanmarine.ca,* northwest of town on Brandy Cover Road, and the **Ross Memorial Museum**, *188 Montague Street; tel. +1 (506) 529-5124; website: www. rossmemorialmuseum.ca,* in an old house filled with antiques, paintings, and curios.

The best place to stay in town is the quirky **Rossmount Inn**, *4599 Route 127; tel. +1 (506) 529-3351; website: www.rossmountinn.com.* The Victorian house is decorated with a mishmash of Persian rugs, English wallpaper, and French art and is set on an 87-acre estate.

The best bird-watching

New Brunswick is an excellent place for bird-watching. More than 350 species of birds can be seen; you need only a pair of binoculars and a North American field guide. During the winter, New Brunswick attracts such rare birds as the Bohemian waxwing, pine grosbeak, common redpoll, and purple finch.

For bird watchers, the event of the year is the **Christmas Bird Count**, sponsored by the National Audubon Society. As many observers as possible are needed on the count day, which usually falls during the last two weeks of December. Write to the **New Brunswick Museum**, *Natural Science Department, 277 Douglas Ave., St. John, New Brunswick E2K 1E5; website: www.nbm-mnb.ca*, for the names and addresses of count compilers.

The New Brunswick Federation of Naturalists sponsors field trips several times a year. For more information, write to the **New Brunswick Museum**, *address above*.

St. John: The oldest town

St. John is the oldest incorporated town in Canada, inaugurated in 1785. Actually, it was founded by Samuel de Champlain on St. John the Baptist Day (June 24) in 1604. The Loyalists turned this city into one of the world's greatest shipbuilding ports. Vessels from every country call here.

The St. John River's **Reversing Falls** will leave you wondering. The falls, which appear to flow backward, are actually rapids beneath the bridge on Highway 100. A Tourist Information Center here shows a film explaining the phenomenon. Usually the river empties into the Bay of Fundy. But as the tide rises, the estuary water reverses the river current, creating climbing rapids.

New Brunswick's best seafood

Shediac, which holds a six-day Lobster Festival every July, is known for its incredibly fresh and inexpensive lobster. The city is also known for having New Brunswick's warmest water, thanks to sand bars and shallow depths.

Paturel Shore House, *tel. +1 (506) 532-4774*, on the ocean next to a seafood packing plant, is the best place in the area to get seafood. Lobster is caught locally and prepared to your specifications. The lobster stew can be a meal in itself.

The best place to stay is **Maison Tait**, *293 Main Street; tel. +1 (506) 532-4233; website: www.maisontaithouse.com*. Private wine-tasting classes are available in the historic mansion built in 1911 it is also but a few minutes away from famous Parlee beach.

NOVA SCOTIA: GAELIC CULTURE

Nova Scotia, a 375-mile peninsula separated from New Brunswick by the Bay of Fundy, preserves Gaelic and Acadian culture in a land of sparkling waters, dramatic coasts, and quaint villages. The province is made up of two main sections, Nova Scotia proper and **Cape Breton Island**, once an island, now joined to the mainland by the Canso Causeway.

Halifax, the capital of the province, is a sophisticated harbor city, with a rich history, many museums, and a beautiful waterfront, where elegant shops, restaurants, and hotels line the piers.

Halifax's best restaurant

Da Maurizio's, *1496 Water Street; tel. +1 (902) 423-0859; website: www. damaurizio.ca*, serves exquisite Italian cuisine made with the superb local seafood, in a lush setting in the historic Alexander Keith's Brewery, near the harbor.

From Halifax, you can head south to the charming town of **Peggy's Cove**, or visit the **Bay of Fundy**, with its astonishing dramatic tides and marine life.

In **Malagash**, visit the **Jost Vineyards,** *tel. +1 (800) 565-4567; website: www.jostwine.com*, where the temperate seaside climate creates an ideal growing season. A tasting room is open daily.

Head northwest to **Cape Breton**, and you enter the heart of Gaelic country. **The Gaelic College of Celtic Arts and Crafts** (*website: www.gaeliccollege.edu.*) offers summer classes in Gaelic language, music, dance, and arts in St. Ann's. Cape Breton fiddlers retain a Scottish style abandoned by most Scottish musicians long ago.

The stretch along the western coast of Cape Breton from the causeway at Port Hawkesbury to Margaree Forks, known as the **Ceilidh Trail**, is the place to go to enjoy traditional music and dance—during the summer season, you can find live music every day in a pub, restaurant, town hall, or at a church dance.

The small fishing village of **Mabou** is at the center of Cape Breton's musical culture. Fiddler Natalie's MacMaster is a native, her uncle, legendary fiddler Buddy MacMaster, was station master for the Mabou trains for decades, and the native Rankin Family are international stars. Two of the Rankin sisters established the Red Shoe, decorated with vintage photographs of Mabou musicians.

Best pub

The Red Shoe, *11573 Route 19, Mabou; website: www.redshoepub.com.* If you haven't caught Natalie at Carnegie Hall, try this place, where the cover charge is between $6 and $8, the chowder is full of lobster and crab from the docks down the lane, the beer is cold and the friendly locals will teach you to step dance if you just stand on the dance floor looking bewildered. Open June-October.

Best music festival

Celtic Colours, *Cape Breton, every October; website: www.celtic-colours.com.* Celtic musicians from around the world perform in venues ranging from little parish halls to pubs to auditoriums.

Best single malt whiskey

Glenora Distillery, *Inverness; tel. +1 (800) 839-0491; website: www. glenoradistillery.com.* This is actually the ONLY single malt whiskey made in North America, and it is excellent. You can tour the distillery, and taste. The Inn offers rooms and cottages; the pub and formal dining room are excellent, often with live music.

Best scenic drive

The Cabot Trail is one of the world's best scenic drives. This stunning circular tour around the dramatic coast of Cape Breton takes you through Cape Breton Highlands National Park, one of Canada's most beautiful wilderness areas. You pass through quiet fishing villages, can stop at swimmable beaches, and may spot pods of whales from atop the rugged cliffs. Fresh lobster restaurants—from down home to fancy—abound. More information and maps at *http://novascotia.com* and click on the "Getting Here and Around" tab.

For more information on Nova Scotia, contact the **Nova Scotia Department of Tourism**, *tel. +1 (800) 565-0000* or *+1 (902) 425-5781; website: http://novascotia.com.*

THE OLDEST COLONY: NEWFOUNDLAND

Newfoundland is at once the newest of the Canadian provinces and the oldest of the British colonies. Sir Humphrey Gilbert landed on this North Atlantic island in 1583 and claimed it for Queen Elizabeth. But it didn't become part of Canada until 1949.

Legions of hunters, hikers, fishermen, campers, boaters, and photographers take advantage of the natural bounties of this northern province's 47 provincial park wilderness areas and two national parks: Terra Nova in the east and Gros Morne in the west.

The **Marine Atlantic Reservations Bureau**, *121 Eden Street, Bar Harbor, ME 04609; tel. +1 (800) 341-7981; website: www.marine-atlantic.ca,* operates a year-round vehicle and passenger ferry service between North Sydney, Nova Scotia, and Port-aux-Basques, Newfoundland. During the summer, an additional service operates between North Sydney and Argentia, 78 miles from St. John's.

Gros Morne: The most beautiful scenery

Gros Morne National Park is a jaw-dropping wilderness area on the west coast of Newfoundland. The 750-square-mile park has the most spectacular fiords in North America. Gros Morne (which translates as *Big Knoll* in French) is a flat-topped extinct volcano rising 2,000 feet front the Gulf of St. Lawrence. Climb the two-and-a-half-mile **Names Callaghan Trail** to the top of Gros Morne for the best view of the tundra and the roaring sea below. Look for moose, caribou, bald eagles, black bears, and beaver.

Hike along the elevated boardwalk through the marshes to **Western Brook Pond**. At the end of the path is a dock, where you can catch a tour boat and cruise the pond. (You can register for a boat tour at the park's visitor center.) Boats sail beneath towering rocky cliffs to a misty 2,000-foot waterfall. Three boat trips depart daily, weather permitting, from mid-June to mid-September. Boat capacity is 25 to 30 people. To get to the pond, drive north of the visitor center on Highway 430 for about 18 miles, past Sally's Cove.

Canada's best archeological sites

The Great Northern Peninsula is the site of some of Canada's most interesting archeological sites. **Porte-aux-Choix** has a 5,000-year-old Red Paint Indian burial mound and the remains of later Inuit cultures. Three Red Paint burial mounds have been excavated here, uncovering the remains of 100 people, weapons, and artifacts. The relics can be seen in the visitor center, which is open from June through Labor Day. (The Red Paint lived here about 2340 B.C. Later, Dorset Eskimos, known for their fine stone tools, lived here for 2,000 years. About A.D. 1100, the Beothuck Indians took over the region.)

At the tip of the Great Northern Peninsula is **L'Anse aux Meadows National Historic Park**, the site of a Viking settlement dating from A.D. 1000 (492 years before Columbus). These early Norse settlers built six thatched houses, three of which have been reconstructed. Historians believe the first European child born in America was Snorri Thorfinnson, born here to Icelandic trader Thorfinn Karlsefni in A.D. 1005. The child is mentioned in Viking sagas.

While visiting the park, stay at the **Tickle Inn**, *P.O. Box 62, Cape Onion, NF A0K 4J0; tel. +1 (866) 814-8567; website: www.tickleinn.net.*

The best of the Beothucks

For a glimpse of the life of the Beothuck Indians, head east on the **Trans-Canada Highway** (Highway 1) to Grand Falls. The **Mary March Museum**, *St. Catherine Street, Grand Falls-Windsor; tel. +1 (709) 292-4522*, is dedicated to the study of these people, who inhabited the region when the first European settlers of the 1600s came ashore. Mary March was the last of the unassimilated Beothucks, and her knowledge was the foundation of the museum.

While in Grand Falls, stay at the **Mt. Peyton Hotel**, *214 Lincoln Road, Grand Falls; tel. +1 (709) 489-2251; website: www.mountpeyton.com.*

Terra Nova: The best wildlife

Terra Nova National Park; *website: www.pc.gc.ca*, southeast of Gander, is famous for its Atlantic beaches and its wildlife (including moose, black bear, red fox, Canada geese, beaver, and lynx). Keep an eye out for the park's unusual pitcher plant, which is carnivorous. You can rent cabins, canoes, and bikes at the park headquarters.

The best of France in the New World

Off the southern coast of Newfoundland are two French islands: **St. Pierre** and **Miquelon**. You must clear customs to travel to these islands, but a passport is unnecessary if you have identification. Both islands truly feel like forgotten French towns, with French architecture, fashion, and culture. French wines are a good buy here, even though the islands lost their tax-free status. For reservations at any of the hotels in St. Pierre, see: *website: www.st-pierre-et-miquelon.com.*

The most romantic town

St. John's, a natural rockbound harbor on the Avalon Peninsula, is Newfoundland's most romantic town. Quaint houses with brightly colored facades recall the town's wild past, when pirates raided and great feasts were held. While St. John's is one of the oldest towns in North America, inhabited by fishermen since the 15th century, its buildings are Victorian. Earlier dwellings were destroyed by fire.

Signal Hill, which looms above the harbor, was the site of the first trans-Atlantic reception of a radio signal, sent by Guglielmo Marconi on December 12th, 1901. About two-thirds of the way up Signal Hill is **Queen's Battery**, built in the late 18th century. Across the narrows from Queen's Battery is **Fort Amherst**. The battery and the fort, together with a chain that stretched across the narrows, were effective in closing the port to enemies.

St. John's has two beautiful churches: the twin-spired **Roman Catholic Basilica** and the **Anglican Cathedral**, one of the best examples of Gothic architecture in North America.

If you're looking for restaurants, shops, and people, stroll downtown along Duckworth and Water streets. **Water Street** is known as the "oldest main street on the continent," because it served as a pathway for the early explorers.

For a wonderful dining experience, try the **Stonehouse Renaissance**, *8 Kenna's Hill; tel. +1 (709) 753-2425*, a lovely 1834 stone house near Quidi Vidi Lake.

For somewhere to lay your head try the **Delta St. Johns Hotel**, *120 New Gower Street*; *tel. +1 (709) 570-1614* and the **Winterholme Heritage Inn**, *tel. +1 (709) 739-7979; website: www.winterholme.com*, which is a gorgeous 1907 Victorian mansion.

THE BEST OF ALBERTA

The peaceful and vast prairies of **Alberta** retain much of the open space and freedom that drew settlers into the Canadian wilderness a century ago. Alberta's prairies stretch for miles, a flat quilt at the foot of the Canadian Rockies.

While Alberta does have thriving, colorful cities, most of this vast 255,285-square-mile province is unpopulated—it has fewer inhabitants than the city of Philadelphia. And most of the population (more than half) lives in Edmonton and Calgary.

Calgary: The best cow town

Calgary is both a colorful remnant of the Wild West and a huge, modern city. Known as Cowtown, because of its cattle industry, Calgary is a thriving business center located less than an hour from the Rockies. This lively, crazy town is best known as the home of the **Calgary Stampede**, a wild rodeo of horse racing and high jinks.

Calgary got its start as a Royal Canadian Mounted Police post in 1875, back in the days when buffalo hunters, whiskey traders, pioneers, and Indians required the likes of Sergeant Preston of the Yukon to keep them in line. The post was founded at the junction of two rivers, the Bow and the Elbow. Colonel J.F. Macloud, the commander of the Mounties who founded the post, named it Calgary after his favorite fishing spot on the Bay of Mull in Scotland. The log fort attracted 600 settlers.

Four years later, the Canadian Pacific Railway reached Calgary in its rush to "save the West from the Yankees." The population of the post promptly doubled, as Chinese were brought in from the Pacific to lay railway tracks and European settlers—mostly English—poured in from the Atlantic Coast. Tremendous beef herds were built up around Calgary, and it soon became a cattle metropolis. With the discovery of oil at nearby Turner Valley in 1914, Calgary boomed.

Outside the downtown area, Calgary is beautiful. The Rocky Mountain foothills begin to the west. The prairie stretches forever to the east. Northeast of Calgary are the **Drumheller Badlands**, where dinosaur skeletons have been found. Southwest is the **Glenmore Reservoir**, surrounded by parks and trails. Farm towns and huge cattle ranches begin south of the city.

The best rodeo

If you want to brave the **Calgary Stampede**, make sure you have reservations—the city swells with participants and spectators. For more information and tickets, contact **Calgary Stampede**, *tel. +1 (403)261-0101; website: www.calgarystampede. com.* The stampede is big and rough, drawing an immense and enthusiastic crowd. Cowboys from all over the continent ride bucking broncos and bulls, rope calves, and wrestle steers for prizes. The **Stampede Stage Show** features chorus girls, clowns, bands, and glamour. The funniest event is the **Chuckwagon Race**, in which old-time cowboy chuck wagons race around the track.

The best view of the city

The observation tower at the top of the 626-foot **Calgary Tower**, *Ninth Avenue and Center Street; tel. +1 (403) 266-7171; website: www.calgarytower.com,* has the best view in town. You can see the Rockies when it's clear. Step out onto the glass floor and feel like you are hovering 525 feet above the ground in the heart of Calgary.

Calgary's top sights

Fort Calgary, *750 Ninth Ave. S.E.; tel. +1 (403) 290-1875; website: www. fortcalgary.ab.ca,* is a 40-acre natural history park on the site of the original

Mounted Police fort. Exhibits explain the history of Calgary. The fort is open daily year-round. Tours can be arranged for a nominal fee.

The **Glenbow Museum**, *130 Ninth Ave. S.E.; tel. +1 (403) 268-4100; website: www.glenbow.org*, has extensive displays of Indian and Inuit art and artifacts. The art gallery has carvings and ceramics from all over the world.

Explore **Heritage Park**, *west of 14th Street and Heritage Drive S.W.; tel. +1 (403) 268-8500; website: www.heritagepark.ca*, an authentic pre-1915 Alberta town. Original pioneer buildings from all over Alberta have been transported here, including a log church, a blacksmith's shop, a newspaper office, and a bakery.

The best shopping

If you have a secret urge to buy cowboy boots, head to **Alberta Boot Company**, *#50 50th Avenue South; tel. +1 (403) 263-4623; website: www.albertaboot.com*. If you're planning to attend the Calgary Stampede, this is the place to pick up your spurs!

The best food

The most elegant restaurant in Calgary is **The Belvedere**, *107 Eighth Ave. S.W.; tel. +1 (403) 265-9595; website: www.thebelvedere.ca*. You will be offered a choice of seafood, wild game and Alberta beef specialties. Try one of their 650 wines served in Riedel Crystal. Reservations are suggested.

The finest of Alberta's beef is served at the **Rimrock Room**, *Fairmont Palliser Hotel, Ninth Avenue and First Street S.W.; tel. +1 (403) 260-1219; website: www. fairmont.com/palliser/GuestServices/Restaurants/TheRimrock.htm*

Calgary's best hotel

The **Fairmont Palliser**, *133 Ninth Ave. S.W.; tel. +1 (403) 262-1234; website: www.fairmont.com/palliser*, is an institution in Calgary, built in 1914 by the Canadian Pacific Railroad. The gracious old hotel has brass doors, marble pillars, and chandeliers.

Canada's most beautiful national parks

Banff and Jasper national parks, on the border between British Columbia and Alberta, are among the most beautiful nature reserves in the world. Together, they comprise 6,764 square miles in the Rocky Mountains. Imagine snow-topped peaks, deep-green forests, cascading rivers, mountain sheep, bears, and silent blue lakes.

Banff is the older of the parks, Jasper the larger. They run together and stretch from Mount Sir Douglas in the south to the Resthaven Mountains in the far north. Many nature trails climb into their remote valleys and peaks. Banff lies 81 miles from Calgary via Highway 1; Jasper is 225 miles from Edmonton on Route 16.

Highway 93, from Banff to Jasper, which passes the Athabasca glacier, is spectacular. You'll see bighorn sheep, mountain goats, and bears from the road.

The 160-square-mile **Columbia ice fields** spread across Jasper. Rent a snowmobile in the park and take off to explore them. Jasper also boasts Alberta's highest peak, **Mount Columbia** (12,294 feet), and the spectacular **Athabasca Falls**, which rush through a narrow gap.

The **Fairmont Banff Springs Hotel**, *Spray Avenue; tel. +1 (403) 762-2211; website: www.fairmont.com/Banffsprings/*, which has views of the mountains and two rivers, is the best place to stay while exploring the parks. Established in 1928 to bring visitors to the nearby hot springs, the castle-like hotel has four dining rooms, an espresso bar, cocktail lounges, and a post office. Its golf course is considered one of the most scenic in the world.

Edmonton: The best boomtown

Edmonton has been a boomtown three times in its life: The fur trade brought hundreds of trappers and trackers in the 18th century, the gold rush attracted thousands in the 1890s, and the discovery of oil and natural gas brought industrial development in the 1960s. Despite its spurts of sudden growth, Edmonton is well-designed, with 11,000 acres of parks. And city leaders have made a tremendous effort to preserve historic buildings.

Edmonton's best festival

Capital EX (formerly called Klondike Days), which celebrate the days of gold prospecting, take place in late July. Everyone must dress in period costumes (those who don't may find themselves temporarily incarcerated in the Klondike clink!), the streets are filled with performers, and parades make their way through the streets. For the full program and ticket information, see *www.capitalex.ca*.

Edmonton's best sights

Fort Edmonton, *tel. +1 (780) 496-6977; website: www.fortedmontonpark.ca*, a replica of the fur-trading post established in 1795, stands in a 158-acre park off Whitemud Freeway in the suburbs. It is complete with a stockade, a fur-processing plant, a clay oven, McDougall's General Store, the Northwest Mounted Police Jail, and a Masonic temple. The original trading post has been replaced with **Alberta's**

Legislative Building, *109th Street and 97th Avenue*, which was built in 1912.

The **Muttart Conservatory and Horticulture Center**, *98th Avenue and 96th Street; tel. +1 (780) 442-5311; website: www.muttartconservatory.ca*, is a complex of four ultramodern pyramid-shaped greenhouses that act as a botanical incubator. Each pyramid has a specific climate and is filled with flora of appropriate regions. The complex is open daily.

The Art Gallery of Alberta, *2 Sir Winston Churchill Square; tel. +1 (780) 422-6223; website: www.artgalleryalberta.com*, is Edmonton's premier public art gallery. Its collection of well over 5,000 works of art includes historical and contemporary paintings, sculptures, installation works and photographs by Canadian and international artists.

Edmonton City Hall, was completed in 1992 and features two steel and glass pyramids, one 141-foot high (ground to peak), on top of a three-story concrete structure. One pyramid provides natural light for the main atrium, the other for the council chambers. The building also features a 200-foot clock tower topped with a 25-bell carillon.

Edmonton's best restaurants

Hardware Grill, *9698 Jasper Ave.; tel. +1 (780) 423-0969; website: www. hardwaregrill.com*, has excellent, inventive food. Try the bacon-wrapped elk paired with red wine short ribs in a raspberry reduction; finish your meal with the lavender panna cotta pistachio-almond cake.

The best hotel

The **Westin Hotel**, 10135 *100th Street; tel. +1 (780) 426-3636; website: www. starwoodhotels.com/westin/*, is where Princess Di and Prince Charles stayed when they visited in 1983. The swimming pool and sauna are inviting, and the restaurant is one of the best in the city.

THE BEST OF BRITISH COLUMBIA

British Columbia, Canada's westernmost province, has snow-capped mountains that rise out of the Pacific, providing backdrops for Vancouver and Victoria. In the north of this region are tiny settlements lost in a stark wilderness; in the center are wide-open ranchlands that cowboys call home. Throughout the area, glacier ice fields jut into birch and maple forests. More than 1 million acres of British

Columbia have been set aside for five national parks. The area also contains 11 million acres of provincial parks.

Throughout this coastal province are **petroglyphs**, rock drawings made by unknown tribes long ago, which are carefully preserved by the government. Mementos of the early fur traders, explorers, and pioneers can be seen at **Fort Langley**, a restored fur trading post in Fort Defiance on Vancouver Island, and at **Fort James**, near Prince George. Artifacts of the Cariboo gold rush of the 1860s are preserved at **Barkerville**. And the Royal Mounted Police left its mark at **Fort Steel**.

Vancouver: A best city

Vancouver is surrounded on all sides by snow-capped mountains, and glass-sided skyscrapers are reflected in the glittering blue harbor. The air is pure, and the climate is mild. At the western edge of the city, cliffs drop to the sea. Totem poles stand near the Strait of Georgia, a reminder of the Northwest Indians, who were the first inhabitants of this region. Canada's third-largest city, Vancouver has over 2 million residents in the greater city area.

The city's main thoroughfare is **Georgia Street**, where you'll find the old Hotel Vancouver, the Vancouver Art Gallery inside an old granite courthouse, and entrances to underground shopping malls.

Near Georgia Street, between Howe and Hornby, is **Robson Square**, a three-block complex designed by Arthur Erickson. Inside the square are international kiosks, a skating rink, and terraced gardens with pools and waterfalls. At the edge of the square is a seven-story glass pyramid—the **Law Courts Building**. During the week, you can wander into an open courtroom, sink into an upholstered chair, and watch a hearing.

Stanley Park, just north of downtown, is a wilderness playground with performing whales and a zoo. The best way to see this immense, 1,000-acre preserve is by bike. (A six-mile scenic drive circles the park.) If you want to hire a bike or roller blades, rental places are just outside the park on Denman Road.

Gastown, east of the Sea Bus terminal, is the birthplace of Vancouver. This renovated 19th-century area is filled with pubs, restaurants, galleries, and boutiques. Stop by **Hill's Indian Crafts**, *165 Water Street*, for baskets, moccasins, carvings, jewelry, prints, and sweaters.

South of Gastown, along Pender Street, is **Chinatown**. Sidewalk stalls sell Chinese food and knick-knacks, and herbalists offer deer horns, dried sea horses, and exotic teas. The **Chinese Cultural Center**, *Pender Street*, has maps of the area. Stroll through the **Dr. Sun Yat-Sen Classical Garden**, two-and-a-half acres of miniature fountains, pavilions, ponds, and bridges.

Granville Island has galleries, theaters, cafés, and an open market. Have dinner at Bridges. Return downtown from Granville aboard the False Creek Ferry, which departs from a dock near Bridges.

The stern-faced totem poles in the **Museum of Anthropology**, *tel. +1 (604) 822-5087; website: www.moa.ubc.ca,* at the University of British Columbia are a sharp contrast to the modern lines of the museum itself, which was designed by Erickson.

The best restaurants

YEW, *Georgia and Howe streets; tel. +1 (604) 689-9333; website: www. fourseasons.com/vancouver,* in the Four Seasons Hotel has a superb menu that features game and seafood. The wine list is extensive. Reservations are highly recommended.

Al Porto, *321 Water Street; tel. +1 (604) 683-8376; website: www.alporto.ca,* specializes in seafood and Italian delicacies, including woodfire pizza served in a rustic Tuscan ambience.

The **Blue Water Café and Raw Bar**, *1095 Hamilton Street; tel. +1 (604) 688-8078; website: www.bluewatercafe.net,* serves a choice of Asian-inspired seafood from sushi to roasted red pepper and lobster bisque.

Vancouver's best beds

Vancouver's best hotel is the **Four Seasons Hotel**, *791 W. Georgia Street; tel. +1 (604) 689-9333; website: www.fourseasons.com/vancouver,* which offers every luxury and convenience imaginable, from a gourmet restaurant to a health club.

The **Westin Bayshore Inn**, *1601 Bayshore Drive; tel. +1 (604) 682-3377; website: www.westinbayshore.com,* once hosted Howard Hughes, who took over the top two floors. Yachtsmen stay here, mooring their boats at the hotel dock. Doormen in red jackets and tall fur hats guard the doors. Rooms have floor-to-ceiling windows with lovely views of the water and the city. Shops, lounges, restaurants, and a pool are available to guests.

If you're watching your budget, stay at the **Sylvia Hotel**, *1154 Gilford Street; tel. +1 (604) 681-9321; website: www.sylviahotel.com.* This nine-story, heritage designated hotel, is located on English Bay. It has a good dining room, and is popular, so make reservations in advance.

Vancouver Island: The most beautiful

Vancouver Island, which stretches 170 miles along the western coastline of British Columbia, is sheltered along its southern border by the state of Washington's Olympic Peninsula. You can take a ferry from Vancouver City to Nanaimo.

Most of the half-million people on Vancouver Island live along its east coast, which is rich in timber, farmland, and fishing streams, or at the southern tip in the city of Victoria. The wild and rugged west coast is sparsely inhabited, with few villages. It is deeply cut by fiords and piled high with mountains. The south end of the island is mountainous, reaching a height of 7,200 feet; the north end is flat.

Victoria, the provincial capital, was first settled by Europeans in 1843. It has been the site of coal mining, logging, fur trading, and fishing. One of the most beautiful sights on the island is **Butchart Gardens**, near Victoria, across the Saanich Peninsula from Sydney. Originally (in 1905), this area was a limestone quarry; today it offers entertainment on summer evenings.

Victoria: The most British city

"A tweedy, daffodilish, green-fingered sort of place, a golfish, fly-fishing, 5 o'clock teapot place." That's how Canadian author Bruce Hutchinson described Victoria, which feels more British than any other city in the Americas. While it is the largest city on Vancouver Island, the atmosphere is relaxed. The air smells of flowers and the sea. The climate is mild, less rainy than on the island's west coast.

Go behind the **Tweed Curtain**, as it is known, along Oak Bay. Enjoy the thick British accents and stop for tea at the **Blethering Place Tearoom** in Oak Bay Village (*website: www.thebletheringplace.com*) or the dining room in the **Gatsby Mansion**, *309 Belleville Street; tel. +1 (250) 388-9191; website: www.gatsbymansion.com*.

Activity in Victoria centers around the harbor, which is surrounded by Victorian buildings, including the Empress Hotel, the Provincial legislative buildings, the old steamship terminal (now a wax museum), and the Belmont Building. The Visitors and Convention Bureau, an art deco building, offers maps and information.

Victoria's **Royal British Columbia Museum**, *tel. +1 (250) 356-7226; website: www.royalbcmuseum.bc.ca*, traces life before and after glaciers covered Vancouver Island with a sheet of ice three-and-a-half miles thick. Walk through the rainforest, which includes a reconstructed 19th-century town and an Indian longhouse.

Outside the Museum complex is **Thunderbird Park**, which has a collection of coastal Indian totem poles. You can watch Indian craftsmen carving reproductions of traditional designs. Just beyond the park is the **Helmcken House**, the oldest house still standing in British Columbia.

The **Tong-Ji Men** (Gate of Harmonious Interest), at the corner of Fisgard and Government in Chinatown, is a 30-foot arch with 4,500 ceramic tiles and 1,008 decorative panels that was made in Taiwan.

Craigdarroch Castle, *1050 Joan Crescent; tel. +1 (250) 592-5323; website: www.craigdarrochcastle.com*, was built in 1885 by the multimillionaire coal baron Robert Dunsmuir for his wife Joan. A non-profit society is refurbishing the castle, which was essentially raffled off after Joan's death.

Along Rockland Avenue is the **Government House**, where the lieutenant governor of British Columbia resides. Its gardens are more than 100 years old.

Most restaurants in Victoria serve mostly bland English fare—fish and chips and the lot. An exception is **Foo Hong**, *564 Fisgard Street*, in Chinatown, a popular and inexpensive lunch spot.

Stay at the **Fairmont Empress Hotel**, *721 Government Street; tel. +1 (250) 384-8111; website: www.fairmont.com/empress/*, which is great fun but rather touristy and expensive. Built in 1906 on the harbor, it has lovely views as well as a bar, a restaurant, and a disco. Have high tea in the afternoon.

A good, moderately priced hotel is **Helm's Inn**, *600 Douglas Street* (near Royal British Columbia Museum); *tel. +1 (250)385-5767; website: www.helmsinn.com.*

The most shopping space

Nanaimo, the second-largest city on Vancouver Island, has the largest amount of retail shopping space per capita of any city in Canada. The city is also filled with preserved pioneer buildings and sites, which you can see on the historic walking tour.

Stroll around Nanaimo's waterfront, where you'll see the **Bastion**, the former Hudson's Bay Company Fort, erected in 1852 by settlers as protection against raiding Indians. **Fishermen's Wharf** has an abundance of fresh seafood.

The **Georgia Park Promenade** leads to the modern seaplane base and on to Swy-A-Lana Lagoon and Maffeo Sutton Park. **Georgia Park** is dedicated to the Indian tribes who first inhabited this area and features a display of authentic Indian canoes and totem poles. **Swy-A-Lana Lagoon** features a man-made tidal pool. Next to the lagoon, native Indians operate a traditional carving shed, where you can watch craftsmen carving masks and other artifacts.

The world's best bathtub race

Nanaimo's annual **Bathtub Race** in mid-July is a zany spectacle. Hundreds of daring tubbers challenge the wild waters of the Georgia Strait in a 30-mile race to the beaches of Vancouver. It's hilarious. See *www.bathtubbing.com* for details.

The best whale watching

You can track the great gray whale each spring as it migrates northward along the west coast of Vancouver Island. The first migrants appear in late February; by mid-April, the waters are filled with hundreds of them. As many as 40 or 50 gray whales like the area so much that they spend the summer here.

The best time for whale watching is from late February through June. The whales can be spotted from the headlands of Pacific Rim National Park, from the restaurant at Wickaninnish Bay, or from the rocky shores of Little Beach, Big Beach, or Amphitrite Point in Uduelet. However, the best way to watch is from the deck of a charter boat that specializes in whale watching trips.

You'll usually see only a small portion of the whale. When spouting, whales roll forward and seem to lift partly out of the water, revealing their scarred gray backs and the bumps of their vertebrae, which are known as knuckles. While diving in deep water, they occasionally show their graceful, barnacle-encrusted tails, displays called fluking. When they poke their heads out of the water for a look around, they are spy-hopping. The most breathtaking sight is when whales breach, jumping almost completely out of the water to land on their backs with a huge splash.

Canadian Princess Resort offers whale-watching cruises that depart from Vancouver and Victoria. For more information, contact the resort at **Oak Bay Marina Ltd.**, *1327 Beach Drive, Victoria, BC; tel. +1 (250) 598-3366* or *+1 (800) 663-7090 (toll free in North America); website: www.obmg.com*. **Subtidal Adventures**, *tel. +1 (250) 726-7336; website: www.subtidaladventures.com*, also offers a whale watching cruise.

The highest city

British Columbia boasts the highest city in Canada: **Kimberley**, in the Rocky Mountains just north of the U.S. border. This mining town-turned-ski resort resembles a Bavarian Alpine village. The townspeople sponsor a **Julyfest** modeled after the German Oktoberfest that includes parades, folk dances, beer tents, and international entertainment. See *www.kimberleyjulyfest.com* for this year's program of events.

Kimberley's real claim to fame is its excellent downhill skiing. The city's mountain rises 2,300 feet and has 80 runs served by chair lifts and T-bars. The mountain also has one of North America's longest lighted ski runs (3.97 miles). For information on ski packages, contact **Kimberley Ski Resort**, *tel. +1 (887) 754-5462; website: www.skikimberley.com*.

Canada's only desert town

Osoyoos is a Spanish-influenced desert town in a 252-mile desert pocket east of Vancouver. It is watered by deep Lake Osoyoos, where you can fish for trout and bass. You can swim here, too, if you don't mind sharing the water with painted turtles. Try your luck panning for gold in the **Okanagan Valley** above Osoyoos.

The most authentic Indian village

Hazelton (known as Kiran-maksh among the Indians), in the heart of British Columbia, is a modern Indian town next to a reconstructed Gitskan Indian village built to look as it did before the arrival of the white man. The village, called **Ksan**, has six longhouses, totem poles, and birchbark canoes. The House of Treasures contains the tribal regalia of Gitksan chiefs. A campground and trailer park adjoin the village.

THE WORLD'S BEST FISHING

Some say Canada, which is bordered by three oceans and the Hudson Bay and dotted with thousands of lakes, rivers, and streams, has the best fishing in the world. Inland waters are filled with major freshwater fish, while the Atlantic and Pacific coasts run with striped bass, bluefin tuna, shark, and other deep-sea fish. Generally, the farther north you go, the better the fishing. In the Yukon and Northwest Territories, the open-water fishing season runs from June to late September. Water in these Arctic regions is ice-cold, and the fish fight harder, making the sport more challenging and exciting.

British Columbia: The best fishing year-round

In British Columbia, which many claim has the best fishing in Canada, you can fish year-round. With so many miles of streams and rivers and thousands of lakes spread across a sparsely populated land, it is a fisherman's paradise. Despite all this, the region isn't crowded.

Five species of salmon can be caught in the coastal waters off British Columbia. Pacific-Gulf Charters offers three-day packages in British Columbia which include accommodation, fishing equipment, and meals.

Contact **Oak Bay Marine Group**, *1327 Beach Drive, Victoria, BC V8S 2N4; tel. +1 (250) 598-3366; website: www.obmg.com.*

You can also visit the **British Columbia Fishing Resorts and Outfitters Association**; *website: www.bcfroa.ca.*

THE HAPPIEST HUNTING GROUNDS

Canada has a profusion of wildlife: brown bears and grizzly bears in British Columbia and the Laurentian Mountains of Quebec, buffalo in Alberta, and elk and moose in Saskatchewan. The Northwest Territories and the Yukon have polar bears, musk oxen, caribou, seals, walruses, and penguins.

Most of the animals are protected. Hunting laws are detailed and involve specific seasons and registrations. For more information, contact the Ministry of Natural Resources of the area where you want to hunt.

CANADA'S BEST SAILING

Nova Scotia is a Shangri-La for boaters. Its calm harbors and rolling hills are a perfect refuge for Atlantic sailors.

Boaters can dock at **Armdale Yacht Club,** *Halifax, North West Arm, website: www.armdaleyachtclub.ns.ca;* **Bedford Basin Yacht Club,** *Halifax, website: www. bbyc.ns.ca;* **Bras d'Or Yacht Club,** *Baddeck;* **Chester Yacht Club,** *P.O. Box 290, Chester, website: www.cyc.ns.ca;* **Dartmouth Yacht Club,** *697 Windmill Road, Darthmouth, website: www.dyc.ns.ca;* **Lennox Passage Yacht Club,** *D'Escousse, Nova Scotia, website: http://lpyc.ca;* **Lunenburg Yacht Club,** *Lunenburg, website: www.lyc.ns.ca;* and **Royal Western Nova Scotia Yacht Club,** *Digby, Nova Scotia, website: www.rwnsyc.ca.*

The rugged island is filled with boat charter and rental companies.

Whale Cruisers Ltd., *P.O. Box 183, Cheticamp, Nova Scotia B0E 1H0; tel. +1 (902) 224-3376; website: www.whalecruisers.com,* offers whale-watching cruises and scenic boat tours and charters that depart Government Wharf at Cheticamp Harbor at 9 a.m., 1 p.m., and 6 p.m. during July and August. Special group rates and charters can be arranged.

THE MOST EXCITING RAFTING

Eau Vive Adventures, *tel. +1 (800) 567-6881; website: www.eauviverafting.ca,* arranges rafting groups on the Rouge River from April through October.

THE BEST ON HORSEBACK

What better way to see the wilds of Canada than on horseback? The best way to go is with **Trail Riders of the Canadian Rockies**; *tel. +1 (403) 874-4408; website: www.trail-rides.ca*, a nonprofit group that leads riders through the uninhabited valleys of Banff National Park. A six-day trip includes accommodation in Indian tepees, horses, saddles, meals, and guides.

THE BEST OF THE
CARIBBEAN

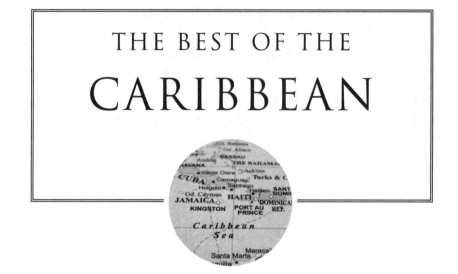

The Caribbean Sea is speckled with dozens of beautiful little worlds—islands rimmed with white sand, coral reefs, and palm trees. Each is unique. Some have volcanoes, others are as flat as pancakes. On some, residents speak French; on others, the people speak Spanish, Dutch, or English. A few of the islands have luxurious resorts with gambling casinos and fine restaurants that draw the jet set. Others are remote, with thick jungles and few inhabitants. Although technically not in the Caribbean, the Bahamas and Bermuda have been included because of their tropical lifestyle and beaches.

THE PUREST OF THE U.S. VIRGINS: ST. JOHN

St. John, the smallest of the U.S. Virgin Islands, seems to be escaping the fate of its overdeveloped sisters. Two-thirds of its mere 20 square miles are set aside as national parkland. Campsites dot the park, just a few yards from the surf.

The favorite pastime on St. John is snorkeling. One of the best places to see a wide variety of coral and watch the fish is **Waterlemon Bay**, past the ruins of the Annaberg sugarcane factory near Leinster Bay. It is best to arrive by boat.

At the tip of Frances Bay is **Mary's Point**, a haunted promontory. Legend has it that during the revolt against the Danes in 1733, slaves leapt to their deaths from the cliff above to avoid being captured. They believed their souls would return to Africa.

Maho Bay, *tel. +1 (800) 392-9004; website: www.mahobay.org*, a 14-acre eco-tourist site, is our favorite place to stay on the island. When Maho Bay was first built, materials were carried to the compound by hand to keep the natural beauty intact. Innovative water and sewage systems help to conserve precious supplies. The 102 cottages at Maho Bay are actually canvas tents on 16-foot platforms connected by a labyrinth of walkways. Each includes a sleeping area with two beds, a living room with one bed, a cooking area, and a porch with a table and chairs. Electric lamps, bed linens, blankets, and towels are provided.

The most luxurious place to stay

The most luxurious place to stay on St. John is **Caneel Bay**, *tel. +1 (340) 776-6111; website: www.caneelbay.com*. The 170-acre, 18th-century sugar plantation is dotted with tennis courts and exotic plants. Cottages are clustered around seven private beaches. The posh cottages don't have air conditioning or telephones.

Best fine dining

Asolare, *tel. +1 (340) 779-4747; website: www.asolarestjohn.com*, is an elegant open-air restaurant overlooking Cruz Bay. Seafood is superb and expensive, but worth it.

Best local (cheap) dining in Coral Bay

Skinny Legs, *website: http://skinnylegs.com*, a no-frills beach bar and restaurant, sits off Coral Bay. Locals eat at the bar; ask for a St. John Ale. A great burger and beer place.

THE BEST OF ST. THOMAS

The island of St. Thomas is 32 square miles of lush tropical paradise, if you stay away from the harbor traffic and tourist mayhem of numerous cruise ship passengers.

Exploring the island will take you up winding hills and along mountainous roadways where each breathtaking panorama is more dramatic than the one before. Visit **Drake's Seat**, the vantage point where Sir Francis Drake used to sit and observe his fleet.

Finest dining in St. Thomas

Built as a residence by a French sea merchant, **Hotel 1829**, *tel.* *+1 (800)524-2002 (toll free in U.S.), +1 (340) 776-1829 (outside U.S.); website: www.hotel1829.com*, is now a registered National Historic Site. Converted into a hotel with a bar and restaurant in 1906, the entire structure—public rooms, terraces, and guestrooms—reflects the architectural style of the Caribbean of the past. Steps and archways lead to landscaped garden patios and delightful nooks where you can enjoy a cool drink and watch the harbor views.

Best place for the kids

Located on the grounds of the Renaissance Grand Beach Resort, **Blazing Villas**, *tel. +1 (800) 581-3800; website: www.blazingvillas.com*, is a unique group of studio suites, each with up to three bedrooms and full kitchens. With full access to the hotel's facilities—white-sand beach, pools, tennis courts, a spa, and dining facilities—Blazing Villas combines the best of a luxury condo with the best of a resort hotel. This is the best place to stay if you're traveling with children.

The best of Old St. Thomas

Located at the west entrance to the St. Thomas harbor in the historic district of Frenchtown, **The Admiral's Inn**, *tel. +1 (340) 774-1376*, is a 12-room B&B.

Frenchtown, a collection of multicolored houses and buildings that gets its name from the French settlers who came from Martinique over 150 years ago, is now the spot where the French fishing boats dock with supplies of seafood for St. Thomas. It's a good place to get a feel for the St. Thomas of the pre-cruise ship era. Plus, some of St. Thomas' finest restaurants are located in this Frenchtown area.

ANGUILLA—THE MOST PEACABLE ISLAND

On **Anguilla**, one of the Caribbean's least-discovered islands, you apologize shyly if you pass someone on the beach. Anguilla has no discos, no casinos, no high-rises—just lots of beach and solitude. The Anguillans are a peaceful people with a peaceful history. Slavery didn't pay here. Cotton and bananas won't grow, and the workers were a strain on the water supplies. So plantation owners left the islanders to lead their own lives.

In 1969, when the English Parachute Regiment landed in Anguilla to put down what was thought to be a revolt, the parachutists were met by Anguillans waving Union Jacks. The islanders wanted to remain a Crown Colony.

Serene beaches border the island. The best is at **Shoal Bay East**, a two-mile stretch that is popular but still uncrowded. The ocean bottom is evenly sloped to a distant string of rocks that attracts sea creatures and snorkelers. Underwater, you can look around for coral gardens, reefs of elkhorn, and star and flower coral, as well as squirrelfish, sergeant fish, and damselfish.

The **Malliouhana Hotel**, *Meads Bay; tel. +1 (800) 835-0796 (toll-free from the U.S.)* or *+1 (264) 497-6111; website: www.malliouhana.com*, is the most exclusive and expensive hotel in the Caribbean. The hotel has Mediterranean and Far Eastern furnishings, hardwood floors, brass fixtures, and balconies off every room. The 30 acres surrounding the hotel are dotted with swimming pools perched high on the cliffs. The restaurant serves great French food in a beautiful open-air space with a lovely view of Meads Bay. It also has an amazing 25,000-bottle wine cellar!

Best restaurants

Blanchards, *tel. +1 (264) 497-6100; website: www.blanchardsrestaurant.com*, is also excellent and boasts a creative menu. Read about the mishap adventures of the owners and how they came to live in Anguilla in their book—*A Trip to the Beach: Living on Island Time in the Caribbean.*

Caribbean's best bird watching

You can expect to see 136 species of birds in Anguilla: the White-tailed tropicbird, Least Bittern, Tricolored Heron, Killy-killy, Lesser Scaup, Killdeer, Greater Yellowlegs, and, of course, the Zaneida Dove, which is the national bird.

ANTIGUA: A BEACH FOR EACH DAY OF THE YEAR

There are 365 beaches on Antigua—one for each day of the year—and all are open to the public.

Antigua has warm steady winds, a complex coastline of safe harbors, and a protective, nearly unbroken wall of coral reef. The trade winds that once blew British men-of-war safely into English Harbor now fuel one of the world's foremost maritime events—Sailing Week; *website: www.sailingweek.com.*

Best hotel in Antigua

Jumby Bay, *tel. +1 (268) 462-6000; website: www.jumbybayresort.com*, the playground of the super-rich and second home for *Livestyles of the Rich and Famous* presenter Robin Leach, is at the top of the line in terms of cost and includes all the expected luxuries. Located on its own 300-acre island reachable by private ferry, 50 suites and villas are offered on an all-inclusive, per-room basis.

THE BEST OF GUADELOUPE

Along with a shimmering aquamarine sea, Guadeloupe has more than 50 beautiful crescent beaches, sleepy rural villages…and wonderful diving and snorkeling.

Best topless bathing in the Caribbean
Don't expect to hear many American or Canadian accents on the beaches of Grand-Terre. Most visitors are from mainland France. Some guidebooks aimed at North Americans take quite a stern moralistic tone. They warn potential visitors that many women sunbathe topless. And, (horror of horrors!), some beaches are "clothing-optional."

Best place to shop for swimwear
On weekend afternoons, the beach at **Saint-Francois** transforms itself into a Parisian catwalk. Nubile wenches from local boutiques arrive with big straw baskets packed with elegant swimwear, sarongs and floppy harem pants. Donning different outfits, they slowly parade like supermodels up and down the water's edge. And they seem to do a roaring trade amongst the captive customers. You can try before you buy—if you don't mind doing it in front of an interested audience!

Most romantic hotel in Guadeloupe
Le Domaine de Malendure, *Morne Tarare Pigeon, Bouillante*; *tel. +590 989-212*, a hideaway set in a jungle-like garden with stupendous views over the Pigeon Islands, is the most romantic hotel in Guadeloupe. Accommodation is in duplexes, built in the style of Creole cottages. Room furnishings are simple, but there's a lovely pool, breakfast is good, and plenty of Creole specialties appear on the restaurant menu.

THE BEST OF MARTINIQUE

Martinique is the most sophisticated and developed island in the Caribbean, with gourmet restaurants and nude beaches. It is lush, covered with flowers. Fort-de-France is known as the Paris of the western Atlantic, with the same wrought-iron grillwork and narrow-street charm as the European city. And Martinique (along with Guadeloupe) has the best Creole food in the region. French luxury goods are sold at bargain prices, and luxury to rock-bottom accommodations are available.

Most flowery island of the Caribbean

Martinique must boast at least $100 worth of fabulously scented blossoms to the square yard. The island's original Carib Indian inhabitants called their lush island *Madinina*, the Island of Flowers. The name is still apt—more than a thousand varieties grow here.

Martinique's most powerful mountain

Climb Martinique's extinct volcano, **Mount Pelée**. Ask for a guide at the town hall. Needless to say, the view from the mountain is spectacular. For a glimpse of the fierce power of Mount Pelée, visit the ruins of the town of St. Pierre, destroyed by the volcano in 1902.

The island's most famous resident

La Pagerie, on the Southwest peninsula, is the birthplace of Empress Josephine. A museum here contains mementos and love letters to her from Napoleon.

Best hotel in Martinique

The best place to stay in Martinique is **La Plantation Leyritz**, *tel. +596 785-392*, an isolated 18th-century French-colonial plantation that has been made into a hotel with a first-class health spa that offers beauty and health therapy, horseback riding, and French food.

Private suite-only hotel

On the eastern coast of Martinique lies **Cap Est Lagoon Resort and Spa**, *website: www.capest.com*, this Relais & Chateaux managed property boasts 50 luxury suites, some with private pools and ocean views. Just 35 minutes from Lamentin airport.

MONTSERRAT—THE BEST REFUGE

Montserrat is a lush green island that was colonized primarily by Irish Catholics from nearby St. Kitts in the early 17th century. Because of its Irish heritage, Montserrat is known as the Emerald Isle. It is now a British colony, but Irish influences remain.

The Caribbean's most active volcano

The **Soufrière Hills** volcano, overlooking Plymouth and the southern end of the island, lurched back to life in 1995. The rumblings increased until 1997, when a violent, ash-filled explosion rose 30,000 feet into the air. Plymouth was evacuated along with all the villages south of Belham Valley…and Montserrat was forever changed. The volcano continues to erupt and spew ash into the air although it has been relatively quiet since the last major eruption in February 2010.

An "exclusion zone" extending from the south coast of the island north to parts of the Belham Valley has been imposed because of the size of the existing volcanic dome and the resulting potential for pyroclastic activity. Visitors are not permitted entry into the exclusion zone, but an impressive view of the destruction of Plymouth can be seen from the top of Garibaldi Hill in Isles Bay.

The best for cultural diversity

The Carib Indians supplied Montserrat's earliest recorded name "Alliouagana," meaning the land of the prickly bush. When Christopher Columbus finally saw the island during his second trip in 1493, its jagged peaks reminded him of the Monastery of Montserrate just outside of Barcelona, Spain—so he renamed it Santa Maria de Montserrate. Over 150 years later, in 1632, Sir Thomas Warner led a group of English settlers to colonize the island. Many Irish, disgruntled at their treatment on St. Kitts, decided to join him. Soon other Irish immigrants arrived from Virginia as well. The settlers concentrated on tobacco, indigo, cotton, and sugar plantations with African slave labor supplying the manpower. With nary a Spaniard in sight, it still took until 1783 for Montserrat to become an English possession by virtue of the Treaty of Paris.

The best St. Patrick's Day in the Caribbean

Art and music festivals and competitions are held throughout the year. Of particular interest is March 17, when both St. Patrick's Day and the slave revolt of over 100 years ago against the wealthy plantation owners are celebrated simultaneously. It's not unusual to find the wearing of the green combined with calypso, soca, and iron-pan music, and the Emerald Singers appearing on the same program as Jumby dancers. Monseratt is one of only four places in the world that marks St. Patrick's Day with a public holiday—the others are the Republic of Ireland, Northern Ireland, and Newfoundland.

THE BEST OF ST. KITTS AND NEVIS

Nevis offers a gorgeous landscape…stunningly rich green clad mountains (dormant volcanoes, thousands of years old), azure seas, balmy breezes, elegant plantation inns…

Best places for a night out on Nevis

The best nightlife is to be found at the **Oualie Beach Bar,** which has Beach Barbeque on Tuesdays, while **Eddy's Bar** (a popular hangout for both locals and expats) in Charlestown is the place to be on Wednesdays for a DJ and dancing. Drop into **Sunshine Bar** for a "Killer Bee" cocktail…their special rum drink. They also open for lunch and dinner.

Best hotel on Nevis

Oualie Beach Resort, *tel. +1 (869) 469-9735; website: www.oualiebeach.com*, is perfect for a romantic getaway if you request one of the cottages farthest from the dining area. Or it's perfect for your whole family. The open-air restaurant and bar offer good Caribbean and continental food, and occasional live entertainment. The informal ambience makes it easy to meet other guests and locals.

Fanciest place to eat on Nevis

The most entertaining evening you'll find on Nevis is at **Miss June's**, *tel. +1 (869) 469-5330*. Miss June cooks at home three times a week by reservation. Limited to 25 guests, diners assemble around 7.30 p.m. for cocktails and hors d'oeuvres in the lounge. At 8.30 p.m., a five-course dinner, with Trinidadian, Caribbean, Indonesian, and European influences is served at formal tables set with fine crystal and pure white napery. The first course is soup and sherry, followed by fish. A tempting buffet beckons and your wineglass is kept full. After dessert, guests retire to the veranda to savor coffee and liqueurs. Miss June joins her guests and the evening sometimes lasts until the wee hours. The price includes all you can eat and drink.

Best rainforest on St. Kitts

The 68 square miles of St. Kitts are mountainous and blessed with expansive soil-rich valleys, natural spring-fed water, and jungle-like rainforests laden with wild bananas, breadfruit, papayas, and mangoes. The highest point is 3,792-foot Mt. Liamuiga, also called "Mt. Misery" by the locals—try to climb it, and you'll probably agree. The island's rich rainforest is the last in the world to be actually increasing in size.

Best shipwrecks for exploration

You can explore one of over 400 wrecks (sunk between 1493 and 1825). St. Kitts has more than any other island in the Caribbean.

ST. MARTIN/ SINT MAARTEN: THE MOST DIVIDED ISLAND

The French and Dutch **St. Martin/Sint Maarten** is the most varied of the Caribbean islands. It has tropical scenery and a European culture. In fact, it has two European cultures.

Sint Maarten, the Dutch half of the island, has luxurious Dutch inns frequented by the royal family of the Netherlands. Cruise ships dock in the Philipsburg Harbor to allow passengers to take advantage of duty-free prices on jewelry, linens, crystal, and cameras.

The French half of the island is more affordable (although several of the large new hotels tend to be expensive) and has better restaurants. Artists come to **Marigot**, St. Martin's waterfront square, to set up their easels. Small fishing boats pull into port with the day's catches; vendors sell their wares under brightly colored umbrellas; and travelers meet at La Vie en Rose to chat over fresh, exquisitely prepared seafood. Accommodation ranges from luxury resorts in the French-Mediterranean style to downright cheap guesthouses.

Away from the main towns, you'll find secluded bays and long sandy beaches protected by coral reefs. In the center of the island, mountain peaks rise sharply. Palm trees grow alongside orange bougainvillea and magenta hibiscus. The sun shines year-round, and temperatures hover around 80° F.

The only international golf course is at Port de Plaisance on the Dutch side. The course runs across the island to the French side.

Thanks to the island's French legacy, dining is a pleasure and worth taking time to enjoy. More than 150 restaurants are spread over both sides of the island.

The best hotels on the island are **La Samanna**; *tel. +590 (590) 876-400; website: www.lasamanna.com*; **Hotel L'Esplanade**; *tel. +590 (590) 870-655; website: www.lesplanade.com* and its sister hotel **Le Petite**; *tel. +590 (590) 290-965; website: www.lepetithotel.com.*

The best way to get a hangover

Guavaberry liquor is a national drink whose secret lies in the rum it's combined with. Stop at the **Guavaberry Emporium**, *tel. +599 542-2965; website:*

www.guavaberry.com, in Philipsburg to learn how to make it—your lesson comes with a free sample.

While on the booze trail, you're apt to come across a **Rum Jumbie** hut on the Dutch side—they also offer a free taste. Local lore says that "Jumbies" are celestial spirits who possess the man who's drunk too much rum, forcing him to dance to the conga drums 'til dawn. You've been warned. By this point on the trail, if you still want a monstrous headache, head over to the Rum Museum on the French side for the finishing touch.

The best way to avoid a hangover

After the Rum Jumbie hut, if you feel you've had enough, save the Rum Museum for another day and visit **La Ferme des Papillons** (Butterfly Farm); *website: www. thebutterflyfarm.com.* Over 1,000 winged beauties in Pucci-like colors (the Blue Morpho is a favorite) fly free, attracted by the many tasty fruits and flowering plants. This is a sure way to avoid any headaches in the morning.

The best restaurants

On the Dutch side, try **Mark's Place** which serves Creole cuisine. Main courses range from seafood (local snapper, conch stew) to chicken and other meats (steaks, Creole chicken, goat stew, pork tenderloin).

On the French side, pay a visit to **Le Cottage**, *tel. +590 (590) 290-330*; *website: www.restaurantlecottage.com,* where hosts Bruno and Stephane spoil you. Choose from their French cuisine and extensive wine list. And they serve the best *fois gras* on the island.

The best nightlife

There's no end to the nightlife—well, actually there is when the sun comes up—on both sides of the island, but especially on the Dutch side, where many people start their evening at the raucous **Sunset Beach Bar** on Maho Bay.

Next, people head to the **Greenhouse Café**, *tel. +599 542-2941*, for dinner and disco, or to the popular **Boat House**, *Simpson Bay; tel. +599 544-5409.* Situated in a bright yellow wooden Creole house, full of nautical inspiration with authentic seafaring trophys, the Boat House is an expat hangout by day and a jumping open-air night-club with live band by night. **Sopranos Piano Bar**, *tel. +599 580-1560, on the first floor of the Sonesta Maho Beach Resort*, is a perfect place to end an evening. The colorful, intimate bar features live piano music (Sinatra to the Beatles), romantic booths, and fine cigars.

THE DOMINICAN REPUBLIC—THE FIRST SETTLEMENT

Columbus called the **Dominican Republic** the most beautiful island in the world when he landed here in 1492. One year later, his brother Bartholomeo established the first permanent European settlement in the Americas, New Isabella (known today as Santo Domingo). Historic monuments, monasteries, and fortresses remain from the colonial days, giving the island a Spanish air.

Unlike most Caribbean islands, where English is widely spoken, few locals in the Dominican Republic outside of the tourist areas speak anything but Spanish. Be sure to learn a few bare essentials.

The Dominican Republic covers 1,900 square miles, approximately two-thirds of the island of **Hispaniola**, which it shares with Haiti. It has lovely beaches, lively nightlife, excellent restaurants, and many hotels. The tallest mountains in the Caribbean (more than 10,000 feet) are here.

The oldest city in the Americas

In Santo Domingo, you can visit **Zona Colonial**, the oldest European settlement in the Americas. Columbus landed here in 1492, after stopping in Cuba, where he believed he had found a shortcut to Japan. In Santo Domingo, Columbus, his brother, and later his son ruled the Spanish colony in the early 1500s. From Santo Domingo, the Spanish launched their conquests of Central and South America. If you're looking for historic colonial architecture in the Americas, it doesn't get any better than this. The colonial district contains the oldest European fort in the Americas, the oldest monastery, the first paved street, ruins from the first hospital, the oldest church…and dozens of buildings that date from the 16th and 17th centuries.

The most posh resort in the Caribbean

The poshest resort in all the Caribbean is the **Casa de Campo**, *tel. +1 (305) 856-5405; website: www.casadcampo.com*, at La Romana in the Dominican Republic. Frank Lloyd Wright designed the main building, and the interior was designed by Oscar de la Renta. A few celebrities have mansions on the grounds. Accommodation at the resort includes private villas along the golf course and sea. You can hire a horse and buggy to take you dining. The nephew of the maharaja of Jodphur introduced polo to the Dominican Republic, and you'll find the best riding horses in the Caribbean at the Casa de Campo resort.

The best whale watching

The town of **Samana** is located on the southern coast of the peninsula. It is built along the water, and up onto the surrounding hills, around a sailboat-filled natural harbor, the Bay of Samana. For several weeks every year (in January, February, and the beginning of March), more than 4,000 humpback whales migrate several thousand miles from distant northern feeding grounds in the Gulf of Maine, the East Coast of Canada, Greenland, and Iceland to breed in the bay's warm, sheltered waters. The 30-ton mammals put on quite a show...males breach 30 feet or more in the air and splash back to the surface. You can watch from shore with binoculars...but will be better off hiring the services of one of the local tour companies.

THE BEST OF THE BAHAMAS

Just a few hours from New York or Miami are the 700 islands of the **Bahamas**, an idyllic chain of islands stretching from Bimini, just 50 miles off the coast of Florida, toward Haiti. The islands are mostly flat and bordered by white-sand beaches. Only 20 of them are inhabited.

Nassau, the biggest tourist center, acts as the seat of government. Nassau has a splendid health club, the **Sandals Royal Bahamian Resort**, *tel. +1 (888) 726-3257; website: www.sandals.com*. This first-class hideaway offers guests use of a gym, a whirlpool, a sauna, steam baths, a massage room, tennis courts, swimming pools, and a private white-sand beach.

The best hotel in Nassau

If you must stay in Nassau, make reservations at the **Wyndham Nassau & Crystal Palace Casino**, *tel. +1 (242) 327-6200; website: www.wyndham.com/ hotels/NASBS*, an oceanfront hotel 10 minutes from the airport downtown. It is on three-quarters of a mile of property, with 11 restaurants and lounges, a spa, fitness center, and of course, the casino.

The world's best planned paradise

The best thing to do when you get to Nassau is leave. Cross the bridge from Nassau to **Paradise Island**, leaving the shabby, graffiti-stained city behind. You will be engulfed in growth as green, thick, and dark as a jungle. This is a planned play-land for vacationers and is best known for the "Vegas-by the-sea" Atlantis resort. All the trappings are here: quick and easy access from the United States; a benevolent

June-like climate year-round; accommodation of every degree of luxury; sandy beaches and calm, clear water; a championship golf course; tennis courts; restaurants and nightclubs; and a large casino. The island has been featured in numerous movies including The Beatles *Help!* and James Bond thrillers *Thunderball* and *Casino Royale*.

One of the most beautiful places on Paradise Island is **Versailles Gardens**. This landscaped series of terraced gardens stretches across the island from the hotel grounds to the water's edge. Work on the gardens began years ago when Dr. Axel Wenner-Gren, who owned the island, set out to recreate the gardens at the Château de Versailles in France. When Wenner-Gren sold the island in 1960, the new owner, Huntington Hartford, continued to develop the gardens, adding statues, fountains, and—the crowning touch—a 14th-century Augustinian cloister transported all the way from France.

Nightlife on Paradise Island is Las Vegas revisited. Most of the action is at the **Atlantis Resort**, *tel. +1 (954) 809-2100; website: www.atlantis.com*, the main resort on the island. It has every type of entertainment you could wish for from a movie theatre to a comedy club to live entertainment in the Bimini Road bar.

The finest (and oldest) hotel on Paradise Island is the **One & Only Ocean Club**, *tel. +1 (242)363-2501; website: http://oceanclub.oneandonlyresorts.com/*. It's a small, tasteful 105-room place. A doorman, in top hat and tails, stands by to greet you. The hotel's restaurant, the Courtyard Terrace, is beautiful and romantic.

The most comfortable hotel on the Exumas

You'll be treated like family at the **Peace and Plenty Hotel**; *website: www. peaceandplenty.com*. The rooms are comfortable and each one looks over Elizabeth Harbor.

TRINIDAD & TOBAGO—THE CARIBBEAN'S BEST CARNIVAL

Trinidad, a cosmopolitan island, oil-rich and industrialized, rivals Rio as host of the world's best **Carnival**. Its Carnival parades have developed into an art form, as carefully choreographed and costumed as any Broadway musical. They have casts of thousands. Participants in Trinidad's spectacular parades are grouped into theme bands. As many as 3,000 people can be part of one costume band, while steel bands have 80 to 100 musicians, playing up to 500 steel pans.

The steel band competition begins about three weeks before the Carnival and culminates on the Saturday before, when the champions are chosen from the island's 100-odd bands. The musicians are so talented (and their drums so well tuned) that they have been known to play classical symphonies with expertise. The Carnival activities climax in the big parade on Shrove Tuesday. Revelers work themselves into a frenzy and join the bands in their dances.

The best place to stay in Trinidad and Tobago is at the **Man of War Cottages**, *Charlotteville; tel. +1 (868) 660-4327; website: www.man-o-warbaycottages.com*. This facility offers truly exceptional accommodation right in the rainforest. Bird watching and hiking are at your fingertips.

Best place to stay in Tobago

Though not on a beach (but just a five-minute walk from it), the small hotel, **Kariwak Village**, *tel. +1 (868) 639-8442; website: www.kariwak.com*, more than makes up for this with a serene warmth and friendliness. Most guests are repeaters, preferring the simply decorated half-moon shaped rooms without TV (never missed), and whole and natural foods served from the well-run kitchen. There are 24 rooms, 18 of which are poolside, with six bordering the garden. A thatch-roofed, open-air *Ajoupa* sits quietly apart, bordered by leafy pathways where daily Hatha Yoga and Qi Dong classes are given.

The best hotel

For something more upscale, try the **Coco Reef Resort and Spa**, *tel. +1 (868) 639-8571; website: www.cocoreef.com*. Near Scarborough, the resort nestles in 10 acres of tropical gardens bordering a beach on the Atlantic side. Of the 135 rooms, suites, and villas, 114 have ocean views.

Best seafood restaurant in Tobago

The **Seahorse Inn**, *Grafton Beach Road; tel. +1 (868) 639-0686; website: www.seahorseinntobago.com*, is considered the best seafood restaurant in Tobago —and besides great food, it's the only place where your dinner may be interrupted by a cry of "turtles sighted." Everyone troops out to watch the six-foot-long leatherbacks come ashore to lay their eggs. Nick Hardwicke, owner and chef, actively protects the glorious creatures during their nesting period of April to August. The restaurant also has four decorative guestrooms, each with an ocean view of Stonehaven Bay.

ST. MARGARITE—THE WORLD'S BEST WIND SURFING

Playa El Yague, on Margarite's southern shores, is the worlds best windsurfing beach and attracts world-class competitors—a lot of them. It now has eight or more windsurfing clubs. The bay is calm and wide, the sea less than waist deep for 1,000 feet out, and the trade winds blow steadily at 15 to 20 mph—qualities made to order for windsurfing. There is a "swim with the dolphins" attraction near Pampatar, called **Diverland**. It features 16 attractions including a giant Ferris wheel, roller coaster, and water toboggan.

THE GRENADINES—THE TAHITI OF THE CARIBBEAN

St. Vincent and the Grenadine Islands are billed as Tahiti of the Caribbean, because of their tropical beauty. Here, Captain Bligh brought the breadfruit that survived the mutiny on the *Bounty*. The 100 islands making up the Grenadines are connected by local mail boats, and all offer inexpensive accommodation.

Mustique is the Grenadine hideout of celebrities, including Princess Margaret. Try the **Cotton House**, *tel. +1 (784) 456-4777; website: www.cottonhouse.net*, a hotel in an 18th-century cotton warehouse built of stone and coral. Rooms are expensive, but the hotel restaurant, Roft, and the Basil's Bar are good.

The crown jewel of the Grenadines

Somehow **Bequia**, the crown jewel of the Grenadines, has avoided becoming another traffic-choked stop on cruise ship itineraries. Its seven square miles of lush, hilly terrain and wide, empty beaches are home to about 6,000 full-time residents who welcome visitors with the friendliest smiles on the planet. And why not? If you're blessed with such near-perfect weather all year-round; you're bound to be happy.

Most of the island's activities center around **Port Elizabeth** on Admiralty Bay, where ferries from St. Vincent come and go and most yachts drop anchor. It's a relatively busy harbor, with several grocery stores, a thriving vegetable market, and a handful of bars and restaurants by the sea. But getting out of Port Elizabeth and exploring around here is easy. If you're in good shape, you can hike the small but well-paved network of roads and see the whole island in just a few leisurely hours.

Alternatively, you can get a rental car or hire a local taxi to take you on a two- or three-hour tour for about $40 to $50, plus tip. Rates should be negotiated in advance, and you can check the tourist office for recommended fares. Bequian taxi drivers are a friendly bunch, so if you choose to take this mode of transportation, be prepared to form a solid friendship during your stay.

The best beds on Bequia

Bequia boasts a handful of luxury accommodations, most notably the **Gingerbread Hotel**, *tel. +1 (784) 458-3800; e-mail: ginger@vincysurf.com; website: www.gingerbreadhotel.com*, and the **Frangipani**, *tel. +1 (784) 458-3255; website: www.frangipanibequia.com*, both of which are located on Belmont Walkway, a narrow, paved path that skirts Admiralty Bay. Well-appointed suites with gorgeous views can be upward of $200 or more, but the comfortable economy rooms are a reasonable $60 to $80. For more about Bequia, go to: *www.bequiatourism.com*.

THE EASIEST—AND CHEAPEST—CARIBBEAN DESTINTION

Puerto Rico boasts the most extensive air service in the Caribbean, with daily flights from all major North American cities. And because it is a U.S. territory, American visitors don't have to worry about passports or changing money.

The island's beaches are lined with modern, self-contained resorts, as well as budget hotels and charming guesthouses. But the island also has a huge modern city with a historic core—**San Juan**. Old San Juan, a cluster of cobblestone Spanish streets with old houses and churches, is built in and around a fort. The city offers posh boutiques, horse races, cockfights (if your tastes run in this direction), casinos, flamenco dancing, Las Vegas-style shows, discos, and brothels.

The most historical hotel in Puerto Rico

El Convento, *tel. +1 (787) 723-9020; website: www.elconvento.com*, located in San Juan, is in a beautiful Spanish-style building with many antiques but modern facilities. A convent dating from 1600, it is a historical landmark in Old San Juan, now restored with most of the original architecture, tiles, and beams left intact.

Puerto Rico's best town

Puerto Rico's most charming town is **Rincon**, on the unspoiled south west coast. Once a drowsy fishing town, it now draws American retirees, while still maintaining its easygoing pace and low prices. Panoramic roads curve down from the green hilltop farms to the beaches. Trade winds from the east dump moisture on the 4,500-foot-high rainforest. In the morning, you can help fishermen pull their nets onto the beach. The main plaza has a supermarket, a bakery, a tropical bar, and restaurants. Palm trees, surrounded by mango, banana, citrus, papaya, and breadfruit trees, shade Rincon's beach.

New investment has increased your choice of accommodations beyond surf shacks. The intimate and luxurious **Horned Dorset**, *tel. +1 (800) 633-1857; website: www.horneddorset.com*, with private villas tumbling down to the water's edge is part of the renowned Relais & Chateaux collection. The Dorset is fast developing a reputation as one of the finest properties in the Caribbean.

For a tropical beach hotel with a villa feel, try the new **Tres Sirenas**, *tel. +1 (787) 823-0558; website: www.tressirenas.com*. Breezy ocean front rooms are $180 to $280 in season, with the owners providing very personal service.

Rincon has an amazing offering of accommodations. New B&B's in town with private patios or balconies are very affordable, and private villas for families are available on the beach or on the hillsides with awe-inspiring views of the sea. See *www.Rincon.org* for everything you need to plan your visit.

Puerto Rico's best-kept secret

Puerto Rico's best-kept secret is **Vieques**, a little known 21-mile-long island due east of the big island. Until 2003 a U.S. Naval base was located here and bomb tests were frequently held on the beautiful beaches. Now much of the island has been designated a National Wildlife Refuge, administered by the U.S. Fish and Wildlife Service.

Island residents are committed to sensitive development in this little paradise. Wild horses and cattle roam on the roads, and enchanting little coves are all but empty. Small boats cruise to **Phosphorescent Bay** on moonless nights, allowing you to see the brilliant streaks emitted by the phosphorescent organisms. Mahogany and rubber trees reach through the ceiling of the small rainforest. And white-sand beaches, some near coral reefs, slip into clear calm waters.

Home to 9,000 Spanish-speaking natives, Vieques is an informal, low-key, and low-cost hideaway. To get to Vieques, either take a plane from San Juan or drive from San Juan to Fajardo and then take the ferry to Vieques. Note, the ferry is a lot of fun but can experience unexpected cancellations and delays.

You can snorkel or scuba the coral reefs, or take a sightseeing charter with **Nansea Charters**, *tel. +1 (787) 741-2390; website: www.nanseacharters.com*. Small guest houses and casas dot the entire island and provide simple beach front rooms $80 and up in the winter.

Try **Casa de Amistad**, *tel. +1 (787) 741-3758; website: www.casadeamistad.*

com, located in the heart of the town of Isabel Segunda, just a block from the main plaza and two blocks from the ferry terminal.

For a contemporary Zen-like experience, **Hix Island House**, *tel. +1 (787) 741-2302; website: www.hixislandhouse.com,* is located in a 13-acre natural refuge, and offers spacious lofts, private terraces and outdoor showers, all with spectacular Caribbean views. Winter rates start at $175 and include Sea Island cotton shirts made just for you, and homemade breads, tropical fruits, and juices delivered fresh to your apartment every day. Be sure to plan for car rental a day or two so you can experience the hidden coves and inlets on your own.

CURAÇAO—THE BEST OF HOLLAND IN THE CARIBBEAN

Curaçao, the largest island in the Netherlands Antilles, is a bit of old Holland in the New World. **Willemstad**, the capital, resembles Amsterdam, complete with canals and 17th-century canal houses; the tallest pontoon bridge in the Caribbean (named after Queen Juliana); Indonesian restaurants; and a museum featuring wooden shoes and Delft tiles.

History buffs should visit the Willemstad forts. **Fort Nassau** is situated in the ramparts above town. **Fort Amsterdam**, on the sea, is the site of the Governor's Palace and the 18th-century Dutch Reformed Church, which still has an English cannonball embedded in its walls.

See **Ronde Klip** in the northeast, a privately owned *landhuis*, or plantation, and **Landhuis Brievengat**, built in 1750 and used as an elegant antique store with a bar and live music on the weekends.

The prettiest natural sight in Curacao is in **St. Christoffelberg**, where wild orchids grow. To see this, you must climb 1,213 feet to the highest spot on the island. For the more active, a mountain bike route will bring you close to the spot. Mountain biking is well organized on Curaçao, with the 2006 World Cup held on the island. Many routes follow surfaced roads but occasionally you will come across narrow tracks or hills.

Wanna Bike Curaçao will rent you the bikes and organizes many tours across the island: *tel. +599 (9) 527-3720; website: www.wannabike.com*

The oldest Jewish settlement in the New World
The Dutch tradition of religious tolerance spread early to the New World, and in 1651 a group of Jews established the oldest Jewish settlement in the Americas on this island. The Jewish graveyard **Beth Haim** is also the oldest in the Americas.

Most exotic cuisine in the Caribbean

Curaçao features a mélange of Dutch, Latin American, and Indonesian cuisines. The greatest seafood restaurants on the island can be found in **Westpunt**, a fishing port just outside Willemstad. Another good place to eat seafood is at the **Astrolab Observatory Restaurant**, *tel. +599 (9) 434-7700.* Although they offer a huge variety of dishes here you should try the Chilean sea bass served with caramelized snow peas and lobster ravioli.

Saba: The most scenic

Although **Saba**, a five-square-mile volcanic island, has no beaches, it is incredibly scenic. This rugged mountainous island is a wall of jagged black and gray rock that shoots up 3,000 feet from the white caps of the surf. Its summit is lost in the clouds. Roads snake through picturesque villages with such names as Hell's Gate and The Bottom. Because most of the houses are built on slopes, each one has a magnificent view. Cultivated crops cut into the sides of hills like steps.

Saba has no casinos and no high-rises, and you won't find air-conditioning. But lush rainforests hug the mountainsides, mist shrouds the summits, and gabled Dutch architecture distinguishes the small towns.

The best place to eat in Saba

After scuba diving and hiking around the beautiful mountains, you'll want a good meal. Try **Scout's Place Hotel Restaurant**, *tel. +599 416-2740; website: www.sabadivers.com.*

BERMUDA—A PERFECT FAMILY GETAWAY

Although most people visit the Caribbean to lie in the sun, this may not be your primary objective if you are traveling with children. If you want to travel in the Caribbean—and you plan to have your family in tow—head for Bermuda, the best place in the Caribbean to entertain kids. Following is a guide to the best things on Bermuda to do with your family.

Ride the ferry. Ferries run from Hamilton Harbor to Somerset and the Royal Naval Dockyard, at the southern tip of the island. They depart Hamilton from 6.15 a.m. until 6 p.m. Monday through Friday, 8.50 a.m. until 11 p.m. Saturday. The ride to the Dockyard takes an hour and costs $4/adult, $2/children. This is one of the best ways to see the harbor and southern section of the island. And children are welcome. Note that cash is not accepted on the ferries. Tokens, passes or tickets are available at the tourist offices, ferry docks, hotels or the post office. The most economical is the daily or weekly pass that can be used on the buses or ferries.

Take the bus to St. George's, at the other end of the island. This is the most historic spot in Bermuda. Settled in 1609, St. George's was the capital of the island until 1815.

Take a ride in a glass-bottomed boat. Many are offered; all depart from Hamilton Harbor.

Ride in a horse-drawn carriage through Hamilton and the surrounding suburbs. Carriages pull up in front of Hamilton Harbor beginning at noon each day and wait for passengers.

Visit the aquarium, the zoo, and the national History Museum, all in Hamilton Parish.

The best way to punish your nagging wife

While at St. George's, you might want to forego a photograph at the stocks and pillory (unless you don't mind waiting in line behind every other tourist on the island), but don't miss the **ducking stool**—a fiendish contraption used to punish nagging wives. Any wife found guilty of spreading rumors or engaging in the crime of gossiping was sentenced to the appropriate number of dunks in the harbor. For the poor disgraced woman, it was a punishment worse than death.

CUBA: WAITING TO BE DISCOVERED—AGAIN

Until Fidel Castro came to power, Cuba was traditionally the Caribbean's most popular vacation destination. Less than 100 miles from Florida, Cuba is also the largest island in the region and has a population of more than 11 million.

Today this island awaits a new influx of tourists. Canadians and Europeans are already enjoying some of the most beautiful beaches in the hemisphere. Five-star hotels have been built on Varadero Beach by Spanish and Jamaican investors.

Most historical hotel in Cuba

The **Hotel Nacional**, *tel. +53 (7) 836-3564; website: www.hotelnacionaldecuba. com*, in Havana, was *the* place to stay before Castro. This other era is still present with memorabilia of famous people like Frank Sinatra or Winston Churchill. Sitting on a hill in the middle of Havana, the Nacional has been restored to its

223

Art Deco glory. Featuring its own water ballet, and 1930's style floor shows, the Nacional has maintained its place of prominence in the newly burgeoning tourism industry. Also every Sunday at 7 p.m. in the garden behind the hotel, guests can enjoy a Highlights of Parisian Cabaret, along with performing jazz musicians.

Havana's best sights

Undeniably the best sight in Havana is its streets. Cars that wouldn't have been out of place in 1950s America trundle through the streets making the roads in Havana a veritable car museum. Due to the trade embargo imposed on the island, it is difficult for ordinary Cubans to import new cars, so they just keep repairing the old ones!

Capitolio Nacional, is Havana's answer to the U.S. Capitol building. It was the seat of Cuban Congress up until 1959. Although this entire (and massive) building is impressive, the most awe-inspiring is the 55 foot statue of the republic. It's the third largest indoor bronze statue in the world. You can also wander around the congress chamber itself.

The **Museo de la Revolucion** is also well worth a look. Housed in the Pavillion Granma this is where the "yacht", *Granma*, that took Fidel Castro and his followers from Miami to Cuba in 1956 and thus marking the beginning of revolution in the country. It is under 24-hour guard as are many of the other vehicles associated with the armed struggle. The museum also has an exhaustive account of the Cuban Revolution (start at the top floor and work your way down).

Hemmingway aficionados should visit the **Hotel Abos Mundos**, *website: www.hotelambosmundos-cuba.com*. This is where the author hid out when in the city and it is said he wrote *For Whom the Bell Tolls* here. Have a mojito in the hotels rooftop bar and gaze down on the city. See his house, *Finca Vigía*, located 12 miles outside of Havana. Filled with Hemmingway's possessions you can't enter the house but you can walk around it and peer in the open windows.

THE BEST OF JAMAICA

Jamaica is a sensuous place, a land of sunshine, ganja, reggae, colonial houses with verandas, and thick tropical jungle. The pace is slow and laidback. The sexiest place on the island is the **Blue Lagoon**, on the northeastern coast at Port Antonio, where Brooke Shields starred in a romantic movie by the same name.

Most beautiful sunset in the Western Hemisphere

At the westernmost point of the island is **Rick's Café**, propped 10 feet from the edge of a cliff. The water below is deep and clear, prompting thrill seekers to dive from the top of the cliff into the water 30 or 40 feet below. Try to get there in time for the sunset, the most fantastic in the Western Hemisphere.

The most beautiful house

The most beautiful of Jamaica's great houses (mansions left from the colonial days) is **Rose Hall** in Montego Bay. Once inhabited by the infamous white witch Annie Palmer, it was said that she murdered three husbands whilst they were sleeping in their beds. It was bought by John Rollins, the former lieutenant governor of Delaware, in the 1960s and restored with meticulous attention to the original detail.

The best places to hear reggae

Jamaica's reggae is an urban outgrowth of the Rastafarian religion, which grew up on this island among poor Jamaicans after Haile Salassie was named King of Ethiopia in 1936. To hear reggae in a perfectly safe tourist environment, visit **Montego Bay** and **Negril**. Appearances by the top reggae artists are advertised in local newspapers, but most often, local events are promoted from loud speakers mounted to vehicles and handbills posted on telephone poles. If you have Jamaican friends, ask them to take you to clubs outside tourist areas. These are cheaper and feature smaller reggae bands. But you shouldn't frequent these clubs unless you are accompanied by a Jamaican (and don't object to the ever-present ganja).

The best hotel in Jamaica

The best thing about Jamaica is there is no "best" hotel! Jamaica has the widest range of accommodations in the Caribbean. From luxurious **Round Hill**, *tel. +876 956-7050; website: www.roundhilljamaica.com*, outside of lively Montego Bay, where the royals stay to a pillar house at funky **Tensing Pen,** *tel. +876 957-0387; website: www.tensingpen.com,* on the laidback cliffs of Negril. Jamaica has something to suit every taste and budget.

Try the JAVA website: *www.villasinjamaica.com*, the official association of villa owners for a $10,000 a week castle in intimate Port Antonio, or a $2,500 a week bungalow with your own staff on the beach near Ocho Rios.

The world's most expensive coffee

Blue Mountain Coffee, the world's most expensive, is grown in Jamaica on the Blue Mountain range. It's also sold here, for far less than you'd pay anywhere else in the world (but still pricey). Be sure to enjoy at least one cup.

THE BEST OF
CHILE

Chile offers a mild climate, friendly people, excellent wines, and some of the best skiing and white-water rafting in the world. In addition, the political situation is stable and the prices are low.

THE BEST PLACE TO EAT IN THE CAPITAL

In Santiago, eat at **Aquí Está Coco**, *La Concepcion 236; tel. +56 (2) 235-8649*. The seafood is especially good. The adventurous should try the national dish, called *erizos*, a mixture of sea urchins that can be quite tasty when prepared in the right sauce. You can also buy head-chef and restaurants owner 'El Coco's' own signed recipe book at the restaurant.

THE MOST ARID PLACE ON EARTH

North of Antofagasta is the small port town to **Taltal**. It lies at the edge of the **Atacama Desert**, which covers the northernmost end of Chile. Reputedly the most arid place on earth, there are whole stretches of this desert where rain does not fall for years at a time. In the interior of the desert, nothing lives—no grass, no cactus, no lizards, and no birds. It is a fascinating landscape.

THE BEST SURFING

Surfers should head to **Pichilemu**, site of the 1990 international surfing and body board championships. Watching from a cliff overlooking the beach, you'll see row after row of breaking waves, as many as 12 to 15 at a time. A primitive beach town, travelers should not expect much as far as accommodation goes. Try the comfortable **Rocas del Pacifico**, *tel. +56 (72) 841-346; website: www.hotelrocasdelpacifico.cl (in Spanish)*.

THE BEST OF THE LAKE DISTRICT

Chile's Lake District is north of Puerto Montt and far south of Santiago. Although Spanish is the official language in the region, many here speak German. The most ambitious trip through the Lake District is to pick up a car in Santiago and drive all the way south to Puerto Montt. However, many car rental companies tack on one-way drop-off charges of hundreds of dollars.

The better option is to fly into Puerto Montt, pick up a car there, and drive a circuit around the region. The main highways are paved and in good condition. The secondary roads vary greatly in condition, from smooth and paved to dirt and gravel. All of the roads are well marked.

In addition to lakes, the Patagonia region is filled with volcanoes and rivers. Given all the waterways and all the rain, the region is incredibly green, reminiscent of New Zealand.

The Lake District's best hotels
The **Hotel Gran Pacifico**, *Urmeneta 719, Puerto Montt; tel. +56 (65) 482-100, website: www.hotelgranpacifico.cl*, is a luxury hotel with a great view of the ocean on the last floor.

Hotel Club Presidente, *Av. Diego Portales 664, Puerto Montt; tel. +56 (65) 251-666; website: www.presidente.cl*, is also good and much cheaper.

CHILE'S BEST LUXURY HOTEL

The luxury hotels in the south of Chile cater to Chilean and Argentine vacationers. The Termas Puyehue Wellness & Spa Resort, *Ruta 215 km. 76 Puyehue, Osorno;*

tel. +56 (64) 331-400; website: www.puyehue.cl, situated next to the Puyehue National Park, has elegant rooms, piped-in Beethoven music, an Olympic-size swimming pool, hot baths, and mud massages.

SOUTH AMERICA'S LONGEST SKILIFT

The longest ski lift in the country is 8,200 feet; it takes 25 minutes to complete the trip. And **Termas de Chillan**, the slope on which the ski lift operates, offers 15,000 acres of challenging runs, with the most varied terrain and snow conditions in Chile. There are volcanoes above, while below are thermal springs belching steam from the mountainsides.

THE BEST WHITE-WATER RAFTING

Though it begins as an emerald green stream, the rapids on Chile's **Rio Bio-Bio** include some of the most challenging stretches of navigable cataracts anywhere in the world.

The Bio-Bio is 400 miles south of Santiago; getting to the river is an adventure in itself. You travel on a 50-year-old train, decorated with mahogany and brass, that rattles slowly south and inland, toward Patagonia and the river. The river begins high in the Andes. Rafters and kayakers meet up with it a few miles from the source, in a little cowboy town called **Lonquimay**. At first the Bio-Bio is little more than a stream, an emerald-green trickle flowing through a valley of flowered meadows and pine scented forests.

The most difficult rapids

When the river approaches **Nireco Canyon**, the narrow path becomes cluttered with boulders. And a few miles downstream from the entrance to the canyon, rising straight up from eye level, is a curving wall of solid basalt. Here are the rapids for which the Bio-Bio is famous: the Milky Way, Lost Yak, Lava South, and Cyclops. The rapids are big and rocky, and to make navigation even more difficult, the force of the river pushes you constantly toward house-sized slabs of volcanic stone. This section of the Bio-Bio has taken its toll, and rafting here is not for the inexperienced.

Flush Canyon, (named after the poker hand, because rafting here is a real gamble) with its five rapids, also offers challenging runs. After the **Valley of the Thousand Waterfalls**, the river's pace slows down.

THE OLDEST LIVING THINGS ON EARTH

Chile's magnificent evergreen giants, called *alerce*, are the largest trees in the Southern Hemisphere. These trees grow only in the temperate rainforests of South America, where the ecosystem is different than in a tropical rainforest. Temperatures are much cooler, the growing season is shorter, and plants and animals must be well adapted to harsh living conditions—or perish.

All of these factors combined to produce an ancient (old growth) forest, with groves of giant old trees, some of which exceed 13 feet in diameter. This is especially amazing when you realize that each tree grows only about one millimeter in diameter each year. These trees were here long before Columbus discovered the Americas.

THE BEST OF
CHINA

China? There lies a sleeping giant. Let him sleep! For when he wakes, he will move the world.

—Napoleon

The People's Republic of China, the largest country in the world, is as big as all the countries in Europe combined. Its civilization flourished when the Occident was struggling its way out of the Dark Ages. It has the world's tallest mountains, the Himalayas, and it controls the world's highest city, Lhasa, in Tibet.

Although 92% of China's population is made up of Han people, the remaining 8% contains nearly 124 million members of minority groups. Tibetans, in their land of monasteries above the clouds, consider the Dalai Lama the head of the Buddhist religion; Mongolian horsemen roam the Gobi Desert; Chinese Muslims (Hui) live in the northwest; the Miao and Dai people in the south are related to the hill tribes of Southeast Asia.

THE BEST OF BEIJING

Beijing (Peking), one of the oldest cities in the world, has been the capital of China for 700 years. People have been living in this area for the last 50,000 years. Peking man, a fossil found in 1918 in a village southwest of Beijing, is one of the oldest relics of early man yet found.

Situated at the end of the route followed by camel caravans for centuries, Beijing is the site of many cities that have come and gone. Kublai Khan built his palace here and called the city Ta-tu (Great Capital). The northern part of the city has remnants of the old Mongol town visited by Marco Polo. Beijing houses are some of the greatest man-made wonders of the world. The Emperor's Forbidden City in the heart of Beijing and the Great Wall on the outskirts of the city are the most notable attractions.

The Forbidden City

The **Forbidden City** (*website: www.dpm.org.cn*), where the emperor of China once lived, is no longer barred to common man. Thousands pass through the Palace Museum every day, gaping at the royal opulence. Surrounded by red brick walls and guarded by tile-roofed towers, the palace was built by Ming Emperor Yung Lo in the early 15th century and covers nearly 250 acres. For five centuries, China was ruled from here by the emperor, who was considered the son of heaven. His every wish was granted. His meals were prepared by 5,000 to 6,000 cooks, and concubines, eunuchs, court favorites, and entertainers were kept here.

Surrounded by 35-foot walls and a wide moat, the city contains six palaces, all roofed in yellow tile, and many gardens and pavilions. See the apartments of the emperor, the empress dowager (the mother of the emperor), and the concubines; the halls of Supreme Harmony, Perfect Harmony, and the Preservation of Harmony; the temples; the libraries; and the art collection. Altogether, the rooms number more than 9,000.

The best way to prepare yourself for touring the palace is to see Bernardo Bertolucci's film *The Last Emperor*, which tells the sad story of China's last ruler who was, as a child, virtually imprisoned in the palace.

The world's largest public square

Tiananmen Square (the Square of Heavenly Peace), where Mao Zedong proclaimed the People's Republic of China in 1949, is the largest public square in the world, covering 100 acres and capable of holding one million people. As they have for centuries, the Chinese people come to hear government proclamations and to rally and demonstrate. Ironically, thousands of students demonstrating here, in the Square of Heavenly Peace, were killed in 1989.

The square is bounded to the west by the Great Hall of the People, which contains a 328-foot-long marble hall and reception rooms where diplomatic meetings are held; to the east by the Museum of Chinese History and the Museum of the Chinese Revolution; to the north by the Tiananmen Gate to the Imperial City, built in 1417 and hung with a portrait of Mao Zedong; and to the south by the Quianmen gate, built in the 15th century. In the center is the 120-foot Monument to the People's Heroes, an obelisk depicting scenes from the revolution and inscribed with quotations by Mao Zedong and Zha En Lai. The mausoleum of Mao Zedong is just south of the obelisk; thousands of Chinese line up to view his body daily. If you are paying Chairman Mao a visit, be sure to bring some form of photo identification with you to gain entry.

Kite flying in the square is a popular pastime and a good way to meet locals. You can buy a colorful Chinese kite in any Friendship Store—an exotic souvenir, unless it gets tangled in the gates to the Imperial Palace. Kites also are available in shops across the street from the square.

The most beautiful temple

The blue **Tiantan** (Temple of Heaven), built in the 15th century, is the finest example of Chinese architecture. Actually a complex of buildings, the temple is surrounded by a walled park. The most beautiful building in the complex is the Qi Nian Dian (Hall of Prayer for Good Harvest), set on three marble terraces, each with a 36-foot balustrade, connected to one another by eight flights of stairs. Supported by 28 columns and topped by 50,000 glazed blue tiles, the 123-foot hall was built of wood with no nails.

Blue-roofed pavilions flank the temple. Nearby is the **Huan Qiu Tan** (Round Altar), where each year for centuries on December 20th (the day before the winter solstice), the emperor made a mysterious animal sacrifice that determined the destiny of the whole nation. The altar is made up of three terraces, each surrounded by a white marble balustrade with 360 pillars.

Beijing's best park

The most famous of Beijing's many parks is **Beihai**, or North Lake. The park has pagodas, formal gardens, and three lakes. Created in A.D. 300, the park is the best-preserved ancient garden in China. Young people row on the lakes and whisper sweet nothings on the shores. Closed during the Cultural Revolution, the park reopened in the 1980s.

In the middle of Beihai is an island called **Jade Islet**, which is crowned by a Tibetan-style white dagoba (a shrine for sacred relics) built in 1651 to commemorate the visit of the Dalai Lama. The lovely **Zhichu Qiao** (Bridge of Perfect Wisdom) leads to the island.

The Empress Dowager's favorite place

Yiheyuan (the Summer Palace) on the outskirts of Beijing was the extravagant summer retreat of the infamous Empress Dowager Ci Xi. Located in the Haidian district and surrounded by a 692-acre, walled park, the palace was built in 1888 to replace an older and supposedly more beautiful palace that was destroyed by British and French troops in 1860. (All that remains of the original are a marble arch, pillars, and a wall.) The existing palace, too, was burned by Western troops, during the Boxer Rebellion in 1900, but it was restored a few years later.

Stroll along the **Chang Lang** (Long Corridor), bordering the lake and exquisitely painted with scenes from Chinese mythology. Visit the royal apartments, which contain jewel-encrusted furniture and beautiful works of art. Climb Longevity Hill, at the heart of the palace.

The best undiscovered sights

The **Gulou** (Drum Tower), near Houhai Lake in central Beijing, is a 15th-century structure in brick and wood, so named because a drum was beat here to summon officials to audiences with the emperor. For some unknown reason, it is seldom visited by tourists. A sign outside the entrance says visitors with heart problems will not be admitted to the tower due to the number and steepness of the stairs.

Just 100 yards behind is the **Zhonglou** (Bell Tower), similar in design, built about 1745. The night watch announced the hour from here until 1924. The two towers are surrounded by a charming maze of residential streets that feel like they belong more in a small village than a large city. The stone houses here are tightly packed, topped with tiled roofs, and entered through doors that are thick, old, and decorated with iron. Clay walls surround courtyards that are broken by doors at irregular intervals. This is one of the few hutong areas (these are narrow streets or alleys) remaining in Beijing, as the city is tearing the hutongs down to make room for high-rise apartment buildings. The area is safe at any hour, but you may get lost and have trouble finding someone who speaks English and can set you back on the right trail.

Another neighborhood worth exploring is a tangle of streets off **Wangfujing**, one of the main shopping streets, where Manchu nobility once lived. The formidable Empress Dowager Ci Xi was raised in one of the mansions on Xila Hutong. Another landmark in the neighborhood is the **East Church**, built in 1666 by the

Jesuits. Pao Fa Hutong is lined with remnants of the **Fa Hua Si Temple** (Temple of Buddha's Glory), built in the 15th century. You can see the original walls, entry gates, and a small antechamber. The rest is gone.

The Great Wall

Forty-six miles from Beijing is the **Great Wall**. It stretches nearly 4,000 miles through the hills of northern China. Contrary to popular myth, you cannot see the wall from the moon. Construction on most of the wall began in 403 B.C. and continued until 206 B.C. Thousands of men, many of whom were political prisoners, carried stones and dirt that make up the gigantic defense. Some of their bodies are buried inside. Once 6,000 miles long, much of it has been destroyed.

The section most visited is at **Badaling**, northwest of Beijing, which was constructed during the Ming dynasty (1368 to 1644). You can walk along the top—it is 18 feet wide and 21 feet tall. Look through the slots in the wall along the top and imagine the barbarians advancing from the north. Special trains and buses connect Beijing and the Great Wall. Badaling is home to the Great Wall Museum, (*tel. +86 (937) 639-6281*) with its dioramas (including one of building the wall), exhibits, and circle-vision theatre.

To avoid all the tourists who gather at Badaling, go a bit farther afield to **Mutianyu**, where a restored section of the wall opened in the 1980s. A great fort with 22 watchtowers was built along this stretch. From the top, you'll have a view of the surrounding mountain slopes, forests, and the town of Mutianyu. To get to Mutianyu, hire a car or take the Dongzhimen Long Distance Bus Line.

The Ming Tombs

On the way to the Great Wall are the **Ming Tombs**, where 13 of the 16 Ming emperors chose to be buried. **Shisanling**, the peaceful valley where the tombs are located, was chosen by the rulers because the winds and the water level ensured that only good spirits wandered the area.

The road to the tombs, known as the **Sacred Way**, is lined with 24 immense statues: 12 animals, real and mythical, and 12 mandarins in ceremonial dress. One of the Qing emperors is said to have wanted to take the statues to line the road to his own tomb. He abandoned the plan after dreaming that the statues are forever loyal to the Ming dynasty and that if he should move them an evil wind would blow across the capital. Only two of the tombs have been excavated, those of Chang Ling and Ding Ling. The best-preserved and largest tomb is that of Chang Ling (the burial name for Yong Le), who died in 1424. It is entered through a red gate that opens into a courtyard. Another gate leads into a second courtyard, where the marble **Ling En Dian** (Hall of Eminent Favors) is supported by 32 giant tree columns. To get to the sepulcher, you must continue into a third courtyard.

The tomb of Ding Ling (the burial name for Emperor Wan Li) was the first to be excavated. A deep marble vault four stories underground contains the coffins of Ding and two of his wives, who were buried here in 1620. A bronze lion and gigantic marble doors guard the tomb. Inside are three coffins and 26 chests filled with jewelry.

Best shopping

Beijing is loaded with upscale shops and malls these days. Wangfujing used to be Beijing's premier shopping street, but no more. Beijing Department Store used to be dowdy and frumpy with mediocre goods, but no more. The building's outside still looks the same, but inside – wow! It's now very upscale and can compete with the best in any international city. FYI: the main shopping area of Wangfujing has now been converted to a pedestrian mall with outdoor cafes, giving off a very European flavor. Other upscale shops can be found at Xi'dan, Kerry Center, World Trade Center, and Chaoyang.

Souvenir shoppers would do well to head to the Panjiayuan flea market, *18, Huaweili, Panjiayuan Road,* just off southeast Third Ring Road and Hongqiao Department Store across from the east gate of the Temple of Heaven. More than 3,000 vendors set up shop selling goods made from all over China. It is open during the week for antique sales in the small shops that surround the outdoor sales area. Weekends are when the arts and crafts vendors show up, as well as tourists by the thousands.

Hongqiao Department Store, *16 Hongqiao Lu*, sells souvenirs on the third floor. It's not as frenzied as Panjiayuan, but still gets a lot of shoppers, including a lot of expats who bring visitors here. One of the better pearl markets in Beijing shares the third floor with the arts and crafts; upscale jewelry is in the basement. There's more arts and crafts items on the upper floors of a back building.

Haggling over the prices is expected at both Panjiayuan and Hongqiao. Never pay more than half of the vendor's initial asking price. With judicious bargaining, you may be able to get the price down to less than 25% of the first asking price.

Beijing's best restaurants

Fangshan (Imitation Imperial), *tel. +86 (10) 6401-1879*, is the restaurant in Beihai Park. The goal of the chefs is to recreate dishes served to the royal families of the past using recipes passed down from the last empress's chefs. The restaurant is set on the shores of North Lake. It can be difficult to get reservations.

On the grounds of the Summer Palace, on Longevity Hill overlooking Kunming Lake, is **Ting Li Guan** (Listening to the Orioles Pavilion) restaurant, *tel. +86 (10) 6288-1955*. This restaurant features dumplings, velvet chicken, and other northern dishes. **The Courtyard**, *95 Donghuamen Ave.; tel. +86 (10) 6526-8883; website: www.courtyardbeijing.com*, is the top elegant restaurant in the city, combining Asian and Western recipes in a most elegant setting.

Quanjude has been serving Peking duck to Beijingers and visitors since 1864. It's grown from one restaurant to a chain of restaurants located throughout Beijing. The largest restaurant is **Hepingmen**, *14 Qianmen Xidajie, tel. +86 (10) 6511-2418,* located near the subway stop on Line 2. It caters to tourists and staff will direct visitors to a special floor which only has set menus. Hold firm if you want to pick and choose what parts of the duck you want, and they'll seat you on the main floor. Quanjude restaurants are usually located in areas tourists frequent, such as Wangfujing Street and Qianhai Lake.

Beijing's best hotels

The **Beijing Hotel**, *33 East Chang'an Ave.; tel. +86 (10) 6526-3388; website: www.raffles.com/en_ra/property/rbj*, was once the only good place in Beijing, and it's still one of the top hotels. Rooms are modern and spacious; some have balconies with views of the Forbidden City. Reservations can be made online.

The **Peninsula Palace**, *8 Jinyu Hutong, tel. +86 (10) 8516-2888; website: www.peninsula.com*, is the ultimate in luxury these days. Renovated in 2002, it oozes elegance and luxury from its basement shops to the top floor. It's been listed by *Conde Nast Traveller* and *Travel & Leisure* as one of the top hotels in the world. The Palace is just a few minutes walk from Wangfujing Avenue and some great shopping.

Xiang Shan (the Fragrant Hills), *Xiangshan Park, Haidian District; tel.+86 (10) 625-91166*. The hotel is located in the western suburbs at least an hour's drive from central Beijing. It was designed by the famous Chinese-American architect I.M. Pei. Jackie Kennedy was one of the hotel's first guests. A grand, white fortress of a place, Xiang Shan has beautifully landscaped gardens and skillfully lit rooms. While the Fragrant Hills is not conveniently located if you want to visit Beijing, it is surrounded by lovely countryside and situated near little-known shrines and monuments. For this reason, it may be the best place to stay if you are looking to relax but not necessarily see Beijing.

Zhu Yuan (Bamboo Garden Hotel), *24 Xiaoshiqiao, Jiugulou Street; tel. +86 (10) 5852-0088; website: www.bbgh.com.cn*, in an attractive residential neighborhood in the central section of the city, has bamboo gardens and rookeries. It is near the Drum Tower and was once home to Kang Sheng, one of the Gang of Four. All the rooms in the hotel are decorated in the style of Ming & Qing Dynasty, simple and elegant.

Metropark Lido Hotel Beijing, *No. 6 Jiang TaiRoad; tel. +86 (10) 6437-6688; website: www.hotel-rn.com*, is Beijing's version of an American resort hotel. It has a bowling alley, restaurants and lounges, a health club, a swimming pool, and rooms with air conditioning and private bathrooms. While it is comfortable, the Lido is outside town on the road to the airport.

The **Shangri-La Hotel**, *29 Zizhuyuan Lu Road; tel. +86 (10) 6841-2211; website: www.shangri-la.com*, is another Western-style luxury hotel. It has an extensive health center with a pool, a sauna, a solarium, a squash court, and tennis courts. The business center is also well-developed, with meeting facilities for up to 1,000.

THE BEST OF GUANGZHOU

Still known to most English-speaking people as Canton, **Guangzhou** is a popular point of entry for foreign tourists visiting China—it is only three hours from Hong Kong by train.

Unlike the rest of China, which stayed free of outside influence until well into the 19th century, Guangzhou began dealing with foreign traders as early as the second century. Thus, a foreigner has never been much of a rarity here. Besides Shenzhen, China's Special Economic Zone, Guangzhou is the most capitalist (and Western-influenced) city in China.

Early on, the Chinese government thought it best to canton the barbarians, as foreign traders were known, so they wouldn't corrupt the rest of the kingdom—hence, the name Canton. Arab, Portuguese, English, French, and American traders who sailed up the Pearl River were isolated and cantoned in their own areas. After their victory in the First Opium War, the Europeans were given an island in the Pearl River off Canton's waterfront, called Shamian. French and Victorian buildings still can be seen here.

Another result of foreign influence: Guangzhou has one of China's largest Muslim communities and the nation's oldest mosque, dating from A.D. 627.

This city remains a trading capital, and the mixture of local and foreign influences is as exotic today as it must have been to residents and traders of the Middle Ages.

Top sights

Zhenhailou (Tower Overlooking the Sea) is a five-story red pagoda originally built in 1380 on the highest hill in Yuexiu Park, originally a temple. Today it is the Guangzhou Historical Museum—fitting, considering the pagoda's involvement in Guangzhou's history. It served as a watchtower during the Opium War, when it was seized by French and British troops, and again during the 1911 revolution.

If you climb all the way to the top of the tower, you will be rewarded with a cup of green tea and a view of the park and the city. The museum's exhibits are displayed in chronological order from prehistoric times to the modern day.

The graceful Five Goats Statue, a reminder of Guangzhou's mythical beginnings, is also in Yuexiu Park. According to legend, the city was founded by five gods bearing stalks of rice who rode to earth on five goats, the rice symbolizing a promise that the city would never go hungry. (That promise wasn't kept.) Guangzhou is still known as Yangcheng, or Goat City.

Cultural Park, near the Pearl River, covers 20 acres and includes an aquarium, an opera house, a concert hall, seven exhibition halls, three television screens for the public, two open-air theaters, a roller-skating rink, a teahouse, a Ping-Pong area, and flower gardens.

Chen Clan Academy, a 19th-century compound, is one of the world's best examples of late imperial southern Chinese architecture. The roof and walls are decorated with terracotta sculptures, and the windows, doors, columns, and roof beams are carved. This family-run school of Confucian studies was built around an ancestral temple where you can still see an altar and a shrine.

At the Academy, you can buy bottles, decorated inside with Shantou paintings, a characteristic art form of southern China. These tiny glass bottles, about three inches high, are elegant and antique in style. Pictures are drawn within the bottles, which have pea-sized mouths. Fine scenery, all sorts of characters, flowers, birds, insects, and fish are painted on the inside surface. Golden patterns on the outside surfaces of the bottles enhance their beauty.

China's largest garden

The largest garden in China, the **South China Botanical Gardens**, is found just northeast of Guangzhou. Covering 750 lush acres, it boasts one of the best botanical collections anywhere in the world. For more information, *tel. +86 (20) 3725-2711* or *website: www.scib.ac.cn/english/index.htm.*

The oldest mosque and the best cathedral
Foreign visitors brought foreign religions to Guangzhou and, as a result, the city has two buildings that may seem out of place in a country with a Buddhist past and a Communist present.

At No. 56 Guangta Road, is the **Huaisheng Mosque**, the oldest in China. It was built in seventh century reportedly by an uncle of the prophet Mohammed, who is said to have brought the first Qu'ran to China in the 630s. It is now the mosque of China's largest Muslim community, which is estimated at 50,000 to 60,000.

On the Yide Road, near the popular Renmin Daxia Hotel, is a Gothic-style cathedral that was designed by the French architect Guillemin. Construction on the cathedral started in 1863; it was dedicated in 1888. During the Cultural Revolution, this building was used as a warehouse; however, it was renovated and reconstructed in 1984, 1986 and 2004-06, and now holds regular Sunday services.

The best shopping
International traders still flock to Guangzhou for the **Chinese Export Commodities Fair**, held for 15 days each spring and fall, usually in April and October, in the big exhibition hall near the Dong Fang Hotel.

If you are interested in more modest retail purchases, wander along Renmin Road, home of the **Nanfang department store** complex, the biggest in the city. It sells more than 50,000 kinds of items.

You can unearth fine antiques on **Hongshu Road**, in an antiques warehouse that has just about anything you could want. The best place for antiques shopping these days is **Antiques Street** in the alleys off Daihe Lu. While this is a fun place to shop, you need to be aware that the antiques may be fake. This is true of any place you shop for antiques in China. If an item truly is antique it will have a red wax seal attached to it; otherwise, it will not be allowed out of the country.

China's best food
Guangzhou's cuisine is the best in China and the best-known in the West, where Cantonese restaurants are common. However, exported Cantonese cuisine is not the real thing. In Canton, the ingredients are exotic, including snake, dog, frogs, and rats. The people of Guangzhou have an expression that explains, "The things

flying in the sky, except the planes, can be eaten. The things on the ground with four legs, except the tables, can be eaten."

If you're feeling adventurous enough to try monkey brain or its specialty, snakes, try **She Canguan**, *43 Jianglan Lu*. Guangzhou's most palatable contribution to the world is dim sum or dyan syin, a Chinese brunch that consists of a long series of small courses, served over one to two hours. Most of the dishes are different varieties of dumplings filled with pork, seafood, or vegetables.

Panxi, *tel. +86 (20) 8181-5955*, is Guangzhou's biggest and best dim sum restaurant, located on the banks of beautiful Li Wan Lake. Try the chicken steamed in Maotai and the crab paste dumplings. If you prefer atmosphere, eat at **Nanyuan**, *No. 142 Qianjin Road; tel. +86 (20) 8444-8380;* it offers dining in a splendid garden.

The best hotels

The **White Swan Hotel**, *tel. +86 (20) 8188-6968; website: www.whiteswanhotel. com*, was one of China's first five-star hotels. Rooms are decorated in jade-colored silk and filled with walnut furniture. The hotel opened in early 1983 and quickly distinguished itself with its many guest services (including a 24-hour laundry), its 30 dining rooms, its trilingual staff, and its astounding variety of fitness activities. The hotel offers its guest the services of a tiny but strong Chinese masseuse, who will give you a great acupressure massage, including walking on your back.

The lobby is one of the most beautiful anywhere. And the hotel has reasonably priced shops selling Chinese silk rugs, hand-painted screens, gigantic carved jade boats, and silk paintings. The building is situated on Shamian Island in the Pearl River, where a legendary hero is said to have been spirited away by a white swan. Free shuttle service is available to the hotel from the train station.

The most romantic temporary address in Guangzhou is the **Dong Fang Hotel**, *120 Liuhua Road; tel. +86 (20) 8666-9900; website: www.dongfanghotel. com*, not so much for its appearance, which is strictly Soviet revival, but for its inhabitants. Journalists, consular personnel, and powerful international businessmen have stayed in the rooms here. The dining room serves everything from Wiener schnitzel to Indian curries, from Japanese tempura to American apple pie.

One of China's most luxurious hotels is outside Guangzhou, on the slopes of Baiyun (White Cloud Mountain): the **Guangzhou Oriental Resort**, *tel. +86 (20) 8663-2888; website: www.oriental-resort.com*. Guests stay in large villas with sunken baths, private gardens, and lovely sitting rooms. Chinese government officials and high-ranking foreigners are among the guests.

The **Garden Guangzhou**, *368 Huanshi Dong Lu, tel. +86 (20) 8333-8989; website: www2.thegardenhotel.com.cn,* combines modern architecture with traditional Chinese decorations in its 30 floors. It's linked with the largest convention hall in Asia, which makes it very convenient for business travelers. The hotel has 14 restaurants serving a variety of international cuisines; on the top floor is a revolving restaurant specializing in seafood.

The best side trips from Guangzhou

Nine miles from Guangzhou is **Bai Yun Shan**, which rises 1,300 feet and has a panoramic view of the city, the countryside, and the river. At the top are teahouses and pavilions, where you can recover from the climb. Don't stray from marked paths—the government doesn't want anyone getting too close to the nearby defense installations.

China's best mineral springs are in **Conghua**, 50 miles north of Guangzhou. The eight springs are about 104° F and are said to cure chronic ailments. They are worth visiting, even if you feel fine, just for the views—they are surrounded by mountains, lichee orchards, plum trees, and bamboo groves.

Zixingyan (Seven Star Crags) is a series of natural rock towers connected by arched bridges and little pathways. Five small lakes and several caves lie in the shadow of traditional pavilions, which provide shelter. You can get to Zixingyan by bus or taxi in three hours.

SHANGHAI: CHINA'S LARGEST CITY

Shanghai was the most powerful city in China before the Communists took over in 1949. Merely a fishing village in the 17th century, it gained its wealth from trades as a treaty port opened by the Europeans during the Opium Wars. Controlled by the British from 1842 until 1949, Shanghai still has a western air and has been compared to New York and Rome. Before the Chinese Revolution, it had a lively stock market and great wealth.

Today, Shanghai is one of the largest cities in the world—and, with more than 15,000 coal-burning factories, the most polluted. Until a few years ago, it was considered China's most important city economically. Covering 2,344 square miles, metropolitan Shanghai remains China's most cosmopolitan city.

The prettiest neighborhood

Shanghai's most charming corner is **Old Town**, the Chinese ghetto during the British occupation. Between Jinling, Renmin, and Zhonghua roads are narrow streets, thatched huts, tiny shops, and outdoor markets with piles of fresh produce. In the northeast section of Old Town is a bazaar where you can buy beautifully carved walking sticks and traditional Chinese handicrafts. A little farther north are the Temple of the Town Gods and the Garden of the Purple Clouds of Autumn. Be careful; it's easy to get lost in this maze.

Forget the fancy restaurants and eat in the area's little food shops. (But don't drink the water.) Chinese lunchtime fare is cheap and fun to eat.

The best opium dens and brothels

Until 1949, the area west of People's Park, off Fuzhou Road, was the heart of Shanghai's world-famous red-light district known as **Blood Alley**. Before it was cleared out, it was inhabited by thousands of opium addicts and prostitutes. Liberation Lane alone, then known as Meet-With-Happiness Lane, had 34 brothels worked by more than 1,000 women. From 1949 until 1954, the brothels and opium dens were closed, the prostitutes given new work and new identities, and the addicts detoxified.

Yu Yuan: The happiest garden

At the heart of the Old Town is **Yu Yuan Garden** (Garden of Happiness), built in 1577 by a city official as a peaceful retreat for his ageing father. It includes more than 30 halls and pavilions, all with charming names: Pavilion for Paying Reverence to Weaving, Fairyland of Happiness, Tower for Observing Waves, and Tower for Appreciating the Moon. A tall, white brick wall topped with stone dragons divides the garden into three separate areas. Each section is designed to create the illusion of space and depth via artificial hills, ponds, bridges, and miniature gardens. A small lake at the center of the garden is crossed by zigzag bridges and bordered by teahouses and pavilions. The scene inspired the famous Blue Willow china pattern.

When you tire of the crowds in Yu Yuan Garden, take a break at **Wuxing Ting** (Five Star Pavilion), a teahouse just opposite the garden.

The Temple of the Town Gods

Not far from Yu Yuan is **Cheng Huang Miao** (Temple of the Town Gods), devoted, as its name implies, to the ancient town gods. Once, every Chinese town had such a temple. This is one of the few that remain. Behind the temple is a garden with a lake, pavilions, and artificial hills. Qiu Xia Pu (the Garden of the Purple Clouds of Autumn) was laid out during the Ming dynasty.

The liveliest promenade

The most delightful place to stroll in Shanghai is **Wai Tan** (the Bund), the area around Zhongshan Park, Zhongshan Road, and the Wiusong River, near the Old Town. The park is green with shade trees and decorated with rock and flower gardens. During the British occupation, the Chinese were forbidden to be in this area. The tall buildings that line the Bund once housed international banks and corporations; now they house the Bank of China and government offices.

Evening is the best time to stroll along the Bund, when city lights reflect in the water. If you are energetic, come here in the morning and join the locals in their daily Tai Chi Quan exercises.

China's best art collection

The three stories of the **Shanghai Museum**, *tel. +86 (21) 6372-5300; website: www.shanghaimuseum.net*, house the finest art collection in China. The first floor has bronzes from the Shang and Western Zhou dynasties (1523 B.C. until 771 B.C.). The most interesting objects are the instruments of torture.

The second floor has ceramics from the Neolithic era to the present, including life-size terracotta statues of warriors and a horse from Emperor Qin Shi Huangdi's tomb in Xi'an. Scrolls from the Tang, Song, Yuan, Ming, and Quing dynasties are kept on the third floor, where good reproductions are sold. It takes at least two hours just to see the highlights; many people spend a full day there or return another day to see everything. The museum is free, which is unusual for one of this caliber.

The best Buddhas

The **Jade Buddha Temple**, in northwest Shanghai, has two statues of Buddha, each carved out of a single piece of white jade. Monks brought them to China from Burma in 1890. Several other statues fill the halls of the temple. Twenty-four monks still live here.

The oldest and biggest temple

Shanghai's oldest and largest temple is **Longhua**, in the southern suburbs. Built before A.D. 687, it has four main halls, drum and bell towers, and a seven-story pagoda next door. The best time to see the temple and pagoda is early spring, when the peach trees blossom.

The best entertainment

The **Shanghai Acrobatic Theatre**, *tel. +86 (21) 278-866,* presents skilled and exciting shows every day except Tuesday. You should see this impressive show, consisting of the very talented Shanghai circus troupe, but realize that it is a production intended entirely for tourists and part of every package tour in the city.

The best undiscovered entertainment

The best place to people-watch and listen to great jazz is at the nightclub in the **Peace Hotel,** *tel. +86 (21) 6321-6888; website: www.fairmont.com.* The band members play as if they have been playing together forever. The music is good and atmosphere unbeatable. You can get the band to play your favorite tunes all night—just give them a small tip of U.S. dollars.

The most exotic foods

Food is sold helter-skelter on the streets of Shanghai. Shortly before New Year's Day, the sidewalks are piled with carcasses of pigs ready for the butcher. The below-freezing temperatures keep the meat from spoiling. On New Year's Day, men sell pancakes cooked over barrel stoves in the streets and set out chickens in cages or baskets of eggs.

Snake is a specialty. Customers choose their favorite snakes from squirming masses on the snakemongers' tabletops. Restaurants devoted exclusively to this delicacy are located throughout Shanghai.

The best Shanghai cuisine

Lao Fandian (Old Restaurant), *tel. +86 (21) 6355-2275,* is a local café serving typical Shanghai food and a good lunch stop after a morning in the Old City. It's beside the parking lot at the entrance to the Old City shopping area.

Meilongzhen, *tel. +86 (21) 6253-5353,* is a well-established spot for Shanghai and Sichuan cuisine, located in the 1930s Communist Party Headquarters.

Gongdelin, *tel. +86 (21) 6327-0218,* is a veteran vegetarian (Buddhist) restaurant with a long history of artistic and savory dishes.

Laozhengxing Restaurant, *tel. +86 (21) 6322-2624; website: www. laozhengxing-sh.com,* meaning Old Prosperity, is a small, well-respected place famous for its turtle, crab, and fish.

The best hotels

The **Heping (Peace) Hotel**, *tel. +86 (21) 6321-6888*; *website: www.fairmont.com,* is part of the last of the metropolitan life Shanghai used to have. The hotel rooms have high ceilings and are spacious 1930s-style suites that even have attached servant rooms.

Another aging hotel is the **JinJiang**, *59 Maoming Road; tel. +86 (21) 3218-9888; website: www.jinjianghotels.com*. It is in a group of mansions surrounded by a wall in the French Quarter. The grounds are beautifully landscaped, with a feeling of sophistication.

The **Broadway Mansions Hotel**, *20 North Suzhou Road; tel. +86 (21) 632-46-260; website: www.broadwaymansions.com*, has average rooms, but its suites are breathtaking. Some come with a private balcony and a grand piano and the view from the rooftop terrace is picturesque.

Hilton Hotel, *tel. +86 (21) 6248-0000; website: www.hilton.com*, offers modern luxury and superior service.

The **Grand Hyatt**, *88 Century Ave.; tel. +86 (21) 5049-1234; website: http://shanghai.grand.hyatt.com*, in the Pudong area is considered Shanghai's most luxurious hotel today. Occupying the 53rd to 87th floors of the Jin Mao Tower in the center of Pudong, it's one of the highest hotels in the world.

SHENZHEN—THE MOST OPEN DOOR IN CHINA

Shenzhen, the coastal region just across the border from Hong Kong, is China's most successful economic experiment. The Special Economic Zone, as it is known, is rapidly becoming a thriving metropolis.

The best miniature recreation of a place

Shenzhen is home to one of the best sites in China: **Splendid Miniature China**, a huge park where all of China is laid out in miniature. It displays models of the best of China, including the Imperial Palace in Beijing (China's largest), Zhaozhou Bridge in Hebei (the most ancient stone arch bridge), the Ancient Star Observatory in Beijing (the oldest astronomical observatory), the Great Wall, and the terracotta soldiers and horses near Xi'an.

In most any other country in the world, we would tell you to shy away from a splendid miniature recreation of a place. Tourist trap, we'd warn. But China is a special case. Travel here is so difficult and slow going that most travelers would never be able to see everything this ancient country has to offer.

For more information contact **China Travel Service Ltd.** *Hong Kong; tel. +852 2998-7888; website: www.ctshk.com.*

Shenzhen's best hotel

As Shenzhen struggles to transform itself into a modern metropolis, beautiful hotels are springing up where chicken coops and rice paddies stood only a few years ago. One of the finest is the **Forum**, *1085 Heping Road, tel. +86 (755) 5586-3333; website: www.china-hotels-asia.com/Shenzhen/Forum-Hotel.htm.* It has seven restaurants and very comfortable rooms, with 24-hour room service.

The **Landmark Hotel**, *3018 Nanhu Road, tel. +86 (755) 8217-2288; website: www.szlandmark.com.cn/eng/index.htm,* offers luxury in the city center. Rooms are fully equipped with modern amenities, including marble bathrooms. The centerpiece of the hotel is its four-story atrium.

HANGZHOU: THE BEST SILKS AND EMBROIDERIES

Hangzhou, which lies on the startlingly beautiful Xi Hu (West Lake), is known for its silks, embroideries, tea, and gourmet restaurants. You can watch silk being made at the Hangzhou Silk Dyeing and Printing Mill, where nearly 5,000 workers produce silk by reeling fibers off silkworm cocoons, and then print designs on the finished fabric. Mulberry trees, where silkworms' cocoons are found, grow in profusion in the surrounding country side. Longjing (Dragon Well) tea is picked and dried at the **West Lake People's Commune**, where you can watch the work or try your hand at tea-leaf picking.

Four islands with pavilions and temples float in West Lake. The largest and most beautiful is **Gu Shan** (Solitary Hill) in the northwest. The second largest, **Three Pools Mirroring the Moon**, is beautiful on moonlit nights, when the pagodas along the water, lit with candles and sealed with thin paper, look like moons on the water.

SUZHOU, THE VENICE OF CHINA

With its maze of canals bordered by small whitewashed houses and weeping willows, **Suzhou**, is the most romantic town in China. China's most famous romantic novel is set here, *The Dream of the Red Chamber*. Gnarled sycamore branches bend low over the town's narrow cobblestone streets, where high walls shield private gardens.

Suzhou's other claims to fame are its gardens—150 in all. The two loveliest are **Zhuozhengyuan** (the Humble Administrator's Garden) and **Liuyuan** (the Tarrying Garden). Both have elements of traditional Chinese gardens: pavilions, ponds, bridges, rock sculptures, and temples. They are two of China's four nationally protected gardens (the other two being the Summer Palace in Beijing and the Imperial Mountain Resort in Changde).

Most of Suzhou's shops are grouped close together in the downtown area. One of the best places to shop is the Friendship Store, which used to cater exclusively to foreigners but is now open to any Chinese with money to spend. Here you find a large and varied selection of silk (Suzhou is known for the quality of its silk), dry goods, and clothing. Collectors will drool over the extensive selection of unusual Chinese antiques. Local handicrafts also are featured, including fragrant sandalwood fans and double-faced embroidery.

GUILIN AND THE LI RIVER: BEAUTY DEFINED

The sharp peaks so often depicted on the Chinese scrolls exist in Guilin, known for its majestic natural beauty. Set in the Karst Hills of southern China, Guilin has shrouded limestone peaks and subterranean caverns.

You can visit some of the spectacular caves in the hills around Guilin. Reed Flute Cave in the northwest suburbs was once a refuge for villagers escaping enemy armies and bandits. Inside is a grotto, **Shuijinggong** (Crystal Palace), which holds 1,000 people.

A Stone Age matriarchal people lived in **Zengpiyan Cave**, where 14 human skeletons have been found, as well as skeletons of elephants, boar, and deer. The cave is open to visitors.

Seven Star Park contains six caves. The most famous **Long Lin** (the Dragon Refuge Cave), has walls carved with ancient inscriptions.

The best hotels

HOMA chateau Hotel, *tel. +86 (773) 3865-555; website: www.guilinhoma.com,* wants its guests to be relaxed! To this end, it combines art and nature, with a spa, sauna and foot spa. It offers massages and Thai herbal compresses to ease away the tensions of the day.

The **Guilin Lijian Waterfall Hotel**, *No. 1 North Shanhu Road, Guilin, tel. +86 (773) 2822-881; website: www.waterfallguilin.com,* lives up to its name, with an artificial waterfall cascading down the outside front of the hotel. The largest five-star in Guilin, it has an ambient setting near the Lijiang River, Shanhu Lake and Elephant Trunk Park.

The best river cruise

The best way to see this region is to take a cruise on the **Li River**. As you float downriver, look for Elephant Trunk Hill, Old Man Mountain, Folded Brocade Hill, and Crescent Moon Hill. You'll be able to recognize each by its name.

You will pass lush tropical scenery—fruit trees, bamboo groves, sugarcane, and rice paddies—as well as a 1,300-year-old banyan tree.

Boats leave at 7:30 a.m. or 8:30 a.m., depending on the season, and sail for five hours, docking for a time at the small village called Yangdi, at the base of two mountains. This is a good place to shop. Local peasants meet the boat, anxious to sell their produce and handicrafts, at bargain prices. For more information on Li River boat cruises stop by the **Tourist Office**, *14 Ronghu Bei Road, Guilin; tel. +86 (773) 2800-318.*

XI'AN: ONCE THE WORLD'S LARGEST CITY

Once the largest city in the world, Xi'an, in north central China, is filled with archeological wonders. The most famous is the tomb of China's first emperor, Qui Shi Huang, which is guarded by 8,000 life-size terracotta soldiers.

Chang'an, as the city was known in ancient times, was the capital of 11 dynasties, and the hills to the north of the city are filled with ancient tombs. Qin Shi Huang Di chose Xi'an as his capital. Under the Tang dynasty, from the seventh through the 10th centuries, it became the largest city in the world, with a population of about one million.

Today, the masses are returning to Xi'an, this time as tourists. In fact, more foreign visitors are appearing in the city than at any time since the eighth century.

While Xi'an is an industrial city congested with throngs of bicyclists, remnants of the city's loftier past remain. A medieval city wall can be seen in places. Two pagodas, Big Wild Goose and Small Wild Goose, watch over the city from a distance. (The view from the top of Big Wild Goose takes in the city.) And the city museum has the Forest of Steles, 1,000 standing stone tablets inscribed with ancient poems, essays, and images.

Xi'an has a large Muslim population and a functioning Great Mosque. This, too, is a remnant of the city's past, when trade routes from all over the world led here. The best day to see the mosque is Friday, when Chinese Muslims arrive to pray in the splendid Ming dynasty prayer hall.

The best collection of ancient artifacts

The **Shaanxi Provincial Museum**, *website: www.chinamuseums.com*, in a former Confucian temple in the south of the city, has the best collection of ancient artifacts in China. It is made up of three main buildings and three annexes and can hold 4,000 separate exhibitions. The Forest of Steles—1,000 standing stone tablets inscribed with ancient poems, essays, and images—is the museum's most important display. Also important is the stone menagerie—a collection of gigantic statues of real and imaginary animals that once guarded royal tombs.

Xi'an top sights

At the center of Xi'an is a Ming dynasty bell tower that provides a convenient vantage point when scouting out street routes. Within sight is Xi'an's drum tower (inside is the city's best antique shop), marking the city's Hui, or Chinese Muslim, neighborhood. The aquiline features and bearded faces of the men here bear witness to their Arab ancestry. Arab and Persian merchants and mercenaries came to Chang'an during the Tang dynasty (A.D. 618 to A.D. 907). The men of this neighborhood often congregate on the tranquil grounds of the Chinese-style mosque.

Throughout old Xi'an are many small shops offering handmade products. Follow the hammer taps to the tinsmith. Simple enamelware, army canteens, straw hats, oilcloth umbrellas, and chopsticks are some of the souvenirs you can buy here. Roast chicken is sold by Hui street peddlers, whose lamp-lit stands dot the street corners in the evenings.

Stop at the **Hua Xing Hot Springs**, outside town, where, according to a local joke, Chiang Kai-Shek left his dentures when running from the Chinese Red army. (He was arrested here in 1936.) The lush oasis was popular with the Chinese emperors, who bathed in the hot springs with their concubines and built a number of palaces in the area. After the court moved from Xi'an, the palaces were turned into a Taoist monastery.

Today, some of the buildings are used as a spa. The springs, discovered 2,800 years ago, have a temperature of 110° F and are said to be curative.

The **Xing Jiao Temple**, located southeast of Xi'an, is the burial site of the Tang dynasty monk, the patron saint of the Silk Route. Xuan Zhuang traveled to India and back in A.D. 627 on a quest for Buddhist scriptures.

China's greatest archeological find

The 8,000 life-sized terracotta warriors found in Lingtong County, 20 miles east of Xi'an, are the 20th century's most exciting archeological find. In 1974, a group of well diggers accidentally unearthed the ancient figures, which stood guard at the tomb of Emperor Qin Shi Huang for 2,000 years.

The first emperor of China, Qin Shi Huang united warring states as protection against northern barbarians. His tomb is divided into three vaults. The first contains the infantry, each statue with an individualized face. The second and third contain an additional 2,000 figures of men, horses, and chariots. The emperor himself is buried a distance away, hidden in a maze of corridors and gates.

The emperor began to build the army of life-sized soldiers when he came to power at age 13. Over a period of 36 years, Qin conscripted three-quarters of a million countrymen to build 6,000 figures and ordered the statues to guard his tomb. (The model soldiers acted as substitutes for real soldiers, who in earlier times would have been buried with their emperor.) The figures have stood for centuries 20 feet underground in an area the size of a football field. Most are lined up in marching positions as they would have been on a military campaign, while others are being pulled in chariots by teams of horses. The painted soldiers are modeled after Qin's live honor guard and carry real swords, spears, and crossbows, set to be triggered by invaders. Despite the decoys and booby traps, however, looters raided Qin's tomb four years after his death.

The best food and spirits

Lao Sun Jia, *tel. +86 (29) 8221-2935*. This family-run restaurant is the best place to taste Xi'an's most famous dishes. Try the coriander noodles and lamb stew served with bread.

De Fa Chang, *tel. +86 (29) 8721-4065*, specializes in dumpling feasts. The restaurant has numerous feasts to choose from, all delicately sweet and rich.

China's best hotel

The **Shangri-La Golden Flower Hotel**, *8 Changle Road W., Xi'an, Shaanxi; tel. +86 (29) 8323-2981; website: www.shangri-la.com*, offers rooms that are vast by present-day standards in China, well-lit, tastefully decorated, and equipped with two queen-sized beds. The staff is impeccable and speaks English. Facilities at the Golden Flower include secretarial and translation services, money changing, and a gift shop. The hotel runs tours and a fleet of taxis, and the concierge can negotiate restaurant reservations, prices, and menus. The local restaurant offers Sichuan and Shaanxi food.

THE MOST EXOTIC DESTINATION: THE SILK ROUTE

The legendary **Silk Route** is far from silken. Ancient caravans following the route braved trackless deserts, towering mountains, and staggering distances to barter with foreign merchants or to spread new religions. Although some of the terrain is paved today, it remains a difficult passage. However, the payoff for undertaking the trip is great: the stark beauty of the landscape; the friendly, freedom-loving Uygurs; the colorful bazaars; and the incomparable religious art.

This 3,720-mile network of routes has spanned Eurasia since the second century B.C. Beginning at China's ancient capital Chang An (modern Xi'an), it snakes to Kashgar in western China and then splits. The main route climbs the Himalayas and continues west to Samarkand (the southern part of what used to be the Soviet Union), Persia (now Iran), and Rome. One alternate route dips down to Pakistan.

The Chinese leg of the route is probably all you'll have the time and fortitude to travel. Guided tours are practical for those with limited tolerance or language skills.

Buddhist bests

Twenty miles from Lanzhou are the **Bilingsi Buddhist Caves**, which are definitely worth visiting. Buddhist monks dug the caves into the face of a 180-foot cliff about 1,500 years ago. They are full of Buddhist statues, sculptures, and murals. From here, the Silk Route crosses the Wei River Valley into the arid province of Gansu, where it flanks the Great Wall for 700 miles. Eventually, it comes to **Jiayuguan**, a fortress built by Ming dynasty rulers in 1372 as their western outpost.

Northwest of Jiayuaguan are the **Thousand Buddha Grottoes** at Dunhuang, an oasis stuck in the middle of the Gansu Desert. In the old days, this dusty little place was a vital staging post for camel caravans going east and west—here the northern and southern branches of the Silk Route met. Only 40 of the 500 cave temples are open to the public. Each enshrines superb paintings and sculptures that were commissioned over a period of 1,500 years by rich and pious pilgrims and merchants as gestures of thanks for a safe journey on the Silk Route. Bring a flashlight to see the details of the works.

The best of the desert

The **Taklmakan Desert**, which the route follows on the southern border, translates from Uygur to mean "Once you go in, you never get out." The desert is haunted not by the specters that the ancients feared but by the sounds of underground nuclear testing. A long, parched trip via bus and train will lead you out of the desert and into Turpan, a cultural oasis where grape arbors shade courtyards.

The friendliest people

Descendants of the Uygurs make up the region's largest—and friendliest—ethnic group (besides the Han Chinese). Their language is Turkish, their religion Islam. Cool evenings, when the people are outdoors, are the best times to meet the Uygurs. Invitations to their adobe huts are not unusual.

The best of the past

Nearby ruins of two ancient Silk Route cities still have recognizable streets, town walls, and buildings. **Gaochang**, the larger of the two cities, was the capital of the Uygur kingdom in the ninth century. It once hosted Marco Polo and is a vast and slightly terrifying place.

    Jiaohe, perched above a riverbed, was a Chinese garrison until it came under local control. Its main road is still clearly visible. Join with other travelers and hire a minibus to take you to the ruined cities.

The Silk Route's best guesthouse

The first leg of the Silk Route is a 13-hour train journey from Xi'an to Manzhou. The best place to stay in Lanzhou is at the megalithic Chinese-built Friendship Hotel. Rooms are comfortable, if cavernous, with well-worn, deep-seated armchairs with lace arm covers, fragile pink lampshades, and heavy velvet curtains. **Friendship Hotel**, *16 Xijin Xi Road, Lanzhou; tel. +86 (931) 268-9999 website: www.sinohotelguide.com/lanzhou/friendship.*

China's least desirable digs

The **Turpan Depression**, which surrounds the town of Turpan, has been called one of the strangest places on earth. It lies nearly 500 feet below sea level and can get so hot in the summer that people live in the underground cellars of their homes. An underground irrigation channel was built 2,000 years ago to bring melted snow from the Tian Shan Mountains in the north (hence the profusion of well-watered melon and grape crops in the middle of the desert).

Ugliest city, loveliest carpets

A few hours beyond Turpan is **Ürümqi**, one of the ugliest, most polluted cities in China. One thing saves this industrial city—it has the country's best carpet market.

To find it, go to the **Overseas Chinese Hotel**, *51 S. Xinhua Road; tel. +86 (991) 2860-793,* head toward the city center, and turn into the fourth lane on the right. At the end is a bustling little market with noodle restaurants, kebab stalls, teahouses, clothes shops, and a magnificent array of carpets.

Urumqi has several five-star hotels, among them the **China Southern Airlines Kepinski Hotel Urumqi**, *No.576, Youhao South Road, tel. +86 (991) 638-8888.* This used to be a Kempinski hotel, and offers the same outstanding service and amenities.

The best of Switzerland in the desert

Once you have visited the market, head out of town toward **Heaven Lake**, a bit of Switzerland halfway up Bogda Shan (the Mountain of God). The trip takes four hours.

Deep Blue Heaven Lake is surrounded by pine forests and snow-capped peaks. The Kazakhs, herders, and horsemen (not to be confused with Russian Cossacks) set up their yurts (dome tents) in the cool meadows here during the summer.

If you can't face returning to Ürümqi, you can rent a yurt from a Kazakh nomad. Or you can stay at the Heavenly Lake Hotel, on the shore of the lake.

The best horsing around

While in Ürümqi, you may be invited to see the ***boz kashi***, a contest of horsemanship. Riders must carry a headless goat or lamb from one end of the field to another. Because this spectacle appears to lack either a referee or rules, it's best to view it from a safe perch.

China's westernmost city

From Ürümqi, you can fly to **Kashgar**, China's westernmost city and the end of the Chinese portion of the Silk Route. (If you continue on from here, you will end up in Pakistan.) But taking the three- or four-day trip in the company of Uygurs, Mongols, Tibetans, and Han Chinese better duplicates Silk Route sojourns of long ago. The buses make frequent stops that give you a chance to sample the area's plentiful melons.

They say Kashgar is farther from the sea then any other town on earth. When you get there, you'll believe it. The streets are narrow and dusty, lined with adobe houses. This is one of the most important cities on the Silk Route; it is at the borders of Russia, Afghanistan, India, and Pakistan. When Marco Polo passed through Kashgar, he called it "the starting point from which many merchants set out to market their wares all over the world."

One thing above all must be seen in Kashgar: the **Sunday Market**. When you plan your trip, make sure you will be in town on a Sunday. Hundreds of thousands of people (mostly Uygurs) swarm to an area on the outskirts of town, where they buy and sell everything you can imagine—and much you can't. The most exciting part of the market is where the Kazakh horsemen test-ride horses in an enclosure full of donkeys, sheep, goats, cows, and camels.

Near the market is **Id Kah Mosque**, one of the largest in China. Built in 1442, it dominates the old town and draws thousands of worshipers every Friday. If you aren't in town on a Sunday, many of the goods available at the market can also be purchased at the bazaar near the Id Kah Square. When you tire, relax over a delicious meal at the **Lao Chayuan Jiudian**, *tel. +86 (998) 282-4467.*

The **Seman Hotel**, *Seman Lu 337; tel. +86 (998) 258-2129*, is more central. Its old wing was once Kashgar's Russian Consulate. Little seems to have been repaired since the Russians left in 1949, but the dilapidated rooms are rather charming. They have the biggest and best bathtubs you'll find within 1,000 miles! What's more, you'll be provided with plenty of hot water. Hong Kong is the best place to arrange a trip along the Silk Route.

DALI—CHINA'S NEWEST VACATION SPOT

Dali is one of the most popular new destinations in Yunnan province. It is a handsome historical city in a spectacular setting. Look one way and you can see the snow-capped Cangshan (White-Haired Mountain), look the other way and you see the blue Erhai (Ear Lake). Between the mountain and the water are well-irrigated green fields dotted with villages.

The majority of Dali's natives—about 80%—are of Bai nationality. For hundreds of years, they formed a kingdom independent from China that flourished until conquered by Kublai Khan in 1253. A stone tablet commemorates the event.

The Bai people are extremely friendly and will greet you constantly with "Hi." Women wear traditional colorful clothing, including ornately decorated backpacks for carrying small children.

When Chinese emperors moved the provincial capital to Kunming, Dali sank into oblivion. Because of this, the town is well-preserved, with narrow cobblestone streets and old buildings of wood, plaster, and stone. A short walk takes you down the main street from one Ming dynasty gate to the other. The gates have been impressively rebuilt, but most of the wall that surrounds Dali is now little more than earthworks with rice planted on the top.

You can buy colorful clothing at the marketplaces in and around Dali. The largest is held every Monday at Shain, on the north side of the lake, about 18 miles from Dali. In addition to pigs, seed, and farming tools, you can buy coins, handkerchiefs, and fabrics. Tailors in Dali can stitch up clothing to order.

Beyond the wall, two competing entrepreneurs rent out bikes. The bikes are crude one-speeds, and the roads are very bumpy.

Finagle a boat ride across the lake and watch the fishermen with their nets. Hike up the mountains, where many old temples are still in use. To relax your tired muscles, get a vigorous massage at Dali's public bathhouse.

April is the best time to visit Dali, when the town holds its **Third Month Fair**, an annual festival that dates back 1,000 years. People come from miles around for their once-a-year trip to town.

Getting to Dali involves a nine-hour bus ride from Kunming, the capital of Yunnan province. Flights to Kunming depart from Hong Kong, Beijing, Guangzhou, Shanghai, and Rangoon.

XISHUANGBANNA: TROPICAL CHINA

The southernmost region of China's Yunnan province, **Xiashuangbanna**, is more like Thailand than China. Bordering Burma and Laos, this is a lush, tropical land with hillside tea and rubber plantations, markets full of exotic fruit, and coconut-palm-shaded villages where women dress in brilliantly colored sarongs.

The liveliest time to visit is during the **New Year Water Splashing Festival** (mid-April). Festivities in Jinghong, the capital, include dragonboat races on the Mekong River, Dai music and dancing, bamboo rockets, and a riot of water splashing. If you plan to visit during the festival, make reservations far in advance. Both flights from Kinming to Jinghong and accommodation become scarce.

A better time to visit is off-season, when you can enjoy the tranquil countryside and the gentle ways of the attractive Dai people (one of Yunnan's largest and most prosperous minority groups).

Jinghong is a small, sleepy town of broad streets bordered by palm trees. Buddhist monks in saffron robes bicycle slowly along the streets, while Dai women carrying pretty parasols congregate in the open markets. If you are lucky, one of the Dai will present you with a sticky cake of glutinous rice wrapped in palm leaves, a common sweet snack in Xishuangbanna.

About 35 miles west of Jinghong lies **Menghai**, one of the great tea regions of China and home of the most famous temple site in the province: the **Octagonal Pagoda**. This tiny gem of intricate architecture was built in the 17th century.

Far to the south, five miles from the Burmese border, lies **Damenglong**, a village with a 13th-century white pagoda and a lively Sunday market. Here you can see a panoply of other minority people, who come to trade with the local Dai: Lahu women in brightly colored bodices; Bulang with colored tufts of wool for earrings; and women of the Hani and Aini tribes (who are similar to Thailand's Akha people) bedecked in breastplates and headdresses of silver and metal coins, embroidered black leggings, belts of cowrie shells, and short black miniskirts that have an alarming tendency to fall off.

Another market is held at **Menghan**, southwest of Jinghon, which you can get to by slow boat on the brown Mekong River. It's a one-hour trip downstream, with stops to pick up villagers. Women can be seen on the river's edge panning for grains of gold.

The life of the Dai in these villages is slow and traditional. They live along the northern shore of Menghan's Virtuous Dragon Lake in large wooden houses built on stilts. You can see men making bamboo baskets and girls weaving cloth. In the Buddhist temple, boy monks learn their sacred texts. Chickens and pigs roam the dusty village paths, and buffalo plow the fields. Inside the thatched-roof wood and bamboo houses, gold-toothed Dai women prepare banquets: purple rice, spiced zucchini, sesame beef, and fried bumblebees.

The easiest way to reach Xishuangbanna is to fly from Kunming to Simao (75 minutes) and then take a bus or taxi the 100 miles to Jinghong. You'll pass spectacular scenery, including rice plains, hillsides of tea and rubber, and dense jungles.

HAINAN, THE RED HAWAII

Hainan Island off the coast of China is the Hawaii of the Far East. The island is off the southernmost part of China, not far from Vietnam, and is nearly as big as Taiwan.

Hainan Island is picturesque with its coconut groves and pristine golden beaches. Sanya is its most famous destination, with more than 100 flights a day landing on the island. Sanya has thousands of hotel rooms in all price ranges. Luxury hotels on the beach include the **Sanya Marriott Yalong Bay Resort Spa**, *tel. +86 (898) 8856-8888; website: www.marriott.com.* Or you can try the **Yalong Bay Mangrove Tree Reort**, *tel. +86 (898) 8855-8888; website: www. mangrovetreeresort.com.* It's a five-star that is the only Balinese style hotel in China.

257

LHASA: THE WORLD'S HIGHEST CAPITAL

Lhasa, **Tibet**, at 12,087 feet above sea level, is the world's highest capital. Set in royal blue skies above the clouds, tourists are given oxygen bags when they arrive. Individual tourist permits are almost impossible to get but it's possible and easier to obtain group permits.

The former seat of the Dalai Lama, the head of Tibetan Buddhism, Lhasa is filled with palaces and temples. Behind these grandiose man-made monuments are towering snow-covered mountains that make the Rockies seem mundane.

The **Potala**, where the Dalai Lama lived until he was ousted by the Communists in 1959, is an enormous 17th-century edifice that dominates the entire valley. The 13-story, 1,000-room palace is a museum today. Inside are gigantic, bejeweled Buddhas, murals illustrating Buddhist legends, and solid gold crypts containing the remains of former Dalai Lamas. The 10,000 chapels are decorated with human skulls and thighbones. Beneath the palace are torture chambers, where criminals and dissidents were kept in dungeons or stung to death by scorpions.

The **Deprung Monastery**, which is about three miles outside Lhasa, is where lesser religious leaders lived. The stone building, constructed in 1416 and set precariously against a mountainside, was once the largest cloister in the world. Although thousands of monks once lived here, the monastery is now inhabited by 300.

The **Jokhang Temple** houses two enormous gold and bejeweled Buddhas. Built 1,300 years ago, it is still visited by pilgrims who can be seen prostrate in front of the temple at dawn and dusk. Beautiful from the outside, the temple is smelly inside, because of the fermented butter burned by monks as part of their religious ceremonies.

One of the best bazaars in all China takes place around the outside. Pilgrims from across Tibet congregate in the Barkhor and walk around it clockwise, praying, shopping, and socializing as they move along. A fantastic variety of goods is sold in the Barkhor, including prayer wheels, silver inlay boxes, and Tibetan musical instruments. Be prepared to bargain fiercely.

The best hotel in Lhasa is the **Kyichu Hotel**, *149 E. Bejing Road; tel. +86 (891) 633-1541; website: www.kyichuhotel.com.* Rooms are air-conditioned and equipped with televisions and telephones.

THE BEST WAY TO TRAVEL

If you have the time, the most pleasant way to travel through China is by boat. Several boat routes allow you to make the circuit of the major Chinese cities. One goes from Guangzhou to Wuzhou, a small town en route to Guilin, in 20 hours.

Everyone on these boat trips gets his own berth, either in an upper with a window view of the Pearl River or on a lower-level berth with easier access. No one sits in the aisles. Thick mats and quilts are provided in the dormitory-like setting. You'll enjoy lovely views and great people-watching opportunities.

THE BEST OF THE
COMMONWEALTH OF INDEPENDENT STATES

"A riddle wrapped in a mystery inside an enigma."
—Winston Churchill

Those are the words that Winston Churchill used to describe the Soviet Union more than 60 years ago. And they are as appropriate today as they were when Churchill first spoke them.

MOSCOW'S BEST SITES

The first thing you must see in Moscow is a ballet at the **Bolshoi Theatre**, *1 Teatralnaya Pl.; website: www.bolshoi.ru.*

The second thing you must see is **Red Square**, one of the most famous squares in the world. The square separates **the Kremlin**, the former royal citadel and currently the official residence of the President of Russia, from a historic merchant quarter. It is home to Lenin's Mausoleum, which contains the embalmed body of the former Soviet leader.

The **Arbat** has become Moscow's Speaker's Corner. Here you can enjoy the local street artists' scathing political cartoons and listen to the speakers, who rant and rave about anything that happens to be on their minds.

Also visit the country's largest department store, **GUM**, *3 Red Square*. GUM boasts an elegant turn-of-the-century interior, comprising three parallel arcades centered on a fountain and overlooked by galleries. Light floods in through the building's glass roof and souvenir stands; foreign stores and designer boutiques fill the arcades.

The best eats

Shesh-Besh, *24 Pyatnitskaya; tel. +7 (95) 959-5862,* has a pleasant serving staff with an incredibly comfortable atmosphere, including quiet music playing in the background. Everyone can enjoy the cuisine, even vegetarians. The food is unique Azerbaijani cuisine with a combination of Turkish, Greek, and Russian flavors. Worth trying is the cutaby, a thin, crepe-like dough stuffed with fresh greens, sheep's cheese, or ground lamb.

White Swan, *Chistoprudny Boulevard, 12; tel. +7 (95) 928-6000,* has been described as a small piece of Venice. In this restaurant choose a table by the window so you can enjoy the fabulous view of the pond, while enjoying outstanding European cuisine. It also offers a sample of its own little bakery at the end of your meal.

CDL, *tel. +7 (95) 291-1515,* specializes in authentic Russian cuisine. This restaurant, housed in a very elegant 19th-century mansion, is one of the very best. It can be a little pricey, but you should go for the unforgettable experience of a real Russian meal.

The best place in the world to buy an original work of art

The best values in Moscow, by far, are in art. Be the first on your block to own an original Russian painting. It will cost you just a few dollars—and there's the chance that it will be worth a small fortune one day. **Arbat Street**, closed to all but pedestrian traffic, is lined with shops and street vendors selling these original pieces of art, as well as souvenirs, clocks, books, linen, and ice cream.

THE BEST OF BELARUS

Belarus is home to **Minsk**, a surprisingly attractive town (although it has the reputation of being one of the ugliest cities in the world). The avenues are wide and tree-lined and a river flows through the town. Many of the public buildings are grand and well-designed. There is a pleasant walkway along the riverbanks (though it is littered by chunks of concrete that have fallen from nearby buildings). There is even a historic section that has been restored and preserved.

The best sites
Walk around the Old Town and along the river; you'll pass the city's hotels and art galleries. Also visit the house where Lee Harvey Oswald lived, the site of the first Communist meeting, and the city's monuments, scattered around town.

An interesting market is the **Storazhovsky Renok**. Here you can find fresh vegetables, fruits, bread, and other good food. There's also a lively pet and live-stock market here.

THE MOST REMOTE REGIONS

Few Westerners have ever seen the remote peaks of the Central Asian Tien Shan and Pamir mountains. Travel here is still highly restricted. The snow-peaked mountains of the **Tein Shan** (Heavenly) mountain range rise out of the hot and arid Central Asian steppelands to heights of 11,500 feet and 13,125 feet, extending into China in the east and the Himalayas in the south. Everlasting glaciers, green valleys, emerald lakes, rapid rivers, and ancient towns and cities are hidden in the mountains' valleys.

The Sairam Valley—The best gateway
The mountain valley of **Sairam**, at 5,580 feet, boasts a dry climate, crystal clear water, unusual rock formations, and birch and juniper woods. It acts as a gateway to the mountains in general. The mountains of Sairam are formed of limestone and basalt. The northern and western slopes are precipitous; the southern ones are more gradual and easily accessible.

The best practice climb
Among the most challenging climbs you can make is up **Ibn Sina Peak** (formerly called Lenin Peak). At 23,400 feet, it is one of the highest peaks in this part of the world. It is a good place to practice before tackling the Karakorum or the Himalayas.

THE WORLD'S MOST EXCITING TRAIN TRIP

Journey 6,152 miles from Moscow to the Pacific port of Vladivostok or take the trip to Beijing from Moscow either via Mongolia (4,735 miles) or via Manchuria (5,623 miles) on the Trans-Siberian Railway journey...certainly the most exciting.

The most interesting route, from Moscow to Beijing via Mongolia uses Chinese rolling stock, replaced in 1990, and cuts across Outer Mongolia and the Gobi desert before entering China and passing through the Great Wall.

We found the following website: *www.seat61.com/Trans-Siberian.htm* very informative. You could also contact the Russian National Tourist Office; website: *www.russia-travel.com*.

THE BEST OF
COSTA RICA

What you'll find most surprising when visiting Costa Rica is that, despite all its natural beauty, despite all the favorable press it has received for years now, despite its low cost of living, despite its Edenic climate, and despite its friendly populace, this tropical paradise has not yet been overrun with tourists.

Yes, there have been many more visitors to Costa Rica in recent years than a couple of decades ago, for example. But, compared with the worlds other tropical paradises, Costa Rica remains largely undiscovered.

The country boasts some of the best-preserved countryside in Latin America. There are acres upon acres of pristine forest and jungle. And there are long stretches of totally deserted and undeveloped beaches, on both the Caribbean and the Pacific coasts.

Two other characteristics set Costa Rica well apart from its Central American neighbors: a high literacy rate (one of the highest in the world) and the absence of an army.

SAN JOSÉ: THE BEST MODERN CITY IN COSTA RICA

The primary drawback to **Costa Rica** is its capital city, **San José**, which is crowded, noisy, run-down, polluted, and crawling with pickpockets. At one time, though, San José must have been beautiful. The old sections of the city are filled with large, ornate buildings that were originally residences but have been converted into office space.

One thing you should take time to see in San José is the **Téatro Nationale**, a beautiful building inside and out. When you walk into the lobby, be sure to look up, to see one of the most beautifully painted ceilings outside Rome.

The best way to get around San José

The best way to see San José is by foot. The city is arranged in a grid, with *calles* running from north to south and *avenidas* running from east to west.

However, if you do decide to walk your way around San José, we offer one caveat: Don't assume that pedestrians have the right of way. Costa Rica has the highest number of traffic fatalities per year of any country in the world. And when you step off a curb in San José, you'll understand why.

The best place to eat in San José

Bakea, *Avenida 11 and Calle 7, Casa 956; tel. +506 221-1051,* serves imaginative and eclectic dishes in a restored colonial mansion with unique features such as the "Japanese room" fitted with a glass floor.

The best beds in San José

The best place to stay in the city is the **Hotel Presidente**, *Central Ave Blvd, 7th Street; tel. +506 2010-0000; website: www.hotel-presidente.com,* where the service is first-rate and it's a good location for exploring the city.

Another good place to stay is the **Marriott**, *700 Metros Oeste De La Firestone; tel. +506 2298-0000; website: www.marriott.com,* set on a 30-acre coffee plantation.

SARCHI: THE BEST WOODEN CRAFTS

Sarchi, a small artisan town, filled with the shops of local craftsmen, exists solely as a tourist attraction. However, the wooden furniture here is so well made and so affordable that touristy Sarchi is worth the visit. Prices are often higher for gringos than for Ticos so, if possible, have your guide or hosts do your buying for you. Haggling is discouraged.

THE MOST DEVELOPED BEACH

Jaco, south of San José, is the most developed beach in the country. Jaco is especially popular with Canadians, who have invested heavily in development here. Construction is evident everywhere; new hotels, restaurants, souvenir shops, and surf shops are springing up every month.

THE COUNTRY'S ONLY JACUZZIS

The **Flamingo Marina Resort** is the only hotel in the country that boasts Jacuzzis in some of the suites. Other amenities include tennis courts, a swimming pool, and a poolside bar. A double room can cost as much as $135 a night during the high season. The hotel can be contacted at: *tel. +506 2290-1858; website: www.flamingomarina.com.*

THE BEST OF
CROTIA
AND
SLOVENIA

Croatia has a spectacular coastline with long sandy beaches, secret coves, and dramatic cliffs. Why battle the crowds and spend a fortune to lie on the beach in Greece, when you can enjoy the same Mediterranean sun and sea for half the price in Croatia? The nations that formerly comprised Yugoslavia, particularly Croatia, Slovenia, and Montenegro, offer stunning landscapes and a rich history.

DUBROVNIK: THE PEARL OF THE ADRIATIC

Dubrovnik, Croatia's medieval showpiece city, was once a city state that rivaled Venice. Dubrovnik's history goes back over 1,300 years. Although access to its walls initially involves lots of steps and costs the equivalent of $10, do make the effort. You won't get better views of the silken Adriatic, the densely wooded Dalmatian coastline, and the distant smudge of islands.

Even at street level, it's obvious why Dubrovnik calls itself "the Pearl of the Adriatic." The drawbridge over Pile Gate leads into a marble-paved street called Stradun. Laid out before you is a treasure house of bell towers, fountains, palaces, and monasteries. Steep alleyways hide cozy restaurants, bars, and hole-in-the-wall boutiques.

Vehicles are banned from the medieval core, mopeds and scooters included. There's none of that annoying put-put-put noise to compete with the clanging bells or strains of classical concertos spilling out of wooden church doors. We like this car-free environment—it's refreshing to sit at outdoor cafés without breathing gas fumes or worrying about risking life and limb whenever you step off a sidewalk.

It's remarkable that anything of Dubrovnik remains. For seven months in 1991 and 1992, it was bombarded by Yugoslavian army shelling. They wreaked immense damage, but under a UNESCO reconstruction plan the city has been meticulously restored.

Europe's second-oldest synagogue

Zudioska Ulica, *tel. +385 (20) 321-028*, near the Ploce Gate on the second floor of a Gothic building, has a 14th-century synagogue, the second-oldest in Europe, and the only Jewish museum in Croatia. In the early 14th century, large groups of Jews found sanctuary in Dubrovnik from persecution in Spain and Italy. Below the synagogue the museum displays historic memorabilia from the Nazi era: armbands and written orders stating that Jews were to identify their businesses.

Best sunset, best swimming

The prettiest place to spend the evening in Dubrovnik is the west end of the city, near the **Fortress of St. Ivan**. Young men often gather by the Porporela jetty below the fortress, where three huge iron spikes jut out from the stone wall. To prove their manhood, they swing from one spike to the other and finally drop into the sea. According to a saying in Dubrovnik, a boy has become a man when he "passes three spikes."

THE BEST OF THE DALMATION COAST

Stretching from Zadar to Dubrovnik is the **Dalmatian Coast**, where the people are loud and friendly. The best beaches along this stretch are between Sibenek and Split.

Split is Croatia's second largest population center and is also one of the oldest cities in the region, thought to be about 1,700 years old. Right in the center of Split you'll find the remains of **Diocletian's Palace**. Built as a retirement palace for the Roman Emperor Diocletian, this opulent palace and its surroundings were at times inhabited by a population as large as 8,000 to 10,000 people. Today the walls of the palace are home to shops, markets, and squares.

For a panoramic view of the city of Split and its harbor, climb **Marjan Hill**.

The most beautiful place along the Dalmatian Coast is the island of **Hvar**, *website: www.hvar.hr*, meaning sun. Listed as one of the world's most beautiful islands by renowned publications such as *Condé Nast*, *The New York Times* and Australia's *Travel & Leisure*, Hvar is surrounded by sapphire blue seas and gets 2,700 hours of sunshine per year. This is an idyll of hidden coves, dense woodlands, and a clutch of quaint towns and villages, and because it's a long, skinny island, you're never too far from the sea. The island is famous for its lavender and wildflowers.

Hvar attracts a good-looking young crowd, which keeps the nightlife lively. After a meal, **Carpe Diem**, *website: www.carpe-diem-hvar.com*, both a bar and a disco, is the place to be seen.

THE CROATIAN COASTLINE

Dubrovnik is certainly the best-known city on the Croatian coastline, but it is hardly the only city along this shore.

Porec, *website: www.to-porec.com,* farther down the peninsula, is the most pleasant town in the region. Located near spectacular fiords, it has narrow, cobblestone streets and a maze of red-roofed stone houses. Galleries and studios fill the medieval towers.

The area on the coast known as the Riviera is the place to stay. Spend your Riviera nights at **Colonia Iulia Parentium**, a popular beach-side club, and your Riviera days sunbathing in the nude at the giant nudist complex south of Porec called FKK Koversada, located at the entrance to the Lim Fiord. Day visitors can enjoy the beach for a few dollars (though groups of men might be barred entry).

The most picturesque town along the coast is **Rovinj**, *website: www.rovinj. info,* an artists' colony. This little town, which has a beautiful old church, is built into a hill. Outdoor cafés and restaurants line the harbor. **Monte Bar,** *tel. +385 (52) 830-203; website: www.monte.hr,* in the Old City serves good Istrian cuisine. The **Hotel Eden** has an informal casino and several discos.

The best place for peace and privacy is **Rab**, a lush town shaded in evergreens. Located south of the Istrian Peninsula, it has deserted coves where you can swim undisturbed. The residents are friendly. Spend an evening enjoying music by a live band on the terrace of the **Hotel Imperial**, *Palit bb; tel. +385 (51) 724-522; website: www.imperial.hr.*

SLOVENIA—THE MOST GLAMOROUS BEACHES

The **Slovenian Riviera**—the area from the Italian border to the end of the Istrian Peninsula's west coast—is the most glamorous stretch along the coast. It feels like Italy.

Izola and **Piran** are the most attractive resort towns along the Slovenian Riviera—both resemble old-style Italian resorts. **Portoroz**, a more modern resort, is the most expensive.

The world's best cream cakes

The Slovenian town of **Bled**—just 15 miles over the Austrian border—claims to have the best cream cakes in the world. Outside almost every café, you'll see a sign depicting the traditional *kremna rezina* (two layers of butter pastry sandwiching an oversized helping of vanilla-custard and cream). This yellow and white cube has become the symbol of the town.

The pastry chefs at **The Park Hotel** on Lake Bled, *website: www. hotel-park-bled.com,* who originally created this delicacy in 1953, are particularly renowned for their produce. From every floor in the hotel, at any time of day, the tantalizing smell of pastry wafts through the corridors. Over the last 50 years, more than eight million of these cream slices have been polished off by the hotel's guests. Many—Slovenians included—come here simply to eat cake.

We recommend the four-star **Park Hotel**, *tel. +386 (4) 579-1600; website: www.hotel-park-bled.com,* as the best place to stay in Bled. Pastries aside, the indoor swimming pool on the hotel's top floor offers magnificent views of the lake (frozen over in winter), snow-capped mountains, and the cliff-top fairytale-like Bled Castle. Rates start at $130 for a double room (buffet breakfast included). Discounts are available for children.

THE BEST OF THE
CZECH REPUBLIC

The **Czech Republic**, at the heart of Europe, has suffered the blows of almost every power to hit the Continent. As a result, it is rich in history and culture and filled with 40,000 monuments and 3,000 castles. Its capital, Prague, is one of the most beautiful cities in Eastern Europe, outdone only by Budapest.

This country is an outdoor-lover's paradise. The Tatra Mountains rise out of the plains to provide excellent skiing and hiking. The 1,000 lakes and ponds that dot the Czech Republic are chock-full of fish. And the deep, wildlife-filled forests attract campers, backpackers, and hunters.

THE CZECH REPUBLIC'S MOST BEAUTIFUL CITY—PRAGUE

Prague, described by Goethe as "the most precious stone crown of the world", is one of the most beautiful cities in Eastern Europe. The best way to see Prague is on foot. Start by climbing the 186 steps to the top of the Prasna Brana (**Powder Tower**) in Old Town. You'll have a panoramic view of the city from the top. A remnant of the old city fortifications, it was built in 1475 and rebuilt in the 19th century.

Old Town's best treasures
Stare Mesto (Old Town) dates to 1120. Celetna Street leads from the Powder Tower through the heart of Stare Mesto. It passes the **Tyl Theater**, where Mozart's

271

Don Giovanni premiered in 1787 and where scenes from the movie *Amadeus* were filmed. Then it skirts the **Church of Our Lady at Tyn**, once a center of early Protestantism. The church's twin spires dominate the skyline.

The street empties into **Staromestske namesti** (the Old Town Square). A medieval astronomical clock, **Orloj**, has kept time here since 1490. On the house, figures of Christ and the 12 apostles appear at two little windows above the clock face. Then the skeleton figure of Death, below, tolls the bell. Legend has it that after its completion, the designer was blinded to prevent him from ever creating such a clock again.

The **Novomestska radnice** (New Town Hall), built in 1378, stands above dungeons. Its 15th-century council chamber, decorated with the shields of Prague's medieval guilds, is still used. Novelist Franz Kafka (1883-1924) was born in the painted house next door to the town hall.

Betlemska kaple (Bethlehem Chapel), *Betlemske namesti 4; tel. +420 (224) 248-595; website: www.studenthostel.cz/betlemen.html,* is a reconstruction of the Gothic chapel where the reformer Jan Huss preached his revolutionary ideas from 1402 to 1415. Huss, who was burned at the stake for his views, became a symbol of freedom to the Czech people. There is a monument to Huss in the Old Town Square.

The most beautiful bridge

The most beautiful bridge in Eastern Europe connects Prague's Old Town and Mala Strana (Small Town). The **Charles Bridge**, built in 1357 by Charles IV, is lined with baroque statues. The bridge is especially lovely at night, when it is illuminated.

The best of Small Town

Small Town, despite its modest name, contains many of Prague's best sights. Much here is baroque, even though the town was founded in 1257. Among other things around town, there are many things to see in the **Maostranske namesti** (Small Town Square), which is dominated by **Kostel sv. Nikulase** (St. Nicholas Church), *Malostranské nam. 1,* a Jesuit church with a beautiful high dome, a belfry, a nave, and ceiling frescoes.

Nerudova ulice (Neruda Street) is the most beautiful street in Small Town. The baroque buildings are identified by signs (a red eagle, for example), as was the custom before numbered streets were introduced.

The magnificent **Valdstejnsky Palac** (Wallenstein Palace), *Valdstejnske namesti,* built in 1624 by Italian architects for the Hapsburg's Gen. Albrecht Wallenstein, now houses the Ministry of Culture. Concerts are held here in the summer. The palace is not open to the general public but the Wallenstein Garden, which borders the palace, is.

New Town bests

Prague's **New Town** is not really new by most standards—it was established in 1348. At its heart is **Vaclavske namesti** (King Wenceslas Square), marked by a statue of King Wenceslas and filled with shops, restaurants, and hotels.

The **Narodni muzeum** (National Museum), *Vaclavské nam. 68; tel. +420 (224) 497-111; website: www.nm.cz*, also on King Wenceslas Square, behind the statue of the king, displays neo-Renaissance paintings, artifacts from Czech history, anthropological and archeological collections, and a famous mineral collection. Closed every first Tuesday of the month.

Prague's oldest pub, **U Fleku**, *Kremencova 11; tel. +420 (224) 934-01920, website: www.ufleku.cz,* has been in existence since 1499. A huge place, it is filled with people singing and drinking its good dark beer. Each room in the old tavern has its own individual design: the Ancient Czech Hall, Academy Hall, Cabaret Hall, Large Lounge, Travelling-Case, Sausage, Vaclav's Room, and the Hop-garden

Karlovo namesti (Charles Square), the biggest square in New Town, is named for Charles IV, who planned the city. Located in this square is the **Novomestska radnice** (town hall), which was the government center from 1398 to 1784. Antonin Dvorak's mementos are housed in the **Dvorak Museum,** *Ke Karlovu 20; tel. +420 (224) 923-363*; *website: www.antonindvorak2004.cz,* near Charles Square. During the summer, Dvorak's music is played in the sculpture garden behind the 18th-century house.

The best-preserved ghetto

Jewish merchants settled in the area north of the old town hall as early as the ninth century. As the area grew, it became a center of Jewish culture. The well-preserved Prague Ghetto is now the **State Jewish Museum**.

The **Altneushul** (Old-New Synagogue), built in 13th-century Gothic style, is the oldest surviving synagogue in Europe. Beside it is the **Old Jewish Cemetery**, *Sikora 3, Josefov; tel. +420 (222) 317-191; website: www.jewishmuseum.cz/en/ acemetery.htm*, which holds 12,000 graves piled in layers. Tombs date from 1439 to 1787. If you lay a pebble on a grave here, it is said your dreams will come true.

The most visited tomb is that of the 16th-century scholar **Rabbi Loew**, who created the mythical, magical being called Golem. Today, visitors place scraps of paper with wishes on them in the crack in Loew's tomb. During World War II, Jews hid their valuables in the tomb's cracks before they were transported to concentration camps.

Franz Kafka is also buried in the cemetery. When the Nazis occupied Prague, they sent Kafka's three sisters to a concentration camp, where they were killed. And they destroyed most of Kafka's letters and manuscripts. However, his diaries were overlooked and are now housed among the treasures of the State Jewish Museum.

Klausen Synagogue, *U stareho hrbitova*, has a moving collection of drawings done by Jewish children in concentration camps. The names of 77,700 Czechoslovak Jews murdered by the Nazis are inscribed on the inside walls of the nearby **Pinkas Synagogue**.

Hradcany, the royal quarter

The **Hradcany Quarter** grew up around Hradcany (Prague Castle), the former residence of the kings of Bohemia and today the seat of government. A city within a city, it holds some of Prague's best treasures.

Three walled courtyards open into each other, progressing in architectural design from medieval to the 20th century. Off the first courtyard is the former chapel, which houses the treasury. Gold, crystal, and jewels can be found inside.

The Hradcany also houses the **National Gallery**, *website: www.ngprague. cz*, which is divided into three chronological sections. The earliest and best, in the former Convent of St. George, houses the state collection of Bohemian Gothic paintings and sculpture.

The third courtyard of the castle contains the imposing **Katedrala sv. Vita** (St. Vitus' Cathedral), the biggest in Prague, and the mausoleum of Czech kings, which holds the crown jewels (including the crown of St. Wenceslas, decorated with a thorn, reputedly from Christ's crown of thorns).

Behind the Hradcany is **Golden Lane**, *Zlata Ulicka*. It supposedly got its name from the story of alchemists living in the street during the reign of Rudolf II who tried to make not only the philosopher stone or the elixir of youth, but also to transform metals into gold. The beautiful cobblestone street, with its small houses and shops, brings the Middle Ages to life. The bookstore at Number 22 was the residence of Franz Kafka in 1917 (who lived here just after he wrote *The Trial* and before he wrote *The Castle*).

Nearby is **Strahovsky Klaster** (Strahov Monastery), *Strahovské nadvori 1; tel. +420 (233) 107-711; website: www.strahovskyklaster.cz*, which houses a museum of Czech literature and beautifully preserved ancient manuscripts and Bibles from all over the world. It is one of the most impressive libraries in Europe.

The **Theological Hall**, a vaulted gallery built in 1671, is lined with 17th-century bookshelves. Its white stucco ceilings are embellished with frescoes.

The **Loreta**, *Loretánské nám.7; tel. +420 (220) 516-740; website: www. loreta.cz*, another monastery, was founded in 1629 by Princess Lobkowitz. It centers around a replica of the Santa Casa in Loretta, Italy. Paired half-columns and relief panels add to its beauty. Its treasury contains saints' crowns and religious objects made of gold and precious stones. Be sure to take a look inside the Chapel of Our Lady of Sorrows which houses a painting of a crucified, bearded lady. This is St. Starosta, or Vilgefortis, who, after taking a vow of virginity, was forced to marry the king of Sicily. It's said that God, taking pity on the woman, gave her facial hair to make her undesirable, after which her pagan father had her crucified. Thus, Starosta went into history as the saint of unhappily married women.

The oldest fortress

Vysehrad Fortress, believed to have been founded in the ninth century, looms above Prague from sheer cliffs facing Hradcany. The Hussites destroyed much of it—apart from the walls, all that remains are an 11th-century rotunda and the Church of St. Peter and St. Paul. Many of the Czech Republic's greatest heroes and artists are buried in Vysehrad's cemetery, including Antonin Dvorak, Karel Capek, Jan Neruda, and Bedrich Smetana.

The world's best crystal

The Czech Republic is known for its fine crystal. **Moser**, *Kpt. Jaroše 46/19; tel. +420 (353) 416-242; website: www.moser-glass.com,* is the best place in Prague to shop for crystal. You can order through the store's catalog, which includes patterns preferred by the world's royalty.

The best restaurants

Bellevue, *Smetanovo Nabr.18; tel. +420 (775) 018-231; website: www. bellevuerestaurant.cz,* Prague's finest restaurant, boasts a great view of the castle, Charles Bridge, and the Vitava River. The cuisine, essentially French with some Czech specialties, is fresh and inventive. Try the duck liver *foie gras* terrine in a pistachio crust served with fresh strawberries, and port wine balsamic vinaigrette.

The **Zlata Praha** (Golden Prague), *Namesti Curieovych 43; tel. +420 (296) 631-111; website: www.zlatapraharestaurant.cz,* on the eighth floor of the Prague Inter-Continental, has a lovely view of the castle. National specialties—roast duck, sauerkraut, and dumplings—are well-prepared.

Kampa Park, *Na Kampe 8b; tel. +420 (296) 826-112; website: www. kampagroup.com,* offers a superb selection of fresh seafood and classic Czech wild game dishes. The restaurant has several dining areas including the winter garden—a heated conservatory overlooking a tributary of the river; and the summer roof terrace—overlooking Charles Bridge.

The best hotels

U Tri Pstrosu (Three Ostriches), *Drazickeho namesti 12; tel. +420 (257) 288-888; website: www.utripstrosu.cz,* is the most charming hotel in town. Located in a 16th-century house at the Small Town end of the Charles Bridge, it has an excellent restaurant. Reservations must be made several months in advance.

Pariz, *U Obecniho domu 1; tel. +420 (222) 195-195; website: www.hotel-pariz.cz,* is an art deco hotel. Its café and restaurant are decorated with blue mosaic tile.

Hotel InterContinental, *namesti Curievyeh 43-5; tel. +420 (296) 631-111; website: www.icprague.com,* is a quick walk from both Wenceslas Square and the Charles Bridge on the New Town side of the Vltava River.

THE BEST CASTLES

The **Czech Republic** boasts 3,000 castles, and most are worth seeing. **Hazmburk**, near Ceske Budejovice in the north, is surrounded by a 30-foot-high wall and guarded by two observation towers. (Peregrine falcons have taken up residence in one of the abandoned towers.) The ruins rise out of sheer rock and are surrounded by a valley filled with wheat fields and plum orchards. Be careful—no railings protect you from the 700-foot drop from the ruins to the valley below. You can take a day trip to this castle from Austria or Southern Germany.

Spilberk Castle, *website: www.spilberk.cz,* in Brno, Moravia, was built in 1287 to fend off invaders and was later used by the Hapsburgs to lock up their opponents. During World War II, the Nazis also used the dungeon as a prison. Take a look at the castle's hair-raising instruments of torture. The castle has a good restaurant that serves game dishes along with Moravian wines.

The little town of **Hluboka** has a gleaming white château that resembles a wedding cake, and has high, crenelated towers. It is a replica of Windsor Castle in England. Brussels tapestries, fine paintings, glassware, china, antique furniture, and medieval weapons can be seen here.

THE BEST SKIING IN EASTERN EUROPE

Slovakia has Eastern Europe's best ski area: **Stary Smokovec**, a national park in the High Tatras with jumps, slalom runs, and long cross-country trails. You won't find the crowds and frenzy of St. Moritz here. In addition to being the best place to ski, Stary Smokovec, which lies in the shadows of the peak called Slavkovsky, is the oldest community in the High Tatras. The first tourist buildings here were built in the late 18th century. The best hotel in town is the **Grand Hotel**, *tel. +421 (52) 4780-000; website: www.grandhotel.sk.*

THE BEST OF
ECUADOR

Ecuador is located between Colombia and Peru on the Pacific coast of South America, directly on the equator (*ecuador* is Spanish for *equator*.) It offers an endless summer, with year-round temperatures of between 65° F and 89° F.

The beauty of Ecuador and its people is stunning…the breathtaking mountain scenery of the Avenue of the Volcanoes…the remarkable detail of Otavalan textiles…the caught-this-minute freshness of the *ceviche* in Puerto López…the exuberance and color of a street festival in Cuenca…the creak of leather and clop of hooves as the Vilcabamba cowboys prance by on their *paso finos*. It's a place you should experience for yourself.

GUAYAQUIL— ECUADOR'S LARGEST CITY

Guayaquil, Ecuador's largest city, bustling with activity year-round, is also one of the country's major exporting ports. Ecuador is the largest exporter of bananas and the second-largest exporter of shrimp in the world.

Guayaquil's best hotel
The best hotel in Guayaquil is the **Hotel Oro Verde**, *9 de Octubre Street; tel. +593 (4) 232-7999; website: www.oroverdehotels.com.* The buffet breakfast will make ensure you are set up for a day of sightseeing.

The best markets

The city's major supermarkets, **Supermaxi** and **Mi Comisariato**, carry abundant fresh fruits, vegetables, fish, and seafood. Excellent fresh milk and European-style yogurt are available from the farmers' Co-op called **Civeria**. And Top Cream makes gourmet ice cream. To shop at either of the two supermarket chains, you must become a member. Simply purchase a *cupo* card, which also entitles you to a 10% discount.

The best day-trips

Within a couple of hours of Guayaquil are **Salinas** and **Playas**, two good weekend getaways. Playas was once a fishing village; today it is a popular beach resort. Salinas is more modern; it, too, is highly regarded by locals for it beaches. It also offers some of the best fishing in the country; for tuna, black marlin, and billfish.

Buses run from Guayaquil to both Playas and Salinas several times a day. **Cuenca**, the country's third-largest city, is four hours away by car. The narrow, winding streets here are filled with *artesinia* shops. And the Old Town area has churches that date from the 16th and 17th centuries.

THE BEST OF QUITO

Quito, the capital of Ecuador, has the feel of an 18th century colonial town; much of its colonial architecture remains. It has been called the "Florence of the Americas."

The best walking tour

Quito's old town center contains some of Latin America's oldest and most spectacular churches, including Church of La Compañía de Jesús, Church of San Francisco, and Basilica del Voto Nacional. This section of town used to be a risky place to visit, but much money and renovation has been devoted into turning Quito's most historic section into a safe, fun, and educational place to spend the day.

Despite its well-preserved historic center, Quito is also a thriving metropolis of 2.5 million people where you can find great hotels, restaurants, shopping, and entertainment.

The best almost-free lunch

Quito is home to the *almuerzito*, the "little lunch" restaurant where security guards and office staffers fill up on local dishes at prices that would make Ebenezer Scrooge dance a jig. There is one every few blocks.

One of the best is **Restaurant Milanesa**, near the corner of Andalusia and Salazar. Despite the name, there is nothing vaguely Milanese about the place. Six small tables and a tiny service counter completely fill the space, but it's clean and well lit. There is no menu—the waiter asks if you want the *almuerzo*, and you either say "yes" or ask for something specific. If they have it, they'll serve it.

An *almuerzo* of fresh pineapple juice, a large bowl of beef and vegetable soup, a plate of tripe and potato stew with a mound of rice, a fresh salad topped with avocado, and a tangerine for dessert comes to a grand total of $2.

The country's best crafts

About two hours north of central Quito is the town of **Otavalo**, situated among several Indian villages. The handiwork of these Indian craftsmen is respected around the world. A market is held every Saturday morning, where you can purchase the Indians' handiwork, including woven goods and gold jewelry.

Ecuador's highest mountain—and greatest adventure

The best adventure in Ecuador is a climb up the country's highest mountain, the 20,670-foot **Chimborazo volcano**. Start your journey on horseback in Pogyos. As you make your way up the mountain, you can make camp at Quebrada Colorado (Red Gorge); Abraspungo; Chuquipogyo, on the volcano's eastern slopes; Riobamba; the Valley of Totoras, on the mountain's southern slopes, and by the Edward Whymper Refuge, at the foot of the Thielman Glacier on the western slopes, where the British mountaineer began the first successful ascent of the Chimborazo volcano in 1880.

En route, your trek will take you across the Valley of Rubbish, where local Indians gather ice from the glacier, wrap it in hay, and then sell it in the mountain villages. Between the Whymper Refuge and the trek's end back at Pogyos, you follow part of the ancient Inca road through El Arenal (the Great Sand Pit), a vast, high desert.

Riobamba, one of the towns along your trek, is the center of an extensive Indian region. The Spanish established their first capital nearby, and Riobamba became the repository of an extraordinary collection of religious paintings, sculpture, and goldwork. (All of it was saved from the 1797 earthquake that destroyed most of the original city.) Riobamba is also famous for its Sunday market, where you can shop for ponchos, shawls, leather goods, and baskets.

The best spa

The little craft village of Cotacachi is 90 minutes north of Quito and an unlikely place to find the best spa in the country, but that's where you'll find **La Mirage Garden Hotel & Spa**, *tel. +593 (6) 2915-237; website: www.mirage.com.ec.* La Mirage is a five-star member of the Relais & Chateaux chain, designed in its every detail to eliminate the harsh sensations of everyday life and induce a state of restful, re-energizing calm. La Mirage's restaurant, bar, spa, and 23 private rooms and suites have been designed with an enlightened blend of European and indigenous architecture, art, and decoration.

THE BEST PLACE TO RELAX

Ecuador is an inexpensive, healthy, safe country; one of Latin America's most popular destinations, with a spring-like climate year-round; and a friendly, polite, laid-back population. But if you already live "away from it all" full-time, where do you go for a vacation? Ecuadorians go to **Baños**.

A four-hour bus ride from Quito, Baños is famous for its hot baths, fed by thermal springs from the base of active volcano Tungurahua (literally "little hell"). Although most visitors come here to relax, there's plenty to do.

You can hike Volcán Cotopaxi, or watch Tungurahua erupt nightly, whitewater raft on class III and IV rivers bike (you can easily cycle downhill to the jungle's edge and return to town by bus for $5), horse ride along the river, or take a rainforest expedition (two to seven days).

THE BEST AMAZON ADVENTURE

On the eastern slopes of Ecuador's Andes, mountains fall away to the vast jungles that form part of the watershed for the Amazon Basin, and the mighty rivers of Ecuador's eastern provinces are a great way to get to know this vast and important ecosystem. There is no better way to tour this amazing country than by a modern, fully equipped riverboat.

The Manatee Amazon Explorer (*website: www.manateeamazonexplorer.com*) plies the Napo River with stops at Cuyabeno Natural Reserve, Yasuni National Park (the largest national park in Ecuador), and Limoncocha Biological Reserve. From the Manatee Amazon Explorer you can canoe into some of the wildest and most abundant habitats on earth, visit hidden jungle Indian villages, and see amazing creatures found nowhere else on earth, then return to the all the modern comforts of home, including air conditioned cabins, Internet, and gourmet meals on board the riverboat.

THE BEST OF
FRANCE

They once said, or rather told us, every man has two countries; his own and France.

—Ernest Hemingway, 1934

If you asked a Frenchman to name the world's most civilized country, he would surely name his homeland. Few in the world would argue. And if you asked a Frenchman to describe himself and his countrymen, he surely would assert that a Frenchman is a wine expert; a gourmet; well-versed in art, history, and literature; dressed in the latest fashion; possessing of impeccable manners; and the world's best lover. Again, few would argue.

The best cuisine, wine, and cheeses in the world come from France. High fashion begins in Paris. And the world's greatest artists and writers are drawn to the land of the Gauls.

The greatest city in the world: Paris

Paris is not only the heart of France but also one of the world's most fascinating cities. Four-star restaurants, cozy cafés, wide boulevards, colorful outdoor markets, and fascinating museums, theaters, parks, squares, monuments, and churches are found in every section of this capital city. The best way to visit Paris is to stroll—past 17th-century houses, butcher shops with whole pigs hanging in the windows, ancient churches, high-fashion boutiques, street performers, art galleries, Africans selling wooden carvings, and Gypsy beggars. The streets are filled with the smells of roasting coffee, expensive perfume, Gauloise cigarettes, crêpes, roasting chestnuts, fresh bread, diesel fuel, and the damp breeze coming from the Seine.

When you get tired, stop in a café for a comforting cup of coffee and a chance to watch the people go by. You can sit for hours. Or buy a pastry at one of the hundreds of patisseries in Paris. Your heart will soar as you bite into the flaky, creamy, or fruit-filled delight.

Paris' most famous sight

The **Eiffel Tower** is the most famous (and unarguably most touristy) Paris landmark. The view from the top is remarkable—if you don't mind waiting in an endless line to get there. Built for the Universal Exposition of 1889, it faced demolition in 1909 but was saved when the French army discovered it could be used as a radio tower.

If you want to prove that you climbed the Eiffel Tower's 1,710 steps (you can cheat if you take the elevator), mail a letter from the mailbox at the top. Letters mailed here are stamped with a special Eiffel Tower postmark. At night the tower is lit up, creating a dazzling effect.

The city's most beautiful church

Notre Dame Cathedral is stunning, especially at sunset, when the splendid stained-glass rose window glows. Druids once worshipped on this site, and the Romans had a temple here before the Christians built Notre Dame in 1163. One of the finest examples of Gothic architecture, the cathedral was used for the coronation of Napoleon. (Napoleon scandalized the world by seizing the crown from Pope Pius VII and crowning himself.) Beneath the church are the foundations of third-century Roman structures. Take a look at the side portals of the cathedral. According to legend, they were carved by the devil after he bought the soul of ironsmith Biscornet. (The devil was unable to decorate the central portal, because that is the one the Host was carried through in procession.)

The world's best museum

The **Louvre** is the greatest museum in the world. It was originally a palace, constructed in the 12th century. The **Louvre** has, however, been a museum since the 18th century. A controversial glass pyramid (three stories high) by I.M. Pei now covers the new underground entrance in the main court that faces the Jardin des Tuileries. Parking arrangements, shops, cafés, and restaurants are underground.

In 1190, the Louvre was one of Philippe Auguste's fortresses. Charles V made it an official residence, and Catherine de Medici had the long gallery built. It was extended under Henry IV and Louis XIII, and the quadrangle was completed under Louis XIV. Today, the museum is divided into six extensive sections: paintings and drawings, Greek and Roman antiquities, Egyptian antiquities, Oriental antiquities, *objets d'art*, and sculpture.

The *Venus de Milo* and the *Mona Lisa* are just two of the 208,500 works of art in the Louvre. The number of masterpieces is overwhelming. So are the crowds, especially on weekends and during the summer. The best way to avoid the masses is to steer clear of the European paintings. Instead, view the collection of ancient art, located in the Cour Carree. Gigantic statues loom above you, the air is cool, and the sounds echo off the walls like long-lost voices of Greek and Egyptian gods. For information *tel. +33 (1) 4020-5760; website: www.louvre.fr*. The museum is open daily from 9 a.m. to 6 p.m. except Tuesdays and certain public holidays. Evening openings are until 9:45 p.m. on Wednesdays and Fridays and admission is free on the first Sunday of every month.

Paris' biggest attraction

Although it is less famous than the Eiffel Tower, the **Beaubourg Centre Pompidou**, in the 4th; *tel. +33 (1) 4478-1233; website: www.cnac-gp.fr*, is the biggest attraction in Paris. More than 25,000 visitors are drawn to this art center each day—twice as many as visit the Eiffel Tower and almost equal to the number who frequent Disneyland. The multicolored modern structure built of steel tubes, concrete, and glass houses the Musée National d'Art Moderne, which displays works by Picasso, Braque, Chagall, Leger, Brancusi, and Calder.

Officially called the Centre National d'Art et de Culture Georges Pompidou, but unofficially known as the Pompidou or the Beaubourg, this arts center also has a 40,000 volume (reference) library, a theater, a restaurant, and temporary exhibits. The library averages 11,000 visitors a day and up to 19,000 a day on weekends. Only 2,000 people are admitted at a time. Outside, street performers breathe fire, perform pantomime, and play guitars. Opening hours are daily (except Tuesdays and May 1st), from 11 a.m. to 10 p.m.

The most pricey café in Paris

Café de la Paix, *5 place de l'Opéra, 9th; tel. +33 (1) 4007-3636; website: www.cafedelapaix.fr*, is a famous corner café that is attached to the Intercontinental Grand Hotel. You can relax for hours over one espresso and people-watch, read, or chat with friends—but at a price. An espresso here will set you back $8.

The world's most beautiful cemetery

Père Lachaise Cemetery, located on the northeastern edge of Paris, is the most beautiful cemetery in the world. The cemetery is housed in a wooded park and is so large that the walkways are given names and maps are handed out at the entrance. The headstones are massive and highly crafted. Many famous people rest there today, including Chopin, Edith Piaf, and the colorful gravestone of Oscar Wilde covered with rouge lipstick marks and letters from admirers is a definite must-see. But the most visited grave is that of rock star Jim Morrison.

Four favorite sights in Paris

Sacré-Coeur, a glowing white Byzantine-style church on a hill in Montmartre, can be seen from almost anywhere in Paris. On summer evenings, a cool breeze wafts across the hill. The church was begun in 1876 to celebrate the end of the Franco-Prussian War. It was completed in 1910. Its interior is decorated with mosaics and stained glass. Nearby is a hokey but entertaining pseudo-artist's quarter.

    La Sainte Chapelle, located in the Palais de Justice on the boulevard du Palais, was built by St. Louis to contain the Crown of Thorns, which he purchased from the Venetians in 1238. (The Crown of Thorns was moved to Notre Dame during the French Revolution.) The Gothic chapel has 15 brilliantly colored stained-glass windows and a graceful 247-foot spire. The stained-glass windows are the oldest in Paris and among the most vivid.

    The Conciergerie, around Sainte Chapelle, is where Marie Antoinette spent her last days before facing the guillotine. It is also where 1,200 less-famous prisoners were held. This fascinating place has dark, dank dungeons. The conciergerie was built by Philip the Fair in the 14th century and contains three Gothic halls in addition to the prisons.

    St.-Germain-des-Prés is the oldest church in Paris, begun in A.D. 558 "in the fields" outside the walls of Paris. The steeple and tower date from 1014, when the monastery was rebuilt after attacks by the Vikings. Enlarged in the 12th century, it was once self-sufficient, housing its own bakers, butchers, law courts, and defense force. All that exists of this today, aside from the church, are street names referring to parts of the ancient abbey. The abbey precincts now form a quarter of small hotels, antique shops, bookstores, publishing houses, and l'Ecole des Beaux-Arts.

The eight best museums in Paris

Musée des Arts de la Mode, *107 rue de Rivoli, 1st*; *tel. +33 (1) 4455-5750*, is the most entertaining museum in Paris. The city that has set fashion for 300 years is an appropriate setting for this institution, which displays the clothing of 19th-century chambermaids as well as 20th-century celebrities.

Musée Carnavalet, *23 rue de Sevigné, 3rd*; *tel. +33 (1) 4459-5858*; *website: www.carnavalet.paris.fr*, is the most Parisian of the city's museums. Located in the Renaissance mansion in the Marais district, Carnavelet covers the turbulent history of the city and its people from the 16th to the 19th centuries.

Musée Marmottan-Monet, *2 rue Louis Boilly, 16th*; *tel. +33 (1) 4496-5033, website: www.marmottan.com,* has the most significant collection of Monet paintings in Europe. Most of the works were painted at Monet's Normandy home in Giverny. This small, private museum near the Bois de Boulogne is hidden away in what appears to be a mundane residence. Inside, it boasts 65 paintings by Monet, the Wildenstein collection of medieval illuminated manuscripts, and Renaissance and Empire works. It is open on Tuesdays, when other museums are closed.

Musée d'Orsay, *62 rue Lille, 7th; tel. +33 (1) 4049-4814; website: www. musee-orsay.fr,* located in the renovated Orsay train station, is the newest museum in Paris. This 19th-century museum houses many Impressionist paintings once displayed at the Jeu de Paume. The enormous vaulted glass ceiling gives a 19th-century industrial atmosphere. The exhibits include 1,500 sculptures, 2,300 paintings, 1,100 *objets d'art*, 13,000 photographs, and works by Dégas, Manet, and Rousseau.

The Picasso Museum, *5 rue de Thorigny, 3rd; tel. +33 (1) 4271-2521*; *website: www.musee-picasso.fr,* in the Marais, is the best place to study Picasso. It contains an intelligent selection of the artist's work and provides a complete, carefully documented and illustrated biography. The collection charts Picasso's artistic development through the rooms of a magnificent 17th-century mansion, the Hôtel Salé.

Musée Rodin, *77 rue de Varenne, 7th; tel. +33 (1) 4418-6110*; *website: www.musee-rodin.fr,* is where the best of Rodin's work is kept. This one-man museum is housed in an imposing 18th-century residence, the Hôtel Biron, where Rodin worked and lived toward the end of his life. He presented his art as payment for rent.

Musée de Thermes (Roman baths) and the **Hôtel de Cluny**, *6 place Paul Painleve, 5th; tel. +33 (1) 5373-7800,* is the most beautiful museum in Paris. A combination of second-century Gallo-Roman remains and an 18th-century mansion, it is set back from the busy corner of the St. Michel and St. Germain boulevards on the Left Bank. The **Hôtel de Cluny**, a Gothic house, once the Paris residence of the wealthy abbots of Cluny, houses one of the world's best collections of medieval art, including the exquisite unicorn tapestries. The lion represents chivalric nobility, the unicorn represents bourgeois nobility, and the lady may represent the Le Viste family from Lyons. The Roman baths were used in the third century as a vast public bathhouse.

Parc de la Villette/Cité des Sciences et Industries, *211, avenue Jean Jaurès, 19th; tel. +33 (1) 4003-7575; website: www.villette.com,* set in a once-upon-a-time run down district near the St Martin canal, this fabulous complex spread out over the largest green area in Paris now boasts the Cité de la Musique music conservatory and museum complex and the Cité des Sciences et de l'Industrie with its planetarium, aquarium and 3D cinema. The canal de l'Ourcq, running through the center of the park, has fountains, ornamental ponds, and waterfalls.

The three most colorful quarters

The greatest pleasures in Paris are its neighborhoods, which most tourists scarcely notice as they rush from sight to sight. Take time to wander through the streets of Paris. Absorb the smells, sounds, and sights. Our favorites for wandering are the **Marais**, the **Latin Quarter**, and **Montmartre**.

The Marais

The **Marais** is vaguely bounded by the rue Beaubourg to the west, the boulevard Beaumarchais to the east, the Seine to the south, and the rues Réaumur and Bretagne to the north. Within its confines are scores of fine old town houses, many built with paved forecourts and walled gardens.

You'll also find several museums; the National Archives; a half-dozen churches; the Jewish Quarter with its little bakeries, delis, and shops; and the Place des Vosges. Tour the Marais during the week, when it is possible to enter most of the buildings. Begin your walk at the St. Paul Metro station.

The Marais (which means marshland) was shunned until the 13th century, when the Knights Templars (a military-religious order) built its headquarters on the rue St. Antoine, a raised highway since Roman times. In the mid-14th century, Charles V built a palace in the area today bounded by the rues St. Antoine, St. Paul, and Petite-Muse. (Some say it was originally Pute-y-Muse, or "whore's muse".)

Place des Vosges was given its current shape in 1605, when Henri IV developed a royal square on the site of the former palace. Uniform houses were built, red-brick buildings trimmed with white stone and slate roofs. After the court moved to Versailles, the quarter began to lose its chic inhabitants, and its popularity. By the end of the French Revolution, it was virtually abandoned. The Marais remained in a declining state until 1962, when the government named the area a historic district. Since then, the Marais has been gradually restored to grandeur.

Don't miss the **Victor Hugo House**, *6 place des Vosges, 3rd,* or the **Museum of French History** at the **Hôtel de Soubise**, *60 rue des Francs-Bourgeois, 3rd*, which contains the National Archives.

Montmartre

Renoir was among the many 19th-century artists who lived in Montmartre and loved it. When traveling in Italy in 1881 he wrote, "I feel a little lost when away from Montmartre. I am longing for my familiar surroundings and think that even the ugliest girl is preferable to the most beautiful Italian." Renoir painted *La Balançoire* sitting in a large garden, actually an abandoned park, behind the house on rue Cortot.

Traces of the artists who loved the quarter can be found throughout Montmartre. A restaurant called **La Mère Catherine's**, looking out on the Place du Tertre, is little changed since it appeared in a painting by Utrillo.

The Bonne Franquette on the corner of rues St. Rustique and des Saules once had a tea garden where Van Gogh painted La Ginguette. If you walk down rue des Saules, you'll pass a tiny vineyard and come to a bar-cabaret called Le Lapin Agile. Here artists and writers, such as Picasso and Vlaminck, kicked up their heels.

The wrought iron gate at 11 avenue Junot marks the home of Utrillo's mother, the beautiful Suzanne Valadon. A painter herself and a model for Renoir, she appears among a group of voluptuous nudes in the painting *Les Grandes Baigneuses*.

The **Moulin de la Galette**, a windmill in Montmartre, has been painted almost as often as the Moulin Rouge. Renoir's painting of the Moulin is well-loved. Corot painted the mill also, and Van Gogh painted it twice. The windmill survives in an altered state—it has been restored and is an architectural feature above the roofs of a new development of apartments along avenue Junot and rue Lepic.

Picasso created cubism in his studio above the *bateau-lavoir* (laundry) that once existed next to Place Emile Goudeau. This tiny space, with a bench and a fountain, is on the downward slope toward the rue des Abbesses.

The most pleasant spot in Montmartre is the vineyard at the corner of rues St. Vincent and des Saules, near the Montmartre Museum. The vines still produce a wine called *picolo*. Every autumn, more than 300 liters of wine are produced and sold, and the proceeds are given to the old age home on the *butte* (hill).

Le Quartier Latin

The **Latin Quarter**, surrounding the boulevards St. Germain and St. Michel, is a bustling student quarter with twisting little streets, street performers and street vendors, restaurants, bookstores, and throngs of people.

The Roman conquerors of ancient Gaul settled here, on the Left Bank of the Seine, 50 years before the birth of Christ. They constructed thermal baths, an arena, and a theater. What is now rue St. Jacques was the Roman road to the south.

The **University of Paris** gave the area its ambience after the departure of the Romans. One of the oldest universities in the Western world, it was established at the beginning of the 12th century. (Its rivals were Bologna, Salerno, Oxford, Cambridge, and Leipzig.) The university was started by Pierre Abèlard, who left the cloisters of Notre Dame to give lessons away from the bishop's influence. He took with him the best students and, at the foot of the Montagne Sainte Geneviève, began new courses taught by liberal masters. Rich benefactors founded colleges to house the students and classrooms. Everyone spoke only Latin; hence, the area was named the Latin Quarter.

In 1792, following the revolution, the University of Paris was discontinued. It wasn't until 1806 that the Emperor Napoleon re-established the university. It exists today pretty much as it was set up then, which is one reason its students riot and strike.

The best bus lines for sightseeing

One of the easiest ways to sightsee in Paris is by bus. And the best buses for sight-seeing purposes are 24, 29, 30, 32, 38, 42, 47, 52, 58, 63, 69, 72, 73, 75, 82, 84, and 87. Use the buses for sightseeing during the off-hours, after 10 a.m. and before 5:30 p.m. In summer, when it remains light later, do your sightseeing from 7:30 p.m. until the buses stop running.

Remember, with your Carte Orange you can get off the bus, visit a museum, walk through a neighborhood, have lunch or coffee, and then get back on and finish your tour without paying any additional charges. For information on the city's bus system, ask at the Metro ticket windows.

The oddest corner of Paris

A place of great faith and pilgrimage is hidden at *140 rue du Bac, 7th*, next to the department store Bon Marché. Most of the inhabitants of Paris, including those who live in the neighborhood, do not know where the high, wooden door leads. But a million-and-a-half pilgrims visit a simple chapel at the back of the court every year.

It commemorates Catherine Laboure, a novice of the Sisters of St. Vincent-de-Paul.

In November 1830, Catherine swore she had a vision. In it she was instructed to have a medal cast of the image she had seen. She was told that those who wear the Miraculous Medal in faith would be blessed. The demand for the Miraculous Medal is so great that a slot machine has been installed in the chapel. When you put in your money, the machine dispenses a medal. An odd twist to the story behind the medal: When the body of Sister Laboure was exhumed in 1933, it was miraculously intact. Her eyes were still blue. Her limbs were still supple, as if she were sleeping. Dressed in the famous white habit of the Sisters of Charity, the body of the saint can be seen today in the rue du Bac chapel.

The most famous gallows

Paris bus number 75 takes you to an intriguing street called *la rue de la Grange-aux-Belles, 10th*. At number 53 stood the 13th-century **Gibet de Montfaucon**, one of the king's gallows. Its 16-yard arms served two purposes: to hang those condemned and to exhibit corpses (often beheaded) as examples. In 1954, while excavating for a garage at number 53, two beams believed to be from the gallows were found.

The most beautiful bridge

The **Pont Alexandre III** is the most beautiful bridge in Paris. It crosses the Seine near the Jardin des Tuileries and the Petit and Grand Palais. The view from the bridge is as beautiful as the bridge itself.

The world's finest *haute couture*

Paris is not only the city of fashion but also the city of *haute couture*. Everyone is fashion-conscious here, from eight-year-old schoolgirls to white-haired grandmothers. To make a splash, you must have an outfit specially made and custom-tailored. Many of the world's finest couturiers are found in Paris. (A couturier, as opposed to a mere dress designer, is one who presents collections of individually made clothes twice a year.) The world's celebrities come to them looking for flair and unique style. The top couturiers in Paris include Chanel, Christian Dior, Givenchy, Yves St. Laurent, Christian Lacroix, and Jean-Paul Gaultier.

The largest collection of secondhand scarves

The best collection of secondhand designer scarves can be found in a tiny shop in the picturesque but hard-to-find Passage Molière that runs between rues Quincampoix

291

and St. Martin in the 4th *arrondissement*, midway between the Pompidou Centre and the Forum des Halles. Thick silk scarves, mostly large squares, with hand-sewn edges, each a veritable work of art, sell for an average price of $200. Steep—unless you compare that price with what you'd pay for a Hermès or Dior scarf, new, which costs more than double that.

The best cures for homesickness

If you feel lonely in Paris and want to hear people speaking English, pop into **Shakes-peare & Co.,** *37 rue de la Bûcherie, 5th; website: www.shakespeareandcompany. com,* an English-language bookstore across the river from Notre Dame Cathedral founded by George Whitman, great-nephew of legendary American poet Walt Whitman. Writers frequent the bookstore. Notable literary figures such as Allen Ginsberg and Anais Nin have been known to have taken shelter in the bookshop in the past, paying their rent through their art. Poetry readings are held on Monday nights.

Also, the **American Library in Paris**, *10 rue du Général Camou, 7th; tel. +33 (1) 5359-1260*; *website: www.americanlibraryinparis.org,* is the oldest and largest English-language library in Europe, with more than 100,000 books and a collection of 350 periodicals. In 1928, Stephen Vincent Benét wrote *John Brown's Body* in the reading room. The library was also used by Gertrude Stein, Louis Bromfield, and Thornton Wilder. It has been an arena for debates by such formi-dable figures as John Kenneth Galbraith, Raymond Aron, and Charles Frankel. It survived and grew through the Great Depression, the Occupation during World War II, the Liberation of Paris in 1944, the street riots of 1968, and the energy crisis of the mid-1970s.

The best flea market

For over 100 years **Le Marché aux Puces de Clignancourt** (flea market) has been operating every Saturday to Monday in the village of St. Ouen, just outside Paris' 18th *arrondissement*. The largest market in Europe, it is a maze of little booths selling everything imaginable, from fine and expensive antiques to cheap, second-hand clothing. To get there, take the metro to Porte de Champerret; take bus 85 to Gare de Luxembourg-St. Denis; or take the metro to Porte de Clignan court.

The best time to browse (if you can manage to wake up early enough) is from 5 a.m. to 7:30 a.m. The buyers at this hour are professionals, looking for really good buys. They move fast, checking every item with an experienced eye and then buying without hesitation. Large amounts of cash are exchanged, and the goods are shipped to warehouses. From 7:30 a.m. until 7 p.m., Le Marché aux Puces is open officially for the 200,000 visitors it receives each week.

The market began in 1890, when sanitation laws first required that used clothing and bedding likely to contain vermin not be sold in the city. The ragpickers moved out to a muddy meadow appropriately called The Plain of the Ill-Seated. They were licensed to sell only to dealers and required to clean all materials before offering them for sale. Over the years, however, the market became fashionable and began drawing large crowds. Today, seven markets make up a large complex. There is less junk and more antiques (both good and fake).

Le Jules Vallès, a covered market, is the best place to find collector items—toys, postcards, medals, dolls, and old newspapers and magazines. **Le Marché Malik** stocks old clothes. The newest markets, **Le Marché Serpette** and **Le Marché Cambo**, specialize in art deco and period furniture, respectively.

The best covered markets

For the true flavor of Paris, visit one of the city's 12 covered markets, where you'll find wonderful displays of fresh fruits and vegetables, meats, cheeses, mushrooms, and furred and feathered game—hare, deer, boar, wild duck, pigeon, partridge, pheasant, and quail. The best remaining covered markets include:

• **Aligre**, *Place d'Aligre, 12th*
• **La Chapelle**, *10 rue de l'Olive, 18th*
• **Enfants Rouge**, *39 rue de Bretagne, 3rd*
• **St. Didier**, *corner of rues Mesnil and St. Didier, 16th*
• **St. Quentin**, *85 bis blvd. Magenta, 10th*
• **Ternes**, *rues Lebon, Faraday, and Torricelli, 17th*

The freshest food in Paris

The open-air markets sell Paris' freshest produce and meats and have the largest selection of cheeses. The supermarkets in Paris just don't compare in price or quality. Our favorite open-air market is on rue de Seine, near St. Germain-des-Pres. Other outstanding open-air markets in Paris include:

Boulevard de Charonne (*between rue de Charonne and rue A. Dumas*; Wednesday 7 a.m.-2:30 p.m. and Saturday, 7 a.m.-3 p.m.), **Bastille** (*blvd. Richard Lenoir between rue Amelot and rue Saint-Sabin*; Thursday and Sunday), **Pere Lachaise** (*blvd. de Menilmontant, between rues des Panoyaux and des Cendriers*; Tuesday and Friday, 7 a.m.-2:30 p.m.), **Monge** (*Place Monge*; Wednesday, Friday, and Sunday), **Raspail** (*boulevard Raspail* between *rue du Cherche-Midi and rue de Rennes*; Tuesday and Friday, 7 a.m.-2:30 p.m.), and **President Wilson** (*avenue Pres. Wilson* between *rue Debrousse and Place d'Iéna*; Wednesday and Saturday, 7 a.m.–2:30 p.m.).

The world's best pastry shops

The best pastries in the world are made in France, where layers of cake, as light as feathers, are molded together with airy, sweet buttercream and topped with curls of fine chocolate. Pastries in France are too beautiful (and too fattening) to eat, but too delicious not to.

Within France, the most tempting *pâtisseries*, or pastry shops, are in Paris, where they adorn every corner. There are 2,300 of them! One of the best known and most honored *pâtisseries* is **Dalloyau,** *website: www.dalloyau.fr*, which specializes in *marrons glacé* (candied chestnuts), *mogador* (layers of chocolate cake, chocolate mousse, and raspberry confiture), and sherbet cakes. Dalloyau shops can be found at *2 Place Edmond-Rostand; 99 rue Faubourg St. Honoré; 69 rue de la Convention; 5 boulevard Beaumarchais; 67 avenue Jean-Baptiste-Clément; 63 rue de Grenelle; 48-52 boulevard Haussmann;* and *16 rue Linois*.

The king of pastry is **Gaston Lenôtre**, who runs Lenôtre shops, throughout Paris. His 350 pastry chefs and cooks use at least 12 tons of butter and 300,000 fresh eggs each month. Lenôtre also has the best chocolates in Paris. He has shops at *44 rue du Bac, 5 rue du Havre, 44 rue d'Auteul*, and *49 avenue Victor Hugo*. For a full list of his Parisian boutiques visit, *website: www.lenotre.fr.*

The best ice cream in Paris

The most delicious ice cream in Paris is sold at **Berthillon**, *31 rue St. Louis-en-l'Ile, website: www.berthillon.fr*. The list of rich, homemade flavors such as toffee popcorn, rum and raisin, and surprisingly delicious brown bread ice-cream is long; so are the lines.

The loveliest gardens in Paris

The **Jardin du Luxembourg**, in the heart of the Left Bank, is an oasis for all ages. Children romp in the park's elaborate playground, watch Punch-and-Judy shows in the outdoor theater, and sail their boats in the fountains. Adults stroll through the formal gardens and read in the sun. During the summer, palm trees line the pebble paths. In winter, they are stored in the Château de Medicis, which also houses the French Senate.

The most elaborate fountain is the **Medicis Fountain**, at the end of a long pool. Scores of statues decorate the lawns. The best are those in the Delacroix group by Dalou. Find yourself a bench and relax. But, unless you are younger than six, don't touch the grass.

The formal **Tuileries Gardens**, which lead from the Louvre to the Orangerie, are also magnificent. Colorful flowers are planted in careful formations. A pleasant day can be spent rambling through the park, from one museum to the next, stopping for a picnic in between.

The best woodland escape

Every large city needs its escape valve—even Paris. The **Bois de Boulogne** is where Parisians let off steam. You can lie on the grass in this immense wooded park (a no-no almost everywhere else in Paris). And you can hike for hours around its 2,500 acres. The Bois de Boulogne offers horseback riding, biking, rowing, and even a zoo. However, don't stay here after dark unless you want to experience Paris' seamy side. When the sun sets, streetwalkers and transvestites work the area.

The deepest tour of Paris

The creepiest but perhaps most fascinating tour of Paris takes you beneath its streets. Eighty-two feet underground is a series of endlessly branching tunnels— 156 miles of them in all. They are corridors left over from when the limestone used in building the city was quarried. In 1785, these tunnels were turned into ossuaries for bones removed from graveyards. The bones of most of the victims of The Terror were transferred here. The southern part of the city beneath Montparnasse and the northern part of the city beneath Montmartre are honeycombed with the old tunnels. It's possible to go from one end of Paris to the other by way of these passages, called *les catacombes* by Parisians.

The section of the catacombs directly under the *Place Denfert-Rochereau, 14th; tel. +33 (1) 4322-4763; website: www.catacombes-de-paris.fr,* is open to the public. The entrance is on the southwest side of the square. Escorted tours of the catacombs (which are not for the fainthearted) are available from Tuesday to Friday 2 p.m. to 4 p.m. and weekends 9 a.m. to 11 a.m. and 2 p.m. to 4 p.m. (Bring a flashlight.)

The best cafés in Paris

Cafés are an institution in Paris. Parisians use them as living rooms. (Apartments in Paris are usually tiny.) All that is required is the purchase of one cup of coffee.

During the summer, tables are set outdoors. Customers soak in the sun while they watch passers-by. In the winter, cafés smell like good coffee and Gauloise cigarettes.

In the 19th century, cafés were gathering spots for artists. Modigliani, the flamboyant Italian painter, frequented the Café de la Rotonde on the boulevard Montparnasse, just around the corner from his *atelier* on the rue de la Grande Chaumière. He and writer Beatrice Hastings often lingered in the café smoking hashish and drinking absinthe (a potent alcohol that up until recently was illegal in France). He eventually died on the steps here. The Café de la Rotonde, with its red awnings, still cheerfully thrives despite its history.

Le Dôme, *108 boulevard Montparnasse, 14th arrondissement*; *tel. +33 (1) 4335-2581,* is decorated with old photos of bygone customers: Picasso, Bonnard, Dufy, Gauguin, and Modigliani. Paris cafés continue to draw celebrities. Many famous faces can be seen at **La Coupole**, *102 boulevard Montparnasse, 14th arrondissement*. This café was a favorite of Gauguin and his Javanese mistress.

Three of the most famous cafés in Paris are across the street from St. Germain-des-Prés Church on the boulevard St. Germain, 6th Métro stop: **Café de Flore**, **Les Deux Magots**, and **Brassérie Lipp**. All three of these cafés have attracted artists, writers, and celebrities for decades. Their notoriety, however, has made them crowded and expensive. Lipp, which is also a restaurant, has art deco décor and attracts the artistic elite. (British wine dealer Steven Spurrier is a regular.) Les Deux Magots is filled with tourists, but it is a good place to people-watch. The lively Flore was Picasso's favorite.

The hottest nightlife

You'll find plenty to do in Paris, regardless of the size of your pocketbook. You can stroll for free through the Latin Quarter or Beaubourg, where lively circles of spectators watch street performers. A beer in one of the little cafés won't cost much, and you can sit for hours watching the crowds. Or you can go all out and have dinner in a fine restaurant and then dance until the wee hours of the morning in a *boîte de nuit*.

The coolest clubs

Les Bains-Douches, *7 rue du Bourg-l'Abbé; tel. +33 (1) 4887-0180; website: www.lesbainsdouches.net,* is a super-stylish club that attracts the trendiest clientele and a large gay crowd. Located in an old public bathhouse, it has a small pool. Celebrities can be seen here from time to time.

In summer when Paris Plage (sand and palm trees are shipped into the banks of the Siene to create a "beach") takes over the city's quays it's hip to be afloat on **Le Batofar**, *opposite 11 Quai François Mauriac 13th; tel. +33 (1) 5360-1700; website: www.batofar.org,* a recently retired lighthouse boat constructed in 1957, which has a superb terrace overlooking the world's most romantic river and a dinky little dance floor where you can get on down till dawn.

The smoothest jazz joints

Le Petit Journal, *tel. +33 (1) 4321-5670,* is a place you can go to hear excellent jazz. This club has been around for years and has featured many famous jazz talents.

New Morning, *tel. +33 (1) 4523-5141,* is another hot jazz club. Live jazz groups from all over Europe and America perform here.

Le Slow Club, *tel. +33 (1) 4233-8430,* based in a cellar that used to be a banana-ripening warehouse, the club is a wonderful place to hear great New Orleans-style jazz under medieval-style vaulted ceilings. It has been around for a while and standards from the 1930s and 1940s are played here. This was an old favorite of jazz legend Miles Davis

The coziest *cave*

Caveau de la Huchette, *5 rue de la Huchette, 11th; tel. +33 (1) 4326-6505*, is a *cave* wine cellar—an ultra-Parisian spot to relax and enjoy good music and wine in an atmosphere that is warm and inviting.

The best cabarets

Paris cabarets can be a lot of fun and many include dinner and drinks with the show. The **Crazy Horse,** *tel. +33 (1) 4723-3232; website: www.lecrazyhorseparis.com,* is one of Paris' most wild and entertaining cabarets. It always puts on a great show, but the late show is best. The principal dancer is none other than cabaret celebrity, Dita Von Teese.

Cultural bests

Classical music and ballet can be found all over Paris, but the best performances are at the **Opera de Garnier**, *8 rue Scribe, 9th*; *tel. +33 (1) 7229-3535* and the **Opera de la Bastille**, *120 rue de Lyon, 12th; tel. +33 (1) 4001-1970; website: www.operadeparis.fr*. There are also many famous music halls around Paris, but if you can, catch a ballet or opera in these halls of perfection.

The cheapest fun

Churches in the Latin Quarter and the Marais offer free concerts. Listen for music wafting out of St. Severin or St. Julien le Pauvre around 8 p.m. The Centre Pompidou also puts on free programs: one night a ballet company, another evening a short play. Street entertainers attract crowds on the plaza outside the building. St. Merry offers concerts Saturday nights and Sunday afternoons. Contribute at the entrance.

The best restaurant in Paris

La Tour d'Argent, *15-17 quai Tournelle, 5th*; *tel. +33 (1) 4354-2331; website: www.latourdargent.com,* has pleased the palate of many a dignitary. Henry III learned to eat with a fork here. Notre Dame is the backdrop of La Tour, which opened 400 years ago. A 120,000-bottle wine cellar graces this time-honored institution, where 150 employees serve 95 people. Until the beginning of this century, the place was modest, with sawdust on its wooden floors. Frederic Delair brought it to fame in 1890, when he began serving *canard pressé*—the duck speciality of the house and still the finest dish on the menu. Each duck was engraved with a serial number. If the *maître d'hôtel* feels you are ordering something you aren't familiar with, he will explain the dish very carefully and recommend gently that you try something else.

First-class restaurants

Le Carré des Feuillants, *14 rue de Castiglione, 1st*; *tel. +33 (1) 4286-8282*; *website: www.carredesfeuillants.fr,* serves the cuisine of southwest France with a generous dash of creativity. Chef Stephane Haissant's delicacies include fillets of pigeon with a mousse of celery.

L'Atelier de Joel Robuchon, *133 avenue Champs-Elyseés; tel. +33 (1) 4723-7575; website: www.joel-robuchon.com,* is a superb restaurant, the reputation of which is due to the finesse of chef Joel Robuchon. Enjoy the truffles, *foie gras*, and seafood.

Alain Ducasse au Plaza Athénée, *Hotel Plaza Athénée, 27 avenue Montaigne, 8th; tel. +33 (1) 5367-6500; website: www.alain-ducasse.com.* Absolutely sumptuous, this dining room is one of Paris' best, thanks to world-famous chef M. Ducasse, whose dishes, such as lobster in spiced wine, always impress.

Taillevent, *15 rue Lamennais, 8th; tel. +33 (1) 4495-1501; website: www. taillevent.com.* Stolidly traditional, this bastion of French cuisine, with a legendary wine list, is the choice of some of the world's most fussy palates. Truffles, frogs' legs, and exquisite soufflés thrill and satisfy.

Macéo, *15 rue des Petits-Champs, 1st; tel. +33 (1) 4297-5385; website: www.maceorestaurant.com,* is a place where everything is good and the service matches the food.

Chez Pauline, *5 rue Villedo, 1st; tel. +33 (1) 4296-2070,* was handed down from father to son, and it has consistently remained first-class. It is one of the few restaurants in France where you can have a soup called Billy By that is made with cream and mussels.

Le Pré Verre, *8, rue Thénard; tel. +33 (1) 4354-5947; website: www.lepreverre.com,* spicy and exciting cuisine from the Delacourcelle brothers in this hip eatery in the heart of the student quarter.

Bistro de l'Oulette, *38 rue des Tournelles, 4th; tel. +33 (1) 4271-4333; website: www.l-oulette.com/baracane.php.* A brand new look for this recently rejuvenated *petit bistro* serving great traditional cuisine from southwest France, in a cosy setting

The fishiest restaurant
Charlot, *12, Place de Clichy, 9th; tel. +33 (1) 5320-4800; website: www.charlot-paris.com,* is known locally as "the king of shellfish" this fishy eatery is the best, but by no means the cheapest, place for good fresh fish in the city. It is closed from mid-July to mid-August.

The best meals for the money
Ambassade d'Auvergne, *22 rue du Grenier St. Lazare, 3rd; tel. +33 (1) 4272-3122; website: www.ambassade-auvergne.com,* serves grilled sausages with aligot (potato purée with Laguiole cheese) and more of the most delicious Auvergnat food in town. It is open Sundays and during the week until 10:30 p.m.

Bofinger, *5-7 rue de la Bastille, 4th; tel. +33 (1) 4272-8782; website: www.bofingerparis.com,* is one of Paris' oldest brasseries and is beautiful to boot. For a midnight seafood craving, this is definitely the place.

Le Pamphlet, *38 rue Debelleyme, 3rd; tel. +33 (1) 4272-3924,* unbeatable value, fresh market menus served with superb wines characterize this recently refurbished restaurant. Try the *prix-fixe* menu for a wonderful value.

Paris' best bistros
The best bistros in Paris are not expensive, and paying more typically means you dine with more tourists than Parisians…not that you enjoy a better meal.

Le Bistrot du 7ème, *56 boulevard de la Tour-Maubourg; tel. +33 (1) 4551-9308,* in the elegant 7th has shockingly reasonable prices, white cloth table linens, pleasant and professional service, and perfectly prepared traditional dishes.

Le Bistrot d'Henri, *16 Rue Princesse 6th; tel. +33 (1) 4633-5112,* on a tiny but important street in the lively Odéon district, also home to the English-language Village Voice bookstore, is always teeming with diners at its (only) 32 seats. For a main course, try the *Fameux poulet de Challans à la crème,* which should be famous if it isn't already (it's the best free-range chicken in France).

La Marlotte, *rue du Cherche Midi, 6th; tel. +33 (1) 4548-8679; website: www.lamarlotte.com,* has terracotta-colored walls and wood beams. A defender of traditional French cooking, La Marmotte attracts politicians, writers, philosophers, and journalists.

Paris' best-kept secret

Le Train Bleu, *20 bd Diderot, 12th; tel. +33 (1) 4343-0906; website: www. le-train-bleu.com,* is one of Paris' best-kept secrets. Most Parisians have no idea it exists. It's a restaurant on the first floor of the Gare de Lyon train station that is as much museum and art gallery as restaurant. The food, service, and ambience are excellent. The place is over 100 years old, built for the Paris Exhibition of 1900. The artwork on the ceilings is so remarkable it's no surprise that Coco Chanel, Brigitte Bardot, Salvador Dali, and many others have been regulars here.

The world's best cigar shop

No, it's not in Cuba—the world's best (and least expensive) cigar shop happens to be in Paris. The head bartender at the Ritz Hemingway Bar buys cigars for his customers at **Le Lotus,** *4 rue de L'Arcade, 8th; tel. +33 (1) 4265-3536.* The shop has a small American clientele who love it for its quality Havanas. Brits cross the Channel to stock up at Le Lotus at comparatively lower prices. For example, at Le Lotus, a cabinet (box in cigar lingo) of 25 Bolivar Belicosos os Finos is 275 euro ($380). A Bolivar in a cedar-lined tube, which keeps about three months, is 15 euro ($21).

Due to its good working relationship with three specialty importers, it has a fabulous range of new cigars—130 different brands for a total of 10,000 in stock. The owner, Regis Colinet, will tell you which brands are pulling and which brands are duds. He says that cigars aren't just for after dinner anymore. The chic thing in Paris these days is to enjoy the smoke during a meal specially made to marry the flavors of the food, the wine, and the cigar.

The best hotels in Paris

Hôtel des Deux Iles, *59 rue St. Louis-en-l'Ile, 4th*; *tel. +33 (1) 4326-1335*; *website: www.deuxiles-paris-hotel.com*, is in a 17th-century building on the other island from the one on which Notre Dame is located. The entrance hall is filled with greenery and flowers, and the popular bar has a fireplace. Rooms are small.

L'Hôtel, *13 rue des Beaux Arts, 6th; tel. +33 (1) 4441-9900; website: www.l-hotel.com*, voted "best urban hotel in the world 2008" by *Harper's Bazaar*, this opulent and stylish hotel is filled with fresh flowers and antiques. The walls are covered with fabric, and the baths are marble. A winding staircase, marble columns, and stone floors make the entrance rather grand. Oscar Wilde died in one of the rooms.

Melia Royal Alma, *35 rue Goujon, 8th; tel. +33 (1) 5393-6300; website: www.solmelia.com*, near the place d'Alma and across the street from the Seine is pleasant. This small, modern hotel has bedrooms with private bathrooms. Prices are reasonable, considering the quiet, elegant neighborhood.

The Ritz, *15 place Vendôme, 1st; tel. +33 (1) 4316-3030; website: www.ritzparis.com*, is elegant and caters to the comfort of its clients, which include many celebrities. The deluxe rooms feature Persian and Chinese carpets, but this luxury is reflected in the price—it is terribly expensive to stay at the Ritz.

Plaza-Athénée, *25 ave. Montaigne, 8th*; *tel. +33 (1) 5367-6665; website: www.plaza-athenee-paris.com*, though not as opulent as the Ritz, is more appealing. It has a 1930s ambience that is more attractive than the other super-deluxe establishments in Paris.

Hôtel Costes, *239 rue St-Honoré, 1st; tel. +33 (1) 4244-5000; website: www.hotelcostes.com*, caters to the high-fashion crowd and celebrity guests, and its lavish interiors and gorgeous employees make you feel like you're in the limelight too (and you'll pay dearly for the pleasure).

The best hotels for the price

Hotel d'Angleterre, *44 rue Jacob, 6th; tel. +33 (1) 4260-3472; website: www.hotel-dangleterre.com*, is a beautiful and inexpensive hotel with a lovely garden and its own classic saloon with a grand piano.

Esmeralda, *4 rue St. Julien le Pauvre, 5th; tel. +33 (1) 4354-1920; website: www.hotel-esmeralda.fr*, is popular with the theater crowd and has charming rooms with views of Notre Dame and St. Julien-le-Pauvre Park.

Best value bed for the night

A private, immaculately clean single room, with shower en suite—in the heart of Paris' Montmartre arts district—can be had for as little as $15 per night.

The **Ephrem** guesthouse, *tel. +33 (1) 5341-8909; e-mail: adoremus@ sacre-cour-montmatre.com; website: www.sacre-coeur-montmartre.com*, which is adjacent to the Basilica on Rue Du Chevalier-dela-Barre, is a 55-room dormitory. Rooms are spartanly furnished, but comfortable and bigger than many single hotel rooms. Rooms are available to those who wish to take part in perpetual adoration and to groups on retreat, or individuals wanting time to reflect spiritually. It's up to you whether to attend mass or simply meditate peacefully as you stroll the streets in the artists' district and gaze out upon panoramic views of Paris. Singles, both men and women, and families are welcome. Most stays are three days or less.

The guesthouse is no Holiday Inn, but it's not a hostel either. If you're new to staying in convents and monasteries, don't worry, no one is monitoring your movements. However, guests are expected to adhere to a curfew. Basilica doors are locked at 9 p.m. All in all, small inconveniences for such an affordable and unique experience.

If you're making reservations, confirm everything precisely, in writing and well ahead of time. E-mail replies take nearly a week.

The world's best subway

The Paris subway, or Metro, will take you anywhere you need to go quickly, efficiently, and cheaply. You can pick up a map of the Metro system at any station and all trains are labeled with the destinations. A single ticket will take you anywhere in the city you want to go with as many transfers as you wish.

The world's most beautiful château

One side trip from Paris that you must make time for is to **Versailles**, the most magnificent of all French châteaux. The palace was created by Louis XIV and has formal gardens that cover 250 acres of land. The grounds also include 600 fountains. The king moved here to get away from the stresses of city life and during his reign 6,000 people lived in the elaborate palace. Be sure to see the Hall of Mirrors, the royal apartments, and the chapel. Le Grand Trianon and le Petit Trianon were smaller retreats for the royal family. Le Hameau was Marie Antoinette's little farm, where she played at being a shepherdess when she tired of the rigors of palace life.

Versailles' greatest rival

The second-best château in France is **Vaux-le-Vicomte**, an hour south of Paris. At the entrance are two enormous stone gods. Beyond the iron gates are pavilions, gardens, terraces, cascades, a statuary, and a forest. Across the moat and at the top of two grand staircases is the château itself, which has five floors and 80 rooms, 27 open to the public.

Nicholas Fouquet, superintendent of France's treasury and protégé of Cardinal Mazarin, dreamed up the château. He bought 12,000 acres and commissioned three artists to design the building, which was completed in 1661. Le Vau is responsible for the architecture, Le Brun for the paintings, and Le Notre for the gardens.

To celebrate the completion of the château, Fouquet made the mistake of inviting Louis XIV to feast there. Three weeks after the visit, the king had Fouquet arrested for embezzlement and imprisoned for life.

The most beautiful cathedral in France

Chartres has the most beautiful cathedral in France—and one of the finest in the world. It once drew thousands of pilgrims, who came to worship at the shrine of the Virgin. Located about 50 miles southwest of Paris, it is known for its stained-glass windows, which date from the 12th and 13th centuries. The present cathedral is the sixth built on the site.

The best French champagne

The best champagne can be found near the cathedral town of **Rheims**, within the Champagne province. The champagne cellars are often found in subterranean caves up to 13 miles long. Two of the best are **Epernay**, about 13 miles south of Rheims on N51, and **Montagne de Rheims**, near the city.

The finest church in the world

The great Gothic cathedral at **Amiens**, north of Paris, was designated the finest religious edifice in the world by UNESCO. For more information, see; *website: www.sacred-destinations.com/france/amiens-cathedral.*

Europe's most expensive theme park

Disneyland Paris opened in April 1992, is complete with roller coasters, castles, and miniature replicas of areas around the world. It is exactly like the other Disneys except for the prices. A one-day pass is 57 euro ($76) for adults and 51 euro ($68) for children under 12. Go to *www.disneylandparis.com* for more information.

LYONS: THE GASTRONOMIC CAPITAL

Although Parisians may disagree, Lyonnais are sure their city is the gastronomic capital of the world.

Sampling the fare

World-famous chef **Paul Bocuse's** restaurant, *tel. +33 (4) 7242-9090; website: www.bocuse.fr,* is excellent. It is located seven miles outside Lyons. Try the superb Bresse chicken and the Elysées soup, served with a flaky pastry cover.

Léon de Lyons, *3 rue Plény, 69001; tel. +33 (4) 7210-1112; website: www. bistrotsdecuisiniers.com/fr/leon-de-lyon,* serves the best Lyonnais specialties. If you are adventurous, try the *Lyonnaiseries en salade* (calf's foot, lamb's trotters, cervelas sausage, brawn, blood pudding, and lentil salad). Chef Lancombe's own inventions are also delicious. Try his *pigeonneau cuit en croûte de sel* (squab cooked in salt).

Nicolas Le Bec, *14 rue Grolée; tel. +33 (4) 7842-1535; website: www. nicolaslebec.com,* the former Maestro of the Cour des Loges, dazzles with imaginative dishes like a grilled slab of *foie gras* in hibiscus juice, with kumquat marmalade and baby spinach, served in a warm, contemporary setting.

Les Trois Dômes, *20 quai Gailleton; tel. +33 (4) 7241-2097; website: www. les-3-domes.com,* is situated on the 8th floor of the Sofitel hotel with gorgeous views of the city. Chef Alain Desvilles serves spectacular all-inclusive menus combining cuisine and wine, such as crab and avocado mille-feuille sprinkled with pink ginger perfumed olive oil and accompanied by a Schlumberger riesling.

The best chocolates

Before you leave Lyons, you have to stop and sample the best chocolates in the world at **Maurice Bernachon**, *42 cours Franklin-Roosevelt, 69006; tel. +33 (4) 7824-3798; website: www.bernachon.com.* Some are sprinkled with gold leaf.

Lyons' finest hotel

The **La Cour des Loges**, *2,4,6,8 rue du Boeuf; tel. +33 (4) 7277-4444; website: www.courdesloges.com,* is a Renaissance palace in the old part of Lyons that was renovated and turned into a modern hotel. It is decorated in an interesting blend of medieval, Renaissance, and modern décor. The interior courtyard, circular stairways, beamed ceilings, and terraced gardens add charm.

PEAK EXPERIENCES: THE ALPS

The Alps are the most beautiful mountains in the world. Like the Rockies, they are snow-capped and dramatically jagged. But unlike their American counterparts, their valleys and slopes are bedecked with picturesque villages. From the peaks, you can look miles down into valleys where tiny church spires are surrounded by gingerbread houses. Stone shepherds' huts offer shelter in the trees. And luxurious hotels pamper tired hikers and skiers.

While the Alps are famous for their tremendous ski slopes, you don't have to be a skier to enjoy them. They are gorgeous year-round. Wild flowers cover the mountains in the spring and summer, and during the fall the leaves turn bright yellow. Hikers, campers, fishermen, and hunters ramble the Alpine peaks long after the ski slopes have closed for the summer.

The prettiest ski resort

Les Contamines-Montjoies is one of the prettiest ski towns in the Alps, and one of the least known. This small ski area is set in a high wooded valley, not far from Chamonix. It has 62 miles of slopes and 15 miles of cross-country ski trails.

The best place to stay is **Le Gai Soleil**, *tel. +33 (4) 5047-0294; website: www.gaisoleil.com/etea.htm.* In the pretty hamlet of Les Contamines-Monjoies at the foot of famous Mont Blanc. It has a cozy atmosphere, which meshes well with the wonderful accommodation.

BRITTANY: THE MOST BEAUTIFUL COASTLINE

Brittany (Bretagne), in the west, has 600 miles of the most ruggedly beautiful coastline in France. Along it are sheltered coves, fishing villages, wide deserted beaches, dramatic cliffs, smart resorts, and lush farmland. The stone-built villages are rich in history.

The Quiberon Peninsula's rocks, caves, and reefs make its coast the most dramatic in the province. Walk to the Cote Sauvage (Wild Coast) from one end to the other, stopping at the strange rock formations: Grottes du Taureau (Bull's Cave), la Fenêtre (Window), and La Vieille (Old Woman). East and south of the coast are wide beaches and fishing ports.

Brittany's greatest sight

St. Malo, a fortified island-city in Brittany that dates back to the 12th century, was bombed during WWII, but has been restored. Visit the castle (which is where you can catch the best view of St. Malo) and the Quic-en- Groigne waxworks museum.

The best seafood and crèpes

Brittany has the most delicious seafood in France—sole, crabs, shrimp, oysters, and mussels served with a bottle of muscadet, the dry white wine of Brittany. Also step into a crèperie and order buckweat crèpes served with potent hard cider.

One of the best restaurants in the region is **Le Relais Gourmand O. Roellinger** in the charming fishing town of Cancale, *1 rue Duguesclin; tel. +33 (2) 9989-6476*. Mr. Roellinger's original, spiced cuisine is fresh from the sea and the garden. Favorites are John Dory steamed in seaweed and coconut milk and wonderful desserts like the assorted spiced chocolates and cookies.

NORMANDY—THE RIVIERA'S COLDEST RIVAL

Normandy's world-famous resorts—Deauville, Trouville, and Cabourg—are the Riviera's coldest rivals. The Gulf Stream warms these elegant towns along the Cherbourg Peninsula in summer. And they are far less crowded than their southern counterparts.

Deauville has great shopping (including branches of the leading Paris jewelers and designers), elegant hotels and restaurants, and a casino. A boardwalk runs the length of the beach.

A peaceful contrast is Honfleur, a small fishing port, where at sunset fishermen bring in the day's catch. A cozy and refined place to stay is **Les Maison de Léa**, *Place Sainte Catherine; tel. +33 (2) 3114-4949; website: www.lesmaisonsdelea. com*, in the heart of the old town.

Incomparable Mont St. Michel

Mont St. Michel is an eighth-century abbey that sits atop cliffs rising from a flat island. It is said to have been built at the command of the Archangel Michael, who appeared on the spot. Guides will show you an indentation in the rock that is supposedly the archangel's footprint. The abbey contains the silver shrine of the archangel, who is supposed to have fought the devil hand-to-hand on a nearby hill. View the Escalier de Dentelle (Lacework Stairway), the Gothic buildings, and the cloister.

Mére Poulard, *Grand Rue, tel. +33 (2) 3389-3212; website: www. mere-poulard.fr,* has an outdoor terrace where you can dine during the tourist season and a stone fireplace where you can huddle in winter. Try the dessert omelet.

CHÂTEAU COUNTRY—THE LOIRE

The **Loire Valley**, Southwest of Paris, puts Disneyland to shame. Known as Château Country, the region is filled with turreted castles. The valley's mild climate, rolling green hills, and lush pastureland attracted French nobility centuries ago. Today these châteaux, once fortresses designed to ward off invaders, are enjoyed by visitors from around the world.

The most beautiful Loire château

Chenonceau is considered the most beautiful château in the Loire Valley. Straddling the Cher River, it was embellished by eight women over a period of 450 years and has been dubbed "The Castle Women Built." It is approached by a promenade of tall trees. The interior is furnished with tapestries, statues, and portraits. The château was built between 1513 and 1521 under the supervision of Catherine Briconnet, a wealthy 21-year-old heiress. After Catherine's death, Chenonceau became the property of Henri II, who presented the castle to his mistress, Diane de Poitiers. She planted fine gardens and had a five-arch bridge built to the far bank of the Cher, where she liked to go hunting. When King Henri died, his wife, Catherine de Medici, forced her rival out of Chenonceau. The queen then added her own touches, including a 197-foot gallery filled with fine paintings. Catherine had elaborate, erotic parties at Chenonceau. One party she had for the Duke of Anjou included regattas, fireworks, and satyrs chasing wood nymphs in the background. The most beautiful noblewomen in France waited on guests—topless!

The largest Loire château

Chambord is the largest of the Loire châteaux. Designed by Leonardo da Vinci for King Francois I as a pleasure palace, it is set in a 13,600-acre game reserve and surrounded by a 20-mile wall, the longest in France. The 440-room hunting lodge is laced with spires, pinnacles, gables, turrets, towers, and 365 chimneys. The palace has 74 stairways, including a double staircase constructed of twin spirals. One person can ascend while another is descending without meeting.

Where to sleep like a king

While you are in the Loire Valley, you can live like a king. The region is filled with lovely château-hotels that are beautiful but not expensive.

The **Domaine de Beauvois**, *tel. +33 (2) 4755-5011; website: www.slh.com/ beauvois/*, dates to the 15th century and has a beautiful, classic style overlooking the beautiful Briffaut Lake. Modern amenities, such as a heated pool, tennis courts, and elevators are also available plus the unique wine tasting in the private trogloditic cellar.

Château de Pray, *tel. +33 (2) 4757-2367; website: www.chateaupray.com,* is a lovely château with moderate prices located two miles northeast of Amboise. It has a beautiful terrace for dining during summer.

The best of the Bordeaux wine region

The region around **Bordeaux** is known for its great red wines—Margaux, Mouton Rothschild, and Saint Emilion. A 30-minute drive from Bordeaux will put you in the heart of the wine country. This region is full of small mansions and splendid castles, all surrounded by acres of vines.

The best wine stores in Bordeaux are **Badie**, *62 allées Tourny* and **La Vinothèque**, *8 cours du XXX Juillet*. The **Maison du Vin of Bordeaux**, *3 Cours du XXX Juillet* offers maps of the wine regions and lists châteaux that receive visitors.

The prettiest wine town

St. Emilion is one of the most picturesque villages in France. The medieval town is perched on a plateau overlooking the valley of the Dordogne. While you are there, visit the 17th-century hermitage, which was hollowed from rock.

Nearby is the entrance to a chapel with a strange underground shrine. It, too, was carved out of rock 900 years ago. A subterranean passage leads to catacombs containing skeletons in ancient tombs. (You must have a guide to visit the shrine.)

At the **Syndicat d'Initiative**, *place Crénaux*, you can get a list of wine châteaux nearby. The Château Ausone produces the St. Emilion's vintage, among others.

BURGUNDY—THE MOST BOUNTIFUL

Burgundy is the most bountiful region in France. The food is sumptuous, the wine rich, and the forests filled with game. The landscape is dotted with tiny

Romanesque churches, old abbeys, canals, and sleepy towns. The area is known for its medieval churches.

Bourgogne is for those who prefer to pamper themselves while slowly savoring the atmosphere, the wine, and the food. Follow the wine route through the region, sampling the vintages. Treat yourself to Burgundy's legendary casseroles, *coq au vin*, or *boeuf bourguignon*, accompanied by a bottle of local red.

Beaune is the wine capital of the region. Typical of Burgundy, Beaune has narrow cobblestone streets and old houses with little gardens. It also has tour buses, tourists, and expensive gift shops.

Known for its fine wines, Beaune is also the center for excursions northward to vineyards and châteaux. Ancient cellars in town include Caves des Hautes Cotes, Domaine Cauvard, and Chanson Père et Fils. Nearby are the wineries around Aloxe-Corton or Nuits St. Georges. The famous Pommard vineyards are just south of the town.

To explore the greatest wine country, drive from Beaune north to Dijon on the Ouche.

Burgundy's best restaurant

L'Espérance, *tel. +33 (3) 8633-3910; website: www.marc-meneau-esperance.com,* is a fine restaurant in an 18th-century luxury hotel. Owner and chef M. Marc Meneau is one of France's most creative and innovative chefs.

The world's best lodge

The best lodge in the world to join is the **Chevaliers du Tastevin** *(www. tastevin-bourgogne.com)*, which inducts new members twice a year in the Clos de Vougeot, the manor house in the midst of the Burgundy vineyards. Only wine produced from those vineyards can bear the prestigious Burgundy label.

The ceremonies begin with the entrance of the *halberdiers* (uniformed men carrying medieval weapons), who are followed by the counsels of the order in their scarlet and gold robes. Each new member, or postulant-knight, is welcomed by a witty poem recited by the grand master in French. He is then dubbed a knight by being struck three times on the shoulder with a grapewood stick "in the name of Noah, the father of the vine; Bacchus, the god of wine; and St. Vincent, the patron of vintners."

The ceremony is followed by a dinner of six courses, each accompanied by a selected vintage—for example, meat pies with 1985 Aligoté from the Hautes-Côtes de Nuits; turbot with 1983 Puligny-Montrachet; wine-cooked eggs with 1982

Savigny-lès-Beaune; mustard chicken with 1981 Beaune Grèves; local cheeses with 1980 Latricières-Chambertin; or pear ice cream and *petits fours* with coffee and Marc or Prunelle from Burgundy. You may smoke only at the end of the meal.

Top places to stay

Along the wine route is the **Château d'Igé**, *tel. +33 (3) 8533-3399; website: www.chateaudige.com*, a hotel in a remodeled 12th-century château near Cluny. Fortified towers, ancient exposed stonework, and a spiral staircase of hewn stone give the hotel a medieval atmosphere. The castle has six rooms and serves gourmet French cuisine.

Another charming old hotel is the **Hostellerie de la Poste**, *tel. +33 (3) 8634-1616; website: www.hostelleriedelaposte.com,* located off Route Nationale 6 halfway between Chablis and Dijon in Avallon. Napoleon stopped at this inn. Established in 1707, it has one of the best restaurants in France, located in old converted stables and on a cobblestone terrace. Most of the 30 rooms have bathrooms. The hotel is closed in January and February.

The Hôtel de la Poste, *5 blvd. Clemenceau, tel. +33 (3) 8022-0811; website: www.hoteldelapostebeaune.com,* on the site of the former ramparts, is the most popular in Beaune. A charming old place with a garden courtyard, it also has the best restaurant in town. (Try the crayfish in cream sauce or the roast quail.)

ALSACE—THE MOST GERMAN REGION

Alsatians describe themselves as *entre deux portes*, or between two gates—France and Germany. This French *département* that stretches between the Vosges Mountains and the Rhine River has been passed between France and Germany five times, and, as a result, its culture is an interesting blend of French and German. Try the local dishes: onion pie, *choucroute* (sauerkraut), and *charcuterie*, accompanied by a glass of the wine or beer of the region. *Kugelhupf*, a yeast-based cake, is the traditional dessert.

Strasbourg: The prettiest old town

Strasbourg is the ancient capital of the province and it contains a centuries-old center enclosed by branches of the Ill River and guarded by the Strasbourg Cathedral. The pink Gothic cathedral was begun in 1176 and completed in the 15th

century.

Ancient half-timbered buildings line the cathedral square and surrounding streets. One of the most striking is the **Maison Kammerzell**, *16 place Cathédrale; tel. +33 (3) 8832-4214; website: www.maison-kammerzell.com,* a restaurant serving regional dishes in a 15th-century house with elaborately carved wood trim. Wander along the rue du Bain aux Plantes to La Petite France. Four massive square towers, remnants of 14th-century ramparts, stand over the covered bridges that cross the Ill.

The best white wines
Regional wines of Alsace, unlike those of the rest of France, are labeled by grape varieties rather than by the name of the village or château. Because they don't understand this German labeling system, the French mistrust Alsatian wines. As a result, vintage Guebwiller Gewurtztraminer is one of the best wine bargains in France.

Along the Alsatian **Route du Vin** (Wine Road), stretching 90 miles from Marlenheim to Thann, are centuries-old towns surrounded by vineyards. Eguisheim is a 16th-century town with half-timbered houses with low doorways. Three medieval towers guarded the town until the 15th century.

Riquewihr is a pretty Alsatian town that clings to a vine-covered hill, within a circle of 16th-century walls. Cars may not enter its cobblestone streets.

DORDOGNE —THE LEAST SPOILED AREA

This *département* is rural, traditional, and relatively unspoiled. But tourists are beginning to discover the area. Dordogne is known for its prehistoric cave drawings and gourmet cuisine. Deep green valleys and river gorges break up the landscape. In the Dronne Valley, walled castles top nearly every hill.

The best country cuisine
The Perigord, a historic province contained within Dordogne, is famous for its cuisine. This is a place to linger over long meals. The area's truffles are famous, and its game and fish are equally delicious. Wash your meal down with a full-bodied Bergerac. A great place to eat in Périgueux is the **Château des Reynats**, *tel. +33 (5) 5303-5359; website: www.chateau-hotel-perigord.com,* which boasts dishes like roasted pigeon stuffed with *foie gras* and served with black truffle risotto.

For a lovely chateau stopover with a friendly welcome near Brantôme, stay in one of the olde worlde rooms at the **Château de la Côte,** *tel. +33 (5) 5303-7011; website: http://chateaudelacote.com.*

The world's finest porcelain

Limoges, the largest city in the region, is famous for its fine porcelain. Cross its Roman bridges, stroll the little streets in the old section, and visit the ancient cathedral of St. Etienne. Notice the half-timbered houses by the river. They have open spaces between the roof and the top floor, held up by wide beams. In the old days, residents dried their laundry and kept food provisions in this airy space below the roof. Tour the porcelain factories or enamel workshops. You can get a list of these from the **Tourist Information Office**, *tel. +33 (5) 5534-4687; website: www.justtourfrance.com.*

The prettiest town in Dordogne

One of the most charming villages in France is **Brantôme**. Bordered on two sides by the Dronne River, it has an 18th-century Benedictine abbey (now the town hall) and a good museum, the Desmoulin. Stroll along the canals past the houses and then visit the Monks' Garden.

The most spectacular town in France

Dordogne boasts medieval castles and walled cities dating back to Richard the Lion-Hearted. The most spectacular of the towns is **Rocamadour**, built into the face of a steep cliff. Narrow, cobblestone streets climb the cliff to its summit, where the Basilica of St. Sauveur is perched along with several shrines. Pilgrims on their knees have climbed the Great Staircase to the shrine since the Middle Ages. See the Black Madonna in Notre Dame chapel.

Medieval musts

East of Le Bugue is the **Château Beynac-et-Cazenac**, a well-preserved fortress atop a cliff. The castle was destroyed and rebuilt twice: in 1189 by Sir Mercadier in the name of Richard the Lionheart and in 1214 by Simon de Montfort during the Crusade against Albigensian heretics.

From the ramparts of the castle, another great fortress, the **Château de Castelnaud**, can be seen. The restored castle was once the headquarters for Simon de Montfort. The village of St. Cirq-La Popie sits beneath the ruins of a 1,000-year old castle and is set in a gorgeous valley. St. Cirq is known for its woodcraft, although the art has largely disappeared.

More than 80 walled cities still stand from Perigord to the Pyrenees, including Monpazier, Domme, Lalinde, Villereal, Beaumont, and Ste. Foy La Grande.

EUROPE'S FAVORITE SUMMER PLAY GROUND

The **French Riviera**, known as the Cote d'Azur, is Europe's favorite summer play-ground. It is hot, crowded, expensive, and super-trendy. The most famous Riviera town is **St. Tropez**, but avoid it in July and August, when it is jam-packed. Visit in September and October, after the summer season and before the winter. Prices drop, the weather is mild and sunny, and the beaches are yours.

The coast is 72 miles long, with 25 miles of long beaches of pebble or sand, from Marseilles to Menton. From Nice to the Italian border, beaches are of gravel or rock. Between Cannes and St. Raphael, the rocks of Corniche are breathtakingly beautiful. But the best beaches are along the coast from St. Raphael to Hyères: Cabasson, Le Lavandou, St. Clair, Cavaliere, Tahiti, Pampelone, and Salins.

The nicest town

Nice is a lovely town with old houses and wide views. Although its beach is rocky, you still can take a pleasant walk along the sea—on Promenade des Anglais. The casino is elegant. Visit the Terra Amata paleontological museum near the old harbor, located on the spot where the remains of a 400,000-year-old mammoth hunters' camp was discovered.

The best casino

In Cannes, the glamorous **Palm Beach Casino**, *tel. +33 (4) 9706-3690; website: www.lepalmbeach.com,* is a huge attraction. The beaches are sandy and luxury yachts line the marina. The Palace of Festivals houses a theater, a casino, a night-club, boutiques, and a convention center. It is also the site of the famous film festival.

The best pastries and market

The late **Gaston Lenôtre**, perhaps France's best-known pastry chef, celebrated his 80th birthday by opening his first shop and tea salon, **Café Lenôtre**, on the Côte d'Azur in 2001. The shop, on *63 rue d'Antibes* in Cannes, features more than 500 pastry specialites. Try the apple douillon and homemade ice cream. The elegant café on the first floor is an ideal place to nibble Lenôtre's stylish breakfasts or afternoon teas.

Don't visit Cannes without paying a visit to the fabulous **Marché Forville** (where the coast's top chefs come to buy their ingredients). The mushroom salesman in the left-hand aisle sometimes has white truffles and Boulangerie Paul has its own traditional bread oven. The Marché Forville is two blocks in from the Hôtel de Ville, on the rue Félix Faure.

A princely resort

Monaco is a separate tiny nation on the Riviera that attracts the world's royalty. The little kingdom is set above the sea and looks like the setting for a fairy tale. But it's far from innocent, with its casinos, decadent hotels, and beaches where the world's best bodies sun topless. Monaco's capital, Monte Carlo, has some of the most glamorous hotels, restaurants, and casinos in Europe.

The finest hotel on the Riviera

The **Hotel de Paris**, *tel. +377 9806-2525; website: www.hoteldeparismontecarlo. com*, attracts jet setters, gamblers, yachtsmen, and the Grand Prix crowd. The hotel's best feature is its magnificent restaurant, **Louis XV-Alain Ducasse**, *tel. +377 9806-8864.*

PROVENCE: THE SWEETEST REGION

The Mediterranean region of **Provence** is a sweet land, literally and figuratively. Its air is scented by the lavender, basil, rosemary, thyme, and sage that grow in its rocky fields. Old traditions and a simple way of life survive here. This is the land of Marcel Pagnol, the beloved French writer, who wrote about his boyhood adventures in these rocky hills, olive groves, and stone houses.

Provence looks like an Impressionist painting. Villages climb the white rocks; the pines are dark green, the soil red, and the olive groves green; and lavender grows in the fields.

Framed by the sea, the Alps, the Rhône and Durance rivers, and the Italian border, Provence stretches from the medieval town of Aigues-Mortes in the west, beyond Marseille to Cassis in the east. It includes the lower Rhône Valley; the flat, windy marshes of the Camargue; and the foothills of the Alps.

Best restaurant in Provence

Les Bacchanales, *10 rue Couronne, Aix en Provence; tel. +33 (4) 4227-2106*, is a small, intimate restaurant with wonderful prices. The restaurant specializes in Provençal food and offers three three-course menus.

The most beautiful walled city

Avignon is one of France's most beautiful walled cities, groaning with history. Every single building seems to tell a story of medieval murder, intrigue, or romance. It also makes an excellent base for exploring the villages of the Rhône Valley. Driving beside the Rhône River, you can see the statue of the Virgin Mary on top of the Palace des Papes, shining in solid gold, and in the distance, the arches of the Bridge of St. Benezet, better known as the Pont d'Avignon of nursery rhyme fame. But forget about dancing across the bridge. Half of it was carried away by flood waters centuries back, and it has never been rebuilt.

The **Hotel d'Europe**, *12 Place Crillon; +33 (4) 9014-7676; website: www.heurope.com*, is almost as ancient as its surroundings. It was built in 1580 as the private home of a Marquess, but has been a hotel since 1799. The guest list of luminaries who have stayed here is long: Napoleon Bonaparte, Pablo Picasso, Salvador Dali, Tennessee Williams, King Edward VII of England. This is one of the most elegant hotels you'll ever stay in.

The oldest houses in France

The road to the golden-hued city of Gordes leads through flat vineyards and steep hills to the **Village des Bories**. This collection of prehistoric stone buildings, or bories, dates back to 3000 B.C. The huts were used by shepherds until the 18th century. They have been restored to look as they did 4,000 years ago and are filled with old cooking implements and tools.

The best Roman ruins in France

Nîmes has the most splendid Roman arena in the country. It has been well preserved and is still used today for bull fighting. Nîmes' Roman temple, known as Maison Carée, is also perfectly preserved.

The most fragrant town

The sweetest smelling town in Provence is **Grasse**, 10 miles from Cannes. It is the perfume capital of the world. Violet, lavender, jasmine, lily, rose, jonquil, and mimosa grow in this town. Once the favorite resort of Queen Victoria, Grasse is a picturesque old village with winding cobblestone streets and weathered houses.

Each year the perfumeries in Grasse process more than 700 tons of roses, 600 tons of orange blossoms, and 800 tons of jasmine. You can take a tour of two perfume factories, **La Parfumerie Fragonard**, *tel. +33 (4) 9336-4465; website: www.fragonard.com* and **La Parfumerie Gallimard**, *tel. +33 (4) 9309-2000;*

website: www.galimard.com, which are open daily. English-speaking guides explain how the perfume is made.

THE MOST SPANISH REGION: ROUSSILLON

West of the Riviera, stretching the length of the Golfe du Lion, from the Pyrénées to the Rhone Delta, is the **Roussillon** region. Medieval walled cities, the peaks of the Pyrénées, Mediterranean resorts, and quaint villages mark this varied region. Also known as French Catalonia, Roussillon has a Spanish air. It belonged to Spain until 1659, and the people are Catalan, as are the people of Barcelona. The red and yellow Catalan flag flies over the region's capital, **Perpignan**. Some Catalans would like to see this region become autonomous.

The least-spoiled coast

Traditional fishing villages can still be found along the western end of the Mediterranean coast. **Collioure** is the most charming fishing port. Matisse painted here. **Sète** also retains its original appeal.

The largest walled city

Carcassonne, Europe's largest medieval walled city, is west of Narbonne. A mighty circle of towers and battlements encircles the hilltop town. Parts of the walls were built by the Romans. In the fifth century, the Visigoths enlarged the fortress. Charlemagne laid siege to the city for five years in the ninth century. And in the 13th century it fell to Crusaders; Simon de Montfort took it over. St. Louis strengthened the fortress. It was rebuilt in the 19th century by Violet-le-Duc to conform to Victorian ideas of how a walled city should look.

The best place to stay in Carcassonne is the **Hôtel de la Cité**, *tel. +33 (4) 6871-9871; website: www.hoteldelacite.com*, located in a former Episcopal palace built into the wall near the Basilica of St. Nazaire. Some rooms have canopy beds, and the dining hall is beautiful. The hotel is open from April through October.

THE MOST EXOTIC REGION: BASQUE COUNTRY

The southwest of France and the northwest of Spain combine to form an exotic region known as **Basque Country**. The Basques have a common language, culture, and history identifiable as neither French nor Spanish. The Spanish Basques, in particular, have struggled for autonomy. A separatist movement exists in France also, but it is milder. The Basque language is related to no other; it is not Indo-European. Some believe that the cavemen spoke Basque.

The mountainous region is known for its cuisine and its specialty dish, the wild dove that migrates from northern Europe to Spain in October.

The most typical town

St. Jean-Pied-de-Port, near the Spanish border, is the most typically Basque town in the region. It was fortified in the time of Louis XIV, and its narrow cobblestone streets are guarded by a tall citadel. The typical Basque houses are stone, sturdy, half-timbered, and whitewashed with red or green trim and chalet-like stucco.

The church's clock tower tolls the hour twice, following local custom. A stone bridge crosses the Nive River to the tower. The *fronton*, or ball court, is always filled with *pelota* players. And flat, round tombstones from pre-Christian times can be seen in the graveyards. *Pelota*, or *jai alai*, is the Basque ball game, played with a hard ball and a racket. It is very fast.

The finest place to surf

Biarritz is a seaside resort on the Bay of Biscay. It has one of France's largest beaches and offers the best surfing on the French coast. A great place to stay while visiting is **Hôtel du Palais**, *tel. +33 (5) 5941-6400; website: www.hotel-du-palais. com*. Visit the Rocher de la Vierge for a good view of the ocean. The lower promenade, along the boulevard du Prince de Galles, leads past the foaming breakers that give the coast its name—Côte d'Argent, the Silver Coast. The lighthouse on the summit of Cap St. Martin has a splendid view.

Biarritz was made famous by the Empress Eugenie (the wife of Napoleon III), who attracted fashionable clientele to the resort. Queen Victoria and Edward VII, among others, slept in Eugenie's villa, now the Hôtel du Palais.

THE BEST OF
GERMANY

We believe Germany is a great all-round travel destination in Europe. As balanced as a fine cuckoo clock, it has something for everyone. Its old cities have museums, concert halls, and gourmet restaurants. Romantic little villages nestle beneath the snow-capped Alps. Its North Sea beaches are edged by 30-foot sand dunes and beautified with goose-pimpled, bronzed (and sometimes nude) bodies. The *avant-garde* lives side by side with folk culture.

BERLIN: THE MOST EXCITING CITY

Berlin has an exciting, devil-may-care atmosphere, and is one of the most exciting cities in the world to visit. Sidewalk cafés, little shops, parks, and offices exist side by side with the remains of the graffiti-covered Berlin Wall.

Berlin is a lively city. Its slogan is *"Berlin weil's Spass macht"* (Berlin because it's fun). It's a fashion center, known for its chic, quality clothing. It has 5,000 restaurants, cafés, and bars situated along its *Kurfürstendamm* (Berlin's Champs-Elysées), some of which stay open all night.

What used to be West Berlin is more modern than its sister, but what used to be East Berlin is often more *avant-garde*. There are lakes, rivers, and forests covering 35% of the city's area. Western Berlin is ablaze with neon and gleaming with chrome and glass architecture. Germany beyond the Berlin Wall was always rich in culture and perfectly preserved historical treasures—now these treasures are easily accessible to visitors. Rather than taking an expensive tour bus, take the bus number 100 to get a good overview of all the sights—its route takes in all the major museums.

Berlin's best museums

The **Museumsinsel** (Museum Island; *website: www.museumsinsel.de*), surrounded by the Spree River and Spree Canal, is one of the world's largest and most magnificent museum complexes. It includes the Pergamon, Bode, and Altes museums, as well as the National Gallery, the Berlin Cathedral, and several ruins. You could spend days, even weeks, here. There is one main website (other than the above, which gives you a good map), *www.smb.spk-berlin.de*. Most museums are open Tuesday to Sunday 10 a.m. to 6 p.m. and Thursday to 10 p.m.

Here is an overview of the major museums:

More than 600,000 people visit the **Pergamon Museum** each year, making it the most popular of the state museums. The Pergamon Altar (180 B.C. to 160 B.C.) is just one of the impressive exhibits reconstructed from the archeological collection of the Prussian court. Also on exhibit are the Gate of Miletus, a two-story Roman market gate (approx. 120 A.D.) and the reconstruction of the gate of Ishtar built during the reign of Nebuchandnezzar (605 B.C. to 562 B.C.), with its magnificent blue tiling. In addition to the classical collection, the Pergamon building contains the collections of the Museum of Islamic Art and the Museum of Ancient Near Eastern Art.

The **Gemäldegalerie**, displays the world's largest Rembrandt collection and is one of several museums that make up the immense Dahlem museum complex, which includes sculpture, prints, the Ethnographical Museum, the Museum of Far Eastern and Indian Art, and the Botanical Museum.

The **Egyptian Museum** houses the most famous piece of art in Berlin—the painted limestone bust of beautiful Queen Nefertiti, created more than 3,300 years ago.

The **House at Checkpoint Charlie,** *Friedrichstrasse 43-45; tel. +49 (30) 2537-250; website*: *www.mauermuseum.de,* open every day of the year from 9 a.m. to 10 p.m., displays many of the ingenious, homemade contraptions used by East Berliners in their attempts to cross the Berlin Wall when it stood as a barrier between East and West. The museum is located in a dilapidated tenement building, near the gate between East and West Berlin in the former American sector. Displays include a miniature submarine created with a motor taken from a motor scooter;

a low-slung sportscar that zoomed beneath the horizontal barrier at Checkpoint Charlie; a homemade bulletproof truck that crashed through the wall; and photos of a 476-foot tunnel that 57 people crawled through to the West.

The **Jewish Museum**, *Lindenstrasse 9-14; tel. +49 (30) 2599-3300; website: www.jmberlin.de*, is the second most popular museum in Berlin. It opened its doors in 2001 and is a stunning piece of architecture designed by Daniel Libeskind. Summer programs are held in the gardens of the museum, including concerts and many other cultural events. Opening hours are 10 a.m. to 8 p.m. (closes at 10 p.m. on Mondays).

The finest opera performances

The **Deutsche Staatsoper**, *Unter den Linden; tel. +49 (30) 2035-4555; website: www.staatsoper-berlin.de*, hosts some of the finest opera performances in the world. The main hall holds 1,500 people and has been presenting opera and concert performances since 1742, having been rebuilt three times. The historic building will be undergoing major renovations from October 2010 to the summer of 2013. During this time, performances will continue to take place at the Schiller Theater, *Bismarckstraße 110* in Berlin-Charlottenburg.

Germany's best park

The **Tiergarten** is Germany's most attractive park. Originally the park was the royal hunting reserve, but is now one of the world's largest urban parks. It has lakes, ponds, and a zoo, which has more species than any other zoo in the world (*website: www.zoo-berlin.de*). At its eastern edge is the Reichstag, Germany's former Parliament building, which burned down in 1933 but was rebuilt after the war. The roof terrace and dome (designed by the architect Norman Foster in 1992) of the Reichstag Building offer an incomparable view of Berlin's parliamentary and government quarter. The Brandenburg Gate at the eastern end of the Tiergarten marks the former border between East and West Berlin.

Berlin's best castle

Schloss Charlottenburg, *Spandauer Damm; tel. +49 (331) 9694-200; website: www.spsg.de*, is the best example of royal Prussian architecture in Berlin. The Schloss was destroyed during World War II, but it has been restored. You can tour the castle, which is surrounded by lovely grounds and a lake, Tuesdays through Sundays, 9 a.m. until 5 p.m.

Schloss Charlottenburg houses the largest collection of French paintings of the 18th century outside of France, a great porcelain collection mostly 17th and

18th century, the museum of arts and crafts, and sumptuously decorated royal apartments, including the splendid white-and-gold rococo gallery. The Charlottenburg Mausoleum contains the tombs of King Friedrich Wilhelm III and Queen Louise.

Counterculture bests

For a taste of Berlin's counterculture, visit **Kreuzberg**, Berlin's answer to New York's East Village. Art galleries, bookstores, used-clothing shops, hip boutiques, and small theaters thrive in this area. Restaurants offering every imaginable cuisine line the streets. A small part of the Berlin Wall, which is covered with colorful graffiti, is the eastern boundary of the neighborhood. A sign here reminds you that you are at the site of Gestapo torture chambers.

The most decadent shopping

Stop in at **Kaufhaus des Westens**, *Tauentzienstrasse 21-24; tel. +49 (30) 212-10; website: www.kadewe.de*, known locally as KaDeWe, Berlin's version of Harrods in London. Located near the Ku'damm, it has an enormous selection of clothing, as well as 450 kinds of bread, 1,000 types of sausage, and 1,000 different cheeses. Open Monday to Thursday, and Saturday 9:30 a.m. to 8 p.m. and Friday to 9 p.m.

The best bargains

The flea market on the Straße des 17. Juni, Saturday and Sunday officially 11 a.m. to 5 p.m., but it is best to get there by 10 a.m. Meissen porcelain, mink coats, old military memorabilia, original artworks, antique bronze door handles, you name it. Get yourself a *Boulette* (hamburger without a bun) from one of the mobile "Imbiss" (snackbars) and drink a pint of *Weisse* (Berlin's own tart beer, brewed from wheat). You may also hear live jazz, hip hop or something entirely new in the streets.

The best nightlife

For night-clubbing, **90Grad**, *Dennewitzstrasse 37, Berlin Schöneberg; tel. +49 (30) 2759-6231,* is one of the city's hottest, and most exclusive, clubs, attracting top DJs and sporting an impressive dance floor, sound and light effects. Dress code is elegant. If you can convince the doorman that you are important/famous/beautiful enough to be admitted, you're in for a night of champagne sipping and celeb spotting.

Once you get past the doorman at **Sage Club**, *Köpenicker Strasse 76; website: www.sage-club.de*, you'll face a fire-breathing dragon over the dance floor. Fortunately, finding a place to sit and talk is less of a challenge. Sage has three dance floors and a special pool area. Check out the website as well-known bands often play here and "underground catwalks" also take place.

For live jazz, **Quasimodo**, *Kantstrasse 12A; tel. +49 (30) 312-8086; website: www.quasimodo.de,* is a cozy basement club appreciated by fans since 1975 as conducive to intimate performances. This venue also features Latin, funk, and rock.

Clärchens Ballhaus, *Auguststrasse 24; tel. +49 (30) 282-9295; website: www.ballhaus.de*, caters to a very mixed crowd, young and old, who like to dance or just watch dancing. You can brush up on your waltzing steps, salsa, tango or even swing. In the summer, afternoon tea is served in the very nice garden. Very in, very retro.

Berlin's top restaurants

Borchardt, *Französische Strasse 47; tel. +49 (30) 8188-6262; website: www.borchardt-catering.de*. High ceilings, elegant paneling, excellent French and Italian cuisine. Most importantly: the place to see and be seen.

Alt-Luxemburg, *Windscheidstrasse 31; tel. +49 (30) 323-8730; website: www.alt-luxemburg.de*. Chef and owner since 1982, Karl Wannemacher creates a sophisticated modern German cuisine focusing on seasonal produce in this intimate and elegant antique-furnished restaurant. A house specialty: Brandenburg duck with pineapple chutney.

Dressler, *Kurfüstendamm 207-208; tel. +49 (30) 883-3530; website: www.restaurant-dressler.de*, is a rare find where both the ambiance and the cuisine delight. Entrées vary according to season, with a focus on seafood, including lobster, cod, and oysters; game is also a house specialty. The welcoming staff is stylish and attentive. They have a second restaurant between Brandenburger Tor and the Staatsoper at *Unter den Linden 39, tel. +49 (30) 204-4422*.

Facil, *Potsdamerstrasse 3; tel. +49 (30) 5900-51234; website: www.facil.de*. Located on the fifth floor of the Mandala hotel, Berliners love the novel architecture, featuring a retractable glass roof that allows for gourmet dining under the stars. Young chef Michael Kempf, who garnered a Michelin star, has created an excellent menu that ranges from *foie gras* to octopus with Venus clams. Closed Saturday and Sunday.

The best hotel

Without a doubt: **Hotel Adlon Kempinski Berlin**, *Unter den Linden 77; tel. +49 (30) 226-10; website: www.hotel-adlon.de*. The hotel dates back to 1907, even then visited by international royalty. Badly damaged during World War II, it has been rebuilt to its original splendor on the same location, directly opposite the Brandenburg Gate.

Bristol-Hotel Kempinski, *Kurfurstendamm 27; tel. +49 (30) 884-340; website: www.kempinski.com.* The atmosphere of this sprawling, old-fashioned hotel is warm and inviting and the staff are ready and willing to help.

Close seconds

The **Hotel Hackescher Markt**, *Grosse Präsidentenstrasse 8; tel. +49 (30) 280-030; website: http://classik-hotel-collection.com/en/hotel-hackescher-markt.html,* is a small boutique hotel, very centrally located in *Mitte*, with a very personal service.

Hotel Q, *Knesebeckstraße 67; tel. +49 (30) 810-0660; website: www. loock-hotels.com,* is the definition of a modern upscale hotel. Offering a range of services such as a personal Berlin club tour, a personal shopper, and a gym. Also try the hotel's specialty chocolate massage. However a membership card is needed for Berlin's "first private membership" hotel bar that attracts models, artists and actors to this lavish establishment.

Hotel Belvedere, *Toni-Lessler-Strasse 4; tel. +49 (30) 826-0010;* is next to a forest as well as the river Havel. The hotel is a huge turn-of-the-century villa with gardens and a peaceful atmosphere, making up for the fact that it is not centrally located. Rooms are furnished with antiques.

GERMANY'S MOST BEAUTIFUL PALACE

Potsdam *(website: www.potsdam.de),* about an hour's drive—also easily accessible with public transportation—from Berlin, is home to Germany's most beautiful rococo palace, **Sanssouci Palace** and its park, *tel. +49 (331) 969-4200; website: www.spsg.de.* It was built by Frederick the Great in imitation of Versailles in 1745. You must wear their felt-soled slippers when you visit to protect the beautiful floors. Paintings by Rubens, Van Dyck, and Caravaggio hang in the palace galleries.

THE BEST OF FRANKFURT

Frankfurt *(website: www.frankfurt.de)* is the logical center for touring Germany. Frankfurt-am-Main Airport is the largest and busiest of Germany's international airports. (All major trains go beyond Frankfurt's main railroad station to the airport train station, allowing incoming tourists to make train connections to all parts of Germany—or Europe for that matter).

A modern, industrial city and Germany's banking and financial center, Frankfurt has a charming old section with good wine bars. The *Altstadt* (Old Town) is ringed by the *Innenstadt* (Inner Town), which developed in the 14th century.

Frankfurt's best restaurants

Weinhaus Bruckenkeller, *Schutzenstrasse 6; tel. +49 (69) 2980-070; website: www.brueckenkeller.de,* specializes in German food served in an arched cellar with candle-lit tables and strolling musicians. The wine cellar contains over 180 German wines. Make sure to try the roasted veal with summer vegetables and white wine spume.

Restaurant Français, in the *Steigenberger Hotel Frankfurter Hof, Am Kaiserplatz; tel. +49 (69) 215-118,* was awarded one of Michelin's coveted stars for its delectable fare. It's a very popular place, so reservations are required. Classical trompe-l'oeil paintings, furnishings and decor create a charming atmosphere à la française. A completely different world awaits you in the Iroha Japanese restaurant. Here you can savor Far Eastern delicacies at the sushi bar, at teppan-yaki tables, or in separate washitsu cubicles.

The two finest hotels

Steigenberger Hotel Frankfurter Hof, *Am Kaiserplatz; tel. +49 (69) 215-02; website: www.steigenberger.com,* has been welcoming guests since 1876. Central and comfortably old-fashioned, it has two cozy bars, three amazing restaurants, and an outdoor café.

Hessischer Hof, *Friedrich-Ebert-Anlage 40; tel +49 (69) 754-00; website: www.hessischer-hof.de,* a five-star luxury hotel located directly across the fairgrounds, it belongs to the Hessian princes' family foundation. The in-house restaurant Sèvres is also excellent and has an important collection of the same-named French porcelain, belonging to the family.

Frankfurt's best undiscovered hotels

About seven miles outside Frankfurt is **Schlosshotel Kronberg**, *Hainstraße 25, Kronberg i. Taunus; tel. +49 (61) 7370-101; website: www.schlosshotel-kronberg. de,* an elegant castle hotel. Built in 1888 as the residence of Kaiser Wilhelm II's mother, it became a gathering place for European royalty. After World War I, French

Occupation officials took possession of the castle. After World War II, American Occupation forces used it as a club for high officers and civilians. Today, the palace is a hotel with 19th-century furnishings. The cuisine is superb and the hotel has an internationally acclaimed 18-hole golf course (*website: www.gc-kronberg.de*) for guests to enjoy.

The best nightlife

Frankfurt, surprisingly for a German town, is not a big beer-drinking city. The preferred drinks are *Ebbelwoi* (from apple wine) and wine. The Ebbelwoi is delicious, but be aware that it carries a much stronger punch than its sweet taste suggests.

Frankfurt is filled with *Weinstuben* (wine taverns). The **Neuer Volkswirt**, *Kleine Hochstrasse 9; tel. +49 (69) 2199-8393; website: www.neuervolkswirt.de,* is popular among young professionals. It has the greatest wine selection in town.

Wein Dünker, *Berger Strasse 265; tel. +49 (69) 451-993*, is a wine bar in a cellar beneath a half-timbered *Fachwerk* centuries-old building in the area of Bornheim. The wine list is long, and the prices are moderate.

Operncafé, *Opernplatz 10; tel. +49 (69) 285-260*, is a trendy place where good-looking people ogle one another before and after concerts, shopping, etc.

Jazz is big in Frankfurt. **Der Jazzkeller**, *Kleine Bockenheimer Strasse 18a; tel. +49 (69) 288-537; website: www.jazzkeller.com*, features top performers.

HAMBURG: THE MOST WORLDLY CITY

Hamburg *(website: www.hamburg.de),* an international port, is Germany's most worldly city, known for the steamy sex shows and wild discos along the *Reeperbahn* in Sankt Pauli and, of course, the starting point for one of the most successful bands of all time—The Beatles. However, Hamburg also has a peaceful section and prides itself in being a stalwart of the best of German traditions. The lakes at its center are bordered by wide green avenues, opulent shops, and hotels.

The best place to take in Hamburg at a glance is atop the tower (your choice: steps or elevator) of the baroque **St. Michaelis Church**, *Krayenkamp 4C, Michaeliskirchplatz; website: www.st-michaelis.de*. The church also presents frequent concerts in its main hall (see website for dates).

Best museum in Hamburg

The **Museum für Hamburgische Geschichte**, *Holstenwall 24; tel. +49 (40) 4281-322-380; website: www.hamburgmuseum.de*, gives an excellent overview of the city's development, from its origins in the ninth century to the present.

Germany's best fish market

The best fish market in Germany is held here on Sunday mornings. This raucous but fun affair is located by the docks in Altona, at *St. Pauli Fischmarkt 2* and goes from 5 a.m. to 9:30 a.m. (Winter starting time 7 a.m. October to March 31).

Hamburg's finest dining

The best restaurant in Hamburg is the **Landhaus Scherrer**, *Elbchaussee 130; tel. +49 (40) 88 3070-030; website: www.landhausscherrer.de*. It specializes in North German cuisine and the restaurant overlooks the Elbe. They are winners of a Michelin star and prices are fairly reasonable.

The **Fischerhaus**, *St. Pauli Fischmarkt 14; tel. +49 (40) 314-053; website: www.restaurant-fischerhaus.de*, serves inexpensive but wonderful seafood. The atmosphere is plain, but the fish is not.

Hamburg's best hotel

The best hotel in Hamburg—some say in all of Germany, in fact—is the **Fairmont Hotel Vier Jahreszeiten**, *Neuer Jungfernstieg 9-14; tel. +49 (40) 3494-3151; website: www.hvj.de*. This elegant establishment on Lake Alster has a grand white facade rising eight stories and decorated with window boxes. Inside, you will find antique furniture, wood paneling, marble floors, brass trim, and modern facilities. The rooms are exquisitely furnished in a traditional way, with all luxury amenities. Founded in 1897, now a member of the Fairmont Hotel Group, it has an especially comfortable lobby, with leather armchairs, oriental rugs, wood paneling, and a huge fireplace. Just off the lobby is a lounge with a large stone fireplace, tapestries, and views of the lake. A staff of 450 caters to the requests of guests staying in the 175 rooms. While you are here, you can have your suits mended or altered by the in-house Italian tailor.

Haerlin, the restaurant of the hotel, is also excellent. Vegetables, fruit, flowers, and poultry come straight to the restaurant from the hotel's farm on the outskirts of town. Choose a fine German wine from the hotel's 65,000-bottle cellar.

Hotel Kempinski Atlantic, *An der Alster 72-79; tel. +49 (40)-288-80;*

website: www.kempinski.atlantic.de, is a first-class, five-star hotel, located close to the center of town with a grand view of Lake Alster.

Charm for less than a fortune
Hotel Abtei, *Abteistrasse 14; tel. +49 (40) 442-905; website: www.abtei-hotel.de*, is a small hotel on a shady street in a quiet residential section of Hamburg. Breakfast is something you don't want to miss.

  Louis C. Jacob Hotel, *Elbchaussee 401-403, tel. +49 (40) 822-550; website: www.hotel-jacob.de*. Originally built in 1791, it is also known for its excellent award-wining restaurant and wine cellar. Very central location, directly on the river Elbe.

BREMEN: THE MOST BEAUTIFUL CITY

Bremen *(website: www.bremen.de)* is Germany's most beautiful city and its oldest port. It became a bishop's seat over 1,200 years ago and in 1358 joined Hamburg and Lübeck as leading members of the Hanseatic League, an association of independent merchant towns. Bremen prides itself on its historic buildings, the oldest of which (some are over 800 years old) are grouped around the Markplatz. The Gothic city hall was built between 1405 and 1410.

The oldest building in Bremen
The massive, twin-towered **cathedral**, built in the 11th century, is the oldest building in Bremen. Its other claim to fame is the mummy in its cellar. According to legend, the body of a roofer, who fell to his death in 1450, was put in the cellar for safekeeping but forgotten. When the body was discovered many years later, it had been perfectly preserved by the cellar's dry air. Outside the cathedral stands the famous bronze **Statue of Roland**, a famous knight of Charlemagne.

Germany's oldest inn
Der Ratskeller, *Am Markt; tel. +49 (421) 321-676; website: www.ratskeller-bremen. de*, west of the town hall, is one of the oldest and most traditional of Germany's inns. It is known for its huge selection of more than 500 German wines, including a 1653 Rüdesheimer.

The best fish dishes

Grashoff's Bistro, *Contrescarpe 80; tel. +49 (421) 147-49; website: www. grashoff.de*, is a little restaurant that does not look like much, but serves the best fish dishes in the region. Reservations are recommended and the bistro is not open on Sundays.

The best ship museum in the world

Just north of Bremen in Bremerhaven (the most important fishing port in Europe) is one of the best ship museums in the world, the **Schiffahrtsmuseum**, *Hans-Scharoun-Platz 1; tel. +49 (471) 482-070; website: www.dsm.museum*. The *Cog*, a Hanseatic tall ship wrecked in 1380, is especially impressive.

Bremen's best hotels

Park Hotel, *Im Burgerpark; tel. +49 (421) 340-80; website: www.park-hotel-bremen. de*, is Bremen's most prestigious hotel, set amid a 400-acre park. It has spacious public rooms, a garden terrace, rooms with balconies overlooking a pond, and a fine restaurant.

Prizeotel Bremen, *Theodor-Heuss-Allee 12; tel. +49 (1805) 697-749 (reservations); website: www.prizeotel.com*. Designed by one of todays most sought after interior designers Karim Rashid, this is a very trendy and inexpensive boutique hotel.

COLOGNE: BEST CARNIVAL, BEST CHURCHES

If you like churches, you'll believe yourself at the gates of heaven when you reach **Cologne** (*website: www.koeln.de*). The number of churches marking the city's skyline is remarkable (13 in all). What's more, many of these churches are among the most beautiful in Germany. While some were badly damaged in World War II, most have been restored to their former beauty and are open to the public.

It's probably a good thing Cologne has so many churches, considering it is also the site of Germany's wildest carnival season. If you like a good bacchanalia, visit Cologne the week before Ash Wednesday. Carnival begins with *Weiberfastnacht*, the Women's Carnival, held on the Alter Markt. Women choose their dancing partners and dance from morning to midnight. (This custom is said to have its origins in 16th-century pre-Lenten orgies.)

Cologne's beautiful churches

Cologne's famous **Gothic cathedral** is a gigantic structure that can be seen from almost any point in the city. Begun in 1248 and completed in 1880, it houses several great works of art, including the 12th-century *Shrine of the Three Magi*, a masterpiece of the goldsmith's art created to house holy relics.

Hlg. Maria im Kapitol was the church most severely damaged during World War II, but it has been beautifully restored. Its extraordinary, carved wooden doors, with 26 reliefs illustrating the life of Christ, date back to 1050. There's also a 12th-century sculpture of the virgin on display.

Hlg. Pantaleon is a twin-towered structure with a nave that dates back to 980 AD. It is the oldest remaining Romanesque church in Germany.

Hlg. Aposteln is the finest example of Rhineland Romanesque architecture. Built between 1192 and 1230, it has a squat nave with ribbed vaults, a trefoil choir, and a tower.

The oldest church in Cologne is **St. Gereon**. Its walls, crypts, and pillars are from the fourth century.

When you tire of touring churches, visit the **Rhein Park,** Cologne's version of Central Park. During the summer, dances and concerts are held here. Concerts begin at 4 p.m.; dancing begins at 8 p.m. You can even indulge in a thermal bath at the **Claudius Therme,** *Sachsenbergstrasse 1; tel. +49 (221) 981-440; website: www.claudius-therme.de*, its mineral waters are said to be especially good against arthritis and rheumatism.

The prettiest part of Cologne is the old section, near the Rhine, where 12th- and 13th-century buildings remain.

Cologne's best restaurant

Seafood dishes and the best German wines are served at **Brauhaus im Walfisch**, *Salzgasse 13; tel. +49 (221) 257-7879; website: www.walfisch.net*, situated in a 350-year-old building. Reservations are recommended, and the restaurant is closed on Sundays.

The coziest hotel

The **Antik Hotel Bristol**, *Kaiser-Wilhelm-Ring 48; tel. +49 (221) 120-195; website: www.antik-hotel-bristol.de*, is a cozy, family-run hotel near the cathedral. Rooms on the lower floor can be noisy. The atmosphere is inviting and the rooms are decorated with carved wooden furniture.

A FAIRYTALE LOVER'S FAVORITE: THE BLACK FOREST

A couple of hours south of Frankfurt is the **Black Forest**—the *Schwarzwald*. Source of scary fairytales, the Black Forest isn't as ominous as it sounds. Although place names include *Hexental* (Witches' Valley) and *Höllental* (Hell Valley), it's not all dense pine forest, but rather a patchwork of mixed woodlands, green valleys, and highlands decorated with waterfalls…and some exceptionally pretty villages and spa towns.

If you enjoy walking or cycling you'll be in your element…and you'll often spy deer grazing at the forest edge, especially at dawn or dusk. For outdoor types, the Black Forest is an all-year-round destination. During winter—invariably cold and snowy—it's a great place for cross-country skiing.

Cuckoo favorite

The woods around **Triberg** *(website: www.triberg.de)* are known as the home of cuckoo birds, which cuckoo like crazy all day. Known as *cuculus canorus*, the bird is shy and rarely seen or heard anywhere else.

If you fail to spot a real cuckoo in the woods, stop at the **Deutsches Uhrenmuseum** in the hamlet of Furtwangen, *tel. +49 (7723) 9202-800; website: www.deutsches-uhrenmuseum.de*, near Triberg, which houses the largest collection of cuckoo clocks in the world.

The oldest castle in Germany

Meersburg *(website: www.meersburg.de)*, an almost vertical village pitched high above a ravine, and directly on the shores of Lake Constance (called *Bodensee* in German), lies in the shadows of the oldest castle in Germany. Locals claim Dagobert built it in A.D. 630. Some of the walls do date back to A.D. 1000 but most of the building is from the 16th century. The entire castle was restored in 1877. The chapel and courtyard are especially worth seeing.

Across from the old castle is the ancient residence of the bishops of Constance. Stand on the terrace and enjoy the view.

Meersburg has a marvelous hotel—the stately **Hotel Romantik Residenz am See**, *Uferpromenade 11; tel. +49 (7532) 800-40; website: www.hotel-residenz-meersburg.com*, which looks out over Lake Constance toward Lindau. Its grand dining room serves delicious meals.

The forest's highest peak

The highest peak in the forest is **Feldberg**. Take a chair lift to the top. The village of Feldberg (*website: www.feldberg-schwarzwald.de*) at the foot of the mountain was the birthplace of German skiing and is one of the oldest winter resorts in Germany.

Baden-Baden: The world's most famous spa

Baden-Baden (*website: www.baden-baden.de*), the world's most famous spa, is known for its curative thermal waters. The spa was built over the ruins of the ancient Roman baths south of Heidelberg in the Black Forest. The best time to visit, if you can stand the crowds, is the last week in August, **Baden-Baden Week**, when horse races, balls, and receptions are held. The magnificent turn-of-the-century Festspielhaus, *Beim Alten Bahnhof, tel. +49 (7221) 3013-101; website: www.festspielhaus.de*, is the place to go for concerts, opera, and ballet performances by international stars year 'round.

Baden-Baden's best hotels

Brenner's Park-Hotel, *Schillerstrasse 4-6; tel. +49 (7221) 9000; website: www.brenners.com*, is the best hotel in the town of Baden-Baden, and one of the best in Europe. This Edwardian hotel is a traditional part of any visit to the spa. It has large, graceful public rooms, excellent service, an indoor heated pool, a sauna, and a solarium. The hotel has views of the park and the river.

      Hotel Steigenberger Europäischer Hof, *Kaiserallee 2, tel. +49 (7221) 9330, website: www.steigenberger.de/baden-baden*, is a slightly more affordable alternative to the rather pricey Brenner's Park-Hotel.

The coziest shelter in the forest

Romantik Parkhotel Wehrle, *Gartenstrasse 24 near Triberg; tel. +49 (7722) 860-20; website: www.parkhotel-wehrle.de*, is a beautiful escape while in the Black Forest. It has a swimming pool, sauna, and an excellent restaurant known for its trout dishes.

      The **Bühler-Höhe Hotel**, *Schwarzwaldhochstrasse 1, Bühl/Baden Baden; tel. +49 (7226) 550; website: www.buehlerhoehe.de*, is a great place to absorb the atmosphere of the forest. It is hidden behind a thick canopy of evergreens in its own 36 acre park. Originally a hunting castle, it is now a luxury hotel with an excellent fitness center.

Germany's 11 wine-growing districts, which stretch from the middle Rhine at Bonn south to Lake Constance (*Bodensee*), produce the lightest white wines in the world. These regions are filled with classic scenery—castle ruins, grand cathedrals, gabled houses, elegant spas, and enchanting little villages.

The world's best Rieslings

The Rheingau region (*website: www.rheingau.de*) on the right bank of the Rhine is the aristocrat of Germany's wine-producing areas. This small region, extending from Hocheim in the east to Lorch in the west, is known for the Riesling grape. Sample the wines at the local wineries for a taste of the best white wines in the world. This is also the place to buy good German wine cheaply. In addition to wine, the Rheingau is also known for its wealth of monuments, monasteries, and wine cellars, some of which date back to the time of Charlemagne.

A good place to sample the local Rieslings is the crowded but exciting town of **Rüdesheim** (*website: www.ruedesheim.de*). The *Drösselgasse*, a narrow, cobblestone alley, is lined with wine taverns and restaurants. Order a *Römer* (a wine goblet with a green pedestal) of the local wine and watch the crowds. Rüdesheim is the site of rousing wine festivals in May and August. One of Germany's best wine museums is in the *Brömserburg* castle at the west end of town.

A fine restaurant that features wine tasting is located in the **Jagdschloss Niederwald**, three miles from Rüdesheim, *Auf dem Niederwald; tel. +49 (6722) 710-60; website: www.niederwald.de*. Delicious game dishes are served in season. This castle hotel is impressive, set on a hill high above the Rhine.

The best German reds

Stuttgart (*website: www.stuttgart.de*) is the perfect base for touring the Württemberg area, which follows the Neckar River south of Baden-Baden. Red wines, such as Trollinger and Lemberger, can be sampled throughout Württemberg. (They are rarely exported, so this could be your only chance to enjoy them.)

Following your wine tasting, round out your visit by going to the old Renaissance palace (*Schillerplatz 6, tel. +49 (711) 8953-5111; website: www. landesmuseum-stuttgart.de*) or viewing the art in the **Staatsgalerie**, in *Konrad-Adenaur-Strasse 30-32; tel. +49 (711) 470-400; website: www.staatsgalerie.de*, with its excellent collection of German expressionist masterpieces, the Roman baths and castle ruins in Weinsberg, or the Palace Gardens of Ludwigsburg.

The best place to eat and sample local Württemberg wines is the **Ratskeller**, *Marktplatz 1; tel. +49 (711) 239-780; website: www.stuttgarterratskeller.de,* right in the middle of Stuttgart.

The wine cellar of the Holy Roman Empire

The elegant wines of the **Rheinpfalz** region (*website: www.rheinpfalz.de*) have been famous since the days of the Holy Roman Emperor Charlemagne. The picturesque *Deutsche Weinstrasse* (German Wine Road, *website: www.deutsche-weinstrasse.de*) runs its length.

Detour, if you can, to nearby **Speyer** (*website: www.speyer.de*), where the town's **Wine Museum**, *Domplatz; tel. +49 (6232) 620-222; website: www.museum.speyer.de,* houses the oldest bottle of wine in the world, dating from the third century. The best place to sample local wine is **Café Hindenburg**, *Maximilianstrasse 91; tel. +49 (6232) 756-81.*

The oldest wine region

Fine wines are produced northwest of Rheinpfalz in the **Moselle Valley**, which has the oldest vineyards in Germany and the steepest vineyards in the world. The Moselle's vines are ancient. The Romans used the *Neumagen* wine ship in the Trier Museum to bring vines to Germany.

Markers along the Rhine describe the wines produced here: Piesporter, Wehlen, Bernkasteller, and Graach. The finest Moselle wines are Bernkasteler Doktor and Wehlener Sonnenuhr. The website *www.msr-wein.de*, unfortunately only in German, is a veritable encyclopedia on this area and its wines.

The most beautiful wine region

The **Ahr Valley** (*website: www.ahrtal.de*), Germany's northernmost wine region, is the most beautiful. Between Altenahr and Bad Neuenahr, the river forces its way in rapid, winding course between rugged slate crags. Vineyards climb steep slopes in the shadows of castle ruins. Wine villages are sandwiched by the hills.

Wine has been made here since ancient Roman times, and today the area produces Germany's best reds and bubbling whites. Try the local wines at the **Weinstube Sanct Peter**, *Walporzheimer Strasse 134; tel. +49 (2641) 977-50; website: www.sanct-peter.de* in Walporzheim or at the lively **Lochmühle**, *Ahr-Rotweinstrasse 62-68; tel. +49 (2643) 8080; website: www.hotel-lochmuehle.de,* at Mayschloss. Hikers can follow the 19-mile Red Wine Trail through vineyards from Lohrsdorf to Altenahr.

The best rosés

The **Baden** region (*website: www.baden-tourismus.de*), located between Heidelberg and the Bodensee, is famous for its whites and Schillerwein rosés. A giant cask holding 52,000 gallons of the region's wine is located in Heidelberg. You can try the local wines at **Perkeo**, *Hauptstrasse 75; tel. +49 (6221) 650-005; website: www.restaurant-perkeo-heidelberg.de*, a restaurant in Heidelberg. A more scenic place to sample the wines is on the terrace of the **Weinstube im Schloss Heidelberg**, *tel. +49 (6221) 654-429,* a restaurant located in Heidelberg castle (*website: www.heidelberg-schloss.de*).

The most charming castle hotels on the Rhine

The Rhineland is a fairy-tale region, home to more than 30 medieval castles. And the best way to soak up the atmosphere here is to stay in a Rhine castle that has been turned into a hotel.

The **Klostergut Jakobsberg**, *Im Tal der Loreley, Boppard; tel. +49 (6742) 8080; website: www.jakobsberg.de,* a monastery turned hotel, is also near the Loreley. Built in 1157 by Kaiser Friedrick I, it is situated on a bluff overlooking the Rhine. The monastery was owned by the archbishops of Trier. In 1640, it became the property of the Jesuits, who used it as a university until the French Revolution. The monastery was later taken over by the Prussians. Today it is a hotel with modern amenities, a good restaurant, an indoor pool, an 18-hole golf course and its own helipad.

The **Hotel Burg Reichenstein**, *Burgweg, Trechtinghausen am Rhein, tel. +49 (6721) 6101; website: www.hotel-burg-reichenstein.de/castle-germany/index,* has a magnificent view of the Rhine. Its 13th-century Gothic arches and rough stonework remain. Robber-knights once watched the river from the castle's towers. Inside the castle is a museum displaying medieval weapons and armor.

Germany's best medieval castle

The best medieval castle in Germany, perhaps in all of Europe, is **Burg Eltz**, *tel. +49 (2672) 950-500; website: www.burg-eltz.de,* nestled in an enchanted forest in the Rhine/Mosel region. It is the epitome of a medieval, fairy tale castle, with its graceful spires and towers. The castle remains incredibly well preserved and, due to shrewd political maneuvering, has remained in the hands of the Eltz family for more than 800 years. They still occupy part of the castle. The best way to see this elegantly furnished castle is with a tour, included in the admission price. From the car park you take a short walk through the forest to the castle. Along the way, there is a scenic overlook where you can view the castle from a distance. Daily tours take you through many of the rooms.

THE STRANGEST HISTORY: WORMS

The city of **Worms** *(website: www.worms.de)* has a strange name and an even stranger history. It was named for a legendary giant worm with fangs and webbed feet that lived in the Rhine and demanded human sacrifices.

Worms was the fifth-century capital of the legendary Nibelungs. The tribe left the area, according to legend, after the wicked Hagen slew their hero, Siegfried, and threw their treasure into the river. A huge statue of Hagen commemorates the story. The town was destroyed in A.D. 436 by Atilla the Hun. Nowadays, it is a popular destination for history buffs on the trail of Martin Luther and for visitors to "Little Jerusalem" and to the oldest Jewish cemetery in Europe.

THE HARZ: THE MOST BEWITCHING REGION

According to legend, witches live in Germany's northernmost mountains, the Harz *(website: www.harzinfo.de)*. They are said to fly on Walpurgis Night, the last night of April. The residents of the area celebrate this night by dressing up as witches, demons, and devils.

However if you miss Walpurgis Night, don't despair—this region is bewitching all year round. The mountains are covered with evergreen forests, inhabited by deer, and brightened by waterfalls, ravines, and rocky streams. One of Germany's highest peaks is the Wurmberg near Braunlage in the Harz. Take a cable car to see the top *(website: www.wurmberg-seilbahn.de)*.

The Harz was made famous by the celebrated German poet Heinrich Heine (1797-1856) in *Die Harzreise* (The Harz Journey), a cycle of poems and prose set to music by Franz Schubert.

BAVARIAN BESTS

Bavaria, which was independent until 1918 (Munich was its capital), is the largest and most visited section of Germany. This southeastern region is touristy, but with good reason—Bavaria is beautiful. The Alps stretch along the region's southern border with Austria, offering wooded slopes, flower-filled meadows, lakes, and castles. The mountain-encircled Königsee is a gorgeous deep-blue lake surrounded by sheer alpine cliffs.

Bavaria's oddest tradition

Each year, mid-April through the end of June, Bavaria celebrates its "royal vegetable," the white asparagus. *Spargel* season includes festivals and markets, an Asparagus Queen, and pick-your-own stalls along the roadsides.

The grandest Spargel festival takes place in Schrobenhausen on Johannistag (St. John the Baptist's Day, June 24) to mark the official end of the season. During Spargel season you can't go wrong having a traditional meal of about six large, white tender asparagus (they are individually peeled prior to cooking), with a butter sauce, new potatoes and very thin slices of cured ham.

Munich: The most fun loving city

Munich is Germany's party town. Every season provides an excuse for celebrating: fall, bock beer time, the opera festival, beer garden days, carnival, and, of course, Oktoberfest.

Munich's best party

If you like a good party and crowds, visit Munich during **Oktoberfest** at the end of September. Make sure you have a hotel reservation; the city never has enough room for all the revelers. If you can't find a hotel call the **Munich Tourism Office**, *tel. +49 (89) 2339-6555; website: www.muenchen.de,* they may be able to help you find a homestay.

Since the first Oktoberfest in 1810, it has been celebrated every year beginning three Saturdays before the first Sunday in October and continuing for 16 days. Festivities start with a parade of the various breweries with sumptuously decorated horse-drawn beer wagons through the streets of Munich to the Theresienwiese. After the wagons arrive here, the mayor taps the first of more than 700,000 kegs; with his cry of "*O'zapft is*" the Oktoberfest officially begins. The next day, another parade takes place, this time with the participation of thousands of visitors from villages large and small, near and far, all in their traditional dress. This parade is so popular, it gets telecast on national television. Over the 16 days, about 6 million visitors quaff the Bavarian brew, enjoy brass band music and spectacular rides.

Enormous beer tents, sponsored by Germany's major breweries, are the hub of activity. Stein-serving waitresses in *Dirndl* folk costumes weave among wooden tables, carrying as many as 16 one-liter glass mugs at a time.

The world's largest science museum

The **Deutsches Museum**, *Museumsinsel 1, tel. +49 (89) 217-91; website: www.deutsches-museum.de*, takes up an entire island in the middle of Munich's Isar River. It's great fun for people who love gadgets. Most of the displays are interactive and lots of fun for any age. The museum is open daily from 9 a.m. to 5 p.m., and on Thursday until 8 p.m.

Munich's top three sights

The **Pinakotheken**; *website: www.pinakothek.de,* open daily except Mondays 10 a.m. to 6 p.m., Thursdays to 8 p.m.: This is actually three world class museums within easy walking distance of each other. To do them chronologically, start with the **Alte Pinakothek**, *Barerstrasse 27; tel. +49 (89) 2380-50,* covering 14th to 18th century European painting and boasting the largest collection of Peter Paul Rubens paintings, Lucas Cranach the elder, Ablrecht Dürer, etc.

Cross the street to the **Neue Pinakothek**, *Barerstrasse 29; tel. +49 (89) 2380-5195*, where the show continues with European painting and sculpture of the 18th and 19th centuries includes works by Manet, Monet, Dégas, Cézanne, Van Gogh, Gauguin, Klimt, and Goya. Its natural lighting sets off the paintings well. Sloping ramps lead past artworks hung in chronological order.

Cross yet another street and go to the **Pinakothek der Moderne**, *Barerstrasse 40, tel. +49 (89) 2380-5360*, and see paintings and sculptures of the 20th and 21st centuries, the museum for design and museum of architecture.

The **Residenzmuseum**, *Residenzstrasse 1, tel. +49 (89) 290-671; website: www.residenz-muenchen.de*, once the palace of the Wittelsbach Kings, it contains rooms from the Renaissance, baroque, and rococo periods. Damaged during World War II, it has been meticulously restored. The Ancestors Gallery houses portraits of all the Bavarian Kings.

The **Schatzkammer** (Treasure chamber) of the Residenz can be accessed separately at *Max-Joseph-Platz 3*. It contains the splendid treasures of Bavarian royalty: jeweled crowns and crosses, goblets, medals, swords, dishes, and jewelry. Perhaps the most beautiful object is in the third room: a statue of St. George slaying the dragon, which was made in 1590 and inlaid with precious stones.

Munich's most inviting park

When you tire of the historical sights and museums, take a walk through the 18th-century **Englischer Garten,** modeled on an English park and set out along the banks of the river Isar, which flows through the city. The park has woods, brooks, and a Chinese tower-turned-beer garden that is a great place to drink huge steins of beer, eat Bavarian pretzels and the veal *Weisswurst* (white sausage) with sweet mustard, and meet people. There is an area set aside for nude sunbathing. End your day by taking a refreshing dip in the ice-cold Isar River, if you dare.

Munich's oldest church

Alte Peterskirche (St. Peter's Church), *Rindermarkt 1*, just off the Marienplatz near the *Rathaus*, is often overlooked, although it's the oldest parish church in Munich. It houses a macabre relic—a gilded and bejeweled skeleton of the martyr St. Munditia (the patron saint of lonely women). Fake eyes look out of her skull, gems glitter where her teeth should be, and a jeweled coronet balances on her head of fake hair. If you climb the 277 steps to the top, you will have a spectacular view of the Alps from the Alte Peter's 300-foot tower.

The world's best Kandinsky collection

Städtische Galerie im Lenbachhaus (Municipal Gallery), *Luisenstrasse 33; tel. +49 (89) 233-32000; website: www.lenbachhaus.de/cms,* has the most comprehensive collection in the world of the works of the founder of the Blue Rider movement, painter Vassily Kandinsky, as well as extensive works by Paul Klee, Alexej von Jawlensky, etc. The gallery is an imitation Italian villa with a small garden.

Note: Due to major renovations, it will be closed until spring 2013.

The best place to buy folk fashions

Loden-Frey, *Maffeistasse 7; tel. +49 (89) 210-390; website: www.loden-frey.de,* is the best place to buy German folk-style clothing (*Dirndls* for girls and *Lederhosen* for boys) in traditional fabrics. This family-run establishment has been in business since 1842.

The most magnificent sight

Schloss Nymphenburg, *tel. +49 (89) 1790-80; website: www.schloss-nymphenburg. de,* in a suburb of Munich, easily accessible with the Nr. 17 tram, is a magnificent 17th-century palace set in a 500-acre park filled with fountains, statues, lakes, waterfalls, and a formal garden. Portraits of the 24 most beautiful women in Europe

200 years ago, commissioned by King Ludwig I, hang in the south pavilion. One of the wings houses an impressive collection of historical royal carriages and a very good collection of Nymphenburg porcelain (Bavaria's answer to the Prussian Meissen porcelain).

Walk to the **Botanische Garten** through the park (or access via *Menzinger Strasse 65; tel. +49 (89) 17861-316, website: www.botmuc.de*), surely one of Germany's finest botanical gardens.

The darker side of Munich

Dachau Concentration Camp, *tel. +49 (8131) 669-970; website: www. kz-gedenkstaette-dachau.de*, now a memorial to those who died in the camp during World War II, is located outside of the city. More than 200,000 people, mainly Jews, were labeled undesirable by the Nazis and imprisoned here between 1933 and 1945. The camp is virtually intact. Several barracks can be seen, as well as the morgue, the crematorium, and the Brausebad (where prisoners were gassed to death). Documentary films of the Holocaust are shown, and photo displays are on view.

Munich's best restaurants

Considered Munich's best restaurant, **Tantris**, *Johann-Fichte-Strasse 7; tel. +49 (89) 3619-590; website: www.tantris.de*, has been winning awards and stars for over 35 years with its consistently *haute cuisine*.

Altes Hackerhaus, *Sendlingerstrasse 14; tel. +49 (89) 260-5026; website: www.hackerhaus.de*, is the best place for Bavarian specialities. (If you have the nerve, try the pig knuckles—*Schweinshax'n*.)

Zum Franziskaner, *Perusa Strasse 5; tel. +49 (89) 231-8120; website: zum-franziskaner.de*, serves the best Munich sausage (*Weisswurst*) and *Leberkäs*, a kind of meat loaf that is made of ground beef, liver, and bacon and eaten with sweet mustard.

Various kinds of Bavarian sausages are also served at **Nürnberger Bratwurst Glöckl**, *Frauenplatz 9; tel. +49 (89) 291-9450*; *website: www. bratwurst-gloeckl.de*, near the cathedral. The décor is charming, featuring large prints, arms, and woodwork. Reservations are a must.

The hottest nightlife

Schwabing is traditionally Munich's student and artistic district and has more than 200 restaurants and cafés, as well as myriad nightclubs and bars.

The **Park Café**, *Sophienstrasse 7; tel. +49 (89) 5161-7980; website: www.parkcafe089.de,* is a '50s-style lounge that has some of the best new music in Munich. It is the place to go.

The best jazz is played at the **Jazzclub Unterfahrt**, *Einsteinstrasse 42; tel. +49 (89) 448-2794; website: www.unterfahrt.de.*

Germany's best beer cellars

Munich is famous for its beer cellars—informal halls where lots of beer is downed at long tables full of friendly people. The city has 12 historic *Bierkeller*, which serve huge steins of beer and Bavarian specialities. Sit anywhere—these are friendly places. Often an oompah-band will play and patrons will sing.

The most famous beer hall in the world is the **Hofbräuhaus**, *Am Platzl 9; tel. +49 (89) 2901-3610; website: www.hofbraeuhaus.de.* Although it is very touristy, the Hofbräuhaus is worth a visit for its friendly atmosphere. In the summer, the beer garden with its big chestnut trees is a nice place to visit.

The **Donisl**, *Weinstrasse 1; tel. +49 (89) 296-264; website: www.bayerischer-donisl.de*, is one of the oldest of Munich's beer halls, popular since 1715.

The **Augustiner-Restaurant**, *Neuhauser Str. 27; tel. +49 (89) 2318-3257; website: www.augustiner-restaurant.com*, has been around since 1328. If you can, get a table in the *Grotto-Halle*—unique décor!

Zum Dürnbräu, *Dürnbräugasse 2; tel. +49 (89) 222-195*, is a little difficult to find as it is tucked away in a small side street, but definitely worth it. This is where a lot of local regulars come—and have been, for over 500 years! Dark paneling, low ceilings and excellent beer and food. When the weather permits, there is a small beer garden in front and another in back.

Munich's best hotel

The **Hotel Vier Jahreszeiten Kempinski**, *Maximilianstrasse 17; tel. +49 (89) 212-50; website: www.kempinski-vierjahreszeiten.com*, is one of the top hotels in Munich. A deluxe, traditional hotel with yellow stucco external walls and blue awnings, the hotel exudes Bavarian hospitality. The hotel's restaurant is excellent.

The **Mandarin Oriental Munich**, *Neuturmstr. 1; tel. +49 (89) 290-980; website: www.mandarinoriental.com,* is located right in back of the Hofbräuhaus and smack in the center of town. A favorite with opera stars and other celebrities.

The **Charles Hotel**, *Sophienstrasse 28; tel. +49 (89) 5445-550; website: www.charleshotel.de*, is Munich's newest luxury hotel and ideally located close enough to the main train station and within walking distance of the major Pinakothek museums.

The best souvenir shop

If you want to take back a trendy souvenir guaranteed not to be made in China, visit **Obacht**, *Lederer Strasse 17; tel. +49 (89) 1890-4260; website: www. obacht-web.de.*

The world's best gingerbread

North of Munich is **Nuremberg**, the gingerbread capital of the world. The best time to visit is Christmas when the local bakers take advantage of the world famous Christmas market (*website: www.christkindlesmarkt.de*) to show off their unrivalled skills in this art. The market also features the largest number of stands with Christmas decorations of all kinds. It goes from the Friday before the first advent Sunday (usually the last Sunday in November) until December 24.

Alpine peaks

The **Alps** stretch along Germany's southern border from the Bodensee in the west to the Watzmann Peak near Berchtesgaden in the east. This mountain range rose from the sea about 80 million years ago. You can find fossils of sea creatures among the peaks. The beautiful lakes in the Voralpenland are remnants of the Ice Age.

Germany's highest peak

The **Zugspitze** (*website: www.zugspitze.de*) Germany's highest peak (9,840 feet), overlooks Garmisch-Partenkirchen and is part of the *Wettersteingebirge*, an ancient formation of hard rock. You can take a cable car or train from Garmisch to the summit. Even when clouded over (about 35% of the time), the view is spectacular. You can see the peaks of other mountains rising above the blanket of clouds. Get a beer at the top, or just breathe in the intoxicatingly thin mountain air.

The best alpine hikes

The German Alps are criss-crossed by 9,000 hiking trails. They are well used by the Germans, who consider *das Wandern* (walking, rambling, exploring the world) a way of life.

The most beautiful walking trail in the Alps is along Bodensee between the towns of Friedrichshafen and Lindau. The snow-capped Alps are reflected in the waters of the lake. The walk is not difficult and can be done in trainers. The entire length takes about two days (longer if you stop in some of the towns along the way). For a map of the trail, stop in at the tourist office in Friedrichshafen or Lindau.

The trail from the town of Füssen to Neuschwanstein Castle is also beautiful. Füssen (*website: www.stadt-fuessen.de*) is a picturesque village in the shadows of the turreted castle. The trail leads past several lakes and into the shadows of the Austrian and German Alps. The walk isn't difficult.

Our third-favorite hike is somewhat more challenging and begins at the path leading from the Olympic Ski Stadium in Garmisch-Partenkirchen to the Graseckbahn cable car, which carries you to the Forsthaus Graseck. At the peak is an inviting little restaurant with panoramic views. From the terrace, you can pick up another trail along the spectacular Partnachklamm, a very narrow and deep gorge filled with torrents of water. You'll be thankful for the guardrails along the path, which is narrow and sometimes slippery.

Hitler's favorite hideout
The **Kehlsteinhaus** (also known as Eagle's Nest); *website: www.eagles-nest.de*, perched on a rocky crag above the town of Berchtesgarden, was Hitler's favorite hideout. No wonder—the view from the hideaway-turned-restaurant is exhilarating. Only open from May to October.

Bavaria's most eccentric king
King Ludwig II, who ruled Bavaria from 1864 to 1886, built the most fanciful and beautiful buildings in Germany, despite (or perhaps because of) his eccentricities. His magnificent creations were extremely costly, and his extravagance nearly bankrupted Bavaria. An important patron of the arts, Ludwig was a great fan of Richard Wagner. He built the Bayreuth Opera House for the composer and lived in a fantasy world based on Wagner's operas. Ludwig's death by drowning has raised many questions over the years. Some say his madness drove him to suicide, others say it was a fatal accident, and still others strongly believe it was murder. Whatever the case, Ludwig died shortly after officially having been declared insane.

Germany's most beautiful castle
King Ludwig II built Germany's most beautiful castle, about a three-hour drive from Munich: **Neuschwanstein,** *tel. +49 (8362) 939-8819; website: www.neuschwanstein. de*. The turreted white castle reaches high into the sky from its perch on a cliff above a valley. Walt Disney liked it so much that he copied it for Disneyland and Disneyworld. It looks enchanted, with its mountain backdrop. Inside, the walls are

decorated with murals of German heroic sagas. In Ludwig's bedroom, stars in the dark blue ceiling light up to look like the night sky.

Ludwig II lived at Neuschwanstein for 102 days before he drowned in the waters of nearby Lake Starnberg at age 40. Guided tours take 35 minutes. You have to walk up and down 170 steps and there is no elevator provided. Open daily April to October.

Germany's smallest castle

The smallest castle in Germany also was the product of Mad King Ludwig's imagination. **Linderhof Castle**, *tel. +49 (8822) 920-30; website: www.linderhof.de*, near Garmisch-Partenkirchen, is an ornate, one-man palace designed as Ludwig's personal residence. The mad king preferred to be alone and went to great lengths to maintain his privacy. He had the dining room built directly above the kitchen and installed a dining table that could be lowered into the kitchen, set by the cooks, and lifted back up to the dining room. Thus, he could be waited on at dinner without having to see the servants. Ludwig lived the longest at this castle.

Up the hill from the castle, Ludwig created an artificial grotto. Entered by way of a hinged boulder, the cave is the recreation of the Venus Mountain from Wagner's opera *Tannhäuser*. Inside the grotto is an artificial lake with a waterfall and Ludwig's boat in form of a swan.

The world's best violins

The world's most perfect violins are crafted in **Mittenwald** (*website: www. mittenwald.de*) a pretty Bavarian town sporting buildings decorated with brightly colored frescoes. The craft of building violins has been passed down through generations of local artisans, who make the instruments to order for famous musicians. The meadows, mountains, and village houses around Mittenwald are so typically Alpine that they were used as location sites for the filming of *The Sound of Music*.

DRESDEN: THE FINEST PORCELAIN

Dresden *(website: www.dresden.de)* and nearby **Meissen** *(website: www. stadt-meissen.de)* are known for their fine porcelain. But Dresden is now becoming known for its newly restored buildings. During World War II, the city was fire-bombed by the Allies during the last days of the war, and 80% of it burned to the ground. It has been beautifully reconstructed. Linden trees again line the banks of the Elbe River, and the city boasts some of the best museums in Germany. Its German nickname is rightly *Elbflorenz.*

Stroll along **Prager Strasse**, once one of the Dresden's most fashionable streets. It is lined with apartments and shops and embellished with fountains and benches. This street connects the new section of Dresden with the old section.

The cathedral **Frauenkirche** (Church of Our Lady) [*website: www. frauenkirche-dresden.de*] dating back to the 11th century, was completely bombed in those last World War II days and had been left in ruins for decades as a memorial to the atrocities of war. However, in 1994 a citizens' petition was successful and reconstruction started. Finally, in October 2005, the Frauenkirche was re-consecrated. Because of its excellent acoustics, many concerts now also take place there.

Dresden's best art museums
The **Dresden state art collections**, *tel. +49 (351) 4914-2000; website: www. skd-dresden.de,* are one of the most important ones in existence. The collections are housed in 11 different museums, of which the most important ones are: the **Zwinger**, *Theaterplatz 1,* and the portrait gallery it contains is Dresden's drawing card. Carefully restored following the bombings of World War II, it retains much of its original structure, including a majestic courtyard where fountains play in the summer. Built as a fortress in the 18th century, it houses Raphael's *Sistine Madonna*, as well as a dozen Rembrandts, 16 Reubens, and several Tintorettos. The bells in its carillon tower are made of Dresden china.

The **Grünes Gewoelbe** (Green Vault) in the **Residenzschloss**, *Taschenberg 2; tel. +49 (351) 4914-2000; website: www.skd.museum/de/museen-institutionen/ residenzschloss/gruenes-gewoelbe/index.html,* is arguably the finest treasure chamber in Europe. Be sure to see the Court of the Grand Mogul, made by the Dresden court jeweler Dinglinger from 1701 to 1718: it is made up of over 150 miniature figurines of princes, dancers and animals made entirely of gold, silver, pearls, enamel and precious stones.

The **Porzellansammlung** (Porcelain collection), located in the Zwinger, *entrance Sophienstrasse, tel. +49 (351) 4914-6612*; *website: www. freundeskreisporzellan.de,* with about 20,000 invaluably beautiful Meissen, Chinese, and Japanese objects.

A music lover's favorite
The **Semper Oper**, *Theaterplatz 2; tel. +49 (351) 491-1705; website: www. semperoper.de,* is where Richard Wagner and von Weber conducted and several

of Richard Strauss' operas premiered. The current opera house was designed by architect Gottfried Semper and completed in 1850. After 1945, it was restored based on original drawings. The building was immortalized in a painting by the 18th-century artist Canaletto.

THE CITY WITH THE MOST CULTURE

Weimar and Goethe are to the German speaking world what Stratford-on-Avon and Shakespeare are to the English speaking world. Weimar (*website: www.weimar.de*), in the province of Thuringia and first mentioned in records in 899, is a jewel of a small city of approximately 65,000 inhabitants, located in the middle of the country and easily accessible by train or car. For centuries, it has rightly held the title of cultural capital and not only since it was European Cultural Capital in 1999.

This city was called home by the paramount German poets Johann Wolfgang von Goethe and Johann Friedrich von Schiller, composers Franz Liszt and Johann Sebastian Bach, the painter Lucas Cranach the elder, the philosopher Johann Gottfried Herder, just to name the most prominent ones. Ludwig van Beethoven, Richard Wagner, Hans Christian Andersen, Lyonel Feininger, and Walter Gropius are no less prominent contributors to the world cultural heritage who spent part of their lives here. It was the cradle of the Bauhaus movement, whose architectural influence is still with us today.

The most beautiful library
The **Duchess Anna Amalia library**, *Platz der Demokratie; tel. +49 (3643) 545-52; website: www.anna-amalia-bibliothek.de*, was built in the 18th century for the erudite duchess. Over the centuries, almost a million books were collected and are now stored in highly modern underground facilities. In 2004, a fire destroyed a large part of the historical Rococo library; thankfully, reconstruction has been swift and the hall can be visited again. Note, however, that access is limited to 250 visitors per day; this means that during the summer season, many are turned away. Best to get there by 9 a.m. and stand in line until the box office opens at 9:30 a.m.

The homes of both **Goethe,** *Frauenplan 1; tel. +49 (3643) 545-400;* and **Schiller,** *Schillerstr 12; tel. +49 (3643) 545-400; website for both: www.klassik-stiftung.de,* are now museums.

BUCHENWALD: THE BLACKEST MEMORY

Just north of Weimar is the infamous **Buchenwald Concentration Camp**, *tel. +49 (3643) 432-00, website: www.buchenwald.de*, where over 250,000 people from more than 50 nationalities were held and over 56,000 people died in World War II. The camp and its museum of torture and extermination devices are chilling. Even in the spring the site is so cold and bleak that you cannot imagine surviving a winter in the scanty barracks. Outside the camp there is a memorial to the victims.

HEIDELBERG: THE MOST ROMANTIC TOWN

Heidelberg *(website: www.heidelberg.de)* is Europe's oldest university town, with students making up one-fifth of today's population of 140,000. It is also a world-leading center for medical research, as well as a technology honeypot attracting swarms of experts in such disciplines as bio-technology, environmental protection, and genetic engineering. And, for the romantics among us it offers a timeless abundance of romanticism to beguile St. Valentine himself.

The most beautiful sight
The **Heidelberg Castle**, *tel. +49 (6221) 654-429; website: www.heidelberg-schloss. de,* is a magnificent red structure with octagonal towers and ruined belfries. From the castle, you have a panoramic view of the city's red roofs, the spire of the Heiliggeist Kirche, and the Neckar River. The castle is open from 9:30 a.m. to 6 p.m.

The best traditional entertainment
At the **Golden Sheep** (*Zum Guldenen Schaf* in German), *Hauptstrasse 115; tel. +49 (6221) 208-79*, you can eat and drink your way through the Bronze Age, Ancient Rome, the Middle Ages, the Renaissance, Baroque, and the Biedermeier periods, accompanied by performances on musical instruments of the various periods. You may also be expected to conform to contemporaneous manners and customs (excluding unauthorized pillaging and ravishing, of course).

Within this 18th-century country inn, proprietor Dr. Karl Kischka has created not just an exhilarating gastronomic experience, but also a museum of musical instruments, an alchemist's kitchen, a facsimile collection of precious medieval documents, a crossbow arena, and even a 19th-century clay pigeon shooting range.

Heidelberg's best hotel

For deeply luxurious five-star opulence, you can't beat the **Hotel Europa**, (*Der Europäische Hof* in German), *Friedrich- Ebert-Anlage 1; tel. +49 (6221) 5150; website: www.europaeischerhof.com*, which has maintained an outstanding position in international tourism for no less than 130 years. In the last 40 years, it has been managed by the urbane Ernst-Friedrich von Kretschmann and his interior-designer wife Sylvia.

Walking into the Europäische Hof feels like going back 100 years in time. Stroll the marbled corridors and fountain-lined terraces, admire its grand dining rooms, and wallow in the opulence of one of its 118 rooms and apartments, all designed by Sylvia with a nod to the Hohenzollern dynasty. European crowned heads check in to this day, even Sweden's King Gustav and his wife Sylvia, a native of Heidelberg, whose signature graces the glittering visitor's book.

Best for youthful spirit

Cantankerous reactionaries who grumble about noisy teenagers will love this relic: the **Student Prison Museum**, *Augustinergasse 2; tel. +49 (6221) 543-554*. From 1778 until 1914, scholars were sent here for up to three days for such common offences as drunkenness and playing tricks on officials, or for up to a month for dueling, all with time off for attending lectures. Bored young prisoners would pass the time decorating the walls, little realizing how fascinating their artwork would one day prove for innocent ticket-buying visitors.

Best souvenir—the Student's Kiss

Not only is the chocolate delicious, so too, is the story behind the sweet "Student's Kiss". It began in 1863 with the opening of the **Café Knösel** in the heart of Heidelberg, *Haspelgasse 16, tel. +49 (6221) 223-45* . The café became a venue for the dashing young students and the young ladies of the city's once-famous finishing schools. Unfortunately, the trysts were silent because the ladies were accompanied by hawk-eyed governesses who intercepted every pass with arctic commitment. Sympathizing with their plight, the pastry chef, Fridolin Knösel, created a particularly ambrosial chocolate pastry which he dubbed the "Student's Kiss." The governesses were unable to prevent them being presented to their charges in lieu—and in anticipation—of the real thing.

Most romantic hotel restaurant

The **Hirschgasse**, *Hirschgasse 3, tel. +49 (6221) 4540; website: www.hirschgasse. de*, was built for romance and retains its fairytale charm under the ownership of Ernst and Allison Kraft. They've retrieved and installed original old lead stained glass windows and antique lamps and lovingly restored wood paneling and prints. A special feature of the Hirschgasse are the pictures of fencing student fraternities and the swords with which they carved dueling scars into their opponents' cheeks. In the rustic *Mensurstube* you can see where Count Bismarck carved his name into a 200-year-old table.

Its restaurants are not just enchanting, but renowned for their regional and international cuisine. Concessions to modern hospitality include Laura Ashley-themed rooms and a hi-tech sound system that can channel music to suit your exact mood to your table.

The most romantic walk

The **Philosopher's Path** is the most romantic walk, just near the Hirschgasse. In spring, it's ablaze with color from Japanese cherries, cypresses, lemons, rhododendrons, yucca trees, and more. And it has the most wonderful view of Heidelberg across the river.

THE BEST OF
GREECE

Greece is a breathtaking country of mountains, islands, and sea. Its special light gives a clarity to the blue sky above and the colors below—colors that include a profusion of wild flowers in early spring. When you visit Greece, forget the packaged tours. This is a do-it-yourself country that should be experienced outdoors. Camp out under Greece's stars to best experience the country. Travel light and be prepared to follow the impulse of the moment.

ATHENS: THE BIRTHPLACE OF MODERN CIVILIZATION

Athens—the birthplace of Western democracy, poetry, drama, art, and philosophy—is no longer at the center of the world it has nurtured. Nonetheless, Athens merits more than a quick visit. It has the world's largest and most remarkable collections of ancient ruins, including the ancient Parthenon and one of the world's finest archeological museums. And beyond these archeological wonders is an exciting nightlife and a unique lifestyle, part European, part Middle Eastern.

The Acropolis: The heart of ancient Athens
You shouldn't miss the **Acropolis**, *Dionysiou Areopayitou; tel. +30 (210) 321-0219*, and the ancient city. It stands in full view on a hill above Athens, adding a majestic dignity and beauty to what otherwise would be a shabby city. Buildings

in Athens are subject to a height limit so that the **Parthenon**, the most important structure of the Acropolis, remains visible from most points in the area. Dedicated to the goddess Athena, the Acropolis was the religious center of the ancient capital. It was reconstructed in the fifth century B.C. by Pericles.

Acro means "top", and *polis* means "city." Together they mean the highest point, or citadel, of the city—which also means a stiff climb. Wear good walking shoes. It is best to visit the Acropolis at dawn or in the late afternoon, because of the play of light. In summer, midday temperatures are too intense.

To the right of the entrance to the Acropolis is the **Temple of Athena Nike**, built to commemorate the victory of the Athenians over the Persians. At the top of the hill is the beautiful Parthenon, temple of the goddess Athena.

The Acropolis is open from 8 a.m. until 4:30 p.m. Tuesdays through Fridays, from 10 a.m. until 4:30 p.m. Mondays, and from 8:30 a.m. until 2:30 p.m. Saturdays and Sundays.

Just 300 meters from the Acropolis is the new and long-awaited glass and concrete **Acropolis Museum** (*website: www.theacropolismuseum.gr*). Located in the historical area of Makriyianni, southeast of the Rock of the Acropolis, on Dionysiou Areopagitou Street, it houses more than 4,000 ancient works that were found on the Acropolis in 20,000 square meters of display space. This is also where Greece hopes to one day display the Elgin Marbles. They are currently on display in the British Museum and the debate continues as to if they should be returned to Athens.

Just beneath the Acropolis on the southern slopes are two ancient amphitheaters. The **Theater of Dionysos** is where the first Greek tragedies were performed, and dates back to the sixth century B.C.

The **Odeum of Herodes Atticus**, which dates to A.D. 161, is the site for performances of theater, opera, ballet, and music during the Athens Festival held between July and September each year. The amphitheaters are open from 8.30 a.m. until 3 p.m. daily. The Odeion is open only for performances.

The ancient **Agora**, or marketplace, is on the eastern slopes of the Acropolis hill, on the north end of the Plaka. Now a major archeological excavation site, this was the downtown area of the ancient city and the main crossroads for routes to other major towns, such as Piraeus. Here you will find the **Stoa of Attalus**, a trading center built in 20 B.C.; the **Roman Forum**, begun during Julius Caesar's reign; the **Kerameikos**, *148 Ermou,* the ancient city cemetery; and **Hadrain's Library**, built in the second century. A museum houses artifacts found during the excavations.

The world's finest sculptures

The **National Archaeological Museum**, *44 Patission; tel. +30 (210) 821-7717; website: www.namuseum.gr,* has the finest collection of sculptures in the world. Treasures include giant figures of Greek gods and men, a world-renowned collection of Greek vases, pieces of ancient Cycladic art, and magnificent frescoes from the Minoan sites of Knossos on Cyprus and Akrotiri on Santorini. The gold Mycaenean death mask here is reputed to be that of Agamemnon, the ancient Greek king of the Iliad.

Athens' main square

Syntagma Square (Constitution Square), in the heart of the business district, is Athens' main square. A favorite pastime of both visitors and native Athenians is to sit at one of the square's outdoor café tables and watch pedestrians walk by. The 3,000 chairs in the square are arranged so that they all face the sidewalk for a better view. Have a coffee, beer, or ouzo and Greek *meze* (snacks) while you watch.

Many of Athens' most important sights and monuments border Syntagma Square. The **National Parliament Building** faces the square on the east side. The changing of the palace guards takes place every hour on the hour each day. On Sundays at 11 a.m., the ritual of the *evzone*, when the guards dress in kilts, white tights, and turned-up shoes, is accompanied by a regimental brass band.

The **Benaki Museum**, *1 Koumbari; tel. +30 (210) 367-1000; website: www. benaki.gr,* to the left of the parliament building. The main building is an old private house crammed with clothes, furniture, and photos dating from Byzantine times to the present. It is closed on Tuesdays.

The **Byzantine Museum**, *22 Vasilissis Sofias Avenue; tel. +30 (213) 213-9572; website: www.byzantinemuseum.gr,* is in a villa not far from the Banaki and is the best place to see Greek icons. Two rooms are replicas of Byzantine basilicas of the 5th and 11th centuries. Open from 8:30 a.m. to 3 p.m. and closed on Mondays.

The **Arch of Hadrian**, on *Leoforos Amalias*, located near the square in the direction of the Acropolis, was erected by the Romans in A.D. 132 to mark the boundary of the ancient city. One side of the arch bears the inscription "This is Athens, ancient city of Theseus." The other side of the arch says, "This is the city of Hadrian and not of Theseus."

The best underground museum

Syntagma Square Metro Station is almost like a small museum. When the lines were being expanded, all kinds of archeological treasures were unearthed—from mosaic floors to pre-Christian graves and hundreds of oil lamps. A number of the finds are displayed around the marble lobby of Syntagma station.

The largest Greek temple

The **Temple of Olympian Zeus**, *tel. +30 (210) 922-6330*, stands directly behind Hadrian's Arch and is the largest temple in Greece. It is open from 8:30 a.m. until 7:30 p.m. every day in summer, 8:30 a.m. until 3 p.m. and is closed on Mondays during the winter months.

Best food and drink in Athens

The best guide to eating, drinking, and current events in Athens is the English-language *Athenian* magazine, which not only lists every restaurant and bar in the city but also critiques them.

The old **Xynos Taverna**, *4 Aggelou Geronda; tel. +30 (210) 322-1065*, serves Greek wine from the barrel and features guitar music in a wonderful and warm atmosphere. Closed Saturday and Sunday.

Athens' most elegant (and among the most expensive) restaurants are **G.B. Corner**, *Constitution Square, at the Grande Bretagne Hotel; tel. +30 (210) 333-0750; website: www.grandebretagne.gr,* the **Balthazar**, *27 Tsoha; tel. +30 (210) 644-1215*; and the **Dionysus**, *43 Roberto Galli; tel. +30 (210) 923-3182*, a first-class restaurant across from the Acropolis.

The best fish restaurants are in Pireaus and along the coast from Glyfada to Sounion. The fish restaurants with the most atmosphere (but also the most expensive prices) are located in the yacht harbor known as Mikrolimano.

Athens *ouzeries* are a dying tradition. Take the time to visit one, where you can sample Greek hors d'oeuvres and the national Greek licorice drink in the company of Greek intellectuals. Stop in at tea time or late in the evening.

Mezedopolio

Mezodopolieon are restaurants that serve only appetizers, which the Greeks call *mezes*. **Ideal**, *46 Panepistimiou; tel. +30 (210) 330-3000,* off Syntagma Square, is a good place to sample a selection.

Bouzoukia concentrate more on music than food. Most of these Greek-style nightclubs are located in an area along the seafront between Athens and Piraeus known as Tzitzines. Ask your hotel which clubs are in at the moment. It usually depends on the artist playing.

The best places to sleep

The grand dame of the city's hotels, the **Grande Bretagne**, *Constitution Square; tel. +30 (210) 333-0000; website: www.grandebretagne.gr*, which features on the 2011 *Condé Naste* Gold List, is located at the heart of things and is touted as one of the world's greatest hotels. It has been welcoming guests since 1862 and is a little rough around the edges today, but holds an air of 1920s splendor. Sit at a café in Syntagma Square and watching the wealthy, famous, and sometimes outlandish-looking people step from limousines and taxicabs to be ushered into the elegant old hotel by fancy-dressed doormen.

St. George Lycabettus, *2 Kleomenous Street; tel. +30 (210) 729-0711; website: www.sglycabettus.gr*, is less expensive and has more atmosphere. Its hilltop location gives it views of the city and the sea. Its location is not convenient, but the views are spectacular.

The best escape islands

The **Agro-Saronic Islands** are the islands closest to Athens. The greenest of all Greece's archipelagos, these islands are virtually untouched. They may not have the best beaches, but their beauty and serenity is what makes them a perfect escape from the pollution of tourism.

THE BEST OF NORTHERN GREECE

Northern Greece is home of the country's tallest mountains, including the magical Mount Olympus; of the Macedonia of Alexander the Great; and of Thessaloniki, the only other city in this essentially rural nation. The farther north you go, the thicker the woods and the more Balkan the atmosphere.

Mount Athos: A misogynist's best

The large Greek Orthodox complex perched on the rocky cliffs of **Mount Athos**, at the end of the Chalkidiki Peninsula overlooking the Aegean, is one of the major wonders of the Christian world. The only self-governing monastic state in Europe, it is made up of about 20 monasteries, many of them individual walled towns. Only adult males are allowed to visit this impressive Byzantine fortress-state. All others

353

are considered temptations. Admission rules forbid women, children, and female animals within the complex.

Mount Olympus: Home of the gods

Mount Olympus is the home of the gods of Greek legend. It's easy to see why—this huge, impressive mountain looming above the clouds, which cut off its tip, captured the imagination of the ancient Greeks. With an altitude of 9,620 feet, Olympus invites skiers in the winter (through May) and mountain climbers and hikers in the summer.

The best Greek cave

The **Petralona Cave** on the Halkidi Peninsula is 30 miles from Thessaloniki. A Neanderthal skull was found here in 1960, and the site appears to have been inhabited half a million years ago.

The best buy on hand-woven rugs

Trikala is a small village in the mountains of northern Greece. This is where the famous shaggy Greek *flokati* rugs originated, thanks to the local sheep population and the crystal clear mountain streams that are necessary for the manufacturing process. Villagers have been handweaving the rugs, now considered an art form, for the last 700 years.

THE BEST OF CENTRAL GREECE

Most of Greece's highest mountains are in the center of the country, where all points are within a few hours of Athens.

Mount Parnassus: The best skiing

About an hour-and-a-half from Athens stands **Mount Parnassus** (8,059 feet), where Greece's most serious skiers spend their winters.

Delphi: The most sacred sight

Just a short drive down from the ski area of Mount Parnassus is one of Greece's most important and impressive ancient sacred sites, **Delphi**, where Apollo was worshiped, Greek games were held, and the famous oracle was consulted about matters of great significance by pilgrims from throughout the ancient world.

Meteora: The best monastery

More accessible than Mount Athos is the monastic complex of **Meteora**, perched on the summits of some precipitous rocks above the valley of the Pineios River, about five miles from Kalambaka. The monasteries here were built in the 14th century. In all, 33 monasteries and cells still stand, but only four are now occupied. In these are housed rare manuscripts, icons, miniatures, and ecclesiastical objects of Byzantine art.

THE PELOPONNESE: THE MOST BEAUTIFUL ISLAND

The **Peloponnese** is a lovely, wild place covered with wild flowers in spring. You will never feel you've wandered long enough among its mountains, rolling plateaus, and numerous ruins. More major archeological sites are located in the Peloponnese than anywhere else in Greece.

Among the must-see ruins are the city of **Corinth**, known for its luxury and decadence during Roman times; **Mycenae**, the main attraction, sites of some of the best archeological finds in the world; **Nafplion**, a pretty town that is the site of a Venetian fortress; **Epidaurus**, where Greek plays are performed in an ancient theater every summer; and **Olympia**, site of the ancient games.

Five miles from the site of ancient Sparta, where only a few stones are left, is the pretty Byzantine town of **Mistra**, once known as the Florence of the East. Its steep, winding streets are full of churches, old mansions, and fragrant flowers and also sport a citadel and a monastery.

The **Summer Festival of Music and Drama at Epidaurus** is one of the world's most exciting performing-arts events. The ancient theater holds 14,000 people and its famous acoustic system enables each of them to hear the tiniest whisper from the stage.

The best hotel in Peloponnese

The **Nafplia Palace Hotel**, *Akronafplia, 2100 Nafplion, tel. +30 27520-70800; website: www.nafplionhotels.gr,* situated inside the walls of the old Venetian fort in Nafplion, is the best of the government-run hotels. Set on the bay, it has gorgeous views all the way to Mycenae.

The best eating in the Peloponnese

The fish tavernas along the waterfront in Nafplion are recommended as much for their views as for their fresh fish and wines served straight from the barrel. **355**

Roadside stands between Corinth and Nafplion sell the Blood of Hercules, the rich red wine famous here.

The most undiscovered, upscale island

The island of **Andros** remains a closely guarded secret, discovered to date only by some Scandinavian and British tourists. Most tourists on the ferry don't pay the island much attention, as they're headed, typically, to Mykonos, two islands away. Many of the streets in the capital city are paved with marble.

Two of the three museums on the island stem from the legacy of the Goulandris family, and you'll find Picassos as well as a sculpture garden. If these don't make you gasp, some of the shipping families' villas will. This northernmost of the Cyclades chain is also the greenest, with streams and even dragonflies.

THE CYCLADES—THE MOST VISITED GREEK ISLANDS

The **Cyclades Islands** are the most visited of Greece's island groups. They offer dramatic beauty and a civilization within a civilization. The Cycladic culture was a subculture of the ancient Mediterranean civilization led first by the Minoans and then by the Mycenaens.

About 17 of the islands are suitable for vacationers. The most famous members of the group are **Mykonos**, **Santorini**, and **Delos**. Others often visited by tourists are **Tinos**, a destination for pilgrims of the Greek Orthodox faith; **Los**, with a dramatic setting and a town built on the side of a mountain; and lovely **Paros**, where you can get away from it all. The island of **Kithnos** has one of the best government-run hotels, **Hotel Xenia**, *tel. +30 (22810) 31217*, situated in a renovated building dating back to 1840, near spas recommended for rheumatism and gynecological disorders.

Mykonos: The island for the jet set

Mykonos, a favorite spot among the jet set, has a reputation for being both wild and flashy and quaint and romantic. It is more open, vivacious, and relaxed than other Greek spots, with a philosophy of live and let live. It is a place where people are allowed and encouraged to do their own things, and where lovers of all persuasions are tolerated—and hardly even noticed. The Greek community itself is more tightly knit and warmer here than perhaps anywhere else in Greece.

356   Like the other islands in the chain, Mykonos is dry, with few trees, but beautiful in a dramatic way. Its whitewashed windmills are its trademark. Mykonians are almost compulsive about the spotlessness of their white houses and cobblestones, which offset nicely the beautiful colors of the potted flowers growing everywhere.

Mykonos' little houses, inns, hotels, and restaurants are hidden in a maze of tiny winding streets. It takes about a week to decipher the layout of the alleyways. Legend has it that the citizens of Mykonos purposely designed their streets in a random pattern to confound pirates. Mykonos' beaches, by the way, particularly Paridis, Superparidis (predominantly gay), and Ilia, are covered with nude sunbathers.

Wining and dining on Mykonos

Alvi Tou Thoodori, *Platys Gialos Beach; tel. +30 (22890) 78100; website: www.avlitouthodori.gr*, serves Greek food with a twist at very reasonable prices and has a great view of the beach.

The hottest nightlife

The **Pierros Bar and Disco,** *tel. +30 (22890) 22177; website: http://pierrosbar.gr/*, on Mykonos is the island's best known gay bar and back-to-the-eighties dance venue and is also the place to see Greek dancing. Get here about midnight. There is a cover charge, which includes one drink.

Staying in Mykonos

Hotel Tago, *Mykonos Town; tel. +30 (22890) 22611; website: www.hoteltagoo.gr*, is the best of the hotels on the island and is located on a hillside with views of the Aegean. Open from May to October.

Hotel Aphrodite, *Chora 84600, tel. +30 (22890) 71367; website: www. aphrodite-mykonos.com*, located on remote Kalafati Beach, is a beautiful place to hide away. The rooms are like bungalows, built in levels stepped up the hill along cobblestone alleyways behind the main building. Each has a balcony. In the flowered central patio is a large warm saltwater swimming pool, just a few yards from the white sandy beach across the driveway. The Aphrodite has a small disco, a nice restaurant, and a couple of private little tavernas at the end of the beach.

DELOS: APOLLO'S BIRTHPLACE

An excursion you must take from Mykonos is to the tiny island of **Delos**, now an archeological park. The god Apollo was born on this sacred island. You can visit this beautiful and eerie island via tour boat from Mykonos, a half-hour away. In spring, wild flowers grow among the impressive ruins.

SANTORINI: THE BEST SUNSETS

Santorini is a volcanic island. The towns of Oia (on the northeastern tip) and Thira (the capital also known as Fira) are situated way up in the clouds, looking down on a dramatic harbor shaped like a huge cauldron. In the evening, people gather along the mountain to watch the magnificent colors of Santorini's sunset.

Ferries pull in at one of two jetties. If you are lucky, your ferry will pull in at the one just below town, giving you the opportunity to be transported to the center of town by donkey.

Akrotiri, at the southeastern tip of the island, is one of Greece's most perfect excavations of a Bronze Age town, thought by many to be the legendary lost Atlantis.

Other things to see on Santorini include churches in Thira; Oia, known for its antiques; the beaches of Kamari, Momolithos, and Perissa (black sand) on the southwest coast; the island's castles; and the active Nea Kaimeni volcano on the small island in the harbor. (Tour boats are available to take you there.)

Buses are the least expensive way to tour the island. You can also rent a car or a moped and go it on your own.

The best beds on Santorini
Villa Renos, *tel. +30 (22860) 22848*; *website: www.villarenos.com,* is located in downtown Thira. It is on a cliff overlooking the sea, and each room has a private balcony.

If you are looking for quiet and romantic on what can be a very busy island, then you need to stay at the **Ikies Traditional Houses** in Oia (*website: www.ikies. com*). This 4-star guest house has a range of luxury accommodations including honeymoon suites and studios, each with their own private terraces. All the rooms have names like the Sailors House, the Winemakers House and the Artisans House.

The **Atlantis Villas**, *tel. +30 (22860) 71214*; *website: www.atlantisvillas-santorini.com,* is the nicest hotel, but also one of the most expensive.

THE BEST OF THE DODECANESE ISLANDS

Situated near the Turkish coast, the **Dodecanese Islands** have a more Turkish atmosphere than other Greek islands, because they were recently ruled by Turkey. Rhodes was a major trade hub of the ancient world. **Patmos** is considered one of the most beautiful. **Kalymnos** offers both a busy harbor town and quiet countryside.

The best island for golfers and gamblers

Rhodes is a favorite among European tourists. It has a more sophisticated atmosphere than other Greek playgrounds. The city is located in and around the walls of the medieval **Fortress of the Knights of St. John**. There are two distinct districts: the New Town (north and west) and the Old Town below it, which is encircled by the medieval fortress walls. Wandering among the shops and restaurants inside the fortress is like visiting Disneyland. Its amusements include an evening sound-and-light show best seen from a boat off the harbor, costumed Greek dances at the summer wine festival, painting and handicraft exhibitions, an aquarium, and a small zoo.

The **Casino Rodos**, *tel. +30 (22410) 97500; website: www.casinirodos.gr,* in the Grand Hotel is open from 7 p.m. to 2 a.m.

Mount Vasiliavias' 18-hole golf course and casino, is located at Afandou.

Rhodes' hottest nightlife

Kontiki, *tel. +30 (22410) 22477*, is a houseboat restaurant/bar with a close-up view of the harbor. Open 6 p.m. to midnight.

The best places to stay

Luxury hotels with huge swimming pools are common on Rhodes. **The Grand**, *tel. +30 (22410) 54700; website: www.mitsis-grandhotel.com,* has great staff and is surrounded by a beautiful beach, and the **Rodos Palace Hotel**, *tel. +30 (22410) 25222; website: www.rodos-palace.com,* is located just outside town and has extravagant amenities.

Patmos: The holiest island

St. John the Divine is said to have written the last book of the New Testament in a mountain cave on **Patmos**. A huge 11th-century monastery atop the rocks marks the spot.

359

THE BEST OF SPORADES ISLANDS

These islands, covered with pine and olive trees, are among Greece's most beautiful. Reached by plane or boat from the mainland port of Vollos, Skiathos is the major destination. Only three other of the islands receive attention from tourists: Skopelos, Ilonissos, and Skyros, all quieter versions of Skiathos.

The best places to stay
The **Skiathos Palace**, on Koukounaries beach, *tel. +30 (24270) 49700; website: www.skiathos-palace.gr,* is the most luxurious hotel on Skiathos—but it's a bit too perfect and not very Greek. But Koukounaries beach is considered to be one of the prettiest in all of Greece.

Savoring Skiathos' cuisine
Skiathos' seafood restaurants offer some of Greece's best meals, prepared with more European subtlety than elsewhere. You can't go wrong at any of the outdoor *tavernas* along the harbor in town. For the best lunch, go where the local fishermen eat—it's a plain establishment, right in the middle of the row of tavernas at the bottom of the hill.

Skopelos: The least discovered
Skopelos is an unspoiled Greek gem smothered in plum trees, where traditional Greek costumes are still the everyday dress. The lack of tourists and their trappings makes this island especially inviting.

THE MOST TURKISH ISLANDS: THE NORTH EAST AEGEAN

Less visited than others, these seven, which include Lesbos, Samos, and Chios, are the most Turkish of Greece's islands.

Lesbos: The prettiest in the group
Lesbos is a large, tree-covered island that is breathtakingly beautiful. It has a Genovese castle in the northern tower of Molyvosa and a petrified forest. The ancient castle above the lovely harbor town of Mytilani is the site of summer concerts performed by international artists each summer. The island's sardines, wine, and locally made ouzo are excellent.

Samos: The best red wine

Dominated by 5,000-foot Mount Kerketeos, **Samos**, has been famous for centuries for its dark red wine. It was considered by the ancients to be the birthplace of Hera, Zeus' wife. The island is popular among Germans and Scandinavians.

CORFU: THE MOST BEAUTIFUL ISLAND IN GREECE

Northern Corfu is said to be the most beautiful island in Greece—which is saying something. Covered with lemon, orange, cyprus, fig, and olive groves, it is a lush place. Many of the island's beautiful villas belong to British expatriates. The main port, Kekira, is a town of Venetian elegance, more Italian than Greek. Corfu offers shops, hotels, restaurants, and nightlife.

The southern and western parts of Corfu have the most striking scenery. Eight miles south of the port is the impressive **Achilleion Palace**, once a summer residence of Kaiser Wilhelm II of Germany and now a gambling casino. Another hangout for the jet set is the **Paleokastristsa**, which is on the west coast. The north coast is the most touristy area, with several resort towns. **Kassiopi** is one of the least spoiled and most reasonable places to stay.

Corfu's best hotel

Cavalieri Corfu, *tel. +30 (26610) 39041; website: www.cavalieri-hotel.com*, an elegant Venetian mansion, was King George II's summer residence in the 1920s. It is expensive, but not the highest priced place on the island.

The best places to eat on Corfu

Corfu food is a combination of Greek and Italian. The island's wine is said to be among the nation's best. **Paleokastritza** is a world-renowned eating spot. After lunch, swim in this beautiful cove where Odysseus is said to have washed ashore.

Crete: The most Middle Eastern of the Islands

Crete is like a small country with its own lifestyle and culture. A huge island of more than 5,000 square miles, it really warrants a separate trip. Crete has some of the world's most impressive ruins. Rent a car to see the island.

The most important sight

The major attraction of Greece and one of the most important archeological sites of the Mediterranean world is the ancient capital of Minoan civilization, **Knossos**. If you're only in port for a day, you can sign up for tours of Knossos in Iraklion. However, the public bus, which leaves from Venizelou Square, is more economical.

Europe's most beautiful gorge

The natural wonder of the island is the **Samarian Gorge**, located in central-western Crete. It is the largest—and many think the most beautiful—gorge in Europe and a popular jaunt for hikers. Buses leave from Hania early in the morning and drop hikers off at the top. The walk down takes about five hours. The gorge exits onto a beach, where you can stop for a swim.

The best hotel

The **Elounda Beach Hotel**, *+30 (28410) 63000; website: www.eloundabeach.gr*, is one of the world's best hotels. It was designed by one of Greece's great architects, Spiro Kokotas. It is on a beautiful beach, set off by lots of flowers. The adjoining Elounda Mare has bungalows with private swimming pools. This resort is outstanding, but pricey.

The best monastery stay

Panormitis Monastery on Symi Island, Greece, is right on the water. Pilgrims are offered free food with wine, as well as a place to stay at no cost. The monastery has an inn attached and, during the summer, rooms (called cells) are full of tourists, mostly from Greece. There are dozens of large rooms set aside for families (a "donation" per family is expected). Visitors and overnight guests must dress appropriately—courtesy clothing may be borrowed. The complex has a pebbled courtyard, a gallery, a Byzantine Museum, and a Folklore Museum. Other on-site facilities include a mini-market, a taverna, a bakery, and a tiny beach.

THE BEST OF
HONDURAS

THE BEST OF THE BAY ISLANDS

The **Bay Islands** today call to mind the Bahamas in the early 1970s. Sufficient infrastructure—phone lines, paved roads, ferry boats from the mainland to Utila, regular flights in and out to the three main islands, restaurants, dive shops, grocery stores—makes life here comfortable.

But the beaches remain pristine and they are not overrun with tourists. Vast swaths of land sit lush with greenery…not a home in sight. Roatan and Utila boast long, white beaches and lush, green interiors. This is quintessential Caribbean with crystal-clear turquoise waters and fiery sunsets. The snorkeling and diving along this hemisphere's largest barrier reef is among the best in the world, and here you avoid the crowds that regularly invade Cozumel, Grand Cayman, Barbados, and the rest.

THE BEST OF ROATAN

Roatan's high green hills, lush with hardwood trees and palms, provide picture-postcard views to the warm, turquoise waters shimmering below. Bright bougainvillea and hibiscus fill gardens, and passion fruit vines tumble over porch railings.

Wide ribbons of white sand cling to the coast in protected coves. Elsewhere, towering rocks jut out into the sea, forming dramatic perches for magnificent homes.

The most affordable diving

Most visitors to Roatan come here to dive. The traveler on a budget heads for **West End**—nice beaches, pleasant posadas, and experienced dive shops. You'll find beautiful beaches and higher-end accommodations at West Bay, a few miles down the road. Here, a full service dive resort, Luna Beach Resort (*website: www. lunabeachresort.com*), caters to every whim.

Other key resorts at the West Bay area are **Henry Morgan Hotel & Beach Resort** (*website: www.hmresorts.com*, and **Anthony's Key Resort** (*website: www. anthonyskey.com*). Anthony's is home to Roatan's Institute for Marine Science where you can visit the reptiles in the museum and swim with dolphins.

Diving off Roatan is popular because it's part of the Belizean Barrier Reef, the second longest barrier reef in the world, abundant with wildlife—schools of colorful fish, sea turtles, sharks, and even octopi—and the intensely beautiful and colorful coral reef.

Staying at West End costs from $15 for a basic room to $50 for a posada with a kitchenette. Many posadas have private beaches with tables and chairs for lounging. If you're self-catering, be sure to stock up on groceries in Coxen Hole, where you'll pay less.

The shuttle from West End to Coxen Hole runs regularly each day—but avoid traveling on Tuesday and Wednesday when the cruise ships dock as it's nearly impossible to get a lift back.

Several small bars offer a daily meal for around $8, usually including lobster. Conch soup is an island specialty at $3 to $5 a bowl, and it's always a filling meal. For a delicious splurge, try the food at Parrot Tree Plantation (*website: http:// parrottree.com/)* and Bite on the Beach. At Bite, visitors can view the giant green eels as a prelude to dinner.

The most affordable diving

Open water diver certification courses start at about $200, making Roatan one of the world's most affordable places to obtain your certification. A typical course includes classroom instruction, contained water dives, and several open water dives. Following certification, additional dives are available from $15 per tank. Specialty night dives may run closer to $45. If you are already certified, you'll still pay under $30 per tank.

Utila has a different feel altogether. Much smaller and flatter, its beaches are just as striking—arguably more so—than those on the big island. Perhaps the swaths of sand here appeal because they tend to take you by surprise. You encounter them, for the most part, by boat. (Precious few roads traverse the island.) Scooters and golf carts are the main means of transportation.

As you round a bend in the coast, squinting in the sun and spray, the tat-tat of the engine and the sound of sloshing water below, you discover in front of you these impossibly picturesque scenes. The small town, with its sand roads and curving pathways, is built of colorful gingerbread houses with well-kept gardens. There you will find two banks, little shops, a cinema, small restaurants, and bars. Excellent food can be found at Café Mariposa, Mango Inn (*website: www.mango-inn.com*), RJ's, and Bundu Café.

As in Roatan, many visitors come to Utila to certify and to dive. There are more than 60 dive shops. Vendors from many of them hang out at the ferry dock, offering discount coupons and telling of their shops.

Utila Dive Center, *tel. +504 2425-3326; website: www.utiladivecenter.com*, pairs up with **Mango Inn**, *tel. +504 2425-3305; website: www.mango-inn.com*, offering excellent accommodations along with certification programs. The Lighthouse offers large rooms, complete with kitchenettes, and is close to the private beach. Prices average $60 per night, with discounts offered for week-long stays. More humble and less expensive housing is readily available most of the year.

A couple of attractions pull tourists to Utila. One is its whale shark. This is the world's largest fish, growing to 15-20 tons. Lucky visitors might spot a whale shark any time of the year, but March to April and August to September are noted for the greater likelihood of a sighting.

Another popular attraction is the **Sun Jam Festival** (*website: http:// sunjamutila.com*). It is held on the first weekend in August at Water Cay, a nearby small island. Loud speakers, campfires, and sleeping bags are the norm for this non-stop musical event.

GUANAJA: THE PERFECT TROPICAL GETAWAY

Guanaja is the most laid-back of the three Bay Islands…the perfect tropical getaway for people who crave the simple life and a return to nature. Thirteen miles long and three miles wide, this is also the tallest island, with mountain peaks crowding the center. The Honduran government declared the central area a national forest. Ninety percent is a forested national reserve.

The island is split into unequal halves by a manmade channel, which you can traverse by water taxi. Next to the channel is a paved airstrip, rated for daytime landings only, with daily service to mainland La Ceiba and an occasional connection through Roatan.

The main community is called Bonacca. It is, in fact, a tiny cay off the main island. Accommodations in Bonacca are cheaper than the spectacular ones on the island, especially **West Peak Inn**, *tel. (for reservations) +1 (831) 786-0406 (in the U.S.); website: www.vena.com/wpi/.*

There are no roads and little nighttime entertainment, besides diving. What do you do here? Hike…ride horses…explore the miles of deserted beaches…and enjoy the silence.

THE BEST OF PICO BONITO

After soaking up the sunshine in the Bay Islands, it is a refreshing change to visit **Pico Bonito**, a lush rain forest, located only 30 to 40 minutes from the coastline city of La Ceiba. A travel agency in La Ceiba can arrange for a shuttle from the airport or the ferry dock. Also, one can rent a car (a 4 x 4 is best) or take a taxi. A taxi would cost $25.

Lodge at Pico Bonito, *tel. +504 2440-0388; website: www.picobonito.com,* is a luxury lodge on 200 acres. It has 22 elegantly furnished cabins with verandas and hammocks. Additionally, it has a pool, spa, and activities and excursions into the jungle: horseback riding, white-water rafting, hiking, bird watching, to name a few.

Less expensive is **Casa Cangrejal**, tel. *+504 2408-2760; website: www.casacangrejal.com,* a B&B inn built from the rocks of the river.

Omega Tours, *tel. +504 9745-6810; website: www.omegatours.info,* is a block away from Casa Cangrejal. At Omega, many adventurous activities are offered, and dorm accommodations are often free with booking of activities.

THE BEST GOLF CLUB IN HONDURAS

Our favorite golf club in Honduras is in **La Ceiba Golf Club** (a two-hour ferry crossing—or an even shorter flight—from Roatan). The club also has a swimming pool and tennis courts. Tee off by 8:30 a.m. if you travel from Roatan by ferry, or 7 a.m. if you fly. At that time of the morning you'll have the course to yourself.

La Ceiba's golf course is only nine holes but there is a second set of tee boxes that makes it 18 holes (only one of Honduras' six golf courses is an 18-hole course). The fairways are tree-lined and the greens are surrounded by plenty of sand. Like all Honduran golf clubs, wearing shorts is acceptable.

We also recommend the course at **Tela** (60 miles west of La Ceiba). The drive from La Ceiba to Tela is a relaxing one, through pineapple plantations and palm groves.

Remember, though, this is Honduras: These aren't U.S. championship quality courses, but they're good nonetheless. La Ceiba club was recently host to the Honduran equivalent of the U.S. Open, a big event for the town.

THE BEST OF
HUNGARY

Hungary is a world unto itself. While it is at the very heart of the European continent, its language, food, and music are not like those of any other European country. Its people are as unique as its culture. The country experienced major political and economic changes from the early 1990s and became a member state of the European Union in 2004. The nicest change has been in the Hungarian attitude toward foreigners. Travelers are now made to feel completely welcome and at ease.

Hungarians, or Magyars, are descendants of migrating tribes from the Ural Mountains and Euro-Asian steppes, who settled down in the Carpathian basin more than 1,100 years ago and established their kingdom. Throughout the centuries the country's stormy history, including long periods of foreign occupations, made the Magyars strong and enriched their culture.

Today, Hungary is a free and democratic country in the family of the European nations. Hungarians speak Magyar, which is distantly related to Finnish and Estonian. Their folk music is passionate; strains of the old tunes can be heard in the works of Ferenc Liszt, Bela Bartok, and Zoltan Kodaly. The abundance of medicinal hot springs all over the country (the second largest thermal water reserve in the world after Iceland) attracts thermal and spa lovers from everywhere.

BUDAPEST: "THE PEARL OF THE DANUBE"

Some also call it the "Queen of the Danube" or the "Paris of the East". And indeed, the capital of Hungary is Eastern Europe's loveliest city and one of the most beautiful cities in the world with its wonderful riverside panorama from the Gellert Hill, which is on UNESCO's world heritage list.

Its 15th-century streets lead past renaissance houses that hide pretty interior courtyards. At night, delicate neon signs glow from the old stone facades of the buildings. Lights from the famous Chain Bridge and the magnificent Royal Palace are reflected in the silent flow of the river. Budapest, a vibrant, dynamic city with 2 million people, welcomes visitors year round through international conferences and exhibitions. Visitors to Budapest can experience the City of Spas, numerous museums, theatres, festivals, elegant hotels, and charming old-world style cafes.

The Danube River divides the City into two sections, **Buda** and **Pest**. Previously two separate settlements, they were united in 1873. Buda, dominated by the spires of the 13th-century Matthias Church, has medieval cobblestone streets, centuries-old houses, and steep little stairways that climb to the castle. Pest, centered around the neo-gothic parliament building, is the more modern business section of the city, with grand 19th-century monuments and memorials.

Budapest is connected with direct flights to most European capitals and major cities. International trains arrive daily to the city's main railway stations. Another way to get there is aboard the hydrofoil that glides from Vienna (Austria) down the Danube and along the border with Slovakia, reaching Budapest at sunset.

The top sights
The Royal Palace or Buda Castle (Kiralyi Palota), *Szent Gyorgy Ter 2,* tops Castle Hill on the Buda side. Generations of Hungarian kings were crowned at this elaborate castle. Demolished during bombing raids in World War II, it has been carefully rebuilt. From the courtyard is a splendid view over the Danube.

The castle houses several points of interest: the **Historical Museum** of Budapest, *Buda Castle, Wing E, tel. +36 (1) 487-8800; website: www.btm.hu*, which contains archeological remains of Old Town and exhibits on the history of the palace.

The **National Gallery**, *Buda Castle, Wing C; website: www.mng.hu*, with an extensive collection of Hungarian works dating from the 10th century.

In the rear wing of the Royal Palace is the **Széchenyi National Library,** *Buda Castle, Wing F; tel. +36 (1) 224-3700; website: www.oszk.hu*, with collections including some surviving parchment manuscript books, called *Corvina* from the time of King Matthias Corvinus, the legendary Hungarian Renaissance king (1458-1490).

However, the most fascinating part of the castle is underground. **Labyrinths**, *website: www.labirintus.com,* running below the castle were used to house troops and a hospital during World War I. The tunnels are now a wax museum depicting Hungary's history: the early Roman settlers, the empire of Attila the Hun (A.D. 434-453), the Mongolian invasion (13th century), the Turkish domination of Hungary from 1526 to 1686, the Austrian (Habsburg) rulers, and modern history.

King Charles (14th c.) and King Matthias (15th c.) were crowned at **Matthias Church,** (*Szentharomsag ter 2; website: www.matyas-templom.hu*) as were Empress Maria Theresa (1740-1780) and Emperor Franz Josef (1848-1916). High Mass is celebrated every day, and organ concerts are held in the church in July and August.

The **Fishermen's Bastion,** a unique structure near Matthias church, was built simultaneously with its last major renovation in the late 19th century. This was a fish market in the Middle Ages, hence the name, paying tribute to the fishermen. A great statue of St. Stephen, the first king of Hungary is located here facing the church.

The **Gellert Hill** on the Buda side with the Hungarian Statue of Liberty, a short distance south of the Castle District, has a fortress called the Citadel on top of it, which was built in 1851. It is now a tourist attraction with terraces offering the famous panoramic view of the city.

The **Houses of Parliament**, *Kossuth Ter 1; tel. +36 (1) 441-400; website: www.parlament.hu*, across the Danube in Pest, are a grand replica of the Houses of Parliament in Westminster. Built between 1885 and 1896, the neo-Gothic buildings are one of the most beautiful and oldest legislative buildings of Europe and the third largest Parliament building in the world. The place is the seat of the Hungarian National Assembly and used for state receptions. One of the most important historical treasures of Hungary that can be seen by visitors to the Parliament Buildings is the so-called Holy Crown of St Stephen I, sent to the first king by Pope Sylvester II in the year 1000.

Also in Pest is the **Hungarian National Museum**, *Muzeum Korut 14; tel. +36 (1) 327-7700; website: www.hnm.hu,* which features a permanent exhibit called "The History of the Hungarian People from the Magyar Conquest to 1849." One room displays a large, lavishly decorated Turkish tent, captured in 1686 when Buda was liberated from the Turkish occupation. Another room shows paintings and sculptures by Hungarian artists from the Middle Ages to the present.

The most impressive square in Budapest is the **Heroes' Square,** *Hôsôk tere,* with the **Millennium Monument** in the middle, which contains the horseback statues of the seven Hungarian leaders, headed by Chieftain Arpad, who led the Magyars into the Carpathian Basin in 896 AD. It was constructed to mark the 1000th anniversary of Hungary as a nation.

Across from the Monument is the **Museum of Fine Arts**, *Dózsa György út 41; tel. +36 (1) 469-7100; website: www.szepmuveszeti.hu,* which holds the world's second largest collection of Spanish Art and has more El Grecos than any institution outside Spain, as well as three Rembrandts and major works by Goya, Raphael, Rubens, Franz Hals, Monet, Renoir, and Cézanne. (It also may have a Leonardo sculpture, depending on whether you listen to the Hungarians or the Italians.)

One of the most impressive buildings is the Italian neo-Renaissance **Hungarian State Opera House**, *Andrassy ut 22; tel. +36 (1) 814-7100; website: www.opera.hu.* Statues of Ferenc Liszt, Ferenc Erkel, and other renowned musicians surround the building. Inside, a visual splendor of ceiling frescoes, a magnificent chandelier, wall paintings, and carved balustrades greets visitors. The State Opera House has presented continuous performances since 1884. The New Year's Eve Opera Gala with popular operettas, ballets, and musicals concluded with on-stage festive dinner offered by the world famous restaurant Gundel is a preferred way of celebration for more and more guests every year. Another event is the Budapest Opera Ball in each February, when the stage is turned into an exclusive grand ballroom to entertain Europe's elite.

Another favorite area, **Vaci utca,** *Vaci street on the Pest side, stretching from Elizabeth bridge to Vorosmarty square,* attracts visitors and locals alike. In this pedestrian shopping area, large department stores and small specialty shops offer beautiful handcrafted goods. Elsewhere, locals and travelers crowd into busy cafés for *espresso-kave,* traditional *somloi galuska* (sponge cake covered with chocolate sauce and whipped cream), and delicious fruit tortes with fresh cream.

The world's best gypsy music

The most famous and unique ensemble is the 100-member **Gypsy Orchestra,** *website: www.100violins.com,* an ambassador for Hungarian and Gypsy music and classical music, giving over 1,000 concerts in venues ranging from the smallest towns in Hungary to many of the world's famous concert halls. Visitors can catch their performance during the Budapest Spring Festival, held in late March to early April every year.

You can also hear Gypsy music year-round at many restaurants and festivals in the city, including Sandor Feher, Sandor Lakatos, Gyorgy Lakatos, and Erno Kallai K. The best Gypsy music while you dine is at the restaurant called **Matyas Pince**, *Marcius 15 ter 7; tel. +36 (1) 266-8008; website: http://eng.matyaspince. eu.* Guests can also watch a 40-minute folk dance performance on Wednesdays and Thursdays starting at 8:30 p.m.

Budapest's best markets

The **Grand Market Hall**, *Vamhaz Korut 1-3; tel. +36 (1) 217-0052,* opened in 1897 and is the city's largest indoor market. An enormous emporium of glass and iron, a special heritage site itself, it sells delicious sausages, salami chunks, and smoked meat, with thick slabs of bread and pickled peppers and infamous Hungarian paprika. Also fine wines and folk arts are on offer. Numerous famous people have taken home souvenirs from Grand Market Hall.

The best restaurants and cafes

The top restaurant in Budapest is **Gundel**, *near Heroes Square in Pest, Állatkerti út 2; tel. +36 (1) 468-4040; website: www.gundel.hu,* which sets the standard for fine dining. Restaurateur George Lang serves the best of Hungarian cuisine at this inviting little restaurant, where many celebrities and famous people enjoyed great food, among them Queen Elizabeth II, Hillary Clinton, Antonio Banderas, and Whoopi Goldberg. Reservations are required and formal wear is a must in the evenings.

Located in a small street across from Matthias Church, restaurant **Alabardos**, *Orszaghaz utca 2, tel. +36 (1) 356-0851; website: www.alabardos.hu,* offers delightful Hungarian specialty dishes for an affordable price. Guests are seated in a huge gothic room with a vaulted ceiling. In the summer, you can sit at tables in the cobblestone courtyard. The menu is presented in six languages.

The nicest café/confectionery in Budapest is the **Gerbeaud**, *Vôrôsmarty ter 7-8; tel. +36 (1) 429-9000; website: www.gerbeaud.hu.* It is also one of the best pastry shops in the city—well worth the usual wait for a table. Built in the mid-19th century, the café boasts crystal chandeliers, heavy drapes, and marble tables that provide an elegant, yesteryear ambience for enjoying some of the best pastries in Budapest. If you have a sweet tooth, the creamy Sacher torte with marzipan-based chocolate butter sponge, home-made apricot jam, and Valrhona chocolate icing is a definite must.

On the ground floor of the Boscolo New York Palace luxury hotel is the famous **New York Café**, *Erzsébet körút 9-11; tel. +36 (1) 8866-125; website: www.boscolohotels.com.* It has been a center for Hungarian literature and poetry since 1894. Be sure to check out the Cigar Bar. Decorated in the style of classic Budapest cafes, this is a place to sit back, relax with a drink and one of the many cigars that are kept in old bank safes.

Where to sleep

There are many lovely B&Bs in Budapest. The city also has one of the most stunning hotels of any city in the world: the **Budapest Hilton**, *Hess Andras ter 1-3, tel. +36 (1) 889-6600; website: www1.hilton.com*, is situated in the historic Castle District next to Matthias Church and built into the restored remains of a 13th century Dominican churchyard. This five-star hotel has over 300 rooms, a fully equipped business center and large conference rooms. While dining, visitors can enjoy the breathtaking panoramic view of the Danube River and the city of Budapest.

The **Duna-Intercontinental**, *Apaczai Csere Janos utca 12-14; tel. +36 (1) 327-6333; website: www.ichotelsgroup.com*, is also a beautifully designed palace in the heart of the city on the Pest side overlooking the Danube and Castle Hill. It is close to shopping (Vaci Street), businesses and attractions such as Chain Bridge, Houses of Parliament, and museums. Facilities include the Atrium, a glass-covered central court, the Corso Restaurant with a show kitchen to witness food preparation, and a state-of-the-art business center and the largest ballroom in Hungary.

Also on the Pest side, the **Grand Hotel Corvinus Kempinkski**, *Erzsebet ter 7-8; tel. +36 (1) 429-3777; website: www.kempinski-budapest.com*, is a five-star luxury hotel with first class conference and meeting facilities. Its Asian-inspired spa and unique art gallery featuring contemporary Hungarian art collection make the place special amongst Budapest hotels.

Budapest's incomparable spa hotel, the **Danubius Hotel Gellert**, *Szent Gellert ter 1; tel. +36 (1) 889-5500; website: www.danubiusgroup.com/gellert*, is famous for its unique historic atmosphere, grand art-nouveau-style building, and medicinal thermal spring baths. The pools are located in mosaic-decorated art deco halls with ornate balconies, massive columns, and skylights. The picturesque Gellert Hill just beside the hotel offers a great hike to admire the fabulous panorama of the city.

Festival city

Bacchus' best for wine-lovers: Every September, the Budapest Castle District is transformed into a wine-lover's dreamland during the **Budapest International Wine Festival,** *Buda Castle District, tel. +36 (1) 203-8507; website: www.winefestival.hu*. Top winemakers from across the country share their best vintages in anticipation of the upcoming harvest, while chefs prepare tasty feasts, cheese masters provide rare cheeses, and violins passionately wail as folk dancers whirl around in colorful costumes. The festival offers art exhibitions, dinners, concerts, and wine competition, at which guest judges taste award-winning wines to see how their opinions compare with those of the professionals. Make sure you buy your favorite Hungarian wine, because you probably won't find many of these ones outside the country.

Throughout the year Budapest hosts numerous other festivals, concerts and events, such as the Budapest Spring Festival, the Budapest Fair, the Budapest Summer Music Festival, the Sziget Festival, which is one of the biggest music festivals in Europe, offering more than 1,000 concerts and other events during August, and the Budapest Parade, a giant summer-end carnival with hundreds of thousands dancing near Heroes' Square.

BESTS BEYOND BUDAPEST

It is now easier than ever before to venture beyond Budapest. Hungary is filled with delightful towns and little-known historic sights outside its capital city.

A popular day-trip destination for visitors just north of Budapest is the **Danube Bend (Dunakanyar),** a region, where the river makes a sharp turn from west to south. Inviting lovely small towns, forested hills along the river gives the region a special charm.

Szentendre, on the right bank of the Danube, offers a Mediterranean atmosphere with a baroque townscape. An artists' town with cobblestone streets and main square, where you'll find shops and market stalls selling embroidered linens, distinctive china and crystal, leather goods, and souvenirs.

Visegrad is another must-see. The Romans built the country's first fortress and watchtower here. It is also famous for the remains of the Early Renaissance summer palace of King Matthias. From the hill visitors enjoy magnificent views of green countryside and the Danube.

Esztergom, a town north west of Budapest up the Danube, is home to the **Esztergom Basilica**, the largest cathedral in Hungary, built between 1822 and 1856. This is the center of the Hungarian Catholic Church and it was the seat of the Magyar kings in the 12th and 13th centuries. The attached Christian Museum contains the largest and richest ecclesial collection in the country. Marcus Aurelius wrote *Reflections* in this town, which was once an important Roman outpost.

To the south-west is **Pecs**, one of Hungary's oldest cities. A Celtic settlement in the third century, Pecs has become a sophisticated university town. Its main claim to fame is a former Turkish mosque from 1580 and the fabulously ornate Pecs cathedral. **Siklos**, in the neighborhood of Pecs has a well preserved medieval castle, which played an important role in conflicts with the Turks and Habsburgs.

To the south-east the city of **Szeged** is famous for its Summer Open-Air Theatre Festivals in July-August (*website: www.szegediszabadteri.hu*). The festival is the most visited summer cultural event in the region. The Szeged Cathedral is part of the spectacular stage scene on Dome square.

HUNGARY'S BEST WINES

If you don't go anywhere else in Hungary, you must not miss **Eger**, the country's best wine region north-east of Budapest. It is a delightful city, rich in history, with yet another castle and the most delectable wines on earth. Visit the tiny wine cellars of Tokaj region bored into the hillside for a leisurely wine tasting. A nearby *csarda* offers magnificent food at incredible prices.

HUNGARY'S FINEST BAROQUE CITY

To the west, half way between Vienna and Budapest, is the city of **Gyõr**, a colorful regional center with rich architectural, cultural and natural treasures. The city has won awards for the protection and reconstruction of the historic buildings of its Baroque center. It is a festival town (Gyor Summer Festival, Baroque Wedding, Autumn Harvest Festival), a city of spas, thermal waters, rivers and fine restaurants, a great place for meeting, business, or relaxation. Near Gyor visitors can find one of the most important sacral monuments, the **Abbey of Pannonhalma**, a symbol of 1,000-year old Hungarian Christianity. Well worth a visit.

HUNGARY'S VERSAILLES

Further West, near to the Austrian border, in **Fertod**, is the **Eszterhaza Palace,** *Fertőd-Eszterháza, Haydn u. 2; tel. +36 (99) 537-640*, the 18th-century home of Prince Nicholaus Esterhazy the Magnificent, who ruled at the height of the

Habsburg monarchy. He modeled the palace after Versailles, which he had visited on a diplomatic trip. Joseph Haydn was concertmaster here between 1762 and 1790. The palace has been restored recently and is open to visitors. It's a must see place for Hayden and classical music lovers.

CENTRAL EUROPE'S LARGEST LAKE

Hungary's **Lake Balaton**, Central Europe's largest lake, is 48 miles long and 36 feet deep in some places. It is known for its sandy beaches, warm waters, resort hotels, and villa quarters, rich folk traditions, excellent wine regions and fine fishing (42 kinds of fish). The tastiest of the fish caught here is the giant pike-perch (*fogas*).

Popular resort places can be found on the south shore of the lake, where the water is warmer and the beaches have a softer grade of sand. The north shore is a good place to get away from the crowds on nice beaches; however, the water is colder and deepens sharper.

Siofok, the largest town on the southern shore, is also the most crowded (long beaches, vivid nightlife). Its famous son is Imre Kalman, composer, the King of Operetta, whose house is a memorial museum today, *Kalman Imre u. 5; tel. +36 (84) 311-287.*

A few good places to stay: **Best Western Janus Atrium Boutique Hotel**, *F u.93-95; website: www.janushotel.hu;* **Hotel Azur**, *Erkel F. u 2/C; website: www. hotelazur.hu;* **Hotel Ezustpart**, *Liszt Ferenc Blvd. 2-4; website: www.ezustpart.com;* **Hotel Panorama**, *Beszedes J. Blvd. 80; website: www.panoramahotel-siofok. hu;* **Residence Conference and Wellness Hotel**, *Erkel F. u. 49; website: www. hotel-residence.hu;* **Hotel Club Siofok** including **Hotel Europa, and Hotel Hungaria**, *Petofi Setany 13; website: www.hotelclubsiofok.hu.*

The healthiest place along the lake is the small spa town of **Balatonfured** on the northern shore. With its 11 medicinal springs and specialized hospital the place is a Mecca for cardiac patients. At its center is **Gyogy Ter** (Spa Square), where waters of mineral springs bubble under a pavilion. Notable guests of town have included Nobel Laureate Indian poet and writer Rabindranath Tagore, who was healed here in 1926. In gratitude, Tagore planted a linden tree in the park, and his example has been followed by celebrities ever since. A lake shore promenade was named after him.

Good accommodations in Balatonfured are **Hotel Annabella,** *Deak Ferenc utca 25; tel. +36 (87) 889-400; website: www.danubiushotels.com;* **Hotel Marina,**

Szechnyi utca 26; tel. +36-87-889-500; website: www.danubiushotels.com; **Hotel Silver Balatonfured,** *Zakonyi u. 4; tel. +36 (87) 583-000; website: www. silverresort.hu.*

A short drive from Balatonfured or a ferry ride from the south shore takes you to the **Tihany Peninsula**. Climb up to the 900-year-old Benedictine Abbey on the hill, one of the oldest churches in Hungary, and enjoy a breathtaking panorama of the lake from the terraces of the Rege Café. For more information contact the **Tourist Office,** *Tihany, Kossuth u. 20; tel. +36 (87) 448-804; website: www.tihany.hu.*

If you want to observe Hungary's famous equestrian traditions with top riders and horses, the annual **August Horse Show and Historical Castle Games** in Nagyvazsony, north-west of Balatonfured, is a must see event. For more information contact **IBUSZ Travel Agency,** *1118 Budapest, 11th district, Dayka G. utca 3, Rubin Business Center, Budapest; tel. + +36 (1) 485-2765.*

You can bathe in a warm-water lake surrounded by rose-colored water lilies in **Heviz**, a town near the west–end of Lake Balaton. Fed by a hot spring, the **Thermal Lake of Hévíz** (*website: www.spaheviz.hu*) is the world's largest biologically active natural thermal lake. Its temperature varies from 82° F to 100° F. The mud from the bottom of the lake is also therapeutic; it is dried and exported for mud packs. The lake turns into a spectacular wonder at the end of summer, when red lilies flower in their thousands. There are numerous therapeutic hotels around the lake.

For further tourist information contact the **Hungarian National Tourist Office,** *447 Broadway 5th Floor, Manhattan, NY 10013; tel. +1 (212) 695-1221; website: www.gotohungary.com.*

THE BEST OF

INDIA

This is indeed India! The land of dreams and romance, of fabulous wealth and fabulous poverty, of splendour and rags, of palaces and hovels, of famine and pestilence, of genies and giants and Aladdin lamps, of tigers and elephants, the cobra and the jungle, the country of a hundred nations and a hundred tongues, of a thousand religions and two million gods, cradle of the human race, birthplace of human speech, mother of history, grandmother of legend, great-grandmother of tradition.

—Mark Twain, 1897

India is an exotic, ancient, multicolored land. The size, variety, and grandeur of this country makes it a feast for visitors. Every region is different. The bordering Himalayas contain the highest peaks in the world, which run over the border to include Mount Everest in Nepal. The Ganges Plain, by the phenomenal river of the same name, is one of the world's greatest stretches of flat land—as well as one of the world's most densely populated regions. There are towns here dating back to 3000 B.C. and temples that draw Hindu pilgrims by the thousands. The country's diverse population shares the land with elephants, tigers, camels, and millions of sacred cows.

The religions of India are as varied as its climate. You'll find Hindus, Muslims, Bahai's, Sikhs, Buddhists, Jains, Jews, Christians, and Zoroastrians. The different groups are lively and colorful, each with their own festivals, dances, culture, and cuisine. Each has left its artistic mark on India—ancient, elaborately carved temples, mosques, and gudwaras are located throughout the country.

We will explore India counterclockwise, beginning with Delhi and moving southwest toward Mumbai (Bombay), southeast to Chennai (Madras), northeast to Kolkata (Calcutta), and finally to the farthest corners of India for a look at the continent's least-known regions.

DELHI: THE OLDEST INDIAN CITY

When Mumbai and Chennai were mere trading posts, **Delhi** was the capital of a 500-year-old empire. India was ruled from Delhi by various Hindu dynasties, then the Moguls, and finally the British. And it was here that India was granted its independence.

Eight cities have flourished where Delhi is today. And each of the city's former rulers has made significant architectural contributions. Today, Delhi is divided into two cities: Old Delhi, once the Mogul capital, which is filled with ancient forts, temples, and monuments; and New Delhi, the present capital, which has wide boulevards, modern office buildings, parks, and hotels.

Tour Delhi from south to north, because growth has moved steadily northward. Bring a sweater if you plan to travel during the winter months, when temperatures drop to 40° F.

The Seventh Wonder of Hindustan

Ten miles south of Delhi is **Qutb Minar,** a 234-foot victory tower known as the Seventh Wonder of Hindustan. One of the earliest monuments of the Afghan period in India, and built in pre-Muslim Delhi, it has stood for 800 years. You can climb the 13th-century tower via a spiral staircase.

At the foot of the tower lies the **Quwwat-ul-Islam Mosque.** The first mosque built in India, it was erected in the 12th century on the foundations of a Hindu temple. The mosque contains the **Iron Pillar,** which has remained rust-free for more than 1,500 years.

Delhi's top sights

East of Qutb Minar is the **Tughlaqabad Fort**, built by the first Tughlaq king. A seven-mile, inwardly sloping wall guards the tombs of the founder of Tughlaqabad and his son. The fortress has a panoramic view of the surrounding countryside.

Following the road back toward Delhi you'll come to **Humayun's tomb**, the mausoleum of Emperor Humayun, erected in the 16th century. This was the precursor of the Taj Mahal, and it features rose-colored sandstone walls inlaid with white marble and surrounded by gardens. Opposite the tomb is a place of pilgrimage, **Nizamuddin Dargah**, the mausoleum of one of the world's most famous Sufi saints, Nizamuddin Auliya. The Dargah also includes a mosque covered with a fine Byzantine dome.

A few minutes away is the **Purana Qila,** a fort standing on the site of Indraprastha, a mythological Delhi of prehistoric times. The present fort, built in the 16th century, frames one end of the two-mile vista leading to the Presidential Palace.

Pass through the **War Memorial Arch** honoring Indian soldiers who died in World War I. This leads to the fabulous **Rajpath,** the broadest avenue of Delhi, lined with government buildings. **Parliament House** is a huge circular structure with an open colonnade. The **Presidential Palace,** built in this century, has 340 rooms and covers 330 acres.

The strange **Jantar Mantar Observatory,** *Parliament Street, Tolstoy Marg,* was built in 1725 by Maharaja Singh II of Jaipur to view the sun, moon, and stars. Every year on the March 21st and September 21st equinoxes, the sun shines through a slit in the wall.

Jama Masjid, India's largest mosque, has three white-marble domes and two 134-foot minarets. Typical of Mogul architecture, its 450-square-foot courtyard is paved with marble.

Facing the mosque is the **Red Fort,** the finest example of Mogul architecture, built in 1648 behind red sandstone walls. Once the imperial palace of Emperor Shah Jahan (1627-1657), today it houses the **Museum of Archaeology**. It is open to the public during daylight hours, usually 9 a.m. to 5 p.m.

Rajghat (Shrine of Mahatma Gandhi), southeast of the Red Fort, is where Gandhi was cremated in 1948 following his assassination. A black marble slab in the garden is inscribed with the leader's last words, "O Ram" or "Oh, God."

The best zoo in India

Delhi Zoological Park (*website: http://nzpnewdelhi.gov.in*), next to Purana Qila on Mathura Road, is a home to rare white tigers. Magnificent gardens brighten the park, which has an especially extensive collection of birds. The zoo closes on Fridays.

India's most colorful festival

Try to time your visit to Delhi to coincide with **Ram Lila,** when gigantic effigies of Ravana and his minions are burned on the last day of the 10-day **Dusseha Festival** to symbolize the destruction of evil. According to Hindu mythology, the evil Ravana kidnapped the wife of the good Lord Rama. Commemorating the story of Lord Rama, Ram Lila is one of the biggest events in Delhi. Dussehra usually falls in October and includes colorful dramas and dances reenacting the stories of gods and demons.

The best dancing

The **Bhangra Dance** of the Punjab, marked by its robustness and energy, is popular in the dance halls of Delhi. Bhangra began as a farming dance to celebrate the coming of spring and was a fusion of music, singing and the beat of the *dhol* drum. Originally it was a male dance but women are increasingly turning to Bhangra, both in India and in Indian communities abroad.

The best hotels in Delhi

The **Ashok,** *tel. +91 (11) 2611-0101; website: www.theashok.com,* is a modern hotel with a pool, miniature golf facilities, gardens, tennis courts, an art gallery, and an open-air theater that features performances by a highly rated contemporary Indian dance company.

The **Imperial,** *tel. +91 (11) 2334-1234; website: www.theimperialindia.com,* at the edge of town is surrounded by a palm garden. Rooms are large, with private bathrooms and air conditioning.

Oberoi, *tel. +1 (800) 562-3764 (toll free in the U.S.) or +1 (866) 377-5241 (toll free in Canada); website: www.oberoihotels.com,* is a gracious old hotel with colonial-style bedrooms and private baths, a swimming pool, tennis courts, and gardens.

THE TAJ MAHAL: ONE OF THE WORLD'S GREATEST WONDERS

South of Delhi, in the town of Agra, is the **Taj Mahal,** one of the world's greatest wonders. Built in white marble by Emperor Shah Jehan Jahan as a mausoleum for his queen, Mumtaz Mahal, it is most beautiful at sunset and under moonlight.

Twenty-two years went into the construction of this palace, which was completed in 1652. Beautiful formal gardens and a reflecting pool lead to the arched entrance. An enormous dome, accompanied by two smaller domes, tops the structure, and four minarets mark the corners. It is said that the architect's right hand was cut off upon completion of the Taj Mahal so that he could not duplicate his creation.

RAJASTHAN: INDIA AT ITS MOST TRADITIONAL

Southwest of Delhi is a desert land broken up occasionally by jungle. Here are some of the most ornate temples in India. **Rajasthan,** which translates as *Abode of Kings,* is the home of the Rajputs, an ancient people whose mythology includes tales of chivalry and romance. You can recognize Rajputs by their colorful clothing: the men wear pink and yellow turbans and sport amazing moustaches, and the women wear full skirts and half-bodices and wrap themselves in long scarves.

The rosiest spot in India, **Jaipur**, the capital of Rajasthan, is known as "the pink city" for its rose-colored buildings in the old city. The city was founded in 1727 by the brilliant Maharaja Jai Sing II, who built a remarkable observatory that is still a key attraction.

The most beautiful building in Jaipur is the City Palace, a complex divided into courtyards, gardens, and buildings. There are several palatial structures within it alone. The Chandra Mahal, or Moon Palace, is a seven-story building where the current Maharaja resides. There are views of the city from its height and on the ground and first floors it houses the Man Singh II Museum. This museum has collections of royal costumes, shawls, rare manuscripts, arms, and paintings.

Next to the palace are the Jai Niwas Gardens, filled with fountains, statues, and artificial lakes where well-fed crocodiles swim.

Near the entrance to the City Palace is the Jantar Mantar observatory, which is worth a look, and the Hawa Mahal (Palace of the Winds), Siredori Bazaar, with its delicate overhanging balconies and perforated windows placed one above the other in a symmetrical pattern. Although it looks like a palace, it is actually a façade behind which women of the court would watch processions secretly.

Guarding the city from the hills above is Naharagarh, or Tiger Fort. You can get there from the Amber Palace by jeep or rickshaw.

Amber: A little-known treasure

The 17th-century palace at **Amber**, known as the Amber Fort or Amber Palace, stands high above a lake, its towers and domes reaching to the sky. An arched gateway leads into the courtyard, where a broad flight of stairs climbs to the royal apartments. Inside are Persian mosaic walls, filigreed doors, fountains, aqueducts, and high ceilings covered with mirrors. Beneath the palace are vaults said to contain the treasures of Jaipur. You can reach the palace by riding up on an elephant for a fee. Musicians play as you make the slow climb to the palace apartments.

Mount Abu: India's most beautiful sunset

While **Mount Abu** is most famous as an archeological and religious landmark, you should come here for another reason as well: to see the sunset. From **Sunset Point** you can see much of Rajasthan illuminated by the pink glow of the setting sun.

Mount Abu, which is in the far south of the state close to the Gujurat border, was originally a center of the cult of Siva. The Jains (a Hindu sect that abhors the killing of animals) still make pilgrimages to this mountain, which is known in Hindu legend as the son of the Himalayas. Between Abu's peaks are five Jain shrines, the most beautiful of which was built of pure white marble by Vimal Shah in the 11th century. Inside, marble elephants carrying statues of Vimal Shah and his family climb from the pavilion to the domed porch, which is intricately carved and supported by eight sculptured columns.

Udaipur: India's most romantic city

Udaipur, known as the City of Dreams, is the most romantic city in India thanks to its beautiful lakeside location, maze of streets, and ornate palaces and *havelis* (mansions). Founded in the 16th-century by Maharana Udai Singh, supposedly a descendent of Sri Ram (the hero of the Ramayana epic), Udaipur is bastioned by a wall and five spiked gates. Inside the walls are white-washed houses painted with murals.

The ruler of the city, known as the Maharana, or Sun of the Hindus, lives in the sparkling **City Palace** overlooking **Lake Pichola**. Amber, jade, and colored glass sparkle on the palace pinnacles. Inside are ivory doors, marble balconies, stained-glass windows, and mirrored walls. You can visit every day, 9:30 a.m. until 4:30 p.m.

Lake Pichola has two islands, **Jagniwas** and **Jagmandir**. On Jagniwas is a summer palace now open as a luxury hotel and used as a set in the James Bond film *Octopussy*, which is shown nightly in restaurants around the city. You can stay here or come over for lunch or dinner.

Another place worth visiting is the **Sahelion-ki-Bari Park,** one of the best examples of Hindu landscaping. The park is filled with ornamental pools, fountains with water spouting from elephant trunks and bird beaks, and black stone monuments.

How to travel like a Maharaja

Maharaja's Palace on Wheels, a reincarnation of the elegant train that once carried maharajas and viceroys, is the most pleasant way to travel through Rajasthan. The plush cars have been restored, and each coach is equipped with individual sleeping cabins, bathrooms, a kitchen, and an attendant dressed in traditional Rajasthani clothing. The train has two dining cars and a library/bar.

Trips range from eight days to 13 days include stops at Jaipur, Udaipur, Jaisalmer, Jodphur, the Taj Mahal, the bird sanctuary at Bharatpur and much more. The train leaves from Delhi Cantt Station every Wednesday from April through September. For more information, see *website: www.palaceonwheels.net.*

Specific rail information is available also on *www.irctc.co.in* and *www. railtourismindia.com.*

Best travels with locals

Camel safaris are the best way for visitors to get a sample of Rajasthani desert life and learn about the lives of locals. Basic meals and beverages, and a blanket are usually included. Camping out at night under the stars is romantic and the camel drivers will sing or chat to you by the fire. Jaisalmer is one of the best places to organize a safari, aim for one between October and February.

Rajasthan's most colorful festival

The annual **Pushkar Camel Fair** (*website: www.pushkarcamelfair.com*) is one of India's biggest livestock fairs. Thousands of people come across the sands to Pushkar to buy and sell camels and horses adorned with ribbons and head dresses. The nomads that come are just as colorfully dressed and converge on the town to meet friends and tourists. You can arrange a camel ride with any of them or watch them dance and sing. The highlight of the fair is the camel racing. The fair goes for five days until Kartik Purnima and coincides with the bright half of the moon in October/November.

Rajasthan's living fort

The **Jaisalmer Fort** is considered the most lively of any in India because there are homes, shops, hotels, and stalls hidden throughout the tangled laneways. From these hang embroidered or mirrored cloths and the family's washing. The fort on the 262-foot high Trikuta Hill contains about a quarter of the town's population. You enter through massive gates into a large courtyard and the former Maharaja's palace. The views from the summit are spectacular.

THE BEST OF AHMEDABAD

Founded in 1411, Ahmedabad was once considered the finest city in India. Of the many Muslim monuments there, the finest is Ahmed Shah's **Masjid Mosque**, which contains his colored marble tomb, 250 massive pillars, carvings, and inscriptions. The Shah's queens lie in ornate tombs across the street.

Another Muslim architectural feat is the **Haibat Khan Mosque**, built in the 16th century by the Rani, one of the two wives of Mahmud Begara, after her son was executed for "misbehavior." Also see the stone carving of a slave of Ahmed Shah in the **Mosque of Sidi Sayvid** and the **Mausoleum of Shah Alam** at Batwa.

The **Sun Temple of Modhera**, 60 miles northwest of Ahmedabad is the best of the many temples built by the Solanki kings of Anhilwad Patan. The grandeur of this temple is enhanced by its wide steps and pillared porch. The shrine was designed so that the image of Surya (the sun god) can be illuminated by the rising sun and the equinoxes.

Best places to stay

The **House of Mangaldas Girdhardas**, *Opposite Sidi Saiyad Mosque, Lal Darwaja; tel. +91 (79) 2550-6946; website: www.houseofmg.com,* is the only boutique hotel in Ahmedabad and is centrally located close to shopping and business districts. It is a real treasure with a Baroque façade, Italian mosaic marble floors, stained-glass windows, intricate passageways, 12 immaculate bedrooms, and two terrace restaurants. It is also part of the Heritage Hotels Association which features places of particular cultural, architectural, or historic interest. For a full list consult the website: *www.heritagehotelsofindia.com.*

KASHMIR: INDIA'S MOST BEAUTIFUL REGION

North of Delhi, wedged between China and Pakistan, is the most beautiful region in India, the **Vale of Kashmir.** At 5,200 feet, it is circled by mountains (the Himalayas to the southwest, the Karakorams to the north).

It feels as if it is cut off from the rest of the world. Snowcapped peaks appear to float above the clouds. Houseboats and lotus leaves bob in spring-fed lakes. The fair-skinned residents look surprisingly European, despite their vales and nose rings.

Mogul emperors (descendants of Genghis Khan) were partial to Kashmir and built lavish palaces and gardens in the valley. In the colonial days, this was one of the few places in India where Europeans were not allowed to build. (They resorted to living in houseboats instead of houses.) For centuries, caravans from China and elsewhere passed through Kashmir on their way to the southern reaches of India, giving it an international flavor.

The best time to visit Kashmir is around April or May when the spring flowers are in bloom. But every time of year has its charms. The leaves turn scarlet in the fall, and the fields are lush during the summer. Winter brings deep snows and good skiing conditions.

Srinagar: The capital of Kashmir

Srinagar, the capital of Kashmir, has flowering rooftops (the roofs are made of earth, which burst into bloom in the spring). Painted shutters and dyed-wool doors brighten the brown houses that line the river. Houseboats with canopied roofs sail the river toward the Dal and Nagin lakes, where they anchor. The men wear fur caps, the women veils to cover their hair. Turbaned old men smoke hookahs on the sidewalks.

Srinagar's most important landmark is a small temple to Siva at the peak of a 1,000-foot hill, which can be climbed by steep stone steps. The view from the top encompasses the town, the river Jhelum, and Dal Lake.

The best places to stay

Hotel Broadway, *Maulana Azad Road; tel. +91 (194) 245-9001; website: www. hotelbroadway.com,* in Srinagar, has a swimming pool and a good restaurant.

The **Lalit Grand Palace,** *Gupkar Road; tel. +91 (194) 2501-001; website: www.thelalit.com,* was formerly the palace of the Maharajas. The hotel has amazing views of Lake Dal. There is a golf course on the property, and the hotel restaurant and bar are recommended.

Garden paradises, beautiful lakes

The Dal and Nagin lakes are bordered by two beautiful gardens: the **Shalimar Bagh** (Garden of Love), which was designed 400 years ago by one of the Great

Moguls for his queen; and the **Nishat Bagh** (Garden of Pleasure), which has terraces of flowers and avenues of cascades.

Lake Manasbal, 18 miles north of Srinigar, is covered with lotus blossoms and adds to the beauty of its clear waters. It is also rich in birdlife.

Lake Wular is the largest lake in the region Kashmir valley.

The holiest spot

In the mountains above the Liddar Valley, 87 miles from Srinigar, is the sacred cave of **Amarnath,** reached by steps cut into the rock by pilgrims. Situated at 13,000 feet, the cave is surrounded by snow and ice most of the year. The night of the full moon in the month of Sravan (July or August) is considered the luckiest time to visit.

India's best skiing

Kashmir has beautiful, pristine ski slopes but its facilities, including the number of lifts and T-bars and the selection of rental equipment, are limited, which can be frustrating to good skiers. The conditions are improving, however, and, for the more adventurous skier, Kashmir offers heli-skiing. For more information, see *www.gulmarg.org.*

THE BEST OF MUMBAI

Mumbai, formerly known as Bombay, is India's most prosperous and cosmopolitan city, an industrial metropolis, and one of Asia's busiest seaports. Despite its industry, Mumbai is also a beautiful city, backed by mountains and hugging the Arabian Sea. Hilly islands dot the harbor.

The best introduction to Mumbai is a cruise along **Marine Drive,** also known as the Queen's Necklace. Tracing the coastline, it is the city's main boulevard and offers views of the sea and the Mumbai skyline.

Wander Mumbai's intriguing neighborhoods on foot. Venture beyond the Colaba market—a village of the Kolis, one of the original fishing tribes of the region. Old traditions are maintained here, and the women dress in colorful saris and flowers.

Chowpatty Beach, with its statue of Tilak, a great political leader of this century, is the political center of Mumbai. This meeting place by the sea is always crowded with people fishing, playing, and eating at food stalls. The entertainment here is free: yogis buried in the sand, soapbox orators, fishermen hauling in their nets. The fortunetellers here are said to be disconcertingly good.

Not far from the beach is **Mani Bhavan** (the Mahatma Gandhi Memorial), which has photographs of the master of passive resistance, along with books he wrote.

The **Chhatrapati Shivaji Maharaj Vastu Sangrahalaya** (to give it its official title), formerly called the **Prince of Wales Museum of Western India** in Fort Bombay, *website: www.bombaymuseum.org*, has a good collection of Nepalese and Tibetan art, as well as 18th-century miniatures, jade, crystal, and china. It is open every day except Monday, 10:15 a.m. to 5:45 p.m.

The **Hanging Gardens**, at the top of Malabar Hill, where you can find respite from the noise of the city, have a beautiful view of the city. Here you can walk among bushes cut to resemble elephants, monkeys, cows, oxen, or giraffes. The greenery on the left as you go beyond the gardens is part of the **Parsi Towers of Silence**, where locals dispose of their dead. The area is concealed by a park, which is surrounded by a high wall. Bodies are carried to the top of towers, where they are left to be devoured by vultures. The Parsis originally came from the city of Pars in Persia, 1,300 years ago. Today their descendants are a key part of the fabric of life in Mumbai.

In Byculla, an old residential area, is **Veermata Jijabai Bhonsel Udyan** (the Victoria Gardens), a park full of trees and plants. The park also includes the city zoo, the Victoria and Albert Museum, and a gigantic statue of an elephant that once guarded the Elephanta Caves outside Mumbai. Visit the park between dawn and dusk but, if you want to see the zoo or the museum, make sure you arrive before 6 p.m., Tuesday through Saturday. You can rent a boat or ride an elephant or camel from 8 a.m. until 9:30 a.m. and 4 p.m. until 5:30 p.m. Compared with the noise and crowds of most of Mumbai, this is a peaceful place to escape for a while.

Best buys in Mumbai

Mumbai's shops display beautiful pure silk saris for $10 to $100 and silver earrings for around $20. Bargain for the best prices.

The city's two most colorful markets are the **Crawford Market**, officially known as the **Mahatma Jyotiba Phule Market** and the **Thieves Market** or **Chor Bazaar,** near Mohammed Ali Road. The first is a good place to buy fruits and vegetables, cotton, animals, and flowers. It is also a good place to take photos. The Thieves Market is a junk-lovers delight, offering everything from old car parts to fine antiques. Both markets are open from early morning until late evening.

The best time to visit

The best time to visit Mumbai is during **Gansh Chaturthi,** a festival that glorifies Ganesh, the god of good omens. Hindus worship images of the deity, which are later sunk in a lake. A spectacular procession follows. The festival is usually held in September.

The best place to stay and eat

The best restaurant, which is also the best hotel, is the **Taj Mahal Palace,** *Apollo Bunder; tel. +91 (22) 6665-3366; website: www.tajhotels.com,* a five-star establishment that has an Indian restaurant with probably the best curry in Mumbai. There are also French and Chinese dishes, but the Indian food surpasses them by far. The hotel has rooms that, while decorated with antiques, are pleasantly modern at the same time.

The Elephanta Caves: The most important site outside Mumbai

The most important side-trip from Mumbai is to the island of **Elephanta,** six miles across the harbor, where five cave temples have been excavated. No one knows who carved the temples, which were created between the 5th and 6th centuries. The caves contain beautiful, life-size sculptures of Hindu gods. The most impressive is a 15-foot sculpture of three-headed Mahesamurti, a trinity made up of the gods Siva, Brahma, and Vishnu. Outside the main cave is an enormous columned veranda, approached by steps and sculptured elephants. To best appreciate the subtleties of the religious statues and carvings here, read up on Hindu mythology before your trip. Bring a flashlight if you want to see anything.

The holiest village

Mahabaleshwar, a tiny village on a hill south of Mumbai was once considered so holy that Englishmen were not allowed on any part of the hill. Five streams of water representing the sources of the five holy rivers flow through the Krishnabai Temple. They combine and travel through a sculpture of a cow's mouth into two cisterns where Hindus take holy baths. Mahashivaratri, a festival of Siva held in February or March, brings throngs of pilgrims.

Climb to nearby **Pratapgarh Fort,** built in 1656, for a view that extends all the way to the coast. On the western side of the fort, a precipice drops 2,000 feet to the Konkan plain below. Prisoners once met their deaths here.

Visit Hollywood of the east

Visiting **Bollywood,** India's thriving film industry is a definite must for film buffs. Experience the colorful sets and sights of some of India's biggest screen hits and maybe even get to be an extra in one of the lively musicals. Package tours are given in India's movie capital, Mumbai and include; a personal audition session, a Bollywood dance class, a stunt man show and a visit to all the famous shooting sights and the homes of the Bollywood starlets. For more details, *tel. +91 (11) 2271-4577*; *website: www.bollywoodtourpackage.com.*

LITTLE PORTUGAL: GOA

South of Mumbai is **Goa,** a Portuguese colony from 1510 to 1961. It has a mixture of local and Portuguese charms and some of the most beautiful ocean and river beaches in India. In addition to all this, Goa has perfect weather (except during monsoon season, June through September). Whitewashed houses and Catholic churches give Goa a Mediterranean look. Traders first traveled to Goa seeking spices.

St. Francis Xavier came here in 1540 and converted many of the people to Catholicism. Although he died in China, his body was returned to Goa. His embalmed remains lie in a silver, gem-encrusted casket in the **Basilica of Bom Jesus** in Panaji. Once every 10 years the saint's body is displayed. If you look closely, you will notice that some of his toes are missing—one was bitten off by a pilgrim and others were removed as religious relics. His arm, too, is gone—it was sent to Rome. Built in 1593, the basilica is Goa's primary example of Portuguese architecture.

Nearby is the magnificent, all-white *sé* (cathedral), noted for its five bells. Its Golden Bell is the largest of its kind in the world. A small chapel in the back of the cathedral contains a crucifix on which a vision of Christ is said to have appeared in 1919.

Goa's delights are physical as well as spiritual. The silvery beaches along the Malabar Coast are incomparable. The best are near Panaji, the capital. **Dona Paula** is the most chic. Across the Mandovi River from Panaji is the spectacular **Calangute Beach. Colva Beach,** on the south coast near Margao, is also beautiful and there is a fine crescent of sand at Palolem in the far south. At some of Goa's beaches, the swimming is spoiled by fierce undertows. Ask around before you test your strength against the sea.

One of the best markets in India is held in Goa on Wednesdays in Anjuna. Anjuna has long been the draw for backpackers and hippies. The weekly flea market has jewelry, carvings, shirts, sarongs, food, didgeridoos, international beers, and plenty of colorful traders.

The best place to stay if you are a beach lover is the **Taj Holiday Village,** *tel. +91 (832) 664-5858; website: www.vivantabytaj.com/Holiday-Village-Goa/ Overview.html,* on Calangute Beach. You can sleep in a cottage near the sea, use the sports facilities, and lounge in hammocks on the beach, as well as visit nearby restaurants and bars.

THE WORLD'S OLDEST BUDDHIST SCULPTURES

The Buddhist caves of **Ajanta** in Maharashtra were carved into the face of a 259-foot rock cliff 2,000 years ago and contain the oldest Buddhist art in the world. Frescoes cover the walls, ceilings, and pillars of the 25 monasteries and temples here.

The **Ellora Caves** form another fantastic complex of Buddhist, Jain, and Hindu temples carved side by side from rock. The 34 elaborately carved and frescoed caves were constructed between A.D. 600 and A.D. 1200.

The Hindu temple **Kailasa** is the most beautiful, with enormous pillars, painted ceilings, and grand statues. It took 100 years to quarry the three million cubic feet of rock here.

Aurangabad, 18 miles away, is the best base for visiting the caves. Stay at the **Rama International Hotel,** *R-3 Chikalthana; tel. +91 (0240) 663-4141; website: www.welcomhotelrama.com.* The staff is efficient and the manager personally meets guests at the airport.

There are daily flights to Bombay and Delhi from Aurangabad. There are two direct trains to/from Mumbai or you can travel by local bus or train to Manmad, 70 miles northwest of Aurangabad, where more services are available. Daily bus service connects Aurangabad with Ellora, Ajanta, and Jalgaon.

Bus tours to the Ellora Caves from Aurangabad are conducted by the Maharashtra Tourism Development Corporation. Tour guides will pick you up at Aurangabad Railway Station at 9 a.m. and return you there at 6:30 p.m.

See the Maharashtra Tourism Development Corporation website for more on the Maharashtra area: *website: www.maharashtratourism.gov.in.*

THE MOST SACRED JAIN HILL

Shatrunjaya (the Place of Victory), a hill by the river of the same name, is the most sacred of five hills considered holy by the Jains and located in Gujurat, 32 miles from Bhavnagar. It is covered by 863 temples. You must remove all leather before you will be permitted to climb the hill. To see the temple jewels or to take photos, you must ask permission from the Munimji, Anandji Kalyanji Trust, in Palitana. Your hotel can give you the daily viewing times for the jewels and help you get permission to take pictures. The temples are closed in the monsoon season (the summer months) and after dark. The best place to stay while visiting the hill is the nearby town of **Palitana,** due south of Ahmedabad in the province of Gujarat.

THE BEST LION VIEWING

The **Sasan Gir National Park,** (it's a long way from the coast) 37 miles from Junagadh in Gujarat, is the last stronghold of the Asiatic lion. The best time to see the king of beasts is during the hot months, from March through May, when they frequently congregate around the water hole, but the forest is open to the public from December until June. To make arrangements to visit the park, contact **Gir Tourism Development Corporation**, *Rang Mahal, Diwan Chowk, Junagad; website: www.india-wildlife-tours.com.*

MOST SPLENDID ANCIENT RUINS

The empty shell of a once-courtly kingdom of **Malwa** sits atop a plateau in **Mandu**, northeast of Mumbai in western Madhya Pradesh. Known centuries ago by the Muslims as the City of Joy, today it is a ghost town. Raj Bhoja first noticed the charms of the location, which is cut off from the world below thanks to its lofty and isolated setting, and built a retreat here in the 10th century. The Muslims took over in the 13th century and expanded the city until it covered eight square miles, and surrounded it with massive walls.

The oldest monument is the mosque, which is to the right as you enter the grand Delhi Gate. The most beautiful is the tomb of Hoshang Shah, a white marble structure with a great dome and four turrets. The buildings are divided into three main groups: the Royal Enclave, the Village Group, and the Reva Kund Group.

The **Taveli Mahal**, once a palace, is located closer to the fort and houses the Archaeological Survey of India's Antiquity Gallery open with fragments found at the site from sunrise to sunset.

You can stay overnight at the modern **Malwa Retreat**, *tel. +91 (07292) 263-221*, which has eight rooms with attached bathrooms. It is located on the main road on the way to the Village Group. For more information, call **Madhya Pradesh State Tourism**; *website: www.mptourism.com.*

THE LEAST-KNOWN BUDDHIST CAVES

A drive through the jungle into central Madhya Pradesh from Mandu brings you to **Bagh,** where sixth-century Buddhist caves rival those at Ajanta (but they're not as crowded). Sadly, the beautiful wall paintings have been somewhat damaged over time.

The river Bagmati flows in front of the humid sandstone caves. The foliage has been cut back to prevent sneak attacks by pythons and tigers. Only four of the nine caves have survived. Hewn from solid rock, each has a veranda, a large central hall, gloomy monks' cells, and a prayer hall. The second cave has a maze of passageways and hidden chambers. It contains larger-than-life sculptures of the Buddha and his disciples and paintings of animals and flowers. The most beautiful paintings are in the fourth cave, Rang Mahal, which on its veranda has a mural of life-size figures.

Sanchi: The best Buddhist art

Northeast of the Bagh Caves, 29 miles from Bohpal, is **Sanchi,** the world's most important center of Buddhist art. Emperor Ashoka built his most beautiful monuments here on a hilltop overlooking the forest. (Theemperor's son, Mahendra, left Sanchi for Sri Lanka, where he worked to spread the influence of Buddhism.)

After the decline of Buddhism in India, the town lay forgotten until 1818, when it was rediscovered. Restoration was begun in 1912 by Sir John Marshall. Of the eight *stupas* (sacred mounds) originally built on the hill, only three remain.

What catches the eye first in Sanchi is the **Great Stupa,** a 106-foot, second-century round burial mound with elaborately decorated gateways. A fence with four ornate gates surrounds it. The bas-reliefs on the yellow stone gates are the most beautiful early Buddhist works of art that exist today. Don't expect to understand the elaborate religious illustrations—one archeologist published three enormous volumes on Sanchi.

The **Gateway Retreat,** *tel. +91 (07482) 266-723*, is a pleasant little inn near the caves with 16 air-conditioned rooms, a restaurant, and a pool. For more information, call **Madhya Pradesh State Tourism;** *website: www.mptourism.com.*

INDIA'S GREATEST MAN

If you head south from Sanchi into Northern Maharashtra, you will come to the tiny town of **Sevagram**, where Mahatma Gandhi established his *ashram* (retreat) in 1933 and began putting his doctrines into practice. The Hindu leader established a self-sufficient community, with a dairy, a tannery, and cloth weaving. He refused to acknowledge the caste system, with its untouchables and "unclean" occupations. His simple hut is preserved exactly as he left it. At the Nai Talimi Sangh School in Sevagram, students continue to follow Gandhi's way of life, growing their own food and weaving their own cloth.

The best place to stay (if you share Gandhi's values of simplicity and modesty) is the guesthouse at the *ashram,* where food is served communally.

If you prefer creature comforts, stay at **Hotel Pride,** *Commercial Road, Nagpur; tel. +91 (712) 2291-102; www.pridehotel.com/nagpur-hotels/index.aspx,* 50 miles away. (Nagpur is known for its fragrant orange groves.)

CHENNAI: THE MOST TRADITIONAL CITY

The state of Tamil Nadu, at India's southern tip, is more traditional than the rest of the country. Because it is so far south, this region was untouched by the many invaders who once assailed the north. Founded by the Dravidians more than 5,000 years ago, Tamil is the home of India's oldest sculptures.

The capital of the region, **Chennai** (formerly called Madras), is as colorful as the brightly colored cotton cloth it is famous for producing. It is also known as the center of the Tamil film industry which almost rivals Bollywood's studios for output in Mumbai. Chennai is the fourth largest city in India, it sprawls across 30 square miles.

The best place to stay

In Chennai, the best place to stay is the **Taj Coromandel,** *37, Mahatma Gandhi Road Nungambakkam; tel. +91 (44) 6600-2827; website: www.tajhotels.com,* a modern building with both Indian and Italian restaurants. It also has an excellent coffee shop.

The best sights

Fort St. George, built in 1640 by the British, is the best sight to see in Chennai. It is also a perfect place to begin a tour of the city. Its 20-foot walls loom over the city, and house the Secretariat and the Legislative Assembly. Inside is **St. Mary's Church,** the oldest Anglican Church in Asia, built in 1680. The Fort Museum contains memorabilia of the East India Company, as well as costumes, coins, and china.

The National Art Gallery houses the famous 10th-century bronze statue of a dancing Nataraja-Siva and rare Mogul, Rajput, and South Indian paintings. Next-door is the **Government Museum,** which has the best bronze collection in India, as well as rare second-century Buddhist sculptures.

Guindy Snake Park in the beautiful **Guindy National Park** is home to cobras, pythons, and other exotic reptiles. The surrounding national park shelters black buck and spotted deer.

Traditions say that the apostle Thomas (Doubting Thomas) came to Chennai as a missionary and was martyred on St. Thomas Mount in A.D. 78. The **San Thome Basilica** is supposedly built atop the tomb of St. Thomas, although only his toe is housed here now—the Portuguese took most of his remains when they left India.

Kapaliswarar Temple, dedicated to Lord Kapaliswarar (Siva), was built by the Dravidians. It was destroyed in 1566 during a war but rebuilt 300 years ago. Its *gopura* (pyramid-shaped entrance) marks the city's horizon.

Chennai is home to the world headquarters of the **Theosophical Society;** *website: www.ts-adyar.org,* an international organization promoting the interplay of religion, science, and philosophy. The banyan tree in the garden of the society's building is the oldest in India, shading 40,000 square feet.

The best dancing

Chennai is the best place to see the classic dance form **Bharata Natya,** in which dancers exhibit perfect control over every muscle in their bodies. (They can actually move their necks while keeping their heads motionless.) They also have distinctive hand, eye, and head movements. Originally a temple dance, this is the most ancient dance form in India, and it is performed to the accompaniment of musical instruments and singing.

The beauty of the Bharata Natya lies in the grace of its symmetrical patterns and in the emotions portrayed by the elaborate gestures and facial expressions of the dancers. Check the local newspapers for show listings.

Chennai's most important side trips

The ancient city of **Mammallapuram (Mahabalipuram)**, 30 miles south of Chennai, has the world's largest bas-relief, *Penance of Bhaghirata,* an 80-by-20-foot work in stone. The city's other claim to fame is its group of seven pagodas, which look like flat-topped pyramids and are guarded by statues of an elephant, a lion, and a bull. The walls of the pagodas are illustrated with images from Hindu mythology. Mammallapuram was once the main harbor of the Pallava Empire, which died out about 1,200 years ago. Hindu sculpture can be found in the cave temples carved from the rock here.

Kanchipuram, 640 miles from Mammallapuram, was the capital of the ancient Pallava Empire from the 6th to 8th century and has 1,000 temples and 124 shrines. It is an important place of pilgrimage for Hindus.

The **Kailasanatha Temple,** believed to be 1,200 years old, contains excellent 7th- and 8th-century paintings. Smaller but prettier is the **Varadarajaswamy Temple.** The best Hindu murals, which illustrate various wars, are in the **Vaikunthanatha Perumal Temple**.

Further south, the coastal town of **Pondicherry** is a popular stop for travelers in Tamil Nadu. The former French colony was settled in the 18th century. It has a number of museums, churches, temples, and beaches. There are plenty of reminders of French culture and even a French/Indian *ashram*.

One of the oldest cities in the south, **Kumbakonam**, in central Tamil Nadu on the banks of the Cauvery River, has 18 temples decorated with lively Hindu sculptures. Once every 12 years pilgrims invade the city for the bathing festival.

A half-hour away is **Thanjavur**, lying at the foot of India's greatest temple, **Brihadiswara**, whose tower rises more than 200 feet. The tower's dome rests on an 80-ton block of granite brought in from a village four miles away.

Forty miles south of Pondicherry (and 155 miles from Chennai) is the breathtaking 9th-century **Temple of Nataraja** at Chidambaram. Two of the temple's four granite *gopuras* are covered with sculptures illustrating the 108 positions of Natya Sastra, the Indian science of dancing. No one knows how the granite was brought to the temple, for there is no granite for 50 miles around.

INDIA'S MOST ELEGANT HILL STATION

Ootacamund, renamed Udhagamandalam (but still affectionately known as Ooty), is a small, elegant hill station in Nilgris, the famed Blue Mountains of southern

India. Situated 8,000 feet above sea level, Ooty appealed to the royalty and the wealthy of many cultures. English is the major tongue here, and Ooty feels for all the world like a Victorian town in the heart of England.

The best way to reach Ooty is to rent a car and driver and travel through the Mudamalai jungle along the intricate hairpin turns that wind through parrot- and monkey-crowded bamboo jungles. It is a dramatic surprise to make the last turn and find yourself in a bit of England. Ooty's flowers are celebrated throughout India. Garden clubs present a floral spectacle each May, mingling familiar English varieties with exotic blooms.

Less than 50 miles away is the **Mudumalai National Park** containing birds, chital (spotted deer), tiger, wild boar, sloth bear, elephants, crocodiles, and otters. There are also large families of monkeys who run off with fruit from both the trees and market stalls.

An excellent and inexpensive place to stay is the **Savoy Hotel,** *77 Sylks Rd*; *tel. +91 (423) 222-5500; website: www.tajhotels.com.* Faded but still elegant in its full Victorian regalia, the Savoy is a treasure. Its gardens are famous throughout India.

ORISSA: INDIA IN A NUT SHELL

For a capsule view of India, visit the state of **Orissa,** on the Bay of Bengal. You can explore mountains, jungles, valleys, plains, tribal villages, coconut groves, and 250 miles of beach in this area of 60,000 square miles.

The recorded history of Orissa begins in 260 B.C., when the edicts of the Emperor Ashoka were carved in rock in Dhauli, five miles from the capital Bhubaneswar. The peak of Orissan civilization was reached between the 4th and 13th centuries, when thousands of temples and monuments were built. The British took over in 1803.

The Adivasi, a tribal group in Orissa, are descendants of the inhabitants of Orissa before the Aryan invasion 3,000 years ago. Over the centuries they have been pushed into the heart of Orissa, the least fertile section of the state. Now they are protected by the government.

Orissa's main sights
The pleasant capital **Bhubaneshwar** is a picturesque town with a myriad of temples, some dating back to 300 B.C. They are covered with spirals, turrets, decorations, and sculptures depicting good and evil, morality and immorality. The

397

Great Lingaraj Temple, built in A.D. 1000, is the finest Hindu temple in India, with a tower that can be seen for miles. Outside town are Udayagiri and Khandagari hills, where caves were carved by Jain monks as far back as the first century B.C.

The Sun Temple at **Konarak** (also known as the Black Pagoda), two hours outside Bhubaneswar, is one of the most beautiful sights in India. More than 1,000 workers took 12 years to build the 100-foot-high temple. Dedicated to the sun, the 13th-century Konarak rests on a base of 24 wheels pulled by seven horses. The roof is topped by a three-tiered spire. The entire temple is covered with carvings and sculptures.

Puri, an hour from Bhubaneswar, is one of the four holiest Hindu pilgrimage places in India. Hindus believe that if you stay here for three days and three nights, you will attain eternal life. The enormous **Jagannath Temple,** dedicated to the Lord of the Universe, was built in the 12th century. While non-Hindus are not allowed to enter the structure, you can get inside the 20-foot temple walls from atop the neighboring Raghunandan Library.

The most colorful (and most crowded) time to visit Puri is June, during the **Rath Yatra Festival,** when the image of Lord Jagannath is taken from its temple and carried in a canopied car by thousands of pilgrims to Gundicha Mandir, the god's Garden House.

Puri is also a great place to shop. If you know how to bargain, you can get good buys on statues, toys, and shoes.

INCREDIBLE KOLKATA (CALCUTTA)

Kolkata is incredible—a huge and growing industrial metropolis inhabited by the Bengalis, an emotional and artistic people who produce many of the best books, dramas, and films in India. In fact Kolkata is often referred to as the cultural capital of India. The city is a convenient base for exploring the Himalayas, Sikh temples, and the temples of Orissa and Bhutan. No one can claim to really know India without visiting Kolkata.

While there is incredible poverty here, Kolkata is also known as the city with a soul, and has been portrayed as such in film and literature such as the famed Dominique Lapierre novel *City of Joy*. If you arrive in Kolkata by train, you will see families camping on the platforms of Howrah Station, water vendors, newsboys, rice peddlers, tea-serving waiters, running children, and shouting porters.

When you leave the station and cross the **Howrah Bridge,** you will encounter cars, bicycles, cows, rickshaws, oxcarts, trucks, and crowds of people. Below the bridge, on the banks of the Hooghly River, live Kolkata's masseurs and barbers.

Kolkata's best sights

On the other side of the Howrah Bridge (the third-largest single-span bridge in the world) is **Old Kolkata,** the core of the city, which grew out of three tiny villages: Sutanati, Govindpur, and Kalikata (anglicized as Calcutta). Kalikata was once a sacred spot with two temples, including the Kalighat or Kali Temple from where the town originally got its name. You can visit this temple still, although it is dedicated to Shiva's destructive side and goats are slaughtered here daily. The temple area is also frequented by the poor who come for free meals at Mother Teresa's nearby Hospital for Dying Destitute.

Victorian Kolkata sprang up around **Fort William,** built in 1780. At the south end of Maidan Park, in front of the fort, is **Victoria Memorial,** completed in 1921 and filled with relics of British rule.

North of **Dalhousie Square** (now called B.B.D. Bagh) and surrounded by busy bazaar streets is the **Nakhoda Mosque,** which holds up to 10,000 people.

The **Indian Museum,** *Chowringhee Road; website: www.indianmuseumkolkata. org,* is the oldest in India and one of the most comprehensive in the Orient. Its archeology section is the largest in Asia and one of the most important in the world, with a large representative collection of antiquities illustrating the cultural history of India from prehistoric times to the Muslim period. The museum also has a fine collection of coins, gems, and jewelry.

Pareshnath Jain Temple, *Badris Temple Street,* built by the court jeweler in 1867, glitters with crystals and precious stones. A French crystal chandelier hangs above the gleaming mosaic-tile floor. The temple lamp has burned continuously for 112 years. A landscaped garden surrounds the structure. You can visit the temple from 6 a.m. until noon and 3 p.m. until 7 p.m.

Kolkata has a fabulous 16 hectare zoo with white Bengal tigers, monkeys, reptiles, and white peacocks, among other exotic beasts and birds.

The **Botanical Gardens** cover 273 acres and stretch along the Hooghly River with mahogany trees, Royal Cuban palms, an orchid house, and other exotic flora. Its crown jewel is its 200-year-old banyan tree, with a circumference of 1,000 feet. It is reported to have the second largest canopy in the world, although the largest is also in India in Andhra Pradesh. The garden was established in 1786 by the East India Company.

In the evening, stroll along **The Maidan,** a two-mile stretch of green lawn bedecked with statues of Indian heroes. During the day it is full of cricket players and kite fliers. When the sun sets, the locals use this as a rendezvous point. If you feel lucky, try out the Maidan Racetrack.

Kolkata's finest hotel

Kolkata's best hotel is the **Oberoi Grand,** *15 Jawaharlal Nehru Road; tel. +91 (33) 2249-2323; website: www.oberoikolkata.com,* which is centrally located and has rooms with beautiful private baths and refrigerators. Guests may use the swimming pool, health club, in-house astrologer, and disco. The hotel has four restaurants and a shopping arcade.

Kolkata's most famous person

Mother Teresa called Kolkata home for 60 years from 1937 to 1997, giving her life to serving the poor of the city. She formed a new order, the Missionaries of Charity, and opened several homes for the dying, lepers, and children. She received the Nobel Peace Prize in 1979 for her work. It is possible to volunteer in these homes and assist the nuns' work. Apply to the Motherhouse, *Missionaries of Charity, Sr. Mercy Maria, MC, 54/AAJC Bose Rd, Kolkata 700 016, India; tel. +91 (33) 2249-7115; website: www.motherteresa.org.*

The most sacred river

The **Ganges River,** considered sacred by the Hindus, is believed to originate in the hair of the god Siva. Regardless of its origins, the water is indeed pure, running downhill from the Himalayas. Hindus believe that washing in the Ganges washes away sin. The holiest place to bathe is **Allahabad,** where the Ganga and the Yamuna (or Jumna) rivers meet. This is also considered a good spot to scatter the ashes of loved ones.

The **Magh Mela,** India's biggest religious bathing ceremony, is held at Allahabad in the spring. During the festival, pilgrims stay in tents along the river, holy men lie on thorns and give sermons, barbers shave the heads of those who intend to bathe in the river, and women throw rose petals and marigolds into the water as part of *puja* (religious ritual). If you wish to join the pilgrims in their holy bath at the confluence you will need to negotiate a price for a boat to take you there.

The bathing festival is largest every 12th year, when millions convene to celebrate the Kumbh Mela, the most important religious ceremony.

The area's best hotel is the **Yatrik,** *33, Sardar Patel Marg, Civil Lines Allahabad; tel. +91 (532) 226-0921; website: www.hotelyatrik.com.*

DARJEELING: FOR THE MOST DARING

The romantic Toy Train ride to **Darjeeling** on the Darjeeling Himalayan Railway (*website: www.dhr.in*) is spectacular and dizzying. The 52-mile trip begins at New Jalpaiguri, near Gagdogra, which is a 55-minute flight from Kolkata, and takes about six hours.

For the first few miles, the train rushes through dense jungle. Then the steep climb begins. The train chugs through lush tea plantations, clinging to the mountainsides. From Kurseong (4,864 feet), about half way, the train climbs to Ghoom, 8,000 feet, to the site of a Tibetan monastery. Monks here worship a 15-foot image of the Coming Buddha and fly prayer flags. This is the highest point in the journey and from here the train descends another four miles to Darjeeling, about 1,000 feet lower. Darjeeling has absolutely amazing views of the Himalayas. **Kanchenjunga Mountain** is especially awe-inspiring; the Hindus believe it is the god Siva lying down.

Darjeeling is built on a hillside and connected by roads and flights of steps. At the top of the hill is the town center with hotels, cafés, and shops. Halfway up are smaller hotels, Indian restaurants, and more shops. The people of Darjeeling live at the bottom. Nepalese, Tibetans, and Lepchas, in their colorful tribal costumes, crowd the bazaars and markets. Women wear nose ornaments and huge necklaces.

At the center of the town is **Observatory Hill,** where the Mahakala Cave is located. The view is beautiful. Also visit the **Lloyd Botanical Gardens,** which are devoted to the flowers of the Himalayas, and the **Bhutia Busty Gompa** and the **Aloobari Gompa,** two Buddhist monasteries.

Darjeeling also boasts Lebong Racetrack, the smallest and highest **racetrack** in the world, five miles from town. The racing season is May-June and September-October.

Seven miles from Darjeeling is **Tiger Hill,** from which you can see Himalayan Peaks and occasionally a peak of Mount Everest on very clear days. The best time to see the mountain is at sunrise, when the white mountain peaks turn rose-colored.

You can learn to mountain climb at the **Himalayan Mountaineering Institute,** *Jawahar Road West; website: www.himalayanmountaineeringinstitute. com,* in Darjeeling. The director of the institute for many years was Tenzing Norgay who climbed Mount Everest with Sir Edmund Hillary in 1953. The institute has a museum that displays climbing equipment.

INDIA'S MOST EXOTIC AREAS

India's most exotic and remote areas are **Assam** and **Nagaland,** located in the extreme northeast corner of the country. Some years ago they were off-limits to foreigners, which makes these two locations all the more fascinating. They are inhabited by indigenous tribes, some of which were headhunters only a generation ago. This is a paradise for wildlife enthusiasts and fishermen. The region has incredible waterfalls, high peaks, and wild rivers.

The **Kaziranga Wild Life Sanctuary** in Assam is one of the best places for spotting wildlife in India. The best way to see the sanctuary is astride an elephant. The reserve protects several species of deer, birds, wild boars, jackals, buffaloes, elephants, and tigers. Note that, for Nagaland at least, you will need a Restricted Area Permit. Contact your travel agent for details on obtaining one.

INDIA'S BEST FESTIVALS

Two of India's festivals deserve special mention. **Holi** or the Festival of Colors, is a spring festival held in late February or early March to welcome the change of seasons and ask for blessings for good harvests and fertility. It is one of India's most exuberant festivals and starts with a bonfire on Holi Eve. On the following day people throw water and colored powder at each other.

Diwali, the Festival of Lights, in October/November is equally colorful. The five-day festival is significant for Hindus, Buddhists, Jains, and Sikhs who celebrate good triumphing over evil by lighting candles and letting off fireworks.

THE BEST TRAVEL PLANNING

India is immense, so it is important to plan your trip carefully. Mumbai, Delhi, Kolkata, and Chennai are the best places to begin your travels. Most travelers to India *must* have a visa. There are five different Indian consular offices in the United States; each issues its own application form and requirements may vary. For further information, visit *website: www.traveldocs.com.*

Foreign visitors receive special assistance and concessions in India. Booking information sections for foreigners, which are located in railway stations and the major offices of Indian Airlines, enable you to avoid the usual long waiting lines and can greatly reduce costs of transportation throughout India. However it is still recommended you book transport as far ahead as possible. To book trains online go to *website: www.indianrail.gov.in*. In states where alcohol is banned, foreigners can apply for a liquor permit. The Indian government is anxious to promote tourism.

Keep in mind that certain parts of India, which are politically sensitive or strategic, are designated by the government as "restricted" or "protected" areas. Foreign tourists can enter them only with special permits from the Foreigners' Regional Registration Offices (in Mumbai, Kolkata, Delhi, and Chennai).

You also need a 30-day permit if you plan to visit the Andaman Islands. This can be obtained through local travel agents in Kolkata or directly from the **Ministry for Home Affairs,** *North Block, New Delhi; website: www.mha.nic.in.*

Western Kashmir is not a recommended destination for travelers, and some areas of the Andamans are restricted. Check at your local consulate or in New Delhi for current restrictions.

In India photography is not allowed of bridges, airports and military installations for security reasons. Permits are also required to photograph railway stations or trains.

THE BEST TIME TO GO

The best time to go to India is between November and the end of March. This avoids the rainy season and the severe heat from April to October in northern India, although hill stations are always cooler. It's wise to plan your travels around the weather. Making your way through India demands tremendous energy; trying to make your way through India during the rainy season or in severe heat can be miserable. Winter can also be more severe than travelers realize. In the mountain areas it can snow and even in capitals like Delhi the temperature drops dramatically. The best areas to tackle in winter are the southern states.

THE BEST OF
INDONESIA

Indonesia is a nation teeming with 237 million people and more than 9,000 islands. Although now mainly Muslim, these islands have a rich history of Buddhism and Hinduism, which can be seen in the ruins of ancient temples and cities scattered among the lush tropical landscape. Its capital, **Jakarta**, located on the main island of Java, is the least attractive of all the cities in Indonesia; its only real claim to fame is that it has more monuments in the city proper than any other city in the world. Once you've escaped Jakarta, you'll discover that Indonesia offers some of the most beautiful scenery in the world.

The best island to visit—Bali

No other island in the archipelago can compare with Bali. Bali has everything: stunning beaches, ancient temples, and several active volcanoes. The best beach is **Nusa Dua**. See it, but don't stop there. Explore the island's lush interior and its temples.

The best base for this is the village of **Ubud**. Discovered by Dutch artists in the 1920s, it is still home to a thriving colony of Indonesian artists and wood sculptors, each with an individual style. It's also the best place to take in the colorful Balinese dance, performed daily in the courtyard of the Ubud Palace.

If your budget can handle it, stay at the ultra-exclusive **Amandari Resort**, *tel. +62 (361) 975-333; website: www.amanresorts.com/amandari/home.aspx*. If it can't, stay at one of the area's many good guesthouses. You can hire a cab to drive you around the surrounding countryside. It's cheaper to negotiate a rate with the driver for an entire afternoon or day than to pay for individual trips. Just tell the driver to show you the temple and the volcano; it will be money well-spent.

The best water activities

The best places for diving and snorkeling on Bali are on the north coast near Amed. The **USAT Liberty shipwreck** at Tulamben is the remains of a U.S. World War II freighter that was torpedoed in 1942. The top of the wreck lies just below the surface and you can easily dive down to it. Tons of fish and an encrusting of animals cover the wreck—marine biologists estimate there are about 400 different species of reef fish living on the Liberty. The Japanese shipwreck east of Amed at Banyuning lies just off shore and is another popular snorkeling excursion. The wreck lies in shallow water (about 16 feet) and is marked by a buoy. Beyond it the real diving starts but even with a snorkel you can admire the relatively unspoiled hard and soft corals and numerous fish.

Surfers usually head to the beaches on the south of the island and the reefs around Kuta, Canggu, Sanur and Nusa Dua.

The world's biggest Buddhist monument

Java's ancient city of **Yogyakarta** is home to the world's largest Buddhist monument, the circular ruin of Borobodur. The stone friezes that circle the monument tell the life story of Buddha and his search for enlightenment. Legend has it that originally only the initiated were permitted to view the higher levels, as they are said to contain the key to a happy life.

The best place to stay is the **Ambarukmo Palace Hotel**, *Jalan Laksda Adisucipto; tel. +62 (247) 566-488.*

The world's heaviest lizards

You'll find these prehistoric beasts on the **islands of Komodo, Flores, Rinca, and Gili Motang**. Komodo Dragons can grow to a length of 10 feet and weigh 200 lbs. You'll also want to keep away from their mouth and 60 teeth which are full of virulent bacteria! They have a good sense of smell, are quite fast and agile and swim well. You can visit them at the Komodo National Park, *website: www. komodonationalpark.org*, between the islands of Sumbawa and Flores.

The most endangered wildlife

The endangered Orangutans, a species of great apes, are now only found in rainforests on Borneo and Sumatra. They live in trees and are known for their intelligence and reddish-brown hair. Estimates put the numbers at between 7,300 in Sumatra and 50,000 in Borneo. Conservation centers in Indonesia are doing their best to assist in saving orphaned babies and rehabilitating them to the wild. The Bukit Lawang Orangutan Rehabilitation Centre in the Gunung Lesser National Park is one of the most famous.

The best volcanoes

Sumatra has a range of mountains that are dotted with volcanoes. These have created fabulous crater lakes—the most famous being **Toba** which is the caldera left from a giant volcano—thermal baths and great diving amidst the lava at sea. The Marapi volcano is the most active, Kerinci is the tallest, and Kaba has seven craters. There are also a number of good hikes to the Sumatran volcanoes including the trek to Gunung Sibayak at Berastagi which you can hike to and then dive into thermal springs afterwards. **Mikie Holiday Resort and Hotel,** *Jalan Raya Medan Berastagi; tel. +62 628-91650; website: www.mikieholiday.com,* is a good option in Berastagi.

The best surfing

The surf-break off **Pantai Sorake** at Lagundri Beach on Nias Island (off Sumatra) is considered the best right-hander in the world. It's well established on the professional surfing circuit (June/July) and the waves go off in July and August when they can reach 13 feet. In Lagundri there are a series of basic bungalows right on the beach. Those across from the surf break are the most popular.

The most relaxing lake

Staying by **Lake Toba**, on Sumatra, is like taking a sedative. It is truly one of the most relaxing places and many people spend far longer than they planned here. Days can be whiled away on Samosir Island in the center of the lake visiting the Batik villages, fishing or swimming, indulging in local food specialties or hiking or cycling. The best place to base on Samosir is Tuk Tuk, which has a number of guesthouses, bookshops, Internet cafes and places to rent motorbikes and bicycles. In Tuk Tuk you can't beat the **Liberta Homestay,** *tel. +62 545-1035; e-mail: liberta_homestay@yahoo.co.id; website: www.sumatra-indonesia.com/liberta.htm,* where the owner Mr. Moon goes out of his way to help guests.

THE BEST OF
IRELAND

When Erin first rose from the dark-swelling flood, God bless'd the green island, He saw it was good. The Emerald of Europe, it sparkled, it shone, In the ring of this world the most precious stone!
—Dr. William Drennan, from the poem "When Erin First Rose"

The good-natured Irish people are a joy to spend time with, so make sure you visit the people of Ireland as well as the Irish countryside. Don't miss the most pleasant occupation in Ireland: sitting in a pub, sipping a pint of Guinness, and chatting.

The best way to tour Ireland's emerald countryside, charming villages, and ancient ruins is to circle around its coast, traveling from Dublin to Wicklow, Wexford, Waterford, Cork, Killarney, and finally Limerick. Venture inland to Kilkenny. Then go to the region the English never conquered: the Burren, Galway, Mayo, and Sligo.

The best ways to explore Dublin

The most pleasant way to visit Dublin is to follow the lines of an old song: "Have coffee in Dublin at 11 and walk in Stephen's Green, and you'll be in heaven." Later, spend time shopping along bustling Grafton, Anne, and Duke Streets. If you are in a hurry, use the **Dublin Trail**. Well posted, it leads past the city's major sights.

Another good way to explore Dublin is to follow in the footsteps of James Joyce. The house where Joyce was born, 41 Brighton Square W., in the agreeable suburb of Rathgar, is marked with a plaque. **Mulligan's**, *Poolbeg Street*, a pub Joyce frequented in his student days, has a special aura, especially in the back parlor, where Joyce often sat and wrote. Joyce once lived at Martello Tower Museum, at Sandycove, as did his characters in *Ulysses*.

Also look for the homes of other famous Dubliners: Shelley lived at 1 Grafton Street; Sheridan lived at 79 Grafton Street; and George Bernard Shaw was born at 33 Synge Street.

Dublin's greatest treasure

The jewel in Dublin's crown is *The Book of Kells*. More than 1,000 years old, it is the most intricate illuminated manuscript in the Western world. See the manuscript on display at **Trinity College**; *website: www.tcd.ie/Library/bookofkells/.*

Ireland's best stout

The **Guinness Brewery**, *website: www.guinness-storehouse.com*, at St. James' Gate on the banks of the Liffey in Dublin produces Ireland's rich and frothy national drink, the brown stout found on tap in every pub. Guinness Storehouse is open from 9.30 a.m. to 5 p.m. seven days a week. The interactive tour takes you through the brewing process, the history of Guinness, and ends in the Gravity Bar, where you get to enjoy a pint of the famous "black stuff" while enjoying 360-degree views of Dublin city.

The oldest pub in Ireland

The **Brazen Head**, *20 Bridge Street, Dublin; tel. +353 (1) 677-9549; website: www. brazenhead.com*, is the oldest pub in Ireland, dating back to the 12th century. It is five minutes away from the antique shops on Francis Street, and it's a perfect break from your shopping. The Guinness here is superb; the brewery is only a stone's throw away, and the smell of hops stays with you for hours after you've moved on.

The pubs with the most atmosphere

Dublin boasts more than 600 pubs, but if you want atmosphere, head to the **Palace Bar**, *Fleet Street, Temple Bar* or the **Long Hall**, *South George's Street*. Both have authentic stained-glass partitions, wood paneling, and collections of Victorian prints. But smokers beware—smoking is now illegal in pubs and restaurants throughout Ireland.

Dublin's best sights

Dublin Castle, *website: www.dublincastle.ie,* restored after a bombing, has handsome state apartments that are open to the public. Castle upon castle has been built on this site. The earliest construction was Celtic. The Vikings later improved upon this; then, in the 13th-century King John of England built a fortress on the site. The British ruled Ireland from this stronghold for 400 years.

The GPO (General Post Office), *O'Connell Street,* was the scene of the 1916 Easter uprising, the major step along Ireland's road to independence. You can read the declaration of Irish independence on the walls. After they proclaimed the free Republic here, the Irish Volunteers were bombed by a British gunboat docked in the River Liffey. Those who surrendered were hanged.

The **National Museum of Ireland**, *Kildare Street; website: www.museum. ie*, has a collection of Irish antiquities from the Stone Age through the War for Independence. It is open daily.

The **National Gallery,** *Merrion Square West; website: www.nationalgallery. ie,* has a fine collection of old masters, including works by Rembrandt, Caravaggio, Monet, and Picasso. It also houses a collection of works by Jack B. Yeats, Ireland's most important 20th-century artist; and the National Portrait Gallery.

Dublin's creepiest experience

Centuries-old bodies lie perfectly preserved in the dry crypt of **St. Michan's Church** on Church Street. The 17th-century church was built on the site of a 10th-century Viking church. Perhaps because of its dryness, the crypt has remarkable preservation qualities. You can actually touch an eight-foot-tall Crusader. It is said to be good luck to shake the hand of one of the corpses here. The crypt is open weekdays and Saturday mornings. The church also contains an organ that Handel is said to have played.

The best park

Phoenix Park in Dublin is the largest public park in Western Europe and the largest enclosed city park in the world. The official residence of the Irish president (Áras an Uachtaráin) is here, as well as the residence of the American ambassador. The 1,760-acre park includes a racetrack, a soccer field, sports grounds, flower gardens, a herd of fallow deer, a lake, and a monument to Wellington, the Papal Cross where over one million people gathered to hear the Pope say mass in 1979, as well as the Dublin Zoo.

Dublin's most picturesque bridge

Peer into the Liffey from the wrought iron **Ha'penny Bridge**, named after the toll once charged for crossing the river. Its southern end brings you through Merchant's Quay into the cobblestone alleyways of Temple Bar. This is Dublin's "left bank," teeming with secondhand bookshops, bars, and cafés.

The best escape from Dublin

If, by some amazing chance, the weather is hot while you are in Dublin, visit the famous seaside resort of **Bray**. It is about 15 miles south of Dublin City, adjacent to the town of Dun Laoghaire (pronounced Dunleary) in County Dublin.

Dublin's best nightlife

The best spots in Dublin are the pubs, with their evenings of Guinness, ballads, and poetry. Busiest from 9 p.m. onward, most pubs open at 11 a.m. and close around midnight. Some of the most famous pubs include **The Brazen Head**, **The Abbey Tavern**, and **Slattery's Pub**.

The world's best pub crawl

Every summer, the infamous "Dublin Literary Pub Crawl" staggers off at 7.30 p.m. every evening between April and October, and every Thursday to Sunday between November and March. First pints are downed at **The Duke**, 9 *Duke Street,* where the owners still display Michael Collins' revolver. At 21 Duke Street, try **Davy Byrne's Pub**, where Leopold Bloom fictionally dined on Gorgonzola and Burgundy. For more information, see *website: www.dublinpubcrawl.com.*

The best Dublin market

For local color head for the **Moore Street Market**, off O'Connell Street. Although you won't meet Molly Malone with her wheelbarrow, you will be able to shop for everything from socks to strawberries, sold out of battered old prams. The language is just as colorful as the people.

The best place to buy antiques

Go to **The Liberties**, the oldest section of the city and the address of its best antique shops. Start at one end of Francis Street and continue to the other. You'll pass a dozen or more quality antique shops. Don't be fooled by their small fronts. The shops stretch back a block or more.

The best seafood restaurant

King Sitric, *East Pier, Howth; tel. +353 (1) 832-5235; website: www.kingsitric.ie*, offers the best seafood in or around Dublin. It is a popular, small restaurant overlooking the harbor at Howth, well worth the 30-minute drive out of the city.

Dublin's finest hotel

The **Shelbourne Hotel**, *tel. +353 (1) 663-4500; website: www.marriott.com*, which graces St. Stephen's Green, is a Victorian hotel where the Irish Constitution was drafted. Inside the hotel's turreted red-brick façade are ultramodern rooms. Don't miss their sumptuous afternoon tea.

The **Gresham Hotel**, *23 Upper O'Connell Street; tel. +353 (1) 874-6881; website: www.gresham-hotels.com*, is ideally located in the heart of the city, close to all sights, shops and restaurants. Excellent service.

For a slightly cheaper alternative, try the **D4 Ballsbridge Inn**, *Pembroke Road; tel. +353 (1) 668-4468; website: www.d4hotels.ie.*

Ireland's greenest county

County Wicklow, which is known as the Garden of Ireland, is the greenest of Ireland's counties. **Enniskerry**, one of Ireland's prettiest villages, is here. Located in a wooded hollow and surrounded by hills, the village is famous for **Powerscourt**, *website: www.powerscourt.ie*, one of Ireland's great estates. The ruins of a Georgian mansion are surrounded by 14,000 acres of grounds, including the 400-foot Powerscourt Waterfall.

Wicklow's other highlight is **Glendalough**, *website: www.glendalough.ie*, a deep valley in the Wicklow Mountains. In the sixth century, St. Kevin took refuge in this peaceful glen between two lakes. However, his refuge didn't remain secret. His disciples followed him and founded a monastery and a famous center of learning here. View the remains of a medieval round tower, as well as buildings from the ninth through 13th centuries. This is a good region for hikers; nature trails head through the valley.

The best antique shopping

R.J. Keighery Antiques, *27a William Street, Waterford City; tel. +353 (51) 873-692; website: www.cityauctionrooms.com*, is the best place to shop for antiques. This country hides antique treasures at bargain prices. In Waterford, Rody's inventory turns over regularly, and his prices are often half what you would pay in the United States for comparable pieces.

Waterford's best restaurant

La Boheme, *2 George's Street; tel. +353 (51) 875-645; website: www. labohemerestaurant.ie,* is the best restaurant in Waterford. Located in the historic Port of Waterford building, the food is exceptional and the service excellent.

The best pubs

Geoff's, *8 John Street,* has little nooks and corners with names familiar to regulars —the Protestants Corner, the Catholics Corner, and the Queen's Chair—that provide a certain intimacy despite its large area.

Downes, *8 Thomas Street,* has been owned by the same family since Henry Downes founded it as a distillery and pub in 1797. The pub is large and rarely crowded, except on Saturday nights when it's a popular local hangout. Don't come expecting to meet tourists, but do taste Downes No. 9, the blended whiskey that has been made and served at Downes since its founding.

If your tastes run toward tourist hotspots, visit **T & H Doolans,** *George's Street.* They feature crowd-pleasing Irish music every night of the week. There's plenty of singing, and you are sure to hear classics like *The Irish Rover* or *Wild Colonial Boy.* The place always has a lively crowd and good atmosphere.

Cork: The Rebel County

Often referred to as the "real capital" by locals, Cork is Ireland's largest county. Its history of rebelliousness dating back to the town's support of the English Pretender Perkin Warbeck in 1491 following the Wars of the Roses, has also earned it the name "the rebel county". The city is a major European sea port and has the second largest natural harbor in the world, after Sydney, Australia.

County Cork's capital, **Cork City,** houses the fascinating **English Market,** a vast covered arcade on Prince's Street that was built in 1788. Here you can soak up a bit of local color and enjoy the unmistakable Cork accent.

Cork's biggest bell

Be sure to climb the pepperpot steeple of **Shandon Church** and ring its bells. Using numbered cards you can even regale the "rebel" city with your own eight-belled version of *Waltzing Matilda.*

Cork's best country restaurant

For country house ambience (including a heated swimming pool), try **Ballymaloe House,** *Shanagarry, Co. Cork; tel. +353 (21) 465-2531; website: www.ballymaloe.*

com. Twenty miles from Cork City and only two from the coast, Ballymaloe is run by the Allen family. Produce for the award-winning restaurant comes from the home farm; members of the Allen family run the Ballymaloe Cookery School, arguably the most prestigious in Ireland.

The blarniest sight

Outside Cork City is **Blarney Castle**, where kissing the **Blarney Stone** is said to give the gift of eloquence or the "gift of the gab" as it is known locally. Doing so is practically an acrobatic feat. You must lie on your back over a sheer drop and stretch backwards to kiss the stone. The legend is that the Lord of Blarney Castle, McCarthy, flabbergasted Queen Elizabeth with his eloquent excuses for having attacked England. She finally dropped the charges against him, calling his excuses "blarney."

The yacht crowd's favorite

Kinsale, about 20-minute drive from Cork City, is an international yachting center overflowing with gourmet restaurants. The *Lusitania* was torpedoed off its coast by a German submarine in 1915. This was also the site of the 1602 Battle of Kinsale, during which the northern chieftains were defeated by the English, establishing English domination of Ireland. The heavy, woolen Kinsale cloak is a popular purchase.

The best wildlife

Fota, *Carrigtwohill, Co. Cork; tel. +353 (21) 481-2678; website: www.fotawildlife. ie,* is Ireland's best wildlife park. Fota is home to free-ranging monkeys, zebras, giraffes, ostriches, flamingos, emus, bison, cheetahs, red pandas, and kangaroos, wandering freely over 70 acres. The park is open all year round.

The best eateries

Greene's Restaurant, *Hotel Issacs, 48 MacCurtain Street; tel. +353 (21) 455-2279; website: www.greenesrestaurant.com,* specializes in seafood, but the menu offers plenty of choice for carnivores and vegetarians. In summer, dine al fresco in the garden, overlooking the floodlit waterfall. Reservations are a must.

    Market Lane, *5/6 Oliver Plunkett Street; tel. +353 (21) 427-4710; website: www.marketlane.ie,* is a great lunch option in the city. The food is made from local produce and the wide menu has everything from soup to seafood and a delicious deep-fried, goat's cheese salad.

If you are looking for a brunch to set you up for a day of exploring the city, eat at the **Liberty Grill**, *32 Washington Street; tel. +353 (21) 427-1049*. Brunch is served from 8 a.m. and they have the best eggs benedict in the city. They also serve an evening dinner menu from 5 p.m. with last orders at 9 p.m. Be sure to get here early for brunch as this small establishment fills up fast.

The best hotels in Cork

If five-star luxury is what you crave, then a stay at the **Castlemartyr Resort,** *Castlemartyr, Co. Cork; tel. +353 (21) 421-9000; website: www.castlemartyrresort. ie*, is a must. Located just a 30-minute drive from Cork International airport, this 18th-century manor-house hotel has all you could need in a luxury hotel. Relax in the spa, tour the manor house and gardens, play golf on the 18-hole course, or take the estate's dogs, Countess and Earl, for a walk around the 220-acre estate.

In Cork City, the **Clarion Hotel**, *Lapps Quay; tel. +353 (21) 422-4900; website: www.clarionhotelcorkcity.com*, overlooks the famous River Lee, which flows through the heart of the city. It is close to shopping, restaurants, and all of Cork's major sights.

Ennis: The best base for exploring Ireland's west

The town of **Ennis** in County Clare is the best base for exploring the west of Ireland, from which so many Americans stem. The old market town has escaped relatively unscathed from the tourist flow, even though Shannon Airport is close by.

The main street in Ennis boasts antique shops selling genuine (if pricey) antiques. But the town's gem is its monastery—the most evocative in Ireland. This roofless, weed-covered ruin's tottering Gothic walls exactly fit Shakespeare's phrase, "bare, ruined choirs."

Bunratty Castle, built in 1425 and restored in the 1950s, is worth a visit. It is the most complete medieval fortress in the country. The folk park on the castle grounds recreates life in 19th-century Ireland.

The **Old Ground Hotel**, *O'Connell Street; tel. +353 (65) 682-8127; website: www.flynnhotels.com/Old_Ground_Hotel/*, is the most charming place to stay in Ennis. Rooms are well-equipped. The restaurant at the Old Ground is splendid and serves Irish specialties, including Dublin Bay prawns (shrimp), mutton chops with kidneys, and apple pie.

Ireland's most spectacular cliffs

The **Cliffs of Moher**, a few miles north of Ennis, are the most spectacular in Ireland, perhaps in all Europe. The 700-foot black cliffs face the constant onslaught of the Atlantic.

Ireland's loveliest lakes

The town of **Killarney** offers a dream-like setting of lush green hills and deep blue lakes. Spend time enjoying the town, but concentrate on the surrounding Lower, Middle, and Upper lakes. At their banks, ferns and mosses grow in the shade of oak, birch, holly, and ash trees. Much of this lake district lies within the 11,000-acre Bourne Vincent Memorial Park.

The Aran Islands: Time's greatest foe

The **Aran Islands** are fascinating, if barely habitable. Gaelic language and traditions survive on these three islands, 35 miles from the mainland. The islanders grow potatoes in a mixture of sand and seaweed and fish in wicker-framed, hide-covered *curraughs*, or boats.

Dun Aengus, an Iron Age fortress built on a cliff on the island of **Inishmore**, has 18-foot-thick walls. The prettiest islands are the two smallest, **Inishman**, which is known for its traditional music and dancing, and **Inisheer**. In good weather, boat service is available regularly to most of the islands. The closest point on the mainland is Doolin, where you can catch a boat to Inisheer. Boats also run daily from Galway to Kilronan on Inishmore.

The best horseback riding

The **Connemara Trail**, which winds its way along the coast of Ireland's County Galway, passes through rugged mountains and along deserted beaches. Beginning near the sea in Barna, the trail goes from village to village and mountain to mountain, leading you eventually to the Atlantic Ocean on the beaches near Clifden.

Biggest horse fair, smallest ponies

Held annually in County Galway, the **Great Fair of Ballinasloe** is Ireland's oldest and biggest horse fair. For the first week of October, Ballinasloe's Fair Green heaves with horseflesh. Many deals are done with a spit and a handshake. Ireland's smallest ponies are found in the wilderness of **Connemara**. Clifden, the color-washed capital of this mountainous region, hosts the annual Connemara pony show during the third week in August.

415

The most delicious oysters

For some of the best oysters in all Ireland, visit **Paddy Burke's Oyster Tavern**, *Clarenbridge; tel. +353 (93) 796-226; website: www.paddyburkesgalway.com.* Oysters are sold by the dozen, or you can sit down for a good meal. To preserve the taste of the sea, you should hold the shell horizontally. With nothing more than perhaps a squeeze of lemon for flavoring, squash the oyster with your tongue, savor its flavor, and then gulp the liquid from the shell.

Yeats' favorite land

The dramatic countryside of **Sligo** is where the poet William Butler Yeats spent his childhood summers. He asked to be buried in Drumcliff Churchyard, five miles from Sligo proper. The area around Sligo claims one of the largest concentrations of prehistoric graves and monuments in Western Europe. Most are neither fenced off nor mentioned in tourist brochures. You must find them by word-of-mouth.

"A pearl, a gem, a jewel in the crown of mother Ireland"

Well, that's how **Hargadons**, *O'Connell Street, Sligo town; tel. +353 (71) 917-0933,* modestly describes itself. Even the atmosphere in this peculiar drinking den is intoxicating. Needless to say, it serves memorable Guinness. But there's more to Hargadons than fine brew—just look around; you'll see a potbellied stove, huge glittering mirrors, open turf fires, and customers who can talk the hind leg off any proverbial donkey. Don't miss it. It also now has a restaurant that serves hearty, locally produced food.

Donegal: The best tweed

"You'll wear out two suit linings," the Irish brag, "before you'll wear out a Donegal tweed." The county of **Donegal**, in northwest Ireland, sells some of the best tweed in the world. **Magee's Tweed Shop**, *The Diamond, Donegal Town; tel. +353 (74) 972-2660; website: www.mageeireland.com,* in Donegal town is a good place to begin your search. If you buy any tweed during your visit, be sure it is labeled "Genuine Donegal Hand-Woven Tweed. Pure New Wool."

The toughest pilgrimage

In the bare blue hills of County Donegal, the **Lough Derg** pilgrimage is a trip to purgatory. Every year, from June 1st through August 15th, pilgrims spend three days on Station Island, the site of St. Patrick's purgatory, depriving themselves of food, sleep, and all physical comforts. The cost to join in is not much, but make sure you know what you're letting yourself in for. The penitential exercises include dragging your bare feet over the jagged remains of monastic cells. It is an excruciating experience.

Ireland's most beautiful ruin

In the northern midlands of Ireland, south of Athlone in **County Offaly**, is the haunting ruin of **Clonmacnoise**, a flourishing monastic settlement more than 1,000 years ago. Still here are ruins of an abbey founded in 541 by St. Kieran, the Seven Churches of Clonmacnoise, a castle, a bishop's palace, and two round towers where townspeople watched for invading Vikings in search of Celtic gold. Celtic crosses from the time when Ireland was the Island of Saints and Scholars also stand here still.

The best riverboat cruising

Winding past Clonmacnoise and cutting through the bogs like a broad silver ribbon is the magnificent **River Shannon**. It's the perfect place for fishing, bird-watching, or simply lazing on a summer afternoon. The river is navigable for 120 of its 220 miles to the sea, and cruising is a popular activity. For more information on expeditions down the river, contact **Emerald Star**, *tel. +353 (71) 962-7633; website: www.emeraldstar.ie.*

The holiest mountain

Ireland's holiest mountain is **Croagh Patrick** in County Mayo. More than 2,500 feet high, it was from here that St. Patrick reputedly banished all snakes from the island. Each Garland Sunday, the last Sunday in July, 60,000 pilgrims clamber to the summit.

The stoniest wilderness

Stark, strange, and almost brutal to the eye, dotted with megalithic tombs and disappearing loughs, **County Clare's Burren region** seems an unlikely place for a flower show. The landscape is lunar: a vast gray sea of rock stretching for mile upon mile. But look closer—hidden in limestone crevices are orchids, vivid blue gentians, and a profusion of other rare wild flowers. It's a real botanist's paradise.

The strangest festival

If you're looking for romance, head for **Lisdoonvarna** on the southern edge of the Burren, where men are men and women are scarce. Each September, this small town hosts a matchmaking festival that boosts the population from 700 to 7,000. And although the matchmaking business isn't as serious as in days gone by, the ballrooms of romance still fill with dancers until dawn.

The best hostel

Ireland's best hostel is the **Valley House Holiday Hostel and Pub,** *tel. +353 (98) 47204; website: www.valley-house.com*, on Achill Island, off the coast of Mayo. The island, about 14 miles across and 19 miles long, is Ireland's largest and only bridged island—you can drive there. Achill has several blue flag beaches, white or golden, plenty of restaurants, and pubs to wet your whistle. The locals are friendly characters. The hostel itself is situated in a huge white manor more than 110 years old. Its bedrooms range from new, comfortable bunks to bouncy twins. The hostel also offers two nicely decorated private rooms, as well as a lawn for tent campers.

Ireland's best accommodation: The castle hotel

The best places to stay in Ireland are the country's castle hotels. Scores of these delightful, historic places dot the countryside. The finest in all Ireland is **Ashford Castle,** *tel. +353 (94) 954-6003; website: www.ashford.ie,* in Co. Mayo. The original castle was built here in 1228. In the 16th century, the troops of Queen Elizabeth battled in the area and stormed through the castle, which later became an English fortress. In the 18th century, a French château was incorporated into the old complex. Nearby are several ancient abbeys, churches, and points of archeological interest.

THE BEST OF THE
ISLE OF MAN

The politically independent **Isle of Man**, located halfway between Ireland and England and only 20 miles south of Scotland, is one of Europe's hidden bests. It is one of the best banking havens in the world. Europe's best ice cream is created here. Manx kippers are world famous, and the Isle of Man has been noted by the World Health Organization for its high-quality lamb and beef. The fishing here is terrific. And some of Britain's prettiest walking trails flank the isle's shores.

The Isle of Man, covering a mere 343 square miles, is probably the least-known country in Europe. Still a member of the British Commonwealth, the Isle of Man has been ruled by Ireland, Wales, Norway, Scotland, and England. Though it is part of the British Isles, it is not part of the United Kingdom. The island has its own representative assembly and courts.

The world's oldest legislature

The **Tynwald**, as the Manx legislature is called, is more than a thousand years old and has the longest continuous history of any legislature in the world. Tynwald derives from the Norse word *tingvollr*, meaning assembly field.

The **Royal Chapel of St. John the Baptist**, in the town of St. John's, is on the field where the open-air Tynwald Ceremony of the Norsemen began 1,000 years ago. Each year on July 5th (or the Monday after, if the 5th falls on a weekend), the Tynwald assembles at the chapel to sign new laws. Any Manx citizen may present a petition on this occasion.

Man's strangest sight

The Isle of Man's strangest monument in stone is a modern tower in **Corrin's Folly** overlooking Peel Bay. It was built around 1806 by Thomas Corrin, who wished to be buried on the hill. But when he died in 1845 this wish was not honored by his son, who believed his father should be buried in consecrated ground. Thomas was briefly laid to rest in the Kirk Patrick Church Yard, until one night when his friends moved his body onto the hill. The rest of the family are also buried here.

Man's best fishing

Sports fishermen adore the Isle of Man because of its variety of fishing: surf casting, river fishing, and deep-sea fishing. Sea fishermen can cast their lines for skate, mackerel, and tope from spring through late summer; pollack (the local name is *calig*), conger, dogfish, plaice (a flat fish that is a bottom eater), coalfish, bass, and mullet from June through October; and whiting, brill, monkfish, and flounder in the fall.

The best place for surf casting is the **Point of Ayre**, where you can fish at any tide. The best time, however, is low tide.

Sea-angling boat services are available from Douglas. Freshwater fishing in the Isle of Man is for salmon, sea trout, brown trout, and rainbow trout, primarily in the rivers that flow through the Manx national glens. The main run of salmon and sea trout starts in late summer.

For information on fishing and licenses, contact the offices of the **Isle of Man Board of Agriculture and Fisheries**, *Government Offices, Douglas; website: www.gov.im/daff/.*

Man's best walking trails

The best walking trail is the **Millennium Way**, established in 1979 to commemorate the millennium of the Tynwald. It follows the Regia Via, or Royal Way, one of the earliest recorded highways. In medieval times, it was used by the king and his attendants traveling to the Tynwald from Ramsey. Clearly marked, the Millennium Way is approximately 21-miles-long and can be walked by an experienced hiker in a full day.

The Way starts approximately one mile from Ramsey Town Square on the main road to Kirk Michael at the foot of Sky Hill. It ends in Castletown at Castle Rushen, the site of the fortification built by the Noresemen to guard the south of the island.

The world's largest waterwheel

Laxey has the largest waterwheel in the world, with a diameter of 72 feet, six inches; a circumference of 217 feet, and a top speed of two revolutions per minute. Built in 1854, it was christened the Lady Isabella after the wife of the lieutenant governor. Originally, it was used to pump water out of the lead mines.

The world's best ice cream

Manx ice cream is the best in the world. This prize-winning concoction is the creamiest and richest we have ever tasted. Visit the **Davisons Manx Dairy Ices**, *Mill Road, Peel; tel. +44 (1624) 844-111; website: www.davisons.co.im/about.html,* or find their ice cream parlor on the Peel Promenade and their new shop on the Douglas Promenade.

The Isle's best coffee shop and restaurants

The best place for a light meal and a great cup of coffee **Copperfields Olde Tea Shoppe & Restaurant**, *24 Castle Street, Douglas; tel. +44 (1624) 613-650.*

One of the best restaurants on the Isle of Man is **JAR**, located in the Admiral House Hotel, *tel. +44 (1624) 663-553.* The cuisine is excellent and the atmosphere is sophisticated.

Hotels with the most charm

Inglewood Hotel, *26 Palace Terrace, Queens Promenade, Douglas; tel. +44 (01624) 674-734; website: www.inglewoodhotel-isleofman.com.* This four-star hotel overlooking the promenade is run by Andy and Pip Cross. The rooms are modern and spacious and Pip's freshly cooked breakfasts must be sampled.

Silvercraigs Hotel, *27 Palace Terrace, Queens Promenade, Douglas; tel. +44 (01624) 677776; e-mail: silvercraigs@gmail.com; website: www.silvercraigshotel. com.* Also located on the waterfront promenade this is another good choice for a stay on the Isle of Man. The rooms are comfortable and the staff welcoming.

The best gambling

The Palace Hotel, *Central Promenade Douglas; tel. +44 (1624) 662-662; website: www.palacehotelcasino.co.im,* has its own casino with over 120 Vegas-style slot machines, roulette and interactive blackjack. Membership is free, just bring photographic id on your first visit.

THE BEST OF
ITALY

Italy is a dream that keeps returning for the rest of your life.
—Anna Akhmatova

The Italians live alongside the world's greatest art the way the rest of the world lives next door to tacky neon signs and billboards. Where else but Italy would an insignificant-looking neighborhood church contain paintings by Botticelli? What city but Rome would go about its business amid the ruins of once-great buildings built by ancestors who ruled the then-known world? What people except Italians can be so surrounded by the greatest vestiges of Western civilization—yet be so unpretentious?

ROME: THE WORLD'S MOST CELEBRATED CITY

Rome has been the world's most celebrated city for more than two millennia. Before Christ was born, Romans watched gladiators fight lions in the Coliseum. For 1,500 years, Rome has been the center of Christianity. Five centuries ago, Michelangelo painted the Sistine Chapel here. Today, Rome is one of the biggest tourist attractions in the world.

The most important sights

The **Colosseum**, *Piazzale del Colosseo*, is the greatest architectural remnant of ancient Rome. Shaped like an oval bowl, it was built by Titus and used for month-long spectacles, including battles between animals and gladiators. Christians were fed to the lions here, according to legend. The structure is well-preserved. Today it is inhabited by hundreds of cats, whose eyes glow from dark archways.

The **Roman Forum**, *Via dei Fori Imperiali*, was the chief public square and a center of government in ancient Rome. Only a few ruins remain.

The **Pantheon**, *Piazza della Rotonda,* is the architectural and civic symbol of the city.

The **Piazza di Spagna** is filled with vendors, tourists, artists, street musicians, and Romans on their lunch breaks—and it truly shows the spirit of Rome. All of these sights are must-sees when visiting Rome and will show the true ambience of the city and the people who live there.

The world's second smallest country

Vatican City, the world's second-smallest country, occupies one square mile within the city of Rome. It is headquarters of the Roman Catholic Church and has its own post office and postage stamps, printing press and newspaper, currency, railway, and radio station. It is governed by the Pope and protected by Swiss Guards, whose colorful blue and gold uniforms were designed by Michelangelo.

The **Vatican Museums**, *website: www.vatican.va*, have the most impressive art collections in the world. The **Sistine Chapel** is one of the great marvels of the Renaissance. The frescoed ceiling was painted by Michelangelo. Some art critics view a recent restoration as a desecration; others applaud it. Judge for yourself. A pedestrian walkway leads through the many museums to the Sistine Chapel, which covers an area of more than 40,000 square yards. En route, keep an eye out for the four rooms painted by Raphael and his assistants in the 16th century, as well as the little Chapel of Nicholas V, with frescoes by Fra Angelico. Check the website for opening times and skip the queues by booking your tickets in advance online.

St. Peter's Basilica, *Piazza San Pietro*, in the Vatican reveals both the grandeur of the Papacy and the impact of Catholicism. When 300,000 people gather together to hear the pope's blessing, you understand his power. The basilica was built by Constantine in A.D. 350 on the site where St. Peter was martyred and then buried. Parts of the original building still exist, underground in the crypt. A cupola designed by Michelangelo crowns the church. Be sure to dress modestly when you visit St. Peter's—shorts are forbidden, and women may not wear dresses without sleeves or with hems above the knee. Many travelers are barred from St. Peter's because of improper clothing.

If you would like a papal audience or to attend a special ceremony in St. Peter's, apply in writing to **Prefettura della Casa Pontifica**, *00120 Citta del Vaticano; website: www.vatican.va/various/prefettura/index_en.html.* When the pope is in Rome, public audiences are held each Wednesday at 11 a.m.

On the edge of the Vatican is an ancient fortress, **Castel Sant' Angelo**, *Lungotevere Castello 50,* built in A.D. 135 as a mausoleum for the Emperor Hadrian. The sixth-century chapel on top of the mausoleum was built to commemorate an angel who appeared to announce the end of the plague. Corner towers and bastions were added in the 15th and 16th centuries. Pope Clement VII lived in the castle in 1527. The fortress is connected to the Vatican by a long passageway.

Rome's best park

In the heart of Rome is the city's most remarkable park—**Villa Borghese**. The gardens around the former estate of Cardinal Scipione Borghese were designed in the 17th century. Rome's zoo is here, as well as two museums housed in the cardinal's palace. The main entrance is at Piazzale Flaminio, just outside the Porta del Popolp. You can also get here by walking up the Spanish Steps and following Via Trinita dei Monti to the left until you can see all seven hills of Rome.

The most macabre sight

The mass of skulls in the church of **Monumental Cemetery of the Capuchin Brothers**, *Via Vittorio Veneto 27,* is the most macabre sight in Rome. Monks at this church maintain a crypt that contains more than 4,000 skulls and bones of past Capuchin monks. Two of the five chapels contain floors of earth brought from Palestine. On November 2nd (All Soul's Day), the crypt is brightly lit, making it even more gruesome.

Rome's best kept travel secret: The Aventine

One of Rome's fabled seven hills, the Aventine, is rarely traveled by tourists. Mons Aventius, as it was known in ancient times, was developed by Caesar's contemporaries into a dignified district of majestic temples, fashionable homes, and plush gardens. The rich vegetation and serene setting that attracted the Romans both remain, untouched by the pollution and crowding of the rest of the city. The Aventine's main attraction however, is its many striking churches.

424   Near the temple to Diana, seven centuries-old churches remain. The most ancient, **Santa Prisca**, *11 Via di Santa Prisca,* was the residence of a Jewish couple, Prisca and Aquila, who allowed Saint Paul and others to worship in their home after their own conversion to Catholicism. The earliest Christians also worshiped at another fourth-century residence nearby, now **Santa Sabina**, *Piazza Pietro d'Iliria*. Along the same street is **Sant' Alessio**, *23 Piazza Sant' Alessio*, named for the son of a prominent Roman senator who fled the city to avoid an arranged marriage. He returned two decades later, a beggar, to die beneath the front stairwell of his parents' home.

The oldest café in Rome

Antico Caffè Greco, *tel. +39 (06) 6791-7000; website: www.anticocaffegreco.eu*, is one of the oldest cafés in the world. Founded on July 24, 1760, it has been frequented by artists, celebrities, and politicians, including composer Hector Berlioz, Mark Twain (in fact, a statue of Twain decorates the café), Hans Christian Andersen, James Fenimore Cooper, Sir Walter Scott, Henry James, Lord Alfred Tennyson, Richard Wagner, Benjamin Franklin, Henrik Ibsen, Goethe, Schopenhauer, Orson Welles, Federico Fellini, Stalin, and Adolf Hitler. The café was declared a national monument by the Italian government in 1953. Homemade ice cream is served, as well as the best cappuccino in Rome.

Rome's most beautiful bridge

The **Fabricio Bridge**, known to Romans as the Bridge of Four Heads, connects Tiber Island, in the middle of the Tiber River, to the rest of Rome. A pillar in the middle of the bridge is carved with four faces representing the four builders of the structure, beheaded for not finishing it by the day promised. Tiber Island has been occupied since 292 B.C., when a temple was built in honor of Aesculapius, the Greek god of health.

The most remarkable fountain

The **Fountain of Rivers**, completed in 1651 by Gian Lorenzo Bernini, is the most beautiful fountain in the city. Located in the heart of Rome's picturesque Piazza Navona, it is a mass of rockwork and grottos. The four colossal figures that create the fountain's four corners represent the Danube, Ganges, Nile, and Plate rivers.

The best places to buy red lingerie

Every December, Romans buy new red lingerie to wear when they usher in the New Year. As a result, the city is home to many shops that specialize in red underwear.

For the finest lingerie in Rome (red and otherwise), visit the via Frattina area. Try **Tusseda**, *via Frattina 25, Rome; tel. +39 (06) 679-3576.*

The world's most beautiful crèches

During the Christmas season, Rome is decorated with crèches rather than lights and Santas. The three most beautiful are on the Spanish Steps, in the Piazza Navona, and in St. Peter's Square. The oldest crèche is in the **Church of S. Maria Maggiore**, *Piazza di Santa Maria Maggiore,* the most beloved crèche is at **S. Maria d'Aracoeli**, *Piazza d'Aracoeli*, and the **Cosma e Damiano**, *Via dei Fori Imperiali*, houses an 18th-century Neapolitan masterpiece, which is on display all year.

The best midnight Mass

The most beautiful Christmas midnight Mass in the world is at **St. Peter's Basilica**. The pope celebrates the Mass with the assistance of dozens of cardinals. The Choir of the Sistine Chapel sings, and the Vatican ushers, known as San Pietrini, turn on hundreds of lights. You can write in advance for tickets to Christmas midnight Mass. Contact the **Prefettura della Casa Pontifica**, *Citta del Vaticano, 00120; website: www.vatican.va/various/prefettura/index_en.html.*

Rome's best hotel

The **Hassler**, *Piazza Trinità dei Monti 6; tel. +39 (06) 699-340; website: www. hotelhasslerroma.com*, which crowns the Spanish Steps, has the best view and the best service. The rooms on the fifth floor have little balconies with tables and chairs and views of the Spanish Steps. If you prefer quiet (the steps can be noisy), the most peaceful rooms are in the back, overlooking the courtyard.

Italy's most prestigious wine

Just a short drive from Rome is a 14th-century castle overlooking the fertile valleys of Ombrone, Orcia, and Asso. Called **Montalcino**, it is surrounded by a medieval stone wall that boasts the ruins of 19 defense towers. But more than medieval artifacts, Montalcino is home to the most prestigious of all Italian wines, the legendary **Brunellow di Montalcino**.

THE BEST PRESERVED ROMAN RUINS IN THE WORLD

Ostia Antica, *Viale dei Romagnoli 717; website: www.ostia-antica.org*, boasts the best-preserved Roman ruins in the world, as well as a beautifully preserved fortress and a *borgo* with history spanning from the fourth to the 15th century. Situated four miles from the Fiumicino airport, it is accessible by car, bus, or by train via Rome.

On arrival in this small town, you'll be welcomed by the imposing view of the Rocca di Giulio II. The fortress was built during the papacy of Giulio II and served as a major defense point for the city of Rome—it was strategically situated on a bend of the river Tiber. A walk around the *borgo*, away from the cars and the chaos, is a good way to start your tour of town. And the fortress itself is worth a visit, giving you a feeling for what life as a soldier must have been like back in those days.

In 1557, the river changed its course and the fortress lost its importance. It was used for a while as a prison, but soon ceased to have any appeal to rulers and enemies alike. The small town and surroundings went into decay and became marsh. In the 19th century, a small group of farmers from Romagna was called in by the Pope to drain the area. Today's town is the result of the hard work of those 500 men.

Although still uncertain, the origins of Ostia have been traced back to the seventh century B.C. The ruins are so well preserved that the amphitheater still stages shows from opera to Roman tragedy and Shakespeare (in Italian). You can spend hours marveling at the mosaics, thermal baths, and imposing structures of the temples. It costs 6.50 euro ($9) to take a look around the ruins, with concessions for pensioners and students. You can get back to Rome easily, too, by train, car, or ferry.

FLORENECE—THE MOST BEAUTIFUL CITY

Florence is the most beautiful city in this country of lovely places. Ringed by hills, its streets are lined with red-tiled houses. Graceful domes rise from curving, narrow, cobblestone streets. The ochre-colored walls of the ancient buildings are decorated with weathered gargoyles and faded coats of arms. Within Florence is some of the greatest artwork in the world. For three centuries, from Giotto to Michelangelo, Florence was the center of the art world. Paintings and frescoes by the great Renaissance masters decorate even the most mundane churches.

The world's finest Renaissance art

The immense **Uffizi Museum**; *website: www.uffizi.com,* has the world's greatest collection of Renaissance art, including paintings by Giotto, Raphael, Titian, and Botticelli. The museum also has a room of modern art. Be sure to see restored *Doni Tondo* by Michelangelo and Botticelli's *Birth of Venus.* The most impressive room holds Botticelli's *Primavera, Birth of Venus, Madonna della Melagrana,* and *Pallas and the Centaur.* For tickets, book them online at the website.

The best-kept secret in Florence

The **Vasari Corridoio** is a long, covered, secret passage built by Vasari in 1565 for Cosimo I de Medici. It links the Uffizi with the Pitti Palace, now one of Florence's great picture galleries but then Cosimo's residence. It crosses the Arno with the Ponte Vecchio and passes through the Church of Santa Felicita, another Vasai masterpiece, where the Medicis attended chapel. It can only be visited by booking in advance. For more information see the Uffizi Museum website.

The largest dome in Christendom

Il Duomo, *Piazza del Duomo; website: www.duomofirenze.it,* one of the world's largest cathedrals, is topped with the largest dome in Christendom. Its marble walls are striped with alternating colors. For this reason, it has been called the Cathedral in Pajamas. Built in 1296 by Brunelleschi, its vast walls are decorated with frescoes illustrating Dante's *Divine Comedy* and works by Ucello. Climb up into the dome for a terrific view of Florence.

The Gates of Paradise

The **Baptistery**, *Piazza San Giovani*, an octagonal building dedicated to St. John the Baptist, is famous for its three sets of gilded bronze doors. Michelangelo called the east door facing the cathedral the "Gates of Paradise." Begun in 1425 by Ghilberti, they weren't completed until 1452, when the artist was 74. They are made up of 10 panels that illustrate the Old Testament. On the Feast of St. John (June 24), the relics of the saint are displayed in the Baptistery, and candles are lit in his honor.

The most important sights in Florence

Pitti Palace, *Piazza Pitti; website: www.museumsinflorence.com,* a huge structure built by Renaissance banker Luca Pitti, is now divided into five museums, including the Palatine Picture Gallery, where works by Titian, Raphael, and Rubens are displayed. The Silver Museum houses Lorenzo de Medici's vases.

Santa Croce, *Piazza Santa Croce; website: www.santacroce.firenze.it*, a striped-marble church, has frescoes by Giotto. The most elegant church in Florence, it contains tombs and monuments to Michelangelo, Galileo, Machiavelli, and Dante. Go through the sacristy into the Leather School started by the monks about 40 years ago.

Accademia Gallery, *Via Ricasoli 58; website: www.uffizi.com/accademia-gallery-florence.asp*, is where the original of Michelangelo's magnificent *David* stands. You'll want to see this, of course, but be prepared to stand in incredibly long lines. The worst days to visit are Sunday and Tuesday; the best times are 8 a.m. and noon, when the lines are shortest.

Bargello, *Via del Proconsolo 4; website: www.polomuseale.firenze.it/english/musei/bargello/*, the national museum, was once a fortress that served as a prison. In centuries past, men were thrown out of the tower for their misdeeds. Today, the building contains the best of Florentine sculpture. Several early Michelangelos are housed here, including his first unfinished *David* and his statue of Bacchus. Upstairs are Giambologna's bronze animals created for a Medici garden grotto. This museum doesn't draw the crowds it merits.

The **Basilica of San Lorenzo**, *Piazza San Lorenzo*, and the **Palazzo Medici** were built by the Medici family north of the Duomo. Brunelleschi began work on the church in 1419, incorporating the coat of arms of the Medicis in the design. Conatello's sculpture fills the church, and Filippo Lippi designed the altarpiece. The Medici Chapel, adjacent to the basilica, can be reached only from outside. Actually a mausoleum, the chapel has two sections: the Princes' Chapel, which contains the tombs of six Medici grand dukes, and the New Sacristy (Sagrestia Nuova), built by Michelangelo.

Santa Maria Novella, *Piazza Santa Maria Novella*, is a grand church with splendid frescoes by Ghirlandaio and Filippino Lippi. They are best seen on a sunny day as the chapels are dark. The wealthy merchants of Florence had special chapels built in their honor in this church. Alberti contains Chirlandaio's most important frescoes, which his student, Michelangelo, helped to create. The cloister of the church is colored with Uccello's frescoes.

Florence's best bridge

Ponte Vecchio, a bridge dating back to Roman times, is lined with goldsmith shops and street musicians. Butchers and tanners originally plied their trades on this bridge, but they were ousted by the Medici family in favor of the more seemly goldsmiths. During World War II, the commander in charge of the German army's retreat refused to blow up the bridge. Instead, he destroyed the buildings at its base so the rubble would block the span.

The prettiest Florentine church

San Miniato al Monte, *Via del Monte alle Croci*, one of the oldest churches in Florence, has an inlaid marble façade with 13th-century mosaics. Inside, the pavement is patterned with astrological signs, lions, and doves. The church contains superb Della Robbia terracottas.

The best dining

Our favorite restaurant in Florence is the **Enoteca Pinchiorri**, *Via Ghibellina 87; tel. +39 (055) 242-757; website: www.enotecapinchiorri.com*. Located in the 15th-century Ciofi-Iacometti Palace, it has a pleasant courtyard for dining and serves nouvelle cuisine. Reservations are required.

The best nightlife

Good nightclubs in Florence are **Yab**, *Via Sassetti 5, 77; tel. +39 (055) 215-160; website: www.yab.it*, and **Tenax**, *Via Pratese 46; website: www.tenax.org*. Yab is a large popular club while Tenax is in an enormous old warehouse on two floors.

Like most major cities, Florence has its fair share of Irish pubs. The one with the best view though has to be **J.J. Cathedral**, *Piazza del Duomo*. If you're lucky you might get a seat on their tiny second-floor balcony which gives a birds-eye view of the cathedral.

The best ice cream in Florence

Vivoli's, *Via Isole delle Stinche 7; tel. +39 (055) 292-334*, behind Santa Croce Square, is one of the best places in the world to buy ice cream. The lines are long, but the choice of flavors is great and the ice cream is out-of-this-world.

The best convent stay

The elegant **Torre di Bellosguardo**, *Via Roti Michelozzio 2; tel. +39 (055) 229-8145; website: www.torrebellosguardo.com*, on the peaceful hills above Florence, was built around a 13th-century tower with nice gardens. The rooms are furnished with antique furniture, the beds are particularly gorgeous.

The best antiques fair in Italy

The city of **Arezzo** is home to one of the best antique fairs in Italy. On the first Sunday of every month, Arezzo's old town streets are closed to traffic and transformed into a great outdoor bazaar/antique fair for both professional and amateur shoppers. Here you can find antiques, collectibles, new articles, or just cool old stuff from all over the world. Artwork, ceramics, apparel, accessories, jewelry, lighting, furniture, collectors' stamps, maps, nutcrackers, dentistry and medical instruments, terracotta vases, planters… You could spend hours here; there are hundreds of stands.

Buyer beware, of course. Some stands sell not-so-authentic antiques at steep prices. You can, however, find good-quality items at good prices. Bargaining hint: If the item is still available at the end of the day, you ought to be able to negotiate a bigger discount.

Arezzo is a charming city strategically located 30 minutes from Florence and accessible by railway or car—it's on the main railway line between Rome/Florence and Milan. If you are driving from Northern Italy, Arezzo is 30 minutes south of Florence on the A1 *autostrada* (freeway).

THE MOST MAGICAL CITY: VENICE

Venice, a city made up of 118 islets held together by a maze of 150 narrow canals and 400 lacy bridges, has a magical air. The interlocking waterways are plied by graceful wooden gondolas. Domed churches look over the shadowed pedestrian streets, where throngs of people (but no cars) roam.

Venetians took refuge in their watery home after centuries of invasions by the likes of Attila the Hun, the Goths, and the Vandals. In A.D. 687, they elected a president, called a *doge*. He was the first in a line of 117 *doges*, each reigning for life, that ended in 1797.

The five most important sights

The heart of Venice is the **Piazza San Marco**, which is dominated by the beautiful basilica on one side and the **Doge's Palace** on the other. This huge square attracts flocks of pigeons as well as tourists. Once the *doge's* private chapel, the **Basilica of San Marco** is now open to the public. Built in the ninth century to house St. Mark's body, the basilica contains the saint's tomb, paintings by Titian, and the Pala d'Oro, a huge panel behind the altar bedecked with rubies, emeralds, sapphires, pearls, topazes, amethysts, and cloisonné figures, all set in gold. The basilica also has Byzantine treasures. These artifacts and the saint's body were the booty of the fourth Crusade, taken from Constantinople by Doge Enrico Dandolo.

The **Palazzo Ducale**, *Piazza San Marco*, is an ornate structure on the water with carved figures symbolizing the trades. On one side are the Quattro Mori, four Moorish warriors embracing one another. Inside are the *doges'* apartments, the senate chamber, and the Room of the Council of Ten, which is covered with beautiful paintings. The sinister box outside is intended to receive denunciations of traitors or criminals.

The **Bridge of Sighs** passes between the Doge's Palace and the prison where Casanova was once held. The covered bridge is so named because condemned prisoners sighed as they were led across it to their deaths. They were allowed one last look at Venice from the bridge before their executions.

The **Grand Canal** has been called the finest street in the world. It is lined with 200 marble-covered palaces built between the 12th and 18th centuries. Wagner died in the Palazzo Vendramin-Calergi, now the Municipal Casino. Lord Byron lived in the Palazzo Mocenigo. Gold leaf was used to coat the balls protruding on the façade of the Ca'D'Oro on the right bank. Its pointed arches were influenced by Islam. A good way to see these palazzos is to take a boat ride along the two-mile length of the canal. Take vaporetto (water bus) 1 or 4.

The **Galleria dell'Accademia** (Gallery of Fine Arts), *Dorsoduro; tel. +39 (041) 520-0345; website: www.gallerieaccademia.org*, houses paintings by Giorgione, Bellini, Tiepolo, Titian, and Canaletto.

The Lido: The most fashionable Adriatic resort

Venice is protected from the rage of the Adriatic Sea by a beautiful sand spit called the **Lido**. A fashionable resort, the Lido draws visitors from around the world to its sandy beaches, elegant hotels, and swank casino. To get there, take vaporetto lines 1 and 2 from Venice across the Lagoon.

Before you go to the Lido, read *Death in Venice* by Thomas Mann. And (if you can afford it) stay at the legendary **Hotel des Bains**, *Lungomare Marconi 17; website: http://desbains.hotelinvenice.com*, where Mann's character, Hans Aschenbach, spent his days. Rooms are expensive.

The romantic islands of the Lagoon

The **Lagoon** is filled with romantic little islands that can be reached by vaporetto. (Boat 12 leaves from the Fondamenta Nuove, near Campo dei Gesuiti, for Murano,

Burano, and Torcello.) Burano and Torcello have especially inviting beaches, fishing villages, and small art museums. Murano is famous for its glassmaking.

Burano Island, actually four tiny islets connected by bridges, is a half-hour water-bus ride from the mainland. Everything here is miniature—the canals and bridges are tiny, and the colorfully painted houses look as if they were built for dwarfs. Burano has its own leaning tower, the bell tower of the **Church of San Martino**, *Piazza Baldassare Galuppi*. However, the island is best known for its lace making. Wherever you go on Burano, you will see old ladies knitting lace and selling it from outdoor tables. You can buy handmade lace doilies, lace table-cloths, lace mats, hankies, baby bibs, and collars. The **Museo del Merletto** (lace museum), *Piazza Galuppi 187*, is open daily.

Murano Island has dozens of workshops where you can watch glass being blown. The **Museo Vetrario**, *Fondamenta Giustinian*, along the main canal, has an immense collection of glass from Roman times to the present. It is closed Wednesdays.

San Francesco del Deserto is a tiny, cypress-covered island inhabited by Franciscan monks. According to legend, St. Francis of Assisi was shipwrecked here in 1220. His wooden staff, which he stuck in the ground, turned into a tree, part of which still can be seen. Gardens and lawns surround the cloister and church. Peacocks and bantams wander the grounds freely.

A surprisingly pleasant island is Venice's cemetery, **San Michele**, which is filled with shade trees, flower gardens, and leaf-covered paths. Ornate tombs and mausoleums are surrounded by gardens and terraces. The ferryboat to San Michele is free on Sundays. The entrance is through the cloister of the island's 15th-century church.

The island of **San Lazzaro** has been the site of an Armenian monastery for 200 years. A priest dressed in a black cassock and sporting a heavy beard will give you a two-hour tour of the cloister, which contains an Egyptian mummy, Armenian paintings, ivories from the Orient, and the room where Lord Byron lived in 1816, when he decided to learn Armenian. One of the rooms contains a collection of rare illuminated manuscripts.

The greatest opera house

Gran Teatro La Fenice, *Campo S. Fantin 1965; tel. +39 (041) 786-511; website: www.teatrolafenice.it*, is one of the greatest opera houses in the world. The 18th-century décor is graceful, with chandeliers, plush armchairs, box seats, mirrored corridors, parquet floors, and a grand staircase with marble columns. The acoustics are flawless. You can book tickets online or by phone.

The most fantastic hotel in Europe

Venice has the most fantastic hotel in Europe, the luxurious **Hotel Cipriani**, *Giudecca 10; tel. +39 (041) 520-7744; website: www.hotelcipriani.com*, on Giudecca Island. A polished motorboat fetches guests at the Piazza San Marco. Rooms have private, flower-bedecked terraces that gaze out over the water. Excellent seafood is prepared in the dining room. The Cipriani has Venice's only tennis courts and its largest swimming pool.

The best Venetian restaurants

Ai Tre Spiedi, *Cannaregio 5906; tel. +39 (041) 520-8035*, is the best place to go for authentic fresh fish Venetian cuisine. **Harry's Bar**, *Sestiere San Marco 1323; tel. +39 (041) 528-5777; website: www.harrysbarvenezia.com*, was one of Hemingway's favorites. Only a few minutes from the *piazzetta* on the Piazza San Marco, it has been owned and run by the Cipriani family for 60 years.

Europe's largest maze

The largest and most complicated maze in Europe is in **Stra**, 18 miles south of Venice. **Il Labirinto**, as it is known in Italy, is part of the stately gardens of the Villa Pisani. This life-size puzzle is one-third the size of a football field and has four miles of paths lined with tall, thick hedges. If you get lost, the caretaker will rescue you. He can reach the tower at the center of the maze in three minutes.

The most colorful day-trip

The **Isle of Burano** is a short boat ride from Venice, but a world apart. The Isle is off the beaten path and the most colorful setting you will ever see—every house is painted a bright and different color. The restaurants offer the most wonderful, fresh seafood in the area, and you can eat at your own pace. There are wonderful little shops in which to browse, and the school of Venetian lace is located within walking distance.

MANTUA: VENICE WITHOUT THE CROWDS

Mantua has the charm of Venice without the crowds. The River Mincio wraps around the ducal city like a cloak and threads its way through the city via little canals. Graceful bridges cross the winding waterways. Once the seat of one of the most brilliant courts of Europe, featured in Shakespeare's *Romeo and Juliet*, today it is one of the best-preserved medieval cities in Italy.

Mantua feels medieval; it has no modern industry and no highrise buildings. The **Ducal Palace**, *Piazza Sordello*, built in the Middle Ages, is actually three interconnected buildings. The palace has 500 rooms, seven gardens, and eight courtyards. Frescoes by Pisanello, depicting episodes from chivalric tales, hang in the Hall of Dukes. Painted in 1440, they were rediscovered in 1969 under two coats of plaster. In Camera degli Sposi (bridal chamber), built in 1474, hang Andrea Mantegna's frescoes of the Gonzaga family.

The **Church of Sant' Andrea**, *Piazza Magenta*, has a coffered ceiling and grandiose arches more reminiscent of the Pantheon than a Christian church. This is a good place to get a feeling for the time when the Pagan and Christian worlds met. The **Palazzo Te**, *Viale Te*, was a pleasure palace for Federico, the favorite son of Mantua's great lady, Isabella d'Este. This palace is filled with artwork depicting early times.

When you tire of sightseeing, enjoy Mantua's fresh fish at the delicious **Ochina Bianca**, *Via Finzi 2; tel. +39 (0376) 323-700; website: www.ochinabianca. it.* The atmospheric art deco interior consists of antique plates on walls, furniture from the 1930's and the 1950's, candles and soft lightning.

A comfortable hotel in Mantua is the **Broletto**, *Via Accademia 1; tel. +39 (0376) 326-784; website: www.hotelbroletto.com.*

NAPLES: THE MOST ITALIAN CITY

Tourists shy away from **Naples**, because of its reputation for crime—although the crime situation here is actually no worse than in New York and other major cities. Because of its rather undeserved bad reputation, Naples is truly an Italian city— free of crowds of gaping foreigners.

A huge, hilly town in the shadows of Mount Vesuvius, Naples is cooled by the breezes of the Gulf of Naples. The city's waterfront is lined with booths where you can stop for a cool drink.

Neapolitans have a lugubrious interest in the macabre. In the **Cappella Sansevero**, *Via F. de Sanctis 19; website: www.museosansevero.it*, for example, are the 16th-century corpses of a man and a woman (called the *Anatomical Machines)* mysteriously preserved by the alchemy of the Duke of Sansevero. Thousands of capillaries can be seen through the skin of the body. The chapel, which is hidden on a small side street off Piazza San Domenico Maggiore, also holds an uncanny effigy of the body of Christ covered in diaphanous veils carved by the sculptor Sammartino.

The most important sight

The cathedral in Naples **Il Duomo**, *Via del Duomo 147*, is dedicated to San Gennaro. It was built in the 13th century on the site of a previous basilica dedicated to Santa Stefania. The original basilica was built on the foundations of a Roman temple dedicated to Apollo. Within the cathedral are an ancient round baptistery, the Byzantine basilica of Santa Restituta, and the 17th-century chapel, which holds San Gennaro's head and blood. The blood has liquefied from its crystalized state the first Sunday in May and on September 19th nearly every year since the Middle Ages. If the blood does not liquefy, it is believed that a disaster will happen. (Great importance is placed on San Gennaro in Naples. When Mount Vesuvius acts up, for instance, the saint's image is taken to the mountain as a pacifier.)

The world's best antiquities

Il Museo Archeologico Nazionale, *Piazza Museo 18-19*, in Naples houses one of the most important collections of Greek and Roman antiquities in the world, including many of the treasures excavated from Pompeii and Herculaneum. Among these treasures are the *Young Satyr*, a graceful figure carrying a wine casket, and the famous statues of Apollo and Diana, which once stood at Pompeii's Temple of Apollo. You can't miss the *Farnese Bull*, the largest surviving sculpture from antiquity, carved out of a single block of marble.

Naples' best Renaissance museum

Outside Naples is the **National Museum and Gallery of the Capodimonte**, *Via Miano 2; tel. +39 (06) 3996-7050; website: www.capodimontegallery.com*, which houses one of Italy's best collections of paintings from the 14th, 15th, and 16th centuries. Located in an 18th-century palace in the hills northeast of the city and surrounded by a park, it contains works by Bellini, Botticelli, Correggio, and Titian. Capodimonte is also a famous brand of porcelain.

Nightlife at its hottest

Naples' nightlife can be found in and around via Caracciono and via Partenope, commonly referred to as the **Margellina Quarter**. Within walking distance is the **San Carlo Theater**, *Via San Carlo 98; tel. +39 (081) 797-2111; website: www. teatrosancarlo.it*, renowned for classical music and dance.

The best ways to thwart thieves

Pickpockets are common in Naples, and they make their living off tourists. Don't drape your purse over your shoulder. Thieves on motorbikes grab bags as they zoom past, often dragging the person along with the bag. Thieves generally work in pairs. They pull up to people carrying shoulder bags or camera bags. One thug hops off the bike, grabs the loot, and hops back on, and the pair then speed away.

Avoid carrying a wallet in your back pocket. Leave all jewelry—including watches—in your hotel. It's best to carry limited amounts of cash and your passport and credit cards in the inside pocket of your pants. When driving, never put anything in the back window of the car. Traffic in Naples is dense, and thieves often break rear windows of cars stuck in traffic jams. And don't leave things in parked cars—not even in the trunks. Most rental cars in Italy have Milan tags, and thieves know to look for them around hotels, restaurants, and museums.

The most delicious fare

Da Peppino Avellinese, *Via Silvio Spaventa 31-35*, is a friendly place with cheap but good seafood. Try the *pesce frigole*, a mixture of crayfish, octopus, squid, mussels, and clams.

La Cantinella, *Via Cuma 42; tel. +39 (081) 764-8684; website: www. lacantinella.it,* is a favorite among Neapolitans. The clams and mussels cooked with garlic, parsley, and tomato and served with linguine are exquisite.

La Fazenda, *Via Discesa Marechiaro; tel. +39 (081) 575-7420*, serves the best Neapolitan dishes, including home-raised chickens. This rustic restaurant has spectacular views of the bay and is decorated with a profusion of flowers. It is closed for two weeks in August.

Il Gallo Nero, *Via Tarquato Tasso 466; tel. +39 (081) 643-012*, is in an antique-filled 19th-century villa. Dine on the terrace, where you'll have a splendid view of Mergellina. The fresh fish is terrific.

Sleeping beautifully

The most luxurious hotels in Naples are the Excelsior and the Vesuvio. The **Excelsior**, *Via Partenope 48; tel. +39 (081) 764-0111; website: www.excelsior.it,* has terraced seaside rooms with views of the Castel dell'Ovo and the bay. The restaurant is good. Rooms are rather old-fashioned and sparsely furnished.

The **Vesuvio**, *Via Partenope 45; tel. +39 (081) 764-0044; website: www. vesuvio.it,* faces the port of Santa Lucia and has a variety of rooms ranging in style from antique to modern.

The strangest sight: The door to the Underworld

Near Naples is one of the strangest sights in Italy—the cave said to have been the door to the Underworld of ancient mythology. Very few people visit the **Grotta della Sibilla**, as it is known.

In the *Aeneid*, the Roman poet Virgil described the cave: "A deep, deep cave there was, its mouth enormously gaping Shingly, protected by the dark lake and the forest gloom: Above it, no winged creatures could ever wing their way. With fuming up from its black throat to the vault of heaven: Wherefore the Greeks called it Avernus, the Birdless Place."

According to the guide, Lago di Avernus was once a volcanic flat with bubbling mud and sulfur fumes that rose into the sky. Because the fumes were poisonous, birds flying over would die and fall into the inferno. (*Avernus* means "no birds" in Latin.) This description matches Virgil's. When Mount Vesuvius erupted, the volcanic action stopped here, and the crater filled with water. The eruption cut off the tunnel leading to the Underworld. The guided tour takes about an hour.

Volcanic bests

Mount Vesuvius, 15 miles southeast of Naples, can be seen from the city on a clear day. It last erupted in 1944. You can take a chair lift up to the top, or you can drive part way and then walk. Take the Ercolano exit from the Autostrada, then drive nine miles up a zig-zagging path across a sort of moonscape. The oval crater, when you finally get there, is 2,000 feet wide and 525 feet deep. Wisps of smoke rise from the top. If you say your name, Vesuvius will echo it back.

Pompeii and Herculaneum: The world's best ruins

Pompeii, *Pompei Scavi; website: www.pompeiisites.org,* and **Herculaneum**, *Corso Ercolano*, once bedroom suburbs of Roman Naples, were destroyed when Mount Vesuvius erupted in A.D. 79. Today, the ruins are preserved in volcanic ash illustrations of everyday life nearly 2,000 years ago. Explore the shops, baths, and houses of ordinary Roman families.

While Pompeii is packed with tourists, Herculaneum is not. What's more, Herculaneum is closer to Naples and is better preserved than Pompeii. Known as *Ercolano* in Italian, Herculaneum once had 5,000 inhabitants. Much of the town remains unexcavated beneath the modern town of Resina. However, among the ruins that have been excavated you'll see cakes in ovens, eggs in cupboards, chicken bones on kitchen tables, fishnets and hooks on a line, and graffiti on bathroom walls. One of the houses has a small cross, the oldest evidence of Christianity in the Roman Empire. The baths are the most interesting sights. You can see cold, warm, and hot water baths, a gym, and a swimming pool. The skeletons of bath attendants have been preserved intact in the men's cloakroom.

The best-preserved Greek temples

The best-preserved Greek Doric temples stand by the sea in **Paestum**, ancient Poseidonia, not far from Naples. The three major temples are along the ancient Via Sacra. The basilica, which is dedicated to Hera, is the oldest, dating back to the sixth century B.C. Next to the basilica is the Temple of Neptune (450 B.C.), one of the most beautiful Doric temples in the world. See the frescoes of a diver and a dinner party, the earliest surviving Greek paintings, in the museum across the street from the ruins.

CAPRI: ITALY'S MOST BEAUTIFUL ISLAND

Capri is a beautiful but crowded island that can be reached by hydrofoil from Naples, Sorrento, or Pozzuoli. After the boat ride, relax and have a pleasant lunch on the terrace of the **Hotel Belvedere Tre Re**, *Via Prov. Marina Grande, 264; tel. +39 (081) 837-0345; website: www.belvedere-tre-re.com*, on the harbor.

Take a funicular from the harbor up to the town of Capri. The best view is from the top of Mount Solaro, where an old monastery stands. To get there, take a bus to Anacapri and then a chair lift to the summit.

The **blue grotto sea caves** are lovely, but touristy. Visit the pagan shrine of the Martomania Cave. Roman Emperor Tiberius built 12 villas on the island to honor the 12 Roman deities. You can best sense his might around Villa Jovis, his headquarters for a decade.

Hotels on the island book up fast, so reservations are a must. One of the most romantic is **Scalanitella**, *Via Tragara 8; tel. +39 (081) 837-0633; website: www.scalinatella.com*, in the town of Capri. Cut into a steep and rocky hill, Scalanitella has a Moorish air. Its glistening marble lobby, winding corridors, classical paintings and busts, carved doors, floor-to-ceiling windows, outdoor garden, and little luxuries create a delightful atmosphere. Its pool is one of the best in Capri. The hotel is open April through October.

The **Grand Hotel Quisisana**, *Via Camerelle 2; tel. +39 (081) 837-0788; website: www.quisi.com,* attracts the jet set with large suites, wide arcades, and an ocean view.

Hotel Luna, *Via Matteotti 3; tel. +39 (081) 837-0433; website: www. lunahotel.com* combines old-fashioned style with modern conveniences.

THE BEST OF THE ITALIAN RIVIERA

The **Italian Riviera**, which stretches from the French border to Tuscany, is less expensive than the French Riviera and just as pretty. It lies within the prosperous northern region of **Liguria**, which has its own lingo and culture. The heart of Liguria is Genoa, a thriving seaport and a good place to stay if you find coastal resorts too pricey. North of Genoa is the Riviera di Levante (Coast of the Rising Sun). Below and to the east is the Riviera de Ponente (Coast of the Setting Sun).

During July and August, rooms are almost impossible to come by. The best time to visit is spring or fall, when the weather is warm and hotel rooms are vacant.

The oldest resort on the Riviera

San Remo, the oldest resort on the Riviera, is overcrowded and overbuilt. But it has a casino and a yacht basin, and the hotels are affordable despite their Edwardian elegance. The tourist office is helpful should you have trouble finding a room.

Where the *crème de la crème* rises

Italy's *crème de la crème* surface in **Portofino** during the summer. Very private and romantic, Portofino is one of the most photographed places in the world. Its remarkably deep natural harbor attracts yachtsmen from all over the world. Hike out to the lighthouse following the footpath marked "al faro" for a spectacular view of the coastline.

Hotel Splendido, *Salita Baratta; tel. +39 (0185) 267-801; website: www. hotelsplendido.com*, is Portofino's most luxurious hotel. It is perched in a spectacular setting above the yacht harbor, set into a cliff. It has an old-fashioned charm despite its modern swimming pool on the terrace.

The Riviera's most charming town

From the docks at the coastal town of Camogli, you can take a boat to **San Fruttoso**, the most charming town on the coast. This tiny fishing village on the Portofino Peninsula is accessible only by sea. It is surrounded by pines, olive trees, and oaks that lead down to the sea. Walk through the cloisters and corridors of the Benedictine Abbey of San Fruttoso di Capo di Monte, which consists of a 13th-century palace, 11th-century church, and a Romanesque cloister.

Camogli has one of the best hotels along the coast, **Cenobio dei Dogi**, *Via Cuneo 34; tel. +39 0185-7241; website: www.cenobio.it*, set in a manor house on the beach. Once the seat of the bishops of Genoa, this manor has lovely grounds, a beach, a swimming pool, tennis courts, facilities for the handicapped, and central heating.

Cinque Terre: The least crowded

At the southern end of the coast is one of the least crowded, most picturesque areas. The mountains, woods, vineyards, and hilltop villages of the Cinque Terre cover 15 miles of coastline. The area's five villages—Monterosso, Vernazza, Corniglia, Manarola, and Riomaggiore—are perched on the rocky coast north of La Spezia. The rare local wine is worth a taste; it is called Sciacchetra.

Monterosso is the largest and most crowded town. But it has a beautiful beach at the southern end of the cove. You can rent boats here. Climb the hill to the **Convento dei Cappuccini**, which houses Van Dyck's *Crucifixion*. After the strenuous climb, relax at Gigante, Monterosso's best restaurant. Hiking trails lead from Monterosso to Cinque Terre's quainter towns. A one-and-a-half-hour hike along a goat path leads through vineyards and olive groves to **Vernazza**. Another hiking trail leads to **Corniglia**, which has a long, pebbly beach.

If you're up to another hour's walk, follow the trail along the jagged coast to **Manarola**, the most beautiful of the Cinque Terre towns. Here, yellow houses balance on cliffs, and artists and writers seek their muses.

THE ALPS AT THEIR CHEAPEST

The **Dolomites** (Italian Alps) are just as beautiful as their French and Austrian counterparts, but visiting them is far less expensive. The skiing is almost as good as it is to the north, and the hiking can be even better.

Valle d'Aosta is just over the border from France. You can take a cable car to the Italian side from Chamonix, France. The panoramic view from the cable car is beautiful—and a bit scary if you fear heights at all.

Alto Badia, 50 miles south of the Brenner Pass through the Dolomites into Austria, is made up of little Tyrolean villages. This region has the beautiful scenery of Austria, but it also has lower prices, summer skiing, and good Italian restaurants. The best-known and largest among the hamlets is Corvara. Less crowded are Colfosco, La Villa, Pedraces, and San Cassiano.

The best hiking

The Dolomites, which are crisscrossed by trails, also boast some of the world's best hiking. Bring hiking boots, a windbreaker, a sweater, socks, and gloves. The best time to hike is in August and September, when the snow has melted completely. Don't hike in April or May unless you are an expert. The melting snow causes avalanches.

Pedraces, near the Austrian border, is one of the best places for hiking. For one of the most scenic routes, take a chair lift to the foot of the Croce Mountains and then follow Trail 7.

The **National Park of Abruzzi**, near Pescasseroli, is another beautiful place to hike. The trails, which are named for animals, wander through a forest of pine trees blanketed with snow.

La Pieja, *Opi; website: www.lapieja.it*, a few miles from Pescasseroli, is one of the best places to stay in the region.

The best base for exploring

Aosta is the best base for exploring the Italian peaks. Near mountain trails and several old castles, it has Roman ruins dating from the time of the Emperor Augustus, including a Roman theater, two Roman gates, the Porta Praetoria, and the Arco di Augusto.

The cloister of the medieval **Church of St. Ursus** dates back to A.D. 1000. St. Ursus, responsible for the first conversions to Christianity in the valley, is buried in a crypt below the altar.

Modern history can be contemplated at the **Istituto Storico della Resistenza della Valle d'Aosta**, *Xavier de Maistre 22*, which documents the Italian resistance during World War II.

Make hotel reservations early if you plan to be in Aosta in July or August or during the Christmas or Easter season. A good place to stay is the **Albergo Mancuso**, *tel. +39 (0165) 060-333.* This family-run hotel is clean and has inviting rooms. The hotel restaurant is good and inexpensive.

Italy's most beautiful national park

The **Gran Paradiso National Park** in the Valle d'Aosta is 363 square miles of protected area set aside for wildlife. The park has breathtaking scenery, wild flowers, and hiking trails. **Cogne** is the best base for exploring the park. You can get there from Aosta by bus. From Cogne, walk to Vanontey and then take Trail 2, which climbs to Rifugio V. Sella. The view from the refuge is mind-boggling. Stop to eat or spend the night before setting out on the six-hour trek to Eau Rousse in Valsavaranche. Again, the views are incredible.

Sleeping like royalty in the Italian Alps

A number of old castles have been made into hotels in the mountains of Italy. **Castle Rundegg**, *tel. +39 (0473) 234-100; website: www.rundegg.com*, is an old castle nestled in the mountains of southern Tyrol. The square towers date back to the 12th century. The main structure dates to 1580. Public rooms have grand staircases, vaulted ceilings, and arches. Private rooms are furnished with antiques. A pool, sauna, solarium, and massage center are open to guests.

THE BEST OF THE ITALIAN LAKE DISTRICT

Italy's Lake Country has steeply rolling hills and a Mediterranean touch. Olive groves and palm trees surround the warm waters.

The largest and clearest lake

Lake Garda is the largest, clearest, and most visited of the Italian lakes. It is surrounded by Mediterranean scenery—rugged, tawny hills dotted with olive and lemon groves and long, shuttered farmhouses. Desenzano, one of the lake's major and most crowded towns, lies on the Venice-Milan train line. From there, it is easy to get to other lake towns by bus or boat. **Torbole**, at the far end of Lake Garda, is the windsurfing capital of Europe because of the steady breezes that blow across the lake.

Europe's deepest lake

Lake Como is Europe's deepest lake. Sadly, it is too polluted for swimming near the main towns of Como and Bellagio. Como is worldly, wealthy, and refined. Its *duomo* is one of the most famous churches in Italy. Built between 1457 and 1485, it has a lovely rose window and houses Bernardino Luini's *Adoration of the Magi*.

The artists' favorite

Bellagio, the Lake District's art center, invites artists to spend a month or more there developing works in progress. Located at the point where Lake Como intersects with Lake Lecco, it has narrow streets and ancient buildings. The beach is next to Villa Serbelloni in the center of town.

The music inspiring waters

The litany of composers who've been inspired by the tranquil waters of Lake Como is staggering. It was here that Verdi wrote *La Traviata*, Bellini penned *Norma*, Rossini wrote *Tancred*, and Franz Liszt composed his *Dante Sonata*. As the American writer Henry James declared, being at Lake Como is like "wallowing in a libretto." Bellagio, Menaggio, Cadennabia, Tremezzo, Lenno…even the names of the villages sound melodious.

The most entertaining restaurant

The most entertaining restaurant in the Lake District is on an island in the middle of Lake Como. To get there, you must take a ferry, but it is well worth the trip. When you arrive at **Locanda dell'Isola Comacina**, *tel. +39 (0344) 55-083; website: www.comacina.it*, introduce yourself to the owner, Benvenuto Puricelli. He will show you to your table and the food will start coming. You do not choose from a menu—a vast selection of fresh meat, fish, and vegetables are simply brought to your table. As a finale, Benvenuto turns out the lights and puts a torch to an alcoholic concoction. Then, as the liquor burns, he ladles the brew into the air in fiery garlands while reciting the history of the island. (According to legend, a curse was laid on the island in the 12th century.)

Europe's finest resort hotel

Villa d'Este, *tel. +39 031-3481; website: www.villadeste.it*, in Cernobbion on Lake Como, is one of Europe's finest resort hotels. Located in a 15th-century villa begun by Cardinal Gallio, it was later used as a palace by an Empress of Russia, a Princess of Wales, and other members of royalty. In 1873 it became a hotel. It is beautifully furnished and offers concerts, dances, tennis, golf, riding, swimming, water sports, and boating.

The gem of the lakes

Floating in the middle of peaceful **Lago d'Orta** is emerald-green **San Giulio Island**, the little-known gem of the lakes. According to legend, St. Julius (San Giulio) ventured to the forested island in the latter half of the fourth century to rid it of an infestation of snakes and dragons. The island, which is 330 yards long and 175 yards across, hides an age-old settlement and an assembly of Romanesque art treasures. Only one family and the 22 nuns who maintain the island's towering convent live here year-round. On Wednesday mornings, while mist is still rising off the lake, nuns cross the lake in small fishing boats, as their predecessors did, to attend the weekly open-air market in Orta.

Each year in July, when the population of San Giulio Island reaches 300, townsfolk gather in the main square to sing popular island songs. This ancient tradition is believed to date back to the time of St. Julius, when early Christians gathered in front of the island's basilica to sing hymns.

On Sundays in September, San Giulio sponsors concerts that combine classical and regional folk music. But the island's most colorful festival is January 31st, St. Julius Day. From midnight until later into the following evening, there are fireworks, music, and dancing.

On San Giulio, among the elegant villas, terraces, clusters of rich green trees, and fragrant flower gardens of the summer, are some of the finest examples of Romanesque art in all Italy. The Romanesque basilica has undergone several renovations. Its history can be traced to the 11th century, but islanders will tell you that it goes back nearly 700 years earlier, to the time of St. Julius.

Inside the basilica is a remarkable collection of frescoes from the 15th century, most by local painters. The masterpiece of the basilica is a 12th-century Pulpit of the Comacine Masters. Gorgeously ornamented with the symbols of the four Evangelists and splendid animals, the polychrome wooden bas-reliefs are supported by marble columns. The bells of the basilica ring on Sunday morning and can be heard for miles around.

Hotel San Rocco, *Via Gippini 11; tel. +39 (0322) 911-977; website: www. hotelsanrocco.it*, is a 17th-century former convent. The restaurant is excellent and boasts a beautiful view of the lake.

UMBRIA: THE BEST OF THE HEARTLAND

Undulating **Umbria** is Italy's heartland, stretching between Rome and Florence. This hilly, forested countryside is dotted with Renaissance architectural gems, ancient farmhouses, vineyards, olive groves, and orchards. Umbria's medieval cities perch on hilltops and hang from mountainsides. St. Francis was born in Umbria, and he left his mark throughout the region.

Umbria's strangest sight

The small town of **Bomarzo** is known for the fascinating but creepy garden at the Villa of Orsini. In the late 15th century, Prince Vicino Orsini created these landscaped gardens, which are dotted with bizarre sculptures. Known as Il Sacro Bosco (the Sacred Wood) or the Parco dei Mostri (Park of Monsters), it is filled with statues of half-human, half-animal monsters.

445

The most beautiful Umbrian town

Orvieto, perched on an enormous rock, is the most beautiful town in the region. It is known for its *duomo*, built in 1229, which has a golden, mosaic-decorated front that glitters when it reflects the sun. Pope Nicholas IV commissioned the *duomo* to commemorate a miracle. According to Church lore, drops of blood appeared on the Host consecrated by a Bohemian priest who had doubted the Doctrine of Transubstantiation (the belief that during the sacrament of communion the bread actually becomes the body of Christ and the wine His blood). The blood-stained chalice cloth is kept in the cathedral and carried through town during the feast of Corpus Christi and again on Easter Sunday. The *duomo* has opaque alabaster windows, a rose window designed by Andrea Orcagna, and frescoes begun by Fra Angelico.

The best place to stay in Orvieto is three miles outside town in La Badia. The **Hotel La Badia**, *Loc. La Badia 8; tel. +39 (0763) 301-959; website: www. labadiahotel.it*, a former abbey that dates back to the 1100s, has comfortable rooms with private bathrooms and a first-class restaurant that features produce from the abbey's own farm. This beautiful complex has a swimming pool and tennis courts, as well as a church of Romanesque-Lombard style and a 12-sided tower. The buildings contain frescoes from the 12th, 13th, and 14th centuries. In the 15th century, the abbey was a retreat for cardinals. It has been in the hands of the family of Count Giuseppe Fiumi for the past century.

Perugia: A historical treasure house

Perugia is a town of historic treasures. The most fascinating sight is the **Baglioni Sotterranea**, an underground street filled with the ruins of the 15th-century houses. Visit the 13th-century **Fontana Maggiore** and stroll along the palace-lined **Corso Vanucci**.

The town's **Collegio del Cambio**, *Corso Vannucci 25*, was frescoed by Perugino and his helpers, one of whom may have been Raphael, in the early 16th century. Upstairs is the **National Gallery**, *Palazzo dei Priori*.

Perugia's best hotel is **Hotel La Rosetta**, *Piazza d'Italia 19; tel. +39 (075) 572-0841; website: http://perugiaonline.com/larosetta/*. Located at the top of the Corso Vannucci, near the main sights, it is friendly and efficient, and the food is delicious. Rooms at the back are quieter.

Umbria's most inviting hotel

Torgiano, a walled town complete with towers, boasts the splendid **Hotel Le Tre Vaselle**, *tel. +39 (075) 988-0447; website: www.3vaselle.it*. Housed in a

300-year-old villa, it has 16th-century wooden doors, thick walls, and hand-hewn ceiling beams and arches. It is a peaceful place on a side street, with spacious bedrooms and views of the countryside. Rooms are decorated with textiles and flowers, and Umbrian specialties are served in the dining room. Try artichoke risotto, sage-and-onion bread tarts baked in a wood oven, and the traditional Umbrian wafer made in 16th-century molds and flavored with anise. The hotel is often used for conferences of oenologists (wine experts), because it is owned by the Lungarotti Wine Company.

IN THE FOOTSTEPS ON ST. FRANCIS

Traces of peace-loving St. Francis are evident throughout **Assisi**, an ethereal mountainside town with medieval houses. Just outside Assisi is the **Basilica Santa Maria**, which includes the fourth-century Chapel of Porziuncola, used by St. Francis and his followers.

St. Francis is buried in the **Basilica of San Francesco**—his remains are kept in the structure's 19th-century crypt. Giotto painted 28 scenes from the life of the saint here. Black-robed pilgrims flock to the basilica from the countryside year-round.

The corpse of St. Clare of Assisi (founder of the Order of Saint Clare or the Poor Clares as they are commonly known) is exposed and can be viewed in its crystal casket in the crypt of the **Basilica of Santa Chiara**, across town.

Outside Assisi, visit the **Convent of St. Damian**, where St. Francis received his holy orders. See the crucifix that supposedly spoke to St. Francis and the rooms where St. Clare lived, worked, and fought off marauders. Go on to the Eremo delle Carceri, a tiny church hollowed out of rock by St. Francis and his followers in a nearby wood.

Hotel Fontebella, *Via Fontebella 25; tel. +39 (075) 812-883; website: www. fontebella.com/home_eng.html*, is located in a 17th-century palazzo in the center of town. Most rooms have a balcony with a view of the city. Guests can play cards and drink cocktails in the comfortable sitting room. The hotel restaurant, Il Frantoio, is expensive.

447

THE BEST OF BOLOGNA

"La grassa, la dotta, la rossa"—fat, red, and brainy. Not the most flattering of descriptions, but that's how Bolognese proudly define their city. Fat, because it's one of the world's leading gastronomic centers; brainy, as home of the world's oldest university, founded in 1088, and as the cradle of such inventions as Marconi's radio; and red, for the dominant terracotta and russet hues of its handsome buildings threaded by its 35 miles of ochre-shaded arcades.

Fat could also refer to the shape of the wallet needed to enjoy much of the best of Bologna. It's a major commercial hub, boasting Europe's fifth-largest exhibition center and hosting major international fairs and conventions such as the **Future Film Festival**, *website: www.futurefilmfestival.org.*

The best hotel: The Grand Hotel Majestic

On arrival, you will be ushered into the 124-room **Grand Hotel Majestic**, *Via Indipendenza, 8; tel. +39 (051) 225-445; website: http://grandhotelmajestic. duetorrihotels.com*, by two gloved doormen, greeted by a concierge, and, having trekked to the end of the hall, welcomed by a small platoon of svelte receptionists. En route, the white pillars and marble floors dazzle, the antique furniture glows and the décor takes the breath away. You are in the footsteps of the global glitterati. The VIP guest book is crammed with grateful messages from concert artistes like Rostropovich and Muti, sporting legends like Pelé, and such show business stars as Liza Minnelli, Bob Dylan, and Diana Ross, and friends and family of the great Pavarotti who had a home nearby. The accommodation is fabulous too—canopied beds, ornate furnishings, 18th-century paintings and elaborate chandeliers.

The best place for people watching

The **Piazza Maggiore** is one of Italy's most imposing sights—a wide pedestrianized square flanked by massive palaces: the Palazzo Comunale, the Palazzo Podesta, and the Basilica di San Petronio. People come here to sit in one of the sprawling cafés and watch everyone else. Sitting not far away is Neptune, a bronze statue complete with bubbly mermaids. Apparently, before its designer, Giambologna, began work on it back in the 1500s, he sought permission from the pope to expose a great deal of the sensual *Il Gigante's* abundant flesh. The pope is said to have replied "For Bologna, it's okay."

The best arts and crafts

Bologna's intriguing backstreets are full of treasures for the specialist, hobbyist, and connoisseur. Interested in buying or restoring a violin? Then drop in on Bruno Liutaio, *Via del Belle Arti; website: www.brunostefanini.it*. To watch iron being wrought into extraordinary shapes, drop in on Pierluigi Prata's ironworks, *Via Caldarese*. And for exquisite collections of antique and modern art, there's the charming Galleria Caldarese, *Via Caldarese*.

Bologna's most impressive towers

Bologna is not short on towers, but there are none more impressive than **Torre Asinelli**, *Piazza di Porta Ravegnana*, whose 498 wooden steps wind upward for 330 feet to a breathtaking view. At its side is the 160-foot-high **Torre Garisenda**, with a Pisa-rivaling tilt. The towers are nicely situated near to the Palazzo dei Congressi, which is itself linked to the Municipal Gallery of Modern Art.

The best restaurant

For a relaxed but professional atmosphere, you can't beat the **Pappagallo**, *Piazza della Mercanzia 3C; tel. +39 051-232-807*, built on the foundations of a 13th-century palace. Serves classical Bolognese dishes, including Pappagallo's own home-made tortellini. Try the gamberoni served with black rice and asparagus tips. If you prefer meat, another specialty is Costola di Vitello alla Bologna, a scintillating blend of marinated veal, ham, and parmesan with zuchinni.

THE BEST OF TUSCANY

Tuscany has historic towns, fashionable beach resorts, and a leading spa favored by the Italian *bene* (elite). The region that gave us Michelangelo and Leonardo da Vinci continues its artistic traditions, creating marble sculpture and fine gold and leather crafts. Yet it is seldom crowded with tourists.

The oldest Tuscan town

Drive up into the hills above Florence to visit **Fiesole**, one of the 12 great towns of ancient Eturia. Long before there was a Florence, this little town sat above the Arno Valley. In 283 B.C., Etruscan Fiesole was conquered by the Romans, who left behind an amphitheater built in 80 B.C. Classical plays are presented in the restored ruins.

An ochre-colored path leads from the Piazza Mino to the San Francesco Monastery in Fiesole. From the path, you can enjoy one of the best views of Florence. The cloister of the Gothic monastery is filled with Chinese art from the era of Marco Polo.

The town's *duomo*, built in A.D. 1000, has gray Corinthian columns and Romanesque arches. Paintings by Fra Angelico and Fra Filippo Lippi are displayed at the Museo Bandini.

The best place to dine in Fiesole is the **Villa Aurora**, *Piazza Mino; tel. +39 (055) 59-363; website: www.villaurora.net.* It has a charming garden and great views, as well as inexpensive Tuscan fare.

Villa San Michele, *Via Doccia 4; tel. +39 (055) 567-8200; website: www.villasanmichele.com*, is a deluxe hotel in a former Franciscan monastery. Monks' cells have been converted into lavishly decorated bedrooms and suites. Michelangelo is supposed to have designed the building.

The best wine-making estate

Not far from Florence, just off Superstrada 67, is the winemaking **Artimino Estate**, *website: www.artimino.com*, with its 740 acres of vineyards, olive groves, and gardens. In the late 16th century, the villa was commissioned by Grand Duke Ferdinand I to house his court. It became known as La Ferdinanda. An excellent restaurant, **Biagio Pignatta**, *tel. +39 (055) 875-1406*, is located on the estate's grounds. It offers Tuscan dishes and the eight wines grown on the estate according to age-old traditions. Wood-burning ovens braise the meats to perfection. The *scaloppina ai carciofi* (veal and artichokes), *bistecca alla Fiorentina* (charcoal-broiled beefsteak), and *faraona alla brace* (broiled guinea hen) are superb.

Hotel Paggeria Medicea, *tel. +39 (055) 875-141*, adjacent to the villa, has 37 rooms with wood beams and enormous fireplaces, as well as 20th-century conveniences, such as telephones, televisions, and refrigerated bars. The hotel is in a 17th-century building formerly called Il Corridoio (the Hallway), because it once separated the court residence from the servants' quarters.

The prettiest Tuscan town

Lucca, a small city enclosed within vast ramparts, is the prettiest town in Tuscany. The 12th-century town is beautifully preserved and maintained. Delightfully cool and shaded green walkways follow the massive 16th-century brick and turf walls that surround the town. The curious towers here are typical of Tuscan towns. In the Middle Ages, most patrician houses were dominated by very high and slender towers often crowned with ilex trees. After exploring Lucca's historic churches, wander through the narrow streets, which are filled with boutiques.

Lucca's grand **San Martino Cathedral,** *Piazza San Martino,* is filled with artistic treasures. Jacopo della Quercia designed the tomb of Ilaria del Carretto, wife of the Lord of Lucca in the early 15th century. A strangely lifelike statue of Ilaria reclines on top of the tomb. Other treasures include Tintoretto's *Last Supper* and Ghirlandaio's *Madonna and Saints.* A life-sized statue of Christ that drifted ashore at the nearby town of Luni is kept in a round chapel in the north nave. Every September 13th, the statue is carried through town in memory of the day it miraculously appeared. The façade of the cathedral is carved with religious allegories and fantastic animals. Nicola Pisano's *Deposition* and *Nativity* are above the door on the right.

Inside the **Church of San Michele,** *Piazza San Michele,* is a painting of saints Sebastian, Roch, Jerome, and Helen by Fra Filippo Lippi.

The **Church of San Frediano,** *Piazza San Frediano,* houses the mummy of Santa Zita. On April 26th, the townspeople place the body in the middle of the church and stroke and kiss its withered limbs.

The best restaurant in town is the **Buca di Sant'Antonio,** *Via della Cervia 3; tel. +39 (0583) 55-881; website: www.bucadisantantonio.it.* Kid roasted on a spit is a specialty here. Try the local wine, Rosso delle Colline Lucchesi.

Lucca has a shortage of hotels. Of the small hotels here, the most comfortable and convenient is the **Hotel Universo,** *Piazza del Giglio 1; tel. +39 (0583) 493-678; website: www.universolucca.com.*

The best-preserved Tuscan town

San Gimignano, with its noble towers, is one of the best-preserved medieval towns in Italy. Unfortunately, tourists flock to this 14th-century gem, crowding the streets. It's difficult to imagine where they all stay—only three hotels are located within the town walls. During the fall, the town is filled with hunters. (Hunting is good in the surrounding hills.)

Fourteen of the 72 towers that once protected this town still stand. At one time, all 72 spires crowded around the main square that surrounds the 13th-century *cisterna* (well). The small square is curiously paved with bricks laid on their narrow sides in a herringbone pattern.

The best hotel in San Gimignano is **La Cisterna,** *Piazza della Cisterna 23; tel. +39 (0577) 940-328; website: www.hotelcisterna.it,* located in the main square. It is an elegant, comfortable, well-run place with an excellent restaurant, **451**

Le Terrazza. Sit on the terrace to watch the lights blink on in farmhouses and peaceful villages as night falls over the valley.

Tuscany's crown jewel: Siena

The jewel in Tuscany's crown is **Siena**, a beautifully preserved town with wide-open spaces and ancient palaces. It is known for its university, its musical academy, and the annual Palio (a centuries-old horse race). Siena's cathedral, a striped marble structure, reaches high into the sky. The 14th-century walls that surround Siena were used during World War II to prevent retreating German troops from passing through the city. When the ancient portals were shut, the 20th-century tanks couldn't get through!

Siena's most beautiful square is the **Piazza del Campo**, which is bordered by the city's magnificent palaces and the 13th-century Palazzo Pubblico (city hall), which houses the town museum. Built of brick, the city hall is a fine specimen of pointed Gothic architecture. The slim, elegant, 334-foot tower (Torre del Mangia) soars high over the city. Its shadow moves across the brick paving as the day progresses. The Sienese Museum is a good introduction to Siena.

In the evening, join the Sienese in their stroll along the *passeggiata,* or promenade, along the curving Banchi di Sopra. The *passeggiata* leads through the banking district. Notice the Monte dei Paschiu di Siena, a bank housed in the 14th-century Palazzo Salimbeni. The bank was founded in 1472 and is still in business. Nearby is Palazzo Tolomei, the oldest private palace in Siena, now home to the Cassa di Risparmio di Firenze, another bank.

The most beautiful Sienese artwork is on display at the **Pinacoteca**, *Via San Pietro 29*, which contains Byzantine paintings and works by Simone Martini.

The most exciting time to visit

The most exciting time to visit Siena is during the **Il Palio**, which is held July 2nd and August 16th each year. This bareback three-lap horse race around the shell-shaped Piazza del Campo is one of the most genuine and fascinating of all Italian spectacles. It lasts 90 seconds but generates feuds that continue for decades.

The Palio is a competition between 10 of Siena's 17 *contrade*, or districts. During the days preceding the race, the people of Siena revert to the venality of the Middle Ages. Bribery, meddling, and skullduggery are not only permitted but also encouraged. *Contrade* captains are expected to indulge in intrigue as part of their efforts to outdo their rivals.

The Palio has roots in the Middle Ages, when Siena was an independent republic. At that time, the 17 *contrade* were separate military societies, each defended by its own military forces. Life in Siena in the Middle Ages was not easy. Homes were small, cold, badly ventilated, and had little light. The streets were narrow and murky and bristled with the threat of ambush. The walls that surrounded the city and those of the high buildings along the streets were blackened by smoke. The danger of epidemic was great, as was the possibility of dying by the sword or dagger. In light of all this, it is no wonder the people looked for escape. The Compagnie Popolari was organized to help provide distraction. These companies, each from a different section of the city, were intended to keep the people happy and free from worries (and thoughts of revolt, no doubt) by initiating games. One of the games the Compagnie Popolari initiated was the Palio.

The best hotels and restaurants

The **Grand Hotel Continental**, *Via Marciano 18; tel. +39 0577-56011; website: www.royaldemeure.com*, is the best place to stay in Siena. Located in a 15th-century villa, it has modern amenities, such as air conditioning, a heated swimming pool, and central heating. Terraces, gardens, and vineyards surround the villa. Situated on Marciano Hill, it has good views.

Pisa: Tuscany's most famous sight

Pisa, which is famous for its leaning tower, has lesser-known sights that are also worth seeing: the cathedral, the baptistery, and the Campo Santo. The *duomo* is fronted by white columns that support five tapered arcades. Winged angels peer out from the corners, and mysterious inscriptions can be found on the walls. Inside are Corinthian columns and striped walls. Art in the cathedral includes an ivory Madonna by Giovanni Pisano, Andrea del Sarto's *Sant'Agnese Mourning*, and Giovanni del Biondo's *Flight From Egypt* and *Presentation at the Temple*.

The **Baptistry**, *Piazza del Duomo; website: www.opapisa.it*, has gables, arches, and stained-glass windows. A white shaft of light shines through the baptistery dome onto the floor. Sounds echo eerily in the dome.

The **Camposanto**, *Piazza del Duomo; website: www.opapisa.it*, is a walled cemetery filled with earth brought back from Calvary by the Crusaders. The cemetery walls are covered with terrifying medieval frescoes: *The Triumph of Death*, *The Last Judgement*, and *Hell*. The last is a picture of snakes, skewered corpses, and demons punishing sinners.

SICILY: ITALY AT ITS MOST EXOTIC

Sicily, an island at the southern tip of Italy, is a land unto itself. In ancient times, Sicily was part of Greece. Later, it became part of the Roman Empire. After the fall of Rome, northern tribes, Saracens, Byzantines, Normans, French, and Spanish invaded it, each group leaving its mark on the island's culture. Sicily didn't become part of Italy until 1860. Sicily's climate is more like that of northern Africa than that of Europe. So the best time to visit is in the spring or fall. (It is blisteringly hot in the summer.)

The best-preserved relics

Some of the best-preserved relics of ancient Greece are scattered across Sicily. **Taormina's Amphitheater**, is spectacular, with **Mount Etna** smoking behind it.

The **Temple of Segesta** (a town in western Sicily) is set on a lonely hill facing a huge amphitheater.

In **Agrigenta**, the temples to Juno, Concordia, and Hercules are awe-inspiring.

Visit **Messina**, founded by the Greeks in the eighth century, and **Siracusa**, which has archeological evidence of the ancient Greeks and Romans.

Europe's highest active volcano

Europe's highest active volcano is in Sicily. **Mount Etna** rises 9,840 feet. Don't take the organized tour of Mount Etna—it is a terrible disappointment. The trip takes all day, and you will see nothing but dirt and rocks. The group never goes near the crater.

The least-changed towns

The smaller hill towns in Sicily are some of the least modern in Italy. Donkeys and mules rather than cars and trucks carry loads. Women carry water from wells in jars on their heads. Each morning, a goat herder follows his goats into town. He milks the goats at each door, delivering fresh milk to the residents. Plumbing in some towns is nonexistent, and water is scarce.

Sicily's most charming resort

Taormina is the most charming resort town in Sicily. Set on a ridge with a spectacular view of the bay, its greatest sight is the Greek Theater carved out of the hillside, which is still used for productions during the summer theater festivals. Palazzo Vorvaia, the site of Sicily's parliament in the 14th century, is on the Piazza

Vittorio Emanuele. Enjoy a glass of wine and a view of the bay from one of the many cafés along the Piazza 9 Aprile.

The best way to get to Sicily

The most beautiful way to get to Sicily is by ferry or hydrofoil from the southern tip of the mainland at Reggio di Calabria or Villa San Giovanni across the Strait of Messina. The crossing is long and often tough, but always lovely. Boats also connect with Naples, Livorno, Genoa, and Cagliari. You can also fly to Palermo and Catania from major Italian cities.

Sicilian cuisine—Italy's most colorful

Sicily is known for its exotic and colorful dishes, which have a slightly Arabic flavor. One typical dish of the region is *pasta con le sarde*, in which pine nuts and currants lend a Middle Eastern touch to *bucatini* (thick, hollow spaghetti) in a sauce of fresh sardines and wild fennel. The combination of pine nuts and currants is common. Eggplant and sun-ripened fresh tomatoes are also commonly used.

Lo Scudeiro, *Viale del Fante 9; tel. +39 (091) 581-628*, one of the best restaurants in Palermo, serves sophisticated Sicilian cooking. It is expensive by Sicilian standards.

The best place to sleep in Sicily

Palermo's luxury hotel is the **Hilton Villa Igiea**, *Salita Belmonte 43; tel. +39 (091) 631-2111; website: www1.hilton.com.* Designed to look like a castle, this hotel is right on the sea. It has lovely flower gardens with palm trees and the ruins of an ancient temple. A swimming pool, tennis courts, an elevator and a bar add to the amenities. All rooms have baths. You can have a car sent to pick you up at the train station.

UNCONQUERED SARDINIA, THE WILDEST REGION

Sardinia is the least-tamed region in Italy. It is still the land of the *banditti*, family clans, and blood feuds. It has produced such rebels as Antonio Gramsci, theorist and founder of the Italian Communist Party. Today, Sardinia attracts movie stars and royalty. Prince Karim (the Aga Khan) bought 35 miles of coastline and established the most luxurious resort in Italy: the Costa Smeralda.

Despite an onslaught of foreign tourists and developers, Sardinia is beautiful —hilly and occasionally tropical. The coast has granite cliffs and long, sandy beaches. The water is the cleanest in the Mediterranean. What's more, Sardinia has fascinating Roman ruins at Nora and Tharros, as well as prehistoric stone towers called *nuraghi*.

Beautiful sights of Sardinia

Very little of Sardinia has been built upon. Most new residential developments have been carefully planned, and there is little that is unsightly. Planning regulations ensure the coastline remains unspoiled. Developers can't build within 330 yards of the sea, and all paintwork must be in natural earthy or ocean colors.

Cagliari, the best bet

Cagliari, on the southern coast, has inexpensive hotels and a charming medieval district called the Castello. Narrow streets and tall towers cover the hills rising out of the harbor. This friendly town is near the *nuraghi* ruins at Barumini and the sandy beaches of the Costa del Sud. Pink flamingos inhabit the lagoons outside town. The tourist office in Piazza Matteotti can help you find a room.

Cagliari has good seafood restaurants. **Dal Corsaro**, *Viale Regina Margherita 28; tel. +39 (070) 664-318; website: www.dalcorsaro.com*, serves fresh lobster, eel, shrimp, and fish.

Trattoria Gennargentu, *Via Sardegna 60; tel. +39 (070) 658-247*, serves enormous plates of lasagne, shish kebab, and squid. The trattoria is comfortable, has plenty of local atmosphere, and serves a good house wine.

Sardinia's oldest city

Nora, a small city near Cagliari, is the oldest city in Sardinia. Settled by Phoenicians, who left the ruins of their temple behind, it became a bustling Roman town before it died about A.D. 500. The Roman roads and theater are well-preserved, and the ruins are being excavated. Climb to the Spanish watchtower for tremendous views of the sea, which breaks on either side of the isthmus.

Sardinia's unique ruins

Don't leave Sardinia without examining its *nuraghi*—ancient stone towers found only in this part of Italy. They were once used as tombs, temples, or forts of refuge. The **Nuraghi of Su Nuraxi** in Barumini, 30 miles north of Cagliari, are the best-preserved in Sardinia. Set on a hill, they are the remains of an ancient village. The huge blocks of stone were designed primarily for defense. The huge central tower dates back to about 1300 B.C. The Nuraghi of Su Nuraxi can be visited every day except Mondays.

The town of **Sassari** has the best Sardinian museum, the **Museo Giovanni Antonio Sanna**, *Via Roma 64*. See reconstructed *nuraghi*, Sardinian paintings and costumes, Roman statues and mosaics, and an ethnographic section where Sardinian music is played.

For basic but comfortable accommodation in Sassari try the **Hotel Carlo Felice,** *Via Carlo Felice 43; tel. +39 (079) 271-440; website: www.hotelcarlofelice.it.*

The best Roman ruins

Near Sassari, **Porto Torres** occupies the site of the Roman town **Turris Libisonis**. Remains of the Roman settlement, including a circular marble altar and the baths of the Palace of the Barbarian King (Palazzo di Re Barbaro), can be seen next to the train station. Seven arches of an ancient Roman bridge span the River Turritano. The Church of San Gavino is one of Sardinia's most notable monuments. Built in the 11th century, it has 28 columns and a wooden truss ceiling.

Sardinia's most beautiful city

Alghero, the most beautiful and best-preserved city in Sardinia, has a Spanish flavor. Sardinia was united with Aragon in 1325, and the Spaniards left their mark on Alghero, which looks somewhat like Barcelona. Alleys are covered with arches, and some restaurants serve *paella*. Starting at the Bastione della Maddalena in the port, walk around the ramparts and the 16th-century Spanish towers to enjoy the view of the shimmering sea.

Outside Alghero are two beaches with clean, clear water—**Spiaggia di San Giovanni** and **Spiaggia di Maria Pia**. Both are crowded. A short boat trip away is the **Grotto di Nettuno**, which puts Capri's Blue Grotto to shame. The large underwater cavern can be visited by boats that leave from docks in front of Bastione della Maddalena.

One of the best restaurants in **Alghero** is **Ristorante Il Pavone**, *Piazza Sulis 3; tel. +39 (079) 979-584.* This family-run restaurant serves excellent soups, antipastos, risottos, and seafood.

The best hotel for royalty

Perched on the sea shore, and once the accommodation of choice for Italian royalty during their vacations in Sardinia, is the **Villa Las Tronas Hotel and Spa**, *Alghero, tel. +39 (079) 981-818; website: www.hotelvillalastronas.it.* Surrounded on three sides by water, the hotel has a sea-water swimming pool, Turkish bath, and a restaurant with stunning views of the Bay of Alghero.

THE BEST OF
JAPAN

A case might be made for Japan as Pandora's box.
—John Gunther, Inside Asia, 1939

Japan is the best-known yet least-understood country in Asia, with a unique combination of Eastern and Western cultures. The Japanese go to great lengths to provide Western travelers with American-style hotels and modern amenities; yet, the Westerner may be excluded from a geisha club or a traditional Japanese inn. In the space of a few miles, you can race with the dizzying traffic of Tokyo's Ginza district and then revel in the silence of a remote Buddhist temple.

An ancient country, Japan is also the most modern nation in Asia. It is at once tranquil and chaotic, trend-setting and traditional. Young people wearing the latest fashions share sidewalks with elderly people in ancient costumes. Japanese businessmen taking the international market by storm also take time to meditate in centuries-old temples.

THE BEST OF TOKYO

Japan's capital and largest city is one of the most expensive cities in the world. Tokyo is not known for its beauty. Indeed, the central districts are an architectural study in neon and chrome. But the city has hidden temples and flower gardens that preserve the serene, traditional side of Japanese culture. The metropolis of Tokyo sprawls to the horizon, covering 800 square miles and comprising 26 cities, six towns, nine villages, and several islands. Curiously, this industrial city also has 20,679 farmers.

The best ways to travel

The subway system in Tokyo is excellent. Its routes are color-coded, and most stations are marked in Roman letters. The bus network is efficient as well, but information is printed only in Japanese. Taxis are luxurious, many with television sets and doors that open and close by remote control.

Despite all this, walking is the best way to see Tokyo. Even at night, the streets in this virtually crime-free city are safe. However, many of the streets are not named, and buildings aren't always numbered, so it is easy to get lost. If you do get lost, you're in luck as long as it's a weekday between 9:30 a.m. and 6:30 p.m. During those times, call the **Tokyo Information Center**, *tel. +81 (3) 5321-3077*. A member of the English-speaking staff will be able to help you.

The number-one sight

At the heart of Tokyo is the **Imperial Palace**, a 28-acre retreat surrounded by a moat filled with swans. The palace stands on the site of Edo Castle, built in the 15th century by Lord Dokan Ota. From the 1500s to 1868, when it was the residence of the Tokugawa *shoguns* (commanders in chief of the armed forces of Japan), it covered 608 acres and was defended by a 10-mile wall with 111 gates, 20 turrets, and 30 bridges. The city of Tokyo grew around the edifice, which has been destroyed and rebuilt several times.

Behind the palace walls there is a silkworm farm, rice paddies, and a mulberry field. Visitors can enter the palace only twice a year: on January 2nd and on the emperor's birthday, December 23rd.

When you visit the **Imperial Palace East Garden**, you'll think you are in the *shoguns'* Japan, not a modern city. Still standing are four gates that once led into ancient Edo Castle. The Kitakibashimon, the entrance to the castle tower, is the most imposing, its stone bulwarks are reflected in the deepest part of the moat.

The **Kitanomaru Koen** and **Chidorigafuchi Suijo Koen** parks are open to the public year-round. The Kitanomaru Koen Park contains the National Museum of Modern Art; the Crafts Gallery, located in the former headquarters of the Old Imperial Palace Guard; the Science and Technology Museum, and the Nippon

Budokan (built for the 1964 Olympics), a concert hall that looks like a Buddhist temple, but hosts performances by such rock stars as Rod Stewart.

The Imperial Palace is encircled by a 4.6-mile bike trail. Five hundred free bikes are available at the police station in the Imperial Palace Plaza if you'd like to take the *tour du palais*. Or you can join the locals in a jog around the palace's perimeter. The Imperial Hotel provides its guests with complimentary running gear and shoes for this purpose.

For the best view of the palace and its gardens, have lunch or dinner in the 23rd-floor restaurant at the nearby Palace Hotel. Another good view is from the Kasumigaseki Building, southwest of the palace. On a clear day, you can see all the way to Mount Fuji.

The loveliest shrines and temples

Beyond the palace grounds and up a hill is the **Yasukuni shrine**, *3-1-1 Kudan Kita, Dhiyoda-ku*, dedicated to the souls of those who have fought and died for Japan. Surrounded by park-like grounds, its entrance is marked by a huge, yoked wooden gateway called a *torii*. Walk through the maze-like shrine, with its many pillars. Toss some coins in the box by the door, clap your hands to awaken the spirits within, and say a prayer. Inside the shrine is a museum containing war memorabilia.

The **Asakusa Kannon temple**, at the heart of the Asakusa neighborhood, is dedicated to Kannon, the Buddhist goddess of compassion. According to legend, the temple was built in A.D. 628 by three fishermen who had discovered a statue of the goddess in their fishing net. It is marked by a 10-foot, red paper lantern that weighs 220 pounds. An enormous incense vat sends sweet-smelling smoke into the air from the courtyard in front of the temple. When cupped in one palm and patted on the body, the smoke is said to cure ailments. The flock of doves that flies around the temple is considered a sacred messenger of Kannon. Many of Tokyo's temples hold annual festivals, but the one held here May 16th to 18th is the largest in the city.

The **Hie shrine**, *2-10-5 Nagata-cho*, is dedicated to Oyamakuni, the money god, who grants fertility and good relationships, and wards off evil. The best time to visit the shrine is every other Juen (i.e. odd years), during the Sanno-sai Festival, when miniature shrines are carried through the neighborhood.

The **Meji Jingu shrine**, *Shibuya-ku*, is one of the most popular Shinto shrines in Tokyo. Founded in 1920, it is dedicated to the Emperor Meiji (1868-1912), who ended the 600-year rule of the *shoguns* and opened Japan to the West.

The shrine is surrounded by a 180-acre garden, and before it stands Japan's largest *torii*. The shrine's best feature is its iris garden, which bursts into color in June and July. Horsemen wearing samurai costumes compete in the yearly archery contest held here.

The **Sengakuji temple**, *Takanawa*, is the burial site of the 47 samurai of Asano Naganoni, Lord of Ako. They died for their master after avenging his death. Naganoni had made the mistake of drawing his sword when the court chamberlain insulted him. As punishment, he was forced to commit suicide. His faithful samurai then cut off the head of the chamberlain, for which they too had to commit suicide. Their story is re-enacted in the Kabukin play *Chushingura*. The faithful still come to lament the death of the samurai by lighting joss sticks on stone memorials in the temple gardens.

Tokyo's best park

On weekends, Tokyo residents flock to busy **Ueno Park**. Weekdays are less crowded. Try to visit during the Cherry Blossom Festival, from late March through mid-April, when the trees are breathtaking. The **Ueno zoo** is worth visiting, if only for its pandas.

Also visit the **Shitamachi History Museum**, *2-1, Ueno-Koen, Taito-ku, tel. +81 (3) 3823-7451, website: www.taitocity.net/taito/shitamachi/*, at the far end of the park, featuring everyday objects donated by Tokyo residents.

Japan's best baseball (*besuboru*)

One of the most popular destinations in Tokyo is in the Korakuen district, southwest of Ueno Park: the **Korakuen baseball stadium**. With two baseball leagues and 12 teams, the Japanese are passionate *besuboru* (baseball) fans, and the stadium is often sold out through the entire season. (The Japanese baseball season is roughly equal to the U.S. season.)

The best theater in Japan

There are three traditional forms of theater in Japan; they are Kabuki, Noh, and Bunraku, all of which can be seen at their finest in Tokyo.

The **National Theater of Japan**, *website: www.ntj.jac.go.jp/english/index.html*, is the best Kabuki and Bunraku. It was designed based on centuries-old Kabuki theaters. Kabuki plays have fantastic plots, elaborate costumes, a lot of action, and singing. All parts are played by men, and performances go on for hours. (You don't have to sit through an entire performance. It is acceptable to leave or arrive in the middle.) Musicians are seated on stage, and stagehands wearing black hoods bring actors their props during performances.

The largest Kabuki theater in Tokyo is **Kabukiza,** *website: www.shochiku. co.jp/play/kabukiza/theater/*, in the Ginza. (However, as mentioned above, the best place to see Kabuki is at the National Theater because performances are translated and explained via earphones.) Kabukiza closed in April 2010 to undergo a major re-build. Until it re-opens in 2013, most of the performances have been moved to nearby Shinbashi Enbujo.

Bunraku—puppet versions of Kabuki—are heroic tales of samurai, enacted by life-size puppets. A small theater in the National Theater is designed especially for Bunraku.

Noh plays, which date back to the 12th century, are highly stylized and symbolic dramas. The stage is bare except for a backdrop showing a huge tree. Actors wear masks and speak in falsetto voices. The best places to see Noh plays are small Noh theaters, including; the **National Noh Theater**, *4-18-1 Sendagoya, Shibuya-ku;* **Kanze Nohgakudo**, *1-16-4 Shoto, Shibuya-ku; tel. +81 (33) 469-5241* and **Hosho Nohgakudo**, *1-5-9 Hongo, Bunkyo-ku.*

The best flower arranging

Ikebana, the Japanese art of flower arrangement, follows strict aesthetic and philosophical principles. Flowers are placed to symbolize heaven above, earth below, and man in the middle. Ikebana was developed in the eighth century, when it was practiced at the Imperial Court. Today, the art can be seen in every temple and many households throughout Japan. The **Ohara School of Ikebana**, *website: www. ohararyu.or.jp*, offers a two-hour course in traditional Japanese flower arranging.

Tea ceremony secrets

The Japanese make even the English look careless when it comes to making tea. O-cha (green tea) is served ceremoniously on important occasions, at the beginning of conversations, at temples, and at the end of meals. The many details of the ceremony have been carefully preserved throughout the centuries. Tea is served without sugar, in small cups without handles, as participants sit silently in a circle. The tea is ground into a fine powder and then, after steeping, whisked until it foams. The cups are held and contemplated before the tea is sipped. Every movement has symbolic significance. You can see tea ceremonies at a number of hotels in the city, including the **Imperial Hotel**, *1-1-1, Uchisaiwaicho, Chiyoda-ku; tel. +81 (3)3504-1111; website: www.imperialhotel.co.jp,* **Hotel Okura**, *2-10-4,*

Toranomon, Minato-ku; tel. +81 (3)3582-0111; website: www.hotelokura.co.jp/tokyo/en/, and **Hotel New Otani**, *4-1, Kioicho, Chiyoda-ku; tel. +81 (3) 3265-1111; website: www.newotani.co.jp/en/tokyo/.*

Super sumo

The best place to witness sumo is the Ryogoko district in northeast Tokyo, home to more than 30 stables for the immense wrestlers who wander the streets dressed in kimonos and topknots. You can watch them competing (wearing slightly less) at the sumo stadium called Kuramae Kokugikan. Sumo tournaments take place in mid-January, mid-May, and mid-September. If you can't make it to the tournaments, have your hotel call a stable to ask permission for you to watch a morning practice session. Two stables to try are **Kasugano-beya** or **Takasago-beya**.

Bathing at its best

Japanese *onsens* (hot springs), *osento* (public baths), or *ofuros* (at home) are the best way in the world to bathe. In Japan, a bath is not just a bath. It is a ceremony. Tokyo has 1,865 public *sento* (bathhouses)—which indicates the importance of the bath to the Japanese. Natural hot-springs feed 16 of the baths. You can enjoy one, but you must follow the rules.

Shoes are left in lockers by the front door, and clothes are exchanged for small towels with which you attempt to cover yourself as you walk to the communal bath. Men and women bathe separately. Before climbing into the steaming water, wash yourself with soap and water using your little towel. Remember to rinse thoroughly. Once you are clean, climb into the *furo* (tub) and soak.

You can also try a mountain *rotenburo* (hot spring outdoors), set in visually stunning locations. Or take your bath as the Japanese do before a mid-evening meal. Wear the crisp pure cotton *yukata* with traditional decorations, navy on white background, and relax on the *tatamiital* mats. It is pure pleasure.

The best restaurants

The best place to get eel is at **Chikuyotei**, *8-14-7 Ginza, Chuo-ku; tel. +81 (45) 465-5785.* You sit on the floor on tatami mats and enjoy the small teahouse atmosphere. **Chinzan-so**, *10-8, Sekiguchi 2-chome, Bunkyo-ku; tel. +81 (3) 3943-1111; website: www.chinzanso.com/english/,* is an enormous restaurant set in a magnificent garden. The food and atmosphere are delightful.

Asia's most dangerous food

If your culinary curiosity is stronger than your common sense, try *fugu* (poisonous blowfish), considered the greatest Japanese delicacy. The meat is fine, but the innards are deadly. (About 30 Japanese per year die from eating *fugu*.) The fish is served as *fugusashi* (raw flakes eaten with a soy, orange, and chive sauce), *birezake* (sun-dried fins dipped in hot sake), and *fuguchiri* (fugu soup). You should eat it only during a month with an R in it (as with oysters), and only when prepared by a licensed *fugu* cook.

Sake at its best

Tokyo has a number of *nomiya* (sake houses), where you can sample this peculiar Japanese brew. **Sasashu**, *2-2-6 Ikebukuro; tel. +81 (3) 3971-9363*, is the best, serving little goodies along with the warm white wine. **Chichibu Nishiki**, *tel. +81 (3) 3541-4777*, is the most attractive sake house, a historic building filled with antiques.

Tokyo's best (and most traditional) hotels

The best accommodation in Japan is at a *ryokan*, a traditional Japanese inn. They are virtually unchanged since the times of the samurai, with translucent paper windows, sliding doors, mat floors, alcoves, polished wood, and intricate gardens. (They do, however, have electricity, running water, and modern toilets.) When you arrive at a *ryokan*, you are greeted at the entrance (where you leave your shoes), then escorted to your room, served tea, and given a freshly laundered cotton kimono. The rooms are furnished with tatami mats and cushions. Sliding-glass walls usually overlook Japanese gardens. After the ritual bath in a sunken wooden tub, dinner is served in your room by a maid in a kimono, who later prepares your futon bed.

Ryokans in Tokyo vary widely. **Hotel Fukudaya**, *4-5-9 Aobadai, Meguro-ku; tel. +81 (3) 3467-5833; website: www.fukudaya.com*, is expensive, but has a wonderful atmosphere and great service.

A slightly cheaper but less intimate version of the *ryokan* is the *minshuku*. These inns are frequented primarily by vacationing Japanese. You are not always given a kimono or served your meals in your room. For reservations, contact the **Japan Minshuku Center**, *website: www.minshuku.jp/english/english.html*.

Tokyo's finest Western-style hotels

Hotel Okura, *2-10-4, Toranomon, Minato-ku; tel. +81 (3) 3582-0111; website: www.okura.com/tokyo/*, next to the American Embassy, offers both Western- and

Japanese-style suites. The hotel is elaborately decorated, and has all needed and wanted amenities.

Imperial Hotel, *1-1-1, Uchisaiwaicho, Chiyoda-ku; tel. +81 (3) 3504-1111; website: www.imperialhotel.co.jp*, is next door to the Imperial Palace, overlooking its grounds and Hibiya Park.

Keio Plaza, *2-2-1 Nishi-Shinjuku, Shinjuku-Ku; tel. +81 (3) 3345-8269; website: www.keioplaza.com*, was the first highrise in Tokyo and has magnificent views.

The **Park Hyatt**, *3-7-1-2 Nishi Shinjuku, Shinjuku-Ku; tel. +81 (3) 5322-1234; website: http://tokyo.park.hyatt.com*, overlooks Shinjuku Central Park, and has views of Mount Fuji.

The best places for romance with a twist

Just outside of Tokyo are **rabu hoteru** (love hotels), where you can choose from rooms with exotic themes: water beds that look like space shuttles, revolving roulette-wheel beds, or beds built into copies of the Sphinx. Most rooms have mirror ceilings and large television screens. Although the tourist boards are not likely to give you the names of specific love hotels, they are not hard to find—they are everywhere. They resemble American motels. And their garages are designed with curtains, in order to hide visitors' cars and protect their privacy.

The best of Tokyo nightlife

Tokyo's liveliest nightlife is in the **Roppongi district**, where clubs stay open until 6 a.m. Wandering the maze of streets, you'll find everything from intimate jazz cafés to huge hostess clubs.

The nightclub hostess, although often clad in a kimono, is not to be confused with the geisha, who presides only at private parties, usually to entertain businessmen. Geishas undergo intensive training in the arts of dance, music, and song. They serve at parties as entertainers, waitresses, and witty conversationalists. Hostesses, on the other hand, are employed by nightclubs to pour sake, provide conversation, and sometimes serve as dance partners. Neither a geisha nor a hostess is a prostitute.

Sweet Basil 139, *6-7-11 Roppongi Minato-ku; tel. +81 (3) 5474-1395; website: http://stb139.co.jp*, is the best place to hear live jazz.

Xanadu, *tel. +81 (3) 5489-3750; website: www.xanadu.ne.jp*, has great DJs, but it is rather small.

The seediest side

The seedy side of Tokyo's nightlife is in the **Shinjuku district**. The streets here are crammed with neon signs for X-rated movie theaters, brothels (often called Turkish baths), and little local bars, where *mama-san* will serve you cheap *mizu-wari* (watered-down whiskey).

These local bars are also the places to experience karaoke. Well-whiskied customers with microphones and accompanying tape recordings entertain the bar with their favorite love songs. Talent is of little consideration in these late-night shows. What counts is volume. (Karaoke has been forbidden in many residential areas.)

Yoshiwara, known as the Turkish massage district, is Tokyo's lust-ridden den of iniquity.

MOUNT FUJI: THE WORLD'S BEST SUNRISE

Those who have seen the sun rise from the top of **Fuji-san** (Mount Fuji) claim it is a mind-altering experience. Mount Fuji—considered by the Japanese to be a goddess—hides her dazzling beauty in a cloak of clouds most days. When the cloak is lifted, the 12,390-foot peak glitters white. You can climb the mountain only from the end of June through the beginning of September. Six trails lead to the top.

A short train or bus ride from Tokyo brings you to **Fuji-Hakone-Izu National Park**. Although the climb takes four to six hours, most of the trails are easy to hike, and the view is spectacular. Fellow trekkers, who sport everything from the latest fashions to the long, white robes of religious pilgrims, are interesting additions to the view.

You can spend the night in communal stone huts along the way and wake up in time to see the sunrise. Or you can begin hiking at night and reach the peak above the clouds just as the rising sun illuminates the sky. Wear sturdy shoes or boots and bring along warm, waterproof clothing and a flashlight. It is windy at the summit.

KYOTO: JAPAN'S MOST BEAUTIFUL CITY

For more than 1,000 years, **Kyoto** was the political, cultural, and religious capital of Japan, and the city's heritage is still evident in its 1,600 temples, 200 shrines, and well-preserved traditions of architecture and craftsmanship. After trying to make your way through Tokyo, you'll find Kyoto's grid-like street plan a pleasure. Kyoto, about three hours from Tokyo, merits a visit of several days. The city's treasures are many.

Kyoto's most important sights

The **Imperial Palace**, and its 220-acre park are the city's central attractions. Built by Emperor Kammu in A.D. 794, it has been destroyed several times by fire, but the existing building follows the original design. To visit the palace, you must get a pass at least 20 minutes, and sometimes up to two weeks, in advance. Register for a pass at the **Imperial Household Agency**, *website: www.kunaicho.go.jp.*

The **Heian shrine**, *website: www.heianjingu.or.jp*, with its impressive *torii* gate, was built to commemorate the 1,100th anniversary of Kyoto's founding. The shrine itself is a replica, 12 times reduced, of the original Chinese-style Imperial Palace, set in Kyoto's most beautiful gardens. In the spring, you can walk among weeping cherry trees and azaleas; in the fall, chrysanthemum displays decorate the stepping stone pond. The shrine is a favorite spot for weddings, and often you will catch a glimpse of a bride and her party, all dressed in kimonos.

Kinkaku-ji (Temple of the Golden Pavilion), in the northwest corner of the city, is Kyoto's prettiest temple. Surrounded by a lake, its exterior walls are gilded. The existing temple is a reconstruction of the original one. Trees shade the structure, and you can see the mountains in the distance.

Southwest of Kinkaku-ji is **Ryoanji** (Temple of the Peaceful Dragon), founded in 1473. Its famous stone garden is simple yet thought provoking. Stones are raked in Zen patterns (the sea, the desert, or the mountains) that are said to aid meditation.

The **Kyoto National Museum**, *website: www.kyohaku.go.jp*, houses an impressive collection of Chinese paintings from the Ming and Ch'ing dynasties, as well as treasures from Buddhist temples and Shinto shrines.

The **Toji temple**, which is five stories and 183 feet high, has the tallest pagoda in Japan. The temple's stone house, built of wood without using nails, houses an unrivaled collection of art treasures.

Nijo Castle, situated on 70 acres and surrounded by stone walls and a moat, was owned by the first *shogun* of the Tokugawa family. Of the palace's five buildings, don't miss the Ohiramai and its Great Hall, decorated with paintings by Tanyu Kano. Corridors in the Imperial Messenger's chamber are constructed so that anyone stepping on the floor will trigger a sound resembling the song of the Japanese bush warbler, warning guards of approaching intruders. The *shogun's*

467

apartments, in the fifth building, contain hidden chambers, where samurai guarded their master out of sight of palace guests.

Sanjusangendo (Temple of 33 Niches), a few blocks east of Kyoto Station, is a national treasure. It is so named because the facade is divided into 33 niches, one for each of the goddess Kannon's 33 personifications. The goddess is embodied here in a 10-foot statue, the *Thousand-Armed Kannon*.

Saiho-ji (Moss Temple), founded in 1339, is an incredible green color. Its pond is shaped like the Chinese character for heart and mind.

The **Katsura Villa** is widely admired as the crowning achievement of Japanese architecture. It is silent, austere, and perfectly balanced.

The **Shugakuin**, a villa in the foothills of Mount Hiei, has three large stepped gardens. Both the Katsura Villa and the Shugakuin can be visited by permission of the Imperial Household Agency.

The craft quarter

Kyoto's old **Nishijin** district is the place to buy famous Nishijin silk brocade, which is still hand-woven. You can hear the sounds of silk looms along the narrow back streets. Displays of the district's handwork can be seen at the **Nishijin Textile Museum**; *tel. +81 (75) 432-6131; website: www.nishijin.or.jp/eng/eng.htm.*

Another Kyoto specialty is Kiyomizuware pottery, produced by a 16th-century technique. Kiyomizuware is sold everywhere in Kyoto, but a concentration of particularly good shops is located along Teapot Lane near the Kiyomizu temple.

A good place to watch a variety of craftsmen at work on damascene metal-ware, wood-block prints, dolls, and porcelain is the **Kyoto Handicraft Center**, *21 Shougoin Entomi-cho, Sakyo-ku; website: www.kyotohandicraftcenter.com.* You'll also see painters, weavers, and goldsmiths here and anything you purchase will be duty-free.

Yuzen cloth, decorated by using a special 300-year-old dyeing process, is another Kyoto specialty. To achieve its perfect color, the cloth must be washed in the cold running waters of the Kamo River. Walk along the river between the Nijo-dori and Shijo-dori bridges for a good view of this activity.

The world's best knives

Aritsugu, *Gokomachi Nishi-iru, Nishikikoji-dori, Nakagyo-ku; tel. +81 (75) 221-1091; website: http://aframestokyo.com/aritsugu.html*, in the heart of the market district in central Kyoto, has been supplying Japan with swords and knives since 1560. Fujiwara Aritsugu, who began the family business, was the sword maker to the imperial household and supplied feudal warriors with their weapons. Today, cooking knives, which are direct descendants of the original Aritsugu swords, form the core of the business. The assortment is bewildering: the *deba-bocho*, for slicing through fish, meat, and bones; the *usuba* and the *nakiri*, for chopping and slicing vegetables; knives with rosewood or black synthetic composition handles; and knives banded with buffalo horn to help prevent cracking.

Kyoto's best restaurants

Kyoto's restaurants tend to be smaller, more old-fashioned, and more intimate than those in Tokyo.

Minoko, *480 Kiyoi-cho, Shimogowara-dori, Gion, Higashiyama-ku; tel. +81 (75) 561-0328*, is the real formal traditional Japanese experience. The food is exquisite, and you will be sitting on a tatami mat in a private room overlooking a pond.

Tousuiro, website: www.tousuiro.com, is famous for its homemade tofu dishes. They have two restaurants in the city, one in Kiyamachi and other in Gion. Reservations by phone are only taken in Japanese so ask your hotel to call if your Japanese isn't up to scratch.

Good places to look for a restaurant is the Kyoto Restaurant Association (*website: www.kyoto-okoshiyasu.com/KRA/index_en.html*).

Japan's best hotel

The **Tawaraya Ryokan**, *Fuya-cho, Anekoji-agaru, Nakagyo-ku, Kyoto-shi; tel. +81 (75) 211- 5566,* on a quiet back street in Kyoto, is a Japanese paradise. Dim and cozy, it has rooms that are booked year-round. You must remove your shoes at the door, where you are welcomed with a warm washcloth, tea, and a *yukata*, a light cotton version of a kimono. (Your street clothes are packed neatly away.) Bedrooms at the Tawaraya open onto a wooden platform overlooking the garden. Guests sit on *zabuton*, square cushions placed on the tatami mats that cover the floor. The bathroom looks out onto its own garden. All utilitarian items, such as televisions, telephones, and tea-making sets, are hidden. There are no room keys, and futons are kept in the closets.

The top Western-style hotels

The most luxurious hotel is the **Grand Prince Hotel**, *Takaragaike Sakyo-ku; tel. +81 (75) 712-1111; website: www.princehotels.com/en/kyoto/*, in the northern suburbs.

Other good western-style hotels are the **New Miyako Hotel**, *tel. +81 (75) 661-7111; website: www.miyakohotels.ne.jp/newmiyako/english/* and the **Kyoto**

Kokusai, *tel. (81)75-222-1111; website: www.kyoto-kokusai.com.*

Three hotels with both Western-style and Japanese-style rooms are the **Kyoto Royal Hotel and Spa,** *tel. +81 (75) 223-1234; website: www.ishinhotels.com/ kyoto-royal/en/;* the **Fujita,** *tel. +81 (75) 222-1511; website: www.fujita-kyoto.com,* and the **Kyoto Hotel Okura,** *tel. +81 (75) 211-5111; website: www.kyotohotel.co.jp.*

The hottest nightlife

Gion district is the place to be. All the best theaters are located there. Gion is also the best place to attend a geisha party. Make arrangements through your hotel or travel agent. Settle on the price beforehand—these are usually costly evenings.

Gion Corner, *website: www.kyoto-gioncorner.com/global/en.html,* was established by the Kyoto Visiting Club. Classes here teach various aspects of Japanese traditional arts. In two evening shows, demonstrations are given of the tea ceremony, flower arrangement, Bunraku puppet plays, *kyomai* (Kyoto-style dance), court music, and *koto* music, which is played on a 13-string instrument.

OSAKA: BESTS BENEATH THE GRIME

Osaka, the industrial center of Japan, seems an ugly city at first glance. But if you look behind the city's utilitarian facade, you will discover its traditional temples and shrines, secluded in their gardens; a mighty castle; and two good museums.

Visit the 10th-century **Temmangu shrine** on July 24th and 25th when the annual Tenjin Festival is held. On these nights, the normally solemn shrine to Tenjin, the god of learning, is transformed, as lantern-lit boats sail down Osaka's canals accompanied by a fireworks display.

The 16th-century **Osaka Castle,** was built by the warlord Hideyoshi, who ordered huge stones for its construction, some of which are still in place. One of the stones, called Higo-ishi, is 47 feet long and more than 19 feet high.

Tennoji Park, in the southern part of the city, contains a zoo, botanical gardens, the Shitennoji temple, and the Keitakuen, one of the best examples of a Japanese strolling garden.

Two excellent museums of Chinese and Japanese art are the **Fujita Art Museum,** *tel. +81 (6) 6351-0582* and the **Masaki Museum of Art,** *website: http:// masaki-art-museum.jp.*

Tree-lined **Mido-suji** is Osaka's best street for strolling and window shopping, but for serious shopping you are better off in one of the city's shopping districts or arcades. An underground labyrinth of stores is located in Kita, near Umeda Station. Shinsai-Bashi-Suji is another well-known shopping street. Also visit the shopping arcade between Shinsai-Bashi-Suji and Ebisu-Bashi-Suji.

Osaka's best restaurants

Benkay, in *Hotel Nikko Osaka; tel. +81 (6) 6244-2468*. If you appreciate Japanese-style red snapper (*tai*), which is served with stewed plums (*ume*), Benkay is the place to go. Sea urchin, squid, and prawns are also on the menu here; tempura and sushi are popular as well. The restaurant uses traditional blond-wood paneling, and there's a sushi bar on one side. Jacket and tie are required.

Chambord, in the *Rihga Royal Hotel, 5-3-68 Nakanoshima, Kita-ku; tel. +81 (6) 6448-1121; website: www.rihga.com/osaka/index.html.* This restaurant specializes in French cuisine. From its perch on the 29th floor of the Rihga Royal Hotel, the restaurant has a panoramic view of Osaka's lights and river activities. There's a pianist providing gentle background music, which makes this one of Osaka's most romantic dinner spots. Reservations are essential.

Fuguhisa, *tel. +81 (6) 6972-5029*. Expect a warm and hearty welcome at this no-nonsense little restaurant that specializes in *fugu ryori*, the blowfish delicacy for which Osaka is famous.

The best accommodation

Two deluxe hotels in Osaka are the **Rihga Royal Hotel**, *5-3-68 Nakanoshima, Kita-ku, tel. +81 (6) 6448-1121; website: www.rihga.com*, and the **Imperial Hotel Osaka**, 8-50, *Temmabashi 1-chome, Kita-ku; tel. +81 (6) 6881-1111; website: www.imperialhotel.co.jp.* Both hotels have great service and wonderful amenities.

The liveliest entertainment

National Bunraku Theatre (National Puppet Theatre) is considered the original home of the 300-year-old art of puppeteering. The best Bunraku shows in Japan are presented here. Bunraku is not just for children, but for all ages.

Kabuki performances are given in the five-story **Shin-Kabukiza**, *tel. +81 (6) 6631-2121*, in the southern part of the city. The Takarazuka All Girls Revue, Japan's most famous all-girl opera, performs at the Grand Theater in Takarazuka City, 40 minutes by train from Osaka.

The best bars and nightclubs can be found in Sonezaki Shinchi in Kita, near the Umeda arcade.

HIROSHIMA: THE WORLD'S MOST SOBERING CITY

Hiroshima, the place where the first atomic bomb was dropped in 1945, is a sobering site. Heiwa O-dori (Peace Boulevard) leads to the **Hiroshima Peace Memorial Museum**, south of Peace Park. The center features the Peace Tower and a museum of objects left after the explosion, as well as photographs of the bombed city and its victims.

The Industrial Promotion Hall, the building believed to have been directly below the center of the blast, is also located here. It has been left standing, gutted from the explosion, as a reminder of the bomb. On August 6, the day of the bombing, Hiroshima holds its annual Peace Festival in the Peace Memorial Park.

You can reach the city of Hiroshima, set on a bay of the Inland Sea, by a two-hour bullet train ride. The stretch between Okayama and Hiroshima (when traveling from Osaka or Kyoto) is considered the most beautiful train ride in Japan.

The best place for singles

A worthwhile excursion from Hiroshima is to the island of **Miyajima** to see the Shinto shrine **Itsukushima**, known among the Japanese as one of Japan's three great sights. (The other two are Amanohashidate and Matsushima.) The island is dedicated to a Shinto goddess who, according to legend, is extremely jealous. For this reason, married couples might want to think twice about visiting the shrine. Singles can take the train or bus from Hiroshima to Miyajimaguchi, where a ferry will take them to the island. Offshore stands the red painted *torii*, the gate of the Shinto shrine. The shrine itself and its smaller galleries are on stilts above the water—when the tide is high, both the shrine and the torii appear to be floating on the water. The sight is most spectacular in April, when the cherry blossoms are out, and in the fall, when the maples turn glowing red. These are also the most crowded times.

For an incredible view of Hiroshima surrounded by mountains and the Inland Sea, take the ropeway from Momiji-dani Park behind the Itsukushima shrine to the highest peak on the island, Mount Misen. From this height, you also can see the ninth-century Gumonjido temple.

Hiroshima's best hotels

Hiroshima Kokusai, *3-13 Tate-Machi, Naku-Ku; tel. +81 (82) 248-2323; website: www.kokusai.gr.jp*, and the **Rihga Royal Hiroshima**, *8 Motomachi, Naku-Ku; tel. (81)82-502-1121; website: www.rihga.com/hiroshima,* are good Western-style hotels.

The best *ryokan* is **Mitakiso**, *1-7 Mitaki-ocho, Nishuhi-ku; tel. +81 (82) 237-1402; website: www.japaneseguesthouses.com/db/hiroshima/mitakiso.htm.*

NAGOYA: JAPAN'S BEST PEARLS

Japan's best pearl farms are in **Nagoya**, between Tokyo and Kyoto. You can get from Tokyo to Nagoya Station in just two hours on the super-express trains on the Shinkansen line. The station is the commercial center of the city, with stores and restaurants located in the network of underground passageways that connect to neighboring buildings.

The heart of the pearl industry is just south of Nagoya in **Ago Bay** and five other bays off Iseshima National Park. To learn about the process of pearl cultivation, visit Toba, where pearls are developed, harvested, and prepared for sale. *Ama* (women divers), ranging in age from adolescence to their early 40s and dressed in white cotton bodysuits, face masks, and caps, collect the oysters, making six or seven dives an hour to depths of up to 100 feet. The oysters are then seeded and suspended in cages from bamboo rafts. More than 200 million pearls each year are harvested after about six months, sorted, and polished. *Ama* demonstrate their diving methods at the Toba Aquarium and on Irukajima, also in Toba Bay. Nearby Pearl Island has a model pearl farm that you can visit.

Nagoya's two most important sights are its castle and the Atsuta shrine. **Nagoya Castle** is topped by a famous pair of golden dolphins, and boasts a five-story inner tower.

The **Atsuta shrine** is considered one of the most important Shinto shrines in Japan, housing the Kusanagi-no-Tsurugi (Grass-mowing Sword), one of the nation's Three Sacred Treasures. (The other two are the Sacred Jewels at the Imperial Palace in Tokyo, and the Sacred Mirror of Ise at the Grand Shrines.) Nagoya also claims to have one of the largest zoos in the Orient, in Higashiyama Park.

Nagoya's best Western-style hotels are the **Mercure Cypress Nagoya**, *2-43-6 Nakamura-Ku, Nagoya; tel. +81 (52) 571-0111; website: www.accorhotels. com;* **Westin Nagoya Castle**, *3-19 Hinokuchicho, Nischi-Ku; tel. +81 (52) 521-2121; website: www.starwoodhotels.com/westin/* and **Nagoya Kanko**, *1-9-30 Nishiki, Naka-Ku; tel. +81 (52) 231-7711; website: www.nagoyakankohotel.co.jp.*

Japan's strangest festival

Japan's strangest festival is the **Konomiya Naked Festival**, held every January 13th in Inasawa City, near Nagoya. This festival, first held in A.D. 780 to ward off the plague, is still thought to drive out devils. Each year one man is chosen to act as a divinity that takes on the sins of others and purges them. The divine man appears naked before the crowd of also naked men at the Owari Okunitama shrine and exorcises spectators' demons. The male worshipers surge forward to touch the holy man and transfer their sins to him.

The best fishing and parasols

The most colorful fishing spectacle in Japan takes place in **Gifu**, 30 minutes by train north of Nagoya. From mid-May to mid-October, cormorant is fished at night along the Nagoya River. Boats are hung with fire baskets to attract *ayu*, a kind of river smelt. The fishermen then command large tame birds, tied to long leashes, to dive in and retrieve the fish from the illuminated river.

Gifu is also famous because it contains one of the few remaining *bangasa*, or Japanese parasol factories, where you can watch paper and silk dancing parasols being made and individually painted. If you buy one, the factory will ship it home for you.

KYUSHU: JAPAN'S BEST SEASIDE RESORT

Kyushu, the southernmost of Japan's islands, is a popular summer resort for Japanese vacationers. Because few Western visitors make their way here, it is a good place to sample Japanese culture as well as sandy beaches. Stay in a *ryokan* in one of the remote towns in the area and explore the secluded coves at your leisure.

Kitakyushu, the largest on the island, is a good place to find a hotel and make travel arrangements. The island's nicest drive is from Kitakyushu to Fukuoka, which takes you along the coast and through Genkai-Quasi National Park. En route are oddly shaped rock formations and pine groves that dot the white sand beaches.

At the southernmost tip of the island is **Ibusuki**, a popular seaside resort. The **Hakusuikan Hotel**, *tel. +81 (993) 223-131; website: www.hakusuikan.co.jp*, a Western-style hotel facing north to Mount Sakurajima, is a good place to stay. A good place to eat and also to stay is the **Ibusuki Royal Hotel**, *tel. +81 (993) 232-211*.

Ibusuki's seawall is lined with small *ryokan*. The beaches cover underwater hot springs, and in certain spots attendants will dig holes so you can immerse yourself from toe to chin in warm sand.

The best of Fukuoka's many parks is **Ohori**, a large open parkland surrounding a tidewater lake formed from the moat of an old castle. Bridges link the surrounding park with smaller island parks in the lake. In the background is a forest with remnants of the stone walls of Fukuoka Castle.

NAGASAKI: JAPAN'S FIRST OPEN DOOR

Curving around the mouth of the Urakami River, **Nagasaki** is considered Japan's first open door. This was the first major port of trade with the Portuguese and Dutch in the 16th century. European influences are still visible in the city's old forts, brick buildings, and cobblestone streets.

Nagasaki was also the first place in Japan to accept Christianity. However, in the 16th and 17th centuries, the Christian communities here were forced underground. Monuments to martyred Christians can be found throughout the city. The most impressive is the **Oura Catholic Church**, built in 1865 to commemorate 26 Christians who were crucified here in the 16th century. The church is the oldest example of ecclesiastical Gothic architecture in Japan.

Glover Mansion is the house where Madame Butterfly (from the opera of the same name) waited for her lover's return. Set on a hilltop, the house has a panoramic view over the harbor.

Nagasaki is also known as the second city on which the Americans dropped the atomic bomb. Peace Park and the **Atomic Bomb Museum** are monuments to the horror.

Good Western hotels in Nagasaki are the **Best Western Premier Hotel Nagasaki**, *2-26 Takara-Machi, Nagasaki; tel. +81 (95) 821-1111; website: www. bestwestern.co.jp/nagasaki;* **Hotel New Nagasaki**, *14-5, Daikoku-machi; tel. +81 (95) 826-8000; website: www.newnaga.com,* and **Sakomoto-ya**, *2-13 Kanaya-cho; tel. +81 (95) 850-0037.*

Suwa-so, on a hillside overlooking the city, is a *ryokan* visited by Japan's royal family.

Nagasaki's most threatening volcano

A short ride by bus or ferry from Nagasaki brings you to the active volcano **Mount Aso** in Aso National Park. A toll road leads most of the way up the side of the volcano. You can reach the rim by foot or ropeway, unless vulcanologists have closed the area. Standing at the rim, you will see white smoke and gases spurting from the bottom of the crater and feel the ground rumbling.

HOKKAIDO'S MINORITY

Hokkaido is known as the home of the **Ainu**, a fast-disappearing people originally from Honshu who have been forced north into the mountains. The Ainu are Caucasians, who unlike other Japanese, have light skin and hairy bodies. The men often have thick beards, and the women have blue tattoos around their mouths. The best place to see their huts and their ritual worship is a small colony in **Asahikawa**, Hokkaido's second-largest city. You can also visit a display village in **Shiraoi**, near Noboribetse Spa on the south coast.

KARUIZAWA: THE BEST MOUNTAIN RESORT

Karuizawa, two hours north of Tokyo, is the mountain escape frequented by Japan's powerful elite. They come here to play tennis or golf, to horse ride, and to sail on the lakes. Since the future emperor Akihito met and married the untitled Michiko Shoda at the Karuizawa Kai tennis club in the late 1950s, Karuizawa has been seen by many as a fairy-tale town where anything is possible—even falling in love with a prince.

The countryside is adorned with waterfalls and streams dotted with elegant villas. In the summertime, classical music concerts are staged outdoors. Generally, the hotels in Karuizawa have great restaurants. The Karuizawa Prince complex holds about 13 restaurants, including an informal Japanese grill and an excellent French restaurant where diners eat overlooking a pond while being entertained by a harpist.

The elegant **Karuizawa Prince**, *Karuizawa, Karuizawa-machi, Kitasakugun, Nagano 389-01; tel. +81 (267) 421-112; website: www.princehotels.com/en/ the_prince_karuizawa/*, offers three types of accommodation: the original hotel, log cabins, and a fancy annex overlooking a pond and a golf course.

The warmest welcome
Originating in Akihabara, Tokyo, *cosplay* restaurants and clubs are highly popular in Japanese culture. The waitress and waiters dress up in various costumes such as

a maid or butler and when a guest comes to the cafe, maids say "Welcome home, Master" even if it is the guest's first time there, with the waiters playing the roles of maids belonging to the guest's mansion. Similarly, they say "Have a nice day, Master" when the guest leaves.

Asia's most alluring women

Geishas are highly talented entertainers, well versed in all traditional arts of Japan. They are good conversationalists who serve food and drinks and provide high-caliber singing and dancing. Geisha parties, often organized by Japanese businessmen, feature pretty entertainers dressed in kimonos, elevated clogs, white face makeup, and elaborate hairdos. Generally these parties are for men, but women can be included.

The Asasaka district in Tokyo has a concentration of exclusive houses where geishas perform. Company presidents and others who can afford the high prices frequent these places.

You can see young apprentice geishas, called *maiko*, near Gion Corner and Ponto-cho in Kyoto. The young women appear at 6 p.m., dressed in colorful costumes, and shuffle in tiny steps from their residences to their places of work.

THE BEST OF
MEXICO

Round the centre of the covered market, where there is a basin of water, are the flowers: red, white, pink roses in heaps, many-coloured little carnations, poppies, bits of larkspur, lemon and orange marigolds, buds of madonna lilies, pansies, a few forget-me-nots. They don't bring the tropical flowers. Only the lilies come wild from the hills, and the mauve red orchids.

—D. H. Lawrence, *Mornings in Mexico*

Mexico is the best choice—especially for those from the U.S. or Canada—for an inexpensive vacation in a warm and exotic foreign country. It is also perfect for sun worshipers, hardy adventurers, high rollers, and those on a tight budget. Mexico offers beautiful beaches, unexplored wilderness, cosmopolitan cities, colonial charm, historic monuments, and good food—all for next to nothing.

MEXICO CITY: THE WORLD'S LARGEST LAND-LOCKED CITY

Mexico City is the cultural, political, and commercial hub of the country. Located on a plateau, it is surrounded by mountains. Colonial architecture gives it a Spanish air. The best place to put the city in perspective is from the rooftop bar on the 44th floor of the **Latin American Tower**, *Eje Central Lázaro Cárdenas*.

The best museums

The best place to begin your tour of the city is the **National Museum of Anthropology**, *Chapúltepec Park; tel. +52 (55) 4040-5300; website: www.mna. inah.gob.mx*. It houses most of Mexico's excavated pre-Columbian treasures, including artifacts from the Palenque tombs, Mexico's most spectacular Mayan site. The architecture and figurines at Palenque strangely resemble those at ancient Oriental sites in Cambodia, which is possible evidence of a direct ancestral link. The museum also houses an Aztec calendar stone that divides the year accurately into a 52-week cycle, providing evidence of early Indian civilizations' ability to use astronomy to divide time. On the second floor, a display depicts present-day Indian lifestyles in Mexico. Bilingual guides are available for tours. The museum is open Tuesday through Sunday 9 a.m. until 7 p.m. Tours in English are conducted daily. On Sundays admission is free to citizens and to resident foreigners.

The **Palacio de Bellas Artes**, *Avenida Juárez y Eje Lázaro Cárdenas; tel. +52 (55) 5512-2593, ext. 217,* has a permanent collection of Mexico's world-famous murals, including a duplicate of the Diego Riviera mural commissioned for the Rockefeller Center in New York City. (Because Rivera depicted John D. Rockefeller as a greedy capitalist, the copy in New York is now covered by another less provocative mural.)

If you visit the Bellas Artes Museum on a Sunday or a Wednesday, you can see a performance by **Ballet Folklórico**, a lively folk ballet company. The glass curtain that hangs across the stage was commissioned from Tiffany's. The museum is open 10 a.m. until 6 p.m. daily except Monday. Admission is free on Sundays.

The best of the Hapsburgs in Mexico

In **Chapúltepec Park**, once the royal hunting grounds of the Aztecs, is Chapúltepec Castle, once the imperial residence of the Hapsburgs, whose quarters are now on display. This unlikely bit of Austria-Hungary in the heart of Mexico was engineered by Napoleon III of France, who in 1864 installed the Hapsburg prince Maximilian as governor of Mexico. Needless to say, this ill-thought-out bit of colonialism didn't work. In 1867, this outpost of Napoleon's empire collapsed, Maximilian was killed, and his widow went mad. The castle, which is a museum today, also displays a collection of 19th-century art and costumes. It is open to the public 9 a.m. until 6 p.m. daily except Monday. A small admission fee is charged.

The best handicrafts

Mexico is known for its regional crafts, including leatherwork, furniture, blown glass, ceramics, pottery, textiles, tinwork, and woodcarving. At the **Museo Nacional de Culturas Populares**, *Avenida Hidalgo 289, Col. del Carmen, Coyoacán; tel. +52 (55) 4155-0920*, you can inspect the country's handicrafts and then purchase your favorites at the museum shop. Prices are relatively cheap, and the quality is usually good. The museum is open every day but Monday, 10 a.m. to 6 p.m. Tuesday through Thursday, and 10 a.m. to 8 p.m. Friday through Sunday. Admission is free on Sundays.

The Zócalo: The heart of the city

Many of Mexico City's attractions are on the Zócalo, the main city plaza. The grandest is the **National Palace**, which houses most of Mexico's government offices. It is a beautiful example of colonial architecture, especially dramatic when illuminated during Mexico's many holidays. Inside are Diego Rivera murals depicting this country's history through the Revolution of 1910. The National Palace is a working building and is usually open to the public Monday through Friday from 9 a.m. to 5 p.m., except during Mexican holidays. Admission is free but foreigners may be asked to show a passport (original, not a copy) to gain admittance.

Mexico's grandest cathedral

The **Metropolitana Cathedral**, the largest in the country, is also on the zócalo. Built over a 200-year period beginning in the 16th century, the cathedral incorporates many architectural styles. Its massive sanctuary houses 16 chapels, 27 altars, and a valuable collection of religious artwork from the Spanish colonial period.

The **Altar of the Kings** is a highly ornamental creation built in the wild baroque style known as *churrigueresque*, which was introduced by Spanish architect and artisan José Churriguera. Popular in the late 17th century, this style ignored the restraint employed by Renaissance artists and used elaborate designs and rich materials, such as gold and silver.

The greatest archaeological find

Located just off the Zócalo is the greatest accidental archaeological find of the last century: the **Great Temple of Tenochtitlán**, *tel. +52 (55) 4040-5600*. Unearthed in 1978 by the Mexican Power and Light Company, it was once the holiest temple of the Aztecs. Although many of the artifacts found here are displayed in museums around the country, the site is still impressive, with intricate, artistic wall sculptures. The site is closed Mondays.

The city's best house
The 17th-century **Casa de los Azulejos** (House of Tiles), *Calle Francisco I.Madero 4, Col. Centro; tel. +52 (55) 5512-1331*, which is completely covered in tiles, was built by the son of one of the counts of Orizaba. The young man became wealthy despite his father's prediction that he would never have a house of tiles (A Spanish saying that meant he would never be successful). To spite his father, he bought a house and had it completely covered in tiles. The House of Tiles is now a department store and café belonging to the Sanborns chain and is open daily.

Mexico City's best restaurants
Hostería de Santo Domingo, *Belisarion Domínguez 7; tel. +52 (55) 5526-5276, www.hosteriadesantodomingo.com.mx*, serves traditional Mexican food and wonderful desserts. The best part about this restaurant is that it is located in a perfectly preserved 19th-century building with beautiful decoration.

The **San Angel Inn**, *Diego Rivera 50 y Altavista, Col. San Angel Inn; tel. +52 (55) 5616-1402; website: www.sanangelinn.com*, is the most beautiful restaurant in Mexico, situated in a 250-year-old building that has been completely restored. It has hosted Pancho Villa, Pavlova, Caruso, and Gershwin. Chef Manual Lozano cooks up a good *pompano en papillote*. Men are required to wear jackets.

The **Hacienda de los Morales**, *Vázquez de Mella 52, Col. Del Bosque, Polanco; tel. +52 (55) 5283-3054; website: www.haciendadelosmorales.com*, is an elegant, reasonably priced restaurant specializing in both Continental and Mexican cuisine. Reservations are a must at this beautifully restored 16th-century hacienda.

La Fonda el Refugio, *Liverpool 166, Col. Juárez; tel. +52 (55) 5207-2732;* is decorated with primitive art and locally blown glass. The menu is exceptional. Try the *enchiladas con mole poblano* (thin tortillas fried and stuffed with shredded chicken and covered with *mole*, a rich sauce made with 25 ingredients, including hot peppers, tomatoes, raisins, and chocolate). Finish your meal with *café de olla* (black coffee served with brown sugar, cinnamon, and cloves). Reservations are recommended.

Mesón del Cid, *Humboldt 61, Col. Centro; tel. +52 (55) 5521-6998*, is a three-level dining room that serves open-hearth cooking. Segovia-style baby suckling pig is the house specialty.

The **Del Lago Restaurant**, *Nuevo Bosque de Chapúltepec; tel. +52 (55)*

5515-9586, has a clear view of Chapúltepec Lagoon through its grand windows. Trees and hanging plants give the interior an outdoor look. The seafood is good. Save room for dessert, and order the *mango flambé au tequila*.

The capital's best hotels
Camino Real, *Mariano Escobedo 700; tel. +52 (55) 5263-8888; website: www. caminoreal.com*, is located at the edge of Chapúltepec Park. Its 7 acres include pools, tennis courts, three entertainment bars, a disco, a coffee shop, and two restaurants.

Hotel Four Seasons, *Chapúltepec Park; tel. +52 (55) 5230-1818; website: www.fourseasons.com/mexico*, is one of the best in the country, with very nice rooms. The staff is attentive.

The **Hotel Majestic**, *Francisco I. Madero 73; tel. +52 (55) 5521-8600; website: www.majestichotel.com.mx*, is another good hotel. From its rooftop terrace, the view of the city is panoramic. The Mexican color guard marches by the hotel every day at 6:30 p.m.

Hotel de Cortés, *Ave. Hidalgo 85; tel. +52 (55) 5518-2181; website: www. boutiquehoteldecortes.com*, a restored 18th-century hacienda, is a moderately priced hotel that is clean, comfortable, and efficient. It is also popular, so make reservations well in advance.

The **Maria Cristina**, *Rio Lerma 31; tel. +52 (55) 5703-1212; website: www. hotelmariacristina.com.mx*, is a small hotel with a pretty garden and a piano bar.

The hottest nightlife
El Hijo del Cuervo, *Jardín Centenario #17, Coyoacán; tel. +52 (55) 5658-7824*, has live music, a local crowd, and a young style.

La Guadalupana, *Higuera Street and Caballo Calco, Coyoacán; tel. +52 (55) 5554-6253*, is known for its ambience and has a wide variety of drinks.

The best day-trips
Midway between Mexico City and Tula, the capital of the ancient Toltec Indians, is the **Tepotzotlán Monastery**, a beautiful example of Spanish architecture, encrusted with intricate gold carvings made by local Indians.

Cholula was the site of thousands of human sacrifices. In fact, although it was built long before the Aztec civilization flourished, this gory monument was still in use when the Spanish came. Hearing that they were to be killed here, Hernán Cortés and his entourage killed thousands of Aztecs. The site is open daily.

The pyramids of **Teotihuacán**, built sometime between A.D. 400 and A.D.

800, make up the largest, most complete archaeological site in this hemisphere, covering more than 35 square miles. The Indians who built the pyramids, who pre-dated the Aztecs marked time in 52-year cycles, building a new pyramid on top of the old one every cycle. The site includes hundreds of small temples, two large ones (the Pyramid of the Sun and the Pyramid of the Moon), and a large enclosed arena that was probably used for religious spectacles or ceremonial ball games. The site is open daily 7 a.m. to 6 p.m.; admission is free on Sundays.

SAN MIGUEL DE ALLENDE: THE BEST ARTISANS' TOWN

Situated in a small valley surrounded by hills, **San Miguel de Allende** has retained its colonial charm while blossoming into a center for the arts. Burros line the streets, and flowers fill every corner. Homes are hidden behind tall, bougainvillea-draped stucco walls. And art galleries, cafés, and restaurants serve the thriving expatriate community.

Located on the high central plateau about 250 miles northwest of Mexico City, San Miguel is in the agriculturally rich Bajio region on the colonial route. The entire town is a historic national monument; all architecture conforms to the colonial style.

La Parroquia, the imposing pink cathedral on the main Zócalo, is a 19th-century Indian mason's interpretation of a French Gothic cathedral. The bells chime every 15 minutes.

Instituto Allende: Largest Latin American fine arts school

San Miguel earned its reputation as an international arts center in 1938, with the opening of the first English-speaking school, the **Instituto Allende**, *Ancha de San Antonio 22; website: www.instituto-allende.edu.mx*. The institute is now the largest Latin American fine arts school for English-speaking students.

Buying handicrafts and antiques

This is one of the best places in Mexico to buy handicrafts. Most shops are within three blocks of the main square. It's a good idea to visit several shops before buying—quality varies. Although you can do some bargaining, most of the prices are set.

Casa Maxwell, *Canal 14*, is one of the best handicraft shops in San Miguel. It's also quite expensive. Don't miss the **Mercado de San Juan de Dios**. And for exquisite leather goods, check out **John Adam Leather**, *Hidalgo #4*.

San Miguel is also a good place to buy antiques. Although no pre- Columbian antiques may be sold legally in Mexico, you can buy Spanish antiques from the colonial period. Try the antique shops that line the main square but be careful, because many items offered are merely convincing reproductions.

The world's best facelift

It is possible to get a 10-day cosmetic surgery vacation package to San Miguel de Allende, with the surgery performed at a private hospital just outside town. The hospital has 20 specialists on staff and surgery is performed in a state-of-the-art operating room, with an M.D. anesthesiologist attending. You are in a private hospital room for three days following surgery, not an outpatient, as is the case in the U.S. The trip is fully escorted, including round-trip transfers by private car from León airport. The price of $6,500 for a complete facelift is one-third the price in the States. And the quality is superior. The cost of the 10-day holiday is an additional $1,800. For more information, visit *www.faceliftmexico.com*.

The best restaurants

There are many great restaurants in San Miguel de Allende. Our favorites include:

Tio Lucas, *Mesones 103; tel. +52 (415) 152-4996.* This is the place for grilled steaks and chicken. Max, the friendly owner will greet you and make you feel welcome. With the majority of the tables set around an open courtyard, the restaurant is inviting and the atmosphere is lively. A hanging tree is the courtyard's centerpiece, which is decorated with hanging red lamps that gives Tio Lucas a magical feel at night. Nights also find great live entertainment.

Romano's, *Hernández Macías 93; tel. +52 (415) 152-7454.* This beautiful old house offers indoor and outdoor settings that are charming and comfortable. The food is delicious and includes pizza baked in a wood-burning oven, old-style lasagna, and daily specials. The ingredients are fresh and often organic, and pastas are home-made.

La Capilla, *Cuna de Allende #10; tel. +52 (415) 152-0698.* The most elegant restaurant in town. Absolutely stunning upstairs terrace that looks up at La Parroquia. The inside dining room is a very romantic setting. You need reservations. This is a definitely the spot for your special occasion.

The restaurant at the boutique hotel **Casa de Sierra Nevada**, *Hospicio 42; tel. +52 (415) 152-7040*, is also very elegant.

La Posada Carmina, *Cuna de Allende 7; tel. +52 (415) 152-8888*, set in a cool, inviting courtyard filled with flowers, is also good. On Thursdays, try the specialty, a cheese and vegetable salad, or the *paella valenciana*. You don't need to make reservations.

The sweetest dreams—accommodation

Las Terrazas San Miguel, *Calle Santo Domingo; website: www.terrazassanmiguel. com*, is our pick as one of the best places to stay in a private apartment or casita in San Miguel. Las Terrazas is a group of four separate residences on hillside terraces with fabulous views, eclectic furnishings, and the most modern amenities.

Right on the main square, **La Posada San Francisco**, *Plaza Principal 2; website: www.posadadesanfrancisco.com*, is within walking distance of just about everything in San Miguel.

Casa de Sierra Nevada, *Hospicio 35; www.casadesierranevada.com*, is an old Spanish villa. The hotel has an excellent restaurant.

Nirvana Restaurant and Retreat, *website: www.hotelnirvana.mx,* is in Atotonilco, about 15 minutes outside San Miguel toward Dolores Hidalgo. It offers a spa, yoga, meditation, and a fusion-style restaurant.

The spiciest nights

Cantinas, nightclubs, and cocktail lounges in San Miguel stay open until 1 a.m., and many will stay open later at the request of guests. **El Ring**, *Calle de Hidalgo 25; tel. +52 (415) 152-1998*, is a popular disco.

Mama Mia, *Umaron 8; tel. +52 (415) 152-3679*, has live music, from Andean folk to jazz, Wednesday through Monday on its patio.

La Cava de la Princesa, *Recreo 5; tel. +52 (415) 152-1403*, is a quiet place where you can listen to music while enjoying an early evening drink.

The steamiest side trips

Just a few miles from San Miguel, in **Taboada**, you can soak in steaming hot springs while a waiter serves you drinks. And at **La Gruta** you can swim in an Olympic-sized heated pool or take a steam bath in a cave of hot mineral water.

The best place to hear the flutter of butterfly wings

A three-hour drive from San Miguel de Allende is the colorful old mining town of **Angangueo**. And only an hour from Angangueo, up a steep, unpaved road, is the **Monarch Butterfly Sanctuary**. The park's 12,000 acres, which includes the butterflies' habitat and migration site, became a protected area in 1986. For information about organized tours to the sanctuary, contact **Rocamar Tours**, *tel. +1*

(866) 762-2627 (toll free in the U.S.) or +1 (613) 821-2147 (in the U.S.); website: www.rocamar.com.mx.

A find...the best personal tour guide and driver

If you'd like a personal tour guide and/or driver, no one is better than **Daniel Hernández**. Contact him at: *danielhr1@yahoo.com or by cellphone at +521 (415) 105-1907.*

TAXCO: THE SILVER CAPITAL

Taxco is a mining town in the mountains. About a day's drive outside of Mexico City and off the main tourist route, it is less crowded than Guanajuato or Cuernavaca. It is also *the* place to buy silver jewelry. William Spratling introduced silversmithing to Taxco in 1929. Now the town has more than 300 fine jewelry shops. And the mines show no signs of cutting off the supply of metal.

Original Spratling pieces are difficult to come by, but most of the jewelry sold throughout Taxco is styled upon his original models. All silver products, from jewelry to candelabras, cost about 25% less than American counterparts and about 50% less than European pieces.

The best jewelry shops are **Los Castillos**, *Plazeula Bernal 10*, and **La Mina**, *Avenida J.F. Kennedy*, on the site of an old silver mine.

The most colorful times to visit Taxco are during Holy Week and the National Silver Fair, at the beginning of December. Make reservations far in advance.

Taxco's best tables

La Ventana de Taxco, *Hotel Hacienda del Solar; tel. +52 (762) 622-0587 or +52 (762) 622-0323*, in a pink stone house on a hill just south of town, serves delicious Italian food for reasonable prices. Tables look out at the red-roofed houses of Taxco and the mountains beyond. The view is loveliest at sunset.

La Pagaduría del Rey, *tel. +52 (762) 622-3467*, serves steaks, seafood, and Mexican food. The menu is limited, and the restaurant opens whenever the staff feels like it, but the food is good.

The best hotels

Rancho Taxco-Victoria, *tel. +52 (762) 622-0004*, is a lovely hotel with large rooms, a pleasant restaurant, a bar, a swimming pool, and beautiful gardens.

Hotel de la Borda, *website: www.hotelborda.com*, is cozy with a pool, restaurant overlooking the city, and large bathrooms.

Hotel Montetaxco, *tel. +52 (762) 622-1300; website: www.montetaxcohotel. com*, a mountainside hotel on the north side of town, has 160 rooms and 50 villas and suites. It offers color television, air conditioning, a pool, spa facilities, a golf course, a tennis court, horseback riding, and a restaurant with nightly entertainment.

And try **Hotel Los Arcos**, *Juan Ruiz de Alarcón; tel. +52 (762) 622-1836.*

CUERNAVACA: WHERE SPRING SPRINGS ETERNAL

Cuernavaca is the city of eternal spring, with temperatures that hover around 75° F year-round, and lush vegetation. The Mexicans were not the first to recognize this city as an ideal resort. The Aztecs also used Cuernavaca (or Cuauhnáhuac, as the city was originally called) as a retreat.

Cortés recognized its appeal as well. He built **El Palacio de Cortés**, his personal residence, here. This massive fortress is now home to the **Cuauhnáhuac Historical Museum**, which houses murals by Rivera, Siqueiros, and Orozco.

See the cathedral that Cortés founded in 1529, the summer palace of the Hapsburgs, and the beautiful Borda Gardens, where a botanical festival is held each year in April.

Cuernavaca has become expensive by Mexican standards, in part because of the year-round expatriate community. Prices are substantially higher than in Taxco or San Miguel de Allende, and the area is more touristy than other cities.

The best hotels

The most luxurious place to stay in Cuernavaca is the **Mision Del Sol Resort and Spa**, *tel. +52 (777) 321-0999; website: www.misiondelsol.com*. Amenities include tennis courts, spa facilities, pools, lounges, two restaurants, and weekend concerts.

Las Mañanitas, *tel. +52 (777) 362-0000; website: www.lasmananitas.com. mx*, is another luxurious hotel with all of the amenities.

OAXACA: THE BEST INDIAN RUINS

Oaxaca, the most indigenous region of Mexico along with Chiapas, is the best place to explore present-day Indian culture as well as ancient Indian ruins. The colonial city of Oaxaca is a good base. Plan to stay at least a few days—there is a lot to see.

The age-old tradition of weaving lives on in the village of **Teotitlán del Valle**. You can watch weavers at work and then buy decorated carpets and serapes.

About eight miles outside Teotitlán del Valle is the **Yagul** site, dating from about A.D. 700. Earlier this century, precious Zapotec artifacts were taken from this series of multiple tombs. The site includes a hill fortress, a group of palaces and temples, and a ball court.

Mitla, the City of the Dead, is 26 miles outside Oaxaca. Built by the Zapotecs, Mitla was later enlarged by the Mixtecs. Although this is a touristy spot (Indian women mill around trying to sell souvenirs), it is also impressive, with intricate mosaics and strange stone carvings on the walls.

In the opposite direction from Oaxaca is another impressive archaeological site: **Monte Albán**. This massive group of Zapotec ruins covers 15 square miles. The Temple of Dancers and the ceremonial ball court are the two most impressive sites. However, you can spend hours wandering among literally hundreds of ceremonial altars, winding staircases, and stone carvings. The site is open daily from 8 a.m. until 6 p.m.

To see what was found in the tombs of Mitla and the ruins of Monte Albán, visit the **Regional Museum in Oaxaca**, *Calle M. Alcalá; tel. +52 (951) 516-2991*, where most of the treasures are kept. Keep in mind that, when exploring the region of Oaxaca, you should use your camera respectfully; not everyone likes to have their pictures taken.

Oaxaca's best buys

The region of Oaxaca is a good place to shop. Prices for textiles, jewelry, and handicrafts are much lower than those in Cuernavaca and Mexico City. Visit the village of **Tlacolula** on a Sunday, when a huge market is set up by Indian vendors and artisans selling clothing, pottery, rugs, wall hangings, and gold jewelry styled upon the original Zapotec and Mixtec patterns. Visit the village of **Atzompa** on a Tuesday for superb green-glazed ceramics. The village of **Ejutla** is famous for its intricately carved knives, **San Bartolo Coyotepec** for its black pottery, and **Ocotlán** for its straw baskets.

If you prefer to shop in stores rather than open markets, visit **Aripo**, *Garcia Vigil 809*.

Oaxaca's best food and lodging

El Asador Vasco, *Portal de Flores No. 10-A; tel. +52 (951) 514-4755; website: www.asadorvasco.com*, overlooking the Zócalo, is the best restaurant in town. Chef Juan Hernández takes cuisine seriously, and his restaurant is worth a special trip. Both Spanish and Mexican dishes are served. Try the house specialty, *cazuelas*, small casseroles of baked cheese, mushrooms, shrimp, or other dishes. The restaurant is closed Sundays.

No matter where you eat, your meal will probably include chocolate. Oaxaca is known for it. Try the famous *mole* sauce (a mixture of chocolate, cinnamon, chili peppers, and other ingredients), which is served on meat and poultry.

There are many luxury hotels in Oaxaca, including the **Hotel Camino Real**, *Calle 5 de Mayo 300; tel. +52 (951) 501-6100; website: www.caminoreal.com/oaxaca*. The hotel is located in the heart of Oaxaca's historic center, in a 16th-century colonial building. Faded frescos have been rescued along the corridors and most rooms look out on colonnaded cloisters and five flower-filled patios.

Atop a hill overlooking town, the **Victoria**, *tel. +52 (951) 502-0850; website: www.hotelvictoriaoax.com.mx,* is one of the best, with a heated pool, tennis courts, a disco, and large breakfasts.

GUADALAJARA: MEXICO AT ITS BEST

Guadalajara is the home of the Mexican hat dance, mariachi bands, tequila, Mexican horsemen, and rodeos. It is also a bustling, sophisticated city with a large U.S. community, attracted by the easy lifestyle and pleasant climate.

This is a good place to admire Spanish colonial architecture. Many of the buildings in the **Plaza Tapatía** have been restored to their former glory. Hospicio Cabañas, built in 1801 as an orphanage, has been renovated and converted into the Cabañas Institute, a center for the arts. Its chapel contains Orozco's famous mural, *Four Horsemen of the Apocalypse.*

Other colonial buildings of interest include the cathedral at the center of the city, the Jalisco Supreme Court, the Government Palace, and the Legislative Hall. Guadalajara is a city of parks. The largest, **Parque Agua Azul**, *González Gallo and Avenida Independencia,* has an open-air theater, a bird sanctuary, and special sections designed for children and the blind. The park also houses the House of Handicrafts, which contains superb examples of colonial furniture, ceramics, blown glass, tinwork, and textiles produced in the state of Jalisco. Most of the products are for sale at reasonable, fixed prices.

Mexico's largest open-air market

The huge **Libertad Market**, *Calzada Independencia*, is the largest open-air market in Mexico. After shopping, retire to the **Plaza de los Mariachis**, across the street, and listen to the strolling musicians while sipping a cool drink.

The best place to eat

If you find yourself hungry in Guadalajara, look for the green building on the corner at 5645 Pedro Simon Laplace. The green is for good luck—and, in this case, good food and good value. **La Gorda**, *5645 Pedro Simón Laplace 5645*, is one of four restaurants whose owner—affectionately known as *"La Gorda,"* or "The Fat One"—has spent over 50 years preserving the traditional culinary arts of Jalisco, the state where Guadalajara is located. Over the years, the *papel picado* (cut paper banners) hanging out front has welcomed a varied and even illustrious clientele, including former Mexican president Vicente Fox, who poses with the owner in a proudly displayed photo.

Through hard work, perseverance, and lots of good food, the original La Gorda kitchen has grown from a street stand to four restaurants, including Las Arboledas, where you're greeted by the appetizing aroma of food bubbling in pots in the open kitchen. All the cooks line up behind the counter wearing white headscarves and aprons, ready to serve specialties such as *pozole* (hominy and pork soup), *mole* (a popular Mexican sauce of chili peppers, nuts, spices, and chocolate), and *pepián* (chicken in spicy green sauce). These cooks are an institution at the La Gorda restaurants, and they preserve the consistent deliciousness of the food.

Try the **horchata** (cold rice milk) served in clay pitchers, *tacos dorados* (tacos with a variety of fillings), and meat enchiladas. The *mole poblano* (a chicken dish made with *mole* sauce) is the best you'll ever eat. The *sopes fritos de pollo*— thick little tortilla pies filled with chicken, is a favorite with the kids.

The best day-trips

Tlaquepaque, a suburb of Guadalajara, has a wide selection of artisan shops selling textiles, blown glass, and brass. Have lunch at the **Restaurante Sin Nombre**, *tel. +52 (33) 3635-4520*, which serves a creative mixture of Provençal and Mexican food. Dress is casual and daily entertainment includes a vocal trio, singing waiters, and mariachis.

XALAPA: THE FLOWER GARDEN OF MEXICO

Xalapa, the capital of Veracruz, is known as the flower garden of Mexico because of its many parks. This small and friendly colonial city is seldom visited by tourists of any kind. The city is 4,700 feet above sea level, and all the streets run at steep angles. Walking is thoroughly exhausting, so hire a taxi to take you sightseeing. Taxis are plentiful, and the rates are regulated.

Begin your tour in the main square. Visit the **Palacio de Gobierno** (Government House), which houses the famous *Liberation* mural by Diego Rivera, depicting man's struggle through life, and the massive colonial cathedral, built in 1773.

El Mercado Jauregui, one of the four local markets, has booths selling food, furniture, clothes, and flowers.

After the crush of the market, visit the small **Barrio Xalitic**, said to predate Christopher Columbus. Women scrub their clothes in the public water trough, and children play in a small park among tapped springs and small Christian shrines.

At centrally located **Parque Juárez**, vendors sell balloons, flowers, and food, and boys offer to shine your shoes. Steer clear of the food sold by vendors; it looks good but is known to cause Montezuma's revenge. Try some of Jalapa's famous coffee at the café in the park, shaded by red-and-white striped umbrellas. The café serves an excellent *lechero*—hot milk poured into rich coffee extract and sweetened.

Mexico's best symphony

Xalapa boasts the best symphony orchestra in Mexico. You can listen to both classical music and contemporary creations in the modern **State Theater**, *tel. +52 (228) 817-3110*. During intermission, members of the audience are allowed backstage to meet the orchestra.

The best hotels

The **Maria Victoria**, *Zaragoza 6; tel. +52 (228) 818-6011; website: www. hotelmariavictoriaxalapa.com*, is the best hotel in Xalapa. It has a good restaurant and a bar.

The **Crowne Plaza Xalapa**, *tel. +52 (228) 842-3400; website: www. ichotelsgroup.com*, is also a good place to stay in the center of town.

CHIHUAHUA: HOME OF THE BEST BANDITO

Chihuahua was home to Pancho Villa (José Doroteo Arango Arámbula), the Mexican Robin Hood. The house where the beloved bandito lived is a museum of the revolutionary era as well as of Villa's life. (In 1910, Villa joined rebels and fought for President Madero and against General Huerta and President Carranza. He and his men killed U.S. citizens in Columbus, New Mexico, in 1916 and were pursued unsuccessfully by the U.S. Army for 11 months.) Villa's house was inhabited until the late 1980s by his aging widow. The featured artifact on display is the bullet-riddled Dodge in which Villa was assassinated in 1923.

Chihuahua's best sites

Also in Chihuahua is the **Museo de Arte Popular**, which has an exhibit on the Tarahumara culture, with woven blankets, full-sleeved blouses, whirling skirts, carved wooden masks decorated with goat hair, and palm baskets. Adjacent to the museum is a gift shop, where you can buy copies of these items as well as books on the indigenous cultures of Mexico and Mexican history.

El Palacio del Gobierno (Government Palace) is noteworthy for its gorgeous murals by Piña Mora, depicting the history of Mexico, including the arrival of the first priests, the Spanish Conquest, and the Mexican Civil War and its heroes.

The **Museo Regional** is housed in a beautiful art deco mansion with well-preserved stained-glass windows and elaborately carved mantels. Parts of the mansion have exhibits of Mormon and Mennonite settlements in Chihuahua.

You can see a replica of an adobe house from the ancient Paquimé Indian culture in the northern part of Chihuahua, at **Casas Grandes**.

The world's grandest canyon—and most exciting train ride

Chihuahua's Barranca del Cobre (Copper Canyon) is four times larger and 300 feet deeper than the U.S. Grand Canyon. Its mountain peaks rise 10,000 feet, and its valleys drop 1,500 feet. Until 1961, when the Chihuahua al Pacífico train line opened, the canyon was inaccessible and known only to isolated Tarahumara Indians living in caves. The train line climbs from sea level at Los Mochis on the Pacific to 8,000 feet before descending to Chihuahua. It passes the most spectacular scenery in Mexico—sheer cliffs that change color as the sun sets, giant rock formations, deep gorges, and mountain peaks. You can catch the train every day in Chihuahua at 7 a.m. or in Los Mochis at 6 a.m.

The best place to stay in the canyon is the **Posada Barrancas Mirador** in

Divisadero, *Est. Posada, MX 33421 TRN STN Km 622, Copper Canyon; tel. +52 (668) 812-1613; website: http://hotelesbalderrama.com/mirador.htm.* The hotel perches on one of the highest points in the area, with spectacular views. The hotel has wheelchair-accessible rooms and regular van service to the train station.

QUERETARO: MEXICO'S (ARGUABLY) MOST BEAUTIFUL CITY

Querétaro's colonial core is crisscrossed with pedestrian walkways, which lead you past lavishly restored homes and shops. Second floors are adorned with iron balconies…from which great bunches of flowers tumble downward—pinks, fuchsias, purples, lavenders, and all seven shades of bougainvillea. European plazas, with manicured gardens and sidewalk cafés, punctuate the downtown.

The best opals in Mexico

Querétaro is famous for its opals—still mined there today—fire opals in particular, in reds and yellows. You can buy them, both set in jewelry and loose, at shops throughout the downtown. However, beware of street vendors hawking low-quality stones that are likely to crumble.

Querétaro's best hotel

La Casa de la Marquesa, *tel. +52 (442) 227-0500; website: www. LaCasaDeLaMarquesa.com,* is a 300-year-old hotel, which was once a dilapidated mansion and is absolutely resplendent today. From the rooms that are furnished with antiques, Persian rugs, and original paintings to the fabulous two restaurants that are housed in the hotel, La Casa de la Marquesa is a grand place to stay. Promotional Internet rates for suites range from $118 to $229. There is also a new extension, La Casa Azul, with similar rates.

The second-best hotel

The **Hotel Mesón de Santa Rosa**, *tel. +52 (442) 224-2623; website: www. hotelmesonsantarosa.com,* another beautifully restored home on the tree-lined Plaza de Armas, has 21 guest rooms and some suites, as well as a heated swimming pool. Its lobby-courtyard, once used to house horse-drawn carriages, still contains a long water trough. The rooms here, with their extravagantly high-beamed ceilings and antique furnishings, are comfortable and inviting.

San Cristóbal de las Casas is a gorgeous colonial city located 6,500 feet high in the mountains of the southern state of Chiapas. Besides market days, the best times to visit San Cristóbal and its mountain villages are during religious festivals. Masked dancers perform to traditional music played on harps, flutes, and drums; farces are acted out mocking the forces of evil; and horse races and fireworks are staged. (Keep in mind that hotel prices are increased during these festival times. And you must make reservations at least a couple of weeks in advance.)

Major festivals are staged during Carnival and Holy Week. In addition, the following holidays are observed: **Martes (Tuesday) of Carnival**, when Chamula (a neighboring village to San Cristóbal de las Casas) enacts a purification ritual, with dancers leaping over open fires; **July 22nd to July 24th**, when Chamula celebrates the festival of its patron saint, San Juan, in ceremonies that are both Catholic and Mayan; **July 24th to July 25th**, when San Cristóbal honors its patron saint with a torchlight parade; and **December 30th to January 1st**, when ceremonies are held to mark the changing of village officials.

The best place to stay in San Cristóbal de las Casas is the **Posada Diego de Mazariegos**, *Calle Ma. Adelina Flores 2; tel. +52 (967) 678-0833; website: www. diegodemazariegos.com.* All the rooms have fireplaces, and the hotel is located just off the main plaza.

The Pacific at its best

Acapulco and Puerto Vallarta are busy resort towns, much changed from the sleepy fishing villages they once were. However, you still can experience the peaceful ways of the Pacific in **San Blas**, 40 minutes south of Mazatlán, off Highway 15.

This is a land of endless summer, with rainforests, orchids, and warm waves. Life is lazy, and no one worries about the time. The cafés serve giant shrimp and fresh fish roasted over coals. For a few cents, you can take a bus from San Blas to **Matanchin Bay**, the most beautiful beach on the Pacific, where the waves are giant and clear and carry surfers miles before breaking. When you tire of the beach, take a jungle boat for a few dollars into the marshy forest. You will see iguanas, blue herons, and parrots. The boat stops at a little cantina overlooking a deep pool. Have a beer and a swim.

The best whale watching

In October, hundreds of gray whales migrate from the Bering Straits to the warm lagoons of the **Baja Peninsula** to mate and have babies. The best place to see them is **San Ignacio Lagoon,** halfway down the peninsula on the Pacific Coast. The whales are so friendly that they'll probably come right up to you.

The bright green lagoon is mirror-like, ringed with sandy hills and rocks. The hazy Santa Clara Mountains stand in the background. Because whale-watching has become so popular here, it is carefully regulated by the Mexican government. San Ignacio, Ojo de Liebre, and Guerrero Negro are official sanctuaries. Boats must have permits to enter, and only two are permitted in at a time.

Baja Discovery, *tel. +1 (800) 829-2252 (in the U.S.); website: www. bajadiscovery.com,* arranges camping and whale-watching expeditions in San Ignacio. Five-day trips include airfare from Tijuana to San Ignacio, all ground transportation, four nights' camping accommodation, and meals.

THE BEST OF THE MEXICAN CARIBBEAN

Until the early 1970s, Mexico's idyllic Caribbean coast was undeveloped, inhabited only by Mayan Indians. Then the Mexican government realized the area's potential as a resort and began developing the Yucatán Peninsula. The empty island of Kankune became **Cancún**—the trendiest resort town in Mexico. Its neighbors, **Cozumel, Isla Mujeres,** and **Playa del Carmen** also have benefited from the exposure, sprouting luxury hotels and restaurants and attracting tourists in larger numbers each year.

Considering their warm, tropical climate, white-sand beaches, and clear waters, it's amazing that these spots took so long to attract notice. The weather is mostly sunny from October through April, and, even during the rainy season (July through September), showers are often only brief afternoon events. If you tire of the sand and surf, you can visit the nearby Mayan ruins at **Tulúm, Cobá,** and **Chichén Itzá**.

While Cancún and Cozumel are developed resort towns, with superb restaurants, luxurious hotels, excellent beaches, and facilities for water sports, Isla Mujeres is less sophisticated—still a place for Mexican families on holiday. Isla Mujeres has a Mayan temple and excellent scuba diving.

The best of the mysterious Mayans

Remnants of the great civilization of the Mayans can be explored near Cancún. Descendants of the Mayan can be seen on the streets of the city and in surrounding villages—friendly, small, dark-eyed people with round faces. Many live as they have for centuries in one-room, palm-thatched huts furnished with hammocks and a table. However, no traces remain of the ancient Mayan priests and mathematicians, who designed and built the great monuments and developed a calendar more accurate than the Gregorian.

Chichén Itzá is worth the three-hour drive from Cancún. The most famous and complete of the ancient ceremonial sites, the 1,000-year-old temple complex includes burial grounds, sacrificial altars, and royal ball courts. Plan to get here early in the day, and wear low-heeled shoes and sunscreen.

The most impressive monument at Chichén Itzá is the **Temple of Kukulcán**, which is a perfect calendar as well as an engineering feat. The 91 steps to the top of each of the pyramid's four faces, plus the one step to the temple at the top, add up to 365, the number of days in a year. Fifty-two panels decorate the sides of the pyramid, one for each year of the Mayan century. The 18 terraces equal the 18 months of the Mayan year. During the spring and fall equinoxes, the sun creates a shadow on one face of the wall that resembles a serpent, the sign of the god Kukulcán.

Another impressive sight at Chichén Itzá is the ceremonial ball court, used by the Mayans to play a game that was a cross between soccer and basketball. The goal was to get the ball through one of two hoops placed 25 feet high on opposing walls. The winning captain was beheaded as a sacrifice to the gods. However, before he was dropped down the 390-foot sacrificial well (which you can still see), the sacrifice was given hallucinogenic drugs and wine. And he was consoled by the fact that he was guaranteed a place in heaven.

To get to Chichén Itzá from Cancún, you can rent a car and drive yourself (but be careful of villagers and their animals, who cross the country roads with abandon). Or you can hire a taxi and a guide to take you there. Another alternative is to join a bus tour at your hotel. Beer and Coke are sold on the bus for a pittance.

The walled city of **Tulúm** is on a cliff overlooking the sea. The piles of ancient rock are brightened by flowering trees. Parts date back to A.D. 500. Climb the steep, narrow steps to the top of the main pyramid, the **Temple of the Descending God**. Below, white-sand beaches stretch in either direction. Human sacrifices were once pushed over this cliff. Note the carving of the upside-down god. Some say it is the god of rain; others claim that it is a being from outer space descending to earth.

You can arrange a bus from Cancún to Tulúm and Xel-Ha. Tours to Tulúm and Chichén Itzá can be arranged from Cozumel. The largely uncharted city of **Cobá**, about 30 miles west of Tulúm, boasts the tallest pyramid in the Yucatan—at 1,150 feet, it is twice the height of El Castillo at Chichén Itzá. Once it has been completely studied, Cobá may prove the most important Mayan city of all. It once had as many as 40,000 inhabitants, and more than 7,000 stone structures have survived. Carvings of the Descending God can be seen on the temple that tops the pyramid. From the summit you can see Cobá's five lakes, surrounded by jungle.

Uxmal is the best preserved of the Mayan cities on the Yucatán Peninsula. It's also one of the prettiest, with reservoirs rather than wells. Built and abandoned three times between A.D. 325 and A.D. 900, it boasts richly carved temples. One of the most intriguing buildings here was named the **Nunnery** by conquistadors, who knew little about the Mayans. Some scholars believe the name is almost correct, because the building housed priestesses, who would be sacrificed to the god Chac. Others say it was just an administrative center.

Note: Uxmal is located between Mérida and Campeche and is several hours (not a day trip) from the Caribbean side of the peninsula.

THE BEST PLACE IN MEXICO TO EXPLORE THE LAND OF THE MAYA

Mérida is a charming colonial city in the heart of the land of the Maya. A town of nearly one million people, Mérida is the capital of the state of Yucatán…about three hours by car west of Cancún. (Conveniently, there is an international airport at Mérida, so it is easy to get here.)

Mérida's shady main plaza is in the heart of the city's central historic district, but there are many other plazas in Merida where you can while away the hours. Many of these offer free live music or other entertainment in the evenings—this is a cultural city, to say the least. Or maybe you'd prefer to spend your time sitting at a sidewalk café…there are many wonderful restaurants to choose from, and Yucatecan cuisine is a completely unique type of Mexican fare. And Mérida is only a 30-minute drive from Mexico's mostly deserted (and beautiful) Gulf Coast beaches.

Mérida's best restaurants

The best seafood restaurant in Mérida is **La Pigua,** *Av. Cupules at Calle 62; tel. +52 (999) 920-1126 or +52 (999) 920-3605, website: www.lapiguamerida.com.* Just blocks away from the main hotels in Mérida, this is a renowned establishment in Campeche that now has a branch in the Yucatecan capital. It serves excellent seafood dishes made with fresh ingredients, free of preservatives and served in mouthwatering presentations. Reservations recommended.

Restaurante La Tradición, *Calle 60; website: www.latradicionmerida.com*, is a favorite pick for traditional Yucatecan food. Many of the hearty (and oh so delicious) entrees made by chef David Cetina cost less than $12. Recommendations include the *papadzules* (hardboiled eggs wrapped in warm tortillas and topped with a pumpkin seed sauce), *cochinita pibil* (deliciously melt-in-your-mouth marinated pork) and the *lomitas de Valladolid* (chunks of tender beef in a rich tomato/garlic broth). There is also a full bar here and mouthwatering desserts. Be sure to try the cool, creamy flan or the *crema española*.

La Casa de Frida, *Calle 61 near 66,* serves good Mexican and Yucatecan dishes at reasonable prices. Try the *chiles en nogada*.

Restaurante Amaro, *Calle 59 between 60 and 62,* just north of the Plaza Mayor. Moderately priced Yucatecan and vegetarian dishes. They have live *trova* music every night starting at about 9 p.m. This colonial mansion also happens to be the birthplace of Andrés Quintana Roo.

Pancho's, *Calle 59 between 60 and 62.* This is the best "theme" restaurant near the *zócalo*. It uses icons of the Mexican Revolution to achieve an ambience like no other. The waiters wear *sombreros* and *bandoleros* stuffed with wine corks instead of bullets. They have a great bar, and their large patio is a lovely place to enjoy the menu.

Villa María, *Calle 68 at 59.* The relaxed but elegant atmosphere, with impeccable service, soft lighting, and white tablecloths, makes this restaurant a great place to spoil yourself without breaking the bank. The Villa María restaurant has both indoor and outdoor seating in a renovated colonial building with tall ceilings, marble floors, and a courtyard open to the sky. The menu features steaks, chicken, pasta, salads, and specials, including soups and entrees, as well as a good choice of desserts and a full bar.

Merida's best lunch spot

Los Platos Rotos (or The Broken Plates) is a little spot with about 10 umbrella-topped tables that spill out onto the sidewalk. It's tucked down a side street around the corner from the CFE (electric utility) and Japay (water department) offices on *Avenida Colón* in Mérida's Garcia Gineres neighborhood. This is *chilango*-style Mexican food. A *chilango* is someone from Mexico City…and that's where the husband and wife who own Los Platos Rotos are from. Every day they offer about six different options of what's called *corrida del dia* (the meal of the day). The price for this is usually around $5. There is always a vegetarian option or two on the menu and other options are usually some type of chicken, pork, or beef in a flavorful sauce. As a starter you get fresh crispy corn chips and a big plate of black bean dip. Then comes your choice of rice or soup.

Best hotel in Izamal

Izamal is one of Mexico's *Pueblos Mágicos* (Magic Towns), a town of historical or religious value. At Izamal, the Maya built the tallest pyramid in the Yucatán, a site rivaled only by Chichén Itzá, 40 miles east. During the Conquest, the Spanish built a city atop the existing Maya settlement and put a small Christian temple atop the great pyramid. They also built a large Franciscan monastery with an atrium second in size only to that at the Vatican.

Izamal today is known as the "Yellow City" because its colonial buildings—the convent, market, municipal building, shops, and homes—are painted a bright egg-yolk yellow. It's a tidy town, with cobblestone streets lined with iron lampposts. *Calesas* (horse-drawn carriages) clip-clop about, carrying visitors on a tour or townspeople about their errands.

The best place to stay in town is **Hotel Macan Ché**, *tel. +52 (988) 954-02-87; website: www.macanche.com*. It's owned by expats Alfred Rordame and Emily Navar. Tropical plants of every size, shape, and color surround you, from orange birds of paradise to bright red gingers, purple ivy, and the tallest, greenest bamboo you've ever seen, rustling magically in the wind. The hummingbirds are buzzing, the parrots are cackling, and sprightly songbirds warble happily. You can smell the garden's loamy richness. Unless, of course, Alfred is in the kitchen cooking… meals at Macan Ché are as extraordinary as the setting.

Mexico's most beautiful Caribbean beaches

Beaches at Tulúm in the Riviera Maya south of Cancún are among the world's most beautiful…bar none. Resorts along this stretch of coastline are small boutique offerings and eco-oriented. They generate their own electricity and are gentle on the earth. One of our favorites is **Posada Margherita**, *Km 4.5 on the Tulúm-Boca Paila beach road; tel. +52 (984) 801-8493; website: www.posadamargherita.com*. The rooms are clean and comfortable, but what's really extraordinary about this place is the food. The restaurant is run by genial Italians who make homemade pasta and bread every day and use only the freshest ingredients in all their dishes. Seafood offerings are exquisite. Evening meals come with a yummy cheese, olive, and bread appetizer, and the wine list features Italian, Chilean, and Argentine wines. Breakfast includes fresh fruit, granola and yogurt, pancakes, French toast, Mexican eggs and omelets.

Best spot for swimming with whale sharks

Laidback **Isla Holbox** is located just off the northeast corner of the Yucatán Peninsula. The island's biggest attraction, drawing the most visitors, is whale shark snorkeling. Every summer, usually from June to September, the giant whale sharks make their migratory stop off the coast here. The distinctively marked whale shark is the largest living fish species and can get as big as 40 feet long and weigh as much as 21 tons. It has a unique checkerboard color pattern of spots and stripes that has earned it the nickname *domino* by locals.

The whale shark is a filter feeder and eats mostly plankton (not people). Because it inefficiently uses its entire body for swimming, it travels only about three miles per hour. Whale sharks are docile and gentle in the water and can actually be quite playful with snorkelers. You can swim with this giant fish without any risk apart from perhaps unintentionally being swatted by a large tail fin. The whale shark is listed as a "vulnerable" species by conservation councils, and Holbox tour operators enforce strict rules for those who swim with these gentle giants. No scuba diving is allowed, nor is touching the whale sharks. Find out more about Holbox, whale shark tours and packages at: *www.holboxisland.com*.

A fisherman's paradise

Fishing is fabulous in the Mexican Caribbean. From March through mid-July, the sailfish run. From May through early June, the bonito and dolphin run. From May through September, it's the wahoo and kingfish. And barracuda, bluefin, mackerel, white marlin, and grouper can be fished year-round.

The best place to arrange a charter is in **Puerto Juárez**. Isla Mujeres also has good rates—you can arrange an all-inclusive deep-sea fishing expedition for four people through **JAX Sport Fishing** (*website: www.jaxsportfishing.com*). Rates are much higher in Cancún and Cozumel.

The world's best luthiers

Ask any guitar player in any Mariachi band where his guitar came from, and he won't tell you about Spain or Italy or New York—places you'd expect great guitar players to find great guitars. He won't even mention Guadalajara, the birthplace of Mariachi music. He'll simply say "Paracho" and expect you to understand.

The story goes that, in the 1600s, a Spanish priest named Vasco de Quiroga came to the Mexican state of Michoacán, high in the south-central mountains, to convert the local Purépecha Indian tribes and teach them economically viable crafts. He taught everyone in one village to make brass kettles. He taught another village to make tables and chairs. He taught yet another to cut stone arches and pillars. And he taught the people of Paracho to make guitars.

A cool story (and maybe it's even true), but, the fact is that today the craftsmen of Paracho make some of the finest guitars in the world. Paracho (30 minutes north of Uruapán) has a population of 17,000, including 2,000 luthiers, many from families who have been making guitars for three generations. Almost half the town's population earns a living in some way from guitar production. Everywhere you go, you see guitars hanging in shop windows; in the back streets, you find workshops in living rooms, old garages, and converted bodegas. Paracho is renowned for the handcrafted artistry that goes into its guitars. Craftsmen carve guitar components with ancient, trusted *cuchillos* (knives), favored over modern equipment.

The result, at least from the best-known and highest-quality shops, is individual works of art composed of exotic woods like Brazilian jacaranda, German spruce, Indian rosewood (or the Mexican variety called *palo escrito*), Canadian cedar, and ebony from Sri Lanka and Cameroon. These instruments take weeks to complete and sometimes years to receive on backorder. Names like Francisco Navarro and Benito Huipe on a guitar can command thousands of dollars apiece. Good-quality Mariachi-style cutaways are easier to get and cheaper to own, as are dreadnought styles, but these too are made one at a time by craftsmen who, in some cases, haven't had to refer to their stencils or cutting patterns for years. For them, it's all look, feel, and instinct.

Paracho produces about 80,000 guitars a year, ranging in price from $50 to $3,000 apiece. The best of these guitars are among the best in the world. But the master builders of Paracho are an independent lot, unwilling to change the old ways or throw in with another shop to increase production or bargaining power. In a world where identical, precision-made, high-quality instruments can be produced by machine in a matter of days, many of the world's players are less inclined to wait for a one-of-a-kind guitar, preferring instead mass-produced models from Japan and China. This means that more of Paracho's youth—the next generation of masters—are leaving to look elsewhere to make a decent living. If you're in the market for a unique, hand-carved guitar from a master craftsman, go to Paracho sooner rather than later.

THE BEST OF
MONTENEGRO

Montenegro (Black Mountain) is a small republic in the heart of the Mediterranean, divided from Italy by the Adriatic Sea. It follows the Adriatic Sea for 200 miles, from Kotor south to Albania. The scenery is dramatic, varying from high mountains to flat meadows to coastline beaches. The drive down the old Post Road (now the coastal highway) to Dubrovnik is especially beautiful.

Herceg Novi, in the north, is the oldest town along the coast. It was founded 600 years ago by Tvrtko, the first Bosnian King. The old part of town has ramparts and towers that contrast sharply with the new villas and hotels. Herceg Novi is known as the rainiest spot in Europe. The Topla area is a good place to stay.

The area around Risan is filled with bays and waterfalls. It is said that Illyrian Queen Teuta, after valiantly trying to fight off the invading Romans in 228 B.C., drowned herself here rather than surrender.

PLITVICE LAKES: NATURE AT ITS BEST

UNESCO has classified the **Plitvice Lakes National Park**, halfway between Zagreb and the coast, as one of the unique natural wonders of the world. Here, 16 magnificent blue-green lakes merge one into the other in a chain of waterfalls that rushes into the Korona River. The highest waterfall is 247 feet. The lakes are surrounded by walking paths, deep forests, beaches, and hotels.

SKADAR LAKE: THE MOST SUPERLATIVE

A list of superlatives describes **Skadar Lake** in the Zetsko-skadarska valley: the last habitat of pelicans in Europe, the biggest bird reservation in Europe, one of the last freshwater marshes at the Mediterranean, and the largest lake in the Balkans. Some parts of the lake bottom are below sea level.

The numerous islands dotted around the lake are interesting not only as bird paradises but also for their cultural and historical monuments. **Starcevo Islet**, for example, has a restored church from the 14th century, a renovated tavern, and the tomb of Bozidar Vukovic-Podgoricanin, the printer of the first Cyrillic books.

THE DEEPEST CANYON IN EUROPE

The **Tara River Canyon** in the Durmitor National Park is the deepest canyon in Europe. The furious Tara River rises in the mountain range in the northern part of the country and for centuries has been hollowing out the soft limestone, creating a 50-mile-long canyon. In some places the canyon is almost a mile deep. Its banks are covered with forest.

THE MOST ATMOSPHERIC RESTAURANT

Kod Miska, *tel. +381 (69) 022-868*, in Ulcinj, is built on a wooden raft on the river Bojana. The restaurant is famous for its food as well as its atmosphere. The surrounding scenery is reminiscent of the Amazon jungle. Fish is a specialty here and the prices are moderate.

SVETI STEFAN: THE MOST EXCLUSIVE RESORT

Off the coast of Montenegro is the island of **Sveti Stefan** (St. Stephen), a 15th-century fishing village that became an exclusive resort in 1960. The original fishermen's cottages have been preserved intact, but the interiors have been renovated in luxury. Flower gardens add color to the stone surroundings. The Duke of Bedford came here on his honeymoon; Adlai Stevenson, Kirk Douglas, and Princess Margaret have also been among the resort's guests.

THE BEST OF
NEW ZEALAND

When George Bernard Shaw visited New Zealand a reporter asked him his impression of the place and, after a pause, Shaw is said to have replied: "Altogether too many sheep" ...

—-George Bernard Shaw, 1934

New Zealand is a land of spectacular scenery: shooting geysers, cloud-shrouded mountain peaks, bubbling hot springs, deep blue fiords, and secluded coves. It is also a land of extremes, with both tropical beaches and icebergs.

The Kiwis, as the people of New Zealand are affectionately known, love their land and are among the most ardent conservationists in the world. They are as varied and interesting as the landscape they seek to preserve.

The Maoris, a Polynesian people who lived here long before the Europeans arrived, maintain their ancient traditions. The Europeans, too, preserve their old ways. Scottish dances seldom seen even in Scotland are danced by kilted sheep farmers.

This is the best place in the world for nature lovers, thrill seekers, and sports buffs. You can raft down a wild mountain river, battle a fighting rainbow trout, explore magnificent fiords, climb or ski the Southern Alps, or hike the awe-inspiring Milford Track.

New Zealand, which is made up of three main islands (North, South, and Stewart) and a number of smaller ones, stretches 1,000 miles along the southern tip of Polynesia. Its nearest neighbor is Australia, 1,300 miles to the northwest.

NEW ZEALAND'S LARGEST CITY

Auckland, huddled on an isthmus separating Waitemata and Manukau harbors, has 14 volcanoes, each with tremendous views. It is known as the Queen City among its inhabitants. Auckland has restaurants, cinemas, shops, theaters, concerts, and art galleries. It also has 102 mainland beaches and 23 secluded islands. The Hauraki Gulf is a favorite among boaters (and Auckland has a lot of boaters—one in every four homeowners also owns a boat). The best panorama is from **Mount Eden**, the highest point in the city. Hike up and picnic in the volcano's grassy bowl while enjoying the view.

The world's best Polynesian museum

The **War Memorial Museum**, *The Auckland Domain; tel. +64 (9) 306-7070 ext. 851 (information); website: www.aucklandmuseum.com*, built in memory of the New Zealanders who died fighting in World War I, houses the world's best collection of Maori and Polynesian artifacts, some dating back to A.D. 1200. The pièce de résistance is a 98-foot war canoe carved from a giant totara tree. It carried 80 Maori warriors at a time.

The best Kiwi art

The world's biggest collection of paintings by New Zealand artists is at the **Auckland Art Gallery**, *Kitchener and Wellesley Streets; tel. +64 (9) 379-1349; website: www.aucklandartgallery.govt.nz*. Especially worth seeing are works by John Webber and William Hodges, both of whom accompanied Captain Cook on his voyages in the South Pacific in the 18th century. The gallery is open 10 a.m. until 5 p.m.

Animal bests

Animal lovers should make time to visit the **Auckland Zoo**, *Motions Road; tel. +64 (9) 360-3805; website: www.aucklandzoo.co.nz,* where the nocturnal, flightless kiwi bird can be seen.

Auckland's best picnicking

The best places to picnic are the **Domain**, a large shaded park, and **Albert Park**, which adjoins the University of Auckland. Pack your picnic basket with mango juice, which is as common here as orange juice is in the United States, and good local cheeses.

The best bargains in town

Lamb is as cheap in Auckland as Kentucky Fried Chicken is in the United States. It can be found on cafeteria lunch menus, on the dinner table several nights a week, and at restaurants.

Good, inexpensive shops are located downtown, near Quay and Queen streets. Just east of the intersection is the **Old Customhouse**, which has been converted into a mall with a movie theater, arts and crafts shops, a tavern, and a bookstore. Built in 1889, the Customhouse is one of the few examples of Victorian architecture in Auckland.

A 10-minute walk west from the corner of Queen and Quay is the **Victoria Park Market** located in the city's former trash dump. (It's quite picturesque, believe it or not!) You can buy kiwifruit for a few cents apiece, fresh fish, and inexpensive clothing. The market is open every day.

Polynesian bests

Karangahape Road (known as K Road) is where Auckland's Polynesian population shops. You can buy brilliantly colored cloth and tropical foods here alongside matrons from Samoa, Fiji, Tonga, and the Cook Islands. (Auckland has the largest Polynesian population of any city in the world. More than 70,000 residents have Maori ancestry, and 58,000 Pacific islanders have immigrated here.)

Auckland's best dining

Most of the better restaurants in Auckland don't have liquor licenses. But you usually can bring your own wine (which brings down the price of dinner considerably).

Auckland's best restaurant is **Antoine's**, *333 Parnell Road; tel. +64 (9) 379-8756; website: www.antoinesrestaurant.co.nz*, a French restaurant in a sun-drenched colonial house with linen-covered tables. Wine is served here. Ring the doorbell to enter.

Other bests include: **The French Café**, *210 Symonds Street; tel. +64 (9) 377-1911; website: www.thefrenchcafe.co.nz*. This restaurant has won the title of Auckland's best restaurant for several years running and with good reason. The service is impeccable, the food delicious and they have an extensive wine list.

The Grove, *St. Patricks Square, Wyndham Street; tel. +64 (9) 348-4129; website: www.thegroverestaurant.co.nz*, is another place with an impressive wine list. Located next to the St. Patrick's Cathedral the setting is relaxed and intimate. Try the duck with chocolate dirt or the fries in truffle oil…fine dining in Auckland doesn't come much better than this.

Cin Cin On Quay, Auckland *Ferry Building, 99 Quay St.; tel. +64 (9) 307-6966; website: www.cincin.co.nz*, is a dining institution in Auckland. Overlooking the harbor this legendary restaurant serves modern European cuisine using New Zealand's finest produce.

Harbourside Seafood Bar and Grill, *First Floor, Ferry Building, 99 Quay St.; tel. +64 (9) 307-0486; website: www.harboursiderestaurant.co.nz*, and **Sails**, *Westhaven Marina; tel. +64 (9) 378-9890; website: www.sailsrestaurant.co.nz*, are also worth a visit.

Other good New Zealand and Polynesian restaurants are located on Ponsonby Road, near K Road.

The best hotels

Aucklands best hotel is the **Stamford Plaza Auckland**, *22-26 Albert Street; tel. +64 (9) 309-8888; website: www.stamfordhotel.co.nz*.

Other good hotels are the impersonal but efficient **Hotel Pullman**, *Waterloo Quadrant and Princes Street; tel. +64 (9) 353-1000; website: www.pullmanhotels. com*, and the **Langham Auckland**, *83 Symonds Street; tel. +64 (9) 379-5132; website: http://auckland.langhamhotels.co.nz*.

The Quay, a key travel hub

The Quay, in addition to offering a view of Harbour Bridge, is a transportation center. You can get a "Bus-About" pass here that allows you to ride public buses at reduced fares. You also can catch a ferry here to take you to the islands and beaches in the Hauraki Gulf.

New Zealand's best train trip

If you want to see the beautiful countryside of New Zealand, buy a ticket on the **Overlander**, one of the best trains in the world. It runs daily from Auckland to Wellington and back. See *www.tranzscenic.co.nz* for more information.

The city of **Wellington**, the capital of New Zealand, sprawls along the southern tip of North Island. For a view of Wellington's harbor and skyline, ascend Mount Victoria. White wooden houses cover the green hills surrounding the city. The beaches of the Inner Harbor are popular, and on summer weekends the harbor is filled with yachts.

Wellington is a cultural center, with two professional theater companies, numerous amateur dramatic and musical societies, the New Zealand Symphony Orchestra, and the Royal New Zealand Ballet Company. The Michael Fowler Center and St. Paul's Cathedral (built in 1866) both sponsor plays and concerts.

From **Lambton Quay**, a bright red cable car carries pedestrians 397 feet over the suburbs to the beautiful **Botanical Gardens;** *website: www.wellington. govt.nz/services/gardens/botanicgardens/botanicgardens.html.*

The **Te Papa Tongarewa Museum**, *Cable Street; tel. +64 (4) 381-7000; website:www.tepapa.govt.nz*, tells the great stories of New Zealand's past, present, and future. Over 20 galleries house exhibitions and interactive experiences that explore the unique natural environment, colonial history, Maori culture, and the diversity of the national art collection.

The best restaurants

Wellington's best restaurants include: **Logan Brown**, *192 Cuba Street; tel. +64 (4) 801-5114; website: www.loganbrown.co.nz*, which is housed in an elegant 1920s banking chamber. Good value options include the three course pre-theatre menu. Sample a drink from the cocktail bar while you wait for your food.

Martin Bosley's Restaurant, *Royal Port Nicholson Yacht Club, 103 Oriental Parade; tel. +64 (4) 920-8302; website: www.martin-bosley.com*, which offers a variety of New Zealand specialties.

For a casual lunch or dinner try Asian restaurant **Chow**, *Level 1, 45 Tory Street; tel. +64 (4) 382-8585; website: http://chow.co.nz*. Choose from a vast menu which includes Thai curry, fishcakes, and a delicious chicken satay.

The best Italian restaurants in Wellington are sister restaurants **Il Piccolo Pizzeria**, *248 Willis Street, +64 (4) 385-2645* and **Piccolo Restaurant**, *105 Vivian Street, +64 (4) 382-8882*. Il Piccolo serves pizza and pasta in a tiny but fabulously atmospheric restaurant run by owners Barry and Ira Bitossi. Piccolo, which serves only pasta dishes is run by Tom Stacey. Slightly bigger than its older sister, this restaurant still maintains the cozy and friendly atmosphere that makes both of these restaurants so great. Both Barry and Tom will pour themselves a glass of wine and pull up a chair at your table for a chat. The food is fresh and delicious and you'll come away from here feeling like you've made new friends.

The best coffee shops
Wellington is famous for its coffee shops. There are more of them in the city per head of population than New York. Some we recommend are: **Fidels**, *234 Cuba Street; website: www.fidelscafe.com*, has a fantastic brunch menu. Get there early though as it's a popular spot.

If you like your coffee with a touch of elegance try **Blondini's Café**, *Embassy Cinema, Kent Terrace; tel. +64 (4) 384-7657*, which is housed in the foyer of the 1920s Embassy movie theatre.

The best desserts
Anyone with a sweet tooth will think they have died and gone to heaven when looking at the menu in **Strawberry Fare**, *25 Kent Terrace; tel. +64 (4) 385-2551; website: www.strawberryfare.co.nz*. This dessert restaurant has an extensive menu (skip the mains and head straight for the sweet treats), but whatever you pick, whether it be Devils Dessert Cake, Chocolate Madness or Succulent Sorbets, you will not be disappointed.

The best beds
The **Intercontinental Wellington**, *2 Grey Street; tel. +64 (4) 472-2722; website: www.ichotelsgroup.com*, is in the business district of the city, close to shops and all major sights.

Museum Hotel, *90 Cable Street; tel. +64 (4) 802-8900; website: www. museumhotel.co.nz*, is located in the city center opposite the harbor front.

THE HIGHLIGHTS OF NORTH ISLAND

North Island is the cradle of New Zealand. It was here that the Europeans first landed and faced off with the native Maori. The island's beauty belies its violent past—it is fringed with beautiful, palm-shaded beaches and blessed with hospitable weather year-round. Explore it from north to south.

New Zealand's northernmost point

Cape Reinga, the country's northernmost point, affords a magnificent view of the Pacific Ocean and the Tasman Sea. Its graceful white lighthouse seems frail and vulnerable, facing the rage of two great bodies of water from the ridge of a narrow point of land.

The Maoris believe this is where spirits of the dead depart for their journey back to the ancestral land, which they call Hawaiki. The cape is a pleasant three-and-a-half-hour drive on Highway 1 or a one-hour flight from Auckland. It is a great place to spend the night if you enjoy camping—the area lacks hotels. Try the campgrounds at Houhora and Taputupoto Bays.

The best boating

Whangaroa Harbor, with its rocky pinnacles with biblical names, is the place to go for boating and deep-sea fishing. This is where the Royal Massacre occurred in 1809. A local tribe did away with the passengers and crew of the *Boyd*, the shell of which still can be seen here.

The largest private museum

The **Wagener Museum**, *tel. +64 (9) 409-8850*, at Houhora Heads, is the country's largest private museum, containing rare pre-European Maori artifacts, an excellent natural history display, and extensive exhibits from the Victorian era.

Best view, best springs

Kailohe has spectacular views of both the Tasman and Pacific coasts, as well as a museum called Pioneer Village. Nearby is **Ngawha Springs**, with waters that have the highest mineral content in the world and are known for their curative qualities.

The most magnificent trees

Magnificent native kauri trees stand along the road that runs through the 6,100-acre **Waipoua Kauri Sanctuary**. The largest is the mighty Tane Mahuta (Lord of the Forest), which is estimated to be 1,200 years old. The oldest is the 2,000-year-old Te Matua Ngahere (Father of the Forest).

Waikato: The best of the Maoris

North of **Hamilton**, which is the capital of New Zealand's rural Waikato region and the largest inland city, is the center of Maori culture.

Turangawaewae Marae is the focal point of a Maori revival movement organized in the 1920s by Princess Te Puea Herangi, who established a complex of buildings on the river. The complex includes traditionally carved meeting houses and a concert hall. It is not generally open to the public, but you can see it from across the river at the bridge downstream. The sacred burial ground of the Waikato Maoris is two-and-a-half miles downstream at **Mount Taupiri**.

The scene of the last battle of the Wakato Land Wars in 1864 is southwest in **Orakau**. Maori Rewi Maniapoto and 300 men, women, and children fought off 1,400 colonial soldiers for three days before they lost their fortified village.

The finest Maori carved meetinghouse is in Te Kuiti in southern **Waitomo**. Maori leader Te Kooti Rikirangi built the wooden structure to thank the local Maniapoto people, who gave him refuge when he was in danger.

King Country, as the region is known, is largely a resort for outdoor enthusiasts. Tour companies based in Te Kuiti and Taumarunui offer canoeing, horseback riding, hunting, jet boating, and fishing expeditions. Safari expeditions operate from Te Kuiti.

The rose of New Zealand

The magnificent rose gardens of **Te Awamutu**, southwest of Hamilton, have earned this town the title Rose Town of New Zealand. The roses are best seen in November during the annual Rose Festival. New Zealand's oldest and loveliest church is here; **St. John's Anglican Church** was built in 1854.

New Zealand's largest lake

Lake Taupo, at the heart of North Island, is the largest New Zealand lake, extending over 232 square miles and filling an old volcanic crater. The trout fishing is terrific in the lake and the rivers and streams that feed it. You can fish here year-round.

One of New Zealand's most attractive lodges is on the banks of Lake Taupo. **Huka Lodge**, *Huka Falls Road, Taupo; tel. +64 (7) 378-5791; website: www. hukalodge.co.nz*, is a five-star hotel with a rustic atmosphere.

The best adventures

At the southern end of Lake Taupo are the renowned trout-fishing and river-rafting waters of the Tongariro and Wanganui rivers, Kaimanawa State Forest Park, and Tongariro National Park, all accessible from Turangi.

Tongariro National Park, *website: www.doc.govt.nz/parks-and-recreation/ national-parks/tongariro/*, with its snow-capped mountain peaks, is a superb ski resort in winter and a scenic place to hike in summer. An extensive network of paths and huts makes it easy to explore the park and its historic Maori sights. The volcanic peaks of Tongariro, Ruapehu, and Ngauruhoe are the focal points.

The **Bayview Château Tongariro**, *Mount Ruapebu; tel. +64 (7) 892-3809; website: www.chateau.co.nz*, is a luxurious hotel at the heart of the park's spectacular mountains.

On the Wanganui River, you can embark on boat trips, guided canoe treks, and white-water rafting expeditions. This is also the site of an annual motorboat race. A luxury paddle boat travels along the river to the Holly Lodge Estate Winery, where wine tastings are held.

Rotorua: A heavenly Hades

"I was pleased to get so close to Hades and be able to return", said playwright George Bernard Shaw after visiting the area around **Rotorua City**—the boiling, bubbling, steaming center of North Island. Located on the volcanic rift that once inspired great fear, Rotorua is New Zealand's number-one tourist spot, surrounded by thermal springs, Maori villages, and 10 trout-filled lakes. Boiling mud, erupting geysers, steaming terraces of sulfur, and colorful silica deposits combine to create an otherworldly landscape.

Rotorua has the greatest concentration of Maori residents of any New Zealand city. The historic Maori village of **Ohinemutu**, on the lake, has a 19th-century traditional meeting house that took 12 years to carve. The Christian church, **St. Faith's** built in 1910, has a window with a Maori Christ, elaborate carvings, and a bust of Queen Victoria presented to the Maoris by Britain for their loyalty to the crown.

On Geyser Flat in Whakarewarewa is New Zealand's greatest geyser, Pohutu (Splashing), which shoots 100 feet into the air several times a day. The smaller geyser next to it usually erupts just before Pohutu does.

Rotorua is popular among trout fishermen. Professional fishing guides are available. If fishing isn't your thing, you can visit wildlife sanctuaries, government gardens, the Buried Village, and the Agrodome, where sheep and dog-handling demonstrations are given.

Rotorua City was established as a sanatorium in 1880, when the New Zealand government leased the land from the Maoris. **The Rotorua Museum of Art and History** (*website: www.rotoruamuseum.co.nz*), which houses a museum and an art gallery, was the original bathhouse. To its right are the **Polynesian Pools**, whose sulphurous waters are still used at the Queen Elizabeth Hospital to treat rheumatism and arthritis. Another good hot pool is **Hinemoa**, on Mokoia Island, in the middle of Lake Rotorua.

The world's only mainland gannet reserve

The world's only mainland gannet (a large yellow-headed seabird) sanctuary is to the south of **Cape Kidnappers**, where large flocks can be seen between April and October. The reserve can be reached by four-wheel-drive vehicles or on foot.

The world's best sheep-shearing contest

Masterton, on the southern tip of North Island, hosts the annual Golden Shears competition—a sheep-shearing contest that attracts shearers from all over the world.

NAPIER: THE ART DECO CAPITAL

Napier is the Art Deco capital of the world, having been re-built after the devastating 1931 earthquake in the prevalent Art Deco style. People come from all over the world for special events and 1930s-style dress-up, many in re-conditioned old cars, for the Art-Deco weekend each February.

SOUTH ISLAND: THE MOST BEAUTIFUL

New Zealand's most spectacular scenery is on **South Island**. At **Punakaiki**, for example, nature has carved limestone rocks into what looks like giant stacks of pancakes. The Tasman Sea rushes into bore holes in these oddly shaped rocks, making great shuddering booms. The island's most memorable sights are described below, starting at the north end, following along the Pacific coast, crossing the Southern Alps, and then following the Tasman coast.

The best boat charters

Ferries from North Island land in **Picton**, a busy little port in South Island's incredibly beautiful Marlborough Sounds, 597 miles of waterways sheltered by bays and coves. Picton is the base for charter boat companies that takes you cruising, fishing, and diving.

The best places to stay on South Island

The **Timara Lodge**, *Dog Point Road, Road #2; tel. +64 (3) 572-8276; website: www.timara.co.nz*, is the best place to say in Blenheim, but it's not cheap.

The **Warwick House**, *64 Brougham Street, Nelson; tel. +64 (3) 548-3164;*

website: www.warwickhouse.co.nz, about 50 miles from Blenheim, in Nelson, is another good place to stay on South Island.

The least-traveled trail

New Zealand is crisscrossed by well-marked trails leading through spectacular scenery. One of the least known, and therefore least crowded, is the **Nydia Trail**, along the Marlborough Sounds. Passing through genuine wilderness, the trail has no access road. A mail boat that serves farms and vacation homes also delivers hikers to any starting point along the 80-mile trail. If prearranged, the mail boat will pick you up again farther north. Check with the ranger station or public information office in the harbor town of Havelock for maps and to arrange transportation.

One of the best routes along the trail begins at Shag Point in Kauma Bay. Heading north, you cross two fast-running jade-green rivers near a deer farm. (The Japanese buy the velvet of the deer antlers and use it as an aphrodisiac). The trail then climbs the first of several 1,000-foot saddles with a view of the valley below. You can quench your thirst at a waterfall before continuing across a stretch of private property. Keep an eye out for wild goats and boars—and take cover if you spot any. At intervals of about five hours, the trail passes a series of bays: Stanley, Duncan, Penzance, and Elaine. The last is a good place to meet the mail boat and return to Havelock.

Don't attempt to travel the Nydia without an accurate map and a compass. The trail is barely marked and rarely tramped.

The wildcat coastline

South of Picton, at **Kaikoura**, the Pacific coast is at its wildest. The town is on a narrow peninsula buffeted by the ocean and protected by rocky cliffs and a narrow beach. Nearby are limestone caves and seal colonies. The Kaikoura Mountains are a dramatic backdrop. The peninsula is popular among fishermen and known for its large crayfish.

The most English town

Nestled at the base of Banks Peninsula on the edge of the Canterbury Plains is the garden city of **Christchurch**, a very English town. The river that meanders through its center, past old stone buildings and terraced houses, is called the Avon.

The **Heartland Hotel Cotswold**, *88-89 Papanui Road, Christchurch; tel. +64 (3) 355-3535; website: www.scenichotelgroup.co.nz*, is pleasant, with its Tudor-style architecture and authentic period furnishings.

Another good place to stay is the **Elizas Manor**, *82 Bealey Ave.; tel. +64 (3) 366-8584; website: www.elizas.co.nz.*

New Zealand's only castle

The Edwardian and Victorian houses of **Dunedin**, on the southernmost Pacific coast, embrace Otago Harbor, a 12-mile fiord. On one of the hills overlooking the city is New Zealand's only castle, **Larnach;** *website: www.larnachcastle.co.nz,* built in 1871 by J.M. Larnach, minister of the crown. The castle took 14 years to build, its ceilings 12 years to carve. The strangely European edifice was built to impress Larnach's French wife. Perhaps it didn't work; she committed suicide in Wellington's Parliament building years later. The castle has been restored, and its 43 rooms are open to the public.

The world's largest flying bird

The world's largest bird of flight, the rare royal albatross, can be seen in all its glory at Taiaroa Head, at the tip of Otago Peninsula near Dunedin. The graceful bird has a 10-foot wingspan and hovers above the sea like a kite. The oldest-known wild bird in the world is an albatross. Since 1937, when she was banded, this albatross has returned here each year. About 20 pairs of royal albatross circle the globe each year, at speeds of up to 66 miles per hour, to roost at Taiaroa. They mate for life and produce one chick every two years. You can observe the birds up close from a newly opened lookout. For more information, call the **Dunedin iSITE Visitor Center***; website: www.dunedin.govt.nz/visitor-centre.*

The world's largest marbles

North of Dunedin, on a beach near the fishing village of **Moeraki**, are the intriguing Moeraki boulders known as **The Devil's Marbles**, strange spherical rocks weighing several tons. The huge round stones were formed 60 million years ago by the accumulation of lime salts.

The shortest route across the Alps

The shortest route across the Southern Alps passes through the Alpine playground that is **Arthur's Pass National Park**. The picturesque mountain village of Arthur's Pass is a great base for mountain climbing, hiking, hunting, skiing, and breathing fresh mountain air.

The Tasman Coast: A nature lover's best

The **Tasman Coast**, on the other side of the island, is a good place to go if you like hiking, mountain climbing, rafting, or watching animals. It has three major national parks and is flanked by rugged mountains and washed by turbulent rivers.

New Zealand's best glaciers

The 217,000-acre **Westland National Park** has New Zealand's two most beautiful glaciers: Fox and Franz Josef. Arrange a (strenuous) guided hike across the icy masses at the park headquarters in the town of Franz Josef. (The native forest is crisscrossed with 68 miles of trails.) Or take a helicopter or ski plane over the shining glaciers.

New Zealand's highest peak: Mount Cook

Mount Cook, at 12,349 feet, is New Zealand's highest mountain. Sir Edmund Hillary, the first man to climb Mount Everest, trained here. The mountain is at the heart of **Mount Cook National Park**, which also features the beautiful 18-mile Tasman Glacier (and four other very high, very large glaciers). Ski planes operate regular flights to the head of Tasman—an exhilarating experience.

The most spectacular park

Fiordland National Park, at the southern tip of South Island, is one of the largest national parks in the world. Much of it remains unexplored. Lonely fiords lap at the mountains, while waterfalls tumble thousands of feet into the densely forested valleys. The fourth-largest waterfall in the world, **Sutherland Falls**, drops 1,873 feet through the forest. The gateway to the park is the town of **Te Anau**, which is the place to go for hotels and restaurants.

    Real Journey's Te Anau Visitors' Center, *tel. +64 (3) 249-7416; website: www.realjourneys.co.nz*, offers boat and bus tours of Doubtful Sound that take you to see Lake Manapouri, the Wilmot Pass, and many beaches in Fiordland National Park.

The eighth wonder of the world

According to Rudyard Kipling, the **Milford Sound**, which leads from Fiordland National Park to the sea, is the eighth wonder of the world. And who are we to argue with Kipling? The scenery is indeed spectacular: misty peaks, white waterfalls tumbling down green cliffs, and cottony clouds reflected in the mirror-like water. The scene is dominated by the 6,247-foot **Mitre Park**, a pyramid-like mountaintop. And it is fed by the spectacular **Bowen Falls**, which drop 531 feet.

The most beautiful walk in the world

The 33-mile **Milford Track**, which makes its way through Fiordland National Park to the Milford Sound, is the most beautiful walk in the world. To get here, take a boat across Te Anau Lake to Glade House. Leading through rainforests, meadows, and mountain passes, the trail passes wild rivers, deep fiords, and crashing waterfalls. The clearly marked track takes five days to hike; it is suitable even for the novice. You can hike independently or join a group. Accommodation is in shelters along the way. You must make a booking to walk the track. This can be done online at *www.doc.govt.nz/parks-and-recreation/tracks-and-walks/ fiordland/fiordland/milford-track/*. Book in advance to be sure you'll get the days you want.

The most southerly Alpine pass

Haast Pass is the most southerly, and the most historic, of the trans-Alpine passages, following an ancient Maori route through a rugged, breathtaking landscape. The contrast between the east and west sides of the pass is dramatic—**Westland** is lush; **Otago**, on the other side of the pass, is a dry region, relieved by lakes.

The pass runs through **Mount Aspiring National Park**, a 100-mile reserve that covers most of the southern Alps. Looming above the park is 9,961-foot Mount Aspiring. Many of the park's activities (hiking and fishing, for example) are centered in its headquarters at Lake Wanaka.

The most beautiful lakes

Mackenzie Country (named for a Scottish shepherd who tried to hide stolen sheep in this isolated area at the heart of South Island) is a rural area known for its six glacial lakes, the largest of which are Tekapo, Pukaki, and Ohau. Lake Tekapo is an unbelievable turquoise color (the result of powdered rock ground by the glaciers feeding the lake). All the lakes offer great fishing.

Queenstown: The most sophisticated resort

Nestled on the shores of clear blue Lake Wakatipu is Tyrolean-style **Queenstown**. Once a sleepy lakeside town, Queenstown has become the country's most sophisticated resort, with restaurants, hotels, an airport, and ski slopes. Any adventure is possible here: jet boating, white-water rafting, canoeing, sailing, jet skiing, water skiing, horseback riding, snow skiing, back-country safaris, and helicopter flights. You can cruise Lake Wakatipu on the TSS Earnsblaw steamer or follow its southern border aboard the Kingston Flyer steam train.

The **Pounamu Apartments**, *110 Frankton Road; tel. +64 (3) 442-4868; website: www.pounamuapartments.co.nz*, are just a 10-minute walk to the town center. Perfect for long or short term stays and has amazing views of Lake Wakatipu.

For something closer to the action, try the **Crowne Plaza Queenstown**, *Beach Street; tel. +64 (3) 441-0095; website: www.ichotelsgroup.com*, located in the center of town.

The **Millbrook Resort**, *Malaghans Road; tel. +64 (3) 441-7000; website: www.millbrook.co.nz*, is a great luxury resort overlooking one of the best golf courses in New Zealand.

STEWART ISLAND, THE MOST UNSPOILED

Across Foveaux Strait from South Island is **Stewart Island**, an untouched haven of dense forest with birds, animals, and flowers. (Its Maori name is Rakiura, which translates as *Heavenly Glow*). The tiny fishing village of **Oban** is the main town on the island. Bush walks and paths spread out from it to strategically placed huts throughout the northern part of the island.

Stewart Island is a bird watcher's paradise. You can see tuis, bellbirds, wekas, tomtits, and wood pigeons. And you can hear their songs year-round from the woods and meadows.

Codfish Island, off the west coast of Stewart Island, is also a great place to view birds. Buffeted by both the Arctic and the Pacific Oceans, Stewart Island's early settlers had a hard life. Many abandoned the island, fed up with the harsh storms and the cold winters, and left behind their homes, sawmills, tin mines, and whaling stations.

The place to stay is the **South Sea Hotel**, *The Waterfront; tel. +64 (3) 219-1059; website: www.stewart-island.co.nz*, in the middle of Oban, where the island's inhabitants meet for a beer. If you're not interested in a beer, just enjoy the view of the harbor.

New Zealand's woolliest bargains

New Zealand supports a flock of 70 million sheep. So it shouldn't be a surprise that fleece is a way of life for many and the backbone of the New Zealand economy. An army of home knitters stands by to turn the raw material into sweaters, gloves, hats, and scarves. The handiwork of New Zealanders pays off in apparel that is sturdy and well-designed. The wool varies from breed to breed, but most is incredibly dense and full of lanolin, which makes it water-resistant (and gives knitters babysoft hands). For those who like their wool still on the hide, New Zealand is also one of the world's greatest marketplaces for sheepskin.

The best food and wine festivals

New Zealand has a host of food and wine festivals every year. Here are the best ones:

Wildfoods Festival, *Hokitika; website: www.wildfoods.co.nz.* The Wildfoods Festival offers tasty and healthy wildfood bush tucker in Hokitika. Over 90 stalls feature not only the classic huhus, possum pies and whitebait in many cloaks, but cows' udders, Chatham Island seagulls, paua titties (roe), bull, lamb and goat testicles, gorse flower wine and gourmet garden snails. Not for those with a weak stomach!

Devonport Food and Wine Festival, Devonport, Auckland; *website: www. devonportwinefestival.co.nz.* Thousands of Auckland residents, New Zealanders, and visitors to the region have enjoyed the Devonport Food and Wine Festival for over 20 years. The festival was the first of its kind in New Zealand. All the money raised from the event is donated to local, regional and national charity organisations, schools and institutions.

New Zealand's premier wine and food event, **The Wine Marlborough Festival,** *South Island; website: www.wine-marlborough-festival.co.nz,* showcases over 200 wines from over 40 wineries. Held over three days in February, it is an opportunity to experience the highly acclaimed wines of the region and indulge in the culinary delights of renowned New Zealand chefs. It also features a line-up of New Zealand's leading performers and wine tutorials with some of New Zealand's leading winemakers.

Toast Martinborough, *North Island; website: www.toastmartinborough. co.nz.* This festival combines the celebration of new release Martinborough wines with culinary delights from some of Wellington's and Wairarapa's finest restaurants and entertainment from some of New Zealand's best performers. Each of the participating vineyards creates its own festival with a resident entertainer and food carefully matched to complement the wine on display. Free shuttle buses provide transport from vineyard to vineyard although most are within easy walking distance. Toast Martinborough has become a key fixture in the New Zealand wine and food calendar.

THE BEST OF
NICARAGUA

LAGUNA DE APOYO: NICARAGUA'S BEST-KEPT SECRET ESCAPE

Laguna de Apoyo, or Lake Apoyo, is a four-and-a-half-mile-wide caldera—a crater formed when the Apoyo volcano exploded about 23,000 years ago during what was probably Nicaragua's strongest volcanic explosion in recent geological history. The steep caldera walls rise more than 300 feet on the eastern rim and up to 1,600 feet on the western rim. The deep lake was formed and is maintained by a series of underground springs. Nicaragua has the largest number of tropical volcanic lake systems outside of Africa, and Lake Apoyo is the largest and cleanest of these crater lakes.

The most healing waters

The clear, turquoise, mineral-dense thermal waters of the lake are said to heal everything from rheumatism to arthritis. Underground vents from the nearly extinct volcano give the lake a high sulfur and mineral content, which helps to keep its water pure.

The best scuba diving in Nicaragua

Laguna de Apoyo is reported to be the cleanest lake in all of Central America. With visibility of up to 100 feet, and colorful fish and underwater wildlife found in very few other places on Earth, it offers the best scuba diving in the country. For more information: *website: www.gaianicaragua.org.*

GRANADA—NICARAGUA'S GRANDEST CITY

Granada is a city with history, charm, and a large central plaza surrounded by traditional Spanish colonial buildings. The city has little streets for meandering, neighborhoods for exploring, and lots of style. Granada has the character and feel of a small town that is friendly and safe. Granada also offers good restaurants, numerous hotels, a movie theater, Internet cafés, and lots of artisan shopping as well as everyday needs.

Granada's best hotels

The **Hotel Colonial**, *tel. +505 2552-7299; website: www.hotelcolonialgranada.com,* located a half-block off the main square, is a beautifully designed and decorated hotel with 26 rooms, including suites and condos for longer-term stays. For $60 a night (for a single room), you can enjoy relative luxury and a prime location.

Another great option in Granada is **Casa San Francisco**, *Calle Corral #207; tel. +505 552-8235; website: www.csf-hotel-granada.com.* This beautiful hotel is perfect for guests looking for a relaxing and friendly place to stay. Each room is uniquely decorated by owners Nancy Bergman and Terry Leary. The rooms open up to balconies that over-look the nearby rooftops, a small swimming pool and a gorgeous courtyard. Offering guests a quiet place to relax. The hotel offers a small bar and a lovely restaurant. The food is amazing and rivals any other local restaurant's fare. The staff is bilingual and incredibly friendly. If you are a repeat guest do not be surprised if the staff remembers you.

The best place to stay—on a budget

The **Hostel Oasis Granada**, *C. Estrada 109; tel. +505 552-8006; website: www.nicaraguahostel.com,* is the first budget hotel in Granada where you wouldn't mind actually spending the night. It has 56 beds, air conditioning, a restaurant, a bar, a swimming pool, a patio, a garden, and is just two blocks from the main square. You can stay in one of the dormitories for just $9 a night. For $23, you can move up to a double room and a private bathroom.

Granada's best restaurant

The best restaurant in town, the **Mediterraneo**, *Calle el Caimito; tel. +505 552-6764,* has a good menu, with daily seafood specials and despite the name, features typical Nicaraguan specialties.

If you get tired of Niacaraguan food, try **Restaurante El Garaje**, *512 Calle*

Corra; tel. +505 8651-7412, for a bit more Latin flavor. Run by a Canadian couple, this is a quiet and cheap restaurant that serves great food.

THE BEST VIEW IN MANAGUA

The **Coyotepe Fort**, just five minutes from Managua airport, offers the best view in Managua. The fort was built in the 1800s, then used in the next century by the Sandinistas as a prison and, for a couple of years, as a place to train their secret police. Today it is managed by the Nicaraguan Boy Scouts. With the help of a flashlight, you can explore the dark, underground maze. Outside, climb up onto the fort walls and you will be presented with a 360-degree view of Managua, the lake and the nearby volcanoes.

NICARAGUA'S FIRST RESORT

Two hours north of Managua, near the city of Matagalpa, is the **Selva Negra Mountain Resort**, *Km 140 Highway Matagalpa-Jinotega; tel. +505 772-3883; website: www.selvanegra.com* (Spanish for *Black Forest*). Owners Mausi and Eddy Kuhl (a well-known Nicaraguan writer) are descendants of a wave of German immigrants who came to Nicaragua in the late 1800s looking for gold, but found their fortune in coffee. When Eddy and Mausi built their German-style mountain lodge on an existing coffee plantation in the 1970s, it was Nicaragua's first real resort.

Today you can tour the coffee plantation and an impressive organic farm. Bump down steep mountain roads, past orchards that produce shade-grown organic coffee, fields and pens filled with cows, pigs, chickens, and food crops, most of which end up on the restaurant menu.

The restaurant serves American, Nicaraguan, and German food, and the beautiful stone chapel at the edge of the rainforest is available for weddings. All this is at Nicaraguan-style prices: rustic bungalows start at $85 a night, and you can get a chalet that sleeps six people for $140.

Selva Negra boasts an annual Oktoberfest celebration. The resort is easy to find: the resort's road marker is a wrecked tank left over from the civil war.

San Juan Del Sur: Nicaragua's best beach town
San Juan Del Sur is on the Pacific Coast and offers amazing beaches and a relaxed tourist scene. This small fishing village offers many amazing beaches, friendly locals and all the amenities you could desire.

San Juan Del Sur's best restaurants
For a variety, head behind the church to **El Colbri**, and enjoy outdoor seating in the courtyard. It is hard to decide whether the ambiance or the food is better. Make sure to take cash, as they do not take credit cards.

If you are in the mood for traditional Nicaraguan seafood, stay on the beach and head to **El Timon,** *Calle Costanera; tel. +505 568-2243; website: www. eltimonsjs.com.* Owned by a traditional Nicaraguan family this restaurant offers fresh seafood, some of the best *ceviche* in town and cold beer. The staff is friendly and the view beautiful.

San Juan Del Sur's best sunset view
Climb the steep path up the mountain-side and make your way to the newly erected Jesus statue. From this vantage point the views are tremendous in all 360 degrees. Enjoy the views of San Juan to the south, the mountains to the east and the coast to the north. The hike is steep, but well worth the effort. Make sure your camera has plenty of batteries.

THE BEST OF
PANAMA

PANAMA CITY: THE CAPITAL CITY

Panama's capital is Central America's only true First World city. It sits on the Bay of Panama, which opens onto the Pacific Ocean. The nightlife and restaurant scene rivals that of any other large cosmopolitan city. There's a burgeoning art scene, a wide range of live entertainment and cultural activities, and of course the gleaming new malls that have South Americans calling Panama a shopping Mecca.

Three cities in one

Panama City is really three cities in one: The first Panama City is now known as Panama La Vieja. Founded in 1519, it was sacked and destroyed by the pirate Henry Morgan in 1671—visit the ruins for an insider's peek at 16th century life. The conquistadors made their second attempt by founding the new city in 1673, on a peninsula today known as Casco Viejo. The golden altar at the San Jose Church, the jewel box that is the National Theater, and the Plaza de Francia are just a few of the historic monuments and areas worth visiting in the "Casco."

For the best in nightlife and restaurants, head to the "third" Panama City—the modern capital whose steel and chrome skyscrapers jut into the sky over the Bay.

The best fare

New and exciting restaurants, cafes and eateries open here every day. Because Panama sits at the crossroads of the Americas, you can find just about every cuisine imaginable, from gourmet Panamanian to Indian, Greek, Thai, Swiss, Japanese, German, Russian, Jamaican and much more. Check local website *www.DegustaPanama.com* for new restaurants, reviews (mostly in Spanish) and the latest food, service, and ambiance ratings on a scale of 1-5.

Here are a few of our favorites:

Luna, *Plaza La Florida, Marbella, tel. +507-263-5862.* For doting waiters and oozing ambiance, head to Luna. Chef Ruben Ortega-Vieto is a star with a Locavore bent. He's been known to use cobia ("black salmon") from Isla Grande, goat cheese from new valley farms, and Panama's famed pork belly for chicharrones…local nosh elevated to new and dizzying heights.

Barandas, *Aquilino de la Guardia St. and 51st; tel. +507 265-7844.* Located in the boutique Bristol Hotel, the Barandas restaurant and adjacent bar evoke an image of genteel Spanish tradition. The little bar offers up excellent Panamanian appetizers and is popular with the white-collar crowd, while the main restaurant is perfect for a leisurely Sunday brunch with white glove service.

La Forchetta, *Calle Pedro J Sosa, Plaza Catedral, Casco Viejo; tel. +507 212-0051.* Currently one of the best restaurants in the colonial Casco Viejo sector of Panama City, La Forchetta (pronounced "for-KEHT-ah") is located on the main plaza, across from the Panama Canal Museum and right by the Cathedral de Panama. The restaurant itself is in a beautifully renovated colonial, with an upstairs room for private parties that looks straight out of the Italian Renaissance. Try the fluffy green pea risotto or the home-made spaghetti, swirled in rich, basil-infused pomodoro sauce.

The best hotels in Panama City

There are so many hotels to choose from in Panama City, you're guaranteed to find exactly what you're looking for. And at time of writing the city has thousands more hotel rooms under construction (many of them nearing completion). Here we have it narrowed down to our favorite three:

The **Bristol Hotel**, *Avenida Aquilino de la Guardia; tel. +507 264-0000; website: www.thebristol.com,* is one of Panama City's finest hotels, with superior food and service. The rooms are luxurious and, to top it off, you're assigned a personal butler upon check-in. The perfect option for excellence right downtown, in the famed financial district.

The Radisson Decapolis, *Avenida Balboa-Multicentro; tel. +507 215-5000; e-mail: reservas@decapolishotel.com; website: www.radisson.com/panamacitypan.* This cosmopolitan hotel is located in the bustling financial district. It's across the street from the MultiCentro Mall complex, which houses a casino, cinema, and restaurants like the Panama City Hard Rock Café. The hotel lobby bar houses a sushi section and is a great place for a drink and *maki* any night of the week.

Baru Lodge, *Calle Elida diez, 2da Norte, El Carmen; tel. +507-393-2340.* For a tropical oasis right in Panama City try the comfortable, inexpensive Baru Lodge. Reserve well ahead as there's only 10 rooms. Despite the central location the lodge is very quiet. Located on a residential street, it has a lush green backyard area with pond and waterfall.

AN ADVENTURE ENCLAVE IN THE BREADBASKET OF PANAMA

Panama's Chiriqui province, known as the breadbasket of Panama, has a growing tourism industry. Yet it still remains one of the best-kept secrets of the tourism world. To take advantage of all Chiriqui has to offer, base yourself in the lush highland town of Boquete.

With the invigorating mountain air and exhilarating views—velvety green polka-dotted with bright flowers of every size and shape—it's easy to see why this is known as the place where Spring reigns eternal. At the weekend market, farmers sell their vegetables, fruits, and more from covered stalls. Get just-picked papaya, pineapple and mango…feast your eyes on the exotic plants and flowers…even bid on the day's catch of sushi-grade tuna.

The perfect haven for the outdoorsman (or woman) in you

In and around Boquete there are hills for climbing, trails for horse riding, streams for fishing, and rivers for rafting.

The famed Amistad International Park and Volcan Baru preserve, both located in the highland region, are filled with rare and exquisite flora and fauna. See the elusive Quetzal, bird of legend—a large, rare breed that is among the most spectacular in the world. The males have fuzzy green-blue heads with charcoal eyes and tiny yellow beaks. Their bellies are royal magenta and their long, ostentatious tails are teal green fringed with white. In flight or perched on a branch above, they are a glorious sight.

For birding tours, try Wilberto Martinez of **Nattur Panama**, *tel. +507 442-1340; website: www.natturpanama.com.*

KUNAYALA: PANAMA'S IDYLLIC ISLANDS

The best of indigenous life on a pristine Caribbean island

Kunayala, also known as San Blas, is a region that stretches from the province of Colon to Colombia, along the Caribbean Coast. It consists of a mainland portion and nearly 400 islands that make up the San Blas archipelago. It's autonomous, governed by the Kuna tribe that inhabits the pristine area, living much the way it did 100 years ago.

You can drive to parts of Kunayala from Panama City, but to experience the Caribbean paradise at its best catch a 30 to 40 minute flight to one of the islands. Spend your days eating fresh seafood (literally from water to table)...boating to tiny deserted islands...snorkeling and swimming...and of course, buying the much sought-after Kuna molas, little tapestries made of cunningly cut appliqué.

The most popular flight destination is El Porvenir, where Hotel El Porvenir provides basic accommodations. Splurge a little and fly instead to Playon Chico to stay at the Yandup Island Lodge (*website: www.yandupisland.com*). Cabins at Yandup are built with local materials by the Kuna residents of the Playon Chico village. The octagonal shape of the cabins is auspicious in the Kuna tradition. Cabins have terraces overlooking the sea and 24-hour electricity powered by solar panels—a big luxury in Kunayala, where some lodges only have power for part of the day. Rates from about $80 per person.

The best surfing

There are popular surfing beaches all over Panama, including island locations like Isla Grande and Bocas del Toro. Try Rio Mar, about an hour's drive west from Panama City, or go all the way to Venao or Cambutal, near the nation's southernmost point, on the Azuero peninsula. In 2011, 200 of the world's best surfers from over 28 countries went to Venao to compete in the Billabong ISA World Surfing Games.

The best adventure-tour specialists

Increasingly more tour companies throughout the country specialize in adventure tours, such as climbing and repelling, surfing, diving, river rafting, and visits to remote indigenous villages. Here are just a few:

- **Aventuras Panama**, *tel. +507 260-0044; website: www.aventuraspanama.com.*
- **Embera Village Tours**, *tel. +6758-7600; website: www.emberavillagetours.com.*
- **Scuba Panama Tours, S.A.**, *tel. +507 261-3841; website: www.scubapanama.com.*

527

THE BEST OF
PERU

Going to Peru is, well if you ever have an opportunity in your life to go there, you should do it because it is absolutely mind boggling.

—Dean Stockwell

Peru is physically spectacular, caught between the Pacific and the stupendous Andes Mountains. Covering 60% of the country is the Amazon basin, located to the east of the Andes; the gateway to this region is the former missionary town of **Iquitos**.

In the southern half of the country is **Cuzco**, a Peruvian region high up in the Andes. From there, the Incas ruled much of South America. Using this as a base, the archeologically inclined can head for the mountains and Machu Picchu.

The most hidden city

Several hours from Cuzco lies **Machu Picchu**. Surrounded by thick jungle, this is the only Inca city that the Spanish invaders never found (although they knew of its existence). This is hardly surprising. Even today, the road to Machu Picchu is not easy. You can make the trip, either by foot or by train, for the most breathtaking scenery in all Peru. On foot, the trip is rugged, taking you along the Inca Trail through the Andean hills—but the view is worth it.

The best tours

Organize your tour arrangements with **Highland Peru Tours**, *Av. Pardo 231, ofic 401. Miraflores. Lima, tel. +51 (1) 242-6292; website: www.highlandperu.com.*

THE BEST OF CUZCO

Cuzco is a small city nestled in a valley against the rugged backdrop of the Andes Mountains. It was once the capital of the Inca Empire, and many Inca vestiges remain. The Spanish retained the superb stonework after conquering the country— they built their homes on top of the original Inca foundations.

The finest church in the Americas

Cuzco's primary site is its Renaissance cathedral, which many believe is the finest church in the Americas. It was built on the site of an Inca temple to the god of creation, Viracocha. Situated in the main square, it is a hub of activity. Here, the people of Cuzco sell everything from handmade turquoise jewelry to hand-woven wool belts. Also see Cuzco's 328 shrines, marvels of masonry built by Indian craftsmen. The shrines correspond to former Inca religious sites (the Inca calendar had 328 days).

PERU'S MOST FAMOUS JUNGLE CITY

Iquitos sprang up overnight in this rainforest nearly 100 years ago, and it garnered such fame that European opera stars risked shipwreck and dysentery to perform in this Amazon city. Today, it is again Peru's largest jungle city, with modern shops, restaurants, and hotels. And it is becoming increasingly popular as a tourist destination.

THE WORLD'S MOST REMOTE JUNGLE

The **Manu National Park** is surrounded by the finest pristine jungle anywhere in South America—if not the world. Comprised of more than five million square acres, the park is located in the Mother of God (Madre de Dios) department in southeastern Peru, at the end of one of the Amazon's tributaries. This park is so remote that two tribes of Peruvian Indians yet to be contacted by the outside world dwell within it. Their villages have only been seen by plane.

THE BEST OF
POLAND

Poland has made great strides in tourism services and infrastructure in recent years—running neck-to-neck with amenities offered in Hungary and the Czech Republic. The country's most outstanding feature is its native inhabitants, a self-effacing and fun-loving bunch, who are among the warmest people in all Europe. If you get lost in Poland, a Pole is likely to take you out for dinner and drinks before he points you in the right direction.

Nature, too, welcomes visitors to Poland. The country's 12 natural parks and 500 wildlife preserves contain animals that have already disappeared in other parts of Europe—bison, chamois, bear, moose, and tarpan (small horses). And Poland's 325-mile Baltic seacoast is lined with long, sandy beaches.

WARSAW: WORST DESTRUCTION, BEST RESTORATION

Warsaw has had the bloodiest history of any Polish city. Hitler ordered that not one stone be left standing in the city following the 63-day Warsaw Uprising against the Nazis. As a result, more than 200,000 people were killed and the city was razed. Between 1940 and 1945, a total of 750,000 of the city's residents died.

The Nazis weren't the first to demolish Warsaw. In the 17th century, the city was razed by the Swedes. It was sacked again in the 18th century. In 1795, Warsaw was given to Prussia. Napoleon took the city in 1806. And the Russians claimed it in 1813.

Although most of Warsaw's old buildings and monuments have been destroyed, many have been beautifully rebuilt. The Old Town section was reconstructed after the war according to prints and old family photographs. It looks much as it did before, with narrow houses, winding streets, and Gothic churches. The district is closed to all traffic except horse-drawn buggies.

At the heart of Old Town is **Market Square**, surrounded by recreated baroque houses, shops, and cafés filled with flowers. The **Negro House**, Number 36 on the square, was once a center of the slave trade. It is marked by a bust of a black man. It is now the home of the **Warsaw Historical Museum**, *Rynek Starego Miasta 28-42; tel. +48 (22) 635-1625; website: www.mhw.pl,* where chamber music concerts are held on Tuesdays. The oldest house on the square is the **Tomb of the Mazovian Dukes**, or St. Anne's House, at Number 31. It has the greatest number of Gothic details.

The **Royal Castle**, *tel. +48 (22) 355-5170; website: www.zamek-krolewski.pl,* blown up during the war, is the most beautiful in Poland. Built between the 14th and 18th centuries, it was restored after World War II. It can be seen from Zamkowsky Square along with **King Sigismund's Column**, a symbol of Warsaw. The slender column was the first monument rebuilt after the war. Originally built in 1644, it honors King Sigismund III, who made Warsaw his capital in the late 16th century.

The old walls surrounding the city and a 16th-century tower called the **Barbican** have also been reconstructed. You can see fragments of the old defensive walls along Kamienne Schodki Street. They are defended by the statue of Syrena, a mermaid with a raised sword. According to legend, the mermaid rose out of the Vistula River and told two children playing on the banks to found the city. Their names were Wars and Szawa, hence the Polish name for the city: Warszawa.

The most frightening sights

The horrors of World War II are evident throughout Warsaw. The most frightening reminder is **Pawiak Prison Museum**, *Ulica Dzielna 24/26; tel. +48 (22) 831-1317,* where 35,000 Poles were executed and 65,000 imprisoned. The walled Jewish ghetto called **Muranow** was flattened by the Nazis.

Today, Spartan modern apartments stand in its place. The **Monument to the Heroes of the Ghetto** stands on a small square at the intersection of Zamenhofa and Anielewicza streets, once the heart of the ghetto. It is a slab of dark granite with a bronze bas-relief.

A high-tech take on wartime destruction can be seen at **The Warsaw Uprising Museum**, *Ulica Grzybowska 79; tel. +48 (22) 539-7905; website: www.1944.pl,* a relatively new museum that diligently documents the 64 days of armed resistance that reduced a large part of Warsaw to rubble.

The **Jewish Historical Institute and Museum**, *Ul.Tlomackie 3; tel. +48 (22) 827-9221; website: www.jewishinstitute.org.pl,* has exhibits of the ghetto uprising. The **Mausoleum to Struggle and Martyrdom**, *Armii Wojska Polskiego Street*, is located at the former Gestapo headquarters and prison.

A less obvious memorial to the war is a manhole cover at the intersection of Dluga and Miodawa streets. Here, 5,300 insurgents left the sewer canal through which they escaped from Old Town during the Warsaw Uprising in September 1944. The horrors of their journey through Warsaw's sewers are graphically depicted in Wajda's film *Canal*.

Poland's prettiest palace

Lazienki Palace and Park, *Ul. Agrykola 1; tel. +48 (22) 506-0024*, is among the most beautiful places in the world. In 1766 King Stanislas Poniatowski bought the neo-classical castle, which stood on an island in the middle of a lake, and had it enlarged and remodeled. The grounds also contain the Myslewicki Palace, the White Cottage, an old orangery, a baroque bathhouse, and a theater by the swan-filled lake, complete with artificial ruins.

The Polish Versailles

Wilanow Palace and Park, *Ulica Stanislawa Kostki Potockiego; tel. +48 (22) 842-8101; website: www.wilanow-palac.art.pl*, called Warsaw's Versailles, was built in the late 17th century by King Jan III Sobieski. The building is crowned with parapets, and the façade is carved with deities symbolizing the virtues of the royal family. Inside is the gallery of Polish portraiture and next door is the world's first **Poster Museum**, *tel. +48 (22) 842-48; website: www.postermuseum.pl*.

Warsaw's most famous residents

Stop by the often-overlooked **Maria Sklodowska Curie Museum**, *Ul. Freta 16; tel. +48 (22) 831-8092; website: http://muzeum.if.pw.edu.pl,* where Madam Curie was born. The scientist was twice awarded the Nobel Prize for her discoveries of the radioactive elements polonium and radium.

Another little-known treasure is the house where **Chopin** was born in 1810. Set in a park in Zelazowa Wola, 33 miles west of Warsaw, the ivy-covered cottage is now a museum. A black Steinway grand piano stands in the corner of the music room. A 19th-century upright grand, which looks something like a harp, stands in another room. Framed musical compositions hang on the walls along with poems Chopin wrote as a boy for his parents. During the summer, Chopin concerts are held here on Sundays.

KRAKOW: THE ONLY UNSCATHED POLISH CITY

Krakow is Poland's city of kings and intellectuals. It was the country's capital from 1039 to 1596. Kracow is also the only Polish city that escaped demolition during World War II.

The city is dominated by **Wawel Hill**, with its fortified castle and Gothic cathedral. UNESCO described the castle, now a museum, as one of the most beautiful in the world. Poland's kings lived here until 1609, when the royal court moved to Warsaw. Even after the move, Polish kings continued to be crowned here.

Wawel Castle, *tel. +48 (12) 42-5155; website: www.wawel.krakow.pl,* looks like a movie set, with gargoyles hanging from walls, elaborately carved doorways, columns, and brightly painted roof tiles. The castle museum contains the "Szczerbiec," a 13th-century sword used in coronation ceremonies, and the world's largest collection of tapestries—356 in all. The 71 rooms of the castle are richly decorated—one is covered entirely in embossed, hand-painted Spanish leather.

The **Czartoryski Palace Museum,** *Ul. Sw. Jana 19; tel. +48 (12) 422-5566; website: www.muzeum-czartoryskich.krakow.pl,* has a collection of tapestries, pottery, weapons, and paintings by old masters, including da Vinci and Rembrandt.

The **Wawel Cathedral**, *tel. +48 (12) 429-3327; website: www.wawel. diecezja.pl,* contains the elaborate tomb of St. Stanislaus, Poland's patron. Lovely 15th-century frescoes decorate the cathedral's **Chapel of the Holy Cross**. **Sigismund Chapel**, an 11th-century crypt, contains red marble tombs of royalty, bishops, and national heroes.

Mariacki Cathedral (the Church of the Virgin Mary) is famous for its bugler. Seven-hundred years ago, a bugler in the church tower was sounding an alarm when he was stopped mid-toot by a Tartar's arrow. Today, a bugle sounds every hour on the hour. The call is cut off suddenly, just as it was centuries ago. The church is also famous for its 500-year-old altarpiece with life-size figures in gold raiment depicting the assumption of the Virgin Mary.

You enter the Old City via the **Florian Gate**, which is next to a round fort called the Barbican, with walls 10 feet thick and pierced by 130 peepholes. Pedestrians can climb medieval staircases here and view the gargoyles. This area is the site of one of the world's oldest universities, **Jagiellonia University**, which was founded in 1364 and counts Copernicus among its alumni.

All streets in the Old City lead to **Rynek Glowny** (the main marketplace). Once the largest municipal square in Europe, it is the site of political rallies, festivals, and public performances. Hundreds of pigeons share the square with crowds of people.

Oldest new market

Nowy Targ, which means New Market, is a town of 10,000 in the foothills of the Carpathian Mountains. The market was new in the 15th century and has operated continuously ever since. Now open every Thursday, the market attracts buyers and sellers from all over Poland. Beginning at the break of day, the market is like a carnival, and fascinates as long as you watch.

CZESTOCHOWA, AMECCA

Every year on Assumption Day (August 15th), hundreds of thousands of pilgrims come to the drab little town of **Czestochowa**, *website: www.czestochowa.pl,* on the Warta River to pay homage to a portrait of the Madonna, said to have been painted by St. Luke. The Madonna's cheeks are marred by two slashes that, according to legend, were made by an enraged Tartar who felt the painting getting heavier and heavier as he tried to steal it. The portrait is kept in a huge monastery called **Jasna Gora** (Hill of Light), *website: www.jasnagora.pl,* founded in 1382 by Paulist monks. Swedish armies were halted here in 1655 and driven out of Poland.

CENTRAL EUROPES LAST PRIMEVAL FOREST

Bialowieza National Park, *website: www.bialowieza.com,* the last primeval forest in Central Europe, covers 480 square miles, half in Poland, half in the Soviet Union. A thick wall of 1,000-year-old oaks, pines, and spruce trees, it is home to Europe's only wild bison, as well as moose, lynx, wild tarpan, bears, foxes, deer, and wild boars. You can explore the forest on four-hour excursions in a horse-drawn carriage.

THE BEST OF
PORTUGAL

*I am very happy here, because I loves oranges, and talk
bad Latin to the monks, who understand it, as it is like
their own. And I goes into society (with my pocket pistols),
and I swims in the Taqus all across at once and I rides on
an ass or a mule and swear Portuguese.*

—Lord Byron, 1809

As beautiful and historic as neighboring Spain, Portugal is far cheaper and less developed. Don't make the mistake of most foreigners and visit only Lisbon. Portugal has much to offer outside its capital city, including quaint old villages surrounded by rolling hills, Moorish cities, long sandy beaches, and mountain vistas.

Portuguese culture has been influenced by the Moors, Catholicism, and seafaring history. The Portuguese sing the *fado*, a heart-rending, wailing sort of blues. Their unique cuisine includes *bacalhau*, a dried codfish served a different way every day of the year. Portugal has its own sweet wines, port and Madeira. And the Portuguese have a version of the bullfight which is gentler than that in Spain. Portuguese matadors wrestle the bull but never kill the animal. At the end of a bullfight, the bull is enticed out of the ring by a cow.

Portugal's cultural center: Lisbon

The capital of Portugal is studded with ancient Moorish quarters and bordered by lovely beaches. Its National Museum of Ancient Art houses one of Europe's best collections. Outside Lisbon are palaces that rival the châteaux of the Loire in France. And at the heart of the city are winding streets that pass medieval churches and inviting cafés.

Built on a series of hills, **Lisbon** has 17 overlooks, called *miradouros*, which offer side views of the city. The best is at the **Castelo de Sao Jorge**, built in the fifth century by the Visigoths and later used as a Moorish stronghold.

Another panoramic view is from the top of the statue of **Cristo Rei**, or Christ the King (a smaller replica of the one in Rio de Janeiro), located on the opposite side of the Tagus River from the city. To get there, cross the Ponte 25 de Abril.

The must-sees of Lisbon

Lisbon's most beautiful landmark is the **Basilica de Estrela**, *Largo da Estrela.* Queen Maria I promised God she would build the basilica if He granted her a son. God kept His part of the bargain, and the basilica was built in the late 18th century of luminous pale marble and topped with an enormous stone dome. Maria's tomb is inside. Look for the life-size manger scene carved by Machado de Castro.

The **Se** (cathedral), *Largo de Se; tel. +351 (21) 886-6752*, is downtown's most imposing structure. It was once a fortress and has battlements, two towers, and massive walls. Behind the austere façade are Gothic cloisters and a burial chapel.

Igreja de São Roque, *Largo Trindade Coelho;* is a Jesuit church with an ornate chapel called Sao Joao Baptista, which is lavishly decorated with amethyst, agate, marble, and entire columns of Chilean lapis lazuli.

The **Gulbenkian Museum**, *Ave. de Berna 45; tel. +351 (21) 782-3000; website: www.museu.gulbenkian.pt*, houses the huge collection of French furniture, Oriental carpets, and great paintings of the eccentric millionaire Calouste Gulbenkian, as well as Beauvais tapestries.

The **Museu de Etnologia**, *Avenida Ilha da Madeira; tel. +351 (21) 304-1160; website: www.mnetnologia-ipmuseus.pt,* has one of the finest collections of African art in the world.

Museu National de Arte Antigua, *Rua das Janelas Verdes 9; tel. +351 (21) 391-2800, website: www.mnarteantiga-ipmuseus.pt,* contains one of Portugal's greatest treasures, the polyptych of the *Adoration of St. Vincent*, painted by Nuno Goncalves between 1460 and 1470. The six-panel work surrounds a statue of St. Vincent, patron saint of Portugal.

Igreja da Madre de Deus, *tel. +351 (21) 814-7747*, has Europe's best display of antique tiles, called *azulejos*, which line the 16th-century crypt.

Belém: An island of bests

Belém, an island in the middle of the Tagus, west of downtown Lisbon, is surrounded by museums and monuments. The **Torre de Belem**, a five-story tower, is the most outstanding landmark. Built between 1515 and 1521, cannons on this Gothic structure protected the Tagus for centuries. A statue of *Our Lady of Safe Homecoming* on the tower's peak welcomes sailors home from sea.

In 1502, the profits of the spice trade were used to build the magnificent **Mosteiro dos Jeronimos**, a celebration of Vasco da Gama and other Portuguese explorers. This was de Gama's point of return after finding the sea route to India. He is buried in this church, which is backed by a decorative cloister with columns, arches, fountains, and cool stone benches. In front is the **Monument to the Navigators**—erected in 1960 in the shape of a ship's prow.

Belém is also home to the **National Coach Museum**, *tel. +351 (213) 610-850; website: www.museudoscoches.pt,* and the **Maritime Museum**, *tel. +351 (213) 620-019*, which houses beautifully restored ships, as well as early airplanes. (The museum has spurred much controversy because it spoils the view from the Torre de Belém.)

Lisbon's oldest quarter, the Alfama

The only neighborhood in Lisbon not destroyed by the great earthquake on All Saints' Day, 1755, is the **Alfalma**, whose tiny medieval streets twist and turn between rows of shops and old houses. Forty-foot tidal waves and fires that burned for a week followed the violent earthquake, which struck while most of the city's residents were in church. At least 60,000 people died. Voltaire wrote about it in *Candide*.

The Alfama existed before the Visigoths arrived in the fifth century. It clusters beneath the Castelo São Jorge on one of Lisbon's tallest hills. The cobblestone streets are so narrow that in some places you must walk single file. Wrought-iron lamps light the streets. Canaries and geraniums brighten the balconies. Laundry waves from lines strung above the streets. Tiles portraying the Virgin Mary, St. Anthony, and St. Martial decorate buildings, some of which date back to the Moors or the Middle Ages.

Walking along **Beco do Mexias**, you pass dozens of tiny shops and come to a doorway that leads to a large fountain where local women do their laundry. Also explore **Rua da Regueira**, which is lined with restaurants and shops, and **Patio das Flores**, a little square with houses faced in tile.

Lisbon's most colorful market

Begin your day in Lisbon wandering through the fish market at the foot of the Alfama. Weathered fishermen bring in their catches here, and *varinhas,* or fishwives, march about with baskets of fish on their heads. The *varinhas* wear black skirts with aprons and go barefoot in the summer, gold hoops dangling from their ears.

Portugal's liveliest country market

If you're in Lisbon on the first Sunday of the month, take a detour to the country fair at **Vila Nogueria de Azeitão**, 21 miles south of the city. Portugal's liveliest and largest marketplace, the Azeitão offers everything from livestock and household furnishings to clothing and food. If you miss the fair at Azeitão, the nearby villages of Pinhal Novo, Coina, and Moita have fairs on successive Sundays. Prices at these fairs are lower than those in city stores. Haggling is expected.

The best dishes

Lisbon is famous for its seafood, and the Alfama and the Bairro Alto are the best places to dine on the local *camaroes* (shrimp), *langosta* (lobster), *pesca espada* (swordfish), *salmonete* (red mullet), *linguado* (sole), and *bacalhau* (dried salt cod), as well as the ubiquitous *sardinas grilhadas* (fresh grilled sardines), which are delicious. If you see *carne de porco com ameijoas* or *ameijoas na cataplana* on a menu, order it. These are uniquely south Portuguese combinations of pork and sausage with clams.

Drink Sumol (lemon or orange soda), Sagres *cerveja* (beer), or local wine, Dão or Vinho Verde. Most of the gin and whiskey in Portugal is faked.

Fado: Portugal's saddest music

Fado, which means *fate*, is as important to Portugal as flamenco is to Spain— although it is more intense and somber. The best *fado* is played in the Alfama, the Mouraria (another neighborhood with Moorish traditions), the Bairro Alto (the old section), and the Madragoa (the fisherman's quarter).

Fado songs range over many octaves, almost always in a minor key, and are usually sung by women dressed from head to toe in melancholy black and carrying red roses. Male *fado* singers or guitar accompanists wear black monks' robes.

Some of the songs date back to the 13th century; others are influenced by

Portugal's Moorish past (and sound atonal) or by Portugal's seafaring tradition (and are reminiscent of sea chanties). Most are about unrequited love.

The places to hear the best fado

Recommended *fado* restaurants include **Adega Machado**, *Rua do Norte 91-1200; tel. +351 (21) 322-4640; website: www.adegamachado.web.pt;* **Lisboa a Noite**, *Rua as Gaveas 69; tel. +351 (21) 346-8557;* and **O Faia**, *Rua da Barroca 54-56; tel. +351 (21) 342-1923; website: www.ofaia.com.* You must make reservations to hear *fado*, and you should go after a late dinner; most shows don't start before 10 p.m.

The hottest nightlife

There are many discos in Lisbon, each with its own character and charm. Included are our favorites: **Alcantara Mar**, *R. da Cozinha Economica; website: www. alcantara-mar.com;* **Incognito**, *Rua dos Poiais de Sao Bento; tel. +351 (21) 390-8755;* **Lux**, *Avenida Infante Dom Henrique; tel. +351 (21) 882-0890;* partly owned by Hollywood actor John Malkovich, this is THE place to spend a night in Lisbon…if you can get past the very selective doormen. These clubs play all kinds of music, including rap, hip-hop, techno, jungle, cool-jazz, funk, and rock 'n' roll.

The cheapest fun

If you're trying to save money, you still can spend a pleasant evening in Lisbon—by strolling through the old sections. You'll find plenty of free entertainment. Student choral groups dressed in caps and gowns sing traditional college melodies to the accompaniment of Spanish and Portuguese guitars.

Lisbon's best hotels

The most luxurious hotel in Lisbon is the **Four Seasons Ritz**, *Rua Rodrigo da Fonseca, 88; tel. +351 (21) 381-1400; website: www.fourseasons.com/lisbon*, set on a hill overlooking Parque Eduardo VII. Rooms at the Ritz are decorated in silks, satins, and suedes.

The least expensive places to stay are off of the Avenida de Liberdade.

Hotel Jorge V, *Rua Silveira 3; tel. +351 (21) 356-2525; website: www. hoteljorgev.com*, has clean, modern rooms and elevators.

Sana Lisboa, *Avenida Fontes Pereira de Melo, 8; tel. +351 (21) 064-300; website: www.sanahotels.com*, overlooks the Parque Eduardo VII and is an easy walk into the old town. The buffet breakfast alone makes a stay here worthwhile.

The best side trips from Lisbon

Queluz, Portugal's version of the Palace of Versailles, is not far from Lisbon. The 18th-century pink rococo palace is filled with Portuguese Empire antiques and surrounded by ornamental gardens.

Cabo Espichel, a windy cape jutting into the Atlantic, is an ancient pilgrimage center. Explore the ruins of the 17th-century baroque church, **Nossa Senhora do Cabo** (Our Lady of the Cape), as well as the arcaded outbuildings that once housed pilgrims. Go around the church to the edge of the cliff, which drops 350 feet into the ocean.

Estoril is a beach resort 13 miles west of the city, famous for its Casino Estoril, *tel. +351 (21) 466-7700; website: www.casino-estoril.pt*. You can take a train to Estoril from Lisbon's Cais do Sodre station. You must show a passport to get into the casino, and men must wear suit coats. The **Hotel Palacio**, *Rua Particular; tel. +351 (21) 464-8000; website: www.palacioestorilhotel.com*, is a gracious old hotel in Estoril near the beach with gardens, a swimming pool, and excellent service.

Nearby is a fishing village that has been turned into a sophisticated resort, **Cascais**. A fine sandy beach lines its beautiful bay. Cascais has had an elegant air since 1870, when the court first moved here for the summer. A royal palace was constructed in the former citadel and is still used by the head of state.

Just outside Cascais is one of the strangest sights on the coast—the **Boca do Inferno** (Jaws of Hell). This great hole, formed by the force of the ocean entering under a rock arch, roars when waves crash into it.

Praia do Guincho, five miles west of Cascais, is a long, sandy beach with dunes. Its massive headland is the westernmost point in Europe. It is famous for good fishing and surfing (but beware of the undertow).

Setubal is a busy fishing port with 16th- and 17th-century churches and a medieval fortress. Inside the walls of the town's castle, São Filipe, is the attractive **Pousada de São Filipe**. Built in 1590, the fortress is 600 feet above the harbor and has many towers and massive battlements. It is entered via a dark, sweeping stone staircase. Underground tunnels and prison cells are now used as wine cellars and storage areas. The chapel is completely tiled.

Just north of Setubal is **Pousada do Castelo de Palmela**, *Castelo de Palmela, 2950 Palmela; tel. +351 (21) 235-1226*, a beautiful castle hotel.

SINTRA: THE MOST ROMATIC TOWN

Sintra is the breathtaking mountain resort made famous by the poet Byron, who wrote, *"The village of Sintra is the most beautiful, perhaps, in the world."* For centuries, Sintra was favored as a summer refuge by Portuguese royalty. It's a 45-minute train ride from Rossio Station in Lisbon.

Once a mountain stronghold of the Moors, Sintra is dominated by a seventh-century Moorish castle. Situated 1,400 feet above sea level, it has crenelated walls and battlements that extend along rocky cliffs. From the walls, you have a view of the cliffs and the sea.

The most romantic sight in Sintra is the **Pena Palace**, a towering pseudo-medieval palace built in the 19th century. From the windows are views of the coast, the cliffs, and the sea. The palace's 500-acre park, which you enter by crossing a drawbridge, has 400 kinds of trees and plants.

EUROPE'S SUNNIEST SPOT—THE ALGARVE

Spanning 200 miles of Portugal's southern coast, from Sagres in the west to the Spanish border in the east, the **Algarve** is Europe's sunniest site, with 300 sunny days per year. During the summer, temperatures range from 68° F to 86° F. The hottest days are tempered by refreshing breezes off the Atlantic. Spring and fall have warm weather just right for swimming.

Separated from the rest of Portugal by a spine of mountains, the Algarve was once considered a separate kingdom. The Phoenicians, Greeks, Carthaginians, and Romans all traded here before the Moors took over and ruled for 500 years. The Algarve was the last province taken from the Moors by Portuguese kings, and many towns still more closely resemble the villages of North Africa than those of Europe.

Albufeira: The hottest town

Albufeira, a Moorish town, has the most beautiful bodies and the hottest nightlife in the region. The real action is along Rua Candido dos Reis, a cobblestone pedestrian street that leads from the beach to the plaza. In the evening, the outdoor cafés, the restaurants, and the bars along here are filled. The discos in Albufeira get going after midnight.

A good, inexpensive place to stay here is the **Hotel Rocamar**, *Largo Jacinto d'Ayet; tel. +351 (289) 540-280; website: www.rocamarbeachhotel.com.*

Nature's best show: Sea caves and rock formations

Between Albufeira and Portimao, near the cliffside village of Praia do Carvoeiro, nature provides one of its most beautiful spectacles. Drive to the **Nossa Senhora da Encarnaçâo**, a chapel at the summit of a steep hill east of Praia do Carvoeiro. Climb down 134 steps through oddly shaped red rocks to see the gaping holes leading into the sea caves, which are engulfed every few minutes by waves. The sights here are simply breathtaking. A path leads to a bluff from which you have a clear view of the entrance to an underwater sea cave.

The **Caves of Cape Carvoeiro** are best seen by boat, which you can do during high season. Ask for information at the tourist office in Praia do Carvoeiro.

Lagos: The saddest past and the sandiest beaches

Ten miles west of Portimao is the town of **Lagos**, once a center of the African slave trade. The **Antigo Mercado de Escravos**, is the site of the first slave trade market established in Europe. Sections of Roman walls remain in the old quarter of Lagos, and you can walk along the walls of the old fortress that guards the harbor. The 18th-century baroque **Chapel of St. Antonio**, *rua General Alberto Carlos Silveira*, is known for its ornate gilded woodcarvings.

South of town is Ponta da Piedad, a headland with fine beaches connected by natural rock tunnels. The scenery is striking—the rocks are a reddish color that contrasts with the green of the sea. The boulders have been carved into strange shapes by pounding waves. Hire a boat to take you to the off shore grottos.

SAGRES: THE END OF THE WORLD

Sagres, the most southwesterly point in Europe, is guarded by the fortress of **Prince Henry the Navigator**. His famous navigational device, the **Compass Rose**, is laid out in the stone.

Prince Henry founded his navigation school here at the beginning of the 15th century. It also was here that he planned his expeditions into Africa and west into the unknown.

Before the great explorations began, sailors believed that **Cabo de São Vicente** (Cape St. Vincent), near Sagres, was the end of the world. The place is marked by a famous lighthouse. Waves crash ferociously on the rocks 250 feet below the lighthouse. If you're going to walk here, bring a windbreaker. Or buy one of the handsome handmade sweaters the women of Sagres are famous for knitting.

Hotel Pousada do Infante, *Sagres; tel. +351 (282) 620-240; website: www.pousadas.pt,* has views of the coast and the lighthouse on the promontory of Cape St. Vincent. Delicious soups are served in the dining room, including *crème de espinafres* (spinach cream soup) and *sopa do mar* (fish soup). The fish is always fresh and well-cooked, and the wine list is extensive.

THE BEST WILDLIFE

Monção is a good base for exploring the **Peneda-Geres National Park**. The National Forest Department can arrange guided trips through the mountainous 170,000-acre park, where wild horses, stags, and boars roam and where you can spot milestones along the ancient Roman Way. For more information, stop at the tourist office in Monção.

The **Pousada de São Bento**, *Canicada 4850; tel. +351 (253) 64-9150; website: www.pousadas.pt*, is a good place to stay if you want to explore the park. A modern hotel with dizzying views of the Minho Valley, it is cozy in the winter, with the atmosphere of a hunting lodge. It has high ceilings, massive rafters, and large picture windows overlooking the mountains. The swimming pool and tennis courts are inviting in warm weather.

PORTO: THE PORT WINE CAPITAL

Originally a Roman settlement, **Porto** has many old palaces, convents, and churches. (The cathedral is famous for its gilded wood altars and grand organ.) However, Porto's true fame comes from port wine. If you wander along the banks of the River Douro, you will see *rabelos*, or barges, bringing the distinctive port wine grapes down from the vineyards.

The area upriver from Porto is the only place in the world that grows grapes for port, and Porto is the only place where it is made. You can try port wine and the local Vinho Verde at any restaurant or café in the city. Also, you can visit the **Port Wine Institute**, *website: www.ivp.pt*. Vila Nova de Gaia, on the south bank of the Douro, opposite Porto, is the center of the port wine trade. You can sample port at the wine bodegas here and learn how it is matured for at least 25 years before being sold. The Tourist Office, *Rua dos Clube Fenianos 25; tel. +351 (223) 393-472; website: www.portoturismo.pt*, is very helpful.

PORTUGAL'S SADDEST LOVE STORY

The **Santa Maria Monastery**, *516 Mosteiro Alcobaça,* in the town of Alcobaça is the final resting place of the ill-fated lovers **Dom Pedro** and **Ines de Castro**. When Prince Dom Pedro married his beautiful mistress Ines de Castro, his father, King Alfonso IV of Portugal, was so outraged by the unequal union that he had Ines assassinated in 1355. When he succeeded to the throne, Dom Pedro got his revenge. He dressed the body of Ines in royal attire and forced the noblemen who had killed her to pay homage by kissing her decomposed hand. The lovers are positioned in their ornate tombs so that they will face each other on Judgment Day. Constructed by Cistercian monks in 1178, the kitchen in the monastery was built above a trout stream so the cooks could have fresh water and fish.

THE OLDEST UNIVERSITY TOWN

Coimbra, where Princess Ines was murdered, is one of the oldest medieval university towns in Europe. The city's streets are dotted with students wearing traditional black capes. A steep cobblestone street leads to the university courtyard, where you can join a tour of the old university buildings, including the Manueline Chapel, with its ornate door and 17th-century *azulejos*, and the library, with its carved and varnished wood embellishments.

THE VENICE OF PORTUGAL

Aveiro, at the northernmost tip of the Costa de Prata, claims to be the Venice of Portugal. It is surrounded by salt flats, beaches, and lagoons and dominated by the Central Canal. Gaily-painted *moliceiros* (boats reminiscent of Venice's gondolas) move through the waters gathering algae to be used as fertilizer.

A good hotel in Aveiro is the **Arcada Hotel**, *Rua Viana do Castelo 4; tel. +351 (234) 421-885; website: www.hotelarcada.com.*

BUÇACO: THE MOST BEAUTIFUL FOREST

Buçaco National Park, which has 700 species of trees from around the world, has been considered a holy place for centuries. Benedictine monks built the hermitage here in the sixth century. In 1622, Pope Gregory XV forbade women to enter the oak and pine forest. And the Barefoot Carmelite monks began the arboretum here in 1628.

In 1810, **Buçaco Mountain** was the site of a battle between the combined British and Portuguese forces under Wellington and the French. (Wellington's forces won.) The Portuguese government took over in 1834 and expanded the arboretum. Today, the park covers 250 acres of woodland. In the center of the park is the royal hunting lodge built by Carlos I (1888-1907). Today it is the **Palace Hotel Bussaco**, *Mata do Bussaco; tel. +351 (231) 937-970; website: www.almeidahotels.com,* an incredibly ornate luxury hotel.

PORTUGAL'S MOST SPECACULAR MONASTERY

Portugal's most spectacular monastery is in **Batalha**. King João vowed to the Virgin Mary that he would build a monastery if she helped him defeat the Castillians. The king's army was indeed victorious against the Castillian army in the Battle of Aljubarrota on August 14th, 1385, ensuring Portugal's independence for the next 200 years. The **Mosteiro Santa Maria da Vitória** (to give it its official title), does justice to the victory, with flying buttresses, turrets, a mass of gables, columns, and elaborate tracery. King João and his wife Philippa of Lancaster are buried here along with their children, including Prince Henry the Navigator.

THE PRETTIEST PORTUGUESE TOWN

Obidos, one of the best-preserved medieval fortified towns on the Iberian Peninsula, has a feminine look, with tiny whitewashed houses and flower-lined streets. The 12th-century **Obidos Castle** dominates the city. **St. Mary's Church**, where King Alfonso V married his eight-year-old cousin Isabella in 1444, is tiled with blue azulejos. The octagonal Senhor da Pedra Church has a remarkable second-century stone cross.

The **Pousada do Castelo**, *Rua Direita; tel. +351 (258) 821-751; website:*

www.pousadasofportugal.com/portugal/pousada/obidos.html, housed within the castle walls, is furnished with antiques and has excellent cuisine and extensive wine cellars. Because it has only six rooms, early reservations are recommended.

The **Estalagem do Convento**, *Rua Dom Joao de Ornelas, 2510-074 Obidos; tel. +351 (262) 959-214; website: www.estalagemdoconvento.com,* is a medieval hotel in Obidos furnished with tables and chairs from the days of the knights and Crusaders. This is a novel place to stay the night, with little rooms and cobblestone courtyards.

MIRACULOUS FÁTIMA

The village of **Fátima**, where Catholics believe the Virgin Mary appeared to three shepherd children in 1917, is a major shrine and place of pilgrimage. Special ceremonies are held on the 13th day of each month between May and October. Make reservations well in advance if you plan to visit Fátima during that time—throngs descend upon the town.

PORTUGAL'S ODDEST DANCE

The mountain town of **Miranda do Douro**, perched on a ravine just across the River Douro from Spain, is famous for its *pauliteiros*, who perform a traditional sword dance each year on the Feast of St. Barbara (the third Sunday in August). Dancers carry sticks representing swords and wear kilts, embroidered shirts, and black hats covered with ribbons and flowers. They move in an ancient pattern to the sounds of tambourines and bagpipes. Another regional remnant of bygone eras is *Mirandes*, a Latin slang that the locals speak among themselves.

The **Santa Catarina Inn**, *5210-183 Miranda do Douro; tel. +351 (273) 431-005; website: www.estalagemsantacatarina.pt,* balanced on the edge of a rocky gorge, has lovely views of the River Douro. Occasionally you'll see a golden eagle. The food, cooked over a wood fire, is good. Try the *guisado de polvo a transmontana*, or octopus ragout.

ÉVORA: THE MOST ROMAN

Évora, one of the oldest towns on the Iberian Peninsula, has the best Roman ruins in Portugal. Originally a Roman settlement, the town was later inhabited by the Visigoths. Under the Moors, it became a major trade and agricultural center. And during Portugal's heyday in the 15th and 16th centuries, Évora's university was a magnet for the best scholars and writers of the time. Now a public high school, the old university's great hall is covered with 17th-century tiles.

The Roman **Temple of Diana**, *Largo do Conde de Vila Flor*, dating from the second century, is well preserved. Before it was excavated in 1870, it was used as a slaughterhouse. The 1975 bloodless revolution was planned beneath its Corinthian columns.

Notice Évora's quaint street designations—streets bear the names of a countess' tailor, a cardinal's nurse, the lisping man, and the unshaven man. And take a look at the macabre **Igreja de São Francisco**, *Rua da Republica*. It contains a chapel built of 50,000 monks' bones. The Franciscans thought this a good way to encourage meditation upon the transitory nature of life. Above the entrance is a warning, *"Nos ossos que aqui estamos pelos vossos esperamos"*—which means "The bones here are waiting for yours."

Évora's **Pousada dos Loios**, *Largo Conde de Vila Flor; tel. +351 (266) 730-070; website: www.pousadas.pt*, is one of the best in the country. It faces the Temple of Diana and is located in what was the St. Eligius Monastery, consecrated in 1491. The cloisters have been glassed in to form a dining room, which has a vaulted ceiling, horseshoe arches, and a marble font. The bedrooms are converted monastic cells. One of the suites has a baroque antechamber.

PORTUGAL'S POTTERY TOWN

Estreméoz has been an artistic center since the 16th century. It is famous for its Alentejo pottery, sold in the main square on Saturdays. Typical wares include narrow-mouthed jars called *barris* and wide-mouthed jars called *bilhas*. Local artists also create clay figurines of people and animals. Local crafts are displayed at the Rural Museum on the main square.

MADEIRA: THE MOST FRUITFUL ISLAND

About 600 miles off the coast of Morocco lies **Madeira**, a garden paradise that belongs to Portugal. The lush, semitropical volcanic island was discovered by Portuguese explorers in 1419 and soon became a regular port of call for seafarers. Ships coming from the New World and Asia stopped here and left behind specimens of exotic plants, which islanders grew in rich volcanic soil with great success. The result is an island abounding in tropical fruits, vegetables, and flowers. Madeira's mild temperature ranges from 60° F in winter to 72° F in summer.

The best footin'

The best way to see the interior of the island is to walk along the *levadas*, or footpaths, which follow ancient Madeiran irrigation channels carrying water from high up in the mountains down through the terraced farms to the fields and villages below. The paths are graded one to four, from easiest to most difficult.

For the most difficult walks, you need more than hiking boots—you also need a good head for heights. On one side of the foot-wide paths is the irrigation stream, which may be running 18 gallons per minute, while on the other is a vertical precipice hundreds of feet high. The natives, often carrying high bundles on their heads, scurry fearlessly up the paths. A map of all canal walking paths is available from the **Direcção Regional de Turismo**, *website: www.madeiratourism.org.*

Portugal's best thrill

If you're brave enough, make time during your visit to Madeira to take an exhilarating ride in a little wicker fruit cart with steel blades from Monte downhill to Funchal, the island's capital. You use levers to control the wooden carts as they roll like bumper cars down the hill. Once used for practical purposes, such as transporting fruits and vegetables, today the carts are used purely as amusement rides. The tourist office will help you arrange a ride.

Bacchus' favorite—Madeira

After such an exploit, you will probably need a drink. Try the island's fortified sweet wine, called **Madeira**. According to legend, when early settlers reached Madeira (which means wood), they burned off the thick forests in a fire that raged for seven years. When vines were planted in the resulting soil, the grapes acquired their characteristic smoky flavor.

During the days of the American Revolution, Madeira could be imported to Colonial America in non-British ships, which made it the drink of independence.

548

It was the favorite tipple of the early American revolutionaries. Tour the wine bodegas in Funchal to see how Madeira is processed and stored. At the end of the visit, you can sample the wine.

Funchal's best sights

Funchal's most famous sights, its **botanical gardens**, *tel. +351 (291) 211-200; website: www.madeirabotanicalgarden.com*, are brightly colored year-round. Against the natural beauty of these gardens, the works of man fade.

The churches in Funchal range from the 15th-century **Capela de Santa Catarina** (in the Manueline style, a Portuguese version of Gothic characterized by nautical-inspired stone carving) to the **Se** (cathedral), with its carved-wood and gilded altars. Church paintings in Funchal and throughout the island show a strong Flemish influence. The **Palace of the Conde de Carvalhal** is now the town hall.

The island's early houses with black stone trim are made of the volcanic rock of Madeira. The customhouse in the harbor (Alfandega) is an often overlooked site; especially noteworthy are the second-floor carved and painted ceiling and the 17th-century illuminated Bible, on which captains had to swear they had nothing to declare.

The world's second-highest sea cliff

Cabo Girão, on Madeira, is the world's second-highest sea cliff. This promontory has extraordinary views. Go at sunset. (The highest sea cliff in the world is the north coast of East Molokai Island, Hawaii.)

Madeira's best festival

One of the best times to visit Madeira is June, during the **Ribeira Brava Festival of St. Peter**. In celebration of the patron saint of fishermen, residents join in solemn processions, which are followed by dances, including the traditional sword dance.

Madeira's best eats

Good restaurants near Funchal include **A Seta**, *tel. +351 (291) 743-643*, which serves barbecued beef and chicken on sword skewers hung from the ceiling, along with mounds of fresh-baked bread and pitchers of red wine.

The most gracious hotel

Reid's Palace, *Estrada Monumental 139; tel. +351 (291) 717-171; website: www. reidspalace.com*, is Madeira's most gracious resort hotel. Set on a cliff overlooking the sea, it has a British colonial flavor. It is surrounded by tropical foliage and flowers and has a private beach, tennis courts, two pools, and boat rentals.

Portugal's best accommodation: the *pousada*

The 25 *pousadas* throughout Portugal offer historic accommodation and fine food. They are housed in converted medieval castles or convents in areas of great natural beauty. For more information: *tel. +351 (218) 442-001; website: www.pousadas.pt.*

THE BEST OF
ROMANIA

Romania is a land for romantics. More Gypsies live here than anywhere else in the world. Romanians claim to be descendants of a lost Roman legion. The Roman poet Ovid was exiled here, on a lagoon north of Constanta. And Vlad the Impaler—the man behind the myth of Dracula—led his bloody life in Transylvania.

BUCHAREST: THE PARIS OF EASTERN EUROPE

Thousands of years ago, a little Stone Age settlement was established on the trade route that crossed the forest-covered Romanian plains. Today, that settlement is Bucharest, the capital of Romania, and the trade route is the chain of grand boulevards that earned the city the title of the "Paris of Eastern Europe."

The boulevards—N. Balcescu, 1848, Magheru, and Ana Ipatescu—are lined with restaurants and brasseries. Along their southern stretch is the **Princely Palace**, which is surrounded by the trading quarter, called **Lipscani**, where narrow medieval streets wind past little shops.

The remains of the **Old Princely Court** (Curtea Veche), built in the 15th century by Vlad Tepes, also known as Vlad Dracula, are at the heart of this area. According to local lore, Vlad kept his prisoners in dungeons which commenced beneath the Princely Court and extended under the city. All that remains today are a few walls, arches, tombstones, and a Corinthian column.

The **Old Court Museum** was established in 1972 when an archaeological dig revealed the remains of the fortress, along with Dacian pottery and Roman coins, evidence of Bucharest's earliest inhabitants. The oldest document attesting to the city's origin under the name of Bucuresti (Bucharest) was discovered here. It was issued on September 20th, 1459 and signed by Prince Vlad Tepes.

Calea Victoriei, Bucharest's most famous street, passes many of the city's major sights. Starting at the **Operetta Theater**, *Piata Natiunile Unite*, it leads north past **Stavropoleos Church** to the **History Museum of Romania**, *Calea Victoriei, nr.12, sect. 3; tel. +40 (21) 315-8207;* in the former post office. The museum displays the 42-pound golden Hen with Golden Chickens, a fifth-century treasure made of 12 gold pieces. It is closed on Mondays.

Like Paris, Bucharest has a triumphal arch. Built in 1922 to celebrate the Allies' victory in World War I, it is located on the wide avenue of Soseaua Kiseleff.

Bucharest's best restaurants

Capsa, *Calea Victoriei nr. 36; tel. +40 (21) 313-4038; website: www.capsa.ro*, is the traditional meeting place for Bucharest's artists. It offers a choice of local or continental cuisine and excellent desserts. It is also a hotel and has its own pastry shop.

Pescarus, *Bulevardul Aviatorilor Nr. 1 (Parc Herastrau); tel. +40 (21) 230-4640; website: www.restaurantpescarus.ro,* located along the Herastrau Park, serves international cuisine on a terrace overlooking a lake in the park.

Bucharest's best hotels

The deluxe **Radisson SAS Hotel Bucharest**, *Celea Vitoriei 63-81; tel. +40 (21) 311-9000; website: www.radissonblu.com/hotel-bucharest*, in the center of town has 800 rooms, two restaurants, two swimming pools, a sauna, and a gym.

The **Athenee Palace Hilton**, *Strada Episcopiei 1-3; tel. +40 (21) 303-3777; website: www1.hilton.com*, a pre-war grand hotel, it was recently restored to its former glory. It has two restaurants, a pastry shop, and very affordable prices.

DRACULA'S CASTLE

While in Brasov, make a day-trip to the town of Poiana Brasov (Sunny Glade) to see **Bran Castle** *(website: www.bran-castle.com),* the legendary home of Count Dracula. It is actually the home of the Prince of Wallachia, who repelled a Turkish invasion by impaling hundreds of his countrymen on tall stakes and lining the route of the enemy's march. The Turks, frightened by the brutal display, avoided the region. In truth, the Prince stayed at this castle only occasionally.

THE BEST OF
SCANDINAVIA

Summer, when the sun hardly sets over Scandinavia, is the best time to visit this northern land. After months of darkness, Scandinavians come out of hibernation to celebrate the golden months of June and July with parties that would go on until dawn—except dawn never comes.

Scandinavia—for our purposes Denmark, Norway, Sweden, and Finland—has both cosmopolitan cities and the most enormous wilderness area in Europe. Lapland, which crosses Norway, Sweden, and Finland, is a stunning region with glittering glaciers and bright blue skies. Lapps herd their reindeer across the tundra as they have for centuries. The region's parks offer well-marked trails and huts, where hikers can sleep in comfort.

DENMARK: THE MOST ACCESSIBLE COUNTRY

The southernmost of the Scandinavian countries has a romantic landscape crisscrossed by waterways and dotted with thatched-roof houses. It is easy to imagine the trolls, werewolves, and sorcerers of Danish legend; Hans Christian Andersen was inspired by these legends to write his famous fairy tales.

The most accessible of the Scandinavian countries, **Denmark** is the only one attached to mainland Europe. North of Germany and south of Sweden and Norway, Denmark is made up of the Jutland Peninsula, which shares a border with Germany, and two major islands, Zealand and Funen. Altogether, the Danish islands number 480. Most are uninhabited.

The best way to meet the Danes

Through the **Meet the Danes** program, you can spend an evening in a Danish home in any one of eight cities: Århus, Aalborg, Esbjerg, Fredericia, Lønstrup, Odense, Roskilde, or Skive. Local tourist offices can arrange the visit if you give them 24 hours notice. For more information, contact the **Danish Tourist Board,** *tel. (in the U.S.) +1 (212) 885-9700; website: www.visitdenmark.com* or see *www.meetthe-danes.dk.*

Copenhagen: The best fun

Copenhagen (København), on the east coast of the island of Zealand, is a city dedicated to entertainment. What other capital city revolves around an amusement park—**Tivoli Gardens,** *website: www.tivoli.dk.* Merrymaking Danes of all ages scream with fear and excitement aboard Tivoli's rides. Try out The Flight, an inter-active ride with a maximum speed of 100 km/h and 360 degree turns, where you are the pilot! The famous Ferris wheel has a far-reaching view.

Built in 1843 on 20 acres in the heart of Copenhagen, Tivoli is more than just an amusement park. It has gardens, lakes, theaters, dance halls, games, bars, and scores of restaurants to suit every budget. At night it is illuminated by 100,000 colored lights, and you can enjoy vaudeville acts, concerts, music, and dancing.

Strøget: The best stroll in Denmark

The longest pedestrian thoroughfare in the world, the **Strøget** (Strolling Place) meanders through the heart of Copenhagen. This mile-long stretch is lined with cafés, banks, department stores, and boutiques selling everything from cheap t-shirts to fine Icelandic sweaters and expensive watches. The Strøget is actually an area made up of five streets: Frederiksberggade, Nygade, Vimmelskaftet, Amagertorv, and Ostergade. It is between the city's two main squares: Raadhuspladsen and Kongens-Nytorv. All this is made more confusing by the fact that "the Strøget" isn't marked as such on city maps.

The most elegant shops are clustered at the eastern end. **Day Birger et Mikkelsen,** *Pilestraede 16; tel. +45 3345-8880; website: www.day.dk*, is Danish design at its best, with stylish clothing for men and women.

The world's largest porcelain factory

The **Royal Copenhagen**, the largest porcelain factory in the world, has a shop on the Stroget at *Amagertorv 6; tel. +45 3313-7181; website: www.royalcopenhagen.com*. It is housed in a 16th-century Dutch Renaissance building and offers a fine collection of all four brand names of china. The Royal Copenhagen has been working at its craft for more than two centuries, producing elegant, hand-painted dinnerware and figurines.

The best amber and silver shopping

The best place on the Strøget to shop for amber and silver is the **Danish Silver Shop**, *Bredgade 22; tel. +45 3311-5252; website: www.danishsilver.com*, which offers unique and elegant Scandinavian jewelry. Small amber heart-shaped pendants and solid amber necklaces are half the price charged in other countries.

The two best museums

Copenhagen has more than 50 public museums and galleries, most within easy walking distance of the Strøget. The largest is the **Nationalmuseet** (National Museum), *Ny Vestergade 10; tel. +45 3313-4411; website: www.natmus.dk*, which has the best display of Viking artifacts in the world. It is located behind the Christiansborg Palace.

Nearby you find **Ny Carlsberg Glyptotek** (art museum), *Dantes Plads 7; tel. +45 3341-8141; website: www.glyptoteket.dk*, which has extensive collections of Roman, Etruscan, and Egyptian art, as well as a respectable number of Impressionist paintings. Its arboretum is a tranquil place where you can sit beneath immense trees and listen to a Gregorian chant.

A beer lover's best

If you love beer and don't mind crowds, visit the **Carlsberg** and **Tuborg** breweries. The tours and beer are free, and it's always a good time—especially after a few tastes. See the website *www.visitcarlsberg.dk* for more information on tours and opening times.

Copenhagen's two castles

Rosenborg, *Oster Voldgade 4A; tel. +45 3315-3286; website: www.rosenborgslot.dk*, a 17th-century castle, houses the crown jewels and the royal treasures of the Danes.

Amalienborg Palace, *tel. +45 3392-6300*, is the residence of the royal family. Witness the changing of the guard daily at noon.

Capital nightlife

Copenhagen is a chic city with a nightlife that is sure to satisfy any traveler; the only problem is keeping up with all there is to do in the capital city. One of the most popular nightclubs is **Rust**, *Guldbergsgade 8; tel. +45 3524-5200; website: www.rust.dk.*

If a nightclub is not exactly your pace, there are plenty of other good night spots to choose from; visit *www.visitcopenhagen.dk* for a list.

The cheapest way to go

The major problem with Copenhagen is that it is expensive. The best way to cut costs is by buying the **Copenhagen Card**, available from the tourist office, train stations, Copenhagen's hotels, and travel agents. The card gives you free entry into museums, free bus and train travel, plus discounts on many of the city's attractions.

The best eating

Krog's Fiskerestaurant, *Gammel Strand 38; tel. +45 3315-8915; website: www. krogs.dk*, across the canal from Christiansborg, is the best seafood restaurant.

For Danish and French cuisine with a skyline view of Copenhagen, try **Aristo**, *Islands Brygge 4; tel. +45 3295-8330; website: www.restaurantaristo.dk.*

For Danish cooking with inspiration from abroad, try **Restaurant Thorvaldsen,** *tel. +45 3332-0400; website: www.thorvaldsens-hus.dk.*

The best hotels

Hotel d'Angleterre, *Konges Nytorv 34; tel. +45 3312-0095; website: www. dangleterre.dk*, is the oldest and most fashionable hotel in Copenhagen, located at the far end of the walking street, Strøget. The hotel also houses a good French restaurant and a popular nightclub.

The **Radisson Blu Scandinavia Hotel**, *Amager blvd. 70; tel. +45 3396-5000; website: www.radissonblu.com/scandinaviahotel-copenhagen,* is a large, ultramodern skyscraper hotel run by SAS (the Scandinavian airline). This hotel caters to those preferring Scandinavian modern over Scandinavian provincial.

The **Savoy Hotel**, *Vesterbrogade 34; tel. +45 3326-7500; website: www. savoyhotel.dk,* is a very old, but modernized hotel that has retained its Old-World charm. Here, style and service with a smile are still the order of the day.

Roskilde: The first capital

The ancient city of **Roskilde**, west of Copenhagen, was the capital of Denmark until 1445. It is also the site of the first Danish church, built in A.D. 960. Members of Denmark's royalty are buried in marble and alabaster tombs in the 12th-century cathedral (known as the Westminster Abbey of Denmark), including Harald the Bluetooth, a 10th-century king; Margarethe, once queen of Scandinavia; and Christian X, the Danish king during World War II who wore a yellow star to demonstrate his sympathy for the Jews.

The **Vikingskibshallen** (Viking Ship Museum), *tel. +45 4630-0200; website: www.vikingeskibsmuseet.dk*, at Havnen displays five Viking ships painstakingly pieced together from hundreds of pieces of wreckage. An amazingly well-preserved seagoing cargo ship from A.D. 1000 sits in the main hall.

Lindenborg Kro, *Lindenborgvej 90; tel. +45 4640-2111; website: www.lindenborgkro.dk,* just outside Roskilde, is one of the most pleasant inns in Denmark. The original inn, built 300 years ago, burned in 1967, but a new one was built on the site.

Denmark's best castles

If you see only one castle in your lifetime, it should be **Frederiksborg**, *tel. +45 4826-0439; website: www.frederiksborgslot.dk.* This 17th-century treasure trove in Hillerød is the largest Renaissance castle in Scandinavia and is surrounded by a moat, a Baroque garden, and has an ornate, gilded chapel with a rare 1610 Compenius organ. Here, Danish kings were crowned. The castle houses the most important national history museum. Every square foot is covered with art and antiques, including four-poster beds, ebony cabinets, coats of arms, and tapestries.

Kronborg Castle, *tel. +45 4921-3078; website: www.kronborgcastle.com*, at **Helsingor** is the bleak and imposing castle where Shakespeare set *Hamlet*. It has secret passages and turrets, exactly as you would imagine. Built in 1574 and restored in 1629, it now houses the Danish Maritime Museum.

Nyborg Castle, *tel. +45 6531-0207; website: www.nyborgslot.dk,* on the island of **Funen**, is the oldest royal castle still standing in Scandinavia and is believed to have been built in the 12th century. Until the 15th century, the moated castle guarded one of the most strategic spots in the country. Be sure to see the knight's hall and the old Danehof, which was used by the medieval parliament, an uneasy alliance between noblemen and clergy. Nyborg can be reached by ferry from Zealand.

Egeskov, *tel. +45 6227-1016; website: www.egeskov.com,* near **Odense**, is the best-preserved moated castle in Europe. A Renaissance structure with magnificent gardens, it was built in 1554 on oak pillars in the middle of a small lake. Legend tells of a maiden who bore an illegitimate child to the young nobleman of the castle and was locked in one of the castle towers from 1559 to 1604. The landscaped gardens are open to the public every day. But the castle itself is a private home and can only be visited during chamber music concerts held in the summer.

Denmark's best bike route

The **Haervejen** (pronounced Hairvayen), a marked bike trail, follows an ancient military road along Denmark's spine. It leads through the center of Jutland past *menhirs* (large monumental stones erected by prehistoric Danes), barrows (mounds of earth or stones over burial sites), rune stones etched with characters from the ancient Scandinavian alphabet, and churches built by the first Danish Christians.

The trail runs 170 miles from Viborg in central Jutland to the Eider River in Germany. For centuries, it was the only road connecting Scandinavia with continental Europe. For more information, contact the **Danish Tourist Board**, *tel. +45 3288-9900; website: www.dt.dk*, or the local tourist board in Svendborg, *tel. +45 6223-5700; website: www.visitsydfyn.dk.*

A kids' best

Families traveling through Copenhagen should set aside at least one day to visit Denmark's unique theme park, **Legoland,** *tel. +45 7533-1333; website: www. legoland.dk.* Specially trained Lego artists used more than 33 million Lego blocks to create 25 acres of colorful fantasy land. Most of the exhibits, displaying historical sights and events from all over the world, are scaled down to one-twentieth of the real-life size.

The two prettiest Baltic islands

Ærø, a tiny island in the Baltic, is the best place to get a glimpse of the traditional Danish seafaring life. A five-hour trip from Copenhagen by train and then ferry, it is one of many Danish islands in the archipelago north of the German coast. Brightly painted little fishing villages fringe this 22-mile-long island. Its picturesque beaches are occasionally dotted with nude sunbathers. Inland, thatched-roof farmhouses break the rolling hills. The villages are tiny, but they usually have hotels and bakeries.

Ærøskøbing, on Ærø, is Denmark's most carefully preserved medieval village, dating from the 13th century. Its narrow cobblestone streets are lined with gingerbread houses roofed with round tiles and painted blue or red. They were once the homes of Ærø's sea captains.

Bornholm, a Danish island between Sweden and Poland, has the world's finest-grained sand and is known for its grandfather clocks and smoked herring.

The island's towns balance on sloping rocks. The ruins of a 13th-century castle can be explored at Hammershus Slot. Half-timbered houses and ancient round churches, once used as protection against pirates and enemy armies, still stand here. The greatest round church is in Ølsker. Built in 1150, the structure is literally round.

The best natural sight on the island is at **Rø**, a 72-foot rock formation filled with columns, caves, and crevices. Its name means Sacred Thing. The most beautiful beach is in Dueodde on the south coast, where the sand is incredibly fine, dunes rise 45 feet, and there is a 145-foot lighthouse. If you tire of the sea, explore Bornholm's forest, Almindingen, the third-largest in Denmark.

The bluest light in Scandinavia

Skagen, a harbor village at the top of the Jutland Peninsula, was discovered by a group of painters in the middle of the 19th century who were drawn here by the unique play of light in this area of Scandinavia. As one Skagen painter said, *"Where two seas meet, the light can't help but be the bluest in creation."*

For the cheapest meals in Skagen, go around the red tackle houses to the opposite side. This is where the Danes purchase their seafood, and anything you get here will be good.

NORWAY: THE MOST RUGGED

Norway, with the second-lowest population density in Europe, is the most rugged Scandinavian country. It has deep-gouged, sharp mountains rising from the jagged coastlines and frigid glaciers glittering beneath the midnight sun. Grass-thatched houses occupy little patches of land on steep hillsides. This is a country that challenges the sportsman, with superb skiing, hiking, sailing, orienteering, hunting, and mountain climbing.

Oslo: The world's most forested capital

Oslo, the capital of Norway, is the most heavily forested capital in the world—encompassing farms as well as nightclubs. The 175-square-mile city was founded in the 11th century by Viking King Oslo. Because it was completely destroyed by fire in 1824, little medieval architecture remains. The finest residences that survived are along Raadhusgate.

Oslo's most dramatic sight

Akershus Castle, *Festnings-Plassen; tel. +47 2309-3917; website: www.forsvarsbygg. no/festningene/Festningene/akershus-festning/*, the ancient protector of the city, looms from atop a cliff that juts out into the eastern half of the harbor. The well-preserved medieval structure (built in 1300 by King Haakon V Magnusson) was an impregnable fortress and royal residence for several hundred years. Although it has suffered through nine battles, it was never conquered and eventually was transformed into a Renaissance palace by Danish-Norwegian King Christian IV. Today, the castle is used by the government for state occasions. The bastions offer tremendous views of Oslo. Inside, some of the works of Expressionist painter Edvard Munch are on display.

Scandinavia's oldest church

The oldest church in Scandinavia, **Gamle Aker Kirke**, *Akersbakken 26; tel. +47 2269-3582*, is still in use after 890 years. Daily services are held May 15th through September 10th, and Sunday services are held year-round (at 10 a.m. and noon). You can visit the church with an appointment Tuesdays and Thursdays. The tour is free.

Top sights

Next to Akershus Castle is the **Norsk Hjemmefrontmuseum**, *Akershus Fortress; tel. +47 2309-3280,* Norway's Resistance museum, which documents World War II and Norway's resistance to the Nazi's.

Domkirke (Oslo's cathedral), *Stortorvet 1; tel. +47 2362-9010, website: www.oslodomkirke.no*, built between 1694 and 1699, has its original altarpiece and pulpit. The stained-glass windows were created by the Norwegian artist Emanuel Vigeland (the younger brother of Norway's most famous sculptor Gustav Vigeland). The bronze doors and ceiling decorations are also impressive, and the cathedral's organ rises five floors. Sunday services are usually at 11 a.m.

Rådhuset, Oslo's city hall, *Fridtjof Nansens plass; tel. +47 2346-1600,* completed in 1950, was embellished in a collective effort by Norway's greatest artists and designers. Inside are more than 2,000 square yards of bold, colorful murals, including Munch's *Life*. The walls are a rainbow of colorful stones and woods.

Norway's most memorable sculptures are at **Frognerparken**, *Kirkeveien; tel. +47 2 49-3700; website: www.vigeland.museum.no/en/vigeland-park,* a 75-acre park devoted to the works of Gustav Vigeland. In 1921, the city gave the sculptor free rein in the park. The result: a 1,150-piece collection of huge, writhing nude figures illustrating the human struggle. The works were once the subject of much controversy.

The best of the Vikings

Three Viking burial ships excavated on the shores of the Oslo fiord (the clay had preserved them since A.D. 800 and A.D. 900) are kept at the **Vikingskipshuset** (Viking Ship Museum), *Huk Aveny 35; tel. +47 2213-5280, website: www.khm.uio.no,* on the Bygdøy Peninsula.

The most spectacular is the *Oseberg*, a 64-foot dragon ship with animals carved on its prow. It is believed to have been the burial ship of Harald Fairhair's grandmother and her slave, who were buried in it along with 15 horses, an ox, four dogs, and some artifacts.

The greatest Norwegian adventure

The balsa-log raft *Kon Tiki*, on which Norwegian scientist Thor Heyerdahl sailed 5,000 miles in 1947, is kept at the **Kon Tiki Museum**, *Bygdøynesveien 36; tel. +47 2308-6767; website: www.kon-tiki.no*, on the Bygdøy Peninsula. The *Kon Tiki*, designed according to specifications for early Peruvian boats, sailed from Callao, Peru to Raroia, Polynesia to prove that pre-Inca Indians could have crossed from South America to populate Polynesia. The museum also houses the papyrus *Ra II*, in which Heyerdahl crossed the Atlantic from North Africa to Barbados in 1970, and artifacts from his voyage to Easter Island.

A close-up view of folk life

Over 100 historic buildings from all over Norway have been transported to the **Norsk Folkemuseum** (Norwegian Folk Museum), *Museumsveien 10, Bygdøy; tel. +47 2212-3700; website: www.norskfolke.museum.no*, a 35-acre area on the Bygdøy Peninsula. Sights there include *Taulandstua*, one of the oldest wooden dwellings in the country; a hand-built wooden stave church that dates back to 1200; historic log cabins; Lapp artifacts; and a reconstruction of the last apartment of Norwegian playwright Henrik Ibsen.

The highest lookout in Scandinavia

For a dizzying view, climb to the lookout tower at **Tryvannstaarnet**. To get there, take the Holmenkollen subway near the National Theater in Oslo to the end of the line, Voksenkollenn. From there, it's a 15-minute walk uphill to Tryvannstaarnet, the highest lookout in Scandinavia.

Another 20-minute walk down the hill leads to the Holmenkollen ski jump, one of the most famous in the world and the site of Olympic competitions in 1952. At the base of the jump is the **Ski Museum**, *Kongeveien 5; tel. +47 2292-3200; website: www.skiforeningen.no*, which displays 2,500-year-old ski equipment and equipment used on polar explorations.

Holmenkollen has the widest network of ski trails in the world (more than 1,300 miles of them, many with floodlights to allow nighttime skiing.) The best skiers in the world gather for **Holmenkollen Ski Festival** each winter to compete in downhill, slalom, cross-country, and ski jumping competitions, drawing thousands of spectators.

Eating well

Norwegian cuisine consists primarily of fish. The smoked salmon (*røklaks*) and mackerel (*røkmakrel*) are delicious. However, the meat, especially during fall hunting season, is equally good—try a reindeer or moose steak. The Norwegian *koldtbord* is a buffet that includes everything from herring to roast beef. In Sweden, it's known as a *smörgåsbord*.

The best seafood restaurants in Oslo are **Lofoten Fiskerestaurant**, *Stranden 75; tel. +47 2283-0808; website: www.lofoten-fiskerestaurant.no*, and **Engebret**, *Bankplassen 1; tel. +47 2282-2525; website: www.engebret-cafe.no*, which is one of the oldest restaurants in Oslo. It specializes in seafood with the Lutefisk as their signature dish.

Étoile Bar, *Karl Johans Gate 31; tel. +47 2321-2000; website: www.grand.no*, on the top floor of the Grand Hotel, has a beautiful view and serves savory French and Norwegian food. It is open daily from 10 a.m. until midnight weekdays and until 2 a.m. on weekends.

Bagatelle, *Bygdøy Allé, 3; tel. +47 2244-4040; website: www.bagatelle.no*. You will appreciate Eyvind Hellstrøm's contemporary Norwegian dishes, which use fresh seasonal produce like wild grouse, deer, or lobster.

Statholdergaarden, *Rådhusgata 11; tel. +47 2241-8800; website: www.statholdergaarden.no*. The ceiling in this elegant 17th-century manor has some of the finest stucco work in Europe. Master chef Bent Stiansen creates imaginative and lush dishes like a guinea fowl fried with Parma ham or Arctic char in nori served with Swedish caviar.

Oslo nights

Oslo doesn't have enough hotels to house all its visitors, so make reservations well in advance, especially if you are visiting during the summer.

The **Holmenkollen Park Hotel Rica**, *Kongeveien 26, Holmenkollåsen; tel. +47 2292-2000; website: www.holmenkollenparkhotel.no*, has cozy, albeit tiny, rooms with views of the city. The public salon has a huge fireplace, and the exceptionally attractive restaurant serves Norwegian specialties.

The **Radisson Blu Scandinavia Hotel**, *Holbergs Gate 30; tel. +47 2329-3000; website: www.radissonblu.com/scandinaviahotel-oslo*, is Norway's largest hotel. Very centrally located near the royal palace, its rooms have views of the city and the fiord. It has a pool, five restaurants, and several bars.

The **Hotel Continental**, *Stortingsgaten 24-26; tel. +47 2282-4000; website: www.hotel-continental.no*, has been owned by the same family for generations. It enjoys an excellent reputation as one of the best hotels in Scandinavia.

Many consider **The Grand Hotel**, *Karl Johanns Gate 31; tel. +47 2321-2000; website: www.grand.no*, Oslo's most prestigious hotel. It has spacious rooms, character suites (if you have the money, stay in its Tower Suite, one of the finest anywhere), and charming eateries. Esther Williams stayed here, as did Diana Ross and Miles Davis.

The best sights outside Oslo

Fredrikstad, a fortified town with ramparts, a drawbridge, and a moat, has a flourishing artists' colony. The cobblestone streets are lined with 18th-century houses and artisans' workshops. You can take an hour-long guided tour of the workshops weekdays between 9 a.m. and 3 p.m. Outside town is the 17th-century **Kingsten Fort**, which has secret passages and dungeons. Contact the Fredrikstad Tourist Office, *Tøihusgaten 41; tel. +47 6930-4600*, for more information.

Tønsberg, Norway's oldest town (founded in A.D. 870), is where Norwegian kings were once crowned. The **Vestfold County Museum**, *Farmannsveien 30; tel. +47 3331-2919*, at the town's entrance contains relics of the once-mighty whaling industry and of Viking chieftains.

Contact the Tønsberg Tourist Office, *Nedre Langgate 36; tel. +47 4806-3333; website: www.visittonsberg.com*, for more information.

A trip to Tønsberg can be combined with a trip to **Sandefjord**, once a great whaling town. This summer resort is just two hours by express train from Oslo. For more information about the area, contact Sandefjord Tourist Office, *Kurbadet, Thor Dahlsgate 7; tel. +47 3346-0590.*

Old whalers work as guides in the **Whaling Museum**, *Museumsgatan 39; tel. +47 9479-3341; website: www.hvalfangstmuseet.no,* relating stories about the whaling days and explaining the sights.

Heddal Stavkirke*; tel. +47 3502-0093; website: www.heddalstavkirke.no,* the biggest stave church in Norway, was built in the 13th-century and is located in **Notodden**, southwest of Oslo. Only 32 of these tiered timber churches with their pointy shingled roofs are still standing.

The **Rica Brakanes Hotel**, at Hardanger Fjord in Ulvik*, tel. +47 5652-6105; website: www.brakanes-hotel.no*, gives you an incredible view of the fjords.

Bergen: A music lover's best

If you like Grieg's music, you'll love **Bergen.** The city's native son left traces wherever he went. And you can hear his music at the ultramodern **Grieg Hall**, *Edvard Griegsplass 1, tel. +47 5521-6100; website: www.grieghallen.no,* which seats 1,420.

Grieg's music is also played during the international arts festival held in Bergen during the last week in May. (The festival also features opera, ballet, and folklore.) Details are available from the **Festival Office**, *Grieghallen, Lars Hilles Gate 3A; tel. +47 5521-6150; website: www.fib.no.*

Climb up to **Troldhaugen**, *Troldhaugvegen 65, tel. +47 5592-2992; website: www.kunstmuseene.no,* the summer villa of the composer in Hop, outside Bergen. The Victorian house contains his Steinway grand piano (which is used for concerts given at the house during the annual festival). The composer created many of his best works in the cottage on the estate. Grieg and his wife are buried in a cliff grotto here.

Bergen was the seat of the Viking kingdom of Norway until the 14th century and was a member of the Hanseatic League, which linked free towns in northern Germany and adjacent countries for trade and protection. Most of ancient Bergen was destroyed by a fire in 1702. A row of Hanseatic timbered houses, rebuilt along the waterfront after the fire, is all that remains. This area, called **Bryggen**, houses the **Hanseatic Museum**, *Finnegaardsgaten 1a, tel. +47 5554-4690*, which illustrates commercial life in Bergen hundreds of years ago.

The oldest building in Bergen, dating back to the 12th century, is a Romanesque church called **St. Mary's Church**, *Dreggen 15; tel. +47 5531-5960.* The baroque pulpit, donated by Hanseatic merchants, is covered with carved figures symbolizing the Virtues. Visit during one of the free organ concerts held at 8 p.m. on Thursday evenings in the summer.

The **Fantoft Stave Church**, *Fantoftveien 46, Paradis, tel. +47 5528-0710*, built in 1150, is covered with both pagan and Christian designs—serpents, dragons, and crosses. It was built to withstand the winter wind and has overlapping roofs and interlocking gables.

THE BEST OF SWEDEN

Progressive, wealthy **Sweden**, the fourth-largest nation in Europe, is sparsely inhabited. This California-sized country is made up of wheat plains, pine forests, thatched and timbered villages, cosmopolitan cities, historic islands, mountains, waterfalls, 95,000 lakes, and miles of rugged coastline. Best of all, its capital, Stockholm, is the least-traveled and least-crowded of all European capitals.

Stockholm: Mother Nature's favorite
While **Stockholm** has museums and fine old buildings, the city's real attractions are natural: the waterways, the beaches, the parks, and the 24,000 little islands of the archipelago that lead to the Baltic Sea (most of them uninhabited). The city is built on 14 islands in Lake Malaren and, believe it or not, the waterways are clean enough for swimming.

The heart of the city
Founded 700 years ago, Stockholm's roots are visible in the twisting streets of the medieval Old Town, **Gamla Stan**. At the heart of the area is the square **Stortorget** (the old marketplace), surrounded by cobbled, narrow streets lined with thick-walled, crooked buildings, as well as boutiques, galleries, and inexpensive restaurants.

Top sights
To the east of Gamla Stan is **Djurgården** (Deer Park), a lake-encircled forested park. Stockholm's great estates and gardens are located here, as is the Royal Flagship *Wasa*, a man-of-war that sank 20 minutes into its maiden voyage in 1628. The **Wasa museum***; tel. +46 (8) 5195-4800; website: www.vasamuseet.se,* is also here.

Skansen, *Djurgårdsslätten 49-51; tel. +46 (8) 442-8000; website: www. skansen.se,* an open-air museum on Djurgården, displays more than 150 18th- and 19th-century buildings from all over Scandinavia, including windmills, manor houses, workshops, and a complete town quarter. At the old workshops, you can see how early printing, silversmithing, glassblowing, and leather making were done. During the summer, chamber music concerts are held at the Skogaholm manor house. At night you can dance in the outdoor pavilion.

The **Nordiska Museet** (Nordic Museum), *Djurgårdsvâgen 6-16; tel. +46 (8) 5195-4600; website: www.nordiskamuseet.se,* is the world's best museum on Scandinavian life, with tools, clothing, and furnishings illustrating life from the 1500s to today.

The **Nationalmuseet** (National Museum), at the tip of a peninsula on Södra Blasieholmshamnen; *tel. +46 (8) 5195-4410; website: www.nationalmuseum.se,* has works by Rembrandt and Rubens and a rare collection of Russian icons, most from the 1400s. Room 45 features the works of Rembrandt, including *Portrait of an Old Man* and *Portrait of an Old Woman.*

Stadshuset (the city hall), *Hantverksgatan 1; tel. +46 (8) 5082-9059,* on the island of Kungsholmen, designed by Ragnar Ostberg, is one of the finest examples of modern architecture in Europe. The poet Yeats said of the building, *"No architectural work comparable to it has been accomplished since the Italian cities felt the excitement of the Renaissance."* Completed in 1923, the city hall is dominated by a lofty tower topped with three crowns, the symbol of the defunct Scandinavian Union. Its Golden Hall is decorated with 19 million pieces of pure gold mosaic. Banquets following the Nobel Peace Prize ceremony are held here. Climb the tower for a view of Stockholm's islands and waterways.

Drottningholm Palace, *Ekerö, Drottningholm near Stockholm; tel. +46 (8) 402-6280; website: www.royalcourt.se,* is the French-style, 17th-century palace of the royal family, surrounded by fountains and parks. The **Drottningholm Court Theater**, the best-preserved 18th-century theater in the world, is located on the palace grounds. Each summer, operas and ballets are staged with full 18th-century regalia. For reservations, contact the theater, *tel. +46 (8) 759-0406.*

The **Moderna Museet** (Museum of Modern Art); *tel. +46 (8) 5195-5200; website: www.modernamuseet.se,* on the island of Skeppsholmen, has works by Andy Warhol, Salvador Dali, Picasso, Braque, and Leger.

The best nights out

If you're interested in meeting someone of the opposite sex, the place to go in Stockholm is the **Café Opera**, *tel. +46 (8) 676-5807; website: www.cafeopera.se,* located in the same buildings as the national opera across from the Grand Hotel and directly across the bridge from the royal palace. The Café Opera has a dance floor, a bar, and a casino, where men toss away thousands of Swedish kronor playing roulette while some of the most beautiful unattached females in the world dance with one another or sit lingering over drinks.

For a different kind of fun, stop by **Gröna Lunds Tivoli** (not to be confused with Tivoli in Copenhagen), *Djurgården; tel. +46 (8) 5875-0100; website: www. gronalund.se.* Enjoy the amusements and go up to the top of the revolving tower for a wide view of Stockholm. Tivoli is open April to September, from noon to midnight.

Stockholm's best hotels

Nobel Peace Prize winners usually stay at Stockholm's finest, the **Grand Hotel**, *Södra Blasieholmshamnen 8; tel. +46 (8) 679-3500; website: www.grandhotel.se.* It is the most exclusive hotel in Sweden and one of the best in the world. The staff is thoughtful and prompt. This luxurious, expensive establishment faces the royal palace and has two restaurants and a bar. Ask for a room facing the water.

Runners-up to the Grand are the **Scandic Sergel Plaza**, *Brunkebergstorg 9; tel. +46 (8) 5172-6300; website: www.scandic-hotels.se,* the **Royal Viking**, *Vasagatan 1; tel. +46 (8) 5065-4000; website: http://royalviking.stockholm.radissonsas.com,* and the **Mälardrottningen**, *Riddarholmen; tel. +46 (8) 5451-8780; website: www.malardrottningen.se.*

Across from the Old City, **Hotel Diplomat**, *Strandvägen 7C; tel. +46 (8) 459-6800; website: www.diplomathotel.com,* located at the edge of the diplomatic quarter, is a small, sophisticated, expensive hotel furnished with antiques. It has a cocktail bar and an elegant teahouse.

Lady Hamilton, *Storkyrkobrinken 5, tel. +46 (8) 5064-0100; website: www. ladyhamiltonhotel.se,* in the old town of Stockholm, has rooms furnished with nautical antiques. Nearby church bells mark every quarter hour, but you get used to them after a couple of nights.

If you are looking for a bargain that's full of charm, try **Hotel Anno 1647**, *Mariagränd 3, on the Island of Södermalm; tel. +46 (8) 442-1680; website: www. anno1647.se.* The old brick building that dates (surprise!) to 1647 was originally the home of a tailor who achieved a senior position in his guild. It has a fine view of Gamla Stan.

Best restaurant

The Swedes like to eat, which is why Stockholm has so many first-class restaurants.

Ulriksdals Wärdshus, *Ulriksdals Slottspark; tel. +46 (8) 85-0815; website: www.ulriksdalswardshus.se,* located on the grounds of a royal park a few miles outside Stockholm, has a sweeping view of gardens stretching down to the water. This might have been the setting for the movie *Elvira Madigan*. The current owner,

Gunnar Ström, is the tenth restaurateur to have run an establishment on this spot. The food here is superb. They serve delicious specialties like the main course deer with quince and mushroom, and the dessert mango yoghurt ice-cream with exotic fruit and coconut panna cotta.

The best side trips from Stockholm

Sigtuna, founded at the beginning of the 11th century on the shores of Lake Malaren, is Sweden's oldest town, containing remnants of Vikings and early Christians. Low-timbered buildings line Storagatan. Sweden's first cathedral, St. Peter's, is here, along with the 13th-century Monastery of St. Maria.

Uppsala, Sweden's major university town, has a famous 15th-century cathedral and a 16th-century castle. The first Swedish university was founded here in 1477. (The university at Uppsala remains a well-respected institution.)

Walpurgis Eve (Valborgsmässoafton), April 30th, is the best time to visit Uppsala. Alumni and students wearing white caps celebrate the rebirth of spring and the death of winter with a torchlight parade and festivities until dawn. Thousands gather to join in hymns to celebrate the arrival of spring and to hear speeches about the end of winter. Walpurgis Eve, according to folklore, is when witches ride. It is the night before the birthday of St. Walpurgis, the medieval protectress against magic.

Gamla Uppsala (the old quarter of Uppsala), two miles north of Uppsala, was once a sacred grove, where animals and people were sacrificed to Norse gods. The Viking burial grounds date back to the sixth century. Nearby, on the site of an old pagan temple, is a 12th-century church. An open-air museum illustrating the life of peasants is open June through August.

While you're in the area, visit **Odinsborg**, *tel. +46 (18) 323-525; website: www.odinsborg.com,* an old wooden inn where you can drink mead from silver-tipped ornamental oxhorns—as the Vikings once did centuries ago. Waitresses wear Viking breastplates over provincial dresses, old murals adorn the walls, the corner fireplace has copper kettles, and the main room is decorated with crude furniture.

Midsummer magic at its best

Dalarna Province in the heart of Sweden has preserved the rites of Midsummer (with a Christian touch, these days) as they were celebrated centuries ago. On **Midsummer Eve (Midsommarafton)**, young people race through forests gathering birch boughs and wild flowers for the maypole. Once the pole is raised, villagers dance around it until dawn, weaving long ribbons that hang from the top.

In the morning, the townspeople go to church in rowboats decorated with greenery. A young girl will dream of her beloved on Midsummer Night if she places a bouquet containing seven wild flowers under her pillow. And if she looks into a reflecting pool on Midsummer Day, the next man she sees will be her loved one. The morning dew supposedly cures all ills.

The most colorful Midsummer celebrations are in the villages around Lake Siljan: Rattvik, Leksand, and Tallberg. In Siljansnas, a church boat race is held on Midsummer Day. In Hjortnas, traditional dancing takes place on the jetty the Saturday night following Midsummer.

Two simple but comfortable hotels in the region are the **Hotel Dalecarlia**, *Tällberg; tel. +46 (247) 891-00; website: www.dalecarlia.se,* and the **Romantik Hotel Åkerblad,** *Tällberg; tel. +46 (247) 508-00.*

The world's oldest cross-country ski race

The town of **Mora**, about four-and-a-half hours north of Stockholm by car, is a peaceful place that comes alive suddenly once a year on the first Sunday in March. This is the day of the **Vasaloppet**, the world's biggest and oldest cross-country ski race. As many as 12,000 cross-country skiers race along the course, fueled by the blueberry soup, lime juice, and Swedish meatballs offered by spectators. If you are brave, a good skier, and in good condition, enter the race. For application forms, contact **Vasaloppet**, *tel. +46 (250) 392-00; website: www.vasaloppet.se.* Arrangements can also be made through major travel agencies. The rest of the year, you can cross-country ski more peacefully. Exquisite trails run along the frozen rivers and fields. Situated on the shores of Lake Siljan, Mora guarantees snow in the winter. It is about as far north as Anchorage.

The **Best Western Mora Hotell & Spa**, *tel. +46 (250) 592-650; website: www.morahotell.se,* is the best place to stay. It is the only 4-star hotel in Mora and the hotel has a spa with swimming pool, a sauna, a solarium, and a good restaurant called Terrassen.

Visby: The most medieval town

A massive, two-mile wall and 44 towers protect Sweden's best-preserved medieval town, **Visby**, on the country's largest island, Gotland (*website: www.selectgotland. com*). Punctuating its skyline are 100 churches, 91 of which were built before 1350. Known as the City of Roses, Visby is filled with the sweet-smelling flowers. Nearby are beautiful sand beaches that are remarkable for their marine stacks— piles of oddly shaped rocks sculpted by wind and water.

FINLAND—THE LEAST SPOILED COUNTRY

Finland is an unspoiled land with the cleanest air in Europe. Its historic towns and cities are simple, elegant, and brightly colored, and its countryside is covered with virgin forests and 62,000 freshwater lakes. Although the population is less than five million, this is the fifth-largest nation in Europe. The lengthy coastline is marked by coves and framed by 20,000 small islands. During the summer, Finland basks in perpetual sunshine.

Finns are known as great sailors and great magicians. Their language is not related to other Nordic tongues, except Lapp. The Finno-Ugric language family is more similar to Hungarian, Turkish, Estonian, and even Eskimo than to Swedish, Norwegian, or Danish. However, Finland has a Swedish-speaking minority, and most Finns have studied English.

Helsinki: Where east meets west

The capital of Finland is located halfway between Russia and Sweden and shows signs of both Eastern and Western influences. It has been ruled by both over the centuries. The skyline is marked by the domes of the Lutheran cathedral and a Russian Orthodox church. A light-colored city built of white granite and surrounded by water on three sides, Helsinki is carefully laid out, with 240 parks and scores of modern buildings, such as the Temppeliaukion Church—an underground church blasted from solid rock and decorated with purple wood and copper.

The city's most imposing sight

The approach to Helsinki by sea is guarded by the 18th-century **Suomenlinna Fortress**, *tel. +358 (9) 6841-880; website: www.suomenlinna.fi.* You can walk the fortress' old ramparts, visit its gardens, and have lunch in its open-air cafés.

A bit of the East

In front of the cathedral is **Senaatintori** (Senate Square), which is so reminiscent of Leningrad that many movies set in that city have been shot here, including the Warren Beatty movie *Reds*. The square even holds a statue of Czar Alexander II, a Russian ruler of Finland who is fondly remembered for allowing the Finns some independence. Also on the square is the oldest building in the city: the Sederholm residence, built in 1755.

The best picture of Finnish history

Finnish history is long and involved. A good place to begin absorbing it is the **Suomen Kansallismuseo** (National Museum), *Mannerheimintie 34; tel. +358 (9) 405-01; website: www.nba.fi*, which has relics of the seafaring life of Viking times and the migration of the Finnish people northward 1,300 years ago. Located in a 22-year-old wooden building on Mannerheimintie, the city's main artery, the museum was designed by Eeno Saarinen. Opposite the museum is the ultramodern cultural center **Finlandia Hall**.

A sacred tradition: The sauna

Don't miss the chance to enjoy a Finnish sauna, a 2,000-year-old tradition that will make you feel euphoric. You take a sauna in a wood-lined room with layers of benches that climb toward the ceiling (the hottest are at the top). A stove heats the room to about 200° F, and water is thrown on a layer of stones in the stove to produce steam. Finns consider the oldest saunas the best. Built by early Finno-Ugric tribes, they are log cabins with earth floors, a pile of rocks above a fire, and no chimney.

Most saunas are built by the water—not surprising considering Finland has 188,000 lakes. Country saunas are stoked for hours, until the stones of the hearth are red-hot and the log walls have absorbed the heat and reflect it back.

If you're lucky, you'll be invited to take a sauna at the house of a native, which is a sign of hospitality. Because a sauna involves certain rules of etiquette, you should imitate your host. Allow him to create the first *loyly*, or vapor, by pouring water on the stove. Always ask other bathers if they are ready for a new cloud of steam before taking it upon yourself to create one.

If you're on your own (nearly every hotel has a sauna), take off your clothes and sweat. Then brush yourself lightly with birch branches. When you've had enough, dive into the frigid waters of a lake, roll around in the snow, or take a cold shower. (If you have a heart condition, you should skip the last step.) The ritual can be repeated three or four times. After the sauna, soap the perspiration off your body.

Don't take a sauna for at least one hour after a meal, and don't drink alcohol before a sauna—it strains the heart. Remove all jewelry, including rings and pierced earrings, because metal gets hot and can burn you. The best saunas in Helsinki are at the Palace Hotel, the Kalastajatorppa, and the Hesperia. You don't have to be a guest, but you must book in advance.

The best—and most affordable—restaurant

The most delightful restaurant in Helsinki, composed of a wine cellar, a coffee-house, and several dining rooms, is **Kappeli**, *Etela Esplanadi 1; tel. +358 (10) 766-3880; website: www.kappeli.fi.* Housed in a glassed-in pavilion on the edge of a park, Kappeli is always crowded with local Bohemians chatting over coffee and enjoying the view. Wander around until a table opens up.

The best Russian restaurant in Finland

Saslik, *Neitsytpolku 12; tel. +358 (9) 7425-5505; website: www.asrestaurants.com,* is a little crowded but very cozy. The *zakuska*, an assorted appetizer for two, includes several smoked, cured, and fresh varieties of fish, caviar with sour cream, meats, cheeses, and vegetables. An order of *zakuska* can be a meal in itself. For dessert, try the homemade Samarkand ice cream.

The best hotel in Finland

The **Hilton Strand Hotel**, *John Stenbergin ranta 4; tel. +358 (9) 393-51; website: www1.hilton.com,* overlooks the harbor of Helsinki and is ideally located next to the exciting Old City. The Botanical Gardens and the market square are also nearby. But more than a prime location, the Strand offers outstanding service and comfort as well as a popular sauna on the top floor.

The best side trips

One of Finland's greatest surviving castles is the **Häme Castle** at **Hämeenlinna**, *tel. +358 (3) 675-6820; website: www.nba.fi.* Built over a long period of time and used for many purposes, including a prison, it displays a collection of Finnish art. Composer Jan Sibelius was born in this town; his house is a museum displaying his violin, his family's piano, and photos. One of the town's centuries-old wooden buildings houses a historical museum.

Operas are staged in the courtyard of **Olavinlinna Castle** in Savonlinna each July by the Finnish National Opera. Begun in 1475, the castle stands on a small island in a passage connecting two large lakes. Contact the Savonlinna Opera Festival: *tel. +358 (15) 476-750; website: www.operafestival.fi.*

The largest wooden church in the world is in **Kerimaki**, near Savonlinna. The 150-year-old church seats 3,600 people. Strange, considering the town's population is 2,900. According to legend, the builders were tipsy when they began working on the church. They misread centimeters as inches, making the structure two-and-a-half times the size planned by the architect.

LAPLAND: EUROPE'S LAST WILDERNESS

Lapland, where the tundra never completely thaws and the winter darkness is broken only by the glimmering aurora borealis, stretches across the northern halves of Norway, Sweden, and Finland. This is Europe's last true wilderness, suffering long, cold, dark winters. During the summer, however, it is eerily beautiful under the Midnight Sun, reflected by glaciers, waterfalls, rivers, lakes, and mountains. For six weeks in June and July, the sun never sets.

A nomadic group, the Lapps (who call themselves Sami), live on this land. They herd reindeer for a living and retain old traditions long forgotten elsewhere in Scandinavia. Some Lapps still wear traditional costume of blue felt with contrasting bands of red, yellow, and green, often decorated with embroidery. Men wear the "caps of four winds," with four floppy points. Women wear red felt bonnets with flaps over the ears. Try the Lapp specialties: *poro* (reindeer meat), *lohi* (salmon), and *siika* (whitefish). Also taste the local liqueurs and desserts made from Arctic cloudberries.

The northernmost point in Europe

Nordkapp, Norway's North Cape, is the northernmost point in Europe, the place where the sun doesn't sink below the horizon for half of May and all of June. This mountain plateau rises 1,000 feet out of the ocean—a bleak but beautiful black cliff. In August, when the sun dips below the horizon for a few minutes, the sky is lit by the Northern Lights, a rainbow of spectacular colors. Even though most people come in July to see the Midnight Sun, August is still the best time to visit. The North Cape is snowbound until early June.

Nordkapp is on Magerøy, an island about 15 miles north of **Honningsvaag**, the northernmost village in the world. During the summer, a Lapp camp with reindeer herds is usually set up at Nordmannset, a little more than a mile outside Honningsvaag.

The northernmost hotel in this northernmost region is the **Arctic Hotel**, *Storgt 12, tel. +47 (78) 472-966*, in Honningsvaag. A modern place, with a nice view of the harbor. Make reservations in advance.

The best of Finnmark

Several towns bring civilization of a sort to **Finnmark** (Norwegian Lapland). **Tromsø** is the best base for trappers, whalers, sealers, and polar explorers. (It is also home to Greenpeace, the international volunteer organization that crusades for the environment.)

The **Arctic Church**, one of the most impressive pieces of modern architecture in the world, is in Tromsø. Built across the longest suspension bridge in Scandinavia (1,100 yards), it is shaped like an iceberg and made of aluminum that reflects the midnight sun.

The best way to visit the Lapps

The town of **Alta** in Finnmark is the best base for excursions into Lapp country. Most Lapps live on the tundra south of here. In Masi, about 44 miles from Alta on the main road to Finland, they wear traditional costumes, although many have taken up a modern way of life.

During the winter, the Lapps live inland. In May and June, they migrate to the coast as they have for centuries, herding thousands of reindeer across rivers and fiords—a spectacular sight. Colorful reindeer roundups usually take place between September and February.

The **Rica Hotel**, *tel. +47 (78) 482-700, website: www.rica-hotels.com*, in Alta, is a good hotel and has the best entertainment facilities in town.

The best of Norrland

Norrland, the Swedish word for Swedish Lapland, covers half the area of Sweden. One-quarter of the country is north of the Arctic Circle, and about 10,000 Lapps live here. It is easier to reach than you might imagine. Trains come here from Stockholm. Postal buses continue even farther north and connect with smaller villages and settlements. You can fly to the airports at Umeå, Luleå, and Kiruna. Or you can drive there on Road E4.

Arvidsjaur is modern but has an old Lappish center, with well-preserved, cone-shaped huts. Reindeer are rounded up here in June and July. Pine forests surround the town.

Norrbotten is a Lapp trading and cultural center. A market is held here the first week of February, when traditional Lapp handicrafts (delicately carved wooden utensils, silver jewelry, and colorful and elaborate woven fabrics) are sold.

Kvikkjokk is the gateway to Sarek National Park, the largest wilderness in Europe. There are no roads or trails in the park.

The best hiking trails

Svenska Turistföreningen (the Swedish Touring Club), *tel. +46 (8) 463-2100; website: www.svenskaturistforeningen.se,* maintains hotels and marked hiking routes for hundreds of miles through Swedish Lapland. The official website for travel and tourist information about Sweden is *www.visitsweden.com*. About 80 cabins are available with beds and bedding, cooking utensils, and firewood. The cabins can be used for one or two nights only.

Swedish hikers prefer the **Kungsleden**, or Royal Trail, the longest marked trail in the world, leading from the resort of Abisko to Jakkvik, a total of 210 miles. Cabins are spaced a day apart along the trail, which follows the old nomadic paths of the Lapps.

The National Swedish Environmental Protection Board owns several basins in **Padjelanta National Park**. The mountain's park is known for its unusual flora and many lakes.

The best of Finnish Lapland

Finnish Lapland, the largest and most northerly of Finland's provinces, occupies one-third the area of Finland and lies almost entirely above the Arctic Circle. It adjoins the Lapland districts in neighboring Norway and Sweden, but the landscape contrasts sharply. Some parts are barren, while others are covered by vast forests of pine and spruce and watered by rushing rivers. There are only about four people per square mile. About 3,500 Sami, or Lapps, live in the northernmost parishes: Utsjoki, Enontekiö, Inari, and Sodankylö. Until the seventh century, Lapps inhabited all of Finland. After the arrival of the Finns from the Volga, they retreated to the north, where they continue their traditional ways.

Finland's best hiking

In the summer, hiking expeditions are led through Lapland by experienced guides. Don't attempt an independent excursion unless you really know what you're doing. And bring the right equipment—boots, protective warm clothing, and maps. Online reservations and useful information can be found on the website: *www. laplandfinland.com*.

A marked 49-mile hiking trail called **Karhunkierros** (the Bear's Ring) runs near Kuusamo, about 124 miles from Oulu, just south of the polar circle. You don't need a guide to follow the clearly marked trail, which passes the most dramatic scenery in the area. You can spend the night in huts along the trail for free. However, in July and August, it is a good idea to carry a tent in case the huts are full. Bring food and mosquito repellent as well. Traveling the entire circle takes four to six days. (Shorter trails are also marked.)

The best base for exploring Lapland

Rovaniemi, the capital of Lapland, is a good base for explorations. This modern town five miles south of the Arctic Circle is easy to reach by train or plane from Helsinki.

The best adventure: Lapland in the winter

If you like romping in the snow, you'll love Lapland in the winter. Days and nights are spent cross-country skiing, taking reindeer rides, and whizzing across the powder in snowmobiles. Light from the stars and moon reflects off the snow, providing enough visibility for these activities 24 hours a day.

The terrain makes for some of the finest cross-country skiing in the world. Competitive skiers come here from around the world to train. Lapland offers a vast network of maintained ski tracks. Seasoned skiers can book a cabin in one of the fell regions and take on the unmarked countryside.

Caution! If you are going out into the wilderness, hire a guide. This is a wild, isolated, and frozen netherworld, and you could easily become lost forever. Arrange guides through the **Finnish Tourist Board**, *297 York Street, Jersey City, NJ 07302; tel. +1 (914) 863-5484 (in the U.S.); website: www.visitfinland.com.*

A reindeer safari is a great way to discover the land. On a guided trip, you are given a sled (a canoe-shaped contraption of wood planks) and a reindeer. The reindeer wears a harness, which is attached to the sled with a colorful braid. Tucked into blankets, you control the critter with a single rope. A reindeer safari can last from 20 minutes to an entire week—it's up to you. The longer excursions are definitely for the hardy—you sleep in a tent or cabin and eat reindeer meat (which can be tough) cooked over an open fire.

To explore Lapland at a faster pace, take a snowmobile safari. You wear enormous Arctic overalls, sled shoes, gloves, and a hat. The cold, dry air is exhilarating as you fly through the forests and across the frozen lakes.

THE BEST OF
SOUTHEAST ASIA

THAILAND—THE MOST EXOTIC ORIENTAL COUNTRY

Thailand can quite rightly claim to be the most exotic Oriental country. Unlike many of its neighbors, it has never been colonized. Nevertheless, Thailand has always been open to foreign influences. Its king plays the jazz clarinet, many of its royals were educated in England and Switzerland, and wealthier Thais speak English.

This openness and friendliness toward foreigners makes Thailand an ideal vacation spot. The Thai people are so friendly and polite that they make you feel right at home. Moreover, Thailand is cheap; it's possible to find accommodation here for as little as $10 a night. (When reading through this section, be aware that many hotels in this part of the world add a service charge and taxes to the prices quoted. Be sure to inquire about these additional charges when making reservations, to avoid an unpleasant surprise when the bill comes.)

BANGKOK—THE MOST SOPHISTICATED CITY

Bangkok, Thailand's largest and capital city is a mix of beauty, crowds, sophistication, and sin. Its downtown is polluted and congested and serenity can be sought in its outlying corners.

Bangkok's best attractions

Bangkok has more than 400 temples and many of them are worth seeing. The most famous include **Wat Pho** (Wat Phra Chetuphon), the oldest and largest in Bangkok, which includes the largest reclining Buddha in Thailand; Wat Pho is open daily from 8 a.m. to 5 p.m.

Wat Phra Kaew, for the Temple of the Emerald Buddha and the adjoining Grand Palace. Wat Phra Kaew is open daily 8:30 a.m. to 3:30 p.m., but is closed between 12 p.m. and 1 p.m.

Wat Arun, also known as the Temple of Dawn is named after the Indian god of dawn, Aruna, and is situated by the Chao Phraya River. Wat Arun is open daily 8 a.m. until 5:30 p.m.

Bangkok's **Floating Market** is also a must, even though it has become tourist-trodden in the last several years. Transfers leave daily from most hotels from 6:30 a.m. A more authentic but lesser-known floating market is at **Khlong Damnoen Saduak**, about 65 miles west of Bangkok. Tours can be arranged from all major hotels. In addition to a floating-market tour, arrange a *klong* (canal tour); for details, ask at any pier in the vicinity of the Oriental Hotel.

Thailand's royal barges

For centuries, visitors have marveled at the sight of Bangkok's royal river barges. Unfortunately today, the breathtaking tradition of the Royal Barge Processions are a rare sighting but you make be lucky to catch one if Thailand has a major occasion to celebrate. But you can still see them on display at the **Royal Barge Museum**, on Klong Bangkok Noi near the Phra Pinkloa Bridge and Arun Amarin Road. The museum and its barges, all restored and reconstructed, are housed in a cavernous shed. The best way to get to there is by river taxi or as part of a general canal trip. The shed is open daily, 9 a.m. until 5 p.m.

The most slithery farm

The **Bangkok Snake Farm**, *tel. +66 (2) 252-0161*, at the Thai Red Cross Society, is by far Thailand's most interesting farm. This is where cobras, kraits, spotted vipers, and other poisonous snakes are fed and milked for their venom. Milking snakes is not an exciting process. The snake's mouth is simply forced open, and the venom squirts out into a small Petri dish. However, it is not meant to be a form of entertainment. It is part of a lifesaving process. The Queen Saovabh Memorial Institute, the scientific division of the Thai Red Cross Society, provides snake-bite serum for much of the world.

What follows the milking process is very exciting. When it's show time, the handlers use long poles to remove the snakes from the pits and place them on the ground. The audience sits only a few feet away, but several feet off the ground, and watches as the handler encourage the snakes to hiss and slither, display their hoods, and strike and spit venom. Although it's all done very casually, rest assured that the handlers don't take their jobs lightly. Open 8:30 a.m. to 4 p.m. on weekdays and 8:30 a.m. to noon on weekends and public holidays.

The best market in Southeast Asia
Be sure to visit the Chatujak (or Chatuchak) weekend market. Take a hotel car to the market and ask the driver to wait, as taxis can be difficult to find or take the BTS Sky Train. Haggle ferociously over the prices and be aware that not all of the antiques are real and that not all the pirated DVDs will work in Western-format players.

The most luxurious places to stay
The **Mandarin Oriental Bangkok**, *tel. +66 (2) 659-9000; website: www.mandarin-oriental.com*, has won countless awards and despite displaying signs of decay, this haunt of the elite is clearly still considered a beautiful place to stay. Situated on the banks of the Chao Phraya River, the hotel is also conveniently located to many of the city's attractions. The hotel is also known for its Thai Cooking School, which conducts classes year-round. Check with the hotel for a current program. Packages include classes, accommodation, materials, and meals.

Close runners-up are the **Grand Hyatt Erawan**, *494 Ratchadamri Road; tel. +66 (2) 254-1234; website: www.hyatt.com*, and the **Sukhothai**, *13/3 S. Sathorn Road; tel. +66 (2) 344-8888; website: www.sukhothai.com*. The **Dusit Thani Bangkok**, *946 Rama IV Road; tel. +66 (2) 200-9000; website: www.dusit.com*, located only minutes from Bangkok's famous Patpong nightlife district, is also a good place to stay. It is less expensive than other luxury class hotels in the city.

The oldest settlement
Chiang Mai is the hill capital of northern Thailand, home to a million people. Founded in 1296, it is one of the oldest continually inhabited settlements in Thailand. It was at one time an independent kingdom, surrounded by a moat and fortified gates. The best way to get to Chiang Mai from Bangkok is by air.

Chiang Mai's greatest attraction

Wat Phra Singh, a temple high on a mountain peak, and **Phuping Palace**, the summer residence of the royal family, are two beautiful and ancient monuments that would alone make the visit to Chiang Mai worthwhile.

The best place to shop

The best place to shop in the city is the **Night Market**, just off Thapae Road. It's also the cheapest: rugs, clothes, and leather goods are all available at bargain prices. This is also the place to buy a pair of boots made out of chicken skin, should your tastes run in that direction, as well as silver and Burmese lacquer and handcrafts.

The best pastime

From Chiang Mai, you can arrange to go elephant trekking. Avoid the big, touristy elephant camp; instead, ask a tuk-tuk or taxi driver to take you to one of the smaller camps, farther up the hills (about 45 minutes outside the city). The driver sits on the elephant's head, and usually two people share the seat strapped across the animal's back. The elephant can go anywhere; they can cross streams on tiny stepping stones with the grace and balance of a gymnast. As they step down, you are tilted at a 90 degree angle to the ground. The motion may make you feel sick at first, but soon your body will become accustomed to it.

The second-best pastime

In a spectacular setting at the foot of the famous Doi Suthep Mountain, just 10 minutes from the center of the city, sits the **Lanna Golf Club**, *tel. +66 (53) 221-911; website: www.golforient.com*. The course is moderately difficult and very popular so booking is essential. There are three 9-hole courses offering more than 20 lakes, water hazards, and elevated greens planted with Bermuda grass.

The best place to stay

Stay at the **Chiang Mai Orchid**, *100-102 Huay Kaew Road; tel. +66 (53) 222-2099; website: www.chiangmaiorchid.com*, a lovely, first-class establishment.

The best place to buy silk in Thailand

Although Jim Thompson's silk shops are the best-known in Thailand—with good reason—they are also the most expensive. (They are easily located all over the major Thai cities.) If you're looking for a bargain, try one of the city's smaller shops. Although the quality is not as good, the prices are much cheaper. We recommend

Chatraporn Thai Silk, *194 Thae Pae Road, Chiang Mai; tel. +66 (53) 234-691,* and **Shinawatra Thai Silk**, *145/1-2 Sankamphaeng Road, Chiang Mai; tel. + 66 (53) 221-076, website: www.shinawatrathaisilk.co.th.*

Asia's hottest resort town

If you're single, and tired of Bangkok's Patpong, there's no better place to vacation than Thailand's **Pattaya Beach**. The nightlife is more outrageous than the wildest London, New York, or Hong Kong has to offer. For centuries Pattaya was a sleepy fishing village astride the invasion routes across the Gulf of Siam. According to local lore, the legendary Thai King Taskin's soldiers were once put ashore here on their way to conquer what is now southern Thailand. Two hundred years later, Pattaya was a favorite destination for American GIs on leave from Vietnam. Today, it is a mecca for sun worshippers and sybarites from all across Asia and Europe.

THE PHILIPPINES—THE FRIENDLIEST NATION

The Philippines has always been known for the friendliness of its people, who speak 67 different dialects. This has not changed in recent years, despite the turmoil the country has suffered.

And the country is certainly as beautiful as ever. The second largest archipelago in the world, it's made up of about 7,100 island paradises stretching toward China and Japan in the north, and Malaysia and Singapore in the south, the Philippines offers a combination of exciting cosmopolitan cities, white-sand beaches, and achingly blue waters.

Manila's best sites

Manila, the capital of the Philippines, is a hustling, bustling international city and is broken up into 16 territorial districts. Although the capital is renowned for its choking smog and traffic, Manila is situated on the island of Luzon, and is a good base for excursions to the surrounding countryside, and is within two hours of beautiful resorts and beaches.

See the **Pagsanjan Falls**, about an hour outside Manila, where you can take a scenic boat tour of the rapids along 330-foot-high falls. Also visit the **Hidden Valley Springs**, a series of mineral springs in Alaminos, Laguna, that are buried in a 295-foot crater and surrounded by lush vegetation.

Other attractions near Manila include the **Malacañang Palace**. Tours are no longer offered as its the official residence of the president, but the gardens are open and the palace is situated by the Pasig River; **Coconut Palace**, which was built, in part, using coconut trees, and is the national symbol of life and abundance; **Makati**, the financial center of the country; and the **San Agustin Church,** the oldest church in Manila, is located in Intramuros, a walled Spanish settlement containing museums, ruins and churches.

The best place to stay in Manila

The **Manila Hotel**, *Rizal Park, One Rizal Park, Roxas Boulevard; tel. +63 (2) 527-0011; website: www.manila-hotel.com.ph*, is a luxury colonial hotel on the edge of Manila Bay. A legacy to the colonial era, the staff is as attentive as ever to its genteel folk.

The best hotel outside Manila

The best place to stay in Laguna, just outside Manila, is the **Villa Escudero**, *San Pablo; tel. +63 (2) 521-0830; website: www.villaescudero.com*, which offers exceptional service, atmosphere, and comfort. This coconut plantation, less than two hours by road from the capital city, gives you a glimpse of typical village life. Even if you can't stay the night, take time to visit the grounds.

The summer capital of the Philippines

The cool, mountainous region of **Baguio City**, located in the province of Benguet, offers a break from the city crowds. Only three or four hours from Manila by car, or 50 minutes by jet, Baguio City is becoming increasingly popular among travelers, who appreciate the region's incredible views and cool climate. The best place to stay in the city is the **Holiday Park Hotel**, *#129 Abanao Extension, Baguio; tel. +63 (74) 619-2807; website: http://holidayparkhotel.com.ph/*.

The most attractive city in the South

Cebu City, the "Queen city of the South," is a beautiful and graceful city, located on the island of Cebu in the Visayas, south of Manila. It is the oldest city in the Philippines founded by the Spanish. Ferdinand Magellan, who landed on its shores in 1521, fell in love with the place and eventually died there. He planted Magellan's Cross, which is now more than 460 years old and still standing. It is the symbol of the Rajah Humabon, and his queen's acceptance of Christianity. The most festive time to visit Cebu City is during its festival of Sinulog, a weeklong religious celebration held every January. Stay at the beautiful **Vacation Hotel**,

35 Juana Osmena Cor. Jose Avila Sts., Cebu City; tel. +63 (32) 253-2766; website: www.vacationhotel-cebu.com, a converted family home originally belonging to one of the prominent Cebu families, and with very friendly staff;

The best of the oldest in Cebu

The image of **Santo Niño de Cebu** is the oldest relic in the country; it was given to Queen Juana by Magellan in 1521.

The **Basilica Minore del Santo Niño**, built in 1565, is the oldest church in the Philippines and was built on the site where the image was found.

The oldest street in the country, **Colon Street**, is also in Cebu. Located in Cebu's Chinatown, in the center of the city, it was built by the Spanish soldiers.

The Philippines' last frontier

The best place in the Philippines to enjoy water sports is on the island of **Palawan**, 70 minutes by plane southwest of Manila. This island is known as the Philippines' last frontier, a paradise for sailors, sunbathers, deep-sea divers, and fishermen.

The island is surrounded by coral reefs, and the waters are filled with tropical fish. Manta rays are common. New marine species have been discovered in the waters off the exclusive El Nido Resort on the island's northern shore.

The best place for water sports

The upscale **El Nido Resort**, *Miniloc Island, El Nido; website: www.elnidoresorts. com*, is the place on Palawan for deep-sea diving. Designed to resemble a native village, this resort was named for the birds' nest (*nido*) found on the surrounding cliffs. El Nido is several hours by car from the airport at Puerto Princesa. You can hire a jeepney at the airport to take you out to the resort. The best way to get there, however, is to charter a plane from Manila.

Another good spot for water sports is the area around Port Barton, which is peppered with beach resorts.

The best time to visit

The best time to visit the Philippines is between December and May, especially April or May. The rest of the year is typhoon season.

LAOS—THE MOST SERENE

It's hard to get to **Laos**, and once you're there, it's hard to get around. Only recently have Americans been able to travel here at all. But it is worth the effort. What you'll remember most about Laos is its serenity: There are no hawkers on the streets; in fact, there are no vehicles on the streets—at least no four-wheeled vehicles. Instead, the streets of Laos are given over to bicycles and tuk-tuks.

The best set for a spaghetti Western

In 1963, UPI war photographer Tim Page described Vientiane, Laos' ancient capital, as resembling *"a set for a spaghetti Western or a Graham Greene thriller."* Forty-odd years later, nothing has changed.

The best restaurant in Vientiane

The best place to eat in Vientiane is the **Kua Lao**, *141 Samenthai Rd; tel. +856 (21) 215-777; website: www.kualao.laopdr.com*, which serves delicious Lao cuisine in a very pleasant setting.

Asia's most beautiful temples

Laos is noted for possessing the most beautiful Buddhist temples in Southeast Asia—temples that have not fallen to explosives, tourism, or redevelopment, as have most of those in Mynamar (Burma), Vietnam, Cambodia, China, and Hong Kong.

Twice daily, weather and inclination permitting, Laos Aviation flies from Vientiane to Luang Prabang, Laos' most beautiful town and the site of **Wat Xiengthong**, one of the most impressive temples in all of Southeast Asia, with its courtyard filled with bougainvillea and its location on the Mekong River.

The best place to arrange your trip

The best place to arrange a trip to Laos is with **Diethelm Travel**, *tel. +856 (21) 213-833 or +856 (21) 215-920; website: www.diethelmtravel.com*. They have a reputation for getting you there—usually on schedule—with the least amount of inconvenience.

The most economical ride

Although daily flights are scheduled in and out of Laos, it's far less expensive and far more adventurous to take the overnight train from Bangkok to Nong Khai in northern Thailand on the Thai/Laotian border. An express train departs Bangkok

Railway Station at 8:30 p.m. and arrives in Nong Khai at 7:30 a.m. the next morning. Save the picturesque daytime ride for the trip home, as the border closes at 5 p.m., and you can't take a day train to Nong Khai from Bangkok and return in the same day.

PALAU: THE MOST UNDISCOVERED IN THE PACIFIC

In the far-western Pacific, about 800 miles southwest of Guam and 500 miles east of the Philippines, is the 36-mile long, 15-mile wide, reef-encircled archipelago known as **Palau.** World-class suba divers and marine experts count it as one of the secret wonders of the world. About 9,000 Palauans live on Koror, the capital of the not-quite-independent Republic of Palau. It boasts 18 miles of paved road, nearly 200 taxis, a speed limit of 25 miles per hour, and no passing. The longest stretch of road wanders eight miles from Palau International Airport to the Palau Pacific Resort. Life on the islands of Kayangel and Angaur, which mark the northern and southernmost tips of the archipelago respectively, revolves around fishing along the reef or in the lagoon and the cultivation of taro, tapioca, coconuts, and bananas.

The jewels of Palau
The pièce de résistance of Palau is the group of 200 Rock Islands, scattered in strings between Koror and Peleiu. Found nowhere else in the world, these jungle-covered knobs of solid coral and limestone, undercut at tide level because of the water-soluble limestone, look from a distance like green mushrooms floating on a turquoise sea. The islands fringed by white sand are ideal for picnicking or snorkeling.

The best places to stay
Stay at the deluxe **Palau Pacific Resort**, *tel. +68 488-2600; website: www. palauppr.com,* or the less expensive **Palau Royal Resort** (Nikko Hotel), *tel. +680 488-2000; website: www.palau-royal-resort.com,* which commands breathtaking views of the Rock Islands. The restaurant offers international foods and seafood specialties daily, 6:30 a.m. until 10 p.m.

The best bargain accommodation
The best buy in town is the **DW Motel***; tel. +680 488-2641 or 488-6788; website: www.palaudwmotel.com,* run by a friendly Palauan named Dave Williams, and

his family. Close to downtown Koror and within walking distance of the central business district, the DW offers large and airy rooms with air-conditioning and refrigerators.

The best restaurants
Take at least one meal at the **Fuji Restaurant,** *tel. +680 488-2918 or 488-3027,* located downtown next to the West Plaza Hotel. The Fuji serves seafood, local specialties, and international dishes Monday through Saturday, 6 p.m. to 10 p.m.

The **Carp Restaurant,** *tel. +680 488-3341,* named after the restaurant owners who also run Carp Island Resort, is located near the government fish dock. Serving Japanese style dishes, in addition to crab and lobster varieties, it's famous for fruit bat soup, which is cooked in coconut milk and spices for hours. Open Monday through Saturday 11 a.m. until 9 p.m., and Sunday 9 a.m. until noon.

MYANMAR: A DESTINATION FOR THE MOST ADVENTUROUS

Myanmar (formerly Burma) is becoming a more accessible destination for the adventurous traveler. It is not a journey to be taken lightly, but an adventure suitable only for the strong of body and spirit. Nonetheless, it is worth the effort it takes to get there. Those who see it invariably describe it as one of the few places left in the world where you can get a feel for what Asia "used to be like."

The busiest city
Yangon (formerly Rangoon), is a gray city of pre-war buildings, faded grandeur, and wide streets cluttered with lampposts, loiterers, and round-fendered cars. Street vendors sell cold drinks made of sugarcane and water, dipping the gray-green liquid from big glass tanks. Myanmar's new capital Naypyidaw, has a somewhat conspiratory connotation since it is rumored to have been built in secret. The sparkling new city sits in a contrast to the rest of the poverty stricken country, and visitors aren't exactly welcomed with open arms.

The best attractions
The glowing **Sule Pagoda** in the center of Yangon is an impressive spectacle at night. But it pales in comparison with the 2,500-year-old **Shwedagon Pagoda.** High on a hill, the Shwedagon is reached either by elevator or by a breathless climb up an enormous stairway lined with hawkers and souvenir vendors. At the

top is a Disneyland-like arena of jeweled spires, gold-plated domes, and gilded statues. People mill about in their bare feet trying to sell flowers, fortunes, and medical advice.

The Strand—Myanmar's oasis

Yangon's **Strand Hotel**, *92 Strand Road, tel. +95 (1) 243-377; website: www. ghmhotels.com*, is considered the best hotel in all Myanmar, and is like what the Raffles Hotel is to Singapore. It is a white-pillared relic from the days of British rule. The ceilings are high, the stairways wide and polished, and the elevator an ornate, wrought-iron cage. In the dining room, waiters in white jackets serve mutton and potatoes from dented silver platters. In the hotel bar, a pianist plays Henry Mancini while sparrows nest in the light fixtures. It is an oasis.

The most historic city

Mandalay is a sprawling, walled city of historic monasteries, bridges, moats, and, of course, more pagodas. Men in sarongs pedal trishaws through the dusty streets. It isn't a beautiful city, but it is a good jumping-off point for excursions along the Irrawaddy River.

The best ruins

Pagan is one of the wonders of Asia, a sprawling landscape littered with thousands of ancient ruins. During the Golden Age of Pagan, in the 11th century, riches were spent on pagodas, shrines, and temples. It is believed that these buildings numbered 13,000 when Kublai Khan sacked the place in 1287. A major earthquake in 1975 caused more damage, but most of the important structures have since been restored.

The ancient city of Pagan is now deserted except for a tiny village. Surrounding the village are the remains of the ancient temples. If you join the other travelers here, moving from one temple to another on foot or rented bicycle, you'll have the opportunity to glimpse dark, cold rooms filled with marble Buddhas and terracotta tiles.

The best resort in Myanmar

The **Candacraig Hotel**, *6th Quarter, Anawrahta St, PyinOolwin (Maymyo); tel. +95 (85) 220-47*, is a 19th-century hill station that used to serve as the officers' residence of the Bombay-Burma Trading Company. Its restaurant serves English food.

The best ways to travel to and through Myanmar

The best way to travel to Myanmar is through Bangkok, where a number of small agents, most with family contacts in Myanmar, specialize in arranging travel to this hard-to-reach country. While independent travel is possible, the amount of time you will be allowed to travel alone varies according to the whims of the government. Nonetheless, it is well worth the trouble to, if possible, avoid the travel agencies and go it alone.

Make your airfare arrangements with **Thai International**, which flies from Bangkok to Myanmar three times a week. Pay for an upgrade to business class on the return flight; the unlimited champagne on this one-hour trip will seem like heaven after roughing it in Myanmar.

Myanmar Airways offers daily domestic flights between Yangon and all other cities open to travelers (which, right now, include Bago, Bagan, Mandalay, Taunggyi, Mawlamyine, Sittwe, Pathein, Pyi, and Pyin Oo Lwin). The alternative is to travel by train, but train travel in Myanmar is time-consuming and sometimes unreliable. It is not possible to rent a car on your own, but day-trips can be arranged with a car and driver. In some areas, you can travel by bus, boat, or horse and buggy (not a tourist treat, but the primary means of local transportation).

SINGAPORE: THE CLOCKWORK CITY

Singapore is an exciting, pulsating place, very cosmopolitan, very well run, and incredibly clean. In fact spitting, smoking, and littering are public offences. But gone are the days of sprawling British colonial homes. Today, space is precious on the 225-square-mile island and it's sparsely dotted with these vestiges of times past, making way for the more prosperous high rises.

Colonial Singapore is north of the Singapore River. **Empress Place** is decorated with the statue of Sir Stamford Raffles (the Brit who founded Singapore and made it the trading port that it is today), overlooking the river where the explorer first stepped onto the island.

The **Raffles Hotel**, *1 Beach Road; tel. +65 6337-1886; website: www. raffleshotel.com*, is a must-see, a symbol of colonial Singapore. Have a Singapore Sling on the terrace (touristy, but fun). Nearby, Chinatown is an interesting area to explore, full of mosques and temples.

The best places to stay

The 90-year-old **Goodwood Park**, *22 Scotts Road; tel. +65 6737-7411; website: www.goodwoodparkhotel.com*, is known for its true Singaporean service and its elegant rooms. Its 13-acre site near the Orchard Road shopping district is convenient.

Another good place to stay is the more reasonably priced **Carlton Hotel**, *76 Bras Basah Road; tel. +65 6338-8333; website: www.carlton.com.sg*. The décor is beautiful, the service good.

The best custom-made clothing

Singapore is also the best place for custom-made clothing. Here, prices are cheaper, the selection of fabrics is greater (you'll find an especially wide selection of cottons, silks, and polyester fabrics), and the workmanship is at least as good as that of anyplace else in the world. And there is certainly no shortage of tailors. (Allow four to five days for a custom-made suit.) **Justmen** in the Tanglin Shopping Center is a good place for men's tailoring.

NEW GUINEA: THE SECOND LARGEST ISLAND IN THE WORLD

New Guinea, the second largest island in the world (Greenland is the largest), looks in profile like a bird taking flight. The head of the bird, a place the Dutch named Vogelkop (bird's head), is now called Irian Jaye and is part of Indonesia. The other end of the island is Papua New Guinea.

Either end of the island makes a perfect destination. But overall, the eastern half, the "bird's tail" has the most to offer. Myriad islands litter the Bismarck Sea off the north coast. And there are mountains, some snow-covered, some with valleys so remote that the life they contain has not changed noticeably since the Stone-Age. Mighty rivers, such as the Fly and the Sepik, coil their way through lowland jungles to the sea in this land that is home to 700 languages and many cultures.

One of the world's greatest adventures

If you're looking for an adventure, you couldn't do better than to set off from Port Moresby, the capital of Papua New Guinea, and fly to Milne Bay, the bird's tail, 250 miles to the east. From there, you can negotiate the coastline all the way from the fabled Trobriands to the upper reaches of the Sepik River.

You can make the journey in two ways. You can either hunt down locally-run trading vessels, take a flight with Air Niugini, and ride a bus from Lae to Madang. Or, if sailing on tiny Spartan vessels and being jolted around on dusty buses doesn't appeal to you, consider the *Melanesian Explorer*, an expeditionary ship that begins its voyages off the northeast coast and heads south after a few days through the D'Entrecasteaux Islands—tiny green places with talcum-white beaches. The journey eventually ends 200 miles upriver, where you can take a plane to the highlands town of Mount Hagan, from which it is another hour by plane back to Port Moresby.

For information on the *Melanesian Explorer* and the newer *Melanesian Discoverer*, contact the **Melanesian Tourist Services**, *PO Box 707, Madang, Papua New Guinea 511; tel. +675 854-1300 or +1 (310) 809 6700 (in the U.S.); fax +675 852-3543; e-mail: melanesian@mtspng.com; website: www.mtspng.com.*

MALAYSIA: THE MOST BOUNTIFUL COUNTRY

Malaysia is known for its extreme beauty, including gorgeous beaches and spectacular mountains. Although it does not have the history of other countries in Southeast Asia, it is one of the most developed and prosperous nations in this part of the world. Kuala Lumpur, the capital (complete with luxury hotels and skyscrapers), is a pleasant stopover from your explorations in other parts of the country. It is a modern city, but colonial-era buildings are evident everywhere.

The most rustic place to eat in Kuala Lumpur

The **Coliseum Café**, *98-100 Jalan Tuanku Abdul Rahman, Kuala Lumpur; tel. +60 (3) 2692-6270*, has seen it all since 1921: The Japanese occupation in World War II, the communist uprising popularized in *The War of the Running Dogs*, Malaysian Independence, and, more recently, the burgeoning of the Malaysian economy and the attendant influx of fast-food joints and yuppie bars. The run-down whitewashed shop/house dates back to its colonial origins when then-owner, Mr. Wong, set the place up. It's now in the hands of the third generation, with his granddaughter, Jo Wong, in charge.

Inside the glass-paneled doors, emblazoned with gold Wild West-style saloon lettering, little has changed. The décor consists of largely bare walls that run up to the high ceilings, kitschy red and green glass light fittings, and whirring ceiling fans. Open daily from 8 a.m. to 10 p.m., the café's 16 or so tables are usually full

of locals noisily tucking into a mix of Chinese, Malay, or Indian specialties…
or indulging in chicken, sausages, or fish. But the reason most still come to the
Coliseum are for its steaks—mouth-watering.

Fifty ringgit ($15) per head is more than enough for a steak and a Tiger Beer.
If you just want to drink, a bar to the left will take care of you—the same bar which
hosted late-night sing-alongs around the piano for hard-drinking rubber planters
who used to pile their weapons on the counter, and has God-knows-what other
stories to tell. For that is the real beauty of the Coliseum—its rustic walls seem to
speak to you.

Best brunch

Prego (The Westin Kuala Lumpur), *199 Jalan Bukit Bintang; tel. +60 (3)
2773-8013*, serves innovative and delicious Italian fare on any day of the week.
However, on Sundays a free flowing Champagne Brunch is excellent value at $45.
Thankfully, if you have overindulged and are a little shaky underfoot, endless platters of pasta, pizza and other delights are brought around or for the more stable the
buffet includes fresh seafood, salads, and roast meats. The waiters are lively, the
champagne offerings generous and there's even entertainment for the little ones.

The best three excursions from Kuala Lumpur

While in Kuala Lumper, you should take three day-trips. First, visit **Malacca**
(Melaka), 93 miles south of the capital city. This splendid old port city on the
infamous, formerly pirate-infested Straits of Malacca, boasting a rich Portuguese,
Dutch, English, Chinese, and Malaysian heritage, is a fertile shopping ground for
antique enthusiasts. To visit, rent a car and driver in Kuala Lumpur or join one
of the day tours that depart from all the major hotels. The journey itself, through
plantation after plantation of rubber trees and oil palms, is worth the trip.

A shorter but equally rewarding journey takes you to the limestone **Batu
Caves**, a Hindu pilgrimage center notable for its swarms of bats, whose guano
adds to the eerie mystical atmosphere inside the caves. Frequent and inexpensive
minibuses from Kuala Lumpur take travelers to the Batu Caves. Or you can hire a
car and driver.

Another must is the island of **Penang**, which lies off the east coast of the
Malaysian peninsula. It is the oldest British settlement in Malaysia. Georgetown,
its major town, is a compact, attractive city, known for its good food. From here,
you have easy access to the rest of the island and its beautiful beaches, rubber-tree
plantations, and forests (filled with monkeys and bananas).

The most romantic colonial-style hotel

Penang's **Eastern & Oriental Hotel**, *10 Lebuh Farquhar Street, Penang; tel. +60 (4) 222-2000; website: www.e-o-hotel.com*, at the waterfront end of Jalan Penang, is unreservedly Malaysia's most romantic colonial-style hotel, a vestige of the former British rule. Even if you're staying in more modest accommodation, stop by the Eastern & Oriental for a gin and tonic on the terrace.

THE BEST OF
SPAIN

I would sooner be a foreigner in Spain than in most countries. How easy it is to make friends in Spain! I defy anyone not to be struck by their essential decency; above all, their straightforwardness and generosity.
—George Orwell, *Homage to Catalonia*

Spain is the most exotic West European nation. Although it is linked to the European continent at the French border, in many ways it feels more like North Africa. Not until the reign of Ferdinand and Isabella in the 15th century did Spain become part of Europe culturally. But when it did finally join hands with Europe, it became a great power, colonizing much of the world.

No longer mighty, Spain still has Roman ruins, Moorish fortresses, and early Christian cathedrals. The landscape is ruggedly beautiful, the traditions colorful, and the art collections among the greatest in the world.

A tour of Spain takes you from Madrid's immense Prado Museum, which rivals the Louvre as one of the greatest art collections in the world, to Granada's unforgettable Alhambra (take a night tour for a magical, once-in-a-lifetime experience). Getting out of the towns and cities reveals ancient forests and soaring mountains iced with snow, extraordinary dessert scenery, golden beaches framed by pine trees, and fishing villages that time forgot. For every cliché—sangria, bullfighting, flamenco—there are a hundred secrets just waiting to be discovered.

MADRID: SPAIN'S MOST COSMOPOLITAN CITY

Madrid is a cosmopolitan city replete with museums, elegant restaurants, and a vibrant nightlife. Yet for all that, it remains a fully functioning metropolis, focused more on business and banking than tourism. Because of this it has a thoroughly lived-in vibe and Madrileños are generally friendly and open to visitors, often inviting them to get caught up in the whirlwind of their lively social intercourses (Madrileños love to go out and you'll find the streets still buzzing well into the small hours).

Situated more than 10,000 feet above sea level, Madrid occupies the vast plains of the Meseta that cover much of central Spain: freezing in winter, with comfortably dry if hot summer highs. It may not have the beaches of its rival, Barcelona, but when the frenetic buzz of life in the capital takes its toll, several lush parks add an unexpectedly green escape.

The most picturesque quarter

The most picturesque section of Madrid is also the oldest; a labyrinth of medieval lanes that criss-cross between **Puerta del Sol** and the **Royal Palace**. Each street has a sign depicting an activity that distinguished it in the past. For instance, Pasadizo del Panecillo has a picture of friars distributing bread to the poor. The best way to explore is on foot. You will find Velazquez's grand statue of Philip IV in the center of the Plaza de Oriente, east of the Royal Palace.

If you want to join in with the locals, eschew the stereo-typical jug of sangria for a *copa de vermut* (artisan vermouth served over ice, a slice of lemon and an olive) with a tapa in Madrid's imposing **Plaza Mayor**, near the Royal Palace. You will be surrounded by 17th-century buildings with balconies and arches. Descend the stairway at the southwest corner of the plaza to an area filled with lively bars.

El Prado: The Louvre's greatest rival

Museo del Prado, *Paseo del Prado; tel. +34 (91) 3302-800; website: www. museodelprado.es*, is Madrid's number-one attraction. One of the greatest museums in the world, the Prado has nearly 9,000 works in its collection, of which some 2,000 are on display at any given time. Take advantage of the museum's one-hour, two-hour, and three-hour routes to get the most out of your visit, and time it for the late afternoon, when the sun adds a diaphanous quality to the somewhat dim interior.

A good many of the works are those collected by Spanish monarchs from the 16th through 19th centuries, including those by Velazquez, Goya, Murillo, El Greco, Breughal, Rubens, and Durer. One of the most famous is that of *Las Meninas*

(Maids in Waiting), painted by Velazquez in 1656. It depicts the artist painting an unknown subject, probably the royal couple, who are reflected in a mirror behind. The artist is surrounded by the royal entourage—the little infants, *las meninas* (ladies-in-waiting), dwarves, and a dog, but there's something unnerving in it as the artist's direct gaze makes the viewer feel that it is they that are being painted.

The "Black Goyas", so named because of their gloomy backgrounds and tragic themes depict the Spanish resistance to Napoleon (1808 to 1814), among the disturbingly poignant *Tres de Mayo* (Third of May) showing the execution of Spanish troops in 1808. They are housed in a special gallery within the Prado. On the ground floor you'll find tapestries designed by Goya for the Escorial (see below).

Also located on the Paseo del Prado, the **CaixaForum Madrid** was incorporated into an old power station by Herzog & de Meuron, and is applauded as much for its vertical botanical garden as for the contents within. Well worth passing by. If you're looking for Picasso's *Guernica* you'll find it along the same cultural mile at the Museo Reina Sofía.

Madrid's mega palace

El Palacio Real (the Royal Palace), *Calle de Bailén 2; tel. +34 (91) 4548-800*, is a baroque structure created under Charles III in 1764. About 50 of the 2,800 rooms are open to the public, each opulently filled with glittering chandeliers, antique wallpaper, and richly patterned rugs. In one room the walls and ceilings are plastered with 400 panels of painted porcelain.

One of the strangest sights in the palace is what appears to be a doll in a glass case in the private Royal Chapel. In fact, these are the bones of St. Felix, a Christian martyr, wrapped in wax and silk and made to look like a small person. The figure was a gift from the pope to Queen Isabella II.

The **Royal Library**, housed in the Palace, holds more than 300,000 books, including 15th-century books, rare manuscripts, and Queen Isabella's prayer book.

You still can see bullet holes and other signs of the bloody Civil War of 1936-1938 in the tapestries, frescoes, and furniture at the Palacio Real. The victorious Franco regime decided to keep these as reminders of the war (but you won't find this information listed in guidebooks).

Madrid's best market

El Rastro, the flea market that starts at the Plaza Mayor and spills down Madrid's streets on Sunday, is the most famous in Spain. Vendors sell fine cotton shirts from India, Moroccan belts of brass and leather, leather bags, alabaster pots, bootleg

CDs and DVDs, semiprecious stones, fossils, and antiques that spill out from the stores that dot the neighborhood. Traditionally you should have walked away with treasures unavailable elsewhere. These days there's an awful lot of tat, knock-offs of designer goods and high street fashions but if you're prepared to dig deep and haggle hard there are still bargains to be had. Get here early. Stalls set up at 7 a.m.

Beware of pickpockets who have a talent for spotting unwary tourists and don't be tempted to buy anything. There's a reason the prices are too good to be true. Above all, the Rastro is a quintessential part of the Madrid experience, especially if you finish up at the Plaza de Cascorro for a *vermut* apertif.

The best jogging

Of Madrid's various green spaces the **Parque del Retiro** is to Madrileños what Central Park is to New Yorkers, and is the perfect place to hit your stride while admiring the intricate network of formal gardens, great open spaces, woodland, and lakes.

The best bull in town

While bullfights may seem barbaric to animal lovers, the Spanish believe that the odds are even, man pitting himself against the untamed elements (the bull). It can seem gruesome to the uninitiated but there are a good deal of *aficionados*— Ernest Hemingway among them—who are mesmerized by the *traje de luces* (the colorful sequined suits of the *torero* [matador]), the ritual, and the strange choreography performed between man and beast. Check it out every Sunday and Thursday from Easter through October at **Las Ventas**, *Plaza de Toros; tel. +34 (91) 356-2200*. Tickets can be purchased at the door. Shows usually start at 5 p.m. or 7 p.m. (It's worth investing in the more expensive tickets for *sombra*— the shady side of the ring.)

Tapas: The world's best snacks

Madrileños don't eat dinner until very late, generally after 9:30 p.m., and it's impossible to order dinner before 8 p.m. unless you're in a very touristy place. The solution is a little snack called a *tapa*. Madrileños, too, get hungry around 6 p.m., so they nibble on tapas—grilled sardines, breaded squid rings, octopus, olives, fried potatoes with brava sauce, sausages cooked in cider, chunks of chorizo (sausage cured with pimentón—the local version of paprika) or morcilla (blood sausage), shell-on shrimp, toasted almonds, and any number of other delicious concoctions—usually washed down with a cool, crisp glass of Fino or Manzanilla (dry sherry) or a *caña* (a small beer on tap). In some bars you'll be offered tapas free when you order a drink, while others charge a modest $1-$4 for the more substantial and creative options they specialize in.

Pinchos come from the Basque Country in the north and generally comprise a small slice of bread with a myriad of toppings skewered on to the top. These can be some of the best tapas in Spain and are worth looking out for. The custom is to have only one drink per *taberna* and then move on to the next one—to spread the wealth so to speak.

Many of the *tabernas* located around the Plaza Mayor specialize in just one thing, be it calamari sandwiches, mushrooms, or prawns. Stroll along the Cava de San Miguel and you won't go far wrong.

Europe's disco capital
Spain's capital has more discos than anywhere else in Europe. They don't get going until midnight. If you enjoy Spanish pop, salsa, meringue, or ear bleeding techno you will have no problem finding your niche in one of the many nightclubs in Madrid.

The finest flamenco
Flamenco dancing has evolved into a unique art form in Madrid. Dinner night-clubs, such as the **Café de Chinitas**, *Torrija 7; tel. +34 (91) 559-5135*; *website: www.chinitas.com,* do a good quality daily show. Flamenco nightclubs can be expensive, however. Alternatively keep your eyes peeled on the side streets around the Plaza Mayor and you might catch an impromptu performance by a traveling troupe of Andaluz gypsies.

Spain's most luxurious hotel
Hotel Ritz, *Plaza de la Lealtad 5; tel. +34 (91) 701-6767; website: www. ritzmadrid.com*, is unrivaled for luxury. The late King Alfonso XIII's favorite hotel was built in 1910 and was restored in 1984 when a British hotel chain took over. It's now owned by the Orient Express Group and all the old luxuries are still there (Limoges china, Persian rugs, crystal chandeliers, and afternoon tea) but a few modern extras have been added such as a gourmet restaurant and in-room massage. The bathrooms at the Ritz are magnificent. Large bouquets of gladioli or exotic birds of paradise give color to the muted green sand grays of the rooms.

Breakfast at the Ritz consists of fresh croissants, Seville marmalade, and hot tea or coffee, served on immaculate white tablecloths accompanied by a little vase of pink carnations, shiny starched napkins, and polished silver.

Twice a day, the splendid bowl of fruit on your dressing table is replenished complete with knife and fork and a finger bowl floating with petals. The location can't be beat either, with the Prado and fabulous boutiques all within walking distance. A night at the Ritz isn't cheap, but you're paying for exquisite service and handsome surroundings.

The closest competition

It's hard to top the Ritz but the **Hyatt Villa Magna,** *Paseo Castellana 22 28046; tel. +34 (91) 587-1234; website: www.hotelvillamagna.com*, comes a close second with beautiful décor and first-class service. It's quiet, despite its central locale. The hotel's garden is gorgeous, set beneath a balconied, nine-story structure. Rooms are large, with bathrooms, individual thermostats, and huge, comfortable chairs. The hotel is decorated with marble, glass, and stainless steel. The bar is cozy. The hotel also has an elegant lounge, a hairdresser, a sauna, and a shopping area.

Westin Palace Hotel, *Plaza de las Cortés 7; tel. +34 (91) 360-8000* or *+1 (800) 325-3535 (in the U.S.); website: www.westinpalacemadrid.com,* is another good luxury option. You still feel pampered and there's plenty to recommend it in terms of maintaining a classical aesthetic. Rooms are plush with *Belle Époque* styling and cost a good deal less than those at the Ritz.

The best contemporary hotels

If you want to hang with the beautiful people look no further than the **Hotel Urban** and **ME Madrid**.

ME Madrid, *Plaza de Santa Ana 14; tel. +34 (91) 701-6000; website: www. memadrid.com,* has the advantage of being situated right on the lovely Plaza Santa Ana and puts you at the heart of downtown action. There's a good fusion restaurant and bar, and rooms decked in dove grey and regal purples. The icing on the cake is the rooftop terrace that affords 360 degree views of the entire city and starts serving champagne and cocktails from around 4 p.m. in the summer. Tip: if you can't afford to stay, members of the public are invited to head on up for a drink.

Hotel Urban, *Carrera de San Jerónimo 34; tel. +34 (91) 787-7770; website: www.hotelurban.com,* is a fabulously designed hotel with lots of edgy features ranging from the soaring glass and steel atrium to the most glamorous cocktail bar in town. Rooms are decadent-feeling with rich velvets and satin throws, charcoal and chocolate color schemes. It also has a roof terrace and what it lacks in views it makes up for in a cooling plunge pool and bar service.

Sweet nights at sweet prices

NH Alcalá, *Calle Alcalá 66; tel. +34 (91) 435-1060; website: www.nh-hotels.com*, is one of the reliable NH chain near the Retiro Park. It's cozy, with a circular hearth in the communal living area giving extra atmosphere in winter, but it can seem a little jaded in daylight. On the plus side rooms are air-conditioned, and double-glazed windows keep out the sounds of traffic. Full-length mirrors and walnut-paneled walls grace the bedrooms. The hotel restaurant is very good also, serving Basque specialties.

Spain's best restaurant

Zalacaín, *Alvarez de Baena 4; tel. +34 (91) 561-4840; website: www. restaurantezalacain.com,* with its 15 cooks is one of the finest restaurants in Europe offering superb avant-garde cuisine at equally avant-garde prices. Expect to pay top dollar and be sure to dress for dinner. Closed Saturday afternoons, Sundays, Holy Week, and in August.

Spain's restaurant capital

You'll probably eat better in Madrid than anywhere else in Spain though it still hasn't attracted the press that goes to Barcelona's new-wave dining scene. As such it's a metropolis brimming with best kept secrets and kitchens serving an even balance of modern and traditional, with enough regional and international cuisines to ensure you'll never have the same dish twice.

The best Castillian cuisine is served at **Casa Botín**, *Cuchilleros 17; tel. +34 (91) 366-4217; website: www.botin.es,* and **Posada de la Villa**, *Cava Baja 9; tel. +34 (91) 366-1860; website: www.posadadelavilla.es*, both in the old part of town. The roast baby lamb and suckling pig is superb at both, though the Casa Botín takes the edge in terms of atmosphere with its warren of old fashioned wood paneled and tiled dining rooms. Both are more than 200 years old and closed on Sunday evenings.

Casa Lucio, *Cava Baja 35; tel. +34 (91) 365-3252; website: www. casalucio.es* (in Spanish), is one of Madrid's oldest restaurants. Despite its unpretentious service and surroundings, this cozy establishment continues to attract the royals and politicians. It is closed Saturday afternoons and in August.

El Amparo, *Callejon de Puigcerda 8, corner of Jorge Juan; tel. +34 (91) 431-6456*, in the exclusive residential neighborhood known as Barrio de Salamanca, serves unique French Basque cuisine. Among the treats are crayfish ravioli with vanilla oil and succulent falling-off-the-bone lamb. The house wines are good and fairly priced.

One of the most elegant restaurants in Madrid, **Horcher**, *Alfonso XII 6; tel. +34 (91) 522-0731; website: www.restaurantehorcher.com*, serves unusual game dishes. The restaurant closes for the month of August.

Jockey, *Amador de los Rios 6; tel. +34 (91) 310-0411; website: www. restaurantejockey.net*, is something of a Madrid institution with a fairly old-fashioned Spanish-French menu running to the odd tub of Beluga caviar and good game dishes such as roast pigeon. Worth it for the experience.

The Spanish passion: paella

If anything could be said to be the national dish it would have to be **paella**—a delicious concoction of rice with seafood, meat or vegetables, or very often a mixture of all three. It is cooked in the vessel from which it takes its name; a flat, wok-style utensil made of stainless steel that should have blackened with age and use. The most popular are the Valenciana (the true home of paella), which generally includes chicken, pork, or rabbit, butter beans and/or green beans; or *de marisco*, which consists of only seafood.

In Madrid head for **El Pescador**, *Calle José Ortega y Gasset 75; tel. +34 (91) 402-1290; website: www.marisqueriaelpescador.net,* an informal restaurant in Old Madrid near the Puerta del Sol. Long communal tables are shared by diners, who serve themselves paella from large pots. If you stop by in mid-afternoon, you will see fishermen with weathered faces peeling freshly-caught seafood for the evening run, though any Spaniard with tell you paella is best eaten before the sun goes down so you have the afternoon to sleep it off.

The best way to get around

The best way to get around Madrid is the city's fast and efficient subway. Buy your tickets at booths and machines in the stations. It costs 1 euro per ride, or you can buy a 10 journey pass for 9.30 euro ($12.40). Tickets are inserted into electronic turnstiles that let you enter the system. Don't throw away your ticket—you'll need it to get back out again. The subway is open from 6:30 a.m. to 1 a.m.

Spain's most intimidating edifice

El Escorial, on a mountain northwest of Madrid, is a 16th-century monastery-palace. It was once the home of Phillip II, who commissioned the Armada to try to conquer England—they failed. A giant, gloomy building with hundreds of rooms and thousands of windows, it is full of history, art, and rare manuscripts. Almost all of Spain's royalty is entombed here, as well as a number of saints, in a cavernous, black-marble room. Trains to the palace leave 20 times a day from the Atocha station in Madrid. A bus takes visitors from the station to the palace.

Spain's best medieval walled town

Avila, Spain's most beautiful walled town, is just 90 minutes from Madrid. Perched on a crest and enclosed within massive 38-foot-high walls, Avila is the highest provincial capital in Spain. Six archways lead into this austere and intimidating town, and 90 towers keep watch over the area. It was also the town of St. Teresa, the 16th-century mystic and reformer. The town has a handful of main tourist sights: the cathedral, the Convent of St. Teresa, and the Basilica of St. Vincent. Visit these first and then explore the streets at random. The best view is from the town walls on the edge of Avila's *parador*, or government-run hotel. Go through the *parador's* garden and climb the flight of stairs to the wall. You will see the River Adaja, the road to Salamanca, and the endless plain. A tourist information office is located opposite the cathedral on the main plaza.

TOLEDO: THE RICHEST HISTORY

Toledo, a city rich in history, is an hour's drive from Madrid. In the words of Gerald Brennan in *2* (1950), *"Like Fez, it reeks of the Middle Ages; like Lhasa, of monks."*

Lording over the city is a fortress called the **Alcazar**, *Calle General Moscardo 4*. El Cid, the Lord Champion of the 11th century, whose courageous deeds were described in Spain's epic poem, lived here. Destroyed during the Spanish Civil War, the Alcazar has been reconstructed. It houses a museum of the Spanish Civil War.

Ferdinand and Isabella built a cathedral at the heart of Toledo in the 15th century and filled it with art, sanctuaries, and chapels. For a great view of the city and a small adventure, climb the cathedral's tower and examine its 18th-century bell, which is still in use.

El Greco left his mark on Toledo as well. His famous painting *The Burial of the Conde de Orgaz* is housed in Iglesia Santo Tome (St. Thomas Church) at Angel Santo Tome. The **El Greco House and Museum** (Casa y Museo del Greco), *Calle Samuel Levi 3*, contains paintings and memorabilia of the 16th-century artist.

A 14th-century synagogue called **El Transito** is down the street from El Greco's house. It was once a house of worship for Jews in Toledo. During the Inquisition, it became a church, and its members were forced either to convert to

Christianity or flee the country. A museum containing Sephardic religious articles is located in part of the synagogue.

The best view of this dramatic city is from the **Circunvalación**, a road that runs parallel to the Rio Tajo.

The best place to stay

Outside Toledo is a highly recommended *parador*. **Parador de Toledo**, *Cerro del Emperador; tel. +34 (925) 221-850; website: www.parador.es*, is one of the most beautiful in Spain. The two-story hotel has a sweeping view of Toledo. Its restaurant serves Castilian cuisine and international fare. Rooms are air-conditioned, and guests can use the hotel's pool.

The best times to visit

The best times to visit Toledo are during the city's festivals: the **Olive Festival**, held at Mora de Toledo on the last Sunday in April; the pilgrimage to the shrine of **La Virgen del Valle**, held on May 1; the **Feast of San Isidoro** at Talavera de la Reina, May 15th to 18th; the annual fair in August that salutes **La Virgen del Sagrario**; and the fiesta known as the **Rosa del Azafran**, held on the last Sunday in October at Consuegra.

BARCELONA: SPAIN'S MOST FLAMBOYANT CITY

Not for nothing was Barcelona nicknamed the "great enchantress"; she is sociable, stimulating, and unabashedly sexy to the point that nearly all who visit fall hopelessly in love. Barcelonín's tend to look more to France than their southern neighbors and residents are fiercely proud of their heritage. To them, the city's ancient hegemony over the Mediterranean is only temporarily in eclipse. The Catalan language is spoken by all and a few words of greeting, *Bon Dia, Bona Tarda, Bona Nit,* (good morning, good afternoon, good evening) will go a long way to endearing yourself to locals. It's not the cheap destination it once was, but there's still a huge amount to love about a city that somehow, manages to retain the community spirit of a small village.

The most romantic quarter

The **Gothic Quarter** (Barri Gòtic), at Barcelona's heart, is a network of narrow streets and stone houses spilling out into quaint little *plaças*. Roman, Gothic, and medieval walls still stand housing a myriad of old-fashioned shops, sweet little bars and restaurants. Wander around and see what you discover; by far the best way to explore it.

The *barrio's* handsome Gothic **Cathedral of Barcelona** on the *Plaça de la Catedral* is a must even if you stop in only to see the white geese in the cloister gardens. Interesting contrasts to the medieval buildings are the street lamps along C/Ferran and in the arcaded, palm filled **Plaça Reial**, which were designed by Antonio Gaudi, an innovative architect known for his strangely organic buildings.

Barcelona's most entertaining avenues

No trip to Barcelona is complete without a stroll along **La Rambla,** although it's worth timing it to miss the crowds—11a.m., when the colorful standing statues have set up for the day, is good. The contiguous segments of Las Ramblas all have their own names—Rambla Dels Estudis, Rambla de Sant Josep—and are each known for different themes: birds and animals, flowers, and arts and crafts.

You'll also find the grand opera house, as well as some iconic bars and cafes such as the cocktail bar **Boadas** (beloved by Sofia Loren and other stars in the 1960s), the elegant **Café Opera**, and the city's best known meeting spot at the top by Plaça Catalunya, **Café Liceu.**

North of here you'll find the **Passeig de Gràcia**, Barcelona's most glamorous shopping street. Filled with the world's top designer names such as Chanel and Dolce and Gabbana as well as Spain's own internationally revered fashion houses, Loewe, Balenciaga, and Manolo Blahnik, it's a shopaholic's paradise. And for those light of wallet, you'll find home-grown Zara and Mango's flagship stores too.

A walk on the dark side

Barcelona's less salubrious side can be enjoyed from the bottom half of the Ramblas heading west into the Raval. Coined the Barrio Chino in the 1920s by a local journalist it represented the underbelly of Barcelona society, in stark contrast to the moneyed classes of the upper *barrios*. Today you still get a glimpse of this darker side of life in the pimps and prostitutes who hang around the street corners here, but many of the places immortalized in Jean Genet's *The Thief's Journal*—an account of his time spent begging and pickpocketing here—have become emblems of old Barcelona. Warning: pick pockets still work this area, so don't walk around here alone at night, and avoid taking any valuables.

Spain's most magnificent opera house

About halfway down Las Ramblas on the right is the **Gran Téâtre del Liceu**, *Rambla dels Caputxins 51-59; tel. +34 (93) 485-9900; website www.liceubarcelona.cat,* where the Barcelona opera is held. This is where Casals first bowed his cello and Caballe hit her first incredible high C. Opened in 1847, it is unassuming on the outside, but inside is one of the most beautiful and state-of-the-art opera houses in all Europe.

A dance with the little green fairy

Absenta, or absinthe, is a potent, bright green colored liquor that is illegal in most countries but perfectly legal in Spain and is credited with giving a number of writers and artists their inspiration (and probably rotted their brains), including Toulouse-Lautrec. The bars **Marsella** and **Pastís** in the Barrio Chino (lower Raval) are some of the most atmospheric in town and offer the chance, should you so wish, to imbibe the infamous absinthe. Traditionally it is poured over a lump of sugar set on the tines of a fork. You then set the sugar alight so that it melts into your glass and top up with water. Limit yourself to two shots at most. After three, you won't know where you are or what you're doing there!

The best of Picasso

Museo de Picasso, *Calle Montcada 15-23, near the Barrion Gotico; tel. +34 (93)256-3000; website: www.museupicasso.bcn.cat/en,* has one of the world's most comprehensive collections of Picasso's works, starting from his childhood and continuing through his entire life. Queues to get in are monumental, but if you get here early in the morning, late in the afternoon and avoid weekends altogether you'll likely find it far more manageable.

Ghosts of the Belle Epoque

Artists like Picasso and Utrillo, along with the Catalan painters Santiago Rusiñol and Ramon Casas, frequented **Els Quatre Gats Café** (The 4 Cats*), Montsio 3; tel. +34 (93) 302-4140; website: www.4gats.com,* in Barcelona at the turn of the century, using it as a place to talk ideas, drink, and exhibit their works. Though designed by the Modernist architect Puig i Cadafalch it was the paintings of these illustrious patrons that earned the place its acclaim, and today, though the food isn't always quite what it should be, it's a magical place nonetheless, especially if you book a table on the gallery level, overlooking the bustling restaurant and piano player.

Gaudi's greatest works

Walking around Barcelona, you can't miss the flagship works of **Antoni Gaudí**. The luxury apartment blocks on and around the Passeig de Gràcia known as the Manzana de Discòrdia comprises the Casa Mila, Casa Batlló (both by Gaudí) as well as others by his contemporaries. They are distinguished by their asymmetrical shapes and lavish colors.

La Sagrada Familia, *Majorca 401; tel. +34 (93) 219-3811; website: www.sagradafamilia.cat*, is Gaudí's never-completed but extraordinary cathedral. Its stonework resembles an enormous dribbled sand castle, a magical folly that literally paints the word of God into stone. Climb the tiny, twisting and turning, steep stairs in the church towers to enjoy the view from the top.

Eventually, Gaudí retired from public life and sequestered himself in the basement, working diligently on his homage to the holy family until the day he died. By then he had become almost unrecognizable and when he stepped off the curb into the road and was hit by the tram that killed him, it was several days before he was formally identified.

Park Güell, *Carrer del Carmel 28; tel. +34 (93) 413-2400*, north of the city, was also created by the imaginative artist and is full of wild and beautiful, sculptures and objects. The benches and walls are studded with pieces of pottery and glass, and caves are hollowed out of a hill. Houses are inspired by Hansel and Gretel and indeed, the whole place has a fairy-tale quality that makes it quite other worldly.

Barcelona's mountain of museums and gardens

Barcelona lies in the shadows of an intriguing hill, **Montjuïc**, crowned by the palace constructed for the 1929 World's Fair. It is a pleasant place to visit—during the day—with innumerable verdant gardens to explore, as well as some of the city's best museums. The walk to the top of Montjuïc and the castle (now home to the Military Museum and outdoor cinema nights through the summer) is long and strenuous (but enjoyable if you are in good shape). If you don't feel up to the hike, take the funicular from the Parallel metro station which whizzes you straight to the top.

The most beautiful of the World's Fair pavilions is a starkly modern structure designed by Mies van der Rohe. It was the first of its kind, with chrome, glass, reflecting walls, and an exterior that played an important part in the interior design of the building. Van der Rohe designed the building for the German exhibit, using green marble and golden onyx in the construction. Inside, scarlet velvet curtains sweep across glass walls. White-kid covered chairs once served as thrones. George Kolbe's statue *Morning*, a classical nude, is reflected in the interior pool. The pavilion is open during daylight hours; entry is free.

Pueblo Español, also designed as a pavilion for the 1929 World's Fair, is still in operation. Typical buildings from all over Spain were reproduced in this village, designed as a miniature view of Spain. Houses are of stone, stucco, or intricately laid brick, topped with Spanish tiles and embellished with elaborate balconies. Typical woodcarvings, metalwork, pottery, glass, leather, and crafts are sold in the village's 35 shops.

Museu Nacional d'Art de Catalunya, (MNAC) *Palau Nacional; tel. +34 (93) 622-0360; website: www.mnac.es,* at the summit of Montjuïc, specializes in Catalan Gothic religious art. The mosaics, frescoes, and artifacts come from isolated churches and hermitages around the region. The museum is open Tuesdays through Sundays.

The **Fundacio Joan Miró**, *Park de Montjuics; tel. +34 (93) 443-9473; website: www.fundaciomiro-bcn.org*, features the work of Joan Miro, whose paintings were inspired by the art and landscape of Catalonia. His painted-bronze sculptures are displayed on the museum balconies, and his stark, late paintings are in alcoves overlooking the courtyard. Perhaps his best work is *Self Portrait*, begun in 1937 and completed in 1960. He drew himself from a reflection in a convex mirror, creating an enlarged, distorted image. His eyes are depicted as star-like.

Barcelona's *"noches locos"* (crazy nights)

As in Madrid, nightlife here begins well after midnight. Then it rolls on full-steam until sunrise. Hundreds of bars and nightclubs are located all over the city, each with its own unique vibe.

The coolest club of the moment is the **Omm Sessions**, *Hotel Omm, Carrer Rossello 265*; *tel. +34 (93) 4454-000; website: www.hotelomm.es*. Here you'll find city slickers shakin' their stuff until the small hours.

Champagne and cocktails

Ever glamorous, when people in Barcelona go for *copas* (drinks) they like to do it in style, opting for old school cocktails at the nautically inspired **Dry Martini**, *C/ Aribau 162-166, Eixample; tel. +34 (93) 217-5072*, or diminutive **Gimlet**, *C/Rec 24, Born; tel. +34 (93) 310-1027*, with its blood red walls and polished wood bar. The other alternative is to pep up with a flute of bubbles at one of the city's many *xampanyerias* (champagne bars). This being Barcelona of course the champagne is cava, the region's own version of fizz, and popular **El Xampanyet**, C/*Montcada 22, Born. tel. +34 (93) 319-7003,* is beloved by tourists and locals alike.

Barcelona's best restaurant

Self-taught chef Jordi Artal just received his first Michelin star for his excellent restaurant **Cinc Sentits**, *C/Aribau 58, Eixample; tel. +34 (93) 323-9490; website: www.cincsentits.com*, which offers sensationally creative dishes. Opt for the tasting menu, which kicks off always with a shot of Canadian maple syrup, Maldon salt and cava sabayon to tickle the taste buds before embarking on a sensory journey you'll be talking about long after the final bite has been eaten.

The finest fish

The old fisherman's quarter of Barcelona is known for its fish and paella restaurants.

One of the best is **Can Majo**, *Almirall Aixada 23; +34 (93) 221-5455; website: www.canmajo.es*, which has terraces onto the beach. Try the *arroz negrè*—a rice dish cooked with squid ink and lashings of *alioli* (garlic mayonnaise). Closed on Monday and Sunday evening.

The best places to sleep

When it comes to service and style, nowhere beats the **Hotel Arts**, *C/Marina 19-21; tel. +34 (93) 221-1000; website: www.ritzcarlton.com*. Situated on the beach at the Port Olìmpic, this was one of the city's first skyscrapers and commands eye popping views of both the Mediterranean and the surrounding city. There's a deluxe spa on the roof, three superb restaurants, and manicured lawns peppered with hammocks.

If your heart is set on being on the Ramblas, the **Hotel 1898**, *La Rambla 109; tel. +34 (93) 552-9552; website: www.nnhotels.es,* is the best on the block, situated in the old Philippine Tobacco Company headquarters. Various black and white photos scattered throughout being testament to its history. Rooms are decorated in fun, candy stripes, it boasts a huge roof terrace with plunge pool and there's a decent dim sum bar in the lobby.

The **Pulitzer**, *C/Begara 8; tel. +34 (93) 481-6767; website: www.hotelpulitzer. es,* offers a high class experience within a lower price bracket than the aforementioned. It too is handily situated smack-bang in the center of Barcelona, has a charming candle-lit roof-terrace for chilling out in the summer, and a comfortable lounge for cocktails in the winter.

If you're on a budget, the **Market Hotel and Restaurant,** *Passatge Sant Antoni*

Abat 10; tel. +34 (93) 325-1205; website: www.markethotel.com.es, is a little out of the way, though still only a 15-minute walk from the center. It has clean, comfortable, Oriental-inspired rooms, and a pleasant, extremely good value restaurant.

Best day trip

A **Benedictine monastery** whose Marian shrine has attracted pilgrims for more than 700 years is located in the Montserrat Mountains, 38 miles northwest of Barcelona. **The Black Madonna (La Morena)**—a 12th-century statue of the Virgin Mary—is the focus of the pilgrims' journey.

SEVILLE'S GREATEST PLEASURES

Seville is a city of simple pleasures: warm sunshine, brightly colored flowers, an expressive river, fragrant orange groves, rustling palm trees, ancient buildings, and shining white houses with patios, flat roofs, and shuttered windows.

In a sense, Seville is the essence of Spain. It has typically ornate and colorful architecture and warm and friendly people. Located on the left bank of the Guadalquivir River, the city is sunny but surrounded by marshland and swamps.

Seville's history is colorful. The Romans conquered the city in 205 B.C. (when it was known as Hispalis), and it became so Romanized that it produced several Roman emperors, including Trajan and Hadrian. Under the Moors it became splendid and the subject of poetry. During the reconquest of Spain, it was the capital. It became the headquarters of trade with the New World in the 16th century. Cervantes spent his youth here, and his famous *Don Quixote* was created in a Sevillian prison.

The old quarters of the city, with narrow winding streets and tiny squares, were built in medieval times in a way intended to provide the best shelter from the heat of the Andalusian summers. The twists and turns of the narrow streets lead to surprises and unexpected views. The houses in the old part of the city have white lime-washed fronts and lots of flowering plants on the balconies.

Spain's most graceful bullfights

Even if you're squeamish, you should see a bullfight in Seville, which is famous for its bullfighters. The Sevillian school of bullfighting teaches a graceful style. Andalusian bulls are bred for the fight and show their stuff in the handsome Maestranza bullring.

Seville's top sight

The most outstanding monument in Seville is the **Giralda**, *Ave. de la Constitucion.* Built on Roman foundations as a minaret in 1184, it is adorned with four huge gilded-bronze apples. In the 1500s, a belfry with 25 bells was added, as well as the enormous statue representing faith, which serves as a weather vane.

The world's third-largest church

Seville's cathedral was built on the site of one of Spain's largest mosques, partly destroyed in the 15th century. It is the third-largest Christian church in the world. The Gothic structure has five spacious aisles, and the main chapel is decorated with a magnificent wrought-iron screen. The tombs of King Alfonso X (the Wise) and his mother, Beatrice of Swabia, are here, as well as an urn containing the remains of King Ferdinand. Many people visit the cathedral without realizing they can also visit the crypt below, which contains the royal coffins of King Pedro the Cruel and Dona Maria de Padilla. The cathedral also contains jewels, vestments, and the sword of King Ferdinand. The Sacristy of the Chalices has paintings by Murillo, Zurbaran, and Goya. Before leaving the cathedral, see the Patio de los Naranjos (Orange Court) and the Christopher Columbus Library. The former was originally the *shan*, or courtyard, of the Mosque. The library contains manuscripts by the discoverer of America.

Best Mudejar architecture

The façade of the old **Alcazar**, *Plaza del Triunfo,* is one of the finest examples of Mudejar art in Spain. (Mudejars were ex-Muslims who remained after the Reconquest.) It was built on the ruins of King Almontamid's palace. After the conquest of Seville, Ferdinand and Isabella and their successors also lived here. Among the remains is the Patio del Yeso. The Alcazar, as it is today, was built by King Pedro the Cruel. Moorish master masons, Sevillian craftsmen, and Toledan decorators took part in creating this building.

The prettiest palace

Casa de Pilatos, *Plaza Pilatos 1; website: www.fundacionmedinaceli.org,* or Pilots' House, a typical 15th-century Andalusian mansion, was built as a reproduction of the Praetorium in Jerusalem. The patio, with a graceful fountain and two ornamental statues of Minerva, is one of the most beautiful examples of Spanish Renaissance art in Seville.

Seville's best museum

The **Museo de Bellas Artes (Museum of Fine Arts)**, *Plaza del Museo 9; tel. +34 (954) 786-500*, located in a monastery, displays Spanish primitives, a magnificent El Greco, and nearly 50 Murillos.

GRANADA: THE MOST ROMANTIC CITY

Granada is one of those romantic towns that makes you feel like you're living a legend or lost in a movie set. It is most famous for its beautiful Moorish palaces and gardens, collectively called the **Alhambra**, *Palacio de Carlo V; website: www.alhambra.org.* The palace is delicate, with multi-colored ceilings carved with stars. Arched windows look out over the water, and private patios open off bathing rooms. The Patio de la Ria and the upper garden are exquisite. The gardens have intricate waterworks, with channels of water that run alongside the steps. Elaborate fountains dance amid the flowering trees.

Patio de los Leones and the adjoining rooms were the heart of the private apartments of the ruler. Light, filtering through the patio, bathes the rooms and glimmers on the patio's fountains and water channels. Washington Irving wrote *Tales From the Alhambra* from his apartment on the Lindaraja patio, which looks out on tall cypress trees and a gently gurgling fountain.

The **Alcazar**, *Pl. Campo Santos de los Martires*, was the guardian of the Alhambra. Its watchtower (Torre de la Vela) is the outstanding feature. In moments of danger, bells rang an alarm. Ferdinand and Isabella flew the banner of Castile from the tower when they took Granada on January 2nd, 1492. From the tower you can see the entire city and the Alhambra.

The ugliest sight in the Alhambra

Charles V decided to plop a huge marble Renaissance palace into the middle of the Alhambra. His imperial majesty felt the Moors' remains were not majestic enough, so he built his monumental palace (now the archeological museum).

The most passionate dancing

Outside Granada at **Sacromonte**, the summit of Mount Albaicin, are famous Gypsy caves, where, to the beating of hands and the sounds of guitars, Gypsies dance the *zambra*, a colorful and passionate dance. The caves sound primitive, but they are warm in the winter, cool in the summer, and often elaborately decorated.

SALAMANCA: SPAIN'S INTELLECTUAL CENTER

Salamanca is the Oxford or Cambridge of Spain—colored greatly by the country's centralization and religious conformity.

The University of Salamanca, *Patio de las Escuelas 1*, the oldest in Spain, was founded at the end of the 15th century, almost at the same time as the Spanish Inquisition, by Cardinal Cisneros, adviser to the monarchs who financed Columbus. The campus is now split between the seminary and the secular university—but many figures on the lay side dress in Roman collars, soutanes, monkish habits, wimples, and coifs.

Perhaps the most telling clue to the way the Renaissance was viewed as both a threat and an opportunity is the large sign at the entrance to the university library, threatening with excommunication those who read books without getting permission from the bishop. All the 16th-century bookshelves lock—and this is not in an effort to stop book thieves!

Near the library is the splendid chapel, which has a painted Renaissance ceiling and is now used for ceremonial occasions. The university buildings are mostly 17th to 19th century, built in tiers around central courtyards. You can visit lecture halls if you enter without disturbing the classes.

Apart from the university, the city also boasts not one but two cathedrals, built partly on top of each other in the local pinkish granite. The older cathedral holds a beautiful retable and the polychrome shrine of Bishop Anaya—both masterpieces.

As is normal in a college town, Salamanca has plenty of cheap eats and cheap digs.

Good eating includes the Michelin-starred **Chez Victor**, *Espoz y Mina 26; tel. +34 (923) 213-123*, which features cockles in *noilly prat* on homemade noodles and *isla flotante* (floating island). Chez Victor is closed in August (when the university closes), Sunday nights, and Mondays.

VALLADOLID: A BEST FOR HISTORY AND ARCHITECTURE BUFFS

A busy provincial capital in the heart of the Meseta Central, **Valladolid** has medieval churches, university buildings, and traces of Spain's greatest writers and artists. The view of the city as you arrive from the highway is memorable—the cathedral, the university buildings, and church spires.

Valladolid's two literary giants

Valladolid produced two famous Spanish literary figures: Zorrilla and Cervantes. The house where poet **Jose Zorrilla** was born, on *Calle Fray Luis de Granada 1*, is a small whitewashed building that contains his letters, manuscripts, and death mask.

The house of **Miguel de Cervantes** (author of *Don Quixote*), *Calle Mayor*, has been converted into a museum. The room that Cervantes used as a study is filled with maps and has a painting of the Battle of Lepanto. One of the writer's manuscripts is exhibited, and the furnishings, carpet, and tapestries were his. Two of his works were written here, *El Licenciado Vidriera* and *El Coloquio de los Perros*.

The most important sights

The **College of San Gregorio**, *Calle Cadenas de San Gregorio 1*, is one of the marvels of pre-Renaissance art. It houses the National Sculpture Museum and contains the finest and most valuable carved figures from the Castile.

Iglesia de San Pablo, *Plaza San Pablo 4*, was originally a Dominican monastery built in the 15th century. Inside are two exquisite small doorways and a vaulted ceiling.

The Cathedral (Catedral), *Calle Arrive 1*, is quite impressive. Begun by the medieval architect Juan de Hererra (who also built the Monastery of El Escorial), it was continued in the 18th century but never completed. The interior is sober and grand, with 32 pillars. Next door is a Diocesan Museum, which contains fine images and jewelry.

Spain's castle country

A great number of castles were built outside Valladolid for its defense. **La Mota**, in Medina del Campo, is one of the most beautiful castles in Spain. Built in the 13th century, it was later home to Ferdinand and Isabella. Over the years it imprisoned Hernando Pizarro, Rodrigo Calderón (the favorite of Philip II), and César Borgia.

Seven miles outside Valladolid stands **Simancas**, originally a bishop's see. It was a Moorish castle until the 11th century, when the Christians reconquered it, and was granted town status in the year A.D. 927. Simincas' cylindrical towers and walls are well-preserved. The inner part of the castle is used as the General Archives of the Kingdom. In its 52 rooms and halls are more than 30 million documents.

Farther down the Douro River is **Penafiel Castle**, a fabulous 14th-century structure that looks down over a historic village. Built in the 10th century, it looks like a huge ship, with 12 buttresses and an interior tower 27 yards high.

SPAIN'S MOST PICTURESQUE CITY—CUENCA

Cuenca is famous for its ancient hanging houses that jut out over a 600-foot gorge. These *casas colgadas*, as they are called, went unoccupied for 200 years before the government restored them. They date from the 14th century, when they were summer residences of kings and queens. Today, they are national monuments. Climb the steep, stony streets to the cobblestone main square with its wrought-iron window grills. Relax in one of the cafés over a glass of *resoli*, the local liqueur made of pure alcohol, coffee, sugar, orange peel, and cinnamon.

A light flickers in the town's lower gate every night in memory of the victory of King Alfonso over the Moors. According to legend, King Alfonso got his troops through the gate by dressing two soldiers in sheepskin and having them slay the gatekeeper. Alfonso's troops then opened the gates and conquered the town without shedding any Spanish blood. A festival is held on September 20th to 22nd every year in celebration of the victory.

The town is prettiest at night when it is lit by hundreds of lights that cast odd shadows on the crooked buildings and winding streets.

MÉRIDA: THE BEST ROMAN RUINS OUTSIDE ROME

Mérida, founded in 25 B.C. as a rest home for retired Roman legionnaires (it was then known as Colonis Emerita August), has the most impressive Roman ruins outside Rome itself. While it was on the main Roman road in antiquity, Merida today is a backwater. It is on a road that goes to the Portuguese border, on a river that you can navigate all the way to the sea at Ayamonte—if you have reason to do so.

Mérida's Roman sights include a multi-tier bridge over the Guadiana River, which carries both traffic and drinking water. The city's monumental aqueduct system, built in granite blocks striped with red clay bricks, is Roman and partially still in use.

The city had both a **Roman theater** (for plays and performances of music for the legionnaires) and a **Roman amphitheater** (for sports events). The Romans were just like modern soldiers—the sports theater is four times as large as the cultural theater.

The theater was built into the slope of a hill, with seats in a horse-shoe shape facing the stage. The stage was made of brick and decorated with marble pillars and columns two stories high. Statues of the Roman gods are visible between the pillars and the wall. Here and there are little doorways cut into the brick, through which entrances and exits were made. In the middle is a two-story doorway used for spectacular effects (*deus ex machina*, for example). Behind the façade you can see the actors' dressing rooms, built into the brick structure. You enter the theater (as you do the Coliseum in Rome) through arched stairways.

The huge amphitheater held 40,000 spectators. On the hillside where both structures stand were Roman notables' houses. The mosaics, paintings, and statuary from these houses can be seen in the Museo Arqueologico. (You pay only one admission price to view the lot.) The bas-reliefs in the museum include depictions of a lute player and of a tavern keeper drawing wine from a barrel.

As if being a major Roman center were not enough, Mérida also was a power center under the Moors. The Moorish fortress by the Guadiana is graced by a lovely colonnaded walk, created of ocher and cream stucco with marble pillars. Even more impressive is the *aljibe*, a set of staircases leading to a bath fed water from a river. Despite the Muslim prohibition against alcohol, the frieze on the entrance to the *aljibe* is decorated with bunches of grapes.

The Romans' greatest engineering feat
The Roman **Aqueduct** in Segovia is the most powerful example of Roman engineering and architecture in Spain. After centuries of use, it still carries water from the River Frio to the town. Running across the center of Segovia, it has 118 arches and rises 96 feet. It was built in the time of uncemented limestone blocks.

Segovia is a beautiful walled town on a rocky ledge above the Eresma River. A 14th-century alcazar (with 19th-century modifications) dominates the town. But the late **Gothic cathedral,** which dates from the 16th century, vies for attention.

Just south of Segovia is the bridge described by Hemingway in *For Whom the Bell Tolls*.

THE MOORS' MOST BEAUTIFUL CITY: CÓRDOBA

Córdoba was the capital of Muslim Spain in the eighth century and one of the major cities of the Muslim world. It once had 500,000 inhabitants and 300 mosques; today 255,000 live here, but most of the mosques are gone.

La Mezquita: A Moorish masterpiece

The city's most amazing monument is **La Mezquita**, *Calles Torrijos*, a masterpiece of Moorish-Spanish architecture topped by a beautiful cupola and boasting an Eastern wall studded with priceless mosaics. Construction of the mosque, which was built on the site of a Visigothic cathedral, was begun in the middle of the eighth century at the orders of Abd-er-Rahman I. Elements of the early cathedral were incorporated into the mosque. Later in the eighth century, Muslims and Christians shared the building, which was also used as a cathedral.

Walk through the Door of Forgiveness into the Orange Tree Patio, an enchanting place with fountains and orange trees. Beyond the patio is a forest of columns—alabaster, jasper, and marble—topped by horseshoe arches. The columns came from North Africa, where they were taken from Roman, Visigothic, and Phonecian ruins. Christians transformed the mosque into an enormous cathedral after they conquered Cordoba in 1236. But they never really got rid of its Moorish look and feel. The interior is vast, large enough to hold hundreds of Muslims facing east. The ceilings are low, with rounded arches. Striped columns hold up the ceiling. Baroque chapels embellish the edges of the cathedral, trying desperately to make it look Christian. In front of the western wall of La Mezquita is the Episcopal Palace, the residence of the Visigothic governors and later the caliph's alcazar.

The most inviting corners

Outside La Mezquita is **Cordoba's Old Quarter**, which is filled with inviting nooks and crannies. Look for good buys in filigree silver and Cordoba leather in the quarter's little shops.

The **Jewish Quarter** (Juderia), northwest of the Moorish structure, has a 14th-century synagogue, located on Calle Judios. Around the corner, on Calle Averroes and Calle Judios, is a patio where you can watch flamenco dancers.

Glance into Cordoba's patios. You will see white-lime walls draped with trailing plants and embellished with wrought-iron balconies. In the center are wells, marble columns, and fountains surrounded by flowers.

PAMPLONA: THE ULTIMATE MACHISMO

Each July in **Pamplona**, the ultimate display of *machismo* takes place. The townsmen pit their lives against hundreds of bulls set loose in the streets and herded toward the bullring. To display their courage, the men run before the bulls, often injuring themselves. Festivities begin when a rocket is fired from the town hall. The streets fill with people who stare in amazement as the race begins. The celebration was made famous by Ernest Hemingway in *The Sun Also Rises*.

All this festivity is in the name of the town's patron saint, San Fermin, a bishop and martyr from Pamplona. Buried in Amiens, France, his body mysteriously disappeared. The body was miraculously found six centuries later, and legend says that, although it was midwinter, the trees burst into leaf.

THE COSTA DEL SOL: A PEOPLE-WATCHING PARADISE

The **Costa del Sol** is the best place in Spain for partygoers, extroverts, and people watchers. The Costa del Sol is for you only if you thrive on the excitement of crowds and nightlife. It's overdeveloped and overcrowded.

Between Malaga and Algeciras are the most crowded resorts—Torremolinos, Fuengirola, and Marbella. Every imaginable language is spoken.

Marbella: The chicest resort
The chicest town on the coast is **Marbella**—it is also the most expensive. Movie stars and oil sheikhs keep prices high. Puerto Banus has a marina that houses yachts from all over the world. Nueva Andalucia, a community within Marbella, has a fancy casino and chic nightclubs. This is nightlife at its best.

Torremolinos: The busiest resort
Torremolinos, once a quiet fishing village, is now the busiest resort on the coast. Germans seem to love Torremolinos, flocking there by the hundreds. Highrise hotels and condominiums line the beaches, and restaurants, nightclubs, and boutiques line the streets. The place is packed with tourists all summer long.

El Torcal: The strangest landscape
When you tire of the beaches, take a trip inland to **El Torcal**, a plain covered with fantastically shaped boulders. The softest parts of the park's limestone rocks have dissolved over the years, leaving the oddly shaped hard sections of rock. You will think you're on the moon.

THE COSTA BRAVA: THE MOST BEAUTIFUL COAST

Spaniards who would rather relax on a secluded beach than gaze at masses of bodies head for the **Costa Brava**, which stretches from Blanes to the French border. The wild coast is known for its ferocious, rugged beauty. Pines fringe the rocky cliffs that drop to the fine, sandy beaches. Little towns are sheltered by the coast's protective coves.

Phoenicians, Greeks, Romans, and Arabs all have taken refuge in the Costa Brava's harbors. Ruins left by these early invaders dot the coast, as do fortified villages from the days of pirate invasions. You'll find Phonecian ruins at Rosas, Greek in Ampurias, and a Moorish fortress at Tossa del Mar.

Girona is the best town for exploring the coast. It is filled with dungeons and ramparts, medieval walls and paintings. The old quarter is dominated by the majestic cathedral, built in the 17th century above Roman ruins. St. Felix Church, next to the cathedral, contains Roman sarcophagi.

The cutest fishing villages

Llafranc, Calella de Palafrugell, and Tamarit occupy the part of the Costa Brava that edges the Baix Emporda—a stunningly beautiful part of Catalonia known for its restaurants and pretty, honey-colored villages. This particular stretch of coast has largely avoided any large scale development and consists of spectacular villas on the cliff tops, white-washed village centers and pristine beaches shaded by pine trees.

Dalí's favorite town

The Costa Brava attracts artists and writers. **Salvador Dalí**, born nearby, was one of the first major artists to live here—at Port Lligat, Cadaques, near the French border. The **Casa-Museu Salvador Dali**, *Portlligat, tel. +34 (972) 251-015; website: www.salvador-dali.org/museus/portlligat/en_index.html,* named after his one true love, is marked by gigantic egg-shaped ornaments and has a whimsical garden. Book in advance to see it as only eight people are admitted at once.

Cadaques is a purely Catalan fishing village where white houses contrast with a dark mountain backdrop. There's no train here, and the road is long and winding, which means it will probably be forever protected from the tourist hoards. As such it's got a wonderfully laid-back air. North of here the spectacular isolated **abbey of Sant Pere de Rodes** is well worth a visit.

In terms of eating, drinking, and sleeping in this neck of the woods, in

Cadaques, **Casa Anita**, *C/Miguel Rosen; tel. +34 (972) 258-471; website: www. cbrava.com/anita/anita.uk.htm,* is a perennial favorite serving excellent fish and Mediterranean dishes. It's where Dalí used to eat.

Casa Nun, *Plaça Portixó 6; tel. +34 (972) 258-856,* is another good bet with a cute terrace onto the front and an excellent value evening menu featuring the day's catch.

Make hotel reservations in Cadaques in advance. The few hotels book up fast. The **Playa Sol**, *Playa Pianch 3; tel. +34 (972) 258-100; website: www.playasol. com,* has great sea views, a pool and tennis courts and is reasonably priced. The hotel is closed in January and February. Alternatively, the **Hotel Port Lligat**, *tel. +34 (972) 258-162; website: www.port-lligat.net,* is modern and comfortable, situated on a secluded by next to the Fundació Gala.

SANTIAGO DE COMPOSTELA—SPAIN'S PILGRIMAGE CENTER

All the roads in northwest Spain (and many roads in France) lead to **Santiago de Campostela**, the greatest pilgrimage center on the Iberian Peninsula. During the Middle Ages, this town was the destination of pilgrims from all over Europe, who came to worship at the tomb of St. James (Santiago), housed in the 11th-century cathedral. Santiago was as important a pilgrimage destination as Rome or Jerusalem.

According to legend, the Apostle James came to this part of Spain to bring Christianity. He landed at Padron on an estuary of the Ulla River. After his death, his remains are said to have been brought back to Spain, where they were lost during invasions by Barbarians and Moors. In the ninth century, a star is said to have appeared marking the point where St. James' remains were buried. They were then taken to Santiago and placed in the cathedral.

Another tale says St. James appeared during a battle against the Moors in A.D. 844, dressed in armor and carrying a white standard with a red cross on it. He fought off the infidels and became known as Matamore, or Slayer of Moors. Later, the saint is said to have fled the Moors by swimming across a river. When he emerged on the other side, he was covered with seashells.

For this reason, pilgrims wear cockleshells to show they have been to Santiago de Compostela. Even if you aren't a pilgrim, Santiago is worth visiting. It is especially beautiful at sunset, when its church spires, hospitals, monasteries, and palaces glint with the sun on their roofs. The town's Romanesque cathedral and Old Town, where ancient houses and little shops fill the streets, are worth exploring.

The best place to stay in Santiago de Compostela (perhaps the best place to stay in all Spain) is **Parador de Santiago de Compostela**, *Plaza de Obradoido 1; tel. +34 (981) 582-200; website: www.parador.es*. Built in the 16th century by Ferdinand and Isabella as a hospice for pilgrims, the *parador* is in the form of a cross, with an interior square and four patios. Bedrooms have high ceilings and ornate furniture.

SAN SEBASTIAN: BASQUE-ING WITH THE BEST

Beautiful **San Sebastian**, bordered by the Urumea River, Bahia de la Concha, and three hills, is where Europe's wealthiest vacationers play during the summer. Drive to the top of Mount Urgall for a long vista of the bay and the sea. An even better view of the city, the bay, and the sea can be seen three miles west of the city at Mount Igueldo.

San Sebastian is known for its Basque cooking with Spanish and French touches and its original use of seafood. The best restaurant in San Sebastian is **Arzak**, *Avda. Alcalde Elosegui; tel. +34 (943) 278-465; website: www.arzak.info*. Chef Juan Mari Arzak won Spain's National Gastronomy Prize for his river crabs with truffles and lobster sauce, his apple pudding with strawberry cream, and his mousse. Arzak specializes in nouvelle Basque cuisine. The restaurant is closed in June and November.

San Sebastian's best hotels
The two most elegant hotels in town are **Londres y de Inglaterra**, *Zubieta 2; tel. +34 (943) 440-770; website: www.hlondres.com*, and **Barcelo Costa Vasca**, *Av. De Pio Baroja 15; tel. +34 (943) 317-950; website: www.barcelo.com*.

GALICIA: THE FISHERMEN'S FAVORITE

Galicia, the westernmost coast of Spain, is a land of fishermen and damp, green landscapes. It has changed little over the centuries and has yet to draw hordes of tourists, probably because of its damp weather. The coastline is beautiful—a great place for romantic walks.

Vigo, the main fishing port

Vigo is the main fishing port of Galicia. Hemingway described this town as *"a pasteboard village, cobble-streeted, white and orange plastered, set up on one side of a big, almost land-locked harbor."* Vigo lies at the end of a swampy river valley. Sheltered bays and quiet inlets surrounding the town produce the shellfish for which Galicia is famous, as well as sardines, tuna, and hake. During the winter, the port is battered by winter gales.

Snug little bars and restaurants can be found on the steep, winding streets of Vigo. Fishermen drink the local wine, *ribeiro*, and chat among themselves in Gallego, the local Spanish dialect, similar to Portuguese. Early in the morning, Vigo bustles. Fisherwomen wearing clogs push cartloads of fish to market. White sandy beaches called Samil and America stretch south of Vigo. A road, lined by vines that produce *ribeiro*, hugs the shoreline, dipping into tiny hamlets and climbing the hills. Narrow one-lane bridges cross muddy creeks.

THE CANARY ISLANDS: ATLANTIS REGAINED

Scattered off the bulge of West Africa, Spain's 13 **Canary Islands** are blessed with 360 days of sunshine. Only on record-breaking days does the temperature dip below 65° F. As a result of this year-round spring-like climate, farmers in the Canaries can harvest four crops a year.

The Canaries have markets filled with an incredible variety of fruits and vegetables.

According to legend, the islands are all that remain of the lost city of Atlantis. Roman discoverers named the islands Canaria, from *canus*, after the wild dogs that lived there.

Tenerife: The largest Canary

Tenerife, which covers 1,231 square miles, is the largest Canary. Through the center of the island runs Mount Teide, the highest peak in all Spain, at 12,192 feet. Throngs of Europeans come here from cold Scandinavia, Germany, and Britain. They romp among the sand dunes and fill the hotels and restaurants all seasons of the year. The burgeoning growth of discos, bars, and multi-sorted highrises, along with planeloads of tourists, makes south Tenerife another Costa del Sol. However, the pace of growth is being checked as building requirements become more stringent.

Cosmopolitan Santa Cruz

The most cosmopolitan city in the Canaries is **Santa Cruz**, on Tenerife, the largest port in Spain. The capital city of 200,000 looks, for all the world, like San Francisco, located at the foot of a gentle slope. It has attractive stores, great restaurants, museums, art galleries, theaters, and even a symphony orchestra. Shopping in Santa Cruz is a special joy. Because the town is a duty-free port, items can be purchased for prices lower than in their countries of origin. Chinese silks, pearls from Japan, watches, designer clothes, and photographic equipment are some of the best bargains.

Puerto de la Cruz, the prettiest town

On the northwest coast, toward Buena Vista, is the small city of **Puerto de la Cruz.** Built on a rocky coast, it has a 600-acre man-made lake and a chain of natural pools that are terrific for swimming. Yellow and red hibiscus, trailing pink geraniums, 30-foot-tall poinsettias, and other tropical greenery surround the pools, and fountains shoot 20 feet into the air. However, the ocean has no beach.

Perhaps the most entertaining thing about Puerto de la Cruz is its underwater nightclub, where you can sip your drink and look through the water to the stars. Stroll along the town's pedestrian street to the best ice cream parlor in the Canaries (if not Spain). It has more than 40 flavors and just as many fresh toppings. Imagine cinnamon ice cream smothered in fresh mango and blueberries!

The best times in Tenerife

The two best times to visit Tenerife are July, when a two-week fiesta attracts people from all over Europe, and February, for Carnival.

The island's best hotel

Tenerife's most attractive hotel is **Gran Hotel Semiramis**, *Leopoldo Cologan Zulueta 12 38400, Puerto de la Cruz; website: www.granhotelsemiramis.com*, an imaginatively designed structure overlooking the ocean.

The best of Gran Canaria

Gran Canaria is a mountainous island with banana trees, coffee groves, sugarcane, and almond trees. Along the southern coast, from the tourist-ridden Playa San Agustin to the quieter and chicer Puerto Mogan, is an unbroken chain of serious sunbathers, windsurfers, campers, and other winter refugees from all over Europe.

Las Palmas, the capital of this 922-square-mile island, is a duty-free port and a shopper's paradise. Although it's difficult to imagine wearing a fur coat in this warm climate, they are a tremendous bargain in the Canaries, where they are available from 30% to 50% less than in European shops.

The most gorgeous resort area in the Canaries is **Maspalomas**. It has long, sandy beaches, lagoons, graceful sand dunes, and enormous palm trees swaying in the breeze. The Oasis Maspalomas shopping center has boutiques, restaurants, bars, banks, car rentals, and book and trinket stalls. Moroccans and other Africans enthusiastically greet you with their wares: camel-skin bags complete with desert aroma, stuffed coiled cobras, and carved ebony elephants.

The most charming village on the island is **Mogan**, a fishing village that rises from the sea on its natural wall of crags and burned earth. Tanned people chat in a half-dozen languages on the streets here. A village artist portrays flamenco dancers on the outside of his house. And the valley is brightened by flowering almond trees and tropical fruits.

Unsurpassable meals

Gran Canaria is a paradise for food lovers. Most restaurants serve delicious meals in gigantic portions for incredibly low prices. This holds true whether you dine in a tiny shack or an elegant restaurant. Choose from a variety of fresh meats and fish, including *chulletas de cordero* (thick, juicy, grilled pork chops); *solomillo pimentas* (steak smothered with roasted sweet peppers); *tuna casuela* (home-style tuna steaks baked with garlic, onions, and red and green peppers); and local fish, such as *salmonetta* (red mullet) and sole, all prepared with fresh parsley and garlic. Tiny island-grown potatoes called *papas arrugadas* are steamed with sea salt and served with a spicy dipping sauce (*mojo picon*) made of chopped chili peppers, garlic, and oil. A good wine is the velvety Lanzarote.

Sleeping in the lap of luxury

Maspalomas Oasis, *Plaza de las Palmeras 2 Maspalomas; tel. +34 (928) 141-448; fax +34 (928) 141-192; website: www.riu.com; e-mail: grandpalace. maspalomasoasis@riu.com*, is a huge resort complex with a nightclub, a golf course, horseback riding, tennis, and a health club. It's popular and expensive.

Meliá Tamarindos, *tel. +34 928 774-090; website: www.solmelia.com*, is a sophisticated hotel with two swimming pools and a nice beach. A full buffet is set up next to one of the pools. A disco and several bars keep the atmosphere friendly.

THE BEST OF THE BALEARIC ISLANDS

The **Balearic Islands** peek sleepily out of the Mediterranean. Europeans love the islands for their perfect summer weather, easygoing inhabitants, and lovely beaches. Mallorca, Menorca, Ibiza, Formentera, and scores of rocky islets make up the Balearics, which lie 100 miles southeast of Barcelona. The trip from Barcelona can be made in 25 minutes by air or in nine hours by boat.

The islands have changed a great deal since the days when Mallorcans stoned George Sand (a woman) for wearing pants. You will see artists and jet setters, punk rockers and tourists, as well as old women in traditional black.

Mallorca: A jet-set getaway

Mallorca offers craggy mountains, Roman temples, and unspoiled beaches. The biggest Balearic island with the starkest contrasts, Mallorca has office buildings and windmills, highways, and ancient villages. Although tourists sunbathe topless, the natives wear traditional costumes. And children inherit thousand-year-old olive trees when family farms get passed down.

About half the island's residents live in Mallorca's capital, Palma de Mallorca. Here, visit the **Cathedral La Seu**, which boasts one of the world's biggest stained-glass windows. Construction of the cathedral began in the 13th century and continued for 300 years.

The prettiest town in Mallorca

The most peaceful town in the Balearics is **Deya**, on the northwest coast. It is a haven for artists and writers who yearn for the romance of the sea, yet despair of spending too much time alone with blank paper or canvas. Robert Graves, who wrote *I Claudius*, lived here for years. A road leads two miles from town through goat fields and over terraces built by the Moors to a beautiful beach. Princess Diana used to vacation here—but it isn't expensive. The aspiring painter can rent a small cliff-side dwelling for very little.

Mallorca's best hotel

The island's most beautiful hotel is **La Residencia**, *tel. +34 (971) 639-011; website: www.hotel-laresidencia.com*. The place holds less than 100 people. The hotel is composed of two huge stone farmhouses, dating back from the 16th and 19th centuries, respectively.

THE BEST OF IBIZA

The cobblestone streets of **Ibiza**, decorated with rainbows of flowers, wind through bright white buildings that lead to the sea. Orange and lemon trees climb terraces to sturdy farmhouses on hilltops. A grove of fig and almond trees curtains sandy beaches. In the evening, lovers stroll to Vedra, the Magic Rock, which reflects the moonlight and is washed gently by the sea.

This island off Spain's east coast has been inhabited by Phoenicians, Greeks, Carthaginians, and Romans. Centuries of invasions by Vandals, Byzantines, and Arabs led to the construction of an enormous fortress here. But the forbidding citadel isn't enough to keep the tourists away.

Despite efforts to enforce zoning restrictions, houses and apartment buildings are going up at a rate that bodes ill for people who like the island's secluded beaches. Already, hotels line some of the island's most languid beach strips. Ancient olive groves are being razed for golf courses. And the visitor's appetites for nightlife have made clubs and bars materialize in out-of-the-way places.

Of course, all this modernizing has its good points (depending on your point of view). Ibiza was the pioneer of nude beaches in Spain, and Agua Blanca beach is an excellent place to get a full-body tan. Cabo Falcon also has a good nude beach called El Cavallet.

Cana Joana, *Carreta Sant Josep; tel. +34 (971) 800-158; website: www. canajoana.com*, is the best restaurant in Ibiza. Local patrons swear by it.

La Marina, *Puerto de Ibiza; tel. (34) 971-310-172, website: www. hostal-lamarina.com* is also good and cheaper.

THE MOST SPANISH TIME TO VISIT SPAIN: HOLY WEEK

The ritual religion of medieval times is resurrected each year in Spain during Holy Week. Candlelight processions mourning the death of Christ file silently through the old quarters of Spain's cities and towns. Statues depicting the life of Christ are carried through the streets. In some areas, residents don the attire of Biblical times and re-enact the life of Jesus.

The biggest Holy Week celebrations are in **Seville**. More than 50 orders of priests and laymen march in procession following an ancient route from the Plaza de la Campana along winding Sierpes Street, past the town hall, and through the Gothic cathedral. They end up in front of the Giralda and the baroque Bishop's

Palace. *Pasos* (platforms of wood and silver) carry statues of the Virgin. They are covered with carnations and rock gently on the shoulders of the bearers to the rhythm of *saetas*, short and fervent prayers or hymns.

Not all the ritual is serious. The **Burial of the Sardine** is a nighttime tradition in Murcia that marks the end of Lent. It includes 25 carriages, each with an accompanying group of merrymakers, bands, and *hachoneros*, or men who carry bras. Little toys are thrown to the spectators from the carriages. At the end of the festival, a huge papier-mâché sardine is burned at the old bridge in Puento Viejo, and fireworks are set off. The Burial of the Sardine dates back to the 19th century, when university students, who could afford to eat nothing but sardines, would bury some to celebrate their graduation.

SPAIN'S BEST WINES

Spanish wines rival French wines and are half the price of their Gallic counterparts. Spain's champagnes are darn good too.

Of the Rioja wines, the two best are **Marques de Murrieta** and **Marques de Riscal**. And the rare **Castillo Ygay Reserva**, made four times a century, is incomparable. The Riscal clarets are delicious; the best of the Riscal reds is the 1922.

Vega Sicilia, which is aged for 10 years, is the best of the Penedes wines (1966 is the best year). Torres is the best brand; the best Torres is the Gran Coronas Black Label.

Spanish sherry too is world-famous, yet underpriced. **Barbadillo's Sanlucar Manzanilla** is the elegant before-dinner drink in Spain. The bestselling dry sherry in the world is **Tio Pepe**.

THE BEST OF
SWITZERLAND

*Exquisite postal service. No bothersome demonstrations,
no spiteful strikes. Alpine butterflies. Fabulous sunsets—
just west of my window, spangling the lake, splitting the
crimson sun! Also, the pleasant surprise of a metaphorical
sunset in charming surroundings.*

—Vladimir Nabokov

Mountainous Switzerland is at the crossroads of Europe. For centuries, its
mountains have protected isolated valleys from marauding armies. Today,
the Alps form a backdrop to orchards and vineyards, lakeside resorts, and picturesque villages. The Rhine, the Rhone, and the Inn rivers all flow from alpine
glaciers. The Matterhorn hovers above Zermatt, and the Berner Oberland mountain range still guards Interlaken. The Swiss Alps challenge the world's top mountain climbers, skiers, and hikers. Nowadays, Switzerland is known as an art center
and setting for Bollywood movies, as well as a tourist destination.

ZURICH: THE WORLD'S BEST QUALITY OF LIFE

Zurich, seat of the Reformation in Switzerland, has attracted revolutionary
thinkers over the years, from Vladimir Lenin to James Joyce, and in the early 20th

century became a center for Dadaism. In Mercer's latest Quality of Living global survey, they rated Zurich as number two in the world for quality of life.

Home to staid bankers, Zurich's German-speaking citizens show a witty, sometimes wild side during the city's annual festivals. In April, its bankers don costumes for **Sechseläuten** and burn an enormous straw dummy, the Böögg, to celebrate the end of winter. The Street Parade held in August is one of the largest techno parties in the world and the largest annual event in Zurich. Most of Zurich's nightlife centers on the **Niederdorfstrasse** and the **Limmatquai**, and features nightclubs bars, and street musicians. For best value, seek out cafes and bars, rather than expensive clubs.

Zurich's top sights

James Joyce once said, *"Zurich is so clean that should you spill your soup on the **Bahnofstrasse**, you could eat it up with a spoon."* The street is best known as Switzerland's premier high-end shopping street.

The **Altstadt** (Old Town), on the right bank of the Limmat River, is a maze of steep cobblestone streets lined with cafés, and nightclubs and sex shops. The arcades of 17th- and 18th-century guildhalls line the Limmatquai and surrounding streets. Most of the guildhalls are now restaurants, decorated with ornate friezes and ceilings.

The Reformation began in Zurich's massive Romanesque cathedral, the **Grossmünster**, *Grossmünsterplatz*. There, Ulrick Zwingli preached against the sale of papal indulgences. His teachings soon spread to the rest of German-speaking Switzerland.

On the left bank of the Limmat River is the **Fraumünster**, its austere Gothic architecture enlivened with stained-glass windows by Marc Chagall and Augusto Giacometti. A few blocks away, the largest clock face in Europe tracks the time of day from the spire of St. Peter's Church, the oldest in Zurich.

The best museums in Zurich

Zurich's **Schweizerisches Landesmuseum** (Museum of Swiss History), *Museumstrasse 2; tel. +41 (44) 2186-511; website: www.slmnet.ch*, in a Neo-Gothic castle behind the railroad station, presents an epic survey of the culture and history of the Swiss people. Collections include medieval religious art and exceptional prehistoric artifacts.

The **Kunsthaus** (Fine Arts Museum), *Heimplatz 1; tel. +41 (44) 2538-484; website: www.kunsthaus.ch*, northwest of the opera house, is known for its collection of 19th- and 20th-century works by Monet, Munch, Giacometti, Rodin, and Chagall. Its temporary exhibitions draw large crowds.

Museum Rietberg, *Gablerstrasse 15; tel. +41 (44) 2063-131*, located in the neoclassical Wesendonck Villa with its private park on the western shore of Lake Zurich, houses Switzerland's only collection of non-European art. Internationally renowned, the Rietberg features works from Asia and ancient America, with the core collection donated by Baron Eduard von der Heydt. Richard Wagner, who stayed here, was said to be so smitten with Mathilde Wesendonck, that he was inspired to compose Tristan and Isolde.

Zurich's best cafés

When you tire of sightseeing, stop in at the **Péclard** (formerly called Café Schober), *Napfgasse 4; tel. +41 (44) 251-5150*, which serves a scrumptious chocolate cake. The cafe is located in a building that dates from 1314, and has been a confectionery since the 19th century.

Another place to appease sweet cravings is the **Confiserie Sprungli**, *Am Paradeplatz 15; tel. +41 (44) 2244-646*. Sprungli is one of Switzerland's most important confectionery producers, famous for white truffles and the delectable *Luxemburgerli* that make such wonderful hostess gifts. Outlets in Swiss train stations and airports make it easy to take a taste of Sprungli home from your travels. The Zurich cafe offers lunch as well as sweets.

Zurich's top restaurants

Rico's Kunststuben, *Seestrasse 160, Küsnacht; tel. +41 (44) 9100-715, website: http://kunststuben.com/wp/*, five miles south of Zurich, is the finest restaurant in German-speaking Switzerland. Chefs Horst Petermann and Rico Zandonella's specialty, seafood, is delicate and refined, but a simple dish of eggs scrambled in truffles, stuffed with liver and artichokes, is also highly recommended. The seasonal menu offers especially good value.

Bierhalle Kropf, *In Gassen 16; tel. +41 (44) 2211-805*, in Zurich's Altstadt, is a popular and lively place to taste Swiss-German staples like liver dumplings, *rösti* (potato cakes) and apple strudel. Der Kropf offers dining in a Teutonic setting, surrounded by wood paneling, boar heads and stained-glass windows.

Kronenhalle, *Rämistrasse 4; tel. +41 (44) 2629-900; website: www. kronenhalle.com* is favored by locals for after-work and after-theater refreshments. Once frequented by James Joyce, the Kronenhalle nowadays is famous for the art that adorns its walls. Sit at a wide table designed by Giacometti and enjoy the works of Braque, Miro, Giacometti, and Leger along with a rather pricey meal, impeccably served.

Zeughauskeller, *Bahnhofstrasse 28; tel. +41 (44) 220-1515, website: www. trymarket.ch/zeughauskeller/index.htm*, an enormous restaurant with outdoor dining in summer, is a happening place, popular among business people from neighboring banks, and less expensive than most Zurich eateries. Located in a converted armory, its house specialties include *Kalbsgeschnetzeltes*, a classic veal dish, and sausages from the different regions in Switzerland, accompanied by a good selection of local wines.

Au Premier, on the upper floor of the main railroad station, *Bahnhofplatz 15; tel. +41 (44) 2171-555*, is an inexpensive restaurant offering a wide selection of Swiss wines in carafes of two, three, or five "decis", or deciliters. Local veal specialties on offer include *Kalbsbratwurst* (sausages), and fancier fare, such as sweetbreads with sherry vinegar or steak with morels.

Hiltl, *Sihlstrasse 28; tel. +41 (44) 227-7000; website: www.hiltl.ch*, was Europe's first vegetarian restaurant. Still housed in its original venue, the restaurant features a fine buffet with Indian specialties, Zurich's largest salad buffet, and an a la carte menu. Hiltl serves freshly pressed juices and has an extensive wine list.

Two of the world's best hotels

The Baur au Lac, *Talstrasse 1; tel. +41 (1) 2205-020; website: www.bauraulac.ch*, located on the edge of Lake Zurich, is consistently rated as one of the best hotels in the world. The service provided by this model of old-fashioned European luxury is superlative, pleasing discerning travelers since 1844. Its Restaurant Français is renowned. Guests at the Baur au Lac join prestigious company, entering their names into a guestbook that has included Kaiser Wilhelm II, Alfred Nobel and countless other movers and shakers. Wagner gave his first performance of *The Valkerie* here.

The Widder Hotel, *Rennweg 7; tel. +41 (44) 2242-526; www.widderhotel.ch*, is an elegant labyrinth of a hotel, located on the left bank of the River Limmat. The hotel was created by joining together eight historical former residences, some dating from the Middle Ages. Staircases, porticoes and courtyards link the buildings seamlessly, creating a sense of intimacy. Service is attentive and discrete, but not stuffy, and food in the two restaurants is innovative.

The best day trip from Zurich

Winterthur is a half-hour's drive or train ride north of Zurich. Dating back to Roman times, it makes for an art-filled day trip from Zurich. Arts patron Oskar

Reinhart's collection is housed in two museums.

The **Museum Oskar Reinhart am Stadtgarten**, *Stadthausstrasse 6; tel. +41 (52) 2675-172, website: http://museumoskarreinhart.ch,* features works by Swiss, Austrian, and German painters from the 18th through the 20th centuries. The **Oskar Reinhart Collection** is housed in the collector's former house, Am Romerhölz, *Haldenstrasse 95; tel. +41 (52) 2692-740*, and features European art from the 14th to early 20th centuries.

Kyburg Castle Museum, *Kyburg; tel. +41 (52) 2324-664*, four miles outside Winterthur, dates from the 11th century, and houses an internationally awarded museum that provides insights into long-ago lives and times. The feudal castle passed from the counts of Kyburg to the Hapsburgs, and now belongs to the canton of Zurich. From the castle's vantage point high above the River Töss, enjoy a panoramic view of the surrounding countryside.

BASEL: INTERNATIONAL ART MECCA

Several of the world's largest pharmaceutical firms have their headquarters here. Basel's world-class museums, medieval old town and new buildings by leading architects, as well as the cultural events, fairs and congresses held here, have also put Basel on the map as a major culture capital.

Art Basel and **Fasnacht** (Basel's unique carnival) draw thousands of visitors each year to this tradition-conscious yet open-minded city. Baselworld is the world's largest and most important event for the watch and jewelry industry. Basel is also Switzerland's oldest university city and has the highest density of museums in the country. Renowned architects Herzog & de Meuron, Mario Botta, Diener & Diener and Richard Meyer have all left their marks here. Located on the banks of the Rhine, at the border between Switzerland, France and Germany, Basel is easily navigated by foot and tram.

Art Basel: The Olympics of the Art World
Art Basel, *Messeplatz; tel. +41 (61) 701-20-77; website: www.artbasel.com,* is the world's premier international art show for modern and contemporary works. Each June, the works of more than 2,500 artists, ranging from the great masters of modern art to the latest generation of emerging stars, go on display for the more than 50,000 attendees. The *New York Times* has called Art Basel the "Olympics of the Art World", while *Le Monde* named Art Basel "The best fair in the world".

A museum city's top three

Kunstmuseum Basel, (Basel Art Museum), *St. Alban-Graben 16; tel. +41 (61) 2066-262; website: www.kunstmuseumbasel.ch*, has the world's largest collection of works by the Holbein family. Owned by the city of Basel since 1661, the collection of the world's first public municipal museum is distinguished by its historic span, from the early 15th century up to the present. Paintings by Basel-born Arnold Böcklin feature among the 19th-century highlights. The accent for the 20th century is on Cubism (Picasso, Braque, Léger), German Expressionism, Abstract Expressionism, and American art since 1950. Its various areas of emphasis give it international standing as one of the most significant museums of its kind. Its smaller contemporary collection is housed in the nearby **Museum der Gegenwartskunst** (Contemporary Art Museum) at *St Alban-Rheinweg 60*.

Fondation Beyeler (Beyeler Foundation Art Museum), *Baselstrasse 101, Riehen; tel. (41) 61-6459-700; website: www.fondationbeyeler.ch*, is the most popular art museum in Switzerland, located just a short tram ride from the center of Basel. It has been called the most civilized art gallery or museum in the world, serene and tranquil both inside and out. The building, designed by the Italian architect Renzo Piano, offers a calm haven for viewing the modern art collection of Hildy and Ernst Beyeler under filtered natural light that streams in from the garden. Artists' works in the collection range from Frances Bacon to Andy Warhol, and they are displayed in direct interaction with 25 works from Africa and Oceania.

The **Tinguely Museum**, *Paul Sacher-Anlage 2; tel. +41 (61) 6819-320; website: www.tinguely.ch*, set in tree-shaded Solitude Park by the Rhine, contains a permanent exhibition of the works of Swiss painter and iron sculptor Jean Tinguely. Tinguely's kinetic art sculptures are on permanent display, and temporary exhibitions bring in works by other modern artists. The building was designed by Ticinese architect Mario Botta.

Basel's most atmospheric dining and sleeping

Les Trois Rois (Three Kings), *Blumenrain 8; tel: 41 (61) 260-5050; website: www.lestroisrois.com*. The first officially documented record of this place was in 1681, and Voltaire, Napoleon, Dickens, Picasso, and Stravinsky, among others, have signed the guest book. The hotel, overlooking the Rhine, was completely restored in 2006 and is a locally prized social center with a piano bar and two restaurants. **Le Cheval Blanc** boasts a Michelin star, with Chef Peter Knogl justly recognized for his edible and seasonal masterpieces. The Italian restaurant features Piemonte cuisine and offers a business lunch menu.

Der Teufelhof, *Leonhardsgraben 47; tel. +41 (61) 2611-010; website: www.teufelhof.com,* is Basel's most creative retreat. It comprises two hotels with a theatre, restaurant, bistro, and a highly rated wine shop. Each room in the Art Hotel is a creation of a contemporary European artist (and the rooms are re-done every three years). The Gallery Hotel is a former convent with stylishly converted rooms. Two excellent restaurants, both popular with prosperous locals, offer innovative cuisine, flawlessly served. A delicious breakfast (cold buffet, with eggs or breakfast meats prepared to order) is included in the room price.

Au Violon, *Im Lohnhof; tel. +41 (61) 2698-711; website: www.au-violon.com,* is a comfortable, slightly offbeat hotel set on a hilltop setting with an elevator down to the town center. Sleeping rooms reflect their origins as cells in a 12th century cloister and more recently, a prison. Diners join the locals for classic French cuisine in the hotel's charming old-world brasserie or outside on a terraced garden in fair weather.

Confiserie Schiesser, *Marktplatz 19; tel. +41 (61) 2616-077; website: www.confiserie-schiesser.ch,* is Basel's oldest tearoom. Situated with a fine view of Basel's medieval town hall and with tables outdoors on sunny days, the place oozes tradition and calories.

GENEVA: SWITZERLAND'S INTERNATIONAL HOST CITY

Geneva, on shimmering Lake Geneva and bordering France, is home to some 200 international organizations.

The European headquarters of the **United Nations** is housed in the Palais des Nations, *14 avenue de la Paix; tel. +41 (22) 9174-1234; website: www.unog. ch,* a testimony to 20th-century architecture situated in the Parc des l'Ariana and built in 1936 to house the League of Nations. The terrace offers a panoramic view of Geneva, the lake, and Mont Blanc. The World Health Organization, the International Red Cross, and the International Labor Office are all located nearby. All offer group visits.

CERN (the European Organization for Nuclear Research), *near Meyrin border crossing; tel. +41 (22) 767-6111; website: www.cern.ch,* is the world's largest particle physics laboratory. Established in 1954 and situated in the northwest suburbs of Geneva on the Franco-Swiss border, CERN is noted for being the birthplace of the World Wide Web. Its scientific work gained new prominence with the development of the Large Hadron Collider (LHC), the world's largest and highest-energy particle accelerator. Visitors are welcome at CERN.

633

The best of Vieille Ville

Most of Geneva's monuments are in old town, the **Veille Ville**. The most prominent of the lot is **St. Peter's Cathedral**, *cours St-Pierre 6; tel. +41 (22) 319-7190.* Completed in the 13th century, the building was partially rebuilt in the 15th century and has an 18th-century neo-Grecian doorway. The predominant décor is plain, befitting a church that turned Protestant in 1536 when St. Peter's became a center of the Reformation. Look for Calvin's seat in the north aisle. Climb the 145 stairs to the north tower of the cathedral for a superb view of the Jura Mountains, Geneva, the lake, and the Alps.

Geneva's Reformation Monument, **Parc des Bastions**, was built in 1917 against a 16th-century rampart in what is today a park. Look for statues of the four Geneva Reformers: Calvin, Knox, Farel, and de Bèze.

Geneva's **Hôtel de Ville** (town hall), *rue de l'Hôtel-de-Ville*, dates in part to the 15th century. The first Geneva Convention (following foundation of the International Committee of the Red Cross) was signed in the Alabama Room in 1864.

The **Maison Tavel**, *6 rue du Puits St-Pierre; tel. +41 (22) 4183-700; website*: *www.ville-ge.ch,* near the cathedral, is the oldest house in Geneva, housing the Museum of Old Geneva and its display of historic engravings.

The deepest Alpine lake

Lake Geneva, or Lac Leman, as it is known locally—the deepest of the Alpine Lakes at 1,000 feet—is also Switzerland's largest. Forty-five miles long and 7.5 miles wide at its widest point, the lake covers 143,323 acres. A "Tour of the Upper Lake," with landing stages throughout Geneva, lasts 12 hours. Look for official timetables and rates, posted at Quai du Mont Blanc, Jardin Anglais, and Eaux Vives, opposite the Parc de la Grange. The **Jet d'Eau**, a fountain spouting 476 feet, presents a striking sight against the southern Swiss and French Alps. It is easily accessible from the Quai du Mont Blanc.

Best hotel

Hotel Le Richemond, *rue Adhémar-Fabri 8-10, Jardin Brunswick; tel. +41 (22) 7157-000; website: www.lerichemond.com,* was completely restyled in 2006. Run by the Armleder family, the imposing building has two fine restaurants, and a wine cellar with over 80,000 bottles. The hotel has long been a Geneva institution.

A short list of Geneva's top French restaurants

Parc des Eaux-Vives, *82 quai Gustave-Ador; tel. +41 (22) 8497-575; website: www.parcdeseauxvives.ch,* is the most famous French restaurant in Geneva. Located in the hotel of the same name, Eaux-Vives has splendid views and classic cuisine. The service is always good, and the wine list is superb.

Perle du Lac, *128 rue de Lausanne; tel. +41 (22) 9091-020*, across the lake, is a superb French restaurant with a view of Mont Blanc. Generous servings come at high prices, but the same fare from the same kitchen at one-third the price can be had from the brasserie next door!

BERNE: SWITZERLAND'S LOVELIEST CITY

Switzerland's capital, **Berne**, is one of the best-preserved medieval cities in Europe, filled with turreted buildings, cobblestone squares and countless fountains. Bounded by the Alps, Berne is divided twice by the Aare River.

Established in 1191 by the duke of Zähringen, Berne was originally a hunting ground. The duke and his cronies named the town after the first animal caught on a day's hunt, a bear (*Bär* in German). Follow the tourist office's mapped walking tour to see Berne's top sights.

St. Vincent Cathedral, *Münsterplatz; tel. +41 (31) 3120-462*, is an impressive Gothic Church with 16th-century statues depicting the Last Judgment. Climb the 254 steps of the 330-foot tower for a bird's eye view of the city and the Alps.

The **Kunstmuseum** (Art Museum), *Hodlerstrasse 8-12; tel. +41 (31) 3280-944; website: www.kunstmuseumbern.ch*, houses the world's largest collection of works by native son Paul Klee. It also features works by Modigliani and Picasso.

The **Historisches Museum Bern** (Historical Museum), *Helvetiaplatz 5; tel. +41 (31) 3507-711; website: www.bhm.ch*, displays booty from the Burgundian wars, including the dramatic tapestries and embroideries of Charles the Bold, Duke of Burgundy, as well as historical replicas of rural Swiss rooms and objects dating back to the Stone Age.

The city's medieval clock tower, the *Zeitglockenturm*, rings several times a day; its mechanical bears, clowns, and kings performing at four minutes before every hour.

MONTREUX: PEARL OF THE SWISS LAKES

Montreux, with its six-mile promenade lined with palm trees and tropical flowers on the shores of Lake Geneva, boasts the mildest climate on the north side of the Alps, where visitors stroll among fig and almond trees, cypresses, and magnolias. Montreux also has an intense cultural life with exhibitions, concerts and, above all, the famous Montreux Jazz Festival. Other music festivals include the International Choral Recitals the week after Easter and the Musical September concerts.

Eden au Lac Palace, *11 rue du Theatre; tel. +41 (21) 9660-800; website: www.edenpalace.ch*, a turn-of-the-century hotel on the lake in Montreux, is the best place to stay. Dine in the hotel garden, right on the lake.

La Vieille Ferme, *40 rue de Bourg, Chailly-sur-Montreux; tel. +41 (21) 9646-465; website: www.laferme.ch,* a rustic restaurant outside town in Montreux-Chailly, is acclaimed for local specialties. Raclette and country music are equally popular here.

La Rôtisserie du Château, *Grand-Rue 91, Villeneuve; tel. +41 (21) 9602-009; website: www.lechateaudevilleneuve.ch,* a towered 17th-century building at the foot of a mountain, was once the residence of the Bouvier family of France's House of Savoy. Wood-beamed ceilings and other antique touches, as well as the outside terrace, add charm to the rotisserie.

Chillon: Swizterland's most poetic castle

Chillon Castle, 1.5 miles south of Montreux; *tel. +41 (21) 9668-910; website: www.chillon.ch*, is perched on a rocky outcropping at the opposite end of the lake from Geneva. The life of prior François Bonivard, imprisoned for four years in this über-romantic stronghold, inspired Byron's lyrical poem *The Prisoner of Chillon*. Bonivard, who sought to bring the Reformation to Geneva, was chained to one of the pillars in the castle's dungeon by the Duke of Savoy, an ardent Catholic. The prisoner's footprints can still be seen traced in the rock. In 1816 Byron carved his name on the third pillar in Bonivard's cell.

Built in the ninth century, the fortress was expanded by the bishops of Sion and embellished by the counts of Savoy from 1150 to the mid-13th century. The Great Hall sports an imposing 15th-century fireplace, a large collection of pewter, and 13th-century Savoyard furniture. To get to the castle, cross a moat on the 18th-century bridge that replaced the original drawbridge. From the castle keep, take in the view of Montreux, Lake Geneva, and the Alps.

LAUSANNE: OLYMPIC CAPITAL

Lausanne, on Lake Geneva between Geneva and Montreux, is a welcoming and cosmopolitan city. Its universities date from the 16th century, but its students keep the atmosphere young. World-class ballet and classical music make it an important center for art and entertainment. The Lausanne municipality of Vedy is home to the International Olympic Committee.

Start your exploration of Lausanne at **Place de la Palud**, in the city's Old Town. This square centers on the 16th-century **Fountain of Justice** and is bordered by the town hall's Renaissance façade. Behind the fountain an unusual covered staircase leads to the town's 12th-century cathedral, one of the finest Gothic buildings in Switzerland. It shelters one of the last night watches in the world, whose duty is to call out the hour during the night. The south door of the cathedral, the **Door of the Apostles**, is covered with 13th-century sculptures. A 700-year-old rose window illustrates the elements, seasons, months, and signs of the zodiac. Climb the 232 steps to the top of the tower for a view of Lake Geneva and the Alps.

Le Musée Olympique (Olympic Museum), *Quai d'Ouchy 1; tel. +41 (21) 6216-511; website: www.olympic.org*, displays memorabilia from games past, along with collections of stamps and coins inspired by the Olympic movement. The museum's terrace has a panoramic view of Lake Geneva.

Collection de l'Art Brut, *Avenue des Bergières 11; tel. +41 (21) 3152-570*, features objects by so-called "fringe" artists, gathered by the artist Jean Dubuffet. The spontaneous paintings, drawings, sculptures, modeling and embroidery are housed in the former stables of the 18th century Beaulieu Chateau.

Restaurant P. Rochat, *1 rue d'Yverdon; tel. +41 (21) 634-0505; website: www.relaischateaux.com/hoteldeville,* is acclaimed well beyond Swiss borders. The chef is precise and inventive with fish and fresh produce. Be sure to leave room for the chocolate soufflé.

Château d'Ouchy, *2 place du Port; tel. +41 (21) 3313-232; website: www.chateaudouchy.ch*, on Lake Geneva, is the most romantic place to stay in the region. It offers dancing, tennis, and excursions in an idyllic setting. This 12th-century stronghold of the bishops of Lausanne became a government customs house in the 1700s. A hotel was built around the castle in 1884, and its Salle des Chevaliers hasn't changed in 800 years.

THE BEST OF THE SWISS ALPS

Matterhorn—Europe's most recognizable peak

The Matterhorn was scaled for the first time on July 14, 1865, in a climb organized by Edward Whymper, a young British illustrator. Whymper, three British friends, a guide from Chamonix, and two guides from Zermatt reached the peak, but four men were killed on the return journey. After the fall, Whymper and the two Swiss guides, the Taugwalders, father and son, reported seeing two crosses shining in a great arc of clouds in the sky.

At 14,692 feet, the Matterhorn is intimidating, but you don't have to be an experienced mountain climber to scale its peak. With the help of a guide, three to five days on the easiest trails can get you to the top. Information on hiking the Matterhorn is available at the **Mountaineering Office**, *tel. +41 (27) 9662-460; website: www.alpincenter-zermatt.ch,* near the Zermatt tourist office.

Zermatt: Switzerland's prettiest ski resort

The Valais-resort of Zermatt is a small, automobile-free village with a picture-postcard tangle of stately hotels. The Matterhorn dominates the town, which has very good skiing, albeit with daunting ski-lift queues. The hotels and restaurants, too, are crowded in ski season.

Lifts in Zermatt travel to 11,500 feet, offering some of Europe's highest slopes and a whopping vertical drop of 6,300 feet. Heli-skiing and snowboarding are popular. And summer skiing here is also tops; offering strong intermediate skiers a morning's run down to Cervinia in Italy.

Excellent (and expensive) hotels are the **Mont Cervin Palace**, *Bahnhofstrasse 31; tel. +41 (27) 9668-888; website: www.seilerhotels.ch/en/mont-cervin-palace/,* which has an indoor pool, a sauna, and day-care facilities, and the **Grand Hotel Zermatterhof**, *Bahnhofstrasse 55, tel. +41 (27) 9666-600; website: www. zermatterhof.ch,* a modern hotel with a swimming pool, saunas, and a fitness center.

Hotel Alex, *Bodmenstrasse 12; tel. +41 (27) 9667-070; website: www. hotlalexzermatt.com,* run by former Matterhorn guide Alex Perren and his wife Gisela, is a center of winter-time social life. Facilities include an indoor swimming pool and indoor squash and tennis courts.

The Hotel Metropol and Spa, *Matterstrasse 9; tel. +41 (27) 9663-566; website: www.metropol-zermatt.ch,* in the center of town on the banks of the Vispa River, has fabulous views. The Taugwalder family, which runs the hotel, bought a meadow opposite the hotel, ensuring unspoiled views of the Matterhorn.

Most scenic alpine train journeys

An elegant and relaxing way to traverse the Alps is aboard the **Swiss Railways' Glacier Express**, which runs from Zermatt to St. Moritz. This train leisurely crosses 291 bridges, passes through 91 tunnels, spans the valleys of the Rhone and Rhine rivers, stops in typical mountain villages, heads into the wild, barren Gotthard region, and then climbs the 6,706-foot Oberalp Pass. The grand finale of the trip is a series of spectacular loops and tunnels that ends at St. Moritz.

From St. Moritz, take the Bernina Express to its final destination at Tirano in Italy. The panoramic cars of the Rhätian Railway pass through 55 tunnels and cross 196 bridges, passing glaciers, picturesque villages and alpine gardens along the way. In summer, a bus brings you back to Lugano, Switzerland, with its palm-lined lake and Italianate buildings.

Canton Valais: Switzerland's most inviting valleys

The canton of **Valais**, situated in the heart of the Alps, is encircled by more than 50 peaks, each at least 13,000 feet high. A prime destination year round, the canton's valleys invite exploration and its mountains offer prime skiing and hiking.

For centuries, the small town of **Brig**, capital of the Valais, has been a center of trade with Italy, but it is perhaps better known for three other characteristics: the Stockalper Castle, Switzerland's largest private residence, built between 1658 and 1678; its position as the starting point for the beautiful Simplon Pass to the south; and hospitality (a huge and colorful sign decorated with a mountain Fräulein welcomes you into this French/German "border town", perched on the canton's linguistic divide).

The Rhone continues from Brig, traveling northeast to tiny towns that give you a true feeling of the region. Stop in **Reckingen** to see its 18th-century Baroque church, possibly the canton's most beautiful building. Visit **Crans-Montana**, which is actually two towns, Crans-sur-Sierre and Montana. Arguably the most tourist place in the entire Valais, this skier's haven attracts jet-setters from around the world.

In summer, the valleys of canton Valais are green with acres of terraced vine-yards and fruit trees. Hike the trails of Val d'Anniviers or wander along ancient aqueducts and the canals known as *bisses*. For maps and hiking route suggestions, see *www.MySwitzerland.com/hiking*.

The Valais is Switzerland's top wine-producing region. The **Château de Villa**, *Rue Sainte-Catherine 4, 3960 Sierre; tel. +41 (27) 4551-896; website: www. chateaudevilla.ch*, offers tastings of wines from more than 70 producers in the region, and to suit every palate. Visit the tasting room to experience the variety of Valais grapes and try raclette and seasonal dishes. The wine shop ships worldwide.

The Valais is as expensive as the rest of Switzerland, but there are less costly ways to enjoy the scenery and sights. One is to stay in a *zimmer-frei* instead of a hotel, in lodgings similar to B&Bs. In the mountains, opt for *cabanes*, or Alpine huts. Some are open only to members of climbing clubs, others welcome everyone. For specifics on where to stay in the Valais, visit the canton's website, *www.valais.ch*.

Most spectacular views of the Alps

One of the most unforgettable views of the Alps—perhaps in the world—is from **Kleine Scheidegg**, near Interlaken. Take a train from Interlaken to Grindelwald and then another train to Kleine Scheidegg, where you can watch mountain climbers in the distance from the lodge's outdoor restaurant. After lunch, hike down to Interlaken through the Lauterbrunnen Valley if you're feeling energetic, or take a train from Wengen to the valley floor.

Travelers on the Swiss Railways' train to **Jungfrauhoch**, Europe's highest railway station, are treated to breathtaking views without the exertion of a hike. Mountaineers depart the train just before it reaches the top, passing through an old railway shaft to the climbing route up the Eiger. Slip and slide through the redoubt's gallery of ice sculptures and step outside and into a swirl of cloud that parts for exhilarating views of the Berner Oberland.

Alpine wilderness at its best, Swiss style

The Swiss National Park, one of the first national parks in Europe, is the place to enjoy a view of the Alps as God made them, untouched by the hand of man. The Swiss obviously want to keep it this way—fires, camping, pets, and mountain climbing are prohibited, and visitors may not leave marked trails. Overnight in the park is allowed only in a designated lodge.

The restrictive rules guarantee wondrous results. The 40,000-acre park is filled with wild, heavily wooded valleys crossed by torrential creeks. You'll spot deer, ibex, chamois, and marmots—but no trash dumps or trailer parks.

Walks through the park are organized by the **Swiss National Park Center, Zernez**; *tel. +41 (81) 8514-141; website: www.nationalpark.ch,* and are offered in summer only. For detailed descriptions of park trails and accommodations, see William Reifsnyder's little book *Footloose in the Swiss Alps*.

Gimmelwald—Switzerland's most picturesque mountain town

Gimmelwald, a sleepy little town in the mountains near Interlaken, is a prime hiking destination, but can also be reached by cable car from Stechelberg or Murren. You'll hear cowbells here and see farmers in lederhosen, but no cars in this peaceful village. From Gimmelwald, take a cable car to the summit of the Schilthorn and take in the view cross the valley to the German border. The revolving restaurant here was the setting for *On Her Majesty's Secret Service*, a 1969 James Bond film.

THE BEST OF THE
UNITED STATES

The genius of the United States is not best or most in its executives or legislatures, nor in its ambassadors or authors or colleges, or churches, or parlors, nor even in its newspapers or inventors, but always most in the common people.
—Walt Whitman

Americans go to great lengths and expense to travel to the far corners of the earth in search of the world's bests. The irony is that they can find many of them right in their own back yards. People from around the world flock to the United States to see New York, Washington, D.C., San Francisco, New Orleans, the Rocky Mountains, the Grand Canyon, and Niagara Falls.

New York is one of the most exciting cities in the world. California is where the world's trends are set. The Grand Canyon is one of the world's major wonders. Texas is a world unto itself. Hawaii has the world's best surfing. Alaska is one of the world's last frontiers. And decisions affecting the entire globe are made in Washington, D.C.

Where to begin? If you like big cities, go to New York or Chicago. If you prefer nature, go to Yellowstone and Yosemite national parks. Beach lovers should head for Southern California.

We will begin our look at the United States on the East Coast with New York City, continue on to New England, and then head south along the East Coast.

Next we will head west through Texas and the Southwest. Then we will explore the Rockies and California, before heading north on the Pacific Coast. We won't overlook the Midwest, including Chicago. And last, but not least, we will describe the bests of Alaska and Hawaii.

NEW YORK CITY: AMERICA'S NUMBER-ONE SIGHT

Ask any foreign visitor where he would most like to go in the United States and his reply most likely will be New York City. People around the globe dream of visiting New York, America's great melting pot, a stew of colorful traditions and peoples. New York is also the creative center of the United States. Ambitious young Americans hoping to make it big make their way to the Big Apple—the country's best dancers, artists, writers, musicians, and fashion designers. This mixture of exotic, ambitious, and energetic people makes New York electric.

Manhattan: The heart of the City

Manhattan, the liveliest of New York's five boroughs, is the heart of the City, as New Yorkers call their town. The famous **Midtown** area, stretching from 31st to 60th streets, contains some of the most famous sights, including the Museum of Modern Art, Rockefeller Center, St. Patrick's and St.Bartholomew's Cathedrals, Times Square, Grand Central Station, the United Nations, Macy's, Saks, and Bloomingdales (three of the most exciting department stores in the world), and the Empire State Building.

The southern tip of the island houses many of the city's historic sights, as well as the financial district. Farther north are ethnic neighborhoods: Little Italy, Chinatown, and the Lower East Side. **SoHo**, a boutique wonderland, is west of Little Italy. North of SoHo is **Greenwich Village**, the famous student, bohemian, and gay district, which has become more polished and expensive in the last 25 years. Andy Warhol and Arthur Miller frequented Chelsea (Manhattan's biggest art scene), just north of the Village. East of Chelsea is **Gramercy Park**, with its 19th-century mansions and brownstones.

The **Lower East Side**, between East Houston and Canal streets and Allen and Essex streets, is a Jewish and Latino community with great bargain clothing stores. The best are on **Orchard Street**. For Jewish treats, visit **Yonah Schimmel's Knishery**, *137 E. Houston Street; tel. +1 (212) 477-2858*, or **Moishe's Bakery**, *504 Grand Street; tel. +1 (212) 673-5832*, open every day except Saturday.

Chinatown, surrounding Mott Street, is the largest Chinese community east of San Francisco, with hundreds of Chinese restaurants and stores. The **Chinese Museum & Chinese Drago**, *8 Mott Street; tel. +1 (212) 964-1542*, explains the history and culture of New York's Chinese community and leads tours through the neighborhood.

For SoHo's best boutiques, check out Rem Koolhaas-designed **Prada**, *575 Broadway*, and **Chanel**, *139 Spring Street*. If you can't afford the real thing, the shops along Canal Street have all the great knock-offs.

Greenwich Village is filled with homes and haunts of American writers, poets, and artists. Louisa May Alcott once lived at *132 MacDougal Street*. Edna St. Vincent Millay, Hart Crane, Bob Dylan, and Allen Ginsberg found inspiration there. Edgar Allen Poe lived at *85 W. Third Street*. Look for Picasso's colossal sculpture *Sylvette* on Bleecker Street.

Washington Square Park is the place to go to see first-class street performances. For a bit of spare change, you can watch comedians, musicians, and other performers do their stuff here. (You'll also see sunbathers, drug pushers, chess players, and lovers.)

Chelsea, the area between 15th and 39th Streets west of Broadway, is the newest art world enclave; all the important galleries are there (walk on Ninth Avenue and up and down the side streets between 23rd and 26th streets).

If money interests you, visit the **Financial District**. Tour the **Federal Reserve Bank** (The Fed), *33 Liberty Street; tel. +1 (212) 720-6130; website: www. newyorkfed.org*, and see the **New York Stock Exchange**, *11 Wall Street*. Unfortunately it's no longer possible to tour the Stock Exchange. Federal Hall, facing the Stock Exchange, is the place where George Washington took his oath of office.

The symbol of freedom

The **Statue of Liberty** (*website: www.nps.gov/stli/*), on an island off the southernmost tip of Manhattan, has become a symbol of America at its best—welcoming immigrants from poor nations and oppressive governments with open arms. The best view of the statue, a gift from France, is from the **Staten Island Ferry**, which leaves from the ferry dock on South Street. For a trip to the statue itself, take a ferry from **Battery Park**.

The best city park: Central Park

New York's **Central Park** is the best city park in the world—and one of the biggest. Here, New Yorkers escape the pace of their frenetic city. This playground for all ages has a zoo, a carousel, an ice-skating rink, a boating lake, gardens, soccer fields, horseshoe courts, baseball diamonds, tennis courts, jogging paths, basketball courts, wading pools, bird-watching, bike rentals, marionette shows, concerts, lawn bowling, horse-and-buggy rides, and refreshment stands. Free "Shakespeare in the Park" plays are performed during the summer. Central Park also hosts two free performances each of the New York Philharmonic and the Metropolitan Opera every summer.

The top sights

The **Empire State Building**, *Fifth Avenue; website: www.esbnyc.com*, between 33rd and 34th streets, was for years the tallest building in the world. Designed by William Lamb, it was built in 1930-31. From the top of this 102-story building, you have a breathtaking view of New York. The building is open from 8 a.m. to 2 a.m. daily.

Radio City Music Hall, *50th Street and Sixth Avenue; website: www.radiocity. com*, next to Rockefeller Center, is New York's most extravagant art deco theater. The long-legged, feathered Rockettes and their can-can are the main attractions.

St. Patrick's Cathedral, *51st Street and Fifth Avenue*, is the largest Roman Catholic cathedral in the United States. Built between 1858 and 1879, it was designed by James Renwick. This Gothic Revival church has 12 side chapels and contains the shrine of St. John Neumann (1811-1860), the first American male to be canonized.

The **United Nations**, *between 42nd and 48th streets*, on the East River, is a large complex with a garden and an esplanade. Guided tours are conducted Mondays to Fridays and last approximately 45 minutes. A limited number of tickets are available each day to the public.

Former Beatle John Lennon lived in the **Dakota Apartments**, *Central Park West*, between 72nd and 73rd streets, until his murder there on December 8th, 1980. This elegant apartment building, home to many celebrities, was built in 1884.

New York's best museums

The **Metropolitan Museum of Art**, *Fifth Avenue at 82nd Street; tel. +1 (212) 535-7710; website: www.metmuseum.org*, houses more than three million works of art, including the Rockefeller Collection of Primitive Art, European paintings, and Egyptian art. The Met, as it is known, is New York's number one museum and a must-see. The museum is closed on Mondays.

The **Museum of Modern Art**, *11W. 53rd Street; tel. +1 (212) 708-9400;*   **645** *website: www.moma.org*, has the best collections of modern art in the world. Permanent shows range from Impressionist to contemporary. It is closed on Tuesdays.

The **Cloisters**, *Washington Avenue and West 193rd Street; tel. +1 (212) 923-3700; website: www.metmuseum.org/cloisters/general,* in a rebuilt medieval monastery in Fort Tryon Park in upper west Manhattan, displays Romanesque and Gothic art. Highlights are the Unicorn Tapestries, the Cuxa Cloister, and the Treasury. It is closed Monday.

The **Guggenheim Museum**, *1071 Fifth Avenue and 89th Street; tel. +1 (212) 423-3500; website: www.guggenheim.org*, a modern spiral building designed by Frank Lloyd Wright, displays the best of contemporary art, including works by Kandinsky, Miró, Calder, and Klee.

The **American Museum of Natural History**, *Central Park West at 79th Street; tel. +1 (212) 769-5100; website: www.amnh.org,* houses the fossilized remains of prehistoric animals, as well as reconstructed homes of present and past civilizations. See the show of stars at the newly renovated planetarium.

The **International Center of Photography**, *1133 Avenue of the Americas at 43rd Street; tel. +1 (212) 857-0000; website: www.icp.org*, is America's foremost museum of photography.

The **Jewish Museum**, *Fifth Avenue at 92nd Street; tel. +1 (212) 423-3200; website: www.thejewishmuseum.org*, is dedicated to all aspects of the Jewish heritage. The Jewish museum is closed Friday and Jewish holidays.

The **Museum of the American Indian**, *One Bowling Green; tel. +1 (212) 514-3700; website: www.nmai.si.edu*, is the largest museum in the world dedicated to the Native American people.

El Museo del Barrio, *1230 Fifth Ave. at 104th Street; tel. +1 (212) 831-7272; website: www.elmuseo.org,* is devoted to Latin American art and culture.

The **Museum of the City of New York**, *1220 Fifth Avenue at 103rd Street and Fifth Avenue; tel. +1 (212) 534-1672; website: www.mcny.org*, is devoted to the complex and rich history of the city.

The **Paley Center for Media**, *25 West 52nd Street; tel. +1 (212) 621-6800; website: www.paleycenter.org*, is one of the least known and most fascinating museums in the city, where you can view your choice of a vast archive of old television shows and radio recordings.

The **Whitney Museum**, *945 Madison Ave. at 75th Street; tel. +1 (212) 570-3600; website: http://whitney.org*, is a contemporary structure housing the work of American greats from Hopper and de Kooning, to Rothko, Warhol, and Judd. The Whitney is known for its innovative special exhibits.

The best entertainment

Midtown, on the west side, is New York at its most entertaining. The **Theater District** stretches from 43rd to 54th streets on Broadway. The most beautiful theaters are the **St. James**, *246 W. 44th Street*, the **Shubert**, *225 W. 44th Street*, the **Booth**, *222 W. 45th Street*, and the **Majestic**, *247 W. 44th Street*.

Lincoln Center for the Performing Arts is one of New York's major cultural centers. More than 13,000 spectators can be accommodated in the center's various buildings: Avery Fisher Hall, the Walter Reade Theatre, the Metropolitan Opera House, the NYC Public Library for the Performing Arts, the Vivian Beaumont Theater, and the Julliard School of Music. The **Metropolitan Opera House**, designed to resemble a jewel box, is as spectacular as its operas, with gigantic Chagall murals, and glittering chandeliers.

The best on and off Broadway

If you're looking for lights, luster, and over-the-top spectacles, see a show on Broadway. For a more intimate or avant-garde evening, see an off-Broadway show. In either case, you'll be experiencing some of the world's best theater.

At **TKTS**, *Duffy Square, 47th Street and Broadway; website: www.tdf.org*, you can get tickets to on- and off-Broadway shows for 25%, 35% and 50% off—but you have to buy tickets for shows that same day. They also have locations at the South Street Seaport and Downtown Brooklyn.

Hit Shows, *630 Ninth Ave.; tel. +1 (212) 581-4483*, offers discount coupons that can be redeemed at the box office.

Rush Tix at **The Public Public Theater**, *425 Lafayette Street; tel. +1 (212) 539-8500; website: www.publictheater.org,* offers a limited number of $20 tickets for every downtown theater performance (as do many others, on and off Broadway).

The Public Theatre's **Shakespeare in the Park** performs at the Delacorte Theater in Central Park from June through September. Tickets are given out free at 6:15 p.m. for the 8 p.m. performance. Fans arrive as early as 6 a.m. on the day of the performance to ensure a ticket, so bring a picnic lunch.

The world's best opera company

The **Metropolitan Opera Company**, *tel. +1 (212) 362-6000; website: www. metoperafamily.org/metopera/,* is the largest in the world, with a stellar roster of performers that includes the likes of Joan Sutherland. The company performs at the Metropolitan Opera House in Lincoln Center. During the summer, free performances are given in city parks.

The best dance and music

The **New York City Ballet**, *tel. +1 (212) 870-5570; website: www.nycballet.com*, is the oldest ballet company in the United States. It presents the classics, including the Nutcracker Suite at Christmas, at Lincoln Center.

The **American Ballet Theater**, *890 Broadway; tel. +1 (212) 477-3030; website: www.abt.org*, is one of the world's most revered and innovative dance companies.

The **Alvin Ailey American Dance Theatre**, *130 W. 56th St, website: www. alvinailey.org*, are innovative troupes that perform in the City Center. Ailey concentrates on modern dance.

The **New York City Opera**, *tel. +1 (212) 870-5570; website: www. nycopera.com*, managed by Beverly Sills, presents bold productions, often in English. Foreign-language operas have subtitles.

The **New York Philharmonic**, *tel. +1 (212) 875-5900; website: http://nyphil. org*, is well-respected, performing works from Bach to Bernstein from September through July at Lincoln Center.

The best jazz joints

Some of New York's best places to hear jazz include the **Blue Note**, *131 W. Third St; tel. +1 (212) 475-8592; website: www.bluenotejazz.com;* **Smoke**, *2751 Broadway; tel. +1 (212) 864-6662; website: www.smokejazz.com;* the **Village Vanguard**, *178 Seventh Ave. South; tel. +1 (212) 255-4037; website: www.villagevanguard.com;* the **Iridium**, *1650 Broadway; tel. +1 (212) 582-2121 website: http://theiridium.com.* Look for young up-and-coming talent as well as classic greats.

The best contemporary music

The Old Knitting Factory, *361 Metropolitan Avenue, Brooklyn, NY 11211; tel. +1 (347) 529-6696; website: http://ny.knittingfactory.com*, features the best in avant-garde, rock 'n roll, jazz, and experimental on several intimate stages. After 14 years in their Leonard Street location, the Knitting Factory has moved to the hip neighborhood of Williamsburg, Brooklyn.

The **Bowery Ballroom**, *6 Delancy Street; tel. +1 (212) 533-2111; website: www.boweryballroom.com*, is a super-cool lounge and concert hall—nowhere better for alternative and Indie-rock.

Joe's Pub, *425 Lafayette Street; website: www.joespub.com.* New York's sexiest venue with world music, jazz, blues, cabaret, and rock. You name it, they got it (and they always have a hip crowd).

New York's best restaurant

Per Se, *10 Columbus Circle at Time Warner Center; tel. +1 (212) 823-9335; website: www.perseny.com.* Having garnered three Michelin stars, chef Thomas Keller's newest venture, after his West Coast triumph with The French Laundry, is taking Manhattan by storm. Adored by even the toughest critics (and they're tough in this city), Keller has reached culinary heights and deserves every one of the tremendous accolades that come his way. Delicate dishes of oysters and caviar, Black Sea bass stuffed with watercress, *foie gras confit* with apple purée…the food is superbly conceived from start to finish.

Other superb restaurants

Le Bernardin, *155 West 51st Street; tel. +1 (212) 554-1515; website: www. le-bernardin.com*, is the seafood lover's dream come true, vying for top spot among restaurant aficionados. Chef Eric Ripert works his magic with seafood of all kinds, interspersed with the staples of great French cuisine (such as seafood broth with lobster, truffles, and *foie gras*) and has a following that considers him a wizard (if not a god).

The **Four Seasons Restaurant**, *99 E. 52nd Street; tel. +1 (212) 754-9494; website: www.fourseasonsrestaurant.com*, is a popular place for lunch. The menu varies with the season, a combination of classic and contemporary cuisines. Save room for the chocolate-chocolate mahogany cake.

Jean Georges, *1 Central Park West; tel. +1 (212) 299-3900; website: www. jean-georges.com.* World-famous chef Jean-Georges Vongerichten never fails to astonish. This drop-dead gorgeous restaurant is outdone only by the lavish cuisine.

Grammercy Tavern, *42 East 20th Street; tel. +1 (212) 477-0777; website: www.gramercytavern.com*, is on the list of top class restaurants in Manhattan, with American cuisine served seasonally. It is famous for grilled meats, with a superb steak and apple tart.

Bouley, *163 Duane Street; tel. +1 (212) 964-2525; website: www.davidbouley. com.* David Bouley confirms his reputation as one of America's finest chefs with his flagship Tribeca eatery. A world-class French restaurant featuring the best of seasonal, local produce.

Masa, *Time Warner Center at 10 Columbus Circle; tel. +1 (212) 823-9800; website: http://masanyc.com.* This is no average sushi joint. With four stars from *The New York Times*, it is the destination of those who love the freshest and most innovative sushi and will pay any price to get it.

The best ethnic restaurants

The best Mexican restaurant in New York (and one of the best in the United States) is **Rosa Mexicana**, *1063 First Ave.; tel. +1 (212)753-7407; website: www. rosamexicano.com*. Try the red snapper in cilantro sauce. The restaurant is closed for lunch but open every night. There are two other locations in Union Square and Lincoln Center.

Babbo, *110 Waverly Place; tel. +1 (212) 777-0303; website: www.babbonyc. com*. If you can get a reservation here, you won't regret it. Some say it's New York's best Italian, period.

Bo Ky, *80 Bayard Street; tel. +1 (212) 406-2292*, is decidedly no-frills and cheap to boot, but it's the real thing when it comes to classic Vietnamese food. New Yorkers in the know flock here.

Barbuto, *775 Washington Street; tel. +1 (212) 924-9700 website: http:// barbutonyc.com*. For a delectable thin-crust pizza East-Coast style, this is your place. It's a stand-out on an island brimming with pizza joints.

The **Second Avenue Deli**, *162 E. 33rd Street; tel. +1 (212) 689-9000; website: www.2ndavedeli.com,* is everything a New York deli should be and more…the helpings are big enough for two, but you won't want to share—everything is too good.

Darbar, *152 E. 46th Street; tel. +1 (212) 681-4500; website: www.darbarny. com,* is the best Indian restaurant in town, an elegant place with white-linen tablecloths and precise service.

New York's best hotels

The best place to stay is the **Carlyle**, *35 E. 76th Street; tel. +1 (212) 744-1600; website: www.thecarlyle.com*, an old-fashioned, Old World hotel with perfect service. The attention to detail is remarkable.

Morgans, *237 Madison Ave.; tel. +1 (212) 686-0300; website: www. morganshotel.com*, is an exclusive hideaway for celebrities. An enthusiastic young staff takes care of guests' needs. Andy Warhol paintings adorn some of the rooms.

The **Algonquin**, *59 W. 44th Street; tel. +1 (212) 840-6800; website: www. algonquinhotel.com*, is a first-class, old-fashioned hotel.

The **New York Palace**, *455 Madison Ave.; tel. +1 (212) 888 7000; website: www.newyorkpalace.com*, is a modern skyscraper rising out of a 19th-century mansion. The lobby and dining rooms are elegant old rooms with antiques. Bedrooms are spacious and modern, with fantastic views of New York.

The **Ritz Carlton**, *50 Central Park S.; tel. +1 (212) 308-9100; website:*

www.ritzcarlton.com, is a very English, very luxurious modern establishment with views of Central Park and a central location near the main shopping areas. The popular Jockey Club dining room is here.

The **Pierre**, *Fifth Avenue at 61st Street; tel. +1 (212) 838-8000; website: www.tajhotels.com/pierre/*, is a peaceful place, where celebrities stay when they want privacy. This recently refurbished hotel has views of Central Park.

The **Michelangelo Hotel**, *152 W. 51st Street; tel. +1 (212) 765-1900* or *+1 (800) 237-0990; website: www.michelangelohotel.com*, is a bit of old Europe in the middle of Manhattan. Each of the 180 rooms is decorated differently, but all have bathrooms of Italian marble. Hotel services include courtesy limousine service to Wall Street and use of nearby health-club facilities. The concierge is especially helpful.

The best budget hotel
The best hotel for your money in New York is the **Paramount**, *235 W. 46th Street; tel. +1 (212) 764-5500; website: www.nycparamount.com*, with a progressive European atmosphere and décor and first-class service. The Paramount is becoming the place to stay in the City.

THE BEST OF NEW YORK STATE

Don't spend all your time in the City; **New York State** is also worth seeing. Unspoiled forest and rolling farmland still exist in this fertile state, which is watered by lakes Champlain, George, Erie, and Ontario, as well as the Hudson River. The Adirondack and Catskill Mountains offer retreat from the noise and pollution of New York City.

The best of the Adirondacks
You can hike in the **Adirondacks** for days without leaving the wilderness. The most beautiful area is between Lakes Placid and Saranac, where the forest is untouched and the streams are pure.

Adirondack State Park is the largest wilderness area east of the Mississippi, bordered by lakes George and Champlain. One of the most beautiful sights in the park is the **Ausable Chasm**, on Route 9 near Interstate 87, a mile-long gorge near Lake Champlain.

Fort Ticonderoga, used during the French and Indian War and the

Revolutionary War, guards the junction of Lakes Champlain and George. A museum today, it is open May through October.

Lakes Placid and Saranac, at the heart of the Adirondacks, offer canoeing, boating, and fishing. Lake Placid has tremendous skiing—good enough for Olympic athletes, in fact, who competed here in 1980.

The best place to stay on Saranac Lake is **The Point**, *Star Route, Saranac Lake, 222 Beaverwood Road; tel. +1 (518) 891-5674; website: www.thepointresort. com*, an 11-room inn with a private beach. Originally a camp, The Point is elegant now, decorated with fine paintings. The bedrooms are enormous. You can sail or canoe on the lake, hike or cross-country ski through the woods, or play tennis, golf, badminton, billiards, Ping-Pong, or croquet.

High Peaks Base Camp, *Springfield Road*, 13 miles from Lake Placid, is situated on 200 acres ringed by the Sentinel Wilderness Range and the Hurricane Mountain Primitive area. It has miles of cross-country ski trails and is just five miles from the downhill ski slopes at Whiteface Mountain. Enjoy a home-cooked meal in the Wood Parlor.

The **John Joseph Inn** (formerly the Rose Inn), *Route 34 North, 813 Auburn Road, Ithaca; tel. +1 (607) 533-0097; website: www.jjande.com,* is also a charming place to stay, 10 minutes outside of Ithaca. The light-rose, Italianate mansion is set on 20 acres of gardens, a pond, and an apple orchard. All the rooms are decorated differently, with a variety of antiques and Victorian furniture.

The Baseball Hall of Fame

Cooperstown, in central New York state, is a small town with a big drawing card—the **Baseball Hall of Fame**, *25 Main Street; website: http://web. baseballhalloffame.org*. Three floors of baseball memorabilia fill this museum, a mecca for baseball fans. You can see enlarged photographs of the world's best baseball players, sculptures of Babe Ruth and Ted Williams carved from single pieces of laminated basswood, and roughly 1,000 artifacts and photos from the early Negro baseball leagues. Also on display are baseball cards from 1900, Lou Gehrig's uniform, and Joe DiMaggio's locker.

Cooperstown has several good restaurants. The best is the **The Hawkeye Bar and Grill**, *60 Lake Street; tel. +1 (607) 547-9931; website: www.otesaga.com/ Dining/*, located at the The Otesaga Resort Hotel, where you can indulge in home-made fare and rich desserts.

Our favorite place to stay is **Angelholm**, *14 Elm Street; tel. +1 (607) 547-2483; website: www.travelguides.com/bb/angelholm/,* a restored home built nearly 175 years ago. This B&B has only four bedrooms, and baths are shared. But a complete breakfast and afternoon tea are included in the price of a room.

Lake Champlain's bests (and beasts)

Between New York, Vermont, and Quebec lies **Lake Champlain**, where more than 200 sightings of a controversial monster called Champ have been reported. Champ's existence is debatable, but the beauty of the lake and its islands is not.

Lake Champlain's major islands—North Hero, South Hero, and Isle La Motte—are dotted with sugar maple and oak trees, red barns, and silos. Although they look serene, they have had a tumultuous history. The French, British, and Americans warred over the lake, because of its importance as a natural highway from New York to Canada.

Samuel de Champlain discovered the islands in 1609, claiming them for the French. Later, the British claimed them, and finally the Americans. The turning-point battle of the War of 1812 was fought at Pittsburgh, where nearly 30,000 British troops were defeated by 2,000 Americans.

Isle La Motte is the site of the first settlement in Vermont, **Fort St. Anne**, which was built by the French in 1666 for defense against the Indians. Today open-air Masses are held here. **Fort Blunder**, built by the Americans in 1777, was so named because its builders didn't realize it was on Canadian soil.

THE BEST OF NEW ENGLAND

One of the oldest and most historic areas of the United States is New England, where quaint, shingled homes and simple churches have a unique charm. Boston harbors intellect, art, ethnic variety, and beauty. Cape Cod has the most beautiful coastline on the Atlantic. And the mountains of northern New England are green and rolling.

The best of Boston

Boston, one of the most livable cities in America, is a collection of inter-connected small towns. Despite its folksy atmosphere, it is sophisticated, with a large intellectual community and many universities and colleges. It is also the best place to trace American colonial history. Historic figures, such as Samuel Adams, Paul Revere, and Ben Franklin, lived here. Walk by the Old North Church, where lanterns were hung to signal an attack by the British during the Revolutionary War. Or climb

Bunker Hill, the site of one of the war's major battles. And visit Fanueil Hall, where the doctrine of "no taxation without representation" was born.

American writers Ralph Waldo Emerson, Henry David Thoreau, Louisa May Alcott, and Daniel Webster found inspiration in Boston. In more recent years, Boston has spawned the Kennedys. And many of America's best minds, including President Barack Obama, have graduated from nearby Harvard University.

The easiest way to see the best of Boston

The easiest way to see Boston is to follow the Freedom Trail—a red brick or painted line that leads past the city's greatest historic landmarks. The trail takes you past the Old State House, where the Boston Massacre occurred; the Old North Church, where the light was hung to signal Paul Revere; the Old South Meeting House, where colonialists rallied before the Boston Tea Party; and the Granary Burial Ground, where the victims of the Boston Massacre are buried.

Boston's must-sees

The best view of the city is from the top of the **Bunker Hill Monument**, but you'll have to climb its 294 steps to enjoy it.

Beacon Hill is an elegant neighborhood with trees, cobblestone streets, and beautiful old brownstones. Louisa May Alcott once lived at 10 Louisburg Square. Blue bloods now live where Puritans originally settled.

The State House, a gold-domed building on Beacon Hill, is open to visitors.

Boston's Public Library, *700 Boylston Street; tel. +1 (617) 536-5400*, is the oldest public library in the world and the third largest in the United States, decorated with murals painted by John Singer Sargent.

Boston's best museums

The Museum of Fine Arts, *465 Huntington Ave.; tel. +1 (617) 267-9300; website: www.mfa.org,* near Northeastern University, has Egyptian, Impressionist, and Americana collections.

The Isabella Stuart Gardner Museum, *280 Fenway; tel. +1 (617) 278-5156; website: www.gardnermuseum.org,* is a small Venetian-style palace filled with great works of art, including Titian's *Europa*, Raphael's *Pieta*, and paintings by Rembrandt, Sargent, Whistler, and Matisse. The museum is closed on Mondays.

Boston's Institute of Contemporary Art, *100 Northern Avenue; tel. +1 (617) 478-3100; website: www.icaboston.org,* housed in a stunning new waterfront building, displays works by contemporary artists.

The museum at the **John F. Kennedy Presidential Library & Museum**, *Columbia Point; tel. +1 (617) 514-1600; website: www.jfklibrary.org*, contains photos and documents about John and Robert Kennedy and Jacqueline Kennedy Onassis.

One of the world's largest fish tanks

The New England Aquarium, *1 Central Wharf; tel. +1 (617) 973-5200; website: www.neaq.org*, is home to a four-story ocean tank, where more than 600 sea creatures live.

Boston's best parks

Boston is a city of parks. The best is the **Boston Common**, with its inviting green lawns, sunbathers, Frisbee players, musicians, picnicking families, and swan-filled ponds.

Boston's Public Gardens, between Arlington, Boylston, Beacon, and Charles streets, are just across Charles Street from the Boston Common.

The Arnold Arboretum, a 265-acre park on the Arborway in Jamaica Plain, is the oldest public arboretum in North America, containing more than 10,000 species of plants.

The **Rose Kennedy Greenway** is Boston's newest park. A block from the waterfront, it stretches from Chinatown to the North End, dotted with sculptures, fountains, green lawns, and great picnic spots.

The most festive times to visit

Patriot's Day (April 19th) is celebrated with the re-enactment of Paul Revere's ride. The hero sets out from the North End and gallops past the Old North Church yelling, "The British are coming, The British are coming." In Concord, Minutemen re-enact the battle of the Old North Bridge. This is also the day of the Boston Marathon.

Boston's best ice cream

Every Boston-area neighborhood has its favorite ice-cream parlor. The best is **Toscanini's**, *899 Main Street; tel. +1 (617)491-5877*, in Cambridge, a small shop serving a myriad of homemade flavors, including grape-nut raisin, malted vanilla, Belgian chocolate, and black bottom pie.

A roster of great restaurants

The best seafood restaurant in Boston is **Mare**, *135 Richmond Street; tel. +1 (617) 723-6273; website: www.marenatural.com.* Although the nautical décor is not the most atmospheric, the cuisine leaves nothing to be desired. Fresh organic seafood is prepared to perfection here. Closed on Mondays

The most romantic restaurant in Boston is also its loftiest, the **Top of the Hub** on the top floor of the Prudential Center on *Boylston Street; tel. +1 (617) 536-1775; website: www.topofthehub.net.*

One of the oldest restaurants in Boston is the **Locke-Ober Café**, *3 Winterplace; tel. +1 (617)542-1340; website: www.lockeober.com,* which opened in 1875. Try the filet of lemon sole *bonne femme.*

The best value seafood and prime rib

The No-Name Restaurant, *15 ½ Fish Pier Street; tel. +1 (617) 338-7539; website: http://nonamerestaurant.com/,* is a little out of the way, but still easily accessible from downtown Boston, especially if you are near the Institute of Contemporary Art. The menu is limited to fried or broiled seafood, and usually a catch of the day. The portions are enormous, and the atmosphere a little crazy. You sit at long tables which seat about 18 people, so this is not the place to go if you're looking for intimacy. It is the place to go if you are looking for great food and cheap prices. Bring your own wine, as they do not serve alcohol here. Reservations are not accepted, so be prepared to stand in line.

Durgin Park, *340 Faneuil Hall Marketplace; tel. +1 (617) 227-2038; website: www.arkrestaurants.com/durgin_park.html,* serves the best prime rib for the money in Boston. Its atmosphere, too, is a little crazy. The portions are enormous—hanging over the edge of the platters—and prices are inexpensive. The décor is rustic or early colonialist.

Boston's finest hotels

The oldest hotel in America and Boston's best is the **Omni Parker House Hotel**, *60 School Street; tel. +1 (617) 227-8600; website: www.omnihotels.com.* Dickens, Emerson, and Longfellow all stayed here. The famous Parker House roll was first baked here more than a century ago. Ho Chi Minh once worked at the Parker House as a busboy.

The **Ritz Carlton Boston Common**, *10 Avery Street; tel. +1 (617) 574-7100; website: www.ritzcarlton.com/en/Properties/BostonCommon/Default.htm,* is an elegant place with a dignified staff and luxurious rooms. The hotel restaurant offers exquisite meals and lovely views of the Common.

The **Copley Plaza,** *138 St. James Ave.; tel. +1 (617) 267-5300; website: www. fairmont.com/CopleyPlaza/,* is an elegant 383-room hotel opened in 1912. While it is grand, it has an intimate air, with a library where you can take tea. The bedrooms are spacious and richly furnished. Dine in the award-winning Oak Room restaurant.

The best of Cambridge

Across the Charles River from Boston is **Cambridge**, a charming area encompassing Harvard University (the oldest in the nation), the Massachusetts Institute of Technology (MIT), and lots of bookstores and movie houses.

The trendiest shops and restaurants are on **Harvard Square**, where you'll also find street performers, ice-cream parlors, and bars. **Harvard Yard**, part of the campus, is quieter and more dignified, and anyone is welcome to stroll the grounds.

The **Harvard University Museum system,** is comprised of four fine and remarkable museums:

> The **Peabody Museum of Archaeology and Ethnology**, *11 Divinity Avenue;*
> *website: www.peabody.harvard.edu/;*
> The **Museum of Comparative Zoology**, *26 Oxford Street;*
> *website: www.mcz.harvard.edu/;*
> The **Mineralogical Museum**, *24 Oxford Street;*
> *website: www.fas.harvard.edu;*
> The **Botanical Museum**, *22 Divinity Avenue;*
> *website: www.huh.harvard.edu/collections/botanical.html.*

The latter museum's Ware Collection of glass flowers is the finest array of decorative glasswork in the world.

One of the largest comic book stores in the United States is the **Million Year Picnic,** *99 Mount Auburn Street; tel. +1 (617) 492-6763.*

The **Grolier Poetry Bookshop,** *6 Plympton Street; tel. +1 (617) 547-4648; website: http://grolierpoetrybookshop.org,* is the oldest poetry bookstore in the country. It is closed on Sundays and Mondays.

Both Grolier and another Harvard Square institution, the **Harvard Bookstore** (unaffiliated with the university), *1256 Massachusetts Avenue; tel. +1 (617) 661-1515; website: www.harvard.com,* are holding their own as strong independent bookstores. They each carry a discriminating selection.

Two historic towns

Just outside Boston are two towns that played essential roles in American history: **Lexington** and **Concord**. Paul Revere rode through Lexington on the night of April 18th, 1775, warning that British troops were approaching. On Lexington Green, the first shots of the Revolutionary War were fired and the first blood was drawn. Founding fathers Samuel Adams and John Hancock slept at the **Hancock-Clarke House,** *36 Hancock Street,* today a museum.

Concord is the town next door, where Minutemen gathered to head off the British. The **Old North Bridge** over the Concord River is the site of the Revolutionary War's first battle. It was made famous by these words: *"Here once the embattled farmers stood and fired the shot heard round the world."*

Concord produced some of America's most famous writers. Louisa May Alcott lived with her family at the Wayside and wrote *Little Women* at the Orchard House. You can visit the **Ralph Waldo Emerson House,** *28 Cambridge Turnpike.* Nathaniel Hawthorne rented the **Old Manse,** *Monument Street,* but bought **Wayside,** *Lexington Road.*

The **Concord Museum,** *Lexington Road and Cambridge Turnpike; tel. +1 (978) 369-9763; website: www.concordmuseum.org,* displays possessions of Emerson and Thoreau.

Cape Cod: The most beautiful coastline

Cape Cod, a hook-shaped sandy peninsula in southeast Massachusetts, has the most beautiful coastline on the Atlantic: sand dunes covered with sea oats, silvery driftwood, seagulls basking in the sun, huge rocks, and the crashing ocean. The Cape Cod National Seashore protects 44,600 acres of the cape from development.

The liveliest town

Provincetown, at the northern tip, is the cape's hot spot, a maze of clapboard houses (some dating back to the 18th century), galleries, guesthouses, and shops. Popular and busy, it draws artists, the gay community, and families. The town lies within the Cape Cod National Seashore and is surrounded by dunes, ocean beaches, marshes, and woods.

Provincetown has a long history. Although Plymouth claims to be the oldest colony, the pilgrims actually landed at Provincetown first, before heading on to Plymouth, where they settled. A monument to these hardy souls sits atop a 100-foot hill at the heart of town. The 252-foot granite column can be climbed via 116 steps. From the top, you can see for 50 miles on a clear day.

Commercial Street, the main thoroughfare, is lined with art galleries, shops, and crowds of pedestrians, bikers, cars, horse-drawn buggies, hawkers, and skateboarders. Here, also, is the **Provincetown Playhouse**, where Eugene O'Neill first produced some of his plays.

Provincetown boasts one of the few links-style golf courses in the United States, the **Highland Golf Club,** *Highland Rd., Truro; tel. +1 (508) 487-9201.*

For dancing, go to **Atlantic House** (also called the A-House), *6 Masonic Place; tel. +1 (508) 487-3821; website: www.ahouse.com.*

Front Street Restaurant, *230 Commercial Street; tel. +1 (508) 487-9715; website: www.frontstreetrestaurant.com,* is recommended by locals and visitors alike for its cozy setting and consistently excellent Italian/Mediterranean fare.

New England's oldest settlement

Plymouth, where the *Mayflower* landed in December 1620, is the oldest European settlement in New England. Half the colony perished the first terrible winter here.

Plymouth Rock, the landmark boulder marking the spot where the pilgrims disembarked, is kept behind bars at **Pilgrim Hall**, *Water Street.* The Plymouth of 1627 and the Wampanoag Indian summer campsite have been recreated here in a Williamsburg-style complex called Plimouth Plantation (*website: www.plimoth.org*), where actors play the parts of the pilgrims and Indians. Explore the Mayflower II, a reproduction of the original.

The **Pilgrim Sands Motel,** *150 Warren Ave.; tel. +1 (800) 729-7263; website: www.pilgrimsands.com*, is a lovely hotel with its own private beach away from the crowds of town. Nice ocean views upon request.

The best whale watching

Whale-watching cruises depart Plymouth and Provincetown for the Stellwagen Bank north of Cape Cod, one of the few areas in the United States where great whales can be seen on a regular basis. Each year, thousands of these beautiful giants take up residence on the 20-mile-long shoal. Fifteen kinds of whales have been seen in these waters, as well as dolphins, porpoises, and rare birds. Marine biologists accompany the cruises to identify and describe the fish and birds and explain their behavior.

Groups offering cruises from Plymouth include **Captain Tim Brady & Sons,** *tel. (508) 746-4809 website: www.fishchart.com.* Whale-watching cruises from Provincetown are available from **Provincetown Whale Watch,** *tel. +1 (508) 240-3636; website: www.whalewatch.com.*

659

Provincetown Inn, at the tip of Provincetown, *tel. +1 (508) 487-9500; website: www.provincetowninn.com*, offers a whale-watching package that includes a cruise, two dinners, two breakfasts, and two nights lodging.

The most beautiful island

Martha's Vineyard Island, off the coast of Cape Cod, is the most beautiful on the Atlantic Coast, protected by bluffs and dunes. Rocky and sandy beaches edge the island. Inland are pine forests and peaceful lakes and ponds, where you can canoe among rare seabirds. At the far end of the island are the brightly colored cliffs of Gay Head and a small Indian reservation. Shingled Cape Cod houses nestle among the island's rolling hills, and bayberry scents the air. You can catch a ferry to Martha's Vineyard from the Cape Cod town of **Woods Hole**. If you plan to bring a car, make reservations well in advance; you'll have to wait in line for hours if you don't.

Edgartown is the most elegant town on the island, its narrow streets are lined with expensive shops and guesthouses.

Oak Bluffs is a honky-tonk town, less stuffy than most of the towns on the island. Gingerbread houses make this slightly seedy town look quaint. The largest carousel in the world, the Flying Horses, is here.

Gay Head is the most beautiful spot on Martha's Vineyard. It is also home to the remaining Indians on the island, who live on a reservation nearby.

Seafood is fresh and plentiful on Martha's Vineyard. For lobster, go to the **Homeport** restaurant, *Menemsha; tel. +1 (508) 645-2679; website: www. homeportmv.com.* Bring your own wine. Reservations are advised.

If you're feeling more adventurous, buy your own fresh lobster and a steamer in **Menemsha**, a small fishing village, and prepare your own feast. Or stop in at any of the restaurants in these towns frequented by the local fishermen; most all of them offer lunch specials including one or two small lobsters, French fries, and salad.

Edgartown is home to the island's two most elegant restaurants: L'Etoile and 28 Atlantic.

L'Etoile, *22 North Water Street; tel. +1 (508) 627- 5187; website: www.letoile. net,* is lovely, the food is truly excellent, and the service is superb.

28 Atlantic, *Route 28, Pleasant Bay, Chatham; tel. +1 (508) 430-3000; website: www.twentyeightatlantic.com*, offers an eclectic menu with excellent international dishes. Elegant and comfortable, it boasts extraordinary views over Pleasant Bay.

Our favorite inn in Edgartown is the **Kelley House,** *23 Kelly Street; tel. +1 (508) 627-7900; website: www.kelley-house.com.* A cozy place decorated in the style of the 1890s, it is open year-round. The dining room is pleasant, the food wonderful and inexpensive.

Nantucket: The most exclusive

Nantucket is a lovely island east of Martha's Vineyard. This wealthy resort has long, sandy beaches and quaint, cobblestone streets. If you love to shop, you'll love Nantucket. Look for Nantucket woven baskets and scrimshaw jewelry (carved from whale teeth). **Seven Seas Gifts** is a pleasant gift shop with enormous variety. The best way to see Nantucket is by bike. Pedal out to **Seaskonset Beach** (pronounced "Skonset") and check out the island's many old lighthouses.

Nantucket was the most thriving whaling town in the United States during the 18th and 19th centuries. Visit the **Nantucket Whaling Museum**, **Hadwen House**, and **Peter Foulger House**, old whaling homes that are open to the public.

The island's best inn and restaurant is the **Jared Coffin House**, *29 Broad Street; tel. +1 (508) 228-2400; website: www.jaredcoffinhouse.com*, which is internationally acclaimed.

Two pleasant old inns are the **Carriage House,** *5 Ray's Court; tel. (508) 228-0326; website: www.carriagehousenantucket.com,* in a converted 1865 carriage house, and the **Ships Inn,** *13 Fair Street; tel. +1 (508) 228-0040; website: www.shipsinnnantucket.com,* in a sea captain's house built in 1812. Both have antique furnishings. Both are seasonal.

New Hampshire's bests

The highest peak on the East Coast is **Mount Washington** in the White Mountains of New Hampshire. Located in the **White Mountain National Forest**, this 6,288-foot mountain is a popular ski resort. Take the train to the top.

Crawford Notch State Park, nearby, has sparkling waterfalls. Take Route 3 to the flume at the southern end of Franconia Notch. This glacier-covered chasm has 70-foot walls. A rock formation called The Old Man of the Mountains looks over Profile Lake.

Mount Washington Hotel and Resort, *Bretton Woods; tel. +1 (603) 278-1000; website: www.mountwashingtonresort.com,* is the most elegant and peaceful of the White Mountain resorts. Excellent stables, a championship golf course, fishing, skiing, and tennis are offered.

Maine's main sights

The best thing about **Portland, Maine** is the area surrounding it. Casco Bay, the Casco Bay Islands, and Sebago Lake are typical New England locales, with quaint houses and good boating and swimming. Portland also has great seafood (especially lobster), good nightlife, and the poet Longfellow's house.

Acadia National Park is surrounded by a 10-mile park road loop. Along the road are **Thunder Hole,** where waves rush into a rocky canyon producing a thundering boom and sending up towers of foam; **Jordan Pond,** an idyllic, mirror-like pond reflecting the "Bubbles" (two rounded mountains); **Jackson Memorial Library,** the world's largest center for mammalian genetic research; and **Sand Beach,** the island's only sandy swimming area.

It's worth rolling out of bed early to see the sun rise from the summit of **Cadillac Mountain**, a windswept bald spot, the highest on the island, with views of forests, ocean, and neighboring islands. If you do get here at dawn, you will be the first person in the United States to see the sun rise.

The best place to dine on the island is the **Jordan Pond House,** *Park Loop Road, Acadia National Park; tel. +1 (207)276-3316; website: www.jordanpond. com,* a rambling old house. You can dine on the lawn when it's warm or by the fireplace when it's not.

A good place to stay is the **Bluenose,** *90 Eden Street, Bar Harbor; tel. +1 (207) 288-3348; website: www.barharborhotel.com,* set on a cliff just outside town. Rooms have French doors that open onto private balconies overlooking Frenchman's Bay. The pool is heated, which is a real asset in chilly Maine. And there is also an indoor pool.

Newport: Best jazz, best sailing

Newport, Rhode Island has New England's finest mansions (which belong to such families as the Astors and the Vanderbilts), as well as the region's top music festival and sailing events. For two weeks every July, Newport hosts a music festival with concerts featuring premier and recently discovered works and thematic programs, such as "Emperor's Court," works composed in Austria-Hungary during the reign of Franz Josef. The spectacular mansions of Newport are converted to concert halls for this 41-year-old event. The long list of debuts by major talents at this festival is indicative of its quality.

The best restaurant in town is the **White Horse Tavern,** *Marlborough and Farewell streets; tel. +1 (401) 849-3600; website: http://whitehorsetavern.us,* America's oldest tavern. Built in 1673, it later became a tavern run by a notorious Red Sea pirate. It doesn't open for lunch on Tuesdays.

A good place to stay the night is **Mill Street Inn,** *75 Mill Street; tel. +1 (800) 392-1316; website: www.millstreetinn.com.*

The most interesting inn in the area is the **Jail House Inn,** *13 Marlborough Street; tel. +1 (800) 427-9444; website: www.jailhouse.com.* Built in 1772, it served as the Newport jail for over 200 years. The 22 "cells" have been converted into modern, sunny suites with views of downtown Newport.

Classic New England in Vermont

Rural Vermont offers the rolling Green Mountains, lovely Lake Champlain, covered bridges, bridle trails, farmland, and little villages.

Stowe, in northern Vermont, is the state's biggest vacation center. It is best visited during its Winter Carnival in mid-January, which includes ice sculpture and winter sport competitions.

Mount Mansfield provides downhill and cross-country skiing and hiking on its Long Trail.

Arlington, in southwestern Vermont, is home to the Norman Rockwell exhibition and to our favorite inn in the area, the **Arlington Inn,** *Historic Route 7A; tel. +1 (800) 443-9442; website: www.arlingtoninn.com.* The feel and décor of the Arlington is pure Victorian; the exterior architecture is Greek Revival. Each of the 13 rooms has a fireplace, as well as a reading chair or sitting area.

The quintessential New England town is **Newfane**, Vermont. North of Brattleboro, this town is gorgeous in the fall, when autumn leaves garland it with color and the air smells of apples. In winter, neighbors gather around the potbelly in Union Hall.

The **Old Newfane Inn** (1787), *Court Street; tel. +1 (802) 365-4427; website: www.oldnewfaneinn.com,* dates back to when Vermont was a republic.

Union Hall, built in 1832, was once a house of worship.

The **Newfane Store** sells homemade cider and fudge.

The famous **Marlboro Music Festival** is held nearby each summer, on the campus of Marlboro College.

One of Vermont's best resorts is **Stratton Mountain Resort**, *tel. +1 (800) 787-2886; website: www.stratton.com*, in the Green Mountains. Lessons are given in downhill and cross-country skiing, golf, tennis, and fishing.

Said to be the most photographed village in Vermont, **Lower Waterford** is home to one of the best places to stay in the entire state. **The Rabbit Hill Inn**, *48 Lower Waterford Road; tel. +1 (802) 748-5168; website: www.rabbithillinn.com,* makes you feel right at home. When you arrive, tea or cider is served in the formal dining room, and dinner is served by candlelight. Many of the rooms include four-poster beds, sitting areas, and fireplaces.

NEW JERSEY: THE MOST MALIGNED STATE

New Jersey is the most maligned state in the Union, probably because most people know only the long and ugly turnpike. Despite odorous industrial cities, such as Newark and Elizabeth, New Jersey does deserve its description as The Garden State. A patchwork quilt of farm communities and historical parks, New Jersey offers the top per-acre value for agricultural production.

The state's beaches are natural and white and extend the entire length of the coast. At the heart of New Jersey are the **Pine Barrens**, an unspoiled wooded area. Northern New Jersey has pretty lakes, and in the northwest are mountains leading into the Poconos. Along the Delaware border are historic towns dating back to the Revolutionary War. More than 100 clashes occurred on New Jersey soil during the Revolutionary War, including pivotal battles in Trenton, Princeton, and Monmouth.

Princeton: New Jersey's prettiest town

Princeton, a beautiful, historic town founded in the 17th century, is the site of an Ivy League university, stately private mansions, and an intimate downtown area. In addition to housing **Princeton University**, the town is the home of the Institute of Advanced Study founded by Einstein, the Princeton Theological Seminary, and Westminster Choir College, famous for its choir.

Built around Princeton University, a center of thought since 1756, the town has been embellished by such wealthy benefactors as Andrew Carnegie (who funded the building of a lake used as a training area for the Princeton rowing crew and as an ice-skating rink in winter). Another benefactor refurbished the central downtown square (called **Palmer Square**) in a Tudor motif, complete with an old-fashioned inn. Palmer Square is especially lovely at Christmas, when the giant pine at its center is decorated. Princetonians gather around the tree to sing carols.

Nassau Hall at the university was the seat of the Continental Congress from June to November 1783.

Bring your lunch and enjoy it on **Princeton Battlefield**, where George Washington's army won a victory on January 3rd, 1777, against the British, or in **Marquand Park**, which has more variety than most botanical gardens. Late in the summer, community theater groups stage plays on the battlefield beside the four marble columns left standing from a home burned down during the Revolutionary War. The cool pines protect the audience from the summer sun.

The **Nassau Inn**, *10 Palmer Square; tel. +1 (609) 921-7500; website: www. nassauinn.com*, at the center of town, has several dining rooms, including the Yankee Doodle Tap Room, which offers live music. Initials carved in the inn's tabletops date back to 1919.

THE BEST OF THE JERSEY SHORE

One hundred miles of boardwalk and beaches trim the New Jersey coast, offering both honky-tonk towns and quiet enclaves.

Atlantic City: A gambler's best

Almost every American knows the streets of **Atlantic City**, a honky-tonk town famous for its gambling—they are on the *Monopoly* game board. Before the Civil War, Atlantic City was the seaside getaway for the high society of New York and Philadelphia. The town fell on hard times during the mid-20th century. However, in 1978, Resorts International opened the first casino here, and since then the town has been revived. A dozen casinos have opened along the boardwalk and on the bay.

The former Million Dollar Pier has been reborn as **Ocean One**, a shopping and dining arcade. Like visitors of 100 years ago, you can ride a canopied wicker chair on wheels from one end of the boardwalk to the other, stopping to see saltwater taffy being pulled.

The best restaurant in town is the **Knife and Fork Inn**, *Pacific and Albany avenues; tel. +1 (609) 344-1133; website: www.knifeandforkinn.com*, near Bally's Grand. Service is fabulous; customers are treated like royalty. The seafood dishes are excellent, especially the *bouillabaisse*, which is chock-full of fish, including large chunks of lobster.

Cape May: A Victorian surprise

At the southern tip of the Jersey shore is a Victorian surprise: **Cape May**. Victorian mansions with wide porches, gables, and elaborate woodwork line the streets. Many are guesthouses. The wide sandy beach is inviting.

The **Summer Cottage Inn**, *613 Columbia Ave.; tel. +1 (609) 884-4948; website: www.summercottageinn.com*, was built in 1867 as a summer home.

Verandas and tall ceilings keep the house cool. This Victorian B&B is decorated with walnut- and oak-inlaid floors and period wallpaper. Afternoon tea is served in the sitting room, where wicker furnishings are placed around the fireplace.

New Jersey's best inn

The **Woolverton Inn**, 6 *Woolverton Road, Stockton; tel. +1 (609) 397-0802; website: www.woolvertoninn.com*, is on the New Jersey/Pennsylvania line at the Delaware River. Shaded by two spacious front porches and big old trees, this stone manor house was built in 1793 by John Prall, who ran a quarry in what is now the garden. In 1957, Sir John Terrell, the owner of the popular Music Circus, bought the property, and many of the celebrities performing in the Music Circus have stayed here. Every room is filled with antiques. Some bedrooms have canopied beds, others have four-poster beds.

PHILADELPHIA: A HISTORIAN'S BEST

Philadelphia is the most historically important city in the United States. Founded in 1681 by William Penn as a Quaker colony, Philadelphia is where Thomas Jefferson wrote the Declaration of Independence, signed at Independence Hall, and where the Bill of Rights was adopted at Congress Hall. The Continental Congress met in Philadelphia, which was the national capital from 1777 to 1800.

All the city's major historic sights are in **Independence National Historic Park:** Independence Hall; the Liberty Bell; Carpenter's Hall, where the First Continental Congress met in 1774; Congress Hall; Graff House, where Thomas Jefferson lived; Old City Hall; and the Betsy Ross House.

Bordering the one-mile-square park is **Society Hill**, Philadelphia's oldest neighborhood, which has been completely restored. Society Hill was named for the Free Society of Stock Traders, a company created by William Penn. However, most people presume it was named for the somewhat snooty residents.

The most important sights

The Declaration of Independence and the Constitution were signed at **Independence Hall,** *Chestnut Street; website: www.nps.gov/inde.* Half-hour tours are offered. Across the street is the **Liberty Bell Pavilion,** where you can touch the cracked bell that rang out in July 1776 to proclaim the Declaration of Independence. (The bell cracked in 1835 and again in 1846.)

The **Betsy Ross House,** *Arch Street between Second and Third streets; tel.* *+1 (215) 686-1252; website: www.betsyrosshouse.org,* is where musket balls were made for the Continental Army and flags were made for the Pennsylvania Navy. In the house are Betsy Ross' spectacles, snuffbox, and Bible.

The **Second Bank of the United States,** *420 Chestnut Street,* houses paintings of great American figures, many painted by artist Charles William Peale. It is open 9 a.m. until 5 p.m. daily; admission is free.

City Tavern, *138 South Second Street at Walnut; tel. +1 (215) 413-1443; website: www.citytavern.com,* a reconstruction of the tavern where delegates of the Continental Congress gathered, is a superb restaurant and pub with indoor and outdoor seating, where a staff in 18th-century dress serves colonial-inspired food and drink. Internationally-acclaimed chef and cookbook author Walter Staib presides over a festive respite from sightseeing. Lunch and dinner served daily.

Penn's Landing is the largest freshwater port in the world. You can visit several ships here, including the *Gazela Primeiro*, a Portuguese square-rigger built in 1883; the *Moshulu*, the largest all-steel sailing ship afloat; and the *SS Olympia*, Admiral Dewey's flagship for the battle of Manila Bay during the Spanish American War.

The **Edgar Allan Poe House,** *532 N. Seventh Street; tel. +1 (215) 597-8787; website: www.nps.gov/edal/,* is where Poe wrote *The Raven, The Tell-Tale Heart,* and *The Murders in the Rue Morgue.*

Germantown: The most historic neighborhood

Philadelphia's most historic neighborhood is **Germantown**. In 1688, its residents made the first formal protest against slavery in the country. The British quartered their troops here during the Revolutionary War. In the 18th century, Philadelphian society built mansions in the area. The most elegant is **Cliveden,** *6401 Germantown Ave.; tel. +1 (215) 848-1777; website: http://cliveden1767.wordpress.com/,* built in 1763 for Benjamin Chew, a friend of the Penns. The mansion is open to visitors Thursday through Sunday, noon-4 p.m., and to groups with advance reservations.

The **Wyck Mansion,** *6026 Germantown Ave.; tel. +1 (215) 848-1690*; open 1 p.m. until 4 p.m. Tuesday, Thursday, and Saturday, April through December, and the **Stenton Mansion,** *Windrim Avenue and 18th Street; tel. +1 (215) 329-7312; website: http://stenton.org,* open Tuesday through Saturday, 1 p.m. until 4 p.m., April through Christmas, (which served as Washington's headquarters for a time), are also beautiful.

The city's best museums

The **Philadelphia Museum of Art,** *26th Street and Benjamin Franklin Parkway; tel. +1 (215) 763-8100; website: www.philamuseum.org,* houses one of the best art collections in the United States. Especially good are the John G. Johnson Collection of European old masters and paintings by Eakins. Don't miss the world's best Marcel Duchamp collection. The building is a 1928 reproduction of the Parthenon. See Rubens's *Prometheus Bound*, Van Eyck's *St. Francis Receiting the Stigmata*, and Brueghel's *Village Wedding*. The museum is open Tuesday through Sunday 10 a.m. until 5 p.m. and until 8:45 p.m. on Friday.

The **Barnes Foundation Museum,** *300 N. Latches Lane, Merion Station; tel. +1 (215) 667-0290; website: www.barnesfoundation.org,* displays a staggering collection of Impressionist paintings, including works by Renoir, Cézanne, and Matisse. Open September to May. Advance reservations are required, and the museum is often sold out 4 to 6 weeks in advance, so call early. At the time of going to press the Barnes galleries are closed in preparation for a move to the new Philadelphia campus, but will reopen in Spring 2012.

The rare book department of the **Free Library of Philadelphia,** *Logan Square; tel. +1 (215) 686-5322; website: www.library.phila.gov,* is a treasure trove of letters, manuscripts, and original prints, including letters by Charles Dickens, folios by Shakespeare, and Edgar Allen Poe manuscripts.

The **Franklin Institute,** *20th Street and Benjamin Franklin Parkway; tel. +1 (215)448-1200; website: www2.fi.edu,* is a hands-on science museum founded in 1824, where you can walk through a giant human heart, check out a steam engine, or watch a giant clock that works by gravity. This is one of the best museums for children in the entire country.

The **Pennsylvania Academy of Fine Arts,** *Broad and Cherry streets; tel. +1 (215) 972-7600; website: www.pafa.org,* contains famous American paintings, including Benjamin West's *Penn's Treaty With the Indians* and Winslow Homer's *Fox Hunt.* The Academy is closed Mondays.

The **Rodin Museum,** *22nd Street and Benjamin Franklin Parkway; tel. +1 (215) 568-6026; website: www.rodinmuseum.org,* has the most complete Rodin collection outside Paris. It is closed Mondays.

The **Rosenbach Museum & Library**, *2008 Delancey Street; tel. +1 (215) 732-1600; website: www.rosenbach.org,* has the Rosenbach family collection of rare books, antiques, paintings, and drawings. The original manuscript of James Joyce's *Ulysses*, first editions of *Don Quixote*, a rough draft of *Lord Jim*, and Keats' famous love letters to Fanny Brawne are kept here. Open Tuesday & Thursday to Sunday 10 a.m.-5 p.m.; Wednesday 10 a.m.-8 p.m.

Three tip-top restaurants

Le Bec-Fin, *1523 Walnut Street; tel. +1 (215) 567-1000; website: www.lebecfin. com,* is an elegant restaurant with only 14 tables and world-class cuisine. Prix fixe and a la carte menus for both lunch and dinner.

The Fountain Restaurant, *Four Seasons Hotel, One Logan Square; tel. +1 (800) 819-5053; website: www.fourseasons.com/philadelphia/dining/,* is one of the country's finest French restaurants serving classic cuisine in a beautiful setting.

Philadelphia's best hotels

The crème de la crème of Philadelphia hotels is the **Four Seasons,** *One Logan Square; tel. +1 (215) 963-1500; website: www.fourseasons.com/philadelphia,* an elegant institution with 24-hour room service, a health spa, an indoor pool, complimentary shoe-shines, valet parking, a superb restaurant, and a lounge.

The **Sheraton Society Hill,** *One Dock Street; tel. +1 (215) 238-6000; website: www.sheratonsocietyhillhotel.com,* is centrally located in Society Hill, near the historic sights. Facilities include an indoor pool, a health spa, a restaurant, an entertainment lounge, and 24-hour room service.

THE BEST OF WASHINGTON, D.C.

Washington, D.C., the capital of the United States of America, has more open space than any capital city in the world. At the heart is the **National Mall**, a two-mile expanse of lawn stretching from the Capitol Building to the Lincoln Memorial and from the Washington Monument to the Jefferson Memorial. The city's main roads are wide as well, giving a sense of that valued American commodity—elbow room.

Capital sights

The **Capitol**, at the east end of the National Mall, is among the most architecturally impressive and symbolically important buildings in the world. Adorned on the top of the dome is the bronze Statute of Freedom, a female allegorical figure who holds a sheathed sword in her right hand and a laurel wreath of victory and the shield of the United States with thirteen stripes in her left hand. She symbolically faces east so that the sun never sets on the face of freedom. The Senate and the House of Representatives have met here for more than two centuries. Open to visitors whenever either body is in session. Visitors may obtain gallery passes from their Senators or Representatives.

The newly-constructed **Capitol Visitor Center,** *First Street at East Capitol Street; tel. +1 (202) 226-8000; website: www.visitthecapitol.gov,* provides a welcoming and educational environment for visitors to learn about the legislative process, as well as the history and development of the architecture and art of the Capitol. Admission is free. Open Monday through Saturday 8:30 a.m. to 4:30 p.m. except Thanksgiving, Christmas, New Year's, and Inauguration Day.

The **Supreme Court,** *One First Street N.E.: tel. +1 (202) 479-3030; website: www.supremecourtus.gov/visiting/visiting.html,* has 16 marble columns that line the front of this classic Greek-style structure. Six-ton bronze doors guard the main entrance, which is flanked by two huge statues: *The Contemplation of Justice* and *The Guardian, or Authority of Law.* Courtroom lectures are held every hour on the half-hour, on days that the Court is not sitting, beginning at 9:30 a.m. and concluding at 3:30 p.m. Open from 9 a.m. to 4:30 p.m. Monday through Friday. Closed Saturdays, Sundays, and federal holidays.

The **White House,** *1600 Pennsylvania Avenue,* is the nation's number-one residence. Public tours of the White House are available for groups of 10 or more people. Requests must be submitted through one's Member of Congress and are accepted up to six months in advance. These self-guided tours are available from 7:30 a.m. to 12:30 p.m. Tuesday through Saturday (excluding federal holidays), and are scheduled on a first come, first served basis approximately one month in advance of the requested date. All White House tours are free of charge; *tel. +1 (202) 456-7041; website: www.whitehouse.gov.* Note that White House tours may be subject to last minute cancellation. All tours are significantly enhanced if visitors stop by the **White House Visitor Center**, *15th and E Streets N.W.; tel. +1 (202) 208-2121.* The Center is open seven days a week from 7:30 a.m. until 4 p.m. and features many aspects of the White House, including its architecture, furnishings, first families, social events, and relations with the press and world leaders, as well as a 30-minute video. Allow between 20 minutes to one hour to explore the exhibits.

The **Library of Congress**, *1010 Independence Street S.E.; tel. +1 (202) 707-5000; website: www.loc.gov.* The Library was founded in 1800, making it the oldest federal cultural institution in the nation. The Library of Congress is the largest library in the world, with more than 138 million items on approximately 650 miles of bookshelves. The collections include millions of books, print materials, recordings, photographs, maps, sheet music, and manuscripts. Only one of three perfect vellum Gutenberg Bibles in the world are housed here, along with a collection of Stradivarius violins, and rare books in 470 languages. Adults may use the facilities for research, but you cannot take books out.

Ford's Theatre, *511 10th Street N.W.; tel. +1 (202) 347-4833; website: www.fordstheatre.org*, where Lincoln was assassinated on April 14, 1865, is still in use today. Plays are presented October through May, although the theatre is open year-round for tours. The box office opens at 8:30 a.m. for distribution of free, same-day, timed tickets. Tours include a presentation by either the National Park Service or Ford's Theatre Society and lasts approximately 45 minutes.

The Smithsonian

Start your visit off at the **Smithsonian Castle**, *1000 Jefferson Dr. S.W.; tel. +1 (202) 633-1000; website: www.si.edu/museums/*, the Smithsonian's first building which houses the Information Center. The Center serves as the focal point for information about the world's largest museum complex and research organization composed of 19 museums and National Zoo. All Smithsonian museums are open daily 10 a.m. until 5:30 p.m. unless otherwise noted; admission is free.

The **National Air and Space Museum**, *606 Independence Ave. at Sixth Street S.W.; tel. +1 (202) 633-1000; website: www.nasm.si.edu*, maintains the largest collection of historic air and spacecraft in the world. It is also a vital center for research into the history, science, and technology of aviation and space flight, as well as planetary science and terrestrial geology and geophysics. The museum has hundreds of artifacts on display including the original Wright Brothers 1903 Flyer, the *Spirit of St. Louis*, the Apollo 11 command module, and a lunar rock sample that visitors can touch.

The **Hirshhorn Museum**, *Seventh Street and Independence Avenue S.W.; tel. +1 (202) 633-1000; website: http://hirshhorn.si.edu*, contains the most comprehensive collection of modern sculptures in the world. The circular building has ramps that lead upward in a spiral past works of art. Outside the Hirshhorn is the museum's sculpture garden, which contains works by Rodin, Matisse and more.

The **Freer Gallery of Art and Arthur M. Sackler Gallery**, *12th Street at Jefferson Drive S.W.; tel. +1 (202) 633-1000; website: www.asia.si.edu/*, displays internationally renowned Far Eastern art and artifacts and is home to the world's largest collection of works by James Whistler. The two museums are connected by an underground exhibition space.

The **National Gallery of Art**, *Fourth and Constitution Avenues N.W.; tel. +1 (202) 737-4215; website: www.nga.gov*, has one of the finest art collections in the world. It was created by accepting the gift of financier, public servant, and art collector Andrew W. Mellon. European and American paintings, sculpture, works on paper, photographs, and decorative arts are displayed in the collection galleries and Sculpture Garden. The collection of paintings spans from the Middle Ages to the present day.

The **National Museum of Natural History**, *10th Street and Constitution Avenue N.W.; website: www.mnh.si.edu*, serves as one of the world's great repositories of scientific and cultural heritage. It contains expertly documented collections of more than 126 million natural science specimens and artifacts, dinosaurs, plants, insects, and the Hope Diamond.

The **National Museum of African Art**, *950 Independence Ave. S.W.; website: http://africa.si.edu,* has one of the best collections of African art in the world, as well as an extensive collection of photos and films about Africa.

The **National Museum of American History**, *14th Street and Constitution Avenue N.W.; tel. +1 (202) 633-1000; website: http://americanhistory.si.edu*, displays the earliest American bicycles, the ruby slippers worn by Judy Garland in *The Wizard of Oz*, a 240-pound brass pendulum, tapes of the Watergate hearings, tapes of old *Superman* television shows, recordings of radio shows from the 1940s, and the original Star-Spangled Banner.

The nation's greatest monuments

The **Washington Monument**, at the west end of the National Mall is the tallest structure in Washington and can be seen from most places in the District. At the top of the 555-foot obelisk, you can see almost 30 miles. The Monument admission is free, but does require a ticket. The Monument Lodge opens at 8:30 a.m. for distribution of free, same day, timed tickets. Open 9 a.m. to 5 p.m., with the last tour at 4:45 p.m.

The **Lincoln Memorial**, *23rd Street N.W.,* is one of the most impressive monuments. The imposing white marble statue of Abraham Lincoln looks over the reflecting pool, with the words of the Gettysburg Address engraved in the marble walls around him. It is most beautiful at night, when spotlights bring out Lincoln's striking features.

The **Jefferson Memorial**, *East Basin Drive S.W.,* is the most beautiful monument. It is a white marble structure softened by a dome and reflected in the Tidal basis. The impressive words of Thomas Jefferson are immortalized on the interior walls for all to see. The memorial is loveliest in the spring when the cherry trees surrounding the tidal basin are in bloom.

The **Kennedy Center for the Performing Arts**, *2700 F Street N.W.; tel. +1 (202) 467-4600; website: www.kennedy-center.org*, commemorates President John F. Kennedy by producing and presenting an unmatched variety of theater and musicals, dance and ballet, orchestral, chamber, jazz, popular, and folk music, and multi-media performances for all ages. Free public tours of the Center are conducted every 10 minutes daily from 10 a.m. to 5 p.m. on weekdays, and 10 a.m. to 1 p.m. on weekends.

War memorials

The most moving monument is the **Vietnam War Memorial,** which lies at the western end of the National Mall. Designed by Maya Lin, it is a striking wall of black marble sunk into the earth on which the names of over 56,000 American soldiers killed or missing in Vietnam are inscribed. War veterans and tourists from around the world make pilgrimages to the site.

Nineteen stainless steel sculptures stand silently under the watchful eye of a sea of faces upon a granite wall—reminders of the human cost of defending freedom at the **Korean War Veterans Memorial,** is adjacent to the Vietnam War Memorial.

The **World War II Memorial** honors the 16 million people who served in the war, the more than 400,000 who died, and the millions who supported the effort from home. A stunningly beautiful tribute of marble and fountains. A nearby kiosk lets you look up family members who served.

The grandest cemetery

Arlington National Cemetery; *tel. +1 (703) 607-8585; website: www. arlingtoncemetery.org,* is the final resting place of over 300,000 soldiers and famous Americans. The tomb of the Unknown Soldier is a popular visiting area. The graves of two presidents, William H. Taft and John F. Kennedy, along with astronauts, chief justices, explorers, and prominent military figures, make this one of the most remarkable cemeteries in the world.

Mount Vernon: The most beautiful home

George Washington's home, **Mount Vernon**, *3200 Mount Vernon Memorial Hwy., Mt. Vernon, VA; tel. +1 (703) 780-2000; website: www.mountvernon.org*, is located in a beautiful spot along the Potomac, in Virginia. The pillared colonial mansion house of the tobacco plantation has a spectacular view of the Potomac River from the piazza, which transports visitors back in time. Four gardens showcase heirloom plants known to have been at Mount Vernon in the late 1700s. Accessible by car, boat, and Metro system. The house is open daily from 9 a.m. to 4 p.m.

The most beautiful parks and gardens

Dumbarton Oaks Museum and Garden, *1703 32nd Street N.W.; website: www. doaks.org,* has the city's most beautiful gardens. The museum has a choice collection of Roman and Byzantine art and a display of Pre-Columbian jewelry. The French and Italian gardens become less formal as they descend the hill toward the woods. The museum is closed on Mondays and federal holidays.

The **National Zoological Park**, *the 3000 block of Connecticut Avenue N.W.; tel. +1 (202) 633-4888; website: http://nationalzoo.si.edu*, is one of the largest zoos in the country. Open daily except Christmas Day, and it's free. The giant pandas were a gift from China. In warm weather, the monkeys play outside on jungle gyms.

Rock Creek Park, *5200 Glover Road N.W.; tel. +1 (202) 895-6070; website: www.nps.gov/rocr,* was founded in 1890 as one of the first federal parks. It's an oasis for joggers, bikers, hikers, and horseback riders to get away from the city, in the middle of the city. Be sure to visit the planetarium.

The **Chesapeake and Ohio Canal National Historic Park**; *tel. +1 (301) 739-4200; website: www.nps.gov/choh/*, provides 185 miles of biking and hiking trails along the Potomac River and stretches from Georgetown in Washington D.C. to Cumberland, Maryland. Millions of visitors hike or bike each year to enjoy the natural, cultural and recreational opportunities available.

The capital's finest fare

Michel Richard Citronelle, at the Latham Hotel, *3000 M Street N.W.; tel. +1 (202) 625-2150; website: www.citronelledc.com*, has become the favorite of Washington's elite. Fine continental cuisine, innovatively prepared, and an impressive array of over 8,000 wines representing 300 distinguished labels, are the hallmark of this famed establishment.

Washington's best ethnic food

The **Makoto**, *4822 MacArthur Blvd. N.W.; tel. +1 (202) 298-6866*. This intimate restaurant takes you straight to Japan. Small dishes gorgeously presented and even better tasting make for a sushi-lovers dream.

Zaytinya, *701 Ninth Street N.W.; tel. +1 (202) 638-0800; website: www. zaytinya.com*, starts every meal with fabulous *mezze*, the traditional Middle Eastern "little dishes." Zaytinya's extensive menu reflects the rich, regional diversity of classical and contemporary Greek, Turkish, and Lebanese cuisine.

Washington's most elegant hotels

The **Washington Court Hotel**, *525 New Jersey Ave. N.W.; tel. +1 (202) 628-2100; website: www.washingtoncourthotel.com,* is located in the Capitol Hill neighborhood. A premier location with perfect views of the nation's capital.

The **Four Seasons**, *2800 Pennsylvania Ave. N.W.; tel. +1 (202) 342-0444; website: www.fourseasons.com/washington/,* situated in a quiet neighborhood in Georgetown, offers an abundance of elegant rooms and suites along with its renowned service.

The **Westin City Center Hotel**, *1400 M Street N.W.; tel. +1 (202) 429-1700; website: www.starwoodhotels.com/westin/index.html,* a vibrant hotel that captures the capital city's dynamic spirit. The atrium lobby offers spectacular skylight views and welcoming staff provide world-class service.

The **Washington Plaza Hotel**, *Massachusetts and Vermont avenues; tel. +1 (800) 424-1140; website: www.washingtonplazahotel.com,* is five blocks from the White House and five blocks from the Convention Center. Retro artwork decorates the lobby of this nine-story building. Everything about the splendid balance of cosmopolitan ambiance and unpretentious hospitality was designed for comfort.

The **Renaissance Mayflower Hotel**, *1127 Connecticut Ave. N.W.; tel. +1 (202) 347-3000; website: www.marriott.com/hotels/travel/ wassh-renaissance-mayflower-hotel.* Locally known as the "Mayflower", this Marriott hotel is pet-friendly. One of the grandest hotels in the world when it opened in 1925, the hotel has sponsored a ball every Inauguration Day since the presidential inauguration of Calvin Coolidge. Presidents John F. Kennedy, Lyndon B. Johnson, and Harry S. Truman stayed here.

The **Capital Hilton**, *16th and K streets N.W.; tel. +1 (202) 393-1000; website: www1.hilton.com,* gracious hospitality refined with neoclassical décor and richly finished mahogany detailing.

The **Hay-Adams**, *H and 16th streets; tel. +1 (202) 638 6600; website: www. hayadams.com,* Washington's most prestigious address with views facing the White House, Lafayette Square, and St. John's Church. The exceptional staff combined with distinctive luxury features create the residence of choice for discriminating visitors.

The **Omni Shoreham**, *Calvert Street and Connecticut Avenue N.W.; tel. +1 (800)843-6664* or *(202) 234-0700; website: www.omnihotels.com.* A true historic Washington landmark, the Omni Shoreham Hotel is nestled on 11 acres of parks and woods, and is just steps from the National Zoo. Built in 1930, the hotel's 834 rooms are exquisitely appointed.

The best nightlife

Blues Alley, *1073 Wisconsin Ave. N.W.; tel. +1 (202) 337-4141; website: www. bluesalley.com*, is the nation's oldest, and D.C.'s foremost, jazz and supper club. This legendary venue boasts an intimate setting and the best acts in town. Specializes in Creole cuisine, steak and seafood dishes.

9:30 Club, *815 V Street N.W.; tel. +1 (202) 265-0930; website: www.930.com*, is definitely D.C.'s top music venue, where thousands go to see the best known and up-and-coming acts in the country. Standing-only venue. The limited bar stools available go quickly.

If you prefer a quieter evening, see a Shakespearean play at the **Lansburgh Theater**, *450 Seventh Street N.W.; website: www.shakespearetheatre.org,* or take in a show at; the **National Theater**, *1321 Pennsylvania Ave. N.W.; tel. +1 (202) 628-6161; website: www.nationaltheatre.org*; or **Arena Stage**, *1101 Sixth Street S.W.; tel. +1 (202) 488-3300; website: www.arenastage.org.*

THE BEST OF DIXIE

The **U.S. South** offers a traditional yet laid-back lifestyle all of its own. Southern hospitality is alive and well below the Mason-Dixon Line.

Williamsburg: America's best colonial town

Williamsburg, Virginia is a completely reconstructed colonial town. Originally, Williamsburg was an outpost of Jamestown, the first permanent English settlement. By the late 1600s, it was the capital of Virginia. However, when the capital was moved to Richmond during the Revolutionary War, Williamsburg was forgotten. In 1926, John D. Rockefeller had the town restored. Today, costumed actors act out the roles of Williamsburg's early settlers.

The College of William and Mary, the country's second oldest college, is located in Williamsburg. The Sir Christopher Wren Building is the oldest class-room building in the United States. Old plantations line the banks of the James River near Williamsburg, remnants of colonial days. **Carter's Grove** is the most beautiful. A dirt road leads from Williamsburg through plantation fields to this Georgian mansion, located on U.S. Route 60.

Berkeley Plantation—not Plymouth—between Williamsburg and Richmond on Route 5 was the site of the first Thanksgiving in 1619. Both Benjamin Harrison and William Henry Harrison were born here.

Charlottesville

Charlottesville, Virginia sits in the foothills of the Blue Ridge Mountains. Its softly rolling countryside is peppered with acres of mature forests. It is less than 20 minutes from the Shenandoah National Park and Skyline Drive and just around the corner from the University of Virginia, founded by the area's most famous resident, Thomas Jefferson. Although the Charlottesville of today has been "discovered" by the world's rich and famous, the city remains at heart a small, Southern town—a place where Southern hospitality, gentility, and even chivalry are alive and well.

The South's best inn

Just 10 minutes from downtown Charlottesville is the **Clifton Inn**, *Route 13, Box 26; tel. +1 (434) 971-1800; website: www.cliftoninn.net.* This 40-acre estate was once part of the Shadwell Plantation, birthplace of Thomas Jefferson. The Clifton possesses not only beauty and history but also a certain charm that truly sets it apart from other inns and hotels. At the Clifton, you are greeted as an old friend and invited to make yourself at home. The main floor of the house is entirely open to guests, who can help themselves to a snack from the kitchen's always-full cookie jar and guest refrigerator.

ATLANTA: THE SOUTH'S MOST VITAL CITY

Atlanta, the city that suffered the most during the Civil War, has become the South's most prominent city. The federal headquarters of Reconstruction following the war is modern and bustling.

Reverend Martin Luther King Jr. began his crusade against racism in Atlanta, which became one of the first southern cities to erase the vestiges of the old slave system. King and his father were pastors at **Ebeneezer Baptist Church**, *407 Auburn Ave. N.E.; tel. +1 (404) 688-7300; website: www.historicebenezer.org.* King's grave is in the churchyard.

Paces Ferry Road is one of the prettiest residential sections in the area. Magnificent estates line the road. The finest is the **Governor's Mansion**, *391 W. Paces Ferry Road*, with its antiques, gardens, and fountains.

The **Atlanta History Center**, *3101 Andrews Drive*, includes the Swan House, an elegant mansion; the Tullie Smith House, a restored antebellum farmhouse and McElreath Hall, which has historic exhibits.

Fans of Scarlett O'Hara and Rhett Butler, should check out the **Margaret**

Mitchell House and Museum, *990 Peachtree Street; tel. +1 (404) 249-7015; website: www.gwtw.org.* This is where Mitchell wrote the Pulitzer Prize-winning *Gone With the Wind*. Also here is the Gone With the Wind Movie Museum, which features photos, storyboards from the film studios art department and the front door of the Tara plantation from the movie set.

Uncle Remus fans should see the **Wren's Nest**, *1050 Ralph David Abernathy Blvd, SW; tel. +1 (404) 753-7735; website: www.wrensnestonline.com*, where Joel Chandler Harris lived.

Atlanta's best restaurants and hotels

The **Dining Room**, *at the Ritz-Cartlon Buckhead, 3434 Peachtree Road N.E.; tel. +1 (404) 237-2700; website: www.ritzcarlton.com*, just outside Atlanta in Buckhead, is a romantic spot with impeccable service and some of the best food in the city, as well as a top wine list. An elegant afternoon tea is also served.

Two of the finest hotels in the South are the **Westin Peachtree Plaza**, *210 Peachtree Street; tel. +1 (404) 659-1400; website: www.starwoodhotels.com/westin*, which has a lake, birds, and floating cocktail lounges and the **Hyatt Regency**, *265 Peachtree Street; tel. +1 (404) 577-1234; website: www.atlantaregency.hyatt.com*, with its 27-story atrium and revolving bars.

Charleston and Savannah: The best of the Old South

Charleston and Savannah retain the charm, beauty, and heritage of the Old South, with pastel houses and tropical greenery.

Charleston is a historic city, with old homes, monuments, and gardens. Mansions line Church, Meeting, and Battery streets. The two most splendid are the **Nathaniel Russell House**, *51 Meeting Street*, and the **Edmonston-Alston House**, *21 E. Battery Street*.

The **Charleston Museum**, *360 Meeting Street; tel. +1 (843) 722-2996; website: www.charlestonmuseum.org*, is the oldest in America.

The **Gibbes Musuem of Art**, *135 Meeting Street; tel. +1 (843) 722-2706; website: www.gibbesmuseum.org*, has a collection of works by American artists.

Also visit **Fort Sumter**, where the Civil War began when South Carolina attacked the Union stronghold.

Stay at the **Maison Du Pre' Inn**, *317 E. Bay Street; tel. +1 (843) 723-8691; website: www.maisondupre.com*, in the historic district of Charleston. A double room includes Continental breakfast, afternoon tea, and newspapers.

Savannah, Charleston's sister city, has a pirate past but an aristocratic

Southern ambience. For two centuries, piracy and shipping flourished here. Today, mansions and gardens dot the town, and the renovated waterfront is filled with shops and restaurants.

The **Ships of the Sea Museum**, *41 Martin Luther King Blvd.; tel. +1 (912) 232-1511; website: http://shipsofthesea.org*, displays ship models and figureheads.

Also see the **Owens-Thomas House**, *124 Abercom Street*, built in 1816 and has formal gardens and a restored kitchen. And the **Davenport House**, *324 E. State Street; tel. +1 (912) 236-8097; website: www.davenporthousemuseum.org*, which is older and has a beautiful china collection. The grave of Tomochichi, the Indian who allowed settlement in the area, is at Wright Square.

The **First African Baptist Church**, *23 Montgomery Street; tel. +1 (912) 233-6597*, built in 1788, is one of the oldest black churches in the country.

Savannah's best restaurant is **Mrs. Wilkes' Dining Room**, *107 W. Jones Street; tel. +1 (912) 232-5997; website: www.mrswilkes.com*. Mrs. Wilkes says grace at each table. Long lines wait to enjoy the food at this inexpensive place.

The **Johnny Harris Restaurant**, *1651 E. Victory Drive; tel. +1 (912) 354-7810; website: www.johnnyharris.com*, serves arguably the best barbecue in the South.

Stay at the **Gastonian**, *220 E. Gaston Street; tel. +1 (912) 232-2869*. With two adjoining mansions built in 1868, the Gastonian is the epitome of Southern inn-keeping.

The best wildlife sanctuary (and swamp): Okefenokee
This huge wildlife sanctuary is home to rare birds and alligators. Immense cypress trees spread their roots in the black water. Known as the Land of the Trembling Earth by Indians, Okefenokee is rife with legends. The northern entrance is south of Waycross, Georgia. For information on swamp excursions, see *website: www.fws.gov/okefenokee*.

The country-western capital: Nashville
Nashville, the town from which most of America's greatest country musicians hail, is a mecca for country music fans.

The **Grand Ole Opry** is where country music achieved its fame. The Opry opened in 1943 at the Ryman Auditorium, drawing country music fans from far and wide. In 1974, it moved to the newer, bigger **Grand Ole Opry House**, *2802 Opry Lane Drive, just off I-40; tel. +1 (615) 871-6779; website: www.opry.com*. The best seats in the house are in high demand, so call early for reservations.

Nashville's top sights

Centennial Park is the place to laze as you listen to local jazz musicians do their thing. The 140-acre park, located on the fringe of downtown Nashville, has a lake and a rose garden and is always filled with people throwing Frisbees and playing soccer.

Centennial Park's reproduction of the Greek Parthenon gave Nashville its nickname, the Athens of the South. This impressive structure was built in 1897 to celebrate Nashville's centennial. Housed inside the Parthenon are a collection of oil paintings by American artists from the late 1800s and a statue of Athena—a Nashville sculptor's rendering of a demolished statue described in a fifth-century B.C. critique. For more information, see *website: www.nashville.gov/parthenon.*

The **Hermitage**, *4580 Rachel's Lane, off Old Hickory Boulevard near I-40; tel. +1 (615) 889-2941; website: www.thehermitage.com,* was the home of Andrew Jackson, the seventh president of the United States, built in 1819. Here, Jackson made the decision to move the Cherokee from their homeland to Oklahoma. Some 18,000 Indians passed not far from his house as they marched the Trail of Tears in 1838. The house escaped harm during the Civil War; it was guarded by Federal troops. The house is open daily.

The **Country Music Hall of Fame**, *222 Fifth Ave. S.; tel. +1 (615) 416-2001; website: www.countrymusichalloffame.com,* houses Elvis' solid gold Cadillac and other memorabilia. Across the street is a pool shaped like a guitar.

Fort Nashborough, *First Avenue below Church Street*, is a recreation of the original settlement of Nashville. It's open daily.

Top entertainment

Although Nashville is home to country music, that's not the only kind of entertainment you'll find here.

The **Tennessee Performing Arts Center (TPAC)**, *505 Deaderick Street; tel. +1 (615) 782-4000; website: http://tpac.org,* offers Broadway road shows and performances by the Nashville Ballet and the Tennessee Repertory Theater.

For live music (including blues, jazz, rock, and country), go to the **Bluebird Café**, *4104 Hillsboro Road; tel. +1 (615) 383-1461; website: www.bluebirdcafe. com*. Get here early or reserve a table.

The best hotel

The most luxurious accommodation in town is at the **Hermitage**, *231 Sixth Ave. N.; tel. +1 (888) 888-9414; website: www.thehermitagehotel.com,* built in 1910.

This hotel, voted the most romantic in Nashville, offers only suites: Choose from contemporary, traditional, and Oriental. Complimentary morning coffee and tea and afternoon cider and cookies are served in the lobby.

Memphis: Home of the king of rock'n'roll

Memphis, located on the banks of the mighty Mississippi, was home to Elvis Presley and is the cradle of blues music. The music lives on, on Beale Street and at Graceland, Elvis' home. Take a guided tour of **Graceland**, *3734 Elvis Presley Blvd.; website: www.elvis.com.* You'll see the King's vast car collection, his trophy room, and the Meditation Gardens, where he is buried. Elvis paid $100,000 for the house in 1957, when he was 22 years-old. Die-hard Elvis fans come here to mourn at the singer's grave, often wearing Elvis costumes (white pantsuits, dark glasses, and slicked-back hair).

NEW ORLEANS: THE BEST PARTY TOWN

New Orleans is famous for its outrageous Mardi Gras, when residents don splendid costumes and hold all-night parties. It is a beautiful city steeped in history and culture with a long musical background and some of the nation's best food.

The **French Quarter** is the oldest, loveliest, and zaniest section of town. Wrought-iron balconies and railings decorate French- and Spanish-style buildings. Female impersonators dance in the bars. Artists, musicians, and partiers roam the streets. Jackson Square, the heart of the French Quarter, is marked by St. Louis Cathedral and a statue of Andrew Jackson.

The **Moonwalk** provides a view of the river. Streetcar tours along the Mississippi are available and excellent river tours are available on the *Cajun Queen* and the *Creole Queen, tel. (504) 524-4567; website: www.creolequeen.com.* You can choose either a day cruise or a dinner and jazz cruise.

The **French Market** has colorful shops with local crafts and fruits for sale.

The **Garden District**, above Canal Street, is also a great place to visit. This was a center of 19th-century Southern aristocracy, and the homes in the area are of Victorian and Greek Revival design.

Bourbon Street, home to lots of bars, many of which stay open 24 hours a day, is an all night party. It is a popular destination for tourists, college students, transvestites, and locals. Stroll up and down the street with a beer in one hand and beads in the other. **Royal Street** is much quieter with many art galleries and high-end shops.

Lafitte's Blacksmith Shop, on Bourbon Street, is New Orleans' most historic saloon. It originally belonged to the pirate John Lafitte, who sold his booty here and plotted to rescue the exiled Napoleon.

Also visit **Café du Monde**, *800 Decatur Street; tel. +1 (504) 525-4544; website: www.cafedumonde.com*, and treat yourself to its famous beignets and café au lait.

The best museums in New Orleans

The **Cabildo**, *website: http://lsm.crt.state.la.us/*, near Jackson Square, houses a death mask of Napoleon along with other historical treasures. The building has been the seat of French, Spanish, and American rule of the Louisiana Territory.

The **Musee Conti Wax Museum**, *917 Conti Street; tel. +1 (504) 525-2605; website: www.neworleanswaxmuseum.com*, tells the story of New Orleans through life-sized wax figures.

The **Voodoo Museum**, *724 Dumaine; tel. +1 (504) 680-0128; website: www.voodoomuseum.com*, has a voodoo altar and educational displays.

Mardi Gras: The biggest party

Mardi Gras is an annual celebration that is marked by the debauchery of Fat Tuesday, before the beginning of Lent. The carnival season leads up to Fat Tuesday and includes balls, parades, and other celebrations in the French Quarter, along Canal Street and on St. Charles Avenue.

The best jazz festival

The **New Orleans Jazz and Heritage Festival** is the last weekend of April and the first weekend of May each year. The festival features jazz, blues, gospel, and Cajun music. Big name performers, such as Fats Domino, Billy Joel, and Wynton Marsalis, have played. For more information go to *www.nojazzfest.com*.

Booklovers' favorite festival

The **Tennessee Williams/New Orleans Literary Festival** is a must for all book-lovers. It takes place each March. For more information see the website: *www. tennesseewilliams.net*.

The best way to dine

The **Grill Room**, at the Windsor Court Hotel, *300 Gravier Street; tel. +1 (504) 523-1994; website: www.grillroomneworleans.com/the-grill-room*, is the most elegant place in town. It has hosted Nancy Reagan and Princess Anne. The menu and wines are superb. The restaurant is open daily for lunch and dinner.

Arnaud's, *813 Bienville Street; tel. +1 (504) 523-5433; website: www. arnaudsrestaurant.com*, in the French Quarter, is one of the best Creole restaurants. The décor glitters: crystal chandeliers, antique ceiling fans, beveled windows, and delicate china. Try the oysters Bienville, but save room for the *crepes suzette*.

The best bars

In the **Napoleon House**, *500 Chartres Street; tel. +1 (504) 524-9752; website: www. napoleonhouse.com*, pictures of Napoleon hang on the wall beneath ceiling fans.

The **Old Absinthe House**, *240 Bourbon Street, tel. +1 (504) 523-3181*, once served absinthe, an extract of wormwood. Here pirates, artists, and gentlemen drank absinthe from a fountain. Today, the bar offers "The Absinthe House Frappe" (now made with Herbsaint), an Old Fashion, an Absinthe Suissesse or the famous Ramos Gin Fizz.

Pat O'Brien's, *718 St. Peter Street; tel. (504) 525-4823; website: www. patobriens.com*, is the home of the famous Hurricane drink, a lively pianist and a beautiful courtyard perfect for sipping drinks and meeting with friends.

Antoine's, *713 St. Louis Street; tel. +1 (504) 581-4422; website: www. antoines.com*, has New Orleans' best wine cellar.

K-Paul's Louisiana Kitchen, *416 Chartres Street; tel. +1 (504) 596-2530; website: www.kpauls.com*, serves gin marinated with jalapeno peppers.

At the **Maple Leaf Bar**, *8316 Oak Street; website; http://mapleleafbar.com*, you can hear zydeco, Jex-Mex, blues, and ragtime music.

The **Preservation Hall**, *726 St. Peter Street; tel. +1 (504) 522-2841; website: www.preservationhall.com*, is famous for its Dixieland Jazz and makes for a perfect night on the town.

The best hotels

A pleasant, affordable place to stay, is the **Frenchmen Hotel**, *417 Frenchmen Street, tel. +1 (800) 831-1781; website: www.frenchmenhotel.com*, in two town-houses built in 1860. Rooms are furnished with antiques and have balconies overlooking the courtyard, the pool, and the patio.

Soniat House, *1133 Chartres Street; tel. +1 (504) 522-0570; website: www. soniathouse.com*, is one of the most elegant and exclusive hotels in New Orleans. The rooms offer imported furnishings, Oriental rugs, fireplace mantels, and hardwood floors.

FLORIDA: THE MOST TROPICAL STATE

Thousands of Americans and Canadians descend on the Sunshine State during the winter and spring to escape the snow and cold of their home states. It's the easiest winter escape, complete with sandy beaches, palm trees, tropical drinks, resort hotels, seafood restaurants, and lively crowds.

The Keys: Florida at its best

The 100-mile chain of gorgeous islands known as the Florida Keys stretches into the Gulf of Mexico from Florida's southern coast. Beaches in the Keys are less commercial, less spoiled, and more relaxed than most of Florida's other beaches. Four towns dot the islands: Key Largo, Islamorada, Marathon, and Key West.

Key West, at the tip of the Keys, is known as a place for all-out parties; **Key Largo** is peppered with beaches in small coves; **Smathers Beach** is the longest; **Memorial Beach** has a 100-yard pier over the water; and **South Beach** is the most peaceful. Tavernier and Plantation islands have pretty Atlantic beaches. Big Pine Key has white sand coves on the Gulf side.

The best place to stay in the Keys is the **Casa Marina Resort**, *1500 Reynolds Ave., Key West; tel. +1 (305) 296-3535 or +1 (888) 303-5717; website: www. casamarinaresort.com*, literally the last resort in the United States, situated at the south end of the southernmost city in Florida, as well as a former stopover for travelers heading to Havana, Cuba. This posh four-story resort hotel has vaulted ceilings, polished mahogany, arched windows, sea views, and landscaped gardens. Hemingway liked this hotel, as did Harry Truman. During the Cuban Missile Crisis in 1962, the hotel housed American troops. In 1978, it was renovated and returned to its original splendor.

St. Augustine: America's oldest settlement

Decades before Plymouth or Jamestown, the Spanish established **St. Augustine**—America's oldest permanent settlement—in 1565. In 1740, the fortified town fought off the English. Its fortress, **Castillo de San Marcos**, built in 1672 of coquina rock, has been preserved and can be visited. The courtyard is surrounded by guardrooms, storerooms, a jail, and a chapel.

The **Oldest Store Museum**, *4 Artillery Lane; tel. +1 (904) 829-9729*, has tools and machines from the 1800s, including high-wheeled bicycles, a steam-powered tractor, a Gibson Girl corset, and animal-powered treadmills.

684 The **Kenwood Inn**, *38 Marine Street; tel. +1 (904) 824-2116 or +1 (800)*

824-8151; website: www.thekenwoodinn.com, is a charming old inn in the historic section of St. Augustine. Built in 1865, it has been restored and is furnished with antiques and reproductions. Guests can use the inn's pool.

Wakulla Springs—America's deepest

Johnny Weissmuller grappled with alligators at **Wakulla Springs** *(website: www. floridastateparks.org/WAKULLASPRINGS/)* in his famous Tarzan role. Located 10 miles south of Tallahassee, this deep spring has no bottom, or so divers claim, which is why the water is so incredibly cold. If you want to get away from the Florida heat, this is the place. Mastadon bones have been found in this spring.

A beautiful old resort hotel, the **Wakulla Springs Lodge**, *550 Wakulla Park Dr.; tel. +1 (850) 421-2000; website: www.wakullaspringslodge.org,* overlooks the spring, surrounded by giant oaks draped with Spanish moss. The lodge is decorated with wood-beamed ceilings, marble floors, massive doors, and antiques.

TEXAS: THE LONE STAR STATE

Texas, the second-biggest state (after Alaska), is a land of extremes. Here, the J.R. Ewings of the world gamble great fortunes, while the women dress in furs, despite the scorching heat, and keep the cosmetics industry in business. At the same time, cowboys roam the stark, wide-open ranges. And Mexicans risk their lives to cross the border illegally. Going to Texas can be as much a cultural experience as visiting a foreign country.

Houston: The fastest-growing city

Houston has grown faster than any other American city, sprawling across 532 miles. Twenty-five oil companies have their headquarters in the city's skyscrapers.

The coolest way to tour hot, humid Houston is through the **Houston Tunnel System**, a series of air-conditioned passageways that connect all the major buildings downtown. For a map of the tunnels, which are lined with shops and restaurants, stop by the Houston Library, Penzoil Place, or the Texas Commerce Bank.

Pennzoil Place is Houston's cultural showpiece. Designed by the prominent architect Philip Johnson, this glass complex includes the **Jesse H. Jones Hall for the Performing Arts** (*website: www.houstonfirsttheaters.com/JonesHall.aspx*) and the **Alley Theater** (*website: www.alleytheatre.org*). The Jesse H. Jones Hall is home of the Houston Symphony Orchestra, the Grand Opera, and the Houston

Ballet Company. Its lobby features Richard Lippold's *Gemini II* sculpture.

Hermann Park contains the Museum of Natural Science and Burke Baker Planetarium, the Houston Zoological Gardens (where you can see a colony of vampire bats), and the Miller Outdoor Theater.

Nearby are the **Contemporary Arts Museum**, *5216 Montrose Blvd.; tel. +1 (713) 284-8250; website: www.camh.org*, which is free, and the **Museum of Fine Arts**, *1001 Bissonet Street; tel. +1 (713) 639-7300; website: www.mfah.org*. Both are worth a visit.

Also notable are the **Bayou Bend**, *1 Wescott Street, off Memorial Drive; website: www.mfah.org/bayoubend*, the former home of Ima Hogg, daughter of the first native-born Texas governor, and the **San Jacinto Museum of History**, *3800 Park Road; website: www.sanjacinto-museum.org*, located at the base of the San Jacinto Monument (which is taller than the Washington Monument) on the San Jacinto Battlegrounds.

The **Menil Collection**, *1515 Sul Ross Street; tel. +1 (713) 525-9400; website: www.menil.org*, is a wide-ranging gallery with prehistoric to modern art and special exhibits on tribal cultures. The gallery is closed Monday and Tuesday.

Houston's best rodeo

Every February, the **Houston Livestock Show and Rodeo,** *website: www.hlsr. com,* is held in Reliant Park. The largest show of its kind in the world, it draws cowboys from all over North America.

Houston's best restaurants

Gravitas, *807 Taft Street; tel. +1 (713) 522-0995; website: www.gravitasrestaurant. com*, has excellent classic and hearty fare. The wine list is very good.

Charivari, *2521 Bagby Street; tel. +1 (713) 521-7231; website: www.chari-varirest.com*, is an elegant establishment with a European flair. The Transylvanian chef trained in the best restaurants of Europe and it shows. The menu changes daily but always includes fresh fish, beef, game, and seasonal produce.

Houston's best hotel

The best hotel in town is the **Saint Regis**, *1919 Briar Oaks Lane; tel. +1 (713) 840-7600; website: www.starwoodhotels.com/stregis*, a beautifully appointed place with a homey feel. Little extras make it special: handmade soaps, fresh fruit and chocolates in the bedrooms, and brass razors.

Dallas: Fact is better than fiction

Dallas is famous for J.R. Ewing of the television series Dallas, the Dallas Cowboys and their cheerleaders, and the assassination of John F. Kennedy. What many people don't know is that it is the most sophisticated city in the South.

Be prepared for the **Dallas-Fort Worth Airport**, the world's largest—larger than Manhattan Island.

The saddest sight

The most sobering sight in Dallas is the spot where John F. Kennedy was shot, a grassy knoll at Market and Main streets marked by a large black granite marker. The **Sixth Floor Museum at Dealy Plaza**, *411 Elm Street; website: www.jfk.org*, opened in November 1988 to commemorate the 25th anniversary of his assassination. It is located on the sixth floor of the School Book Depository, where Lee Harvey Oswald hid and took aim at the president.

Dallas' best sights

Dallas City Hall, *1500 Manila*, rises 560 feet and surrounds a pleasant plaza.

The **Dallas Zoo**, *650 South R.L. Thornton Freeway (I-35E); tel. +1 (469) 554 7500; website: www.dallaszoo.com*, has the finest collection of rare birds in the nation. It is open daily.

Thanksgiving Square has a bell tower, the Chapel of Thanksgiving, and the Hall of Thanksgiving, which exhibits costumes and artifacts from seven continents.

The **Museum of Fine Arts**, *1717 N. Harwood Street; tel. +1 (214) 922-1200; website: http://dallasmuseumofart.org*, displays classic, pre-Columbian, European, and American paintings and sculpture. The museum is closed Mondays; admission is free.

The best collection of museums

Fair Park, *off I-30 East; website: www.fairpark.org*, has a number of museums within walking distance of one another. The Aquarium and Hall of State are currently undergoing renovation.

The **Museum of Nature and Science** is one of the best science museums in the United States, housing exhibits on astronomical phenomena, human anatomy, shells, and the workings of radios, along with specimens of birds, insects, and mammals.

The **Museum of the American Railroad** exhibits an old Dallas depot, a streetcar, an old passenger train, and the world's largest steam locomotive.

Dining bests in Dallas

Lawry's The Prime Rib, *14655 Dallas Parkway; tel. +1 (972) 503-6688; website: www.lawrysonline.com*, serves the best roast beef in Texas, carefully dry-aged for 14 to 21 days and then roasted on a bed of rock salt. It is carved and served warm at your table. When it was founded 50 years ago, Lawrence Frank and Walter Van de Kamp agreed that their restaurant should be elegant but friendly—no snooty waiters and no foreign languages on the menu.

The **Mansion Restaurant,** *in Rosewood Mansion on Turtle Creek, 2821 Turtle Creek Blvd; tel. +1 (241) 443-4747; website: www.mansiononturtlecreek.com*, in a renovated prairie-style house has an art deco decor. For a really intimate dinner, book the Chefs Table which overlooks the chef's garden. Reservations are required.

Dallas' best digs

Rosewood Mansion on Turtle Creek, *2821 Turtle Creek Blvd.; tel. +1 (214) 599-2100; website: www.mansiononturtlecreek.com*. For that once-in-a-blue moon big splurge, this is a good place for over-the-top luxury and even more extravagant food. A star-studded clientele adds to the already significant dazzle.

Austin: The most laid-back city in Texas

A large student population and a rebellious history make Austin the most laid-back and freethinking city in Texas. It is also one of the prettiest.

Austin's top sights

The **Texas State Capitol**, *Congress Avenue*, built in 1888, is colossal and the largest state capitol building in the U.S. It has over 400 rooms and nearly 900 windows. It is open 24 hours a day when the legislature is in session.

The **AMOA-Laguna Gloria Art Museum**, *3809 W. 35th Street; tel. +1 (512) 458-8191; website: www.amoa.org*, has the city's best art collection. Concerts, plays, and festivals are held on the grounds, which are lovely. The museum is closed Mondays.

The **Lyndon Baines Johnson Library**, *2313 Red River St.; website: www. lbjlibrary.org*, contains the president's speeches and fascinating memorabilia from an important time in U.S. history.

Austin's Area Garden Center, *2220 Barton Springs Road; website: www. zilkergarden.org*, in Zilker Park, has gardens, a 19th-century pioneer cabin, a log-cabin school, and an old blacksmith shop.

A country-western Hollywood

Second only to Nashville, young country-western musicians flock to Austin to make it big. Willie Nelson and Jerry Jeff Walker are among those who have succeeded.

La Zona Rosa, *612 West 4th Street; tel. +1 (512) 651-5033; website: www.lazonarosa.com*, the hot spot for big acts and a great venue all around, has a funky garage-like interior.

The **Broken Spoke**, *3201 S. Lamar; tel. +1 (512) 442-6189; website: www.brokenspokeaustintx.com*, is the best place for foot stompin' to Western honky tonk.

A bed for the night

The best place to stay in Austin is the **Driskill Hotel**, *604 Brazos Street; tel. +1 (512) 474-5911; website: www.driskillhotel.com*, a renovated 19th-century building with all the amenities.

San Antonio: The best of Tex-Mex

San Antonio is the site of the battle of the **Alamo** between 200 Texans (including Davy Crockett) and 4,000 Mexicans led by Commander Santa Anna. The Texans turned a mission building into a fort and fought to free Texas from Mexico. When the siege ended, all but six Texans were dead. Crockett survived, but he was later killed on the orders of Santa Anna. "Remember the Alamo" became a battle cry. The people of San Antonio still commemorate March 6, the day the siege ended.

Founded in 1718 as a Spanish military mission, the city is now more than half Mexican-American. The Tex-Mex atmosphere is thick and spicy. The best Mexican food north of the border is prepared in San Antonio.

Try **Acenar**, *146 E. Houston Street; tel. +1 (210) 222-2362; website: www.acenar.com*. Don't let the crowds deter you—this large Tex-Mex joint has some of the best fare around.

Or for fabulous American regional cuisine, try **Francesca's at Sunset**, *16641 La Cantera Pkwy.; tel. +1 (210) 558-6500; website: www.westinlacantera.com/dining.html*, which has the best wine list in the city and absolutely superb south-western cuisine.

The best of the missions

Spanish Franciscan missionaries built five missions in San Antonio to convert local Indians to Christianity. Two of them, the Alamo and Mission San Jose, are downtown.

The **Alamo**, *Alamo Plaza*, is actually the San Antonio de Valero Mission, with a chapel and barracks. The **Mission San Jose**, *6539 San Jose Blvd.*, is the largest. It has its own irrigation system, built by the Spaniards, and a beautiful rose window. Mass is still held here, and a mariachi band plays on Sundays.

The **Mission San Francisco de la Espada**, *10040 Espada Road*, has a beautiful chapel. A mile-long aqueduct, built between 1731 and 1745, supplies it with water. The **Mission San Juan Capistrano**, *9102 Grof Road*, built in 1731, differs from other, more architecturally elaborate missions in its simplicity.

The best museums

The **Witte Museum**, *3801 Broadway; tel. +1 (210) 357-1900; website: www. wittemuseum.org*, is San Antonio's premier museum, with acclaimed exhibits and traveling shows. It is good for children and adults alike, along with a remarkable tree house and stunning grounds.

The **San Antonio Museum of Art**, *200 W. Jones Ave.; tel. +1 (210) 978-8100; website: www.samuseum.org*, is housed in the restored Lone Star Brewery building, which has towers, turrets, ornate columns, and huge rooms. The collection includes pre-Columbian, American Indian, Spanish Colonial, Mexican, and European art as well as locally made furniture.

The best restaurant and hotel

San Antonio's most elegant hotel is **Hotel Valencia Riverwalk**, *150 East Houston Street; tel. +1 (210) 227-9700; website: www.hotelvalencia-riverwalk.com*, which is beautifully decorated and includes twice daily maid service.

Bullis House, *621 Pierce Street; tel. +1 (210) 223-9426; website: www. bullishouseinn.com*, is a great budget option, considering its wonderful downtown location in a historic mansion.

THE SOUTH WEST: NATURE AT ITS MOST POWERFUL

The **Southwest** region of the United States is an area of awe-inspiring natural beauty, much of which is preserved in the region's national parks. The most famous is the **Grand Canyon** in Arizona. If you think the reality can't possibly match the Grand Canyon's reputation, you're wrong. This is a sublime place, carved over the course of eons by the Colorado River. The descent to the bottom is rugged. From the base, the canyon looks like some otherworldly Shangri-La, a rainbow of colors and powerful bastions.

The park contains seven different lodges, with distinct features and historic character. **El Tovar Hotel;** *tel. +1 (303) 297-2757; website: www.grandcanyonlodges. com*, on the South Rim, is an elegant but rustic lodge perched on the edge.

For more information about the park, contact the **Grand Canyon National Park,** *tel. +1 (602) 638-7888; website: www.nps.gov/grca/.*

Zion National Park, in Springdale, Utah, is less famous. It is so named because its beauty reminded Mormon pioneers of paradise. The best view in all the Southwest is from **Angel's Landing,** a two-and-a-half-mile trail from the Grotto picnic area in the park.

Bryce Canyon National Park; *tel. +1 (435) 834-5322; website: www.nps.gov/ brca/index.htm,* five hours south of Salt Lake City, has a delicacy that differentiates it from other canyons. Some consider it the most beautiful, with its lacy rock formations.

Phoenix: The best oasis

The power of nature in the Southwest—the giant rocks and the lack of water—is unrelenting. Phoenix is a welcome oasis in the middle of this desert. The capital of Arizona is actually a chain of resort towns. The Valley of the Sun, ringed by mountains, is inhabited by one-and-a-half million people—many of them wealthy retirees. Outside Phoenix are 23 Indian reservations, home to 50,000 native Americans.

Frank Lloyd Wright was the architectural consultant on the valley's greatest hotel, the **Arizona Biltmore,** *2400 East Missouri Avenue; tel. +1 (602) 955-6600; website: www.arizonabiltmore.com.* Gold leaf lines the ceilings. The color scheme and décor are Southwestern, with stained glass, murals, paintings, and Indian tapestries. The Biltmore has two 18-hole golf courses, 18 tennis courts, three swimming pools, a health club, and a sauna.

The best of Tucson

Tucson, surrounded by the Sonora Desert, has both the easygoing atmosphere of a small town and the cultural offerings of a big city, including opera, a symphony, theater, and art. With an influx of newcomers from the East Coast, Tucson is losing some of its Hispanic and Southwestern flavor. But old Spanish festivals are still held, and good Mexican restaurants can be found throughout the town.

Most of Tucson's sights are within walking distance of the University of Arizona campus. The **Arizona State Museum,** *1013 E. University Blvd, tel. +1 (520) 621-6302; website: www.statemuseum.arizona.edu,* for example, has a collection of Southwest Indian artifacts and exhibits on area plants and animals. It is open

Monday through Saturday and is free (although donations are requested).

The **Arizona History Museum**, *949 E. Second Street; tel. +1 (520) 628-5774; website: http://arizonahistoricalsociety.org/museums/tucson.asp*, illustrates the state's history, with colorful exhibits about early settlers and outlaws.

El Presidio is a walled fortress built by Spanish settlers. Nearby are the **Spanish Colonial Pima County Courthouse**, built in 1928, and the **Tucson Museum of Art**, *140 N. Main Ave., tel. +1 (520) 624-2333; website: www.tucsonmuseumofart. org*. The museum is closed Monday.

Old Town Artisans, *201 N. Court Avenue, tel. +1 (800) 782-8072; website: http://oldtownartisans.com,* occupies a city block in El Presidio, with restaurants, and shops offering Western handicrafts, including Navajo rugs, in 19th-century adobe buildings. Open daily.

Fourteen miles west of Tucson is the spectacular **Arizona-Sonora Desert Museum**, *2021 N Kinney Rd, Tucson; tel. +1 (520) 883-2702; website: www. desertmuseum.org*, an educational, research, and conservation center and botanical garden where you can see jaguars, mountain lions, beavers, and bighorn sheep in natural habitats.

The **Mission of San Xavier del Bac,** *1950 W. San Xavier Road, San Xavier District; tel. +1 (520) 294-2624; website: www.sanxaviermission.org*, nine miles south of Tucson on Mission Road on the Tohano O'Adham Indian Reservation, was founded in 1692 by the Jesuits. It is one of the most beautiful churches in the Southwest, a white Mexican Renaissance structure surrounded by brown desert. This adobe structure has frescoes, carved figurines of saints, and two lions that wear satin bow ties.

The best place for closet cowboys

If you've always dreamed of riding horses across the desert, visit the **Tanque Verde Guest Ranch**, *14301 E. Speedway Blvd.; tel. +1 (520) 296-6275; website: www. tanqueverderanch.com*. Located 12 miles from Tucson, this hostelry, a working ranch until the 1920s, welcomes you into ranch life. You can eat well, swim in the indoor pool, and ride horses; it is great for families.

The best cliff dwellings

Most travelers head to Machu Picchu and Chichen Itza to see ancient Indian ruins. However, some of the most extraordinary pre-Columbian ruins are to be found in the United States. The mysterious Anasazi Indians built beautiful, complex cliff dwellings in the **Four Corners** region of the American Southwest long before

Europeans arrived. Great cities were carved out of reddish-gold sandstone cliffs by these unknown people, whom the Navajo named the Anasazi, or Ancient Ones. Their civilization flourished from the time of Christ until 1300, then disappeared without a trace.

No one knows exactly what became of the Anasazi, but you can explore their ancient dwellings, perched in gigantic cliffside caves on plateaus in the open plain, at times five stories high with as many as 800 rooms. (The caves are tiny when compared with the sheer cliffs that loom above them.) The caves went unseen by the white man until December 1888, when they were discovered by two cowboys searching for stray cows.

The most extensive cliff dwellings (4,000 in all) are in the 52,000-acre **Mesa Verde National Park** in Colorado. The largest and most famous cliff dwelling is **Cliff Palace**, where about 250 people lived in the 13th century. Its towered ruins look like a fantasy castle protected by a gigantic cave 100 yards wide and 30 yards deep, almost perfectly preserved because it is shielded from the elements by the cliff overhang. It is one of the five dwellings in the park that you can visit.

Hiking is limited in the park, but you are permitted to walk along five marked trails. The best is the loop called **Petroglyph Trail**.

During the winter season, ranger-guided tours of **Spruce Tree House,** one of the cliff dwellings, are conducted daily, and the **Archaeological Museum** is open from 8 a.m. to 5 p.m. For more information, contact the Park Superintendent, *Box 8, Mesa Verde National Park, CO 81330; tel. +1 (970) 529-4465; website: www.nps. gov/meve.*

Mesa Verde National Park is a two-hour drive from the airport at Durango, Colorado, where rental cars are available.

The best place to stay is the **Far View Lodge***; tel. +1 (602) 331-5210; website: www.visitmesaverde.com/accommodations/far-view-lodge.aspx,* near the cliff dwellings. Each room has a private balcony with a view.

You also can see Anasazi dwellings at the Navaho National Monument in **Monument Valley Tribal Park**, near Kayenta, Arizona. Unfortunately, overuse is wearing down the three dwellings there—Inscription House, Betatakin, and Keet Steel. Inscription House has been closed, and entrance to Betatakin and Keet Steel houses is limited. Monument Valley is geographically spectacular—you will recognize iconic images from classic John Ford westerns, and many other movies, which have been shot here.

The best of modern-day Native American country

Modern-day Indians maintain their traditions throughout the Southwest. Their *pueblos* are living communities, not museums.

The **Navajo reservation** in Monument Valley covers 16 million acres, mostly in northeastern Arizona. Over 260,000 people make up the Navajo nation. They are shepherds, silversmiths, weavers, and tour guides. One of the oldest (active) Navajo trading posts in the area is **Hubbell's**, a national historic site. For more information on the Navajos, contact **Navajo Parks and Recreation Department,** *tel. +1 (928) 871-6647; website: www.navajonationparks.org.*

The **Hopi** reservation is surrounded by Navajo country. The 10,000 Hopis (whose name means Peaceful Ones) occupy 1.4 million acres of land. Believed to be the descendants of the Anasazi, the Hopis are farmers and craftspeople, who honor the spirits that live in the nearby San Francisco Peaks.

The Hopis live on three main mesas. The Native Americans who live on **First Mesa** produce what is considered the best pottery. Those on **Second Mesa** create beautiful baskets, kachina doll carvings, and silver jewelry. The Hopis on **Third Mesa** are known for their decorative wicker plaques. **Old Orabi** on Third Mesa vies with Acoma Pueblo in New Mexico as the oldest inhabited town in the United States. The centuries-old village of **Walpi,** high on the edge of First Mesa, has tiny winding streets and houses crowded into the cliffs. For more information, contact the **Hopi Cultural Center,** *Box 67, Second Mesa, AZ 86043; tel. +1 (928) 734-2401; website: www.hopiculturalcenter.com.*

Santa Fe: The nation's oldest state capital

Set atop a 7,000-foot plateau at the base of the Sangre de Cristo Mountains in northern New Mexico is **Santa Fe**. The air is pure, the adobe homes are ancient, and the people are a mixture of Spanish, Indian, and Anglo.

The oldest state capital in the nation is inhabited by families who have been here for 14 generations. Outside the city are weathered mountains and old Indian pueblos. The desert is dotted with cacti and piñon pines.

Spanish conquistadors arrived here 400 years ago and named the town La Villa Real de la Santa Fe de San Francisco. The Spanish town was built on the site of abandoned pueblo Indian villages that had been built 300 years before the arrival of the conquistadors. In the early 20th century, artists from the Eastern U.S. and Europe traveled to New Mexico, attracted by the light, the desert landscapes and adobe architecture, and the Native culture. Santa Fe and Taos became important artist's colonies, and writers and poets followed the painters and printmakers.

Today, Santa Fe is a world-class art destination, where Native American, Hispanic, and Western arts flourish. The city boasts several important museums and dozens of influential commercial galleries.

The central plaza of Santa Fe was laid out by the Spanish in 1610. **The Palace of the Governors**, built of adobe in 1610, is the oldest public building in North America. It houses the **Museum of New Mexico,** *105 West Palace Avenue; tel. +1 (505) 476- 1140; website: www.museumofnewmexico.org,* and occupies the entire north side of the plaza. Along its porch, Native Americans from the surrounding pueblos spread blankets from which they sell handmade jewelry and pottery. All of the vendors here are vetted by the museum: if you want to buy Native American arts and crafts, this is an excellent place to start. You can speak with the artists, and learn about the styles of the different pueblos.

The **New Mexico Museum of Fine Arts**, *107 West Palace Avenue; tel. +1 (505) 476-5072; website: www.mfasantafe.org*, contains a rich collection of art native to the region, and work by the artists who immigrated or sojourned here, including celebrated woodcut master Gustave Baumann, and contemporary artists.

The **Georgia O'Keefe Museum,** *217 Johnson Street; tel. +1 (505) 946-1000; website: www.okeefemuseum.org/*, celebrates the life and career of one of the most famous painters who migrated to New Mexico. The Museum houses a large permanent collection of O'Keefe works, and mounts exhibitions of work by contemporaries of O'Keefe. The museum also maintains O'Keefe's home and studios outside of Santa Fe in Abiquiu and at Ghost Ranch. Contact the Museum for touring information.

Across the plaza from the museums is **St. Francis Cathedral,** completed in 1886. The two gold towers of this stone structure glow in the sun. Inside is a 16th-century wooden statue called *La Con quistadora,* said to be the oldest Madonna in North America. A block away is the **Loretto Chapel**, which houses the circular miraculous staircase built without nails or other visible means of support by an unknown carpenter. Legend says the carpenter was St. Joseph. The chapel itself was modeled after the Sainte Chapelle in Paris.

The best fiesta
The **Fiesta de Santa Fe** (*website: www.santafefiesta.org*), held in September, has music, dancing, and candlelight processions that begin at the cathedral. Zozobra, a 40-foot puppet representing Old Man Gloom, is burned to the delight of the crowds.

The biggest bomb

The scientists responsible for the atomic bomb met at 109 E. Palace Street beginning in 1943. A plaque on the wall says, "All the men and women who made the first atomic bomb passed through this portal to their secret mission at Los Alamos. Their creation in 27 months of the weapons that ended World War II was one of the greatest achievements of all time."

The best restaurants

The **Old House,** *Eldorado Hotel, 309 West San Francisco Street; tel. +1 (505) 988 4455; website: www.eldoradohotel.com.* The hacienda-like dining room and the inspired cuisine make this one of the area's top restaurants, with a wonderful list of wines by the glass.

Bumble Bee Baja Grill, *301 Jefferson Street; tel. +1 (505) 820-2862; website: www.bumblebeesbajagrill.com.* Locals love this casual eatery for its straight-forward southwestern and Mexican cuisine. Always fresh and plentiful, mouthwatering tacos and burritos, as well as other Cal-Mex specialties, draw crowds daily.

Café Pasquals, *121 Don Gaspar; tel. +1 (505) 983-9340; website: www. pasquals.com.* This festive restaurant a few blocks off the plaza, serves breakfast, lunch, and dinner, with creative New Mexico fusion cooking, using local and organic ingredients. If you want to make friends in Santa Fe, ask to sit at the large community table in the center of the dining room.

The best accommodation

An inn has existed at the site of the **La Fonda Hotel**, *100 E. San Francisco Street; tel. +1 (505) 982 5511; website: www.lafondasantafe.com*, off the plaza, since before the opening of the Santa Fe Trail. This hotel is a masterpiece of Southwest Style, with an historic bar and restaurant.

Ten Thousand Waves, *3542 Hyde Park Road; tel. +1 (505) 982-9304; website: www.tenthousandwaves.com*, is a Japanese-style spa a few miles outside of Santa Fe, with outdoor hot tubs, complete spa services, and Japanese-inspired lodging.

The **Bishop's Lodge,** *1297 Bishop's Lodge Road; tel. +1 (505) 983-6377; website: www.bishopslodge.com*, is set on 1,000 acres in the foothills of the Sangre de Cristo Mountains and offers horseback riding, tennis, swimming, and a fine dining room.

Taos: An artists' best

Artists and writers flock to **Taos**, the most picturesque town in the Southwest. About 3,000 people live here at the foot of Taos Mountain, sacred to the Native Americans at Taos Pueblo, *tel. +1 (575) 758-1028*. The pueblo, just north of town on Route 68, has been continuously inhabited for over 1,000 years, painted by generations of artists, and influenced architecture throughout New Mexico. Native guides offer tours of the pueblo, and some tribal dances are open to the public. The pueblo contains some excellent shops for Native crafts. It is usually open daily from 8 a.m. to 4:30 p.m., but can close for tribal rituals and funerals, and closes for about 10 weeks during the winter.

The **Taos Plaza** is the heart of the town, filled with restaurants, shops, and fine commercial art galleries. Museums around the plaza include the 200-year-old **Blumenschein House**, in LeDoux Street, where pioneer artist Ernest Blumenschein lived from 1919 to 1962.

The **Harwood Foundation Museum and Library**, *238 Ledoux Street, tel. +1 (575) 758-9826; website: http://harwoodmuseum.org/the_museum.php*, contains the paintings of early Taos artists.

The **Fechin House**; *website: http://taosartmuseum.org*, is a beautiful pueblo-style home designed by Russian artist Nicolai Fechin, and holds a collection of his work and works of other early 20th-century Taos painters.

A few miles north of town is the **Millicent Rogers Museum of Southwestern Arts and Crafts**, *website: www.millicentrogers.org*, with one of the world's best collections of Native American pottery and jewelry and colonial Hispanic Arts.

About 20 miles north of Taos is **D.H. Lawrence Shrine and Ranch**, where the writer lived for two years in the 1920's. His widow, Frieda, interred his ashes in a small rustic shrine here, and Frieda was buried here after her death in 1956. The ranch has not been well maintained for many decades, and a pilgrimage is only recommended to real Lawrence devotees—but they will be very glad they made the trip. The University of New Mexico owns the property, and plans are afoot to improve its accessibility. Take Highway 522 north to Forest Service Road 7, and follow signs up the mountain to the Ranch. Then follow a short hike to the cabin where the Lawrences and painter Dorothy Brett lived, and then up hill to the shrine.

The best place to stay in the area is the **Sagebrush Inn**, *1508 Paseo Del Pueblo Sur; tel. +1 (575) 758-2254; website: http://sagebrushinn.com*. The adobe walls are 24 inches thick and the interior ceilings are supported by log beams. Spanish-tile floors and fireplaces give the inn a rustic look. Navajo Indian rugs and works by Taos artists decorate the lounge. The inn has a swimming pool and tennis courts.

697

The **Taos Inn**, *125 Paseo del Pueblo Norte; tel. +1 (575) 758-2233; website: www.taosinn.com*, is another fine choice, with rooms in the main building, or arranged around courtyards. Some of the rooms have working fireplaces. Doc Martin's Restaurant, in the Inn, is an excellent choice for breakfast, lunch, or dinner, and the Adobe Bar has live music many nights and an extensive margarita menu.

The best restaurant in Taos—and one of the best in the Southwest—is **Joseph's Table**, *108A South Taos Plaza; tel. +1 (575) 751-4512; website: www. josephstable.com*, in the lovely and historic **Hotel La Fonda de Taos**. Open seven days a week for dinner, 5:30 p.m. to 10 p.m. And while you're at La Fonda, visit the hotel's small and rare collection of erotic D. H. Lawrence paintings.

THE BEST OF THE ROCKIES

Glacier National Park, in northwest Montana contains some of the most spectacular and least-touched scenery in the **Rocky Mountains**, including glaciers, high peaks, lakes and streams, and a great variety of wildlife (including grizzly bears, so be careful). The park straddles the Continental Divide.

Going-to-the-Sun-Road (*website: www.nps.gov/glac/planyourvisit/going-tothesunroad.htm*) is a 50-mile stretch leading to hiking trails.

Glacier Park Lodge, *website: www.glacierparkinc.com*, in the park, draws nature lovers, fishermen, hikers, and backpackers. This scenic resort also offers naturalist programs, golf, horse-back riding, swimming, cruises, and nightly entertainment.

Rocky Mountain National Park, *website: www.nps.gov/romo,* is the best place in Colorado for hiking and horseback riding. Two hours from Denver, the park has 20 peaks rising more than 12,000 feet. You'll see bighorn sheep, deer, and elk on the park grounds. Admission to the park is $20 per automobile, and the ticket is valid for seven consecutive days.

Yellowstone National Park is the world's greatest geyser area, with more than 200 geysers and 10,000 hot springs. The most famous geyser is **Old Faithful**, which erupts at regular intervals. Steamboat is the largest geyser in the world, lasting 20 minutes and shooting higher than 300 feet.

The **Yellowstone River** has carved a canyon through the rock at Yellowstone National Park. Waterfalls and lakes reflect the blue sky. More than 1,000 miles of trails crisscross the park. Be careful if you hike the backcountry; grizzly bears have become a problem. You'll also see moose and bison. Park employees say swimming in the warm waters of Firehole River can be exhilarating; however, this isn't encouraged, because you can be scalded. Yellowstone is the oldest national park in the United States, established in 1872.

THE BEST OF CALIFORNIA

During the past century, Americans have flocked to **California** with visions of fame, fortune, and freedom. They have been drawn by dreams of striking it rich or of making it big in Hollywood. The energy created by these imaginative and ambitious people has made this state one of the most productive in the Union—and one of the most unusual.

The best of San Francisco

San Francisco is the most inviting city in the United States—even if it also is one of the most expensive. It's beautiful, surrounded on two sides by water—the Pacific Ocean and San Francisco Bay. When the fog rolls in, the city becomes mysterious and soft. When the sun shines, the city glitters.

Situated atop steep hills, San Francisco has been the setting for many a chase scene in the movies. Nearly every neighborhood has a hill with a spectacular view. This city is remarkably clean—and very cosmopolitan.

The **Golden Gate Bridge**, which crosses the Golden Gate Strait between the Pacific Ocean and San Francisco Bay, is the city's most famous landmark. Actually a reddish color, the bridge is especially beautiful when partially shrouded in fog. The bridge connects the city to exclusive Marin County, home of Sausolito's artists' colony. It is also one route to the Napa Valley wineries.

The **Golden Gate Promenade** in Aquatic Park is a three-and-a-half-mile hike to the bridge that passes beaches, a yacht harbor, the Palace of Fine Arts, the Presidio Army Museum, and Fort Point.

Golden Gate Park, *website: www.nps.gov/goga/,* offers 1,017 acres of hiking trails and bridle paths. Visit the Nike Missle Site (an operational site from 1953 to 1979, the height of the Cold War). One of the city's major art museums, the **MH de Young Memorial Museum**, *website: http://deyoung.famsf.org/,* which has a splendid Rodin collection, is in the park.

The **California Academy of Sciences**, *55 Music Concourse Drive; tel. +1 (415) 379-8000; website: www.calacademy.org,* which features the Steinhart Aquarium, the Morrison Planetarium, and a four-story rainforest is also located here. Every Thursday night the academy hosts Nightlife, where you can wander around with a cocktail in hand while listening to live bands and DJs.

The **Asian Art Museum,** *200 Larkin Street; tel. +1 (415) 581-3500; website: www.asianart.org*, is devoted exclusively to Asian art.

The most interesting neighborhoods

San Francisco's **Chinatown** is the largest Chinese community in the United States. Walking these streets, you can almost imagine you are in China, with all signs in Chinese. Little shops sell silk Chinese jackets and little black slippers. Food stores have unidentifiable items in their windows. And the architecture of the buildings is Chinese; many were built long ago by the first Chinese immigrants, encouraged to emigrate to America to help build the railroad. The best time to visit is during the Chinese New Year celebration in January or February. The highlight is the Dragon Parade, but there also are marching bands, fireworks, and a beauty pageant.

Nob Hill, an area with plush hotels and a lovely park, is San Francisco's most elegant neighborhood. The **Stanford Court Hotel**, *905 California Street; tel. +1 (415)989-3500; website: www.marriott.com,* serves high tea and delicious dinners. Leland Stanford, a railroad mogul, once owned this mansion.

Huntingdon Park, between Taylor and Mason streets, with a lovely view of Grace Cathedral, is the most romantic place for a picnic.

North Beach, between Chinatown and Fisherman's Wharf, is home to hippies, the Italian community, and many of the city's best restaurants and bars. **The Cathedral of Saints Peter and Paul** looms above the neighborhood, making sure its residents keep their faith. You are likely to see elderly men playing *boccie* (Italian bowling game) in the parks. The most colorful time to visit is during the Blessing of the Fishing Boats, the first weekend in October, when the community parades from the cathedral to Fisherman's Wharf.

Superb restaurants

The Top of the Mark, *The Mark Hopkins Hotel, One Nob Hill, 999 California Street; tel. +1 (415) 392-3434*, is one of the best in San Francisco. It has a superb view of the city and is famed for its 100 Martinis menu. Treat yourself to the champagne brunch. Opens for breakfast and lunch Monday through Saturday, dinner nightly and brunch on Sunday.

Zuni Café, *1658 Market Street; tel. +1 (415) 552-2522; website: www. zunicafe.com.* This stylish, eclectic café reflects the best San Francisco has to offer. Reasonably priced, the Mediterranean menu offers game, fish, and oven-roasted specialties. Dozens of varieties of fresh oysters are served daily. Make a reservation, this place draws crowds.

Restaurant Gary Danko, *800 N. Point Street; tel. +1 (415) 749-2060; website: www.garydanko.com*, is the city's best French restaurant. With an impeccable menu, a stellar wine list, and nearly perfect service, this might be your most perfect meal out in the city.

Kokkari, *200 Jackson Street; tel. +1 (415) 981-0983; website: www.kokkari. com*. The Greek/Mediterranean cuisine here is famous citywide for its freshness, variety, and innovation. The restaurant offers anything from classic moussaka to fabulous grilled fish and meats. Always a crowd-pleaser.

Favorite inns

Our favorite inn in San Francisco, home to some of the best inns in the United States, is the **White Swan Inn**, *845 Bush Street; tel. +1 (415) 775-1755; website: www.jdvhotels.com/white_swan_inn/*. Each room is individually decorated, with four-poster beds, fireplaces, antique chairs and desks, and shelves and shelves of books. Guests are provided with thick terry bathrobes, and at night the sheets are turned down and chocolates are left on the pillows. Soft teddy bears lounge on the beds, and the air smells of the homemade cookies being baked in the kitchen. Breakfasts are enough to keep you going until dinner. Afternoon cocktails and hors d'oeuvres are served in the cozy sitting room. The staff is extremely helpful and friendly.

La Petite Auberge, *863 Bush Street; tel. +1 (415) 928-6000; website: www. jdvhotels.com/hotels/sanfrancisco/petite_auberge*, has a French motif. Fresh flowers scent the rooms, and floral wallpaper, French country antiques, quilts, handmade pillows, and working fireplaces make them cozy. Continental breakfast and afternoon tea are served in the dining room.

The **Ritz-Carlton**, *600 Stockton Street, Nob Hill; tel. +1 (415) 296-7465; website: www.ritzcarlton.com*, is the most elegant place to stay in the city and one of the top hotels in the world. It is drop-dead gorgeous with the type of luxury rarely seen in the U.S. With every amenity at your fingertips, there's no doubt about it: you'll feel like royalty here.

The **Four Seasons**, *757 Market Street; tel. +1 (415) 633-3000; website: www.fourseasons.com/sanfrancisco/*. Although pricey, this exquisite modern hotel is an oasis in the downtown area. Elegant and spare, it caters to your every whim and then some. Hang out in one of the wonderfully atmospheric lounges.

The best side trip

Sausalito, *website: www.sausalito.org*, across Golden Gate Strait by bridge or ferry, is a pretty port and beach resort. The population of this former Bohemian haven doubles on summer weekends. Situated between San Francisco and Mount Tamalpais, Sausalito has lovely views, unusual crowds, great bars and restaurants, and a profusion of shops.

While in Sausalito, stay at the **Casa Madrona**, *801 Bridgeway; tel. +1 (415) 332-0502; website: www.casamadrona.com*, a beautiful historic landmark hotel (with suites and cottages) that boasts wonderful views of the area.

Los Angeles: The most eclectic city

Although **Los Angeles** is often obscured by smog and deafened by the din of traffic, it has the stuff of which dreams are made: Hollywood, Beverly Hills, Malibu, and Marina del Rey. This is the stage for the jet-set world of the Beautiful People.

Hollywood: The best of the limelight

Northwest of downtown Los Angeles is the center of the entertainment world: **Hollywood**. Major film and television studios are here, as well as great cinemas and theaters. **Hollywood Boulevard** is a fascinating mishmash of shops and people. **Grauman's Chinese Theater** is a garish building. Outside the theater, in the cement, are the foot- and handprints of famous Hollywood movie stars.

Sunset Boulevard, or The Strip, is lined with nightclubs, bars, and performance halls, and **Melrose Avenue** is lined with vintage clothes shops and pleasant restaurants, where you can stargaze. Hollywood is seedy at night, frequented mainly by prostitutes.

The best studios

Universal Studios, *Universal City; website: www.universalstudioshollywood. com*, the birthplace of box-office hits and prime-time television shows, offers a behind-the-scenes studio tour and a theme park with rides, shopping, and photo opportunities with Universal's most popular characters.

NBC Television Studios, *3000 W. Alameda Ave., Burbank; website: www. nbc.com*, is smaller, but you can sit in on TV tapings free. Free tickets to some show tapings are offered by all the television studios on a first-come, first-served basis. See the NBC website for ticket details.

L.A. sights

The oldest buildings in the city are in the **Pueblo de Los Angeles State Historical Monument**, *website: www.ci.la.ca.us/elp/,* a 19th-century area in the northwest section of downtown. Bring your lunch to the Plaza and enjoy Aztec dancing, Peruvian music, flute players, and salsa, Monday through Friday, from 11 a.m. to 4 p.m.

The **Old Plaza**, with 100-year-old trees, stands at the center. You can tour the Avila Adobe, the Pico and Sepulveda houses, and ancient Chinese gambling and opium dens.

Visit the **Huntington Library, Art Gallery, and Botanical Gardens**, *1151 Oxford Road, San Marino; tel. +1 (626) 405-2100; website: www.huntington.org.* The library houses one of the world's most important collections of rare books, including a Gutenberg Bible and original editions of *The Canterbury Tales*, Thoreau's *Walden*, and Benjamin Franklin's autobiography. The art gallery contains 18th- and 19th-century British paintings, including Thomas Gainsborough's *Blue Boy* and Sir Thomas Lawrence's *Pinkie*. The botanical gardens are immense, with desert, Japanese, and Elizabethan sections. The complex is closed on Tuesdays.

The **J. Paul Getty Museum at the Getty Center**, *2100 Getty Center Drive; tel. +1 (310) 440-7300; website: www.getty.edu,* located in the lofty Richard Meier-designed Getty Center, houses an opulent collection of 18th-century French decorative art, European paintings, sculpture, furniture, and antiquities. Admission is free. Also visit the Getty Villa in Malibu, which houses works of art from the museums Greek, Roman, and Etruscan antiquities.

The **Museum of Contemporary Art/Geffen Contemporary at Moca**, *Downtown; tel. +1 (213) 626-6222; website: www.moca.org.*

Disneyland: The world's best theme park

Disneyland, *website: http://disneyland.disney.go.com,* located just south of Los Angeles, is the world's original theme park. (Disney World in Florida, was built later.) The oldest and still the best, it brings Mickey Mouse to life, offers trips through the stars, and creates a disconcertingly convincing haunted house. Millions visit every year and it's a child's paradise.

The best song and dance

The **Los Angeles Philharmonic** plays at the **Walt Disney Concert Hall**, *111 South Grand Avenue; tel. +1 (323) 850-2000; website: www.laphil.com,* designed by architect Frank Gehry, throughout the season. It is reputed to be one of the most acoustically sophisticated concert halls in the world.

The **Troubadour**, *9081 Santa Monica Blvd.; website: www.troubadour.com*, hosted the likes of Linda Ronstadt, Miles Davis, Joni Mitchell, and Blood, Sweat, and Tears before they hit the big time.

The **Roxy Theatre**, *9009 Sunset Blvd.; website: http://theroxyonsunset.com*, is a fashionable night spot as well as a testing and recruiting ground for the music industry.

The **Comedy Store**, *8433 Sunset Blvd.; website: www.thecomedystore.com*, has played host to top comedians, including Richard Pryor, Steve Martin, and Robin Williams.

The best restaurants

The **Polo Lounge**, at the Beverly Hills Hotel, *9641 Sunset Blvd.; tel. +1 (310) 276-2251; website: www.thebeverlyhillshotel.com/restaurants_bars/polo_lounge. html*, is where celebrities are made—and then fade. The many windows of this fishbowl offer views of a swimming pool and tropical plants. The Polo Lounge attracts the likes of Barbra Streisand, Gore Vidal, and Joan Collins. If the celebrities don't interest you, concentrate on the food, which is very good.

Spago Beverly Hills, *176 N. Canon Drive; tel. +1 (310) 385-0880; website: www.wolfgangpuck.com*. No doubt you've heard of it as its fame has spread worldwide, and for good reason. Great décor, consistently top-rated food and wine, and best of all, the people watching. You'll get a true LA experience dining here.

L.A.'s heavenly hotels

Celebrities who don't live in Beverly Hills stay at the Beverly Wilshire or the Beverly Hills hotels. The **Regent Beverly Wilshire Hotel**, *9500 Wilshire Blvd.; tel. +1 (310) 275-5200; website: www.fourseasons.com/beverlywilshire/*, has cobblestone pavements and Louis XIV gates. The older wing, called the Wilshire, is a lavish neo-Renaissance building. The newer Beverly Wing is decorated with French tapestries, Spanish furniture, and Italian marble. Prince Charles stayed in the most opulent suite, the Christian Dior.

The **Beverly Hills Hotel and Bungalows**, *9641 W. Sunset Blvd.; tel. +1 (310) 276-2251; website: www.thebeverlyhillshotel.com*. Arguably the best in town, this hotel is housed in a pink-stucco Spanish villa, and is surrounded by palm-shaded lawns where movie stars lounge. Less-famous folks have a hard time getting a room here. Movie fans will recognize this as the *Pretty Woman* hotel.

The **Hotel Bel Air**, *701 Stone Canyon Road, Bel Air; tel. +1 (310) 472-1211; website: www.hotelbelair.com*, is an elegant pink mission building with red-tiled roofs and a courtyard fountain. This beautiful historic hotel has all the modern luxuries. Dolly Parton stays here.

Bacchus' favorite: Napa Valley

The beautiful **Napa Valley**, 40 miles north of San Francisco on Highway 101, produces America's best wines. September through November, the area's wineries are busy harvesting grapes. More than 60 wineries in Napa and Sonoma counties invite visitors to tour their facilities and sample their wines.

The best tour is the three-hour exploration of the **Robert Mondavi Winery**, *7801 St. Helena Hwy; tel. +1 (888) 766-6328; website: www.robertmondaviwinery. com.* It is a great place to start whether you know a lot about wine or nothing at all.

A lovely place to stay in the valley is **Auberge du Soleil**, *180 Rutherford Hill Rd., Napa; tel. +1 (707) 963-1211; website: www.aubergedusoleil.com*, a thoroughly gorgeous hotel nestled in olive groves, with views of the valley from each room's private deck. Peaceful and calm, the fresh flowers and fireplaces, swimming pool, and a private Jacuzzi in the spectacular cottage suite, all make for an unsurpassed visit.

The tallest tree in the world

Redwood National Park in northwest California contains the world's tallest tree, at 367 feet high. Magnificent stretches of virgin redwood forest, many with trees 2,000 years old or older, are the main attraction. The park borders the Pacific coastline, where sea lions, seals, and birds live unthreatened.

The highest falls in North America

The falls located in **Yosemite National Park**, in east central California, are the highest in North America (dropping 2,425 feet). They are among many natural spectacles in the **Sierra Nevada**, the cliffs and pinnacles of which were formed by glaciers. The nature photographer Ansel Adams took many of his best-known photographs in this park.

The **Ahwahnee Resort**, *website: www.yosemitepark.com*, in Yosemite, built in 1927, has views of the falls and Glacier Point. The six-story pseudo castle is decorated with Western and Native American motifs. Movie stars and heads of state have stayed here. The 77-foot Great Lounge has two fireplaces. Facilities include a pool, tennis courts, horseback riding, hiking trails, and winter sports.

THE NORTHWEST: NATURE AT ITS BEST

The **Pacific Northwest** has managed to keep its natural beauty from being commercialized and overdeveloped. The rugged, untouched coasts of Washington and Oregon are breathtaking. The mountains are protected as national parkland. The cities are lively without polluting the countryside.

The Northwest gets a lot of rain. If you can put up with the drizzle, you'll love the experience here. This is the greenest place in North America: the grass is the color of emeralds; pine trees grow straight and tall, to heights unheard of on the East Coast.

Seattle: Where the grass is greenest

Seattle is one of the nation's most beautiful cities. Surrounded by mountains on nearly all sides, it sits on Puget Sound and Lake Washington. The Cascade and Olympic mountains are only two hours away, and the lone white peak of Mount Rainier can be seen from anywhere in the city. In addition to all its natural wonders, the city also offers fabulous restaurants, bars, and cultural activities.

The best view of the city is from the **Space Needle** in Seattle Center, a remnant of the 1962 World's Fair.

The most bizarre place in Seattle is **Ye Olde Curiosity Shop**, *1001 Alaskan Way #54; tel. +1 +1 (206) 682-5844; website: www.yeoldecuriosityshop.com*, where shrunken heads and mummified humans are displayed.

The best place for restaurants and nightlife is **Pioneer Square**, the reno-vated section of Old Seattle. **Grand Central Arcade**, *First Avenue and Occidental Street*, has the best shops.

The best tour of the city is the **Underground Seattle Tour**, *website: www. undergroundtour.com*, which leaves from 608 First Ave. and shows you the remains of the original city, which burned in 1889.

Seattle's finest food

Pike Place Farmer's Market, *First Avenue and Pike Street*, has stalls filled with colorful fresh vegetables and fruits. It also has good restaurants. One of Seattle's best is **Chez Shea**, *94 Pike Street; tel. +1 (206) 467-9990; website: www.chezshea. com*, a cozy room on the top floor of the Corner Market Building. You can enjoy gourmet food while looking out over Puget Sound and the Olympic Mountains.

Etta's Seafood, *2020 Western Avenue, Pike Place Market; tel. +1 (206) 443-6000; website: www.tomdouglas.com/restaurants/ettas*, is the place to go for seafood and is a popular standout among the many eateries at Pike Place.

Canlis, *2576 Aurora Ave. N.; tel. +1 (206) 283-3313; website: www.canlis. com*, is a Seattle institution. Open since 1950, it has consistently provided excellent food in a lovely atmosphere. Traditional dishes, like steak and local seafood blends well with more contemporary cuisine.

Rover's, *2808 East Madison Street; tel. +1 (206) 325-7442; website: www. rovers-seattle.com*. Don't be deceived by the modest clapboard house, this is assuredly one of Seattle's most acclaimed restaurants. The French cuisine by its award-winning chef is noted for making the very best of the region's famously fresh local products.

Seattle's best stay

The Sorrento Hotel, *900 Madison Street; tel. +1 (206) 622-6400; website: www. hotelsorrento.com*, is one of Seattle's oldest hotels and, with its wrought iron gates, plush lobby, and opulent guest rooms, it's surely one of the finest places to stay… period.

The best of the wilderness

Mount Rainier, a 14,410-foot mountain in **Mount Rainier National Park**, has more glaciers than any other mountain on the U.S. mainland. The four-and-a-half-mile **Skyline Trail** is the longest loop trail on the mountain. From Panorama Point, you can see glaciers and the summit. Mount Rainier was sacred to the Yakima and Klickatt Indians, who believed evil spirits inhabited a crater lake at the summit and caused storms and avalanches.

You can stay in Mount Rainier National Park at the **Paradise Inn**, *Highway 706; tel. +1 (360) 569-2275; website: www.mtrainierguestservices.com*, which looks out over Mount Rainier and the valley below. This rustic inn was built in 1916 of notched cedar logs, with no nails. The open-beamed lobby has 50-foot cathedral ceilings and two stone fireplaces. The inn is open May through October.

The **Olympic National Forest** has wildly beautiful beaches along the Pacific Ocean. Inland, the Hoh, Queets, and Quinault river valleys have non-tropical rainforests. Up to 140 inches of rain fall here each year, and moss covers everything. **Mount Olympus** rises 7,915 feet, challenging mountain climbers.

Stay at beautiful **Lake Quinault Lodge**, *345 South Shore Road; tel. +1 (360) 288-2900; website: www.visitlakequinault.com*, a grand old inn on Lake Quinault in Olympic National Park. Facilities include fireplaces, a pool, sauna, boats, hiking trails, and fishing.

To truly understand the power of nature, visit **Mount St. Helens**, a volcano that erupted in 1980 and caused serious destruction. You can tour the barren, lava-scorched area around the mountain. This peak is 50 miles northwest of Portland, Oregon.

America's deepest lake

Crater Lake in Oregon, which fills a 1,932-foot crater, never freezes, because of its depth. Located 6,000 feet above sea level, it is surrounded by snow-capped mountains. This beautiful, deep blue lake is five hours south of Portland. While the park is open year-round, only the south and west entrance roads are open during the winter. And Rim Drive is open only from July 1 through late September or October, depending on the snowfall. For more information, see, *website: www. nps.gov/crla.*

You can spend the night by the lake in rustic cottages operated by **Crater Lake Lodge**, *tel. +1 (888) 774-2728; website: www.craterlakelodges.com.* The cottages are minimally equipped with cold running water, blankets, and electricity.

THE BEST OF THE GREAT LAKES

In America's northeast are the **Great Lakes**, the world's largest freshwater bodies. Surrounding these five mammoth lakes are some of the nation's best farmland and most populated cities. **Lake Superior** is the deepest, the most treacherous, and the most beautiful. **Lake Michigan** is the best for fishing, swimming, and sailing. And its high western dunes are excellent for hang gliding.

Chicago: The prettiest skyline

Chicago's architecture is among the most sophisticated in the country. The second-largest city in the United States, Chicago has some of the world's tallest buildings. And its neighborhoods are wonderfully diverse, filled with different ethnic groups. An unexpected aspect of this rough-and-tumble town is its beautiful clean beaches.

The best architecture

Chicago was the birthplace of modern architecture as developed by Louis Sullivan, his disciple Frank Lloyd Wright, and other members of the unofficial Chicago School of Architecture. Many of this group's first skyscrapers are still standing, next to taller, more modern buildings designed by the likes of Mies van der Rohe and Helmut Jahn. The **Archicenter**, *224 S. Michigan Ave.; tel. +1 (312) 922-3432; website: http://caf.architecture.org/*, is the place to learn about Chicago's diverse architecture.

The tallest building

Standing proudly over Chicago is the **Sears Tower**, *233 S. Wacker; website: www.searstower.com.* Covering an entire city block, its 110 stories are reached by 103 elevators and lit by 16,000 windows. You can visit the sky deck on the top floor, from which, on a clear day, you can see as far as Wisconsin to the north, Indiana to the south, and Michigan to the east.

Shopping's best mile

The 16-block stretch of Michigan Avenue between the Chicago River and Oak Street is called the **Magnificent Mile**—with good reason. Here are Chicago's best and most exclusive department stores, boutiques, and specialty shops as well as many of the best restaurants in Chicago.

Along the Magnificent Mile is **Water Tower Place**, *835 N. Michigan Ave*, by far Chicago's best and most beautiful indoor shopping mall—eight stories of shops and restaurants.

See the **Chicago Water Tower and the Pumping Station**, *Michigan and Chicago Avenues*, the only buildings that survived the Great Chicago Fire of 1871.

The best museums

The **Art Institute of Chicago**, *111 Michigan Avenue at Adams; tel. +1 (312) 443-3600; website: www.artic.edu*, is a world-class art museum with the finest collection of Impressionist paintings in the country and an outstanding collection of Renaissance, Oriental, and post-Impressionist art.

The **Field Museum of Natural History**, *1400 South Lake Shore Drive; tel. +1 (312) 922-9410; website: www.fieldmuseum.org*, is an interesting museum with a collection of jewels, Egyptian mummies, and freestanding dinosaur skeletons.

The **Museum of Broadcast Communications**; *website: www.museum.tv*, pays tribute to Chicago's glory days, when many national radio and television broadcasts originated here. You can watch or listen to more than 400 classic radio shows and over 900 television shows. It is currently closed as it prepares to move into a new facility at State and Kinzie in downtown Chicago. Check the website for updates.

The **Museum of Contemporary Art**, *220 East Chicago Avenue; tel. +1 (312) 280-2660; website: www.mcachicago.org*, features art being created today.

The museum is closed on Mondays.

With more than 2,000 displays—including a coal mine, a World War II German submarine, and the Apollo 8 command module—the **Museum of Science and Industry**, *57th Street and South Lake Shore Drive; tel. +1 (773) 684-1414; website: www.msichicago.org*, is a world-class museum and the most popular in the city. Its Omnimax Theater features a five-story domed screen that puts the viewer in the middle of the action. The theater boasts wonderful exhibits for kids of all ages, with life-sized robots and an exquisite fairy castle dollhouse.

The **Oriental Institute**, at the University of Chicago, *1155 E. 58th Street; tel. +1 (773) 702-9520; website: http://oi.uchicago.edu*, is a first-rate museum of artifacts from the ancient Near East (Egypt, Mesopotamia, Iran, and the Holy Land). Highlights are Egyptian mummies, fragments of the Dead Sea scrolls, and a huge winged bull from the throne room of King Sargon II of Assyia. Admission is free. The institute is closed Monday.

The most colorful neighborhoods

Hyde Park, the home of the University of Chicago, is an intellectual's dream, with six bookstores (four new, two used) and hundreds of people itching for a good conversation. Hyde Park is also home to the Museum of Science and Industry, the Oriental Institute, and Frank Lloyd Wright's famous Robie House. Every June, Hyde Park hosts its annual **57th Street Art Fair** (*website: www.57thstreetartfair.org*).

The wealthiest part of town, known as the **Gold Coast**, is an area of old mansions and luxury apartment buildings, conveniently close to Lake Michigan, Oak Street Beach, and the Magnificent Mile.

Chicago's old Bohemia was Old Town, where many of the city's artists and hippies lived. But as Old Town gentrified, rising rents drove the artists, actors, and writers out. The new Bohemia is **Lake View**, the neighborhood around Belmont and Clark, which is filled with restaurants, bookstores, small theaters, coffee shops, and used-clothing stores.

Chicago's newest neighborhood is **River North**, an old warehouse district that in the past 15 years has become a chic loft area. Bounded by the Chicago River on the south and Chicago Avenue on the north, River North is an area of fashionable shops, trendy nightclubs, and popular new restaurants.

An art gallery district—not unlike SoHo in New York City—thrives along West Erie, Huron, and Superior streets, between Wells and Sedgwick.

The best parks and zoos

Chicago has 29 miles of lakefront parks. Lake Michigan offers clean water and pleasant swimming. The most popular beaches are **Lincoln Park** and **Oak Street**. Smaller, rockier, and less crowded are the beaches in **Hyde Park**, between 49th and 57th streets.

Grant Park, on the waterfront between Roosevelt Road and Randolph Street, east of Michigan Avenue, is attractive. The Grant Park Music Festival is held here every year in Millennium Park, the northwestern corner of the park. See *www.grantparkmusicfestival.com* for details. At night, a light display dances across the Buckingham Fountain, which sprays 90 feet into the air.

On the grounds of the **Lincoln Park Zoo**, *2200 N. Cannon Park; tel. +1 (312) 742-2000; website: www.lpzoo.org*, are beaches, yacht harbors, and the Lincoln Park Conservatory, which is the city's music capital. Good music can also be heard in the bars and theaters along Clark Street and Lincoln Avenue.

The **Brookfield Zoo**, *First Avenue and 31st Street; tel. +1 (708) 688-8000; website: www.brookfieldzoo.org*, in Brookfield, re-creates the Sahara Desert and the Australian Outback, as well as the habitat of the Siberian tiger.

The best town for theater

Thirty years ago, Chicago had no live theater to speak of. However, today more than 100 groups perform in the city. In fact, Chicago's theater scene rivals even those of New York and London. Although many are shoestring operations performing in storefronts and church basements, Chicago also has a respectable number of strong, well-established theaters.

No other Chicago theater group comes close to the **Steppenwolf Theater**, *1650 N. Halsted Street; tel. +1 (312) 335-1650; website: www.steppenwolf.org*. Many of its best shows have gone on to perform off-Broadway in New York City.

Chicago's best laughs

Since 1959, **Second City**, *1616 N. Wells; tel. +1 (312) 337-3992; website: www.secondcity.com*, the best comedy theater in the city, has provided Chicago with consistently popular comedy revues. John Belushi, Shelley Long, Gilda Radner, and Alan Arkin all began their careers here. If you want to go, make reservations at least a week in advance.

The most outrageous entertainment

One of Chicago's most popular night spots is the **Baton Lounge**, *436 N. Clark Street; tel. +1 (312) 644-5269; website: www.thebatonshowlounge.com*, an outrageous club, where funny, ravishing female impersonators attract an eclectic crowd. Straight and gay, young and old all come to see such local legends as Chili Pepper and Leslie. Reservations are essential.

The best jazz and blues

For music lovers, Chicago is synonymous with jazz and blues. And Joe Segal's **The Jazz Showcase**, *Dearborn Station, 806 S. Plymouth Ct.; tel. +1 (312) 360-0234; website: www.jazzshowcase.com*, has been the place to hear all the jazz greats in Chicago for decades.

No blues bar comes close to the **New Checkerboard Lounge**, *5201 South Harper Ct.; website: www.checkerjazz.org*, where such blues greats as Buddy Guy and Junior Wells performed regularly and rock stars such as Mick Jagger and Keith Richards drop by. (Sometimes they even jam with the old bluesmen.) The club itself is friendly and safe, but it is located in a dicey neighborhood—so park near the club or take a cab. Don't take a bus or the subway—Chicago's South Side is rough.

If you love the blues but prefer to stay in a safer neighborhood, visit the **Kingston Mines**, *2548 N. Halsted; tel. +1 (773) 477-4646; website: www.kingstonmines.com*, in the heart of Lincoln Park. The Kingston Mines attracts many of the acts that play at the New Checkerboard Lounge as well as newer bands during the week.

The best classical music and opera

Under the leadership of its conductor, Daniel Barenboim, the **Chicago Symphony Orchestra**, *website: www.cso.org*, has become a world-class orchestra, popular not only in its home city but worldwide. The CSO performs at **Symphony Center**, *220 S. Michigan Ave.*, across the street from the Art Institute.

The **Lyric Opera**, *20 N. Wacker Drive; tel. +1 (312) 332-2244; website: www.lyricopera.org*, is world-famous for its grandly staged operas.

The best deep-dish pizza

A quick way to start an argument in Chicago is to ask who has the best pizza in town. Everyone has his favorite place for pizza. The world-famous Chicago-style pizza was first served in the late 1940s at **Pizzeria Uno**, *29 E. Ohio Ave.; tel. +1 (312) 321-1000; website: www.unos.com*. And everyone agrees (even in Chicago) that Pizzeria Uno and sister restaurant **Pizzeria Due**, *619 N. Wabash Ave.; tel. +1 (312) 943-2400*, still serve great pizza.

The best barbecued ribs
Chicago, not the South, has the best barbecued ribs in the world. At **Ribs'n Bibs**, *5300 S. Dorchester Ave.; tel. +1 (312) 493-0400*, tuck into a whole slab of hickory smoked ribs with BBQ sauce, fries, coleslaw, and bread. Delicious!

The best ethnic restaurants
A city of ethnic groups—Poles, Irish, Lithuanians, Serbs, Croatians, Italians, and Hispanics—Chicago has hundreds of great ethnic restaurants.

The best is a Mexican restaurant called the **Frontera Grill & Topolobampo**, *445 N. Clark Street; tel. +1 (312) 661-1434; website: www.fronterakitchens.com*, which serves authentic Mexican cuisine at its very best, and not at all what you'd expect. This is truly gourmet dining, with organic ingredients and meats, like pork loin in mole sauce and a bread soup that's to die for. A fun bar scene too.

The best gourmet restaurant
Charlie Trotter's, *816 Armitage Ave.; tel. +1 (733) 248-6228; website: www.charlietrotters.com*. Celebrity chef Charlie Trotter has made his Chicago outpost a must-visit for gastronomic tourists and lovers of fine dining. Opt for one of the tasting menus where you'll get the best sampling of the chef's wildly innovative cuisine; all organic too. Plus, Trotter's boasts a stellar wine list and an elegant dining room.

The best grand hotel
The **Drake**, *140 E. Walton Place; tel. +1 (312) 787-2200; website: www.thedrakehotel.com*, is Chicago's answer to a classy downtown hotel. Open since the 1920s, the landmark building has loads of character and rooms with a lake view are worth asking for. Although a historic hotel, it has been renovated to bring it completely up to date.

The best little hotel
The **Tremont Hotel**, *100 E. Chestnut Street; tel. +1 (312) 751-1900; website: www.tremontchicago.com*, just off the Magnificent Mile, is one of Chicago's most elegant little hotels. This reasonably priced lodging is just a short walk from Michigan Avenue and the Oak Street Beach, making it a favorite for guests looking to traverse the city on foot.

The Great Lakes' best resort

Mackinac Island, Michigan, where Lake Huron meets Lake Michigan, is a beautiful, peaceful place with no automobiles, just horse-drawn carriages and bicycles. Indians once lived here in lodges that are preserved in an open-air museum. During the Revolution, British forces built a fort here, now restored and open to the public. The island became a fashionable resort in the late 19th century, and it was the second area (after Yellowstone) to become a national park. Today, the island is a refuge for city dwellers, a place for sailing, golfing, horseback riding, and tennis. Victorian homes and white church steeples dot the town. Sailboats bob in the lakes, and the waterfront is filled with shops and restaurants.

The **Grand Hotel**, *1 Grand Ave.; tel. +1 (800) 334-7263; website: www. grandhotel.com*, on Mackinac Island, was built in 1887 by railroad and steamship companies. Constructed in Greek Revival style, with a long veranda supported by columns, it has a lovely pool (where Esther Williams swam in *This Time for Keeps*), as well as a golf course and tennis courts. The food is great, but the main dining room is slightly stuffy. Tea is served in the parlor.

The **Island House**, *tel. +1 (906) 847-3347; website: www.theislandhouse. com*, is an old Victorian resort on Mackinac Island. The enormous white building is ringed with shaded porches and topped with corner turrets and dormer windows. Built in 1852, it is the island's oldest hotel. Breakfast and dinner are served in the hotel dining room. You can sleep late and then have brunch on the front porch while savoring a view of the straits.

Mission Point Resort, *6633 Main Street; tel. +1 (800) 833-7711; website: http://missionpoint.com/*, is set on 18 acres of Lake Huron shoreline. It has a heated outdoor swimming pool, two hot tubs, three tennis courts, a fully equipped health and fitness center, a pool hall, and an arcade. The main lobby is a spacious circular room with five huge stone fireplaces and a soaring, vaulted ceiling of 40-foot hand-hewn timbers. Rooms overlook Lake Huron.

ALASKA: THE WILDEST (AND COOLEST) STATE

Alaska is the last frontier in the United States. Having more unexplored territory than the rest of the 49 states combined, Alaska's virtues lie not in its few major cities but in the beauty of its frozen landscape, home to only 300,000 fishermen, prospectors, and Eskimos. The largest U.S. state has excellent fishing, unlimited trails, and an endless reserve of wildlife.

Alaska is a land of superlatives. **Mount McKinley**, at 20,320 feet, is the tallest mountain in North America. Astounding amounts of gold and oil have been discovered in this state. And Alaska is the last area in the country where native populations keep their traditional ways, undisturbed by the white man. Alaska has the longest winter in the United States, lasting from October to April. June and July have days of continuous light. This is the best time to visit—unless you really like the snow.

Alaska's most spectacular sight

The most spectacular sight in Alaska is **Glacier Bay National Park and Preserve**, where myriad of ice boulders float in fiords bordered by thick forests. The park was covered by ice thousands of feet deep until just 200 years ago. Nowhere else can you get so close to glaciers. In this ever-changing area, humpback and killer whales spout, porpoises and seals play, and bears, mountain goats, and more than 200 species of birds, including the bald eagle, live. The waters are filled with trout, salmon, and halibut. During the summer, Glacier Bay is a rainbow of flowers.

The top of the world

Across the **Arctic Circle** is the land of the Eskimo, where the sun never sets during summer. All you can see for miles is vast, gently rolling tundra.

Barrow is the northernmost point of the continent, located 330 miles north of the Arctic Circle. North America's largest Eskimo settlement is here—Barrow covers 88,000 square miles. This is also the whaling capital of the Arctic.

Kotzebue is the trading center of the Arctic. Part of the ancient land bridge that once joined Siberia and North America, it has been a major settlement and trade center for 6,000 years. **Front Street**, the city's main street, is also the beach, where fishing boats pull up and fish and meat are hung on racks to dry. You can shop here for jade, ivory carvings, furs, native handicrafts, and artifacts.

The Pribilof Islands

The **Pribilof Islands**, in the Bering Sea, are home to North America's largest seal herd and the biggest seabird colony in the world. (More than 190 bird species have been sighted.) Each summer, 1.7 million northern fur seals migrate here to bear their young.

The best of the Alaskan panhandle

The history of Alaska began in its panhandle, a scenic fishing, timber, and mining area filled with thousands of wooded islands, mountains covered by glaciers, and waterfalls. The entire southeast of the state is the huge, wild **Tongass National Forest**. One of its glaciers, the Malaspina, is 40 miles wide and 28 miles long, with an area of some 1,500 square miles…that's the same size as Rhode Island. Lonely, isolated towns are blocked from the mainland by the Coastal Mountains.

Juneau: The capital

Juneau, the capital of Alaska, was founded 100 years ago as a fishing and gold-mining town. It has just over 30,000 residents, who are watched over by Mount Roberts and Mount Juneau. Behind the state capitol is **Gold Creek**, where a mining museum shows what it was like to tunnel through the mountains. North of town is the splendid **Mendenhall Glacier**.

Juneau's best hotel is the **Westmark Baranof Hotel**, *127 North Franklin Street; tel. +1 (907) 586-2660; website: www.westmarkhotels.com/juneau.php*, located downtown.

Therapy in Alaska

Rest your weary bones in the hot-springs resort area of **Tenakee Springs** on Chichagof Island. The springs (about 107° F) are therapeutic. The town is made up of wooden houses on stilts connected by plank walkways.

Sitka: Where Russia meets America

Alaska's tourist center is **Sitka**, at the base of Mount Edgecumbe. When Alaska was part of Russia, this was its capital. You can still see the Slavic influence, especially in the Russian Orthodox cathedral. Visit the **Sitka National Historical Park,** at Lincoln Street and the Indian River. Here, Russians captured a Tlingit Indian stronghold in 1804. You can see totem poles, the battlefield, and a museum with displays of Tlingit and Russian culture.

Stay at the **Westmark Sitka**, *330 Seward Street, Sitka; tel. +1 (907) 747-6241; website: www.westmarkhotels.com/sitka.php*, which is decorated with native art, including a wall mural illustrating Tlingit history. A sunken living room surrounds the fireplace. The best views are from the rooms on the fifth floor.

Where the people are: Anchorage

Half of Alaska's population (about 280,000 people) lives in **Anchorage**. This big city boasts two daily newspapers, performances by celebrities and internationally recognized orchestras, theater, fast-food joints, glass and steel buildings, supermarkets, and department stores.

The best thing about Anchorage is its nightlife. This is where those with cabin fever go to let off steam. Bars, massage parlors, restaurants, nightclubs, and strip joints keep the money changing along Fourth Avenue and Spenard Road.

Visit the **Anchorage Museum**, *625 C Street; tel. +1 (907) 929-9200; website: www.anchoragemuseum.org,* which has recently been renovated and expanded.

Shop for the soft, warm clothing of Alaska at the **Oomingmak Musk Ox Cooperative**, *604 H Street; tel. +1 (907) 272-9225; website: www.qiviut.com.*

Alaska's best restaurants and hotel

Even hotel restaurants in Alaska, which is known for its seafood, are surprisingly good. The best restaurant is the **Crow's Nest**, at the Hotel Captain Cook, *939 W. 5th Avenue; tel. +1 (907) 276-6000; website: www.captaincook.com,* in Anchorage.

Other good restaurants include **Jen's Restaurant**, *36th Avenue at Arctic Blvd.; tel. +1 (907) 561-5367; website: www.jensrestaurant.com,* where everything—food, service, ambiance, wine list, etc.— is absolutely wonderful.

Simon and Seaforts Saloon and Grill, *410 L Street; tel. +1 (907) 274-3502; website: www.simonandseaforts.com,* offers not only great straight-forward seafood and steaks, but also some good raucous fun in a real saloon atmosphere

One of the state's best hotels is the **Hotel Captain Cook**, *939 W. 5th Avenue; tel. +1 (907) 276-6000; website: http://captaincook.com/,* which will seem like paradise after the rough cold of the Alaska wilderness. This is a world-class destination where anyone from movie stars to visiting royalty stay.

The largest island: Kodiak (with the biggest bears)

Kodiak, the largest island in the United States, is also the largest fishing port and the home of the king crab. This island, where you will see Russian architecture, has the oldest European settlement in Alaska. The Kodiak bear is the world's largest species of bear.

A heavenly sight

One of the most beautiful sights in Alaska can be seen from anywhere in the state. Electromagnetic fluctuations in the atmosphere and the magnetic pull of the North Pole create the magnificent spectacle of the **Aurora Borealis**, a rainbow of colors that glimmer on the horizon.

HAWAII: AMERICA'S PARADISE

The most beautiful place in the United States is halfway around the world—**Hawaii**. Long, sandy beaches, palm trees, jungles, exotic people, luxurious resorts, and the some of the world's best surfing combine to make this state a true paradise.

Maui, the second-largest of the Hawaiian Islands, has both luxury resorts and large undeveloped areas. The **Kaanapali Beach Hotel**, *2525 Kaanapali Parkway; tel. +1 (808) 661-0011 or +1 (800) 262-8450 (worldwide); website: www.kbhmaui.com*, has restaurants, shops, and a myriad of amenities.

The **Hyatt Regency Maui**, *200 Nohea Kai Drive; tel. +1 (808) 661-1234; website: http://maui.hyatt.com,* is basically an enormous spa with every facility imaginable for pampering yourself.

On the east coast of Maui is **Hana**, a ranch town (the drive here is breathtaking). Maui's best adventure is a helicopter ride over the **Haleakala Volcano**. You will see waterfalls and sacred pools, as well as the grave of Charles Lindbergh. You also can join a bicycle tour down Mount Haleakala. A van carries you to the rim of the volcano, where you enjoy breakfast and the sunrise. Then you coast downhill for 38 miles.

The most civilized island is **Oahu**, where Honolulu is located. The **Kahala Hotel and Resort**, *5000 Kahala Ave, Honolulu; tel. +1 (808) 739-8888; website: www.kahalaresort.com*, is superb, as is the **Halekulani**, *2199 Kalia Road; tel. +1 (808) 923-2311; website: www.halekulani.com*, arguably the islands most lavish and lovely hotel. While on the island, visit the Iolani Palace, the Bishop Museum, and Pearl Harbor.

Hawaii: The biggest island

Waterfalls, black-sand beaches, cliffs, surf, soft trade winds, and beautiful views make **Hawaii** gorgeous. The Big Island, as it is known (to avoid confusion with the state as a whole), is also the most historic, settled by Polynesians more than 1,000 years ago. The island has plantation towns, royal homes, missionary churches, and burial grounds. Its extraordinary resort hotels, which draw people from around the world, lie on the **Kohala Coast**. Hawaii is a 93-mile-long diamond-shaped island with four active volcanoes. A trip around the island leads past fields of sugarcane, rainforests with wild orchids, steam vents, volcanoes, black-sand beaches, petroglyphs, ancient temples, coffee trees, shacks, grasslands, and cacti. While exploring Hawaii, you may also see the Night Marchers, ghost warriors who chant along the ancient **King's Trail**, which winds through several resorts.

The **Puuhonua O Honaunau National Historical Park** was a place of refuge, where Hawaiians could escape the king's wrath in ancient times. Near the town of **Hawi** is the birthplace of Kamehameha, the first king to rule all the islands. Nearby is the **Mo'okini Heiau**, a temple dating back to A.D. 480, still cared for by the Mo'okini family, which has watched over it since it was built.

The beach town of **Kailua** has reasonably priced hotels, fishing charters, shops, and stone churches built in the 1800s. **Hulihee Palace**, now a museum, provides a view of the harbor. Built as a summer palace for Hawaiian royalty, its architecture is a curious blend of elements from New England, France, England, and Hawaii.

Hawaii Volcanos National Park encompasses the island's two active volcanoes: **Kilauea** and **Mauna Loa**. An 11-mile drive circles Kilauea's huge collapsed summit, or caldera, which passes near man-size lava tubes and the **Halemaumau**, a fire pit where the goddess Pele is said to live.

The most beautiful drive is along the **Chain of Craters Road**, which winds 25 miles down Kilauea and takes you as close as you are permitted (and as close as you would want to get) to **Puu Oo Vent**, which erupts regularly.

Mauna Kea is the best place on earth to conduct infrared studies. This peak is 13,796 feet above a huge, dark ocean, protected from the lights of civilization; it is also above 40% of the earth's atmosphere.

The **Mauna Kea Observatory,** *website: www.ifa.hawaii.edu/mko/ maunakea.htm,* has 13 working astronomical telescopes, operated by astronomers from 11 countries.

Kauai: The lushest isle

Kauai, the fourth-largest Hawaiian island, is the most beautiful. *The Thorn Birds*, *Raiders of the Lost Ark*, and *South Pacific* were filmed here. The **Na Pali Coast**, which can be reached by helicopter, is the island's most spectacular area. Even the air seems green on this lush island. Waterfalls cascade down sharp peaks into the **Hanalai River**. Orchids and ginger plants line the river, which meanders through taro fields toward the sea. Three beautiful parks line Hanalei Bay: Hanalei Beach Park, Hanalei Pavilion, and Waioli Beach Park. Two large peaks, Hihimanu and Namolokama, watch over the valley.

Waimea Canyon is often called the Grand Canyon of the Pacific. It is 3,600 feet deep and 10 miles long. Its valleys are green, and its ridges are blanketed with flowers. The **Kukui Trail** leads down 2,000 feet to the fertile canyon floor, where you can explore ancient Hawaiian ruins.

The wettest place on earth is **Mount Waialeale**, where 450 inches of rainfall each year.

On the western slope of this 5,080-foot peak lies the **Alakai Swamp**, a 10-mile area where birds and plants (but no mosquitoes) flourish.

The **Pihea Trail** (which translates as *Din of Voices*) leads to the swamp, where giant ferns and tree-size violets grow.

Hawaii's most luxurious resorts

Honolulu has two grand hotels: the **Moana Surfrider Resort** and the **Royal Hawaiian**.

The **Moana Surfrider**, *2365 Kalakaua Ave.; tel. +1 (808) 922-3111; website: www.moana-surfrider.com,* one of Hawaii's first hotels, opened in 1901. Robert Louis Stevenson came here to write. The 75-room white clapboard hotel is of classic South Seas design, with several verandas overlooking the beach.

The **Royal Hawaiian,** *2259 Kalakaua Ave.; tel. +1 (808) 923-7311; website: www.royal-hawaiian.com,* is a pink Moorish-style palace built in the 1920s. The hotel's first guest was Princess Kawanakoa, who would have been queen of Hawaii if the islands had been left alone. The hotel is on the beach and has a pool.

The **Kahala Hotel and Resort**, *5000 Kahala Ave., Honolulu; tel. +1 (808) 739-8888; website: www.kahalaresort.com,* is a first-class hotel where presidents and celebrities like to stay. Along with every amenity under the sun, it also has a pool where you can swim with the dolphins.

The **Mauna Kea Beach Hotel**, *62-100 Mauna Kea Beach Drive, Kohala Coast; tel. +1 (808) 882-7222; website: www.princeresortshawaii.com/ mauna-kea-beach-hotel*, was built in July 1965 by Laurence Rockefeller on the white sands at Kaunaoa Bay.

THE BEST OF
URUGUAY

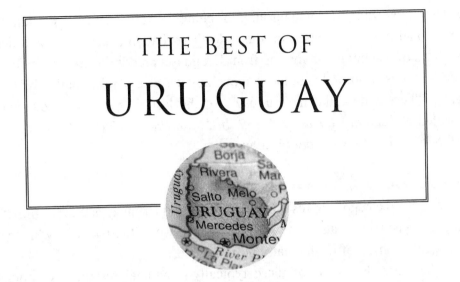

Uruguay has been a well-kept secret in South America, but the secret is getting out quickly. Every year that goes by, more and more people come to visit, and many even stay on to live in this tiny country.

Nestled on the South Atlantic coast between Argentina and Brazil, Uruguay sits between 30° and 35° southern latitude, which is about the equivalent of both the Carolinas and Georgia in the northern hemisphere. The seasons in Uruguay of course, are the opposite of those in the northern hemisphere.

With only three million people, Uruguay is one of South America's smallest countries; about the size of the U.S. state of Missouri. Uruguay was in turn a Portuguese, Spanish, and Brazilian territory. Yet while the language in Uruguay is Spanish, the largest cultural influence in the country is Italian…something you'll readily spot in Uruguay's food and customs.

Some people come to Uruguay to enjoy the elegant city life…or perhaps visit a beautifully-restored Portuguese-Spanish colonial city. Others come to see the vast stretches of rolling *pampas*, with gauchos still tending their herds…or maybe to enjoy the high life at South America's premier beach resort.

That's the beauty of Uruguay…it's all here, among First-World conditions, friendly people, and at reasonable prices.

The best restaurant in Montevideo's old city

Montevideo's Ciudad Vieja is known for its fine dining, charming cafes and night spots. So it's a tough call to pick a single best restaurant here. But time after time, the elegant **Panini's** has come through for being the "best in class". Its sumptuous international menu is focused on their Northern Italian specialties…and despite the wealth of restaurants stemming from Uruguay's predominantly-Italian culture, Panini's stands head-and-shoulders above anyone else. And remarkably, they've won the "best wine cellar in Uruguay" for the last six years in a row. Panini's is located at *Peatonal Bacacay #1339, in Montevideo's Ciudad Vieja; tel. +598 2916-8760; website: www.paninis.com.uy.*

The best *Parrilla* in Montevideo

A special category of restaurant found around Uruguay is the *Parrilla*. It's an eating establishment that, at its heart, has a huge wood-fired grill on which you'll find a sizzling array of fresh meats and vegetables.

There are thousands of these typically-provincial restaurants throughout Uruguay. But the best in Montevideo is an upscale version; **Locos de Asar,** *San José #1065, Centro district; website: www.locosdeasar.com.* Their great menu, quiet, romantic ambiance and excellent service distinguish them from anyone else.

Montevideo's best tango club

The tango culture is big in Uruguay, and there are a number of clubs where this signature regional dance is featured. But you won't find anything like the tiny club called **Fun Fun**; *Ciudadela #1229; tel. +598 2915-8005; website: www.barfunfun. com/funfun_eng.htm*; an institution in Montevideo since 1895. It's possible to live in downtown Montevideo for years and not even know it's there…since by day, Fun Fun looks like an abandoned building. But for over a century, nighttime has attracted some of the city's best tango singers and professional dancers, along with a handful of internationally-famous names. Fun Fun is not fancy…but it's the best place to go to enjoy a great evening of local tango.

If you want an even simpler version of local tango, walk up Avenue 18 de Julio a few blocks to **Plaza del Entrevero,** *Avenida 18 de Julio,* between *Julio Herrera y Obés* and *Rio Negro.* Here in this beautiful park on Saturday night, you'll find a boom box set up, playing old tango favorites from years gone by. As the sound of old scratchy records fills the neighborhood with music, couples from the area will dance the tango as most of the neighborhood gathers around and looks on.

Uruguay's best beach resort

Uruguay is home to South America's premier beach resort, **Punta del Este**. It's a town that boasts miles of sandy beaches bordering deep blue waters…not to mention the country's hottest nightclubs, the best casinos and shows, and its highest concentration of fine restaurants.

The world's rich and famous have descended on Punta de Este each summer for more than a century, with today's part-year residents including the likes of actor Michael Caine, rock star Shakira, and even Carlos Slim, the world's richest man. Punta del Este is accessible via its own international airport, as well as Montevideo's, about 1.5 hours to the west.

Punta del Este's best restaurant

There are plenty of elegant restaurants around Punta del Este, and you can easily spend over $400 for lunch if you're so inclined. But the best town has long been **Isidora**, *Rambla and Calle 21 (overlooking the marina); tel. +598 4244-9646; website: www.isidora.com.uy*, a waterfront restaurant that offers excellent cuisine at reasonable prices…along with a peaceful view of the marina, Gorriti Island, and the dazzling evening sunset.

When you visit, be sure to sample their *chipirones a la plancha*, a local signature dish of sautéed baby calamari that Isidora prepares better than anyone. Another unique favorite is *Pollo Manhattan*, a rich, creamy chicken dish that we haven't seen elsewhere. The service here is the best in the city.

Uruguay's best colonial city

Founded by the Portuguese in the 1680s as a trading post offering contraband priced lower than neighboring Buenos Aires, **Colonia de Sacramento** is Uruguay's most-treasured colonial gem. Colonia is a UNESCO World Heritage Site, and when you see it you'll understand why.

The 17th-century Portuguese stone architecture is in a splendid state of preservation and restoration. And you can even see some interesting architectural modifications made by the Spanish, when they settled the area in the following century.

Colonia is the perfect town for strolling. You can spend a leisurely afternoon walking its old cobblestoned streets, admiring its fine stone buildings, or shopping in its elegant boutiques. The fine dining and sidewalk cafes in Colonia are among the best in the country.

Located just 28 miles across the river from Buenos Aires (a 50-minute ferry ride), Colonia also has a quiet marina, over which you can watch some of the country's best sunsets.

South America's best football

In 2011, Uruguay's football team (soccer team) once again proved their superiority in the region by winning the *Copa América*—for a record-setting 15th time—defeating the far-better known powerhouses of Brazil and Argentina.

THE BEST OF
VENEZUELA

Venezuela is a land of contrasts that has remained unchanged for thousands of years. The country boasts the world's largest falls, Angel Falls (3,212 feet), impenetrable rainforests, and an abundance of wildlife and lush vegetation. Then there's Caracas, Maracaibo, and other coastal towns, where the concrete and skyscrapers remind you that you are still in the 21st century.

THE FASTEST-GROWING CITY—CARACAS

Caracas, Venezuela's capital, is modern, boasting an efficient and inexpensive metro system, as well as theaters, concert halls, and sports arenas. See the **Casa Natal del Libertador**, *Calle Traposos*, the birthplace of Simon Bolivar and a museum; the **Museo de Bellas Artes**, *Plaza Morelos, Parque Los Caobos*, which has an excellent collection of contemporary art; and the **Museo de Arte Contemporaneo**, *edificio Anauco, Parque Central*, which has an exceptional display of cyber-kinetic art.

The best hotels in Caracas
The best place to stay in the city is the **Hotel Paseo Las Mercedes,** *Avenida Principal de Las Mercedes; tel. +58 (212) 993-2387; website: www.hotelpaseolasmercedes.com.*

The best cuisine in Caracas

For a Venezuelan meat fest, try **Maute Grill**, *Av. Rio de Janeiro, between Calles New York and Trinidad, Quinta el Portal, Las Mercedes; tel. +58 (212) 991-0892.* With a huge central indoor courtyard, this is a popular spot and will serve your steak to your exact specifications.

Another favorite is **Barba Roja**, *Avenida Tamanaco; tel. +58 (212) 951-1062,* in the Rosal section. The food is Spanish with an emphasis on fish dishes. Try the *hayaca navidena*, a pastry made of light corn flour.

MERIDA: VENEZUELANS' FAVORITE CITY

If you ask a Venezuelan what his favorite city is, nine out of 10 times he'll name **Merida**. The climate in this city, which is located about an hour west of Caracas at the foot of the Andes, is close to ideal. Merida lies in the Chama River Valley, where small farms bordered with ancient stone walls are still cultivated by oxen. Local craftsmen who sell alpaca blankets, sweaters, and other handicrafts line the roads. Merida is also home to an impressive, though austere, cathedral and the University of the Andes.

THE BEST BONE-JARRING TRAILS—THE GRAN SABANA

The journey through **Canaima National Park** in Venezuela's Gran Sabana is a succession of surprises. There are no tour buses, no airplanes, and no schedules. There are also very few tourists. The only thing you can count on here is the scenery, which is world-class. The Gran Sabana is the remains of an ancient plateau in southeastern Venezuela. The heart of the savanna is almost uninhabited and is protected by Canaima National Park, the third largest national park in the world.

Journeying the Gran Sabana

Do not attempt to make your way through the Gran Sabana without a guide who knows his way across this unmarked and unmapped terrain. To arrange a trip through the Gran Sabana, visit *www.lastfrontiers.com*.

ANGEL FALLS: THE WORLD'S LARGEST FALLS

The most famous landmark in Canaima National Park is **Angel Falls**, which plunges 3,280 feet from Auyan-Tepui (Devil's Mountain). Thousands of tourists fly by Angel Falls every year—or fly to stay at the comfortable Canaima camp a few miles from the falls.

SECTION TWO

THE WORLD'S BEST HONEYMOON DESTINATIONS

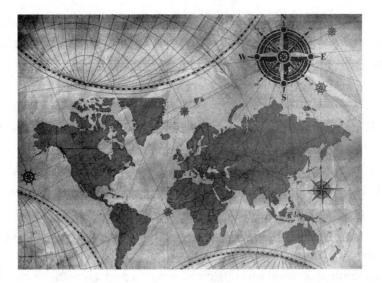

PARIS: THE WORLD'S MOST ROMANTIC CITY

Few would argue that Paris is not the most romantic city in the world, and one of the best destinations for lovers.

The most romantic restaurants in Paris

The number-one most romantic restaurant in Paris is **Le Grand Vefour**, *17 rue de Beaujolais; tel. +33 (1) 4296-5627; website: www.relaischateaux.com/vefour*, a three-star restaurant built in 1784 at the north end of the Palais Royal. Napoleon is said to have courted Josephine here. Chef Guy Martin's cuisine has been described as "inventive flights of fancy reaching new heights." Expensive…but a good ambience. It is closed on Saturday and Sunday.

    The Jules Verne, *tel. +33 (1) 4555-6144*; *website: www.lejulesverne-paris. com*, on the second level of the Eiffel Tower offers, without question, one of Paris' finest views. And the dark interiors are perfect for romance. Unfortunately, the food doesn't live up to the price, and you may be intruded on by tourists who don't know how to whisper. Nevertheless, the atmosphere is as romantic as it gets.

THE MOST ROMANTIC TOWN ON THE FRENCH RIVIERA

Antibes, the center of the perfume market, has lovely beaches, a small port, and a colorful fruit and flower market. The best place to stay in this romantic town is the **Hotel du Cap-Eden Roc**, *tel. +33 (4) 9361-3901; website: www. hotel-du-cap-eden-roc.com*. It was a favorite of Scott and Zelda Fitzgerald because of its glamorous and romantic atmosphere.

THE MOST ROMANTIC HOTEL ON THE AMALFI COAST

Hotel San Pietro, *tel. +39 (89) 875-455; website: www.ilsanpietro.it*, is a cantilevered castle built into a cliffside in **Positano** on the Amalfi Coast. Every room faces the sea and has a sweeping view. While each room is different, they all have private gardens. Balconies with painted tiles, arches, antiques, and bouquets of flowers give you your own view of the foaming sea. You can descend through the mountain to swim and sunbathe, watch the fishermen come and go in their boats, shop for Italian pottery, or sit back and relax by the bay. A double room is $550 a night.

THE MOST ROMANTIC HOTEL IN AUSTRIA

The **Schloss Durnstein**, *tel. +43 (2) 711-212*; *website: www.schloss.at,* presides over a wide curve of the Danube River. Located deep in the wine district of Wachau, this magnificent castle is surrounded by distinctive vine-clad hills, age-old ruins, and timeless picturesque villages with one-lane streets. According to legend, it was here that the imprisoned Kind Richard the Lionhearted was reunited with his faithful minstrel, who had sung his way across Europe searching for his master. Also intriguing is the wine cellar (which can accommodate 8,000 "buckets" of wine), the arch-crossed cobbled courtyard, and the 33 chandeliered chambers fronting the Danube.

ENGLAND'S MOST ROMANTIC B&B

Hope End, *Ledbury; tel. +44 (1531) 635-890; wesite: www.hopeendhouse.com,* is one of the most alluring B&Bs in England. Located in the coach house and stables of the house where Elizabeth Barrett Browning lived for 23 years, it is cozy and serves delicious meals.

MENORCA, SPAIN'S MOST ROMANTIC ISLE

Menorca, the most romantic of the Balearic Islands, is the kind of spot you might want to escape to on your honeymoon, as Princess Grace and Prince Rainier did. Traveling from one end of the island to the other on its narrow, winding roads, you will probably encounter no one, save the unobtrusive sheep on the hillsides. Menorca is lush and hilly but not mountainous. Menorca is said to have 120 coves with beaches, most unpeopled. The most deserted beach is **Sambal**, which is four miles long. Lobster and bouillabaisse are served at **Es Pla**, *tel. +34 (971) 376-655,* a restaurant famous for its breathtaking setting on the waterfront. The best hotel on the island is **Port Mahon**, *tel. +34 (971)362-600; website: www.sethotels.com/en/ hotel-port-mahon-menorca.php.*

NIAGARA FALLS: AMERICA'S BEST HONEYMOON SPOT

You'll hear **Niagara Falls** long before you see it. This 180-foot waterfall, which pours 40 million gallons of water a minute, is actually made up of three great torrents: **Canada's Horseshoe Falls**, the **American Falls**, and **Bridal Veil Falls**. Horseshoe is the most spectacular, so you should definitely see this natural wonder from both the U.S. and Canadian sides.

The best way to see Niagara is aboard the *Maid of the Mist*, which departs Prospect Park and the landing on the American side. Another good way to see the falls is from the Observation Tower in Prospect Park. You can also view the cascade from below. Take an elevator 125 feet down to the **Scenic Tunnels**, which lead to a two-level observation deck near Horseshoe Falls. Wear a slicker; it's wet. Bridges and wooden walkways lead across the base of Bridal Veil Falls, within 25 feet of the river, to the **Cave of the Winds** below Goat Island. The roar of the water and the heavy spray are overwhelming.

THE MOST ROMANTIC TOWN ON VANCOUVER ISLAND

One of the loveliest places on the island is **Parksville**, a little town off Route 19 on the east coast. From the highway, the town doesn't look like much—a few trailers and gift shops. But behind the ever-present towering pines are wide beaches with calm, clear waters. On the horizon are purple, snow-topped mountain ranges. The beach extends out for nearly a mile at low tide, and sea lions cavort not far from land. The water is surprisingly warm as early as May.

Tigh Na Mara Resort, *tel. (800) 663-7373; website: www.tigh-na-mara. com*, has the most romantic accommodation on Vancouver Island. You stay in log cabins (with fireplaces) next to the beach and have use of a Jacuzzi, canoes, paddleboats, and rowboats.

THE MOST ROMANTIC RESORT IN ST. THOMAS

Each of the 25 rooms at the St. Thomas resort known as **Pavilions and Pools**, *tel. (800) 524-2025; website: http://pavilionsandpools.com*, has its own freshwater pool set inside a private and secluded garden. All units are one-bedroom villas with kitchenettes, and all are within walking distance of two beautiful white-sand beaches. This is undoubtedly the best place on the island for a romantic getaway or honeymoon.

THE MOST ROMANTIC HOTEL IN THE CARIBBEAN

Tucked into Maunday Bay on Anguilla is the ultimate Caribbean hideaway. With its villas of soft white arches, tiled roofs, and covered terraces that face long, creamy beaches, **Cap Juluca**, *tel. +1 (264) 497-6666; website: www.capju-luca.com*, offers secluded island beauty. The sunset sail on Cap Juluca's yacht to offshore cays, with a silver service picnic prepared by seven members of the crew, is particularly recommended. Other noble pursuits include Sunfish sailing, Hobie cat voyages, windsurfing, deep-sea fishing, and water-skiing.

THE MOST ROMANTIC RESORT IN THE BAHAMAS

Fernandez Bay Village, *tel. +1 (954) 474-4821; website: www.fernandezbayvil-lage.com*, one of only three establishments on **Cat Island**, is nothing less than spectacular. With no major towns, and only occasional hamlets on the island's one main road, Fernandez Bay is a focal point for the area. But it's more like a sailor's retreat than a social center. Before bags are unpacked, guests are pointed toward a thatched-roof circular bar and veranda just a few feet from the water's edge. The bar, like all the resort's facilities, happily goes unmanned most of the time. The Armbristers (the owners) invite guests to help themselves on the "honor system." The best part of the day is dinnertime. Just before nightfall, barefoot guests begin their nightly stroll to the dining area to join the Armbristers and staff for cocktails. Travelers from all over the world meet at the open-air restaurant by the sea to trade tales of the day's events. The food is delicious and served buffet-style in a relaxed atmosphere.

THE BEST HONEYMOON SPOT IN BERMUDA

The **Elbow Beach Hotel**, *tel. +1 (441) 236-3535; website: www.mandarinoriental.com/bermuda*, is a jet set—and romantic—place to stay on the island. You can choose either a spacious room in the main hotel or an ocean-view suite tucked away in the hotel's botanical gardens. A private ocean beach is at your doorstep, as well as a beautiful pool, a health club, and six distinctive bars.

THE BEST PLACE TO HONEYMOON IN MACAU

Pousada de Sao Tiago, tel. *+853 2837-8111; website: www.saotiago.com.mo*, became a hotel in 1980 and every historical feature was preserved during the transformation, including the Portuguese marble, hand-painted tiles, ancient stone walls, gentle cascades, hand-covered mahogany, and even the trees that shade the multilevel terraces. This hotel overlooks the South China Sea and is enveloped in warm, salty breezes.

SECTION THREE

THE WORLD'S BEST BEACHES

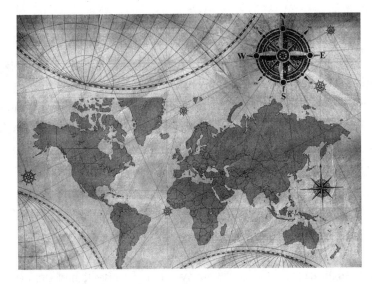

BRITAIN'S MOST REGAL BEACH RESORT

The seaside town of **Brighton** became popular with aristocrats in the mid-18th century. (It later lost standing and became a big favorite of P.G. Wodehouse's Jeeves, the butler, who liked to fish here.) Brighton was originally a tiny fishing village that is mentioned in the Domesday Book. The best walks in Brighton are along Old Steine, which is the center of activity; out to the Palace Pier, a Victorian structure that juts nearly a third of a mile into the English Channel; and along the Marine Parade, an attractive promenade with 19th-century terraces.

The biggest attraction in the town is the restored **Royal Pavilion**, a pseudo-Oriental structure built by the Prince Regent, George, Prince of Wales (later King George IV) from 1787 to 1822. The pavilion graphically demonstrates the excesses and extravagances of the Regency period.

If you tire of the sun—or rain—the most inviting places for tea are the lounge of the Hilton Brighton Metropole (*website: www.hilton.co.uk/brightonmet*) and the veranda of The Grand (rebuilt after the IRA bombed it in 1984 in an attempt on the life of Margaret Thatcher); *website: www.devere.co.uk/our-locations/the-grand.*

FRANCE'S MOST BEAUTIFUL BEACH

The most beautiful beach in France is **Étretat**, in Normandy. Two magnificent white cliffs loom above the wide, rocky beach. While the beach is gorgeous, it's not particularly comfortable but, because of this, it's never crowded.

GERMANY'S BEST BEACHES

Few visitors realize that, as well as medieval villages and deep forests, Germany boasts beautiful beaches. The **East Frisian Islands**, which fringe the North Sea coastline, have long sandy beaches guarded by dunes and frequented by nude sunbathers. The islands also have fishing villages, seal-covered rocks, and an ancient language and culture. For more information on the East Frisian Islands, visit the tourist office in the railroad station in Oldenburg.

THE BEST BEACH IN SARDINIA

La Costa del Sud, about 31 miles southwest of Cagliari, has unspoiled beaches and hidden coves. The water is turquoise and perfectly clear. Buses run to the coast from Cagliari as far as the beach near the Torre di Chia. But the next beach over, Capo Spartivento, is larger and has two lovely islands that are great for sunbathing.

SPAIN'S BEST BEACHES

Costa de Almería: The most peaceful beaches
Spain's most peaceful beaches are along the relatively undiscovered **Costa de Almeria**. Stretching 120 miles between Almeria and Cartagena on the south-eastern edge of Spain, the coast retains much of its original charm and still has reasonable prices.

CROATIA'S BEST BEACH

The nicest beach on the entire coastline is at the south end of the island of **Krk**, a half-hour boat ride from Rijeka. Krk is a strangely beautiful place with a barren valley surrounded by stern, stony hills. The island has numerous small hotels.

SLOVENIA—THE MOST GLAMOROUS BEACHES

The **Slovenian Riviera**—the area from the Italian border to the end of the Istrian Peninsula's west coast—is the most glamorous stretch along the coast. It feels like Italy. **Izola** and **Piran** are attractive resort towns along the Slovenian Riviera—both resemble old-style Italian resorts. **Potoroz**, a more modern resort, is the most expensive.

INDIA'S BEST BEACHES

Hugging the coast of the Bay of Bengal, **Marine Beach**, is the most beautiful beach in Madras, if not the world. It has fine sand and is lined with walkways and gardens.

GREECE'S BEST BEACHES

Skiathos has the best sand beaches (most beaches in Greece are pebbly) and its Old Town section is charming. Not as tourist-trodden as the other, better-developed islands, such as Corfu, Rhodes, and Mykonos, Skiathos is said to be the Greeks' favorite island. Its large British expatriate community colors its cultural atmosphere. A few of the resident artists are British. English pubs are sprinkled among the alleyways of the Old Town. Vacation amenities include water-skiing, windsurfing, and boating; yet those who want to get away from it all will find a sense of privacy. Small boats gather on the town waterfront each morning to offer tourists excursions to nearby islands, beaches, and the Kastro, a castle ruin on the other side. The best-organized trip is to an uninhabited island across from the town, which has a beautiful beach with flowers growing in the sand and a myriad of butterflies.

THE BEST OF AFRICA'S BEACHES

Kenya's best beach
Kenya has 300 miles of glorious beaches along the Indian Ocean. The white-sand beaches, edged with palms, are protected from pollution and sharks by reefs. Beyond the palm trees is the forest, inhabited by leopards, Colobus monkeys, and brightly colored birds.

South Africa's best beaches

With more than 100 gorgeous white-sand beaches to choose from, the Cape Peninsula has some of the best coastline in Africa. Discerning sun worshipers prefer **Clifton** beach, with its mountainous backdrop. Another favorite is **Muizenberg**, a seaside resort town within 22 miles of beach.

Senegal's best beach

Cap Slurring in Joal is an unspoiled, dazzling white beach fringed by coconut trees. **Club Med** has a highly recommended outpost here. Watch out for sharks (not just the human kind). The resort is closed during the summer (monsoon season).

The least expensive place to stay is **Le Campement**, a government-run accommodation made up of little concrete huts on the water. For a few dollars, you can spend the night on foam pads under clean sheets and enjoy good local food.

The Egyptian Riviera

In the summer, Muslim Egyptians crowd Alexandria's beaches, where the temperature is an average 15 degrees cooler than in Cairo. The beaches are beautiful and the water clear, but Egypt's **Riviera** is crowded and cluttered. And remember, this is a Muslim beach, so don't wear bikinis or daring swimsuits. **Corniche**, the 15-mile road along the coast, is lined with houses, hotels, shops, and palm trees. At the eastern tip of Alexandria's stretch of beaches is the **Montaza Palace and Gardens**, a huge complex that includes gardens, beaches, and hotels. Just east of Montaza is **Ma'amura**, a cleaner, relatively isolated beach where the people have more Western tastes in swimwear. However, true beach lovers will best enjoy Egypt's beach resorts along the Sinai and Red Sea.

The best beaches in Morocco

Agadir, in southwest Morocco, is the country's playground. It has a white-sand beach and all the sun and water sports anyone could want. And, unlike most of the world's beach towns, Agadir doesn't scream commercialism and tourism. Destroyed by an earthquake in 1960, Agadir has been completely rebuilt. But its main attraction is still its beach, which is a pleasant 10-minute walk from the center of town. To get there, you meander down a terraced hillside covered with greenery and flowering plants. Along the beach runs a wide walk of marble, which is lined with open-air cafés facing the water. In the background are the **Anti-Atlas Mountains**.

Agadir enjoys more than 300 days of sun a year. And the temperature is always between 66 and 82 °F. Its white-sand beaches are as beautiful as you'll find anywhere, and its water as blue. It is easy to see why European sun seekers flock here year-round. Agadir can be expensive and crowded because of its thriving tourist industry, however. If you're looking for space and a bit of private beach, head north from Agadir, where you'll find sandy coves every few miles.

ISRAEL'S BEST BEACH

Acre is one of the oldest (it existed more than 3,500 years ago) and most picturesque cities in the world. Surrounded by thick seawalls on the tip of a point of land, the city is fringed with palm trees and punctuated with minarets. Only 14 miles north of Haifa, it was an important Phoenician port and later served as a capital for the Crusaders.

On the southern edge of Acre is the **Argaman**, or purple beach, the most beautiful beach on the coast, with crystal-clear water. Acre was the site of the largest prison break in history. On May 4, 1947, 251 prisoners were freed from the prison known as the Fortress by Jewish underground fighters. The movie *Exodus*, which is about the escape, was filmed here. Part of the prison, known as the Museum of Heroes, contains Jewish memorabilia and the cell where prophet of the Bahai Faith, Bahá'u'lláh, was imprisoned in the 1860s.

THE BEST BEACHES IN AUSTRALIA

Sydney's best beach

Sydney has 34 ocean beaches, each with its own style. If you are looking for peace and quiet, try Whale, Avalon, or Bilgola. But if you want to see a Sydney beach at its best—filled with perfect bodies, sun-streaked blonds, surf bums, and joggers, all in a sunny mood—go to Bondi.

Bondi (pronounced Bond-Eye) has produced many world-champion surfers. The half-mile crescent of sand and surf is filled from dawn to dusk with surfers, sunbathers, and swimmers. Snacks and drinks are available at Bondi Junction, near the beach. Bondi's neighbor, **Tamarama Beach**, is smaller, prettier, and more peaceful.

Surfer's Paradise: The best of the Gold Coast

Just south of Brisbane is **Surfer's Paradise**, the largest and liveliest resort on Australia's 20-mile Gold Coast. The sandy beaches are perfect, the water warm, the surf, as you would expect, terrific—and behind it all are the MacPherson Mountains. Believe it or not, the beach here is even better than in Hawaii. However, the crowds can be unbearable, especially around Christmas and Easter.

NEW ZEALAND: NORTH ISLAND'S BEST BEACHES

Doubtless Bay is a crescent of perfect sandy beaches that draws throngs on holidays. Houhora is a beach favored by fishermen, picnickers, campers, and smugglers.

Ninety Mile Beach (which is only 57 miles long) is a seemingly endless stretch of golden sandy beaches lined with dunes and embroidered with seashells. This is the scene of a popular fishing contest each summer and the prime spot to find toheroa, a much sought-after shellfish.

The hottest beach

The **Coromandel Peninsula,** on the east coast of North Island, has New Zealand's hottest (and strangest) swimming spot: **Hot Water Beach**. Named for the hot springs that seep through its sand, the beach literally steams. You can create your own thermal pool by digging into the sand.

The peninsula is also a mecca of alternative lifestyles and naturalists. The back-to-nature movement remains as healthy here today as it was in the United States in the 1960s. You can see how hippies have evolved over the past 40-odd years—bringing communal life into the electromagnetic age by constructing recording studios on their farms, for example.

THE BEST OF THE U.S.'S BEACHES

New York's best beaches

While New York isn't known as a beach town, it does have 20 miles of beaches. The best are **Rockaway Beach** (not Far Rockaway, which is seedy) and **Jones Beach**; the worst is **Coney Island**, which has become a slum.

Take the A or CC subway train to Rockaway, the Long Island Railroad to Jones. **Brighton Beach** is a Russian enclave called Odessa by the Sea.

Florida's most peaceful beaches

Most people think of the Atlantic Coast when they think of Florida. But some of the prettiest and least crowded beaches are along the Gulf of Mexico. **Pensacola Beach**, on the panhandle, has fine, white sand and temperate, clear water. **Fort Walton Beach** is attractive and has a 1,200-foot observation pier. Farther south are the white-sand beaches of **Belleair** and **Clearwater**. The finest sand is at **Madeira** and **Redington** beaches.

Long Boat Key is posh and not too crowded. **Point O'Rocks**, an isolated beach near Siesta Key, is famous for its colorful rocks. **Venice Beach** is known for the sharks' teeth that wash up on shore. **Fort Myers Beach** has the most beautiful sunsets. And **Sanibel** and **Captiva** islands are the best places in the state to look for seashells.

Our favorite hotel on the Gulf of Mexico is the **Don CeSar** on St. Petersburg Beach, *tel. +1 (727) 360-1881 website: www.doncesar.com*; an amazing pink Spanish-style castle surrounded by palm trees overlooking the ocean. Once the hideaway of F. Scott Fitzgerald, it is the playground of celebrities.

Where the action is: The Atlantic Coast

The Gulf of Mexico is nice, but the surf and the crowds are more exciting on the Atlantic. **Daytona Beach** has 23 miles of sandy beach and a boardwalk. Highrise hotels and condominiums line the ocean. Alas, cars can drive on the beach (a real nuisance).

The most beautiful dunes and beaches along the Atlantic Coast are at **Ponte Vedra** and **South Ponte Vedra** beaches, where two exclusive resorts are located: the Sawgrass and the Ponte Vedra Inn.

The quietest East Coast beach is **New Smyrna**, between Daytona Beach and Titusville. One of the state's last unspoiled beaches is **Playalinda**, part of the Canaveral National Seashore.

Southern Florida's Atlantic Coast has some of the world's most famous resort towns: **Palm Beach**, **Fort Lauderdale**, and **Miami Beach**. College students flock here for spring vacation, and Americans in general migrate here during the winter.

Our favorite place to stay on Florida's Atlantic Coast is the **Breakers**, *One South County Road, Palm Beach; tel. +1 (561) 655-6611; website: www.thebreakers. com.* The lobby of this grand Italianate resort has frescoed vaulted ceilings and 15th-century Flemish tapestries. The original Breakers, built in 1903, burned, as did the second. The present building was built in 1926. The National Register of Historic Places lists the Breakers as "culturally significant in its reflection of

20th-century grandeur." It has two 18-hole golf courses, a private beach with cabanas, 14 tennis courts, an outdoor saltwater pool, a sauna, lawn bowling, croquet, and programs for children. The hotel dining room is large, and its 100,000-bottle wine cellar is one of the world's biggest.

Fort Lauderdale has some of the finest beaches south of Daytona—and the best nightlife. **The Hyatt Regency Bonaventure**, *250 Racquet Club Road, Weston; tel. +1 (954) 616-1234; website http://bonaventure.hyatt.com*, is surrounded by palm trees and waters. You can put your body through a Swiss needle shower, a Shiatsu massage, or an herbal wrap.

Miami Beach is the most famous resort, drawing 13 million visitors each year to its luxurious beachfront hotels. South Beach's **Lummus Park** is the best beach area. Eighth Street in **Little Havana** is lined with great Cuban restaurants. The affluent **Coral Gables** neighborhood has more elegant restaurants.

Venice: Los Angeles' craziest beach

Venice, a crowded, crazy, somewhat seedy beach area on the edge of Los Angeles, is the best place in the city to people watch. **Ocean Front Boulevard**, a coastal walkway, is lined with vendors, street musicians, roller skaters, drug addicts, lovers, beach boys, gay people, senior citizens, artists, and tourists from all over the world. Venice was so named because of its many canals and Italian-style buildings. Abbot Kinney attempted to build an American Riviera here at the turn of the century, with canals and gondoliers.

MEXICO'S BEST BEACHES

Acapulco: Mexico's most sophisticated resort

Since the 1920s, the rich and famous have retreated to **Acapulco** every winter. The tropical Pacific Coast resort is famous for its fine beaches, luxury hotels, and deep-sea fishing facilities. Slim, tanned bodies line the beach, and colorful parasails float above it. Acapulco isn't quite as nice as it used to be. It has become a smoggy, crowded city with bumper-to-bumper traffic. And on the hills above the city, crowded, dirty barrios have developed that house the cheap labor serving the many hotels and restaurants.

Villa Fiore, *ave. Del Prado 6; tel. +52 (744) 484-2040*, serves good Italian food in a tropical garden. The place to stay, if you can afford it, is **Las Brisas**, *Carretera Escenica Clemente Mejia 5255; tel. +52 (744) 469-6900; website:*

www.brisashotelonline.com. Guests stay in individual casitas on a hill overlooking Acapulco Bay, surrounded by bougainvillea and hibiscus. Each little cottage has its own pool.

Mexico's most secluded beach

The most secluded, pristine stretch of white powder beach is at the **Si'aan Kaan Biosphere**, a nature preserve just outside of Tulum, on the Yucatan peninsula. These deserted beaches—dotted with coconut palm trees, populated by curious iguanas and sea birds, with azure blue water and total silence but for the roar of the surf—cannot be matched for tranquility and natural beauty.

The most seductive beaches

The Caribbean side of Cancun has the best beaches, with sand as soft as talcum powder, aquamarine water, and exhilarating waves. The beach in front of the **Hyatt Caribe Internacional Hotel**; *Av. Yaxchilan and Sunyaxchen*; *tel. +52 (998) 884-3999; website: www.caribeinternacional.com*, is especially pretty, shaded by coconut palms and studded with lounge chairs that can be used by anyone, not just guests at the hotel.

On Cozumel, the beaches north and south of San Miguel are superb. Most of the island's hotels hug these beach coves, so guests walk directly from their rooms onto the beach each morning. Because the currents off Cozumel are so unpredictable, you should never swim alone.

Isla Mujéres' most beautiful beach is **El Garrafón**. The beaches at Tortugas and Marias are less crowded, though.

SOUTH AMERICA'S BEST BEACHES

Rio de Janeiro in Brazil has spectacularly beautiful beaches—Botafogo, Copacabana, Ipanema, Leblon, São Conrado—where women, wearing the world's skimpiest bikinis, bask in the sun. Called tangos, the bikinis here consist of three tiny triangles of fabric held in place by lengths of string.

The prettiest beach is the one most distant from the center of the city, **São Conrado**, where the Hotel Intercontinental has taken root. This beach is not as crowded as Copacabana and Ipanema, and the water is cleaner. São Conrado is also the best place to go hang gliding—or just to watch the colorful gliders hover in the air for hours, held aloft by updrafts coming off the ocean and up the mountainside. They look like huge butterflies leisurely enjoying the afternoon sun.

Copacabana, lined with luxury hotels, restaurants, and nightclubs, is the chicest beach in South America. It is the longest and widest in Rio. Stroll along Avenida Atlântica, which is tiled with mosaics and lined with first-class hotels and expensive shops.

Close rivals of Copacabana are Ipanema (which is less congested and draws a younger crowd), Leblon, and Barra da Tijuca. The southern part of Ipanema is a fashionable residential area.

About 90 miles north of Rio is Cabo Frio, where forts and a 17th-century convent provide a dramatic backdrop to a wide, almost deserted beach. A word of caution: never take valuables to the beach—leave them in your hotel safe. Thieves from the nearby *favelas* (slums) roam the beaches looking for easy pickings, and they move quickly.

THE STANN CREEK DISTRICT: BELIZE'S NICEST BEACHES

If you're looking for a relaxing getaway where you won't see many other tourists and where you can sun yourself on the nicest beaches in the country, go to Placencia. The one dirt road that runs the length of the peninsula helps to make the area seem far away and a real escape.

COSTA RICA'S BEST BEACH

Cahuita beach is notable for its split personality: it has one beach of white sand and one of black sand. A wrecked Spanish galleon lies on a nearby coral reef; you can swim out to explore it.

The best place to eat in Cahuita

Cha Cha Cha, *tel. +506 8394-4153*, is a family-run restaurant in Cahuita. With local art adorning the walls the atmosphere here is laid back and relaxed in this open-air establishment. Their freshly caught seafood is delicious and the menu includes everything from jerk chicken to pasta and fajitas.

The best place to stay in Cahuita

Down the road from the Cahuita National Park Restaurant is a place called Atlantida Lodge, *tel. +506 2755-0115; website: www.atlantida.cr*. It's hidden back off the road but worth going out of your way to find. Each of the 30 cabins comes with a private bathroom, breakfast, and the use of a bicycle (necessary for beach hopping). Picnic tables and hammocks are set up on the grounds. There's even a mascot—a spider monkey who roams freely.

THE BEST BEACHES IN THE CARIBBEAN

St. Barthélemy: The beaches of the rich and famous

St. Barthélemy has the most gorgeous beaches in the Caribbean. This million-aire's island is dotted with vacation homes of such illustrious families as the Rockefellers and the Rothschilds. Mick Jagger, Peter Jennings, Beverly Sills, Mikhail Baryshnikov, and Billy Joel frequent this island. They are drawn to St. Barts (as the island is affectionately known) by the seductive languor of its lifestyle and its sophisticated French atmosphere.

The island's most beautiful beach is **Anse du Gouverneur**, on the south coast. The sand is as soft as talcum powder, and jagged cliffs protect the beach on two sides, giving it a secluded air. It is never crowded. Despite the jet-setters who frequent the island, life on St. Bart's is homey and small scale. However, it has become pricey. St. Barthélemy is one of only two completely free trading ports in the Caribbean (the other is St. Martin), and it sells French perfume and champagne at prices lower than in Paris.

St. Thomas's most beautiful beach

Magens Bay Beach, below Drake's Seat, is one of the most beautiful beaches in the world, according to *National Geographic*.

Martinique's best beaches

Martinique has both silvery beaches and rocky cliffs. Inland are rainforests and a volcano. The island's most appealing beaches, as well as several petrified wood savanna forests, are in **Ste. Anne**. The church in the center of town is planted with beautiful tamarind trees.

Off Martinique's coasts are the wrecks of 13 ships, which can be explored by scuba divers. For equipment, visit the Carib Scuba Club in Carbet.

Aruba: The world's most beautiful beaches

The southwest coast of the island of Aruba is fringed by seven miles of white-sand beaches, considered the most beautiful in the world. In fact, *Sports Illustrated* was so impressed that it featured the beaches in past Swimsuit Issues.

749

The best hotels in Aruba

The **Hyatt Regency Hotel,** *tel. +1 (297) 586-1234; website: www.aruba.hyatt.com,* is an elegant and dramatic-looking hotel. Though expensive, it definitely offers Aruba's best beds.

The most beautiful beach in Jamaica

Jamaica's longest, most beautiful white-sand beach is **Negril**, discovered by hippies almost two decades ago. The hippies have gone, but Negril is still a place for the younger crowd. Nude sunbathing is allowed on a section of the beach.

ROATAN'S BEST BEACH

West Bay Beach is arguably the best beach on the island…maybe the best beach in all the Bay Islands. The aqua blue water that is home to a large population of tropical fish surrounds the crescent-shaped, two-mile-long, gleaming white stretch of sand. Accommodation on this beach can be found by contacting *www.westbayvillage.com.* They can also arrange scuba diving and car rentals for you.

VENEZUELA'S BEST BEACHES

The beaches of **Tucacas** on the Caribbean Coast are part of Morrocoy National Park, and finding a nearly deserted stretch of sand is not a problem. **Cumana** has an isolated coastline protected by Mochimo National Park and is an important fishing center of Venezuela. Here you can find many undiscovered beaches while adventuring. Other great beaches in Venezuela include Cauataro, Cautarito, Los Matos, Puerto la Cruz, and Margarita Island. Rocky cliffs make them accessible only by sea.

SECTION FOUR

THE WORLD'S BEST
SPORTING DESTINATIONS

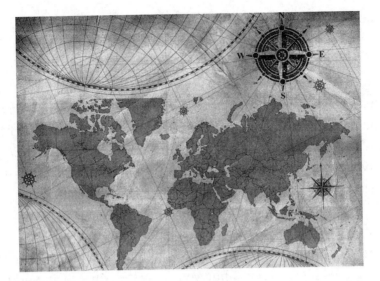

THE WORLD'S BEST SKIING

Austria's best skiing

The **Arlberg** region of Austria is the best place in the world for skiing. It offers a combination of features not duplicated anywhere else: a high altitude, which guarantees good snow; slopes for skiers of all levels of experience; interconnected villages that range from quaint to crowded to exclusive; serious ski instruction; and a cheery dose of Gemutlichkeit, or coziness. Some of the villages are large, such as Lech or St. Anton; others, including Zurs, are small and exclusive.

Innsbruck: The prettiest Alpine city

One of the prettiest Alpine cities, Innsbruck is also one of the biggest ski centers in Europe. The towering Alps can be seen from almost every street corner. Miles of cross-country skiing can be found outside Innsbruck, as well as the Olympic bobsled run, a ski jump, and a large ice-skating rink and hockey arena.

 Stubai Glacier, 25 miles from Innsbruck, is said to be the most exciting summer skiing around. For tickets, prices, and other information, view their website: *www.stubaier-gletscher.com.*

The best ski school

St. Anton is the best place to go for ski instruction, thanks to tradition and the city's 300 instructors. This is the cradle of modern skiing, where Hannes Schneider began teaching the now-accepted Arlberg School ski technique. The runs from the top of the Galzig and the Valuga (9,216 feet) are superb—as are the views. St. Anton is also a good place to go for nightlife.

The most exclusive resort

Zürs is a first-class ski resort where tour groups are discouraged. This place is for the skiing purist who also likes fine living. All the hotels in Zürs are first-class or better. The **Zürserhof**, *tel. +43 5583-25130; website: www.zuerserhof.at*, is an expensive five-star deluxe establishment that regularly attracts celebrities. It may be the best ski hotel in Austria.

The French Alps: The mightiest Alp and best resort

The mightiest Alp is **Mont Blanc**, Europe's highest peak, which rises 15,772 feet into the sky. A good place to stay while you enjoy the Alps is **Chamonix**, a convenient train ride from Paris. Many hiking trails and cable car rides radiate from this posh and expensive ski resort. For more information, see *www.chamonix.com*.

The best ride is from the téléphérique to the Aiguille du Midi. You'll hover thousands of feet above rocky drops and seas of ice. Try to take the ride in the morning, when the view is clearest. Wear warm clothes because it's chilly at the top! If you'd rather hike through the mountains, you can follow the miles of signposted trails. For more information, contact **Compagnie des Guides de Chamonix**; *tel. +33 (4) 5053-0088; e-mail: info@chamonix-guides.com; website: www.chamonix-guides.com;* the most popular ski resort in the French Alps.

The deep-powder snow and the variety of runs in the 13,000-foot mountain range attract experts from all over the world. The 12.4-mile glacier run down the Vallée Blanche is one of the most exciting in the world. For those who find skiing too tame, Chamonix also offers one of the newest thrills: parapente, which involves parachuting off steep vertical cliffs high in the mountains. You can also hang-glide in the mountains.

The best skiing in the German Alps

Garmisch-Partenkirchen; *website: www.gapa.de*, the most popular resort in the German Alps, offers Germany's best skiing. The powdery peaks are accessible via an assortment of lifts. Trails are geared toward every level of skier. A pretty town with gaily-painted alpine houses, Garmisch has après-ski entertainment, a casino, and concerts. Proximity to the American Army base, however, is causing the town to lose some of its Germanic charm. Nearby are Ludwig II's Linderhof Castle and the domed Benedictine abbey of Ettal.

The best bargain skiing in the Italian Alps

Cortina d'Ampezzo; *website: www.cortina.dolomiti.com,* in the eastern Dolomites, is Italy's most popular ski resort. Although it is very crowded, it has some of the best ski facilities in Italy. The area is huge—you can ski for days without doubling back to redo the same runs. When you tire of skiing, you can ice skate in what remains of the Olympic Stadium, shop in the town's many boutiques, or dine in one of its many restaurants.

Accommodation here is more expensive than in Mount Livata or Pescasseroli, nearby. The **Cristallo Hotel Spa & Golf**, *via R. Menardi 42; tel. +39 (0436) 881-111; website: www.cristallo.it,* has spacious, well-appointed rooms and a good restaurant. It is open from July to September and December to April.

In **Courmayeur** and **Cervinia**, you can ski in the summer as well as the winter. These towns are well known—and pricey for Italy. The Val dAyas is undiscovered and has lower lift prices (and more challenging runs).

Colfosco, a small, quiet ski village with numerous runs, attracts ardent downhill skiers. The area is best suited to beginning and intermediate skiers—it offers little cross-country skiing and no deep-powder skiing. Its major advantage over the larger, more crowded ski resorts is that it is part of the **Alta Badia**, a five-village ski association. With a Colfosco lift ticket you have access to 75 miles of trails and 53 lifts. You can also buy the Super Dolomite lift pass, which gives you access to 10 major ski areas that include 650 miles of trails and 430 lifts. For more information, see *www.altabadia.info*.

The cheapest skiing in Western Europe

Spain is famous for sunshine and bullfights, not snow-covered mountains and ski slopes. However, the skiing in Spain can be quite good, and it's far less expensive and less crowded than in the Alps. Although the Spanish Pyrenees may not have the kudos of the Alps resorts of France, Italy, Switzerland, and Austria, that is also one of its advantages, for it remains pretty much off the radar of the package holiday firms. Instead, the slopes are almost wholly for the locals.

The most popular ski resort is **Baquiera-Beret**, in Lerida province in the Pyrenees. The long ski season here lasts from late November to late April. You can choose from seven slopes of varying difficulty. Facilities include six chair lifts, eight ski lifts, and one baby lift. Ski instruction and equipment rental are available. For more information about the area, see *www.baqueira.es*.

The largest of the string of resorts that run along Spain's border with France is Alp 2500, just a two-hour drive north from the mild Mediterranean climes of

Barcelona. Strictly speaking, it is two resorts—**La Molina** and **Masella**—occupying adjacent pine-clad valleys which have been linked by lifts to form a combined ski area of 68 runs, totaling 67 miles of pistes.

The two-star **Hotel Solineu**, *tel. +1 (866) 332-3590 (in the U.S. and Canada); website: www.hotel-solineu-la-molina.com*, in La Molina village is a leisurely five-minute walk from the cable car station. Though basic, the rooms are clean and comfortable, and the eat-as-much-as-you-like dinner in the restaurant is a definite hit after an appetite-inducing day on the slopes.

Up on the slopes there is also plenty to entice. Both Alp 2500 resorts offer a good range of pistes that will test all skill levels, from beginner to advanced. There are also the additional attractions of a cross-country circuit, dog-sledge track, and quad bike area around the winter-wonderland setting of la Molina's lake. Alp 2500 boasts a good snow record, too, with more than 600 artificial snow cannons on standby in case of any shortfall.

St Moritz: The world's most famous ski resort

St. Moritz, Switzerland, is the most famous, most elegant ski playground in the world. Princess Ira von Furstenberg and Gunther Sachs are among the celebrities who have skied here. And it's easy to understand why—the five mountains at St. Moritz have great slopes. However, as you might expect, skiing here in peak season is expensive.

Where to stay on the mountain

Badrutt's Palace, *Via Serlas 27, 7500 St. Moritz; tel. +41 (81) 837-1000; website: www.badruttspalace.com*, is the finest hotel in town and, in February, the most elite skiers stay here.

Hotel Waldhaus am See, *Via Dim Lej 6, 7500 St.Moritz; tel. +41 (81) 836-6000; website: www.waldhaus-am-see.ch*, is much cheaper and also very nice.

Zakopane: Poland's best ski resort

Zakopane, *website: www.zakopane-life.com,* in the Tatra Mountains near the Czech border, a half-hour south of Nowy Targ, is the top ski resort in Poland. At 2,625 feet, it has good ski conditions November through May. Zakopane is also a center for sheep-herding mountaineers and has been a mecca for sports and nature enthusiasts since the turn of the century. Summer is for rafting, hiking, fishing, and mountain climbing. And the numerous health spas are popular regardless of the season.

Hokkaido: Japan's best skiing

The 1972 Winter Olympics were held in **Hokkaido**, Japan's northernmost district. It was then that the world discovered the region's ideal skiing conditions. Skiing in Japan is luxurious. Everything is civilized and efficient. For your après-ski enjoyment, try a relaxing *o-furo* (hot bath) with a massage and hot sake.

The two best places to ski are **Teine**, good for slalom skiing, and **Eniwa**, good for downhill skiing. **Mount Moiwa**, 30 minutes southwest of the city by bus, is also popular, overlooking the capital and the Sea of Japan.

The best places to stay

Numerous lodges and *minshuku* (guesthouses) are located throughout Japan's ski country. Accommodation is Japanese-style—which means you sleep on a futon and share a room with three or four other people. Rooms are heated and often have televisions. Baths are communal and toilets are down the hall. The food, Japanese country cooking served boarding house-style, is plentiful and good. You can rent ski equipment at most Japanese resorts, and it is easy to book a ski trip once you are in Japan.

Australia's best skiing

The **Snowy Mountains**, 300 miles southwest of Sydney, are much higher than the Blue Mountains. Covered with snow from June to late August, they are a great place to ski. Australia's highest peak is here, Mount Kosciusko (known as Mount Kozzie locally), which rises 7,314 feet.

Although skiing in Australia is as spectacular as skiing in the Alps (Australia has more snow than Switzerland), it is much less expensive. And it's one big party. Aussies drink until dawn, and then manage to ski the 25 miles of trails flawlessly.

The Snowy Mountains are worth a visit off-season as well, when prices are even lower and you can take a mile-and-a-half chair lift to the top of Mount Crackenback. The fishing, swimming, and hiking can't be beaten.

New Zealand: The world's best summer skiing

Summer skiing in New Zealand is much cheaper than winter skiing in the United States or Europe. Lift tickets are about half the price of those at U.S. or European ski resorts. And hotels and restaurants are much less expensive.

The largest ski area

One of the most popular ski areas in New Zealand is the **Whakapapa Skifield** in Tongariro National Park on North Island. The slopes descend from Mount

Ruapehu, a dormant volcano. Skiers are warned that part of the ski area is in a mudflow danger zone. The park is a comfortable one-day drive from Auckland. If you arrive early in the morning, the road to the top of Ruapehu is usually clear of snow and ice, allowing you to drive all the way to the parking area. Midday, however, usually brings fresh snow, and you may be forced to leave your car below and ride up the hill on a goat (a comfortable, four-wheel-drive bus).

Whakapapa has slopes for every level of skier, including a superb national downhill course for experts. Skiing across the top of the last face of the High Traverse, you can look up into the chimney at the end of the run. The chimney isn't very long, but when you drop in from the top you can't see the slope below—and you have no retreat. It's a bit like stepping into an empty elevator shaft—a thrill for even the most jaded of skiers.

New Zealand's newer ski fields are around the town of Queentown on the South Island. **The Remarkables** and **Coronet Peak** are popular with both skiers and snowboarders. On-going investment in these ski areas means that the facilities are excellent. Catch a bus from town (free when you have a day or multi-day pass) to get up the mountain. See *www.nzski.com* for more information. Queenstown is very much a party town so the après-ski here goes loud and long each night through the winter.

The best skiing in the United States

Taos, New Mexico, and **Jackson Hole, Wyoming**, are challenging ski areas that are remote enough to not attract big crowds. Both have serious ski schools, but neither has much après-ski activity. Taos does have French-run inns and an Indian culture. Jackson Hole has views of the magnificent Tetons, and from time to time you'll see a graceful elk leaping through the snowfields. **Grand Targhee**, the backside of the Tetons, offers world-class powder and empty slopes. The resort at **Sun Valley, Idaho**, has all the amenities but little charm. Snowbird, Utah, has the best powder skiing in the country.

Canada's best skiing

Skiing in Canada is as exhilarating as skiing in the Alps. British Columbia and Alberta have some of the most spectacular peaks in the world, beginning on the Pacific coastline. The Canadian Rockies are rugged, wild, and challenging. And Quebec's Laurentians offer après-ski activities with a French flavor.

The best heli-skiing

Heli-skiing, a relatively new sport, uses helicopters instead of chair lifts to allow you to avoid lift lines and to reach empty slopes in remote places. Canada boasts some of the best heli-skiing opportunities in the world.

CMH Heli-skiing, *website: www.cmhski.com/heli-skiing/trips*, has been operating heli-ski trips for over 40 years so these guys know what they're doing. They offer helisking and heliboarding trips of varying lengths.

Whistler Heli-skiing, *P.O. Box 368, Whistler, BC V0N 1B0; tel. +1 (604) 905-3337; website: www.whistlerheliskiing.com*, offers packages out of Whistler and Bralorne that take you into the four surrounding mountain ranges.

Mike Wiegele Helicopter Skiing, *P.O. Box 249, Banff, Alberta, Canada T0L 0C0; tel. +1 (800) 661-9170; website: www.wiegele.com*, takes you to the Cariboos and Monashees in the Canadian Rockies.

The best powder skiing: British Columbia

British Columbia's ski slopes are a sparkling, powder-covered paradise. And they are varied, including the Rockies, Bugaboos, Purcells, Selkirks, Chilcotin, Cariboo, and Monashees. The longest fall-line runs in North America are here, as is the highest serviced vertical drop.

Whistler, a trendy resort with gorgeous powder-bowl skiing above the tree line, has the longest vertical drop in the Americas (4,278 feet). Used as one of the venues for the 2010 Winter Olympics means that amenities here are top class. Nearby is **Blackcomb Mountain**. For more information, contact **Tourism Whistler**; *tel. +1 (604) 932-0606; website: www.whistler.com*.

Alberta's best slopes

Calgary, Alberta, the jumping-off point for some of the world's finest downhill and cross-country skiing, hosted the 1988 Winter Olympic Games. About an hour from Calgary are the magnificent Rocky Mountains and **Mount Allan**, the site of many Olympic events. Thirty minutes farther into the mountains is **Banff National Park**, with beautiful terrain reminiscent of Lake Tahoe and Yosemite National Park.

Banff: The best ski area

The area around the town of **Banff** has some of the best skiing in Canada, *tel. +1 (403)705 4000; website: http://skibanff.com*, with both the easiest and most difficult trails as well as superb facilities. The three most popular ski resorts close to Banff are **Mount Norquay** (*website: http://banffnorquay.com*), **Sunshine Village** *(website: www.skibanff.com)*, and **Lake Louise Mountain Resort** *(website: www. skilouise.com)*. Mount Norquay has some of the best beginner trails in the park, as well as three of the most difficult runs in North America: the North American, the Bowl, and the Lone Pine. The Lone Pine is a favorite among residents of Calgary, but it often intimidates tourists. The North American and the Bowl have acted as training grounds for many of Canada's world-class downhill racers. The mountain rises from 2,680 feet to 7,005 feet; the longest run measures 1.6 miles.

The best time to visit Banff (unless you dislike crowds) is during the winter festival, which has been held every January since 1917. Teams from around the country meet for the Mountain Madness Relay Race—a pentathlon of downhill skiing, running, skating, snowshoeing, and cross-country skiing.

The **Banff Springs Hotel**, *405 Spray Avenue, Banff; tel. +1 (403) 762-2211; website: www.fairmont.com/Banffsprings*, is the best ski lodge in Canada. Built in 1888, it was once the world's largest hotel. Not only does it look like a castle, but it operates like one, too. A medieval banquet—complete with period costumes and mead—is staged once a week in the imposing two-story Mount Stephen Dining Hall.

The world's biggest ski jump

The world's biggest ski jump is in **Thunder Bay, Ontario,** a hot spot for ski-jump fans. Four major Alpine areas have scores of slopes, including dozens of cross-country trails, for both beginners and experts. Canada's famous ski-jump champions practice here. Daily air service is available from Toronto, Winnipeg, Sault Ste. Marie, and Minneapolis.

North America's oldest ski slopes

The **Laurentians** (*Laurentides* in French), 40 minutes north of Montreal, boast the oldest ski areas in North America. The world's first rope tow was installed here in 1932 in the Quebec village of Shawbridge. Since then, these mountains have catered to skiers from around the world.

Mount Tremblant, the highest peak in the Laurentians, has a spectacular view of lakes, valleys, and forests. Its 3,000-foot vertical drop makes all kinds of skiing possible.

Gray Rocks also offers tremendous skiing. **St. Sauveur** is the place to ski and be seen.

If you're looking for accommodation in the Laurentians, try **Fairmount Tremblant**, *tel. +1 (819) 681-7000; website: www.fairmont.com/tremblant.*

Pinoteau Village Resort, *tel. +1 (819) 425-2795; website: www.pinoteau.com,* has the best view of Tremblant and serves excellent food.

Chile: South America's best summer skiing

In Chile, the snow begins to fall in June and July, and from mid-August through September the weather and snow conditions are dependable, the slopes are not crowded, and all the ski resorts offer their lowest prices of the year. Furthermore, the scenery of the Andes is as spectacular as any in the Alps.

The safest slopes

At **La Parva**, only 35 minutes from Santiago, you can ski right from your door to the base of the lift. From there you can choose from nine Poma lifts and two chair lifts. Wide-open and friendly, this is a safe place to be adventurous. Snowboarders can twist and turn over the edges of wind-curled cornices, and the miles of treeless mountains are perfect for heli-skiing.

The biggest slopes

Valle Nevado is the biggest, newest, and most talked about ski resort in South America, with 33 square miles of skiable terrain. These slopes offer the solitude of cross-country skiing and the conveniences of a downhill resort.

The granddaddy of ski resorts

The first skiers at **Portillo**, the granddaddy of South American ski resorts, were Norwegian mountaineers who arrived in 1890 to study the construction of a railroad between Chile and Argentina. The first lift was built in 1937 and had wooden towers. In 1947, this was replaced by a chair lift, and in 1949 the first hotel was built.

Portillo offers some of the most challenging terrain and ski lifts in South America. Because avalanches periodically wiped out lift towers on the steep upper slopes (where the best skiing is), the French invented the Va et Vient lift. Also known as the Sling Shot, this contraption shoots people standing four abreast on a Poma lift, straight up 2,442 feet.

THE WORLD'S BEST GOLFING

Scotland's best golfing

The **Gleneagles** in Perthshire has a guest list that comprises the who's who of golfing and is a favorite with golf-loving celebrities. Gleneagles has four courses: the nine-hole Wee Course, the King's Course (tricky), the Queen's Course (beautiful), and the PGA Centenary Course (stunning), designed by Jack Nicklaus. It cost more than $11 million, so it's not surprising that it's rated one of the best in the world. The **Gleneagles Hotel**, *Auchterarder, Perthshire, Scotland PH3 1NF; tel. +44 (01764) 662-231; website: www.gleneagles.com.*

The world's oldest golf course

The **Old Course** in St. Andrews, Scotland, is the oldest and most venerable golf course in the world. It dates back to the 15th century and has been the site of numerous British Opens. It is a difficult course, with ever-changing winds and sandy greens. Contact the **Links Management Committee of St. Andrews**, *tel. +44 (1334) 466-666; website: www.standrews.org.uk.* You will need a certificate of handicap or a letter of introduction from your club.

Ireland's best golfing

Ireland is internationally recognized as a major golfing destination, and in recent years has hosted such major competitions as the American Express World Championships and the Ryder Cup and the ladies Solheim Cup.

Ireland is best known for its wonderful links courses. Links land is literally the ground that connects (or "links") the sea to the farmable soil. Its sandy, treeless, and windswept. This is the kind of terrain on which golf was first played by the Scots in the middle of the 19th century. Because no trees or crops could grow on the sandy soil, Scottish farmers used it to play golf. In Ireland, the game was introduced by the ancestors of British aristocrats, who supplanted Irish peasants to make way for their games. Links courses are common in the western regions of Ireland, mainly Sligo and Donegal. Ireland possesses 40% of the world's links courses, but also has a range of parkland courses that offer a real test of golfing skills.

Some of Irelands best golf courses include **The K Club** in Co. Kildare which hosted the 2006 Ryder Cup (*website: www.kclub.ie*); **Druids Glen** in Co. Wicklow known to be a tough course (*website: www.druidsglenresort.com*); **Slieve Russel** in Co. Cavan has been the venue for many PGA tournaments (*website: www.slieverussell.ie*).

Europe's best golf course

Portugal's Algarve has the best golfing in Europe, combining emerald greens and perfect weather year-round. And the best of the Algarve's many courses is **Quinta do Lago**, *tel. +351 (289) 390-700; website: www.quintadolagogolf.com.* Lush fairways of Bermuda grass invite international golfers. The clubhouse and the pool are both welcoming.

Hotel Dom Pedro Golf, *Rua Atlantico-Vilamoura, 8125-478 Quarteira; tel. +351 (289) 300-780; website: www.dompedro.com,* has a swimming pool and tennis courts. It is popular with golfers.

The world's highest golf course

The highest golf course in the world is at **Gulmarg** (8,700 feet), in India, once a summer hill station popular with British colonialists. Gulmarg's seven-mile Circular Path offers a dizzying view of the Vale of Kashmir and Srinagar.

Thailand's best golf course

Thailand is fast emerging as a favorite year-round venue for the world's golfers. The country already boasts some 50 courses, and additional courses are in the works.

The best golf course in Thailand is the **Rose Garden Golf Course**, *53/1 Moo 4 Sampran Nakorn Pathom 73170; website: www.rosegardencountryclub.com,* 45 minutes from Bangkok. It has been awarded a Silver Medal by *Golf Magazine USA* for being one of the best golf courses in the world. It is renowned as Thailand's best managed and most attractive, and the caddies are exceptionally well trained and savvy.

America's best golf resort

Pebble Beach, 120 miles south of San Francisco and 337 miles north of Los Angeles, has America's best golf course. **Pebble Beach Golf Links,** *tel. +1 (800) 654-9300; website: www.pebblebeach.com;* has hosted five U.S. Open golf tournaments (1972, 1982, 1992, 2000, and 2010), two U.S. Amateur Golf Championships, and the annual AT&T Pebble Beach National Pro-Am. It is 6,357 yards long, very narrow, and draped across a magnificent landscape.

The **Cypress Point Club**, *website: www.montereypeninsulagolf.com/ Cypress+Point+Club,* also in Pebble Beach, is the most exclusive golf course in the world and one of the prettiest. You must be invited to play here. This area is worth a visit even if you aren't a golfer.

Carmel, a quaint beach town with chic shops and inviting inns, is nearby.

The best view of the sun setting over the Pacific Ocean is from the beach in Carmel. Residents flock here each evening to watch the red orb sink behind the sea. And the **Del Monte Forest**, stretching along the coast, offers some of the most scenic—and expensive—real estate in the world. The forest is surrounded by **17-Mile Drive**, a loop that passes beaches, sea lions, blowholes, grand estates, and scenic overlooks.

The **Lodge at Pebble Beach**, *17 Mile Drive, Pebble Beach; tel. +1 (800) 654-9300; website: www.pebblebeach.com*, is a gorgeous resort with tennis, swimming, horseback riding, saunas, hiking, fishing, and hunting.

The premier auto show in the world is the **Pebble Beach Concours d'Elegance**, *website: www.pebblebeachconcours.net*, held on the lawn of the Lodge at Pebble Beach.

THE WORLD'S BEST DIVING

Eilat, Israel: The world's best scuba diving

During the winter, fashionable Israelis flock to this port town at the southernmost tip of Israel, on the coast of the Red Sea. The beaches are filled with tanned bodies; the water just offshore is filled with marine life that exists nowhere else—tropical fish, the origin of which is lost in time. The Red Sea is part of the African Rift, which runs through East Africa to the gold mines of the Rand in South Africa. **Eilat** has marvelous facilities for skin and scuba diving. One of the best places to rent gear is the **Lucky Divers' Eilat Scuba Center**, *tel. +972 (8) 632-3466, website: www.luckydivers.com*.

Eilat has one of the best underwater observatories in the world for viewing exotic aquatic life. In spring, the city becomes a bird watcher's paradise, as dozens of migrating species make a stopover here. The colorful annual festival at Eilat (usually held in March) is marked by water sports and moonlight pageants.

Palau's best dive sites

Scuba divers in Palau should head straight for the outer reefs, including the Big Drop-off, Blue Corners, Blue Hole, and Turtle Cover, where you can descend to incredible depths in search of dazzling coral formations and exotic sea life.

The best dive shop in Palau

Koror has no shortage of dive shops or tour operators, but you can't go wrong with **Sam's Tour Service**, *tel. +680 488-7267; website: www.samstours.com*. Sam

Scott is the American stepson of Ibedul, high chief of Koror. He can help you arrange it all—diving in the coral reefs of Rock Islands, exploring shipwrecks from World War II, sightseeing, fishing, boat charters, or even a night search for alligators in the mangrove swamps of Babeldop.

The best diving and snorkeling in Belize

In **Ambergris**, Belize, you'll find some of the very best diving and snorkeling in the world. Ask at your hotel for a captain they recommend. Fishing is worthwhile, too. A good guide will know all the secret spots to try, and you'll come back with dinner, guaranteed.

The almost perfectly round "Blue Hole" of Belize, in the center of the Lighthouse Reef Atoll, is one of the world's most intriguing dive destinations. At more than 400 feet deep and 1,000 feet in diameter, it's visible from outer space. The Blue Hole, a two-hour boat ride off the island of Caye Caulker, used to be a cave that rested atop the sea, and was made famous by Jacques Cousteau in the 1970s. Melting ice from the end of the last Ice Age engulfed the cave, which now delves 480 feet into the sea.

The Cayman Islands: A mecca for scuba divers

The most varied scuba diving in the Caribbean is off the Caymans, three islands (Grand Cayman, Cayman Brac, and Little Cayman) surrounded by almost continuous rings of reefs. This spectacular underwater frontier contains 325 coral-encrusted shipwrecks, some rumored to contain pirates' treasure. The water is crystal clear, with a visibility of 200 feet. Craggy coral formations extend to the North Canyon Wall, where the ocean floor drops off a mile deep. More than 20 diving companies offer scuba-diving lessons and gear rental in the Caymans.

The inhabitants of the Caymans are among the best seamen in the world and are heavily recruited by international freighting companies. Until tourism became their bread and butter (beginning in the 1960s), every able-bodied man went to sea at age 18. Aside from scuba diving, the national pastimes are barhopping and church going.

Blue laws close bars at midnight on Saturday. Bars can open again at noon on Sunday; however, on Sunday, live music can't be performed.

The best diving in Guadeloupe

Underwater explorer Jacques Cousteau once described Basse-Terre's western coast as being among the world's top 12 dive sites. Attracting a daily pilgrimage of divers and snorkelers, the **Pigeon Islands** lie just off Malendure village. Warmed by hot springs, the bright turquoise seas around these three islets boast some of the Caribbean's most varied marine life. The islets are protected as part of the Cousteau Marine Reserve, but even non-divers can see the corals, sponges, and vividly colored shoals of tropical fish. A glass-bottomed boat, the Nautilus, sails from Malendure four times daily. The first boat leaves at 10.30 a.m. and the trip takes 90 minutes.

Saba's best diving

The Caribbean island of **Saba** is world-famous for its scuba diving, with more than 25 different diving areas. Diving instruction and certification are offered at **Saba Deep**, *tel. +1 (866) 416-3347; website: www.sabadeep.com*, a diving shop at the LAI Chance Harbor, which is owned and operated by two Americans.

Mexico's best diving and snorkeling

Outside Cancun, on the road to Tulum, is an idyllic lagoon called **Xel-Hà**, where you can enjoy the best snorkeling in the Mexican Caribbean. Netting keeps the sharks out, while letting all the colorful fish in. You can glide among rocks, circle around the edge, or explore coves on the far side. You will see electric-blue fish, yellow fish with black stripes, and schools of tiny darters moving in unison. Although the lagoon is deep, the water is so crystal clear that you can see to the bottom. You can rent equipment here, but the flipper sizes are limited.

Cancun's best scuba diving is in the waters off its southern point. You can arrange guided diving expeditions and equipment rental through your hotel.

THE WORLD'S BEST FISHING

Australia's best fishing

For decades, **Cairns** has been a fishing capital of the world, abounding in barramundi, shark, and marlin. It's also the stepping-off point for the world's best black marlin fishing grounds. Although they aren't particularly good eating, black marlin put up one heck of a fight, making for a good battle.

New Zealand's best fishing

The **Canterbury** region, especially the town of Methven, is a mecca for salmon and trout fishermen. During the summer, quinnat salmon run in the Rangitata and

Ashburton rivers near Geraldine. Three major salmon-fishing contests are held each year on the Rangitata, Rakaia, and Waitaki rivers.

Man's best fishing

Sports fishermen adore the Isle of Man because of its variety of fishing: surf casting, river fishing, and deep-sea fishing. The best place to go surf fishing is the **Point of Ayre**, where you can fish at any tide. The best time however is low tide.

SECTION FIVE

THE WORLD'S BEST SHOPPING

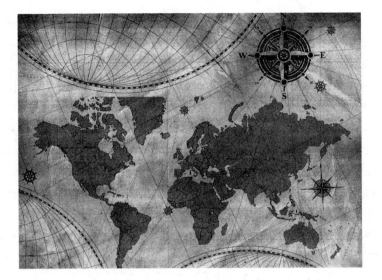

SINGAPORE: THE WORLD'S GREATEST SHOPPING

There are two reasons Singapore offers the best shopping in the world. First, a better selection cannot be found anywhere else. Second, the government's harsh policy toward unscrupulous merchants makes this a safe place to spend your money.

Tanglin, **Orchard**, and **Scotts** roads are the obvious places to begin a shopping spree. Prices are fixed, charge cards are welcome, and shopkeepers are friendly and speak English. Bring your walking shoes—or better yet, buy a pair at one of the shops in the area.

The best place to buy a carpet
The best place to buy a carpet in Singapore is at an auction. Open to the public, auctions are announced in the local paper. They are usually held in hotel ballrooms. Attend several auctions before purchasing anything; it pays to listen and learn. The carpets sold are from Afghanistan, Turkey, and Pakistan. Weavers tend to depict their everyday experiences in their works.

ATHENS' BEST SHOPPING

The **Plaka,** where you can buy any kind of handicraft made in Greece, is the best place for shopping. However, if you're heading out to the islands, where goods are cheaper, wait.

Monastiraki, better known as the Athens flea market, is a special part of the Plaka. It runs from Monastiraki Square to Ifestou Street and includes shops offering both antiques and old junk. The best time to visit is Sunday morning.

Kolonaki has posh boutiques, modern art galleries, expensive antique shops, and good dress designers.

Omonia Square is where the locals shop. The Greek-style department stores here offer better prices than Kolonaki. Goods are sensible rather than stylish.

Pandrossou, the Street of Shoes, also has shops selling brassware, peasant costumes, Greek dolls, and good imitation antiques. (You can't take real ones out of the country.)

The **National Archeological Museum** sells copies and castings of Greek museum pieces.

THE BEST SHOPPING IN ROME

Luxury shops fill the Piazza di Spagna and line the adjoining streets. Less expensive shops can be found along Via del Corso, and there are also department stores that employ their own designers and feature stylish collections. Leather goods, gloves, shoes, purses, wallets, belts, and luggage displayed in windows draw credit cards from the pockets of passersby like magnets.

FLORENCE: THE MOST INTERESTING SHOPPING

The **Oltrarno**, or artisan quarter on the left bank of the Arno, is a maze of streets spreading out from the Pitti Palace and around the Church of Santo Spirito. Stop in at the workshops, where picture frames are gilded, furniture is restored, and metals are forged.

BOLOGNA'S BEST FOOD SHOPPING

Tamburini, tel. *+39 (051) 234-726; website: www.tamburini.com*, on Via Caprarie, has been in business for over 70 years purveying over 150 foods, including the best of the region's delicious cheeses, pastas, sausages, hams, patés, preserves, balsamic vinegar, Vignola cherries, and wines. There's an attached bistro too, with a vast lunch menu.

Around the corner from the Tamburini is the thriving **Mercato di Mezzo** food market for meat and fish, fresh fruit and vegetables, and the ubiquitous parmesan cheese. Make sure your parmesan is marked Parmigiano-Reggiano to prove it's the genuine article from Bologna's Emilia-Romagna region.

LISBON'S BEST SHOPPING

Veer off the grand Avenida da Liberdade onto the Rua do Carmo and Rua Garrett. This is **Chiado**, Lisbon's shopping district, where you'll find jewelry, Portuguese tiles, leather goods, and wine for reasonable prices. Lisbon's other main shopping area, **Baixa**, is located between Rossio Square and the river. Here you'll find old bookshops and antique stores. The best place for gold and silver filigree is **Sarmento**. **Por-fi-ri-os Contraste** sells the skimpiest bikinis around. **Helio Cinderela** has good prices on Charles Jourdan shoes and smart leather bags. **Saboia** sells fine men's suits. Brightly colored *azulejos* are sold at **Fabrica Sant'Anna**.

Where to find a real steal

A cheap, offbeat place to shop is the **Feira da Ladra** (Market of Female Thieves). This 300-year-old market is similar to huge flea markets in Rome and Paris. Originally, it was literally a market of *sovaqueiras*, or female thieves. The *sovaqueiras* hid illegal wares in their armpits and sold them at stalls then located in Lisbon's central Rossio Square. You can buy just about anything you want at this market. Be on the lookout for bronze, copper, and gold—sometimes you can find great bargains.

ZURICH'S BEST SHOPPING

The Bahnofstrasse is also known as **Luxury Mile**, because of its expensive, first-class shops. While it's fun to look at 18-carat gold shoehorns and watches, you're better off doing your shopping in Zurich's department stores or along **Marktzplatz Oerlikon**, a pedestrian district near Bahnhofstrasse.

BEIJING'S BEST SHOPPING

Qianmen-Dashalan Business Street lies in the southern city of Beijing. It is to the south of Zhengyangmen and to the west of the central line. This is an old shopping street with a long history. It has a lot of famous shops, such as Liubiju sauce and pickle shop, Tongrentang drugstore, Ruifuxiang silk shop, Neiliaansheng shoe shop, and Zhangyiyuan teashop.

Wangfujing Business Street lies in Dongcheng District, the center of Beijing. It is a beautiful walking street. On this street are the well-known Beijing Department Store, the famous Dong'an Market, the biggest arts and crafts shop in China, the biggest Xinhua Bookstore, the Foreign Languages Bookstore, Lisheng Sports Shop, and a Medical Appliances Shop. Also here are some famous old shops, such as Shengxifu hat shop, Tonghesheng shoe shop, New World silk shop, Hengteli watchmaker's shop, Baicaoshenrong drugstore, and Jiguge historical relic shop.

Xidan Business Street is in Xicheng District, the center of Beijing. This district is where the famous Xidan Market, Xidan Shopping Center and some old shops, such as Shengxifu hat shop and Jingyi glasses shop, are located.

Some popular shopping centers are **Yansha Friendship Shop**, *No.52 Liangmahe Road*, **Chaoyang District**; *Saite Shopping Center, Jianwai Street, Chaoyang District;* **Friendship Shop**, *No. 17 Jianwai Street, Chaoyang District.*

Flea and antique markets are also very popular. Some good ones to attend are the **Panjiayuan Flea Market** (the third eastern and southern circle), **Haiwangcun Flea Market** (Liulichang), **Hongqiao Flea Market** (the northern gate of the Temple of Heaven).

For arts, pearls, and jewels, China's arts and craft shops are lovely. **Yuanlonggu Silk Shop**, *No. 55 Tiantan Road*, is a famous old shop, where you can buy original color silks, green satins and brocades, as well as carpets and tapestries.

THE WORLD'S MOST EXOTIC MARKET

In China, Guangzhou's **Quingping Market,** just over the bridge from Shamian Island, has an incredible assortment of animals intended for the table. It is divided into two sections: one for vendors of traditional Chinese medicines and one for vendors of produce, meats, and live animals to be butchered. Dogs hang from hooks. Kittens are sold by the pound. Dead rats are sold as food. Wild boars are caged. Owls, mice, and snakes await slaughter. Small, Bambi-like deer are slaughtered before your eyes. And internal organs you have never heard of are for sale.

THE GINZA: TOKYO'S BEST SHOPPING

The **Ginza district**, southeast of the center of the city, is world-famous for its enormous department stores and exclusive little shops. Cars and trucks are barred from this area on weekends, when shoppers take over the streets and merchandise is moved onto the sidewalks. Ginza (which translates as *Silver Mint*) is named for the Japanese mint, which was once located south of Kyobashi Bridge.

In addition to the usual fare, Takashimaya, a department store in the Ginza, has restaurants, tearooms, boutiques, a kimono department, and an art gallery that exhibits shows from top international museums. The best time to experience the formal hospitality of this store is at 10 a.m., when it opens and the salespeople line up and bow to you.

For an experience in high-tech shopping, visit **Seibu**. In addition to designer clothes and imported ice cream, Seibu has 177 closed-circuit televisions that entertain shoppers with rock music videos, breaking waves, and cherry blossoms.

The most colorful place to shop in the Ginza is the Tsukiji fish market, a 50-acre stretch of wholesale fish stalls. This is a great place to take photos. You will see all the fish that make their way into Tokyo's sushi bars, some familiar, some not. Wear waterproof shoes.

THE BEST SHOPPING FOR GEMS

Hong Kong boasts more jewelry shops per square mile than any other city in the world, and it's the world's third-largest diamond-trading center. You'll find good buys on not only diamonds but also on gold, pearls, emeralds, sapphires, coral, jade, and lapis lazuli.

The best-known street market

The most famous of Hong Kong's many street markets is the **Stanley Market** (*website: www.hk-stanley-market.com*), on the south side of the island. Stanley is an old fishing village with a large expatriate community. Silk dresses, sunglasses, fresh fruits, rattan furniture, porcelain ware, shoes, and luggage are available for bargain prices.

DELHI'S BEST SHOPPING

Chandni Chowk, the city's marketplace, is a web of narrow streets that surround the Red Fort. Here you can shop for shoes, cows, pungent oriental spices, jewelry, ivory carvings, and rich brocades, and then have your stars read or your hair cut.

THE BEST SHOPPING IN CALCUTTA

New Market is one of the largest markets in India, with 2,500 stalls selling everything from cheap tin pots to fine silks. The market's real name, the Sir Stuart Hogg Market, is, not surprisingly, seldom used. The market is open from early morning until about 8 p.m.

NAIROBI'S BEST SHOPPING

In the center of Nairobi is the **Nairobi City Market**, where you can barter for animal carvings and usually come out ahead. The **African Heritage Shop**, *Kenyatta Avenue*, sells animal carvings, textiles, and jewelry.

Colpro, *Kimathi Street*, is the place to go for safari gear.

Here are some of the Swahili words that may prove useful:

Bei gain? (How much?)
Ni ghali (It's expensive)
Taf adhali nipunguzie bei (Please give me a discount)

THE MOST INTERNATIONAL SHOPPING

Dakar, in Senegal, Africa, is filled with fascinating markets that combine African, Arabian, and European traditions. The one drawback is that all the city's markets are expensive.

The most colorful is **Sandaga**, an enormous place covering several city blocks with little stalls selling everything from fruit and meat to cloth and sandals. This is where the locals shop—it is about as authentic as you'll get.

Another typical market is **Marché Tilène**, *Avenue Blaise Diagne*. Local designers create garments decorated with batik and embroidery and then sell their clothing in boutiques throughout the city. Recommended boutiques include **Fara**, *rues Assane N'Doye and Wagane Diouf*, and the **Deco Shop**, *rues Carnot and Blanchot*.

Marché Kermel, *near place de l'Indépendence*, is Dakar's European-style market, where you can buy high-quality imported goods, as well as clothing and souvenirs. Haggling is not recommended. The market is open daily.

SYDNEY'S BEST SHOPPING

Paddington, or Paddo as it is called, is the best place to shop in Sydney. The area is much like Washington, D.C.'s Georgetown, with restored town houses and colorful little shops.

The major draw is the **Village Bazaar**, held each Saturday from 9 a.m. to 4 p.m., on the grounds of the Uniting Church in Australia. The bazaar feels like California in the 1960s, filled with lots of long-haired youths. But look closer and you also will see busy matrons searching for dinner. More than 120 stalls sell handicrafts, antiques, clothing, imported goods, and art. This is one of the best places in Australia to find authentic Australian-made goods at bargain prices. Although the bazaar can be a shopping spree in itself, it should be considered only the starting point of a shopping journey through Paddington. Along Oxford Street, the main thoroughfare, and its side streets, you will discover antique shops, boutiques, art galleries, bookstores, craft shops, jewelers, and record shops.

MELBOURNE'S BEST SHOPPING

Melbourne's center for shopping buffs is located between Swanston and Elizabeth Streets, on Collins and Bourke. This is where you'll find **Myers**, *website: www. myer.com.au*, Australia's biggest department store. Bourke Street is a pedestrian mall, but be careful; trams pass through here at alarming speeds.

Aboriginal Handcrafts, *130 Little Collins Street*, is the best place for honest-to-goodness handicrafts, including paintings and drawings, made by Australia's oldest residents.

777

NEW YORK CITY'S BEST SHOPPING

Fifth Avenue is lined with some of the world's chicest and most fashionable, elegant, and expensive stores. Make like Ms. Hepburn and admire the stunning gems in Tiffany's windows. Take stock of the latest fashions on display at Henri Bendel, Bergdorf Goodman, and Saks Fifth Avenue. Or stop in at F.A.O. Schwartz, the world's most fabulous toy store, where you can drop anywhere from $20 to $20,000 for a toy. Also look for Cartier, Gucci, Steuben Glass, and the famous Trump Tower mall.

Other remarkable shopping streets include Madison Avenue, lower Fifth Avenue between 14th and 23rd Streets, and all of Soho. If you prefer savings over elegance, check out the Orchard Street area or for bargain basement prices (and quality) try 14th Street.

But for the best finds, New Yorkers in the know head to the financial district where **Century 21**, *22 Cortlandt Street; website: www.c21stores.com*, has designer and high-end fashions at excellent prices for this year's models, and outstanding buys for last-year's still-happening trends. **Burlington Coat Factory** (*website: www.burlingtoncoatfactory.com*) and **Daffy's** (*website; www.daffys.com*), are great for steeply discounted designer duds too and have stores all over New York.

The world's best diamond market

The **New York Diamond Exchange**, *tel. +1 (877) 693-4239; website: www.nydex.com,* is responsible for more than 80% of the world's wholesale diamond trade. The exchange is dominated by the Orthodox Jewish community.

New York's best food markets

Zabar's, *2245 Broadway (at 80th Street); tel. +1 (212) 787-2000; website: www.zabars.com*, has the greatest variety of delicacies and the biggest crowds, attracting 35,000 customers per week. The coffee is roasted by Saul Zabar himself. Twenty-six kinds of salami, 42 kinds of mustard, and 30 varieties of honey are sold. Zabar's is open every day.

Dean & Deluca, *560 Broadway; tel. +1 (212) 226-6800; website: www.deandeluca.com*, is another deli with an incredible variety, including edible ferns in season. The Italian foods are good. There are also Dean & Deluca cafés in several exclusive New York neighborhoods, including Greenwich Village, Times Square and the original café at 121 Prince Street in Soho.

UNDERGROUND MONTREAL: THE WARMEST SHOPPING

Because Montreal can be buried in as much as 100 inches of snow during the winter, many of the city's shops have taken refuge in a seven-mile mall beneath the city. Designed by architect I.M. Pei and developer William Zeckendorf in the 1950s, the underground complex has shops, sports facilities, theaters, exhibits, restaurants, apartments, hotels, and banks. Best of all, it's all heated.

The nucleus of the complex is **Place Ville Marie**, where shops surround a sculptured fountain. Corridors link Ville Marie with similar complexes at Place Bonaventure and Place du Canada. The three areas together contain 280 shops, 20 restaurants and bars, and entrances to three hotels. Place des Arts is a lavish performing-arts center, home of the Montreal Symphony Orchestra and the Montreal Opera. To get there, take the metro to the Place des Arts stop.

TORONTO'S BEST SHOPPING

Eaton Centere *(website: www.torontoeatoncentre.com),* an 860-foot-long shopping center docked on Yonge Street, is the hub of downtown shopping. The mall is shaped like a large ocean freighter, with a series of railings, big exposed ducts, greenhouse glazing, and three-dozen sculptured geese swooping from the glass-domed ceiling. The Eaton Center does more gross sales than any other shopping mall in North America. The mall has 300 shops, banks, boutiques, and fast-food outlets on three levels.

RIO'S BEST SHOPPING

The best shopping in Rio is for leather goods. You'll find good deals at all the city's department stores, including **Rio Sul**, on the west side of the tunnel leading from Avenida Princesa Isabel. Or stroll along Avenida Atlantica in the evening, where you'll find a wide assortment of leather products.

Feirarte (formerly known as the Hippie Market) is a good place to buy arts and crafts. It is held Sundays at Praça General Osorio in Ipanema.

THE BEST SHOPPING IN THE MEXICAN CARIBBEAN

Shopping in the Caribbean takes patience, persistence, and a poker face. The basic rules of haggling apply. First ask the price of something. Your best response is to shrug your shoulders and walk away. The shopkeeper will probably follow you.

In Cancun

Cancun's major market area is downtown along Avenida Tulum. As you walk by this open-stall market, which stretches for about two blocks, the shopkeepers call to you—some even reach out and grab you by the arm as you pass. Blankets, sweaters, silver bracelets, and straw hats are thrown in boxes and tables in the stalls, and nothing is marked with a price. Feel free to rummage, but wait to ask for help until you're sure of what you want to buy. Once you have the attention of a salesperson, you won't get rid of him easily.

The sweaters and blankets at this market are good quality, but the gold and silver may be less so. Buy a piece of jewelry (if you can get a good price) because you like it, not because you think you're investing in gold. Real silver is marked with a government symbol that shows an eagle with a snake in its mouth leaning against a cactus. If you'd rather avoid the market, good shops are located along Avenida Tulum. Little boys on the streets sell marionettes dressed in Mexican costume that make good gifts for children and cost next to nothing.

In Isla Mujéres

The place to go for handmade, brightly embroidered cotton dresses is **Isla Mujéres**. As you step from the boat onto the deck, you'll be bombarded by people selling blankets, lace tablecloths, necklaces, and conch shells. However, the better merchandise is in the shops in town. These shops keep their doors open to the sun, and the maracas and hats seem to pour from the shops onto the streets and sidewalks.

In Cozumel

In Cozumel you will find good Mexican folk art stores on *Boulevard Rafael E. Melgar*, selling high quality items, including silverwork, tapestries, and pottery at good prices. And **Plaza del Sol** has about a dozen craft and jewelry shops.

SHOPPING BESTS IN SÃO PAULO

São Paulo is known for its shopping. The best buys include clothing, antiques, and Brazilian jewels. The steep Rua Augusta, lined with little boutiques selling native art and unusual clothing, is a good place to begin your shopping spree. In addition, the city has many large shopping malls, which offer a glittering array of high-quality merchandise. The two biggest are **Iguatemi** and **Ibirapueraon**. The jeweler Henry Stern has an office in São Paulo as well as in Rio.

A huge Sunday fair is held along the **Praça da Republica**. A colorful street fair is held Tuesday and Thursday through Saturday in Pacaembú Stadium. Unrecognizable tropical fruits and vegetables are sold, as well as such exotic items as octopus and orchids.

THE CAYMAN ISLANDS: THE WORLD'S BEST DUTY-FREE SHOPPING

The Cayman Islands have recently expanded into a bargain center for high-quality goods. Shopping centers have arisen to accommodate the needs of the Caymans' relatively affluent population—and to cater to tourists. You'll find fashion boutiques, scuba equipment shops, beauty salons, and gift stores. Better yet, prices of goods in duty-free shops are often as much as 40% cheaper than those in U.S. shops.

THE WORLD'S BEST SCENIC DRIVES

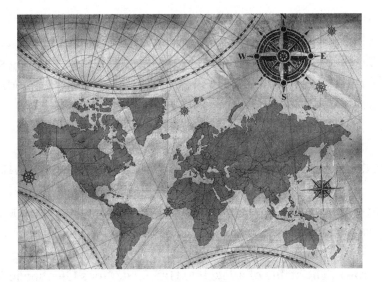

IRELAND'S MOST BEAUTIFUL DRIVES

County Kerry is known for the spectacular **Ring of Kerry**, a 110-mile drive that hugs the coast of the Inveragh Peninsula. Highlights of the drive include **Rossbeigh Beach**, near Glenbeigh on the north coast, which offers the best view of Drung Hill; **Glencar**, near Caragh Lake, a good place to hike; cells carved from solid rock by monks escaping the Vikings at **Skellig Rocks**; **Ballaghisheen Pass**, which takes you through scenic mountains; and the peaceful beaches that line the southern half of the ring. You can make the drive in a day, but don't be surprised if you take longer—all the beautiful sights along the road make it hard to pull yourself away.

The wild and Gaelic **Dingle Peninsula** is another beautiful drive in County Kerry. Begin the drive in the town of Dingle, on the ocean. Surrounded by hills, this fishing town is protected by an ancient wall. From Dingle, take the road to Ventry, which has an inviting beach. Outside **Ventry** are beehive huts built by monks of early Irish monasteries. **Slea Head**, at the tip of the peninsula, has a lovely view of the seven Blasket Islands. And the beach at Slea Head has water warm enough for swimming, thanks to the Gulf Stream.

Northeast of Slea Head is **Gallerus Oratory**, an unmortared stone building from the ninth century. After 1,000 years, it is still watertight. From the **Conair Pass**, you can see the lakes and Brandon, Tralee, and Dingle bays. **Sybil Head** has high green-sodded cliffs topped by thatched cottages and washed by the Atlantic below.

While in Kerry stay at the **Ballyseede Castle Hotel**, *tel. +353 (66) 712-5799; website: www.ballyseedecastle.com.* Acres of greenery surround this 15th-century castle. Or stay at the ideally situated **Parknasilla Great Southern**, *tel. +353 (64) 75600; website: www.parknasillahotel.ie.* It offers outstanding atmosphere, great service, beautiful room décor, and extensive facilities, including swimming, tennis, golf, and horseback riding, all on 300 acres of beautiful grounds. The hotel overlooks Kenmare Bay.

SCOTLAND'S MOST SCENIC DRIVES: THE HIGHLANDS

The Road to the Isles, A830, follows the spectacular Atlantic Coast. One of the most beautiful passes en route is **Glenfinnan**, where in 1745 Bonnie Prince Charlie, the 25-year-old son of the exiled Stuart Pretender, launched his campaign to reclaim the British crown. The statue of a Jacobite Highlander tops Glenfinnan Monument on the shore where the prince raised the Stuart standard.

The tiny town of **Arisaig** is also steeped in history. Bonnie Prince Charlie landed here to begin his uprising. He hid in a cave in the region. The rocky coast is a short walk away. While here, stay in **Arisaig House**, *Beasdale; tel. +44 (1687) 450-730; website: www.arisaighouse.co.uk*, an outstanding hotel with a walled rose garden.

On the route to Mallaig from Arisaig is an unpaved track leading to a remote and beautiful hamlet called **Bracora**. The road follows Loch Morar, Scotland's deepest lake, which is 1,017 feet.

THE BEST DRIVE ON THE FRENCH RIVIERA

The drive along the **Grande Corniche** on France's Côte d'Azur, the high road along the crests of the mountains, is spectacular. At times you will see the high snow-covered peaks of the Alps. At other places, you will see the sea. On the way down, visit Roquebrune, where a château was hewn from the rock. The Corniche is where the Monte Carlo Grand Prix car races are held and where the spectacular chase in the James Bond movie *Casino Royale* was filmed.

ITALY'S MOST SPECTACULAR DRIVE: THE AMALFI COAST

The **Amalfi Coast**, a mountainous peninsula between the Gulf of Naples and the Gulf of Salerno, is a land of legends. Pirates once used the secluded inlets as hideouts. Spectacular views can be enjoyed from the dizzying summits of the mountains. Serpentine roads wind through cliffside villages. Olive groves and grapevines dot the plains. In July or August, the Amalfi Coast becomes a madhouse, and it is nearly impossible to drive. The spring and fall are idyllic—warm and uncrowded.

The best coastal views

One of the most breathtaking views on the coast is from the old **Capuchin Monastery** perched on a cliff above Amalfi. An elevator takes you up to the 12th-century building, which today is an inexpensive hotel. Theodore Roosevelt and Henry Wadsworth Longfellow have stayed here. You still can visit a chapel and cloisters within the hotel. The foundations of the convent, which is perched on a sheer cliff, date back to A.D. 1000. Bus service connects the hotel with the beach. If you ask, the staff will pack you a picnic lunch.

Another spectacular view is from the little town of **Ravello**, above Amalfi. A bus will take you to this summit via narrow, twisting roads. **Hotel Rufolo**, *via San Francesco 4, 84010 Ravello (Salerno); tel. +39 (089) 857-133; website: www. hotelrufolo.it*, is a lovely 11th-century building now used as a hotel. It has gorgeous gardens filled with hydrangeas and a Moorish cloister overgrown with flowers. During the summer, concerts are staged here. The villa was once the residence of Pope Adrian IV, the only English pope, who reigned from 1154 to 1159. Lord Byron, Greta Garbo, and composer Richard Wagner have stayed here.

The cathedral in Ravello has sculptures of strange-looking animals and contains a reliquary with the skull of Santa Barbara. The blood of the town's patron saint, San Pantaleone, is preserved in a cracked vessel that never leaks (or so it is said).

The **Hotel Caruso**, *via San Giovanni del Torro 52, 84010 Ravello (Salerno); tel. +39 (089) 858-801; website: www.hotelcaruso.com*, set 900 feet above the Mediterranean coast, has sweeping views of the sea through its arched terrace. This well-known hotel is in the 11th-century d'Afflito Palace. Wines from surrounding vineyards are served in the restaurant. Most rooms have private bathrooms and private balconies.

Hotel Palumbo, *via S. Giovanni del Toro 28, 84010 Ravello (Salerno); tel. +39 (089) 857-244; website: www.hotelpalumbo.it*, perched 1,200 feet above the coast, also has tremendous views. The 12th-century building was once the Palazzo Confalone. It is a pretty building, with arch and pillar vaulting, stone staircases, tile-inlaid floors, and good paintings. The hotel restaurant serves its own Ravello wines.

Germany is known for its beautiful scenic drives. The longest is the **Alpen-Ostsee**, stretching from the Baltic Sea island of Fehmarn to the Bavarian village of Berchtesgaden. The most unusual is the Windmill Road in the marshy area of Minden/Lubeck. The roads overlap in many of the most picturesque places. For instance, the Romantic and the Alpine roads both lead to Mad Ludwig's castle Neuschwanstein.

The Romantic Road

The **Romantic Road** runs from Wurzburg in the north to Fussen in the south. The road, which follows a medieval trade route, is about 200 miles long and passes vineyards, ruined castles, and wooded hills. Begin by heading east from Heidelberg along the Neckar River on the Castle Road (Route 37). At Nedkarelz, turn left on Route 27 and go through Mosbach. Take Route 292 to Bad Mergentheim. Stop in Weikersheim to visit the town's castle, which has a marvelous Hunting Hall and baroque gardens.

The German Alpine Road

The **Deutsche Alpenstrasse** (German Alpine Road) leads from Bodensee through the Bavarian Alps. It passes Germany's highest peak, the Zugspitze; the limestone massifs of the Alpine National Park; the ski resorts of Garmisch-Partenkirchen; Berchtesgadener Land, where the mighty Watzmann Mountain drops down suddenly to the deep-blue Konigsee; Mittenwald; and the castles of Hohenschwangau and Neuschwanstein, where Mad King Ludwig lived out his fantasies. The natural scenery along the route is consistently awe-inspiring.

The best place to stay along this route is the Atlas Posthotel Partenkirchen, *Marienplatz 12, 82467, Garmisch-Partenkirchen; tel. +49 8821-7090; website: www.atlas-posthotel.com*. This 15th-century family-run hotel overflows with Bavarian atmosphere. The exterior of the three-story building is covered with paintings. Inside are oil portraits, dark wood furniture, beamed ceilings, and wood paneling.

The Road of the Nibelungs

The **Nibelungenstrasse** (Road of the Nibelungs) is a favorite among devotees of the Siegfried sagas. (Wagner used these tales for his Ring operas.) The route, which goes from Worms to Wertheim, passes through the Odenwald, an inhospitable forest region in the time of the Nibelungs. Today, the hilly, wooded region

The World's Best SCENIC DRIVES

is much more welcoming, with a series of health spas (Amorbach, Bad König, Beerfelden, Erbach, and Michelstadt).

The **Bergstrasse-Odenwald Nature Park** is a good place to stop and appreciate the rocky forest. The park is covered by an extensive network of footpaths.

The Fairy-Tale Trail

The **Fairy-Tale Trail** leads from Bremen through Hamelin to Steinau, the home of the Brothers Grimm. The road leads 360 miles south, through medieval towns and past castles, palaces, and seemingly enchanted forests. It takes you to the 13th-century castle of Neustadt, where Rapunzel was locked in a tower by a witch; the town of Schwalmstadt, where Little Red Riding Hood lived; and Kassel, where the brothers Grimm collected their first book of fairy tales in 1812.

The most magical place to stay en route is Sleeping Beauty's castle, **Dornröeschenschloss Sababurg**, *website: www.sababurg.de*. Built in 1334 to protect pilgrims heading for Gottsbüren, the castle has two massive towers.

THE LOVELIEST DRIVE FROM NAIROBI

The best way to see the countryside around Nairobi is by car, at your own pace. Following is the best itinerary, recommended by an old Kenya hand. Drive three hours north of Nairobi to **Nanyuki**, stopping along the way to see the grave of Lord Baden Powell, founder of the Boy Scouts, in Nyerere. On his tomb is a circle with a dot in the middle, the scout symbol for "gone home." Nanyuki is situated 8,000 feet high on the slope of snow-topped Mount Kenya, which sits smack on the equator. Once you have become acclimated to the altitude, you will find this an ideal base for observing Kenya's wildlife.

From Nanyuki, head north to **Archer's Post**, a spring in the middle of the desert. If you are traveling independently, this is the end of the line. Solo travelers are not permitted to venture farther out into the Northern Frontier district. (This is for your own protection).

To venture deeper into the desert, join an organized tour and continue north to **Marsabit**, a tree-covered mountain in the middle of the Kaisul desert; this is where game animals come to drink during the dry season. Backtrack to Nanyuki and then take the road to **Nakuru**, which runs along the edge of the Rift Valley. You will see flamingos and views of mountains and the plain. This is where early traces of man were discovered.

En route, stop at the **Nyahururu Waterfall** (formerly called Thomson's Fall). Stay at the **Thomson's Fall Lodge**, a bit of old England, where you can take tea on the lawn while watching the waterfall. A few miles away is the courthouse where Jomo Kenyatta, leader of the independence movement, was tried.

NEW ZEALAND'S MOST BEAUTIFUL DRIVE

The road around the **East Cape** on North Island is one of the most rugged yet beautiful coastal drives in New Zealand, passing small historic settlements, pleasant coves and beaches, and wild countryside that remains rich in Maori tradition and culture. Some of the finest Maori carvings can be seen in the traditional meeting-houses of this district, which is the first in the world to greet the morning sun.

AMERICA'S MOST BEAUTIFUL DRIVE

The drive along the Pacific Coast, from San Francisco south to Big Sur, is the most spectacular in the United States. **Highway 1** is a dizzying twisting ribbon edging high cliffs above the pounding surf. Many movie chase scenes have been filmed on these precipitous roads. Stop from time to time to look over the edge at the deep blue water and empty beaches below. Because the undertow along the coast is so fierce, swimming is usually forbidden. In places, you'll hear colonies of sea lions barking on the rocks. The most spectacular scenery is at **Big Sur**. Waves crash through holes worn in giant rocks, and fierce winds whip along the sand. When you get here, ask how to get down to the beach. The roads often aren't marked.

The **Ventana Inn**, *48123 Highway 1, Big Sur; tel. +1 (831) 667-2331, website: www.ventanainn.com*, is a modern cedar structure. Rooms have carved arched headboards and handmade Nova Scotian quilts. Some have fireplaces, saunas, and Japanese hot tubs. The hotel has a heated swimming pool. Continental breakfast is served in the lobby, and a complimentary cheese and wine buffet is offered in the afternoon. The inn's restaurant has good food and a view of the ocean and mountains.

Alaska's best drive
The most spectacular drive from Juneau is north to **Haines**. Forty miles of road wind through the mountains to the border. **Klukwan**, near Haines, has the largest

concentration of bald eagles in North America. The **Chilkoot Trail**, which begins in the gold-rush town of Skagway, is littered with wagon wheels, horse skeletons, and commemorative plaques that trace the steps of gold-crazed miners.

CANADA'S LOVELIEST DRIVE

Canada's most beautiful drive is **Highway 430,** north of Gros Morne, on the coast of the **Great Northern Peninsula**. The waters of jagged fiords lap at the steep Long Range Mountains. At the northern tip of the peninsula, hundreds of icebergs rise as much as 300 feet out of the water. You can get more information from the Information Center in Wiltondale, which is open 9 a.m. until 9 p.m. in the summer.

RIO'S BEST DRIVE

The road that winds through Rio's mountain backdrop, passing through Itatiaia National Park toward Visconde de Maua, is breathtaking. En route is **Petropolis**, once the emperor's summer palace, which has been preserved complete with royal belongings, including the Brazilian imperial crown. You must remove your shoes to visit the interior of the palace. About an hour farther along is **Teresopolis**, a national park that attracts mountain climbers.

APPENDIX ONE

LIST OF CONTRIBUTORS

Peter Abraham

Zenaida des Aubris

Cynthia Baughman

Anita Breland

Becky Brych

Patty Fortin

Heidi Fuller-Love

Eileen Hartman

Carmen Jenner

Charlotte Kihlstroem

Anna Kutor

Debi Lander

Joanne Lane

Anne Lesnet

Gregory Long

Ken Lovering

Bonnie Lynn

John O'Regan

Gary May

Roisin Ni Dhonncha

Cheryl Probst

Anya Quiggin

Cynthia Stark

Linda Steinmuller

Tara Stevens

Emma Weldon

APPENDIX TWO

PHOTO CREDITS

©iStockPhoto.com/Elena Elisseeva

©iStockPhoto.com/Keith Binns

©iStockPhoto.com/Kyu Oh

©iStockPhoto.com/PeskyMonkey

©BigStockPhoto.com/FER737NG

©iStockPhoto.com/Nicholas Belton

©iStockPhoto.com/Mike Bentley

©iStockPhoto.com/Chanyut Sribua-rawd

©iStockPhoto.com/Pawel Gaul

©iStockPhoto.com/Lauri Wiberg

©iStockPhoto.com/zennie

©iStockPhoto.com/Nathan Watkins

©iStockPhoto.com/Pontus Edenberg

©iStockPhoto.com/Jean Assell

©iStockPhoto.com/Chris Pecoraro

©BigStockPhoto.com/gemenacom

©iStockPhoto.com/teekid